D0145860

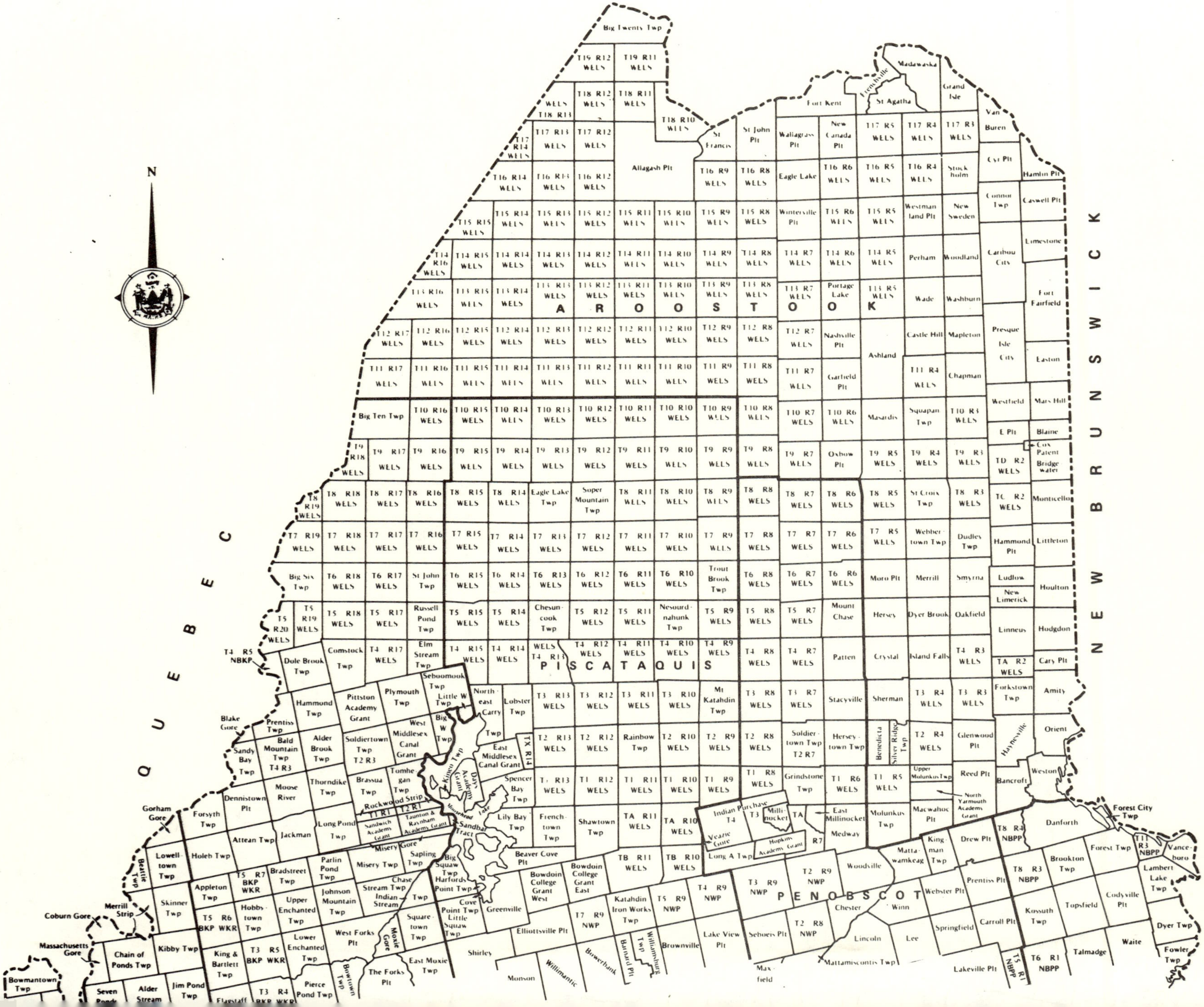
NEW BRUNSWICK
QUEBEC
AROOSTOOK
PISCATAQUIS
PENOBSCOT
N

MINOR CIVIL DIVISIONS

STATE OF MAINE

PREPARED BY THE
STATE OF MAINE
DEPARTMENT OF TRANSPORTATION
BUREAU OF PLANNING
IN COOPERATION WITH THE
U.S. DEPARTMENT OF TRANSPORTATION
FEDERAL HIGHWAY ADMINISTRATION

1975

SCALE

0 5 10 15 20 25 MILES

0 10 20 30 KILOMETERS

LEGEND

MD	Middle Division
NBKP	North of Bingham Kennebec Purchase
NBPP	North of Bingham Penobscot Purchase
ND	North Division
SD	Southern Division
WELS	West of the Eastern Line of the State

Pl.	Plantation
Twp	Township
T 2 R 3	Township 2 Range 3
T 27 MD	Township 27 Middle Division
BKP	Bingham Kennebec Purchase
BPP	Bingham Penobscot Purchase
ED	Eastern Division

W.E.S. West of the Kennebec River

Revised March 1975.

ATLANTIC OCEAN

NEW HAMPSHIRE

WASHINGTON
HANCOCK
KNOX
LINCOLN
WALDO
SOMERSET
FRANKLIN
OXFORD
KENNEBEC
ANDROSCOGGIN
CUMBERLAND
SAGADAHOC
YORK

Maine

A Bibliography of Its History

Maine

A Bibliography of Its History

Volume Two of Bibliographies of New England History

Prepared by the

COMMITTEE FOR A NEW ENGLAND BIBLIOGRAPHY

JOHN BORDEN ARMSTRONG
Boston University
Chairman

Edited by
JOHN D. HASKELL, JR.

UNIVERSITY PRESS OF NEW ENGLAND
Hanover and London

University Press of New England
Brandeis University
Brown University
Clark University
Dartmouth College
University of New Hampshire
University of Rhode Island
Tufts University
University of Vermont

*This volume has been
made possible in part by a grant
from the Research Materials
Program of the National Endowment
for the Humanities*

With the exception of minor corrections in the front matter, this volume, originally published by G. K. Hall in 1977, is reprinted by the University Press of New England with no revisions.

Printed in the United States of America on permanent/durable acid-free paper.

LIBRARY OF CONGRESS CATALOGING IN PUBLICATION DATA

Haskell, John D. (John Duncan)
    Maine, a bibliography of its history.

    Reprint. Originally published: Boston: G. K. Hall, 1977.
(Bibliographies of New England history; v. 2) With minor corrections in
the front matter.
    Includes index.
    1. Maine—History—Bibliography—Union lists. 2. Catalogs,
Union—New England. I. Committee for a New England Bibliography.
II. Title. III. Series: Bibliographies of New England history; v. 2.
Z1291.H24 1983 [F19] 016.9741 83-19868
ISBN 0-87451-281-6

Sponsors

American Antiquarian Society
Amherst College Library
Bangor Public Library
Bay State Historical League
Boston Athenaeum
Boston College
Boston Public Library
Boston University
Bowdoin College
Brown University Library
William L. Bryant Foundation
Helen P. Burns
Colonial Society of Massachusetts
Randolph P. Compton
Connecticut Historical Society
Connecticut Library Association
Fred Harris Daniels Foundation, Inc.
Dartmouth College Library
Essex Institute
Faust and Louisa Fiore Memorial
Historic Deerfield, Inc.
Janet Wilson James
Maine Historical Society
Maine State American Revolution
Bicentennial Commission
Maine State Archives
Maine State Museum
Massachusetts Historical Society
Mount Holyoke College
Museum of Our National Heritage
New England Historic Genealogical Society
New England Library Association
New Hampshire American Revolution
Bicentennial Commission

New Hampshire Historical Society
Old Sturbridge Village
Providence Public Library
Putnam Foundation
Rhode Island Historical Society
Smith College
Society of Colonial Wars in Massachusetts
Abbott and Dorothy H. Stevens Foundation
Stoddard Charitable Trust
Trinity College Library
University of Connecticut Foundation
University of Maine
University of Massachusetts
University of New Hampshire
University of Rhode Island Library
University of Vermont Library
UpCountry Magazine
Vermont Bicentennial Commission
Vermont Department of Libraries
Vermont Historical Society
Warren Brothers Company
Wellesley College Library
Wesleyan University
Williams College

Officers

Committee for a New England Bibliography

Contents

CITIES, TOWNS, AND OTHER CIVIL DIVISIONS

CONTENTS

CONTENTS

CONTENTS

CONTENTS

CONTENTS

CONTENTS

Preface

Users of this volume who are interested in the origins and early history of the Bibliographies of New England History project will find an account in my preface to the first volume in the series, *Massachusetts: A Bibliography of Its History*. In brief, beginning in 1968 a group of college history teachers, librarians, and historical society and museum personnel concerned at the lack of bibliographical keys to the vast historical resources of the region formed a committee to compile and publish a multivolume bibliography of New England history. The committee formulated a publication plan, editorial guidelines, and a strategy for securing financial support. By 1972, the committee had acquired funding that enabled it to obtain an editor and commence work on the first volume. The complexity of the project, the absence of models, and the prevailing economic stringency made for slow progress on the road to publication.

In that same preface, I expressed the opinion that the publication of the first volume indicated that the committee had reached a turning point in the project. Now, less than two years later, the second volume in the series has been completed. Many individuals and institutions have contributed time and money to this end. They are too numerous to list, but their contributions should be acknowledged.

The committee itself, with a growing membership, has evolved an effective structure for administering and overseeing the project, and its members continue to give close attention to its many details. Working in close harmony with the committee, the editor and his assistants have developed an increasingly effective editorial process.

The favorable reception accorded the Massachusetts volume has been gratifying. Some reviewers have noted how the bibliography reveals the unevenness of historical coverage of subjects and locales in Massachusetts. This is a welcome observation, since one of the committee's goals has been to encourage research and writing by demonstrating the "needs and opportunities" in historical writing on New England. Reviewers and users have also made suggestions for improving the bibliographies. Those consistent with the committee's general plan and guidelines have been incorporated into this volume. I should like to emphasize the request made in the editor's introduction to this volume for corrections and such addenda as fall within the guidelines and terminal dates for inclusion in the volumes. The committee hopes to publish these corrections and addenda in a section of the New England volume, which will be the final volume in the series.

The committee continues to seek financial support from both individuals and institutions. A contribution of five hundred dollars or more qualifies the donor as a "sponsor" of the Bibliographies of New England History series. In the last two years, the number of our sponsors has risen from forty-three to fifty-eight; except for two who wish to remain anonymous, they are listed herein. Some contributors have given much more than the amount stipulated for a sponsorship, others have given less. All have helped to demonstrate a commitment to the project, and have thereby assisted the committee's efforts to secure major foundation support. The National Endowment for the Humanities has provided funding for the project since 1972 on the basis of the committee's continuing to raise matching funds. Once again, it is my pleasure to express the committee's gratitude to the Endowment for its aid, and for the guidance and encouragement provided by the Endowment's staff. I should also like to acknowledge the generous editorial assistance and financial support that has come from within the state of Maine, especially from the Maine State Archives and the Maine State American Revolution Bicentennial Commission.

Great efforts must still be made to complete the Bibliographies of New England History according to schedule in the next five or six years. The editor will continue to need editorial assistance. The matching funds must be raised for the grant from the National Endowment for the Humanities. Nonetheless, prospects for success are good, and they will become increasingly so with each volume. Work on New Hampshire and Vermont is now underway; when complete, it will take the project to its half-way point.

In the preface to the Massachusetts volume, I stated that this publication project contained a moral. The series should serve as an instructive example of how scholarly projects of merit but with no special allure or modishness can be accomplished even in difficult times by the voluntary, cooperative efforts of individuals and institutions. That moral, that larger value of the Bibliographies of New England History, is restated more emphatically with the appearance of this second volume in the series.

John Borden Armstrong
Associate Professor of History
Boston University

1 May 1977

Acknowledgments

The compilation of a bibliography is a rewarding experience because so many people are interested in its development and betterment. Many have proffered aid, others have responded wholeheartedly when asked for opinions, and all have given generously of their time.

Initially, work on this volume was undertaken in appropriate Boston area libraries. The greater part of the compilation process, however, was conducted in Maine, where detailed searches were made of the four most helpful collections for the study of Maine History: the Bangor Public Library, the Maine Historical Society, the Maine State Library, and the University of Maine at Orono. The following staff members of institutions visited by the editorial staff were most helpful and hospitable: James C. Agnew and Gary B. Roberts, New England Historic Genealogical Society; Helen Atchison, Cary Library, Houlton; Esta J. Astor, Thomas L. Gaffney, E. Virginia Gronberg, Julieanne B. Irving, and Gerald E. Morris, Maine Historical Society; Karen Berg, Bonnie Hunter, Steven Robbins, Hilda Russ, and Margaret Taylor, Maine State Library; Eric S. Flower and Frances C. Hartgen, Fogler Library, University of Maine at Orono; Edith L. Hary, Maine State Law Library; Robert W. Lovett, Baker Library, Harvard University; Edith H. McCauley, Portland Public Library; Arthur Monks, Bowdoin College Library; Peter C. Schmidt, Grand Lodge of Maine (Freemasons), Portland; Evelyn Vradenburgh, American Congregational Association, Boston; and Robert C. Woodward, Bangor Public Library. The collections of the Boston Public Library and Widener Library, Harvard University, were also utilized, particularly for the examination of runs of periodicals.

The following individuals were more than willing to meet with the editor in order that he might draw upon their specialized knowledge of Maine and its history: Ronald F. Banks and Alice R. Stewart, University of Maine at Orono; Edwin A. Churchill, Maine State Museum; Richard F. Dole, South Portland, Maine; Charlotte L. Melvin, Ricker College; James B. Vickery, III, Brewer, Maine; and Margaret A. Whalen, Maine State Archives.

For bibliographical contributions, gratitude is expressed to John Borden Armstrong, Boston University; John E. Frost, New York University; and Irene M. Simano, University of Maine at Orono.

The following individuals corresponded with the editor regarding particular bibliographical questions: Marjory Bryant, Wilton Free Public Library; Natalie S. Butler, Farmington Public Library; Geraldine Chasse, Madawaska Historical Society; Priscilla Harrman, Newagen Memorial Library; Mary B. Howard, Rice Public Library, Kittery; Claire Lambert, Jesup Memorial Library, Bar Harbor; Frances M. Parker, Colby College Library; Martha P. Perkins, Waldoboro Public Library; Marlene Pooler, Fort Kent Public Library; Mary Riley, Bates College Library; Michael J. Sheehy, University of Maine at Orono, and Anne D. Stimpson, Turner Memorial Library, Presque Isle.

Jonathan Randolph and Margaret M. Meehan, Editorial Assistants for this volume both made immeasurable contributions. Margaret Landy typed the final copy, Webb Dordick proofread it, and Neil H. Aronson assisted with preparation of the index.

Cities, Towns, and Other Civil Divisions within Counties*

Androscoggin County

AUBURN
Durham
Greene
Leeds
LEWISTON
Lisbon
Livermore
Livermore Falls
Mechanic Falls
Minot
Poland
Sabattus
Turner
Wales

Aroostook County

Allagash Plantation
Amity
Ashland
Bancroft
Benedicta
Big Twenty Township
Blaine
Bridgewater
CARIBOU
Cary Plantation
Castle Hill
Caswell Plantation
Chapman
Connor Township
Cox Patent
Crystal
Cyr Plantation
Dudley Township
Dyer Brook
E Plantation
Eagle Lake
Easton
Forkstown Township
Fort Fairfield
Fort Kent
Frenchville
Garfield Plantation
Glenwood Plantation
Grand Isle
Hamlin Plantation
Hammond Plantation
Haynesville
Hersey
Hodgdon
Houlton
Island Falls
Limestone
Linneus
Littleton
Ludlow
Macwahoc Plantation
Madawaska
Mapleton
Mars Hill
Masardis
Merrill
Molunkus Township
Monticello
Moro Plantation
Nashville Plantation
New Canada Plantation
New Limerick
New Sweden
North Yarmouth Academy Grant
Oakfield
Orient
Oxbow Plantation

Perham
Portage Lake
PRESQUE ISLE
Reed Plantation
St. Agatha
St. Croix Township
St. Francis
St. John Plantation
Sherman
Silver Ridge Township
Smyrna
Squapan Township
Stockholm
Upper Molunkus Township
Van Buren
Wade
Wallagrass Plantation
Washburn
Webbertown Township
Westfield
Westmanland Plantation
Weston
Winterville Plantation
Woodland

Cumberland County

Baldwin
Bridgton
Brunswick
Cape Elizabeth
Casco
Cumberland
Falmouth
Freeport
Gorham
Gray
Harpswell
Harrison
Naples
New Gloucester
North Yarmouth
Otisfield
PORTLAND
Pownal
Raymond
Scarborough
Sebago
SOUTH PORTLAND
Standish
WESTBROOK

Windham
Yarmouth

Franklin County

Alder Stream Township
Avon
Beattie Township
Carrabassett Valley
Carthage
Chain of Ponds Township
Chesterville
Coburn Gore
Coplin Plantation
Dallas Plantation
Davis Township
Eustis
Farmington
Freeman Township
Gorham Gore
Industry
Jay
Jim Pond Township
Kibby Township
Kingfield
Lang Township
Lowelltown Township
Madrid
Massachusetts Gore
Merrill Strip
Mt. Abram Township
New Sharon
New Vineyard
Perkins Township
Phillips
Rangeley
Rangeley Plantation
Redington Township
Salem Township
Sandy River Plantation
Seven Ponds Township
Skinner Township
Stetsontown Township
Strong
Sugarloaf Township
Temple
Tim Pond Township
Township D
Township E
Township 6
Washington Township

Weld
Wilton
Wyman Township

Hancock County

Amherst
Aurora
Bar Harbor
Blue Hill
Brooklin
Brooksville
Bucksport
Castine
Cranberry Isles
Dedham
Deer Isle
Eastbrook
ELLSWORTH
Franklin
Gouldsboro
Great Pond Plantation
Hancock
Lamoine
Long Island Plantation
Mariaville
Mount Desert
Orland
Osborn Plantation
Otis
Penobscot
Sedgwick
Sorrento
Southwest Harbor
Stonington
Sullivan
Surry
Swans Island
Tremont
Trenton
Verona
Waltham
Winter Harbor

Kennebec County

Albion
AUGUSTA
Belgrade
Benton

Chelsea
China
Clinton
Farmingdale
Fayette
GARDINER
HALLOWELL
Litchfield
Manchester
Monmouth
Mount Vernon
Oakland
Pittston
Randolph
Readfield
Rome
Sidney
Unity Township
Vassalboro
Vienna
WATERVILLE
Wayne
West Gardiner
Windsor
Winslow
Winthrop

Knox County

Appleton
Camden
Cushing
Friendship
Hope
Isle au Haut
Matinicus Isle Plantation
North Haven
Owls Head
ROCKLAND
Rockport
St. George
South Thomaston
Thomaston
Union
Vinalhaven
Warren
Washington

Lincoln County

Alna
Boothbay
Boothbay Harbor
Bremen
Bristol
Damariscotta
Dresden
Edgecomb
Hibberts Gore
Jefferson
Monhegan Plantation
Newcastle
Nobleboro
Somerville
South Bristol
Southport
Waldoboro
Westport
Whitefield
Wiscasset

Oxford County

Adamstown Township
Albany Township
Andover
Andover North Surplus
Andover West Surplus
Batchelders Grant
Bethel
Bowmantown Township
Brownfield
Buckfield
Byron
C Surplus
Canton
Denmark
Dixfield
Fryeburg
Gilead
Grafton Township
Greenwood
Hanover
Hartford
Hebron
Hiram
Lincoln Plantation
Lovell
Lower Cupsuptic Township

Lynchtown Township
Magalloway Plantation
Mason Township
Mexico
Milton Township
Newry
Norway
Oxbow Township
Oxford
Paris
Parkertown Township
Parmachenee Township
Peru
Porter
Richardsontown Township
Riley Township
Roxbury
Rumford
Stoneham
Stow
Sumner
Sweden
Township C
Upper Cupsuptic Township
Upton
Waterford
West Paris
Woodstock

Penobscot County

Alton
Argyle Township
BANGOR
Bradford
Bradley
BREWER
Burlington
Carmel
Carroll Plantation
Charleston
Chester
Clifton
Corinna
Corinth
Dexter
Dixmont
Drew Plantation
East Millinocket
Eddington

Edinburg
Enfield
Etna
Exeter
Garland
Glenburn
Grand Falls Plantation
Greenbush
Greenfield
Grindstone Township
Hampden
Hermon
Herseytown Township
Holden
Hopkins Academy Grant
Howland
Hudson
Indian Island Penobscot Indian Reservation
Kenduskeag
Kingman Township
Lagrange
Lakeville Plantation
Lee
Levant
Lincoln
Long A Township
Lowell
Mattamiscontis Township
Mattawamkeag
Maxfield
Medway
Milford
Millinocket
Mount Chase Plantation
Newburgh
Newport
OLD TOWN
Orono
Orrington
Passadumkeag
Patten
Plymouth
Prentiss Plantation
Seboeis Plantation
Soldiertown Township
Springfield
Stacyville
Stetson
Summit Township
T3 Indian Purchase
T4 Indian Purchase
Veazie

Veazie Gore
Webster Plantation
Winn
Woodville

Piscataquis County

Abbot
Atkinson
Barnard Plantation
Big Squaw Township
Blanchard Plantation
Bowdoin College Grant East
Bowdoin College Grant West
Bowerbank
Brownville
Chesuncook Township
Cove Point Township
Days Academy Grant
Dover-Foxcroft
Eagle Lake Township
East Middlesex Canal Grant
Elliottsville Plantation
Frenchtown Township
Gore A2
Greenville
Guilford
Harfords Point Township
Katahdin Iron Works Township
Kineo Township
Kingsbury Plantation
Lake View Plantation
Lily Bay Township
Little Squaw Township
Lobster Township
Medford
Milo
Monson
Mt. Katahdin Township
Nesourdnahunk Township
Northeast Carry Township
Orneville Township
Parkman
Rainbow Township
Sangerville
Sebec
Shawtown Township
Shirley
Soper Mountain Township
Spencer Bay Township

Trout Brook Township
Wellington
Williamsburg Township
Willimantic

Sagadahoc County

Arrowsic
BATH
Bowdoin
Bowdoinham
Georgetown
Perkins Township
Phippsburg
Richmond
Topsham
West Bath
Woolwich

Somerset County

Alder Brook Township
Anson
Appleton Township
Athens
Attean Township
Bald Mountain Township (2)
Big Six Township
Big Ten Township
Big W Township
Bigelow Township
Bingham
Blake Gore
Bowtown Township
Bradstreet Township
Brassua Township
Brighton Plantation
Cambridge
Canaan
Caratunk Plantation
Carrying Place Town Township
Carrying Place Township
Chase Stream Township
Comstock Township
Concord Township
Cornville
Dead River Township
Dennistown Plantation
Detroit

Dole Brook Township
East Moxie Township
Elm Stream Township
Embden
Fairfield
Flagstaff Township
The Forks Plantation
Forsyth Township
Hammond Township
Harmony
Hartland
Highland Plantation
Hobbstown Township
Holeb Township
Indian Stream Township
Jackman
Johnson Mountain Township
King & Bartlett Township
Lexington Township
Little W Township
Long Pond Township
Lower Enchanted Township
Madison
Mayfield Township
Mercer
Misery Gore
Misery Township
Moose River
Moscow
Moxie Gore
New Portland
Norridgewock
Palmyra
Parlin Pond Township
Pierce Pond Township
Pittsfield
Pittston Academy Grant
Pleasant Ridge Plantation
Plymouth Township
Prentiss Township
Ripley
Rockwood Strip
Russell Pond Township
St. Albans
St. John Township
Sandbar Tract
Sandwich Academy Grant
Sandy Bay Township
Sapling Township
Seboomook Township
Skowhegan
Smithfield

Soldiertown Township
Solon
Squaretown Township
Starks
Taunton & Raynham Academy Grant
Thorndike Township
Tomhegan Township
Upper Enchanted Township
West Forks Plantation
West Middlesex Canal Grant

Waldo County

BELFAST
Belmont
Brooks
Burnham
Frankfort
Freedom
Islesboro
Jackson
Knox
Liberty
Lincolnville
Monroe
Montville
Morrill
Northport
Palermo
Prospect
Searsmont
Searsport
Stockton Springs
Swanville
Thorndike
Troy
Unity
Waldo
Winterport

Washington County

Addison
Alexander
Baileyville
Baring Plantation
Beals
Beddington
Brookton Township

CALAIS
Centerville
Charlotte
Cherryfield
Codyville Plantation
Columbia
Columbia Falls
Cooper
Crawford
Cutler
Danforth
Deblois
Dennysville
Devereaux Township
Dyer Township
East Machias
EASTPORT
Edmunds Township
Forest City Township
Forest Township
Fowler Township
Grand Lake Stream Plantation
Harrington
Indian Township State Indian Reservation
Jonesboro
Jonesport
Kossuth Township
Lambert Lake Township
Lubec
Machias
Machiasport
Marion Township
Marshfield
Meddybemps
Milbridge
Northfield
No. 14 Plantation
No. 21 Plantation
Pembroke
Perry
Pleasant Point State Indian Reservation
Princeton
Robbinston
Roque Bluffs
Steuben
Talmadge
Topsfield
Trescott Township
Vanceboro
Waite
Wesley
Whiting
Whitneyville

York County
Acton
Alfred
Arundel
Berwick
BIDDEFORD
Buxton
Cornish
Dayton
Eliot
Hollis
Kennebunk
Kennebunkport
Kittery
Lebanon

Limerick
Limington
Lyman
Newfield
North Berwick
Old Orchard Beach
Parsonsfield
SACO
Sanford
Shapleigh
South Berwick
Waterboro
Wells
York

Serial Abbreviations

AASP	American Antiquarian Society. Proceedings
AgricHist	Agricultural History
AHR	American Historical Review
AIrHSJ	American-Irish Historical Society. Journal
AJHQ	American Jewish Historical Quarterly
Am Heritage	American Heritage
AmJLegalHist	American Journal of Legal History
AmJSoc	American Journal of Sociology
AmNep	American Neptune
AmPolSciRev	American Political Science Review
AmQ	American Quarterly
AmSocRev	American Sociological Review
Atlantic	Atlantic Monthly
BA	Bowdoin Alumnus
BBHS	Bulletin of the Business Historical Society
BHistMag	Bangor Historical Magazine
BHistMed	Bulletin of the History of Medicine
BHSSC	Berkshire Historical and Scientific Society. Collections
BSM	Bay State Monthly
BTJ	Board of Trade Journal (Portland)
BULRev	Boston University Law Review
CanHistRev	Canadian Historical Review
CanJHist	Canadian Journal of History
CathHistRev	Catholic Historical Review
CCJM	Chamber of Commerce Journal of Maine
CEAIA	Chronicle of the Early American Industries Association

ColbLibQ	Colby Library Quarterly
CongQ	Congregational Quarterly
CSMP	Colonial Society of Massachusetts. Publications
DARMag	Daughters of the American Revolution Magazine
EconHistRev	Economic History Review
EEH	Explorations in Entrepreneurial History (became Explorations in Economic History with second series, volume seven)
EIHC	Essex Institute. Historical Collections
FR	Freemason's Repository
GeogRev	Geographical Review
Granite Mo	Granite Monthly
HistEdQ	History of Education Quarterly
HistMag	Historical Magazine
HMPEC	Historical Magazine of the Protestant Episcopal Church
HPHR	Hyde Park Historical Record
JAH	Journal of American History, (1964-)
JAmHist	Journal of American History, (1907-1935)
JEconHist	Journal of Economic History
JHistMed	Journal of the History of Medicine and Allied Sciences
JLibHist	Journal of Library History
JMS	Journal of Medicine and Science
JNegroHist	Journal of Negro History
LabHist	Labor History
LJ	Library Journal
MagAmHist	Magazine of American History
MagHist	Magazine of History
Maine Dig	Maine Digest
MASB	Massachusetts Archaeological Society. Bulletin
MassLQ	Massachusetts Law Quarterly
MassMag	Massachusetts Magazine
MeArchSocB	Maine Archaeological Society. Bulletin
MeCathHM	Maine Catholic Historical Magazine
MeCP	Maine Christian Pilgrim
MeHistMag	Maine Historical Magazine
MeHSC	Maine Historical Society. Collections

MeHSN	Maine Historical Society Newsletter
MeHSP	Maine Historical Society. Proceedings
MeHSQ	Maine Historical Society Quarterly
MeLAB	Maine Library Association Bulletin
MeLB	Maine Library Bulletin
MHGR	Maine Historical and Genealogical Recorder
MHSC	Massachusetts Historical Society. Collections
MHSP	Massachusetts Historical Society. Proceedings
MNEH	Magazine of New England History
Moravian HST	Moravian Historical Society. Transactions
MPAP	Maine Press Association. Proceedings
MVHR	Mississippi Valley Historical Review
NEG	New England Galaxy
NEHGR	New England Historical and Genealogical Register
NEJMed	New England Journal of Medicine
NEM	New England Magazine
NEQ	New England Quarterly
OTNE	Old-Time New England
PCHSC	Piscataquis County Historical Society. Collections
PejHSC	Pejepscot Historical Society. Collections
PolSciQ	Political Science Quarterly
Potter's AmMo	Potter's American Monthly
Putnam's HM	Putnam's Historical Magazine
PVMA	Pocumtuck Valley Memorial Association. History and Proceedings
QH	Quaker History
RLHSB	Railway and Locomotive Historical Society. Bulletin
SJMH	Sprague's Journal of Maine History
SocArchHistJ	Society of Architectural Historians. Journal
UHSP	Unitarian Historical Society. Proceedings
WMHJ	Worcester Magazine and Historical Journal
WMQ	William and Mary Quarterly
Worcester HsProc	Worcester Historical Society. Proceedings of the Worcester Society of Antiquity
WPSAM	White Pine Series of Architectural Monographs

Location Symbols

MB	Boston Public Library
MBC	American Congregational Association, Boston
MBNEH	New England Historic Genealogical Society, Boston
Me	Maine State Library, Augusta
MeB	Bowdoin College, Brunswick
MeBa	Bangor Public Library
MeFarP	Farmington Public Library
MeForK	Fort Kent Public Library
MeForF	Fort Fairfield Public Library
MeHi	Maine Historical Society, Portland
MeHoC	Cary Library, Houlton
MeHoR	Ricker College, Houlton
MeMaHi	Madawaska Historical Society
MeP	Portland Public Library
MePGLM	Grand Lodge of Maine, Ancient Free and Accepted Masons, Portland
MePriT	Turner Memorial Library, Presque Isle
MeU	University of Maine, Orono
MH	Harvard University, Cambridge
MH-BA	Baker Library, Harvard University
MWA	American Antiquarian Society, Worcester

Introduction

In keeping with the guidelines established by the Committee for a New England Bibliography, the entries in this volume are arranged by geographical units. Subject access is provided by means of the index. The initial section of the bibliography contains works relating to the state as a whole, or to more than one of its counties. Sections then follow for the individual counties and, after these, for the subordinate political units, which in Maine are known collectively as minor civil divisions. Within each section, entries are arranged alphabetically.

For the purposes of this bibliography, Maine has been considered in terms of its present boundaries. Although Maine was part of Massachusetts until 1820, writings relating to Maine appear in the present volume regardless of the period of time to which they pertain. Works relating to the separation of Maine from Massachusetts appear both in the present volume and in the Massachusetts volume, which was published in 1976.

Maine's civil divisions below the county level comprise four types: cities, towns, plantations, and unorganized townships. All told, there are 909 such civil divisions, but of these only 666 are named. The remainder are designated by township and range numbers, e.g., T15 R10, and generally have little or no population. In the preparation of this volume, the search was limited to materials relating to named civil divisions. For many of these, particularly plantations and unorganized townships, it will be noted that no items were located. This is not surprising when one considers the meager population of much of the state. According to the 1970 census, there were only forty-two civil divisions with a population of over 5,000, and only fifteen with more than 10,000 inhabitants. In population density, Maine ranked thirty-eighth among the fifty states, with thirty persons per square mile. Information on some of the civil divisions for which no items were located can be gleaned from county histories (where they exist), gazetteers, and guidebooks.

Works that deal explicitly with more than one civil division are treated in the following manner. If the divisions are all within the same county, the work is listed under that county, with SEE ALSO cross-references under the particular civil divisions. The entry is also indexed under the names of the civil divisions treated. Works pertaining to civil divisions in more than one county are entered under the first-named civil division, with cross-references under the others and, again, full indexing. Thus a reader who wishes to locate all of the entries pertaining to a particular county or civil division is urged to consult not only the entries listed under that heading but in addition the SEE ALSO references at the end of the section. All of the entries pertaining to a particular county or civil division may also be located by means of the index. The index also provides access to materials pertaining to centers of population within civil divisions, such as villages, hamlets, and localities. It should be noted, however, that no attempt has been made to list or index the material on particular civil divisions that may be found within county histories.

The general terminal date established for listings in this volume is December 1975. Some later titles, however, have been included when they have come to the editor's attention. Spelling of place names follows the *Standard Geographic Code for Minor Civil Divisions by County and Planning Development District*, a 1974 publication of the Maine State Planning Office.

One general rule for this bibliography series should be mentioned. Works that deal with more than one New England state, as, for example, an article on a boundary dispute between two states, will appear in the final volume on New England as a whole rather than in the volumes for the particular states involved.

In coverage, as in arrangement, this volume follows the guidelines established by the Committee for a New England Bibliography. It is confined to published works—principally books and magazine articles—written in whole or in part with a conscious historical purpose. These may be scholarly monographs or a more informal review of the history of a local church or business firm. Within these listings may be found material on political, economic, social, and intellectual history, along with natural history, literary history, historical archaeology, folklore, and military history. Practical and budgetary considerations made it necessary for the committee to set some limits to the types of material covered. Government documents are exluded, except for edited series of published archival and vital records; but published diaries, personal papers, journals, account books, and travel narratives that are significant for the history of a locale are listed. Works of collected biography have been included, but not biographies of individuals. Books and periodical articles, however, on aspects of an individual career related to the state or to a locality within it are included. Examples are a periodical article on Oscar Wilde's visit to Bangor, or a book on the governorship of Kenneth Curtis. Other categories left out, sometimes regretfully, are unpublished doctoral dissertations, works of genealogy, maps and atlases, guidebooks, fiction, and works that are primarily pictorial. Although the editorial search has been limited to American libraries and catalogs, foreign-language titles have been included when found.

Birth and death dates of authors are given only when necessary to distinguish those persons from others of the same name who appear as authors or subjects in this bibliography. Pseudonymous works are entered under the author's autonym, with a cross reference from the pseudonym in the index. Authorships attributed by individuals or libraries other than the Library of Congress are noted.

Writings by the same author which appear consecutively are arranged alphabetically, regardless of whether they were written by the author alone or jointly. In those few entries where a multivolume work was written by several authors who did not write contemporaneously, this distinction has been noted. Title changes are indicated in a note. For works of more than one edition, the latest edition is cited, with the date of the first edition, if known, indicated in parentheses immediately following the title. Place of publication and dates supplied by the editor appear in square brackets. Variant imprints for multivolume works appear in a note. For broadsides, dimensions are given in inches, height before width.

A location is given only for those works which do not appear in the published catalogs of the Library of Congress or in the *National Union Catalog*. The symbols are those used in the *National Union Catalog*, except for those supplied by the editor, in square brackets, for works in libraries which do not have an assigned symbol. See page xlvii for location symbols. No locations are given for periodicals. Users should refer to the *Union List of Serials, New Serial Titles*, or regional lists as available. For a union list of serials in Maine libraries, see entry 173.

Index listings are given for authors, editors, compilers, subjects, and geographical places, including earlier names of localities. Histories of institutions are indexed both under collective subjects, such as railroads and insurance companies, and under the institution's proper name. Entry numbers for bibliographies relating to a particular place or subject appear in the index immediately after the heading for that place or subject; they are set off by a semicolon from the other entry numbers for that place or subject.

The reader should make particular note of the fact that since index references are to entry numbers, the reader can choose those entries under a subject which refer to a particular place by first referring to the inclusive numbers for that place in the table of contents.

The committee will welcome both corrections and such addenda as fall within the guidelines for inclusion and within the terminal date for a particular volume. The terminal date for the Massachusetts volume was 1972, and for the present volume, as noted, 1975.

Beyond the published material which these volumes bring to notice, the serious student of a locale is urged to make a personal visit to the local library and/or historical society, since, by their very nature, many local history materials are not widely distributed beyond the place to which they pertain. Often these institutions also have collections of mounted newspaper clippings, prints and photographs, scrapbooks, and typescripts prepared by members of the community. Inquiry should also be made about possible materials which may be yet uncataloged.

Maine

1 ABBOT, EDWARD. "The Androscoggin lakes." Harper's New Monthly Magazine, 55 (1877), 23-38.

2 ABBOTT, JOHN STEVENS CABOT. The history of Maine. (1875) Revised throughout and five chapters of new matter added by Edward H. Elwell. 2d ed. Portland: Brown Thurston, 1892. Pp. 608.

3 "THE ABENAQUIS Indians." MeHistMag, 9 (1894-1895), 147-148.

4 ADAMS, EPHRAIM DOUGLASS. "Lord Ashburton and the Treaty of Washington." AHR, 17 (1912), 764-782.

5 ADAMS, WILLIAM CUSHING. Jonathan Edwards Adams, D.D., and Maine Congregationalism. Portland: Southworth Pr., 1933. Pp. xvi, 164.

6 AHLIN, JOHN HOWARD. Maine Rubicon: Downeast settlers during the American Revolution. Calais: Calais Advertiser Pr., 1966. Pp. xi, 224.

7 ALBION, ROBERT GREENHALGH. "Suggested readings in Maine history: the forest." MeHSN, 1 (January, 1962), 6-8.

8 _____. "Suggested readings in Maine history: the sea." MeHSN, 1 (September, 1961), 7-8.

9 ALDRICH, PELEG EMORY. "Massachusetts and Maine, their union and separation." AASP, No. 71 (April 24, 1878), 43-64.

10 ALEXANDER, DE ALVA STANWOOD. The Alexanders of Maine. Buffalo, N.Y.: Peter Paul Book Co., 1898. Pp. 129.
   Alexander family.

11 ALLEN, C. F. H. "The end of steam on the Maine Central." RLHSB, No. 108 (1963), 39-48.

12 _____. "The ten wheeler on the Maine Central Railroad." RLHSB, No. 66 (1945), 51-52.

13 ALLEN, CHARLES EDWIN. "Huguenot settlers in the Kennebec Valley, Maine." MNEH, 3 (1893), 17-30.

14 _____. "Loyalists of the Kennebec." NEM, New Ser., 37 (1907-1908), 623-629.

15 _____. "A short romance of Arnold's Kennebec Expedition of 1775." MNEH, 3 (1893), 227-232.

16 ALLEN, FREDERIC. "The early lawyers of Lincoln and Kennebec counties." MeHSC, 6 (1859), 39-81.

17 ALLEN, JAMES P. "Franco-Americans in Maine: a geographical perspective." Acadiensis, 4 (Autumn, 1974), 32-66.

18 _____. "Migration fields of French Canadian immigrants to southern Maine." GeogRev, 62 (1972), 366-383.

19 _____. "Variations in Catholic-Protestant proportions among Maine towns." Association of American Geographers. Proceedings, 3 (1971), 15-18.

20 ALLEN, JOSEPH, JR. "The steamer J. T. Morse--her history and adventures." OTNE, 27 (1936-1937), 79-98, 129-147.
   Rockland to Bar Harbor.

21 ALLEN, STEPHEN and WILLIAM HACKET PILSBURY. History of Methodism in Maine, 1793-1886. Augusta: C. E. Nash, 1887. 2 v. in 1.
   Pilsbury is the author of volume two which has the title: History of Methodism in East Maine....

22 ALLEN, WILLIAM, 1780-1873. "Bingham land." MeHSC, 7 (1876), 351-360.

23 _____. "Sandy River." MeHSC, 4 (1856), 31-40.
   Economic conditions along the river.

24 ALLEN, WILLIAM, 1784-1868. "Account of Arnold's Expedition." MeHSC, 1 (1831), 387-416.

25 ALLIS, FREDERICK SCOULLER, ed. William Bingham's Maine lands, 1790-1820. Boston: The [Colonial] Society [of Massachusetts], 1954. 2v.

26 "AMERICAN Home pilgrimages, No. 4--Maine."
American Home, 20 (August, 1938), 8-11,
54-56.
    1750-1890.

27 AMORY, THOMAS COFFIN. Life of James Sullivan: with selections from his writings.
Boston: Phillips, Sampson, 1859. 2v.

28 ANASTAS, PETER. Glooskap's children: encounters with the Penobscot Indians of
Maine. Boston: Beacon Pr., 1973. Pp. 216.

29 "ANCIENT land grants east of Penobscot
River." BHistMag, 1 (1885-1886), 29-31,
33-39.

30 ANDERSON, MIRIAM SYLVIA. The history of
secondary education in Waldo and Piscataquis
counties in Maine. Orono: University Pr.,
1939. Pp. viii, 111.

31 ANDREWS, L. A. "Squeaker Guzzle." The Rudder, 63 (November, 1947), 18-19, 68.
    Place names.

32 "THE ANTI-SLAVERY movement in Maine." SJMH,
1 (1913-1914), 38-39.

33 APPLETON, DANIEL FULLER, ed. The origin of
the Maine law and of prohibitory legislation,
with a brief memoir of James Appleton. N.Y.:
The National Temperance Society and Publication House, 1886. Pp. 52.

34 ARCHER, GLEASON LEONARD. "Maine's place in
early colonial history." Maine State Bar
Association. Proceedings, 30 (1936-1937),
26-50.

35 _____. "Pioneers of the rock-bound coast."
Americana, 32 (1938), 239-283, 486-524,
653-697; 33 (1939), 42-88, 349-414, 488-547.

36 "ARE Maine's Indians a disappearing race?"
Yankee, 17 (March, 1953), 38-40.

37 ARMSTRONG, LEBBEUS. The temperance reforma-
tion: its history, from the organization of
the first temperance society to the adoption
of the liquor law of Maine, 1851; and the
consequent influence of the promulgation of
that law on the political interest of the
State of New York, 1852. (1853) 2d ed.,
enlarged and improved. N.Y.: Fowlers and
Wells, 1853. Pp. xvi, 465.

38 "THE AROOSTOOK War and the volunteer troops
therein." BHistMag, 2 (1886-1887), 121-124.

39 ARSENAULT, BONA. History of the Acadians.
Québec: Conseil de la vie française en
Amérique, 1966. Pp. 265.
    A translation and revision of the author's
Histoire et généalogie des Acadiens.

40 "ART in Maine." Colby Alumnus, 52 (Fall,
1962), 1-5.

41 ARTHUR, ROBERT. "Coast forts in colonial
Maine." Coast Artillery Journal, 57 (1922),
217-238.

42 "ARTISTS born in Maine." MeLB, 13 (1927-
1928), 3-17.

43 "ARTISTS not born in Maine but having defi-
nite residence in this state." MeLB, 13
(1927-1928), 17-23.

44 "ASSOCIATION history." MeLAB, 20 (November,
1959), 21-22.
    Maine Library Association.

45 "THE ATLANTIC and St. Lawrence Railway."
Pine Tree Magazine, 6 (1906-1907), 127-134.

46 ATTWOOD, STANLEY BEARCE. The length and
breadth of Maine. Orono: Univ. of Maine,
1973. Pp. 279, 12, 30.

47 AUSTIN, HARRY B. "Salmon, shad and alewives,
rivers of Maine in olden days." SJMH, 6
(1918-1919), 158-160.

48 AVILA, LILIAN and ALICE ROSE STEWART. "French
in Maine." French Review, 27 (1953-1954),
460-466.
    French language, 1785-1954.

49 BABB, CYRUS CATES. Bibliography of Maine
geology. Waterville: Sentinel Publishing,
1913. Pp. 68.

50 BACON, GEORGE FOX. Northern Maine, its points
of interest, and its representative business
men, embracing Houlton, Presque Isle, Caribou,
Ft. Fairfield, Danforth, Lincoln, Mattawamkeag, Winn and Kingman. Newark, N.J.: Glenwood Publishing, 1891. Pp. 87.

51 BAGLEY, MARION MILLER. Maine history. [Port-
land]: J. Weston Walch, 1964. Pp. vi, 106.
MeBa.

52 _____. Maine history can be fun: an activity
text.... Portland: J. Weston Walch, 1956.
Pp. 81. MeBa.

53 _____. Maine history can be fun. Supplement.
Teacher's guide. Portland: J. Weston Walch,
1956. Pp. 16. MeBa.

54 BAILEY, DUDLEY PERKINS. "The Maine savings
banks and the late crisis." Banker's Magazine, (October, 1880), 257-268.

55 BAKER, ORVILLE DEWEY. Addresses and memorials
of Orville Dewey Baker (1847-1908). Manley H.
Pike, ed. Augusta: Kennebec Journal, 1909.
Pp. vii, 172.

56 BAKER, WILLIAM AVERY. "The Boston boats from
sail to steam." MeHSN, 9 (1969-1970), 5-16,
39-44.
    Steam navigation between the Kennebec River
and Boston.

57 _____. Maine shipbuilding: a bibliographical guide. Portland: Maine Historical Society, 1974. Pp. 22.

58 BALDWIN, J. R. "Ashburton-Webster boundary settlement." Canadian Historical Association. Report, (1938), 121-133.

59 BALLARD, EDWARD. "The early history of the Protestant Episcopal Church in the Diocese of Maine." MeHSC, 6 (1859), 171-202.

60 _____. "Geographical names on the coast of Maine." U.S. Coast Survey. Report, (1868), 243-259.
   Also issued as a separate in 1871.

61 BANASIAK, CHESTER F. Deer in Maine. Augusta: Department of Inland Fisheries and Game, 1961. Pp. 159.
   Includes history, 1623-1959.

61A BANGOR, ME. PUBLIC LIBRARY. Bibliography of the State of Maine; compiled in the Bangor Public Library. Boston: G. K. Hall, 1962. Pp. v, 803.

61B BANGOR AND AROOSTOOK RAILROAD COMPANY. History of the strike of engineers, firemen and hostlers on the Bangor & Aroostook Railroad, winter of 1913. n.p., [1913]. Pp. 36. MeBa.

61C _____. 75 years: the Bangor and Aroostook, 1891-1966.... n.p., 1966. Pp. 48.

62 BANKS, CHARLES EDWARD. "The administration of William Gorges, 1636 to 1637." MeHSC, 2 Ser., 1 (1890), 125-131.

63 _____. "The early settlements in Maine, prior to 1620." MHGR, 2 (1885), 207-216.

64 _____. "Martha's Vineyard and the Province of Maine." MeHSC, 2 Ser., 9 (1898), 123-127.
   1641-1664.

65 _____. "Sir Robert Carr in Maine." MagAmHist, 8 (1882), 623-626.
   1665.

66 BANKS, RONALD FILLMORE. "The great and the good: a course that explores Maine's oft neglected history." Maine Alumnus, 58 (Fall, 1976), 9-11.

67 _____, comp. A history of Maine: a collection of readings on the history of Maine, 1600-1976. (1969) 4th ed. Dubuque, Iowa: Kendall/Hunt, 1976. Pp. vii, 460.

68 _____. Maine becomes a state; the movement to separate Maine from Massachusetts, 1785-1820. (1970) 2d ed. Somersworth: New Hampshire Publishing, 1973. Pp. xx, 266.

69 _____. Maine during the Federal and Jeffersonian period: a bibliographical guide.

Portland: Maine Historical Society, 1974. Pp. 49.

70 _____. "The Maine economy: 1820-1860." Thomas Business Review, 3 (Fall, 1975), 6-10.

71 BARKER, LEWIS A. "Great Maine conspiracy." NEM, New Ser., 37 (1907-1908), 371-382.
   Gubernatorial election of 1879.

72 BARLOW, MRS. JAMES E. "The activities and a brief history of the Josselyn Botanical Society." Josselyn Botanical Society of Maine. Bulletin, No. 9 (1957), 34-39.

73 BARNES, CHARLES P. "A glimpse at Maine." SJMH, 12 (1924), 141-147.

74 BARR, ANNIE L. "Some who served." MeLAB, 3 (November, 1941), 5-6.
   Maine librarians.

75 BARROWS, HAROLD KILBRITH. Water resources of the Kennebec river basin, Maine. Washington: Govt. Print. Off., 1907. Pp. vi, 235, iii.
   Includes historical statistics.

76 _____ and CYRUS CATES BABB. Water resources of the Penobscot river basin, Maine. Washington: Govt. Print. Off., 1912. Pp. 285.

77 BARRY, PHILLIPS, FANNIE HARDY ECKSTORM and MARY WINSLOW SMYTH. British ballads from Maine: the development of popular songs with texts and airs. New Haven: Yale Univ. Pr., 1929. Pp. xlvi, 535.
   Contains music.

78 BARTER, J. MALCOLM. "Spring freshet." Down East, 15 (April, 1969), 48-51.
   Floods.

79 BARTLETT, ARTHUR. "Cruising Down East." Holiday, 14 (August, 1953), 48-53, 104-105.
   Yachting.

80 BARTLETT, ARTHUR C. "The cradle of prohibition." Outlook and Independent, 156 (1930), 48-50, 76-77.

81 BATEMAN, LUTHER C. "The Indians of Maine: history and present condition." Red Man, 5 (1913), 443-447.

82 BATES MANUFACTURING COMPANY, LEWISTON, ME. Do you know Maine? Vol. I. How Maine became a state. Vol. II. Maine holidays by Robert P. T. Coffin. Augusta: Kennebec Journal, 1948. 2v. Me.

83 BAXTER, JAMES PHINNEY. "The Abnakis and their ethnic relations." MeHSC, 2 Ser., 3 (1892), 13-40.
   Indians.

84 _____, ed. The Baxter manuscripts. Portland: Maine Historical Society, 1889-1916. 19v.
   Documents relating to the early history

85 MAINE

of Maine gathered from the Massachusetts Archives; the Public Record Office, London; and the Bureau of Marine and Colonies, Paris.

85 _____. "The beginnings of Maine." MeHSC, 2 Ser., 2 (1891), 273-300.

86 _____. "The campaign against the Pequakets: its causes and results." MeHSC, 2 Ser., 1 (1890), 353-371.
1703-1713.

87 _____. "Reminiscences of a great enterprise." MeHSC, 2 Ser., 3 (1892), 247-263.
John A. Poor and the Atlantic and St. Lawrence Railway.

88 _____, ed. Sir Ferdinando Gorges and his Province of Maine, including the Brief Relation, the Brief Narration, his defence, the charter granted to him, his will, and his letters. Boston: The Prince Society, 1890. 3v.

89 _____, ed. The Trelawny papers, ed. and illustrated with historical notes and an appendix. Portland: Hoyt, Fogg and Donham, 1884. Pp. xxxi, 520.
Correspondence and other papers of Robert Trelawny, of Plymouth, England, relating to his Maine grants.

90 BAXTER, SYLVESTER. "The redevelopment of an old state." American Monthly Review of Reviews, 33 (1906), 55-61.

91 BAYLEY, WILLIAM SHIRLEY and FRANCIS PLAISTED KING. Catalogue of the Maine Geological Collection with a brief outline history of the two surveys of the state. Waterville: Geological Department, Colby Univ., 1890. Pp. 32.

92 BEARD, FRANK A. 200 years of Maine housing. [Augusta]: Maine Historic Preservation Commission, [1976]. Pp. 15. MeU.
Architecture.

93 BECK, HORACE PALMER. The folklore of Maine. Philadelphia: Lippincott, 1957. Pp. 284.

94 _____. "Folksong affiliations of Maine." Midwest Folklore, 6 (Fall, 1956), 159-166.
Since the eighteenth century.

95 _____. Gluskap the liar, & other Indian tales. Freeport: Bond Wheelwright, 1966. Pp. ix, 182.

96 BEEDY, HELEN COFFIN. Mothers of Maine. Portland: The Thurston Print, 1895. Pp. 451.

96A "BELFAST & Moosehead Lake." Trains, 4 (April, 1944), 4-5.
Railroad.

97 BENNETT, RANDY L. "The Rumford Falls and Rangeley Lakes Railroad." Down East, 21 (March, 1975), 48-51.

98 BERCHEN, WILLIAM. Maine. Boston: Houghton Mifflin, 1973. Pp. 112.

99 BESTON, HENRY. Northern farm, a chronicle of Maine. N.Y.: Rinehart, 1948. Pp. viii, 246.

100 _____, ed. White pine and blue water, a State of Maine reader. N.Y.: Farrar, Straus, 1950. Pp. xxii, 410.

101 "BIBLIOGRAPHY of eastern Maine." BHistMag, 5 (1889-1890), 221-225.

102 BIBLIOGRAPHY of studies of the Maine economy, 1945-1973, as found in Fogler Library, University of Maine at Orono, summer 1973. Prepared by Wayne M. O'Leary and David L. Bridgham, under the supervision of Arthur M. Johnson. Orono: Balanced Growth Project, Univ. of Maine at Orono, 1974. Pp. ix, 107 leaves.

103 BICKNELL, HENRY S. "Along the Kennebec." NEM, 4 (1886), 197-207.

104 BILLIAS, GEORGE ATHAN. "Misadventures of a Maine slaver." AmNep, 19 (1959), 114-119.
Samuel Patterson.

105 "BIOGRAPHIC glimpses of some Maine men." SJMH, 6 (1918-1919), 79-104.

106 BIOGRAPHICAL encyclopaedia of Maine of the nineteenth century. Henry Clay Williams, ed. Boston: Metropolitan Publishing, 1885. Pp. 441.

107 BIOGRAPHICAL review ... containing life sketches of leading citizens of Sagadaboc, Lincoln, Knox, and Waldo counties, Maine.... Boston: Biographical Review Publishing, 1897. Pp. 422.

108 BIOGRAPHICAL review ... containing life sketches of leading citizens of Somerset, Piscataquis, Hancock, Washington, and Aroostook counties, Maine. Boston: Biographical Review Publishing, 1898. Pp. 738.

109 BIOGRAPHICAL review; this volume contains biographical sketches of leading citizens of Oxford and Franklin counties, Maine.... Boston: Biographical Review Publishing, 1897. Pp. 639.

110 "BIOGRAPHICAL sketches of deceased members of the Maine bar." Maine State Bar Association. Proceedings, 15 (1906-1907), 120-160; 16 (1908-1909), 81-89.

111 BIOGRAPHICAL sketches of representative citizens of the State of Maine.... Boston: New England Historical Publishing, 1903. Pp. 452.

112 BIONDI, ARNOLD S. and FREDERICK W. LYMAN. Abandoned railroads in Maine: their potential

for trail use. [Augusta: Department of Parks & Recreation], 1973. Pp. 108.

113 BIRD, HARRISON. Attack on Quebec: the American invasion of Canada, 1775-1776. N.Y.: Oxford Univ. Pr., 1968. Pp. 255. Arnold's Expedition.

114 BISBEE, ERNEST EMERSON. The State o' Maine scrap book of stories and legends of "Way Down East." Lancaster, N.H.: The Bisbee Pr., 1940. Unpaged.

115 BISHOP, WILLIAM HENRY. "Fish and men in the Maine islands." Harper's Magazine, 61 (1881), 336-352, 496-510.

116 _____. "The lobster at home." Scribner's Monthly Magazine, 22 (1881), 209-218. Lobstermen.

117 BLANDING, EDWARD MITCHELL. Maine State Board of Trade, historical sketch ... delivered ... at Waterville, Me., September 24th, 1913. n.p., [1913]. Pp. 32. Me.

118 BOARDMAN, SAMUEL LANE. Agricultural bibliography of Maine: a list of Maine writers on agriculture, with biographical sketches and a catalogue of their works. Also an index to the volumes on the Agriculture of Maine from 1850 to 1892. Augusta: Burleigh & Flynt, 1893. Pp. 117.

119 _____. "A family of printers--George V. Edes." Maine Genealogist and Biographer, 1 (1875-1876), 56-60.

120 _____. Maine cattle: some materials for a history of the cattle of Maine; with facts concerning early breeders, and notices of the thoroughbred herds at present kept in the state. Augusta, 1875. Pp. 48. MeBa.

121 BOLTON, CHARLES KNOWLES, ed. "A journey to Maine in 1859: a diary of Charles Edward Bolton." NEQ, 9 (1936), 119-130.

122 A BOOK for the children of Maine, for the use of families and schools. Portland: Samuel Colman, 1831. Pp. 118.

123 BORNS, HAROLD W., JR. "Late Wisconsin fluctuations in the Lawrentide ice sheet in southern and eastern New England." Geological Society of America. Memoir 136, (1973), 37-45.

124 "THE BOSTON and Mt. Desert Limited." RLHSB, No. 82 (1951), 72-73.

125 BOURQUE, BRUCE J. "Aboriginal settlement and subsistence on the Maine Coast." Man in the Northeast, 6 (1973), 3-20.

126 BOWLER, ERNEST C. An album of the attorneys of Maine, with a portrait and brief record of the life of each. Bethel: News Publishing, 1902. Pp. vii, 316.

127 _____. An album of the executive and legislative departments of Maine. Bethel: News Publishing, 1901. Pp. 196. MeHi.

128 _____. An album of the legislative departments and seventy-first Legislature of Maine, with portrait and brief record of the life of each. Bethel: News Publishing, 1903. Pp. 209.

129 BOYLE, JAMES. "Review of legislation in Maine from 1820-1915, relating to the exemption of wages." Maine Law Review, 8 (1914-1915), 100-113.

130 [BRACKETT, GEORGE EMERSON.] "The school master fifty years ago." Maine Teacher and School Officer, 3 (1860-1861), 265-269; 4 (1861-1862), 39-42. Author attribution by the editor.

131 BRADBURY, JAMES WARE. "Railroad reminiscences." MeHSC, 2 Ser., 7 (1896), 379-390.

132 BRADFORD, CHARLES. "Arnold's march to Quebec through the State of Maine." Maine Trucking News, (March, 1964), 12-15, 26.

133 BRADFORD, PETER AMORY. Fragile structures: a story of oil refineries, national security, and the coast of Maine. N.Y.: Harper's Magazine Pr., 1975. Pp. xiii, 392.

134 BRADMAN, ARTHUR. A narrative of the extraordinary sufferings of Mr. Robert Forbes, his wife, and five children, during an unfortunate journey through the wilderness--from Canada to Kennebeck River, in the year 1784 ... taken partly from their own mouths, and partly from an imperfect journal; and compiled at their request. Portland: Thomas Baker Wait's Office, 1791. Pp. 23. See also entry 916.

135 BRAULT, GÉRARD J. "The Franco-Americans of Maine." MeHSN, 12 (1972-1973), 3-28.

136 BRAZER, ESTHER STEVENS. "Zachariah Brackett Stevens: founder of the japanned tinware industry in Maine." Antiques, 29 (1936), 98-102. Author's name appears incorrectly as Fraser.

136 BRICKETT, GEORGE EDMUND. History of ovariotomy in Maine. Portland: S. Berry, 1877. Pp. 26.

138 BRIEF biographies, Maine: a biographical dictionary of who's who in Maine. Vol. I, 1926-1927. Lewiston: Lewiston Journal, [1926]. Pp. 284. No more published.

139 "BRIEF history [of the Maine Department of Health and Welfare."] Maine. Department of Health and Welfare. Report, (1942-1944), 6-7.

140 "BRIEF history of the wild lands of Maine." The Northern, 2 (April, 1922), 9-10, (May, 1922), 12, (June, 1922), 6.

141 BROWN, EVERETT S. "Maine's election date." AmPolSciRev, 29 (1935), 437-441.
History of the legislation establishing the date.

142 BROWN, JOHN MARSHALL. "Coasting voyages in the Gulf of Maine, made in the years 1604, 5, and 6, by Samuel Champlain." MeHSC, 7 (1876), 243-266.

143 _____. "The Mission of the Assumption on the River Kennebec, 1646-1652." MeHSC, 2 Ser., 1 (1890), 87-99.
Mission of the Jesuit priest Gabriel Druilletes located at various points along the Kennebec including the Augusta vicinity and Moosehead Lake vicinity.

144 BROWN, PHILIP GREELY. First editions of American authors, Americana, historical, biographical and genealogical works, books about Maine, exploration and sports; the library of the late Philip Greely Brown, Portland, Maine, sold by order of the National Bank of Commerce of Portland, executor. Public sale ... October 15 and 16.... N.Y.: American Art Association, Anderson Galleries, Inc., 1935. Pp. 99.

145 BRYANT, H. W., FIRM, BOOKSELLER, PORTLAND, ME. A check list of Maine town histories, for the use of librarians and collectors. (1902). [Portland], 1904. Pp. 4.

146 BURGESS, GEORGE. "A discourse delivered before the Maine Historical Society, at Brunswick, August 2, 1854." MeHSC, 4 (1856), 67-91.
Church history.

147 BURNHAM, HORACE M. "Pharmacy of the red man." SJMH, 6 (1918-1919), 69-71.
Medical practices among Indians.

148 BURRAGE, HENRY SWEETSER. "The attitude of Maine in the Northeastern Boundary controversy." MeHSC, 3 Ser., 1 (1904), 353-368.

149 _____. The beginnings of colonial Maine, 1602-1658. Portland: Marks Printing House, 1914. Pp. xv, 412.

150 _____. "Capt. John Wilson and some military matters in Maine in the War of 1812-15." MeHSC, 2 Ser., 10 (1899), 403-429.

151 _____. Centennial discourse, one hundredth anniversary of the Maine Baptist Missionary Convention, Waterville, Oct. 5, 1904. Portland: Marks Printing House, 1904. Pp. 21.

152 _____. "Charter rights of Massachusetts in Maine in the early part of the eighteenth century." MeHSC, 2 Ser., 6 (1895), 392-414.

153 _____. George Folsom, John A. Poor and a century of historical research with reference to early colonial Maine.... n.p., 1926. Pp. 62.

154 _____. Gorges and the grant of the Province of Maine, 1622; a tercentenary memorial. [Portland?]: Printed for the State, 1923. Pp. xv, 178.

155 _____. History of the Baptists in Maine. Portland: Marks Printing House, 1904. Pp. viii, 497.

156 _____. Maine at Louisbourg in 1745. Augusta: Burleigh & Flynt, 1910. Pp. viii, 143.

157 _____. Maine in the Northeastern Boundary controversy. [Portland]: Printed for the State, 1919. Pp. xiv, 398.

158 _____. "The Plymouth colonists in Maine." MeHSC, 3 Ser., 1 (1904), 116-146.
Kennebec Patent.

159 _____. "The St. Croix Commission, 1796-98." MeHSC, 2 Ser., 6 (1895), 225-251.
Northeast Boundary.

160 _____. "Waymouth's voyage to the coast of Maine in 1605." MeHSC, 2 Ser., 2 (1891), 225-250.

161 BUTLER, EVA L. and WENDELL STANWOOD HADLOCK. A preliminary survey of the Munsangan-Allagash waterways. Bar Harbor: Robert Abbé Museum, 1962. Pp. 31. MeHi.

162 BUXTON, HENRY [JAMES]. Assignment Down East. Brattleboro, Vt.: Stephen Daye Pr., 1938. Pp. 204.

163 BYERS, DOUGLAS S. "'Red Paint tombs' in Maine." MASB, 15 (1953-1954), 2-8.

164 BYRNE, FRANK LOYOLA. Prophet of prohibition: Neal Dow and his crusade. Madison: State Historical Society of Wisconsin for Department of History, Univ. of Wisconsin, 1961. Pp. vii, 184.

165 "THE CABOT expedition." SJMH, 3 (1915-1916), 123.
1497.

166 CALHOUN, JOHN C., JR. "Yachts of the golden era." Down East, 6 (August, 1959), 42-46.

167 CALHOUN, PHILO. "Charles Dickens in Maine." ColbLibQ, 6 (1962-1964), 137-158.
1868.

168 CAMMETT, STEPHEN. "Early homes of Longfellow." Century, 73 (1907), 647-657.
In Portland and Hiram.

169 CAMPBELL, FREDERIC L. "A legend of Jefferson Davis." Sun Up, 9 (January, 1931), 9.
His visits to Maine.

170 ____. "With Arnold in Maine." Sun Up, 9 (May, 1931), 16, 29, (July, 1931), 6, 26.
   "To be continued," but no more appeared.

171 CAMPBELL, THOMAS JOSEPH. Three historical events in Maine. N.Y.: America Pr., 1910. Pp. 46.
   Golden jubilee of St. John's, Bangor; laying of cornerstone of Church of Our Holy Redeemer, Bar Harbor; reconsecration of the Rasle Monument.

172 CAMPBELL, W. E. "Seventy-five years of waterworks progress in Maine." New England Water Works Association. Journal, 72 (June, 1958), 98-105.
   1830-1957.

173 CAMPO, CHARLES A., comp. and ed. Maine union list of periodicals, 1974. Orono: Univ. of Maine, 1974. 456 columns. MeU.

174 CANAVAN, FRANCES EBBS. "The Catholic Indians of Maine." Catholic World, 135 (1932), 81-84.

175 "CAPT. George Weymouth's pond, discovered on coast of Maine, 1605." BHistMag, 4 (1888-1889), 201-202.
   Controversy as to the location.

176 "THE CAPUCHINS in Maine." HistMag, 8 (1864), 301-304.

177 CARLES, REGINALD E. "Governors of Maine, 1860-1900." Pine Cone, 5 (Autumn, 1949), 11-15.
   Biographical sketches.

178 ____. "Governors of Maine, 1900-1948." Pine Cone, 4 (Autumn, 1948), 34-37.
   Biographical sketches.

179 CARR, JOSEPH WILLIAM and GEORGE DAVIS CHASE. "A word list from eastern Maine." Dialect Notes, 3 (1907), 239-251.

180 CARTER, ROBERT GOLDTHWAITE. "Col. Thomas Goldthwait--was he a Tory?" MeHSC, 2 Ser., 7 (1896), 23-44, 185-200, 254-274, 362-379; 8 (1897), 31-53.

181 CARY, AUSTIN. "The forests of Maine." Paper Trade Journal, (April 25, May 9, and May 16, 1896).

182 ____. "Forty years of forest use in Maine." Journal of Forestry, 33 (1935), 366-372.

183 ____. "Maine forestry in retrospect and in prospect." Maine Naturalist, 2 (1922), 148-154.

184 ____. "Notes on timber history of the Kennebec River." Maine. Forest Commissioner. Biennial Report, 12 (1933-1934), 133-147.
   1896-1933.

185 "THE CATHOLIC Church in Maine." MeCathHM, 1 (July, 1913), 39-54, (August, 1913), 29-40, (September, 1913), 5-12, (October, 1913), 49-54, (November, 1913), 37-45, (December, 1913), 52-57; 2 (January, 1914), 40-45, (February, 1914), 38-43, (March, 1914), 33-42, (April, 1914), 50-54, (May, 1914), 32-39; 3 (July, 1914), 36-46, (August, 1914), 39-43, (September, 1914), 43-48, (October, 1914), 39-48, (November, 1914), 42-48; 4 (January, 1915), 25-28, (February, 1915), 46-50, (March, 1915), 45-48, (April, 1915), 27-30, (May, 1915), 32-39, (June, 1915), 46-51; 5 (August, 1915), 45-48, (September, 1915), 40-48, (October, 1915), 42-47, (November, 1915), 19-23, (December, 1915), 38-41; 6 (January, 1916), 41-47, (February, 1916), 49-52, (March, 1916), 46-48, (April, 1916), 42-48, (May, 1916), 50-56; 7 (1916-1917), 79-88, 158-166, 272-278, 339-350.

186 "CATHOLIC footprints in Maine." MeCathHM, 7 (1916-1917), 97-101.

187 "THE CATHOLIC Indians of Maine in the Revolution." MeCathHM, 2 (May, 1914), 11-16.

188 "CATHOLIC landmarks in Maine." MeCathHM, 7 (1916-1917), 72-74.

189 CHADBOURNE, AVA HARRIET. The beginnings of education in Maine.... N.Y.: Columbia Univ., 1928. Pp. vi, 135.

190 ____. "Early social libraries in Maine." MeLAB, 31 (February, 1970), 3-16.

191 ____. A history of education in Maine, a study of a section of American educational history. Orono, 1936. Pp. xiii, 544.

192 ____. "Indian names in Maine." The Northern, 2 (September, 1922), 7.

193 ____. "Indian names in Maine towns." Pine Cone, 5 (Spring, 1949), 21-24.

194 ____. Maine place names and the peopling of its towns. Portland: Bond Wheelwright, 1955. Pp. 530.

195 ____. "Names of Maine cities." Pine Cone, 3 (Autumn, 1947), 16-19.

196 ____, comp. Readings in the history of education in Maine: a collection of sources and readings concerning the history of Maine and the development of educational theory and practice. Bangor: Burr Pr., 1932. Pp. 104.

197 CHADBOURNE, WALTER WHITMORE. A history of banking in Maine, 1799-1930. Orono: Univ. Pr., 1936. Pp. ix, 211.

198 CHADWICK, JOSEPH. "An account of a journey from Fort Pownal--now Fort Point--up the

Penobscot River to Quebec, in 1764." BHist
Mag, 4 (1888-1889), 141-148.
Notes by Joseph W. Porter.

199 CHAMBERLAIN, JOSHUA LAWRENCE. Maine. Boston:
Little, Brown, 1882. Pp. 22.

200 _____. Maine: her place in history, address
delivered at the Centennial Exhibition,
Philadelphia, Nov. 4, 1876, and in convention
of the Legislature of Maine, February 6,
1877.... Augusta: Sprague, Owen & Nash,
1877. Pp. v, 129.

201 CHAMPLIN, JAMES TIFT. "Educational institutions in Maine, while a district of Massachusetts." MeHSC, 8 (1881), 157-180.

202 CHAPMAN, J. K. "The mid-nineteenth-century
temperance movement in New Brunswick and
Maine." CanHistRev, 35 (1954), 42-60.
1830-1856.

203 CHAPMAN, LEONARD BOND. "Rev. Caleb Bradley
on the Madawaska War." MeHSC, 2 Ser., 9
(1898), 418-425.
Northeast Boundary, 1839.

204 CHASE, EDWARD EVERETT. Maine railroads, a
history of the development of the Maine railroad system. Portland: A. J. Huston, 1926.
Pp. 145.

205 CHASE, GEORGE DAVIS. "Further word lists--
Maine." Dialect Notes, 4 (1914), 151-153.

206 CHASE, HENRY, ed. Representative men of
Maine, a collection of portraits with biographical sketches of residents of the state,
who have achieved success ... to which is
added the portraits and sketches of all the
governors since the formation of the state....
Portland: Lakeside Pr., 1893. Pp. 250, liii.

207 CHASE, MARY ELLEN. A goodly heritage. N.Y.:
Henry Holt, 1932. Pp. 298.
Social life and customs.

208 _____. "My novels about Maine." ColbLibQ, 6
(1962-1964), 14-20.

209 CHASE, VIRGINIA. "Shipwreck ... the 'Portland' disaster." Down East, 4 (January,
1958), 16-18, 39-40, 42-43.

210 "CHIEF Justices of Maine." MeLB, 16 (1930-
1931), 54-64.

211 CHISHOLM, HUGH JOSEPH, 1847-1912. "History
of papermaking in Maine, and the future of
the industry." Maine. Bureau of Industrial
and Labor Statistics. Annual Report, 20
(1906), 161-169.

212 CHITTENDEN, ALBERT D. The story of the early
years of the State of Maine Board of Osteopathic Examination & Registration. Bangor:
Maine Osteopathic Association, [1964].
Pp. 15.

213 "CHRONOLOGY of the Sisters of Mercy in the
Diocese of Portland." MeCathHM, 4 (June,
1915), 5-6.

214 CHURCH, BENJAMIN. The history of the eastern
expeditions of 1689, 1690, 1692, 1696, and
1704, against the Indians and French. Henry
Martyn Dexter, ed. Boston: J. K. Wiggin and
W. P. Lunt, 1867. Pp. xxxii, 203.

215 CHURCHILL, EDWIN A. Maine communities and
the War for Independence: a guide for the
study of local Maine history as related to
the American Revolution. Augusta: Maine
State Museum, 1976. Pp. vi, 110.

216 _____ and JAMES S. LEAMON. "Maine in the
Revolution, a reader's guide." MeHSQ, 15
(1975-1976), 145-195.

217 "CHURCH'S expeditions into Maine, 1689-1690-
1692-1696-1704." BHistMag, 6 (1890-1891),
252-256.
Benjamin Church.

218 CILLEY, JONATHAN PRINCE. "Regimental his-
tories." Maine Bugle, 1 (1894), 175-178.
Includes a bibliography of histories of
Maine Civil War regiments.

219 CLARK, CALVIN MONTAGUE. American slavery and
Maine Congregationalists: a chapter in the
history of the development of anti-slavery
sentiment in the Protestant churches of the
North. Bangor, 1940. Pp. ix, 198.

220 _____. History of the Congregational churches
in Maine.... Portland: Southworth Pr., 1926-
1935. 2v.

221 CLARK, CHARLES E. Maine during the colonial
period: a bibliographical guide. Portland:
Maine Historical Society, 1974. Pp. 38.

222 _____. "The wonderful world of John Josselyn,
Gent., a glimpse of seventeenth-century
Maine." Bates College Bulletin, 73 (April,
1976), 28-30.

223 CLARK, CORNELIUS EDWARDS. "Provincial conditions in Maine in 1807." MeCP, 45 (January 15, 1958), 6-8, (February 15, 1958), 4-6.
Maine Missionary Society.

224 CLARK, LEWIS E. Trends in Maine agriculture,
1954-1964. Orono, [1966]. Pp. 20.

225 CLASSEN, H. GEORGE. Thrust and counter-thrust: the genesis of the Canada-United States boundary. Toronto: Longmans, 1965. Pp. 386.

226 CLEVELAND, GEORGE ARTHUR. Maine in verse and story. Boston: R. G. Badger, 1915. Pp. 275.

227 CLIFFORD, HAROLD BURTON. Maine and her people. (1957) With a supplement by Charlotte L. Melvin on The Story of Aroostook, Maine's last frontier. 2d ed. Freeport: Bond Wheelwright, 1963. Pp. iv, 346.

228 CLOUDMAN, S. B. "Early recollections of the Cumberland and Oxford Canal." MeHSC, 3 Ser., 1 (1904), 397-405.

229 _____. "Recollections of the old time militia and the general muster." MeHSC, 3 Ser., 2 (1906), 331-341.

230 CLOUGH, BLANCHE COLE. Grandma spins Down-East yarns. Portland: Fred L. Tower, 1953. Pp. 214. MH.

231 _____. More Down-East yarns by grandma. Book 2. Portland: House of Falmouth, 1956. Pp. 187.
Sequel to previous entry.

232 CLUBB, HENRY STEPHEN. The Maine liquor law: its origin, history, and results, including a life of Hon. Neal Dow. N.Y.: Fowler and Wells, 1856. Pp. 430.

233 CLUFF, DOHN A. "Lobster fishing on the Maine coast past and present." AmNep, 14 (1954), 203-208.

234 COATSWORTH, ELIZABETH JANE. Country neighborhood. N.Y.: Macmillan, 1944. Pp. 181.
Social life and customs.

235 _____. Maine memories. Brattleboro, Vt.: Stephen Greene Pr., 1968. Pp. ix, 165.
Social life and customs.

236 _____. Maine ways. N.Y., Macmillan, 1947. Pp. 213.
Social life and customs.

237 COBURN, LOUISE HELEN. Canal projects for the Kennebec, 1825 to 1832. [Skowhegan?, 1927?]. Pp. 21.

238 _____. "The Josselyn Botanical Society of Maine." Maine Naturalist, 1 (1921), 18-21.

239 CODMAN, JOHN. Arnold's Expedition to Quebec. (1901) 2d ed. N.Y.: Macmillan, 1902. Pp. ix, 340.

240 COE, HARRIE BADGER, ed. Maine, resources, attractions, and its people: a history. N.Y.: Lewis Historical Publishing, 1928. 4v.
Volumes 3 and 4 contain biographical material.

241 COFFIN, HAROLD WILHELM. Assignment in military intelligence. Old Town: Penobscot Pr. Associates, 1972. Pp. v, 210.
World War II.

242 COFFIN, ROBERT PETER TRISTRAM. Coast calendar. Decorations by the author. Indianapolis: Bobbs-Merrill, 1949. Unpaged.

243 _____. Kennebec, cradle of Americans. N.Y.: Farrar & Rinehart, 1937. Pp. x, 292.
Kennebec River.

244 _____. Maine, a state of grace; commencement address delivered at the University of Maine, June 14, 1937. Orono, 1937. Pp. 10.

245 _____. Maine doings. Indianapolis: Bobbs-Merrill, 1950. Pp. 266.
Social life and customs.

246 _____. "The State of Maine." American Mercury, 66 (January, 1948), 66-73.
1608-1947.

247 _____. Yankee coast. N.Y.: Macmillan, 1947. Pp. 333.
Social life and customs.

248 COLBY, (GEORGE N.) & CO. Atlas of the State of Maine including statistics and descriptions of its history.... 4th ed. Houlton, 1888. Pp. 111. MeU.

249 COLBY COLLEGE, WATERVILLE, ME. Artists active in Maine in the twentieth century. Waterville: Archives of Maine Art at Colby College, 1963. Pp. 12. Me.

250 _____. Exhibition of Maine art ... April 22-May 21, 1944. Waterville: Colby College, 1944. Unpaged.

251 COLBY COLLEGE, WATERVILLE, ME. ART DEPARTMENT. Exhibition of Maine architecture, from the 17th century to the Civil War, arranged by the Art Department of Colby College, Waterville, Maine. [Waterville, 1945]. Unpaged.

252 COLBY COLLEGE, WATERVILLE, ME. ART MUSEUM. Maine and its artists, 1710-1963, an exhibition in celebration of the sesquicentennial of Colby College, 1813-1963. Colby College Art Museum, Waterville, Maine, May 4-August 31, 1963.... [Waterville, 1963]. Pp. 31.

253 MAINE

253 COLE, JOHN N. In Maine: "Of all the winds that blow I like the northwest best...." N.Y.: Dutton, 1974. Pp. 143.

254 COLE, WILLIAM I. "Maine in literature." NEM, New Ser., 22 (1900), 726-743.

255 COLE'S EXPRESS, BANGOR ME. Connecting Maine with the nation. 40th anniversary, 1917-1957. n.p., [1957]. Pp. 44.
A history of Cole's Express.

256 COLLIER, SARGENT F. Down East: Maine, Prince Edward Island, Nova Scotia, and the Gaspé. Boston: Houghton Mifflin, 1953. Pp. 148.

257 COLLINS, W. E. "Arnold's Expedition to Quebec." BHSSC, 2 (1894-1897), 59-67.

258 "COLONEL Thomas Westbrook's expedition to Penobscot River, 1722-23." BHistMag, 5 (1889-1890), 101-103.

259 CONGDON, ISABELLE. Indian tribes of Maine. Brunswick: Brunswick Publishing, 1961. Pp. 22. MeU.

260 CONNOLLY, DONALD F. X. "A chronicle of New England Catholicism before the Mayflower landing." American Catholic Historical Society of Philadelphia. Records, 70 (March-December, 1959), 3-17, 88-108.
Voyages of explorers and fishermen and their attempted settlements in Maine, 1497-1620.

261 CONSERVATIVE BAPTIST ASSOCIATION OF MAINE. The Conservative Baptist Association of Maine, 1955-1957. n.p., [1957?]. Pp. 28. MeU.

262 COOK, JULIA ANNA. "Maine's forest fires of twenty years ago." Down East, 14 (October, 1967), 34-36, 44-47.

263 COOK, WALTER LEONARD. The story of Maine Baptists, 1904-1954. Waterville: City Job Print, 1954. Pp. 163.

264 COOLIDGE, AUSTIN JACOBS and JOHN BRAINARD MANSFIELD. History and description of New England. Maine. Boston, 1860. Pp. iv, 406.

265 COOLIDGE, PHILIP TRIPP and W. C. WHEELER. "Growth of pulpwood in Maine." Journal of Forestry, 29 (1931), 907-914.
1917-1927.

266 COOLIDGE, PHILIP TRIPP. History of the Maine woods. Bangor: Furbush-Roberts, 1963. Pp. 805.

267 COREY, ALBERT BICKMORE. The crisis of 1830-1842 in Canadian-American relations. New Haven: Yale Univ. Pr., 1941. Pp. xi, 203.
Northeast Boundary.

268 CORLISS, CARLTON JONATHAN. Railway developments in Maine; an address at Ricker Classical Institute and Ricker College Alumni Association banquet, Houlton, Maine, June 8, 1953. n.p., [1953 or 4]. 19 leaves.

269 CORNISH, LESLIE C. "A century of the Supreme Judicial Court of Maine." Maine State Bar Association. Proceedings, 22 (1920-1921), 109-144, 242-251.

270 COSTRELL, EDWIN. How Maine viewed the war, 1914-1917. Orono: Univ. Pr., 1940. Pp. v, 101.

271 CRAM, HAL. "Horses, horses, horses." Sun Up, 3 (August, 1926), 30, 76.
Horseracing since 1850.

272 _____. "The long trail of transportation in Maine." Sun Up, 2 (February, 1926), 6, 16-17.

273 _____. "The why, when, and where of Maine names." Sun Up, 3 (June, 1926), 14, 19-21.
Geographical names.

274 CRANE, ABIJAH ROBINSON. The Baptist ministers in Maine from 1804 to 1904; paper read at Waterville, October 5, 1904, at the centennial of the Maine Baptist Missionary Convention. Portland: Marks Printing House, 1904. Pp. 20.

275 CRANE, J. R. "Ships and sawmills." American Forests, 63 (August, 1957), 24-26, 54-56.
Colonial period to 1955.

276 CRITTENDEN, HENRY TEMPLE. "Wiscasset, Waterville & Farmington Railway." RLHSB, No. 57 (1942), 114-135.

277 CROWELL, MARNIE REED. "Maine Indian baskets." Down East, 21 (October, 1974), 40-43.

278 CRUMB, LAWRENCE N. "The Anglican Church in colonial Maine." HMPEC, 33 (1964), 251-260.
1605-1820.

279 CUMMINGS, EPHRAIM CHAMBERLAIN. "The Rasles Dictionary." MeHSC, 2 Ser., 6 (1895), 144-152.
A manuscript Abnaki dictionary presently in the Houghton Library, Harvard University.

280 CUMMINGS, OSMOND RICHARD. "A history of the Atlantic Shore Line Railways." Transportation, 4 (June, 1950), 1-37.
Street railroad.

281 _____. "Portland - Lewiston Interurban." Transportation, 10 (May, 1956), 1-28.
Street railroad.

282 _____. Toonervilles of Maine, the Pine Tree State. Newburyport, Mass., 1955. Pp. 52. MeBa.

283 CURRENT, RICHARD N. "Webster's propaganda and the Ashburton Treaty." MVHR, 34 (1947), 187-200.

284 CURRIER, ISABEL. "The Belfast and Moosehead Lake RR." Down East, 10 (October, 1963), 36-44.

285 CUSHMAN, DAVID QUIMBY. "Weymouth's voyage." MeHSC, 6 (1859), 307-318.
George Waymouth.

286 CUTLER, ALEXANDER MUNRO. Bent sails, a sail-making saga written in the words of a New England craftsman of square rigger days. Cincinnati: Mail It, 1962. Pp. 81.

287 DAGGETT, WINDSOR PRATT. A Down-East Yankee from the District of Maine. Portland: A. J. Huston, 1920. Pp. 80.

288 DALE, THOMAS NELSON. The granites of Maine. Washington: Govt. Print. Off., 1907. Pp. iv, 202.

289 DANA, SAMUEL TRASK. Forest fires in Maine 1916-1925. Augusta: Maine Forest Service, [1926?]. Pp. 73.

290 DANIELS, L. R. "Early Maine Conference of Unitarian Churches." Maine Unitarian, (1947), [12-14].

291 DARRAH, WILLIAM C. "A checklist of Maine photographers who issued stereographs." MeHSN, 6 (May, 1967), special supplement.
1863-1890; alphabetical and geographical listings.

292 DAUGHTERS OF THE AMERICAN REVOLUTION. MAINE. A brief history of the Maine Daughters of the American Revolution, to March 1, 1925.... Mabel Goodwin Hall, ed. [Waterville, Me.? 1925]. Pp. 60.

293 _____. History of the Maine society, Daughters of the American Revolution.... Farmington: Knowlton & McLeary, 1946. Pp. 147. MeBa.

294 DAVIAU, JEROME G. Maine's life blood. Portland: House of Falmouth, 1958. Pp. 139.
Industrial uses of water resources, 1820-1957.

295 DAVIDSON, JACQUELINE. "Maine and American artists, 1710-1963." American Artist, 27 (December, 1963), 32-39, 63-67.

296 DAVIS, GHERARDI. Alice and I go Down East again.... N.Y.: Gillis Pr., 1924. Pp. 48.
Yachting.

297 DAY, CLARENCE ALBERT. Farming in Maine, 1860-1940. Orono: Univ. of Maine Pr., 1963. Pp. v, 306.
A continuation of the next entry.

298 _____. A history of Maine agriculture, 1604-1860. Orono: Univ. Pr., 1954. Pp. ix, 318.

299 _____. How extension work in Maine began. Orono: Univ. of Maine, 1937. Pp. 23. MeBa.

300 _____. "Suggested readings in Maine history: agriculture." MeHSN, 1 (May, 1962), 4-5.

301 DAY, HOLMAN FRANCIS. "The queer folks of the Maine coast." Harper's Monthly Magazine, 119 (1909), 521-530.
Social life and customs.

302 DEANE, CHARLES. "Indians kidnapped from Maine in 1605." MHSP, 2 Ser., 2 (1885-1886), 35-38.
George Waymouth.

303 DEARBORN, VANCE E. and RONALD J. DAIGLE. A data file; Maine: population, natural increase, and migration trends, 1940-1970; births, deaths, migration, 1960-1969 (for counties and towns). Orono: Maine Cooperative Extension Service, 1971. Unpaged. MeU.

304 DE COSTA, BENJAMIN FRANKLIN. Ancient Norombega, or The voyages of Simon Ferdinando and John Walker to the Penobscot River, 1579-1580. Albany: J. Munsell's Sons, 1890. Pp. 12.
A revision of the author's "Simon Ferdinando and John Walker in Maine, 1579-1580." NEHGR, 44 (1890), 149-158.

305 _____. "Champdoré in New England, 1608." NEHGR, 45 (1891), 137-141.
Pierre Angibaut.

306 _____. The Northmen in Maine: a critical examination of views expressed in connection with the subject, by Dr. J. H. [i.e. G.] Kohl, in Volume 1 of the New Series of the Maine Historical Society, to which are added criticisms on other portions of the work, and a chapter on the discovery of Massachusetts Bay. Albany: J. Munsell, 1870. Pp. 146.
See also entry 656.

307 _____. Sketches of the coast of Maine and Isles of Shoals, with historical notes. New York, 1869. Pp. 221.

308 DECROW, GERTRUDE. "Folklore from Maine." Journal of American Folklore, 5 (1892), 318-320.

309 DEEMS, MERVIN MONROE. Maine--first of conferences: a history of the Maine Conference-United Church of Christ. Bangor: Furbush-Roberts, 1974. Pp. vii, 168.

310 _____. The Maine Missionary Society, 1807-1957. Portland: Marks Printing House, [1957]. Pp. 31.

311 MAINE

311 DE LASKI, JOHN. "Glacial action about Penobscot Bay." American Journal of Science, 87
(1864), 335-344.

312 DEMERITT, DWIGHT BURGESS. Maine made guns
and their makers. Hallowell: Published for
the Maine State Museum by P. S. Plumer, Jr.,
1973. Pp. vii, 209.

313 DENIS, MICHAEL J. Maine towns and counties:
what was what, where and when. n.p., 1973.
63 leaves. MeHi.

314 DE PEYSTER, JOHN WATTS. The Dutch at the
North Pole and the Dutch in Maine. A paper
read before the New-York Historical Society,
3d March, 1857. N.Y.: Printed for the Society, 1857. Pp. 80.

315 [_____]. Proofs considered of the early
settlement of Acadie by the Dutch; being an
appendix to The Dutch in Maine. Poughkeep-
sie, N.Y.: Platt & Schram, 1858. Pp. 19.

316 DESJARDINS, PHILLIPPE E. "French Canadians,
central and southern Maine." Church World,
21 (June 1, 1951), 4, 8-10.

317 "THE DEVELOPMENT of our telephone system."
The Northern, 5 (June, 1925), 3-5.
Great Northern Paper Co.

318 DIBNER, MARTIN. Seacoast Maine: people and
places. Garden City, N.Y.: Doubleday, 1973.
Pp. 208.
Social life and customs.

319 DIETZ, LEW. "The character of Maine." Down
East, 21 (August, 1974), 78-80, 85, 93-94.
Social life and customs.

320 _____. "Kennebec log drive." Down East, 15
(August, 1968), 52-56, 61.
Kennebec Log Driving Company.

321 _____. "Man on the Maine frontier--the Maine
Finn." Down East, 19 (January, 1973), 36-39,
66, 68.

322 _____. "The unabashed apostles of the Allagash." Yankee, 31 (March, 1967), 88-93,
110-112, 114-115.

323 DILLINGHAM, CHARLES A., comp. The Penobscots.
Bangor: Record Print, [1900?]. Unpaged.
MeBa.
Indians.

324 DINGLEY, EDWARD N., JR. "The ship, the man,
and the lady." Steamboat Bill, 28 (1971),
200-203.
S.S. Governor Dingley named after Nelson
Dingley, Jr. and christened by Mrs. Edward N.
Dingley.

325 DINGLEY, NELSON, JR. "The State of Maine."
NEM, New Ser., 4 (1891), 547-570.

326 DINGLEY, ROBERT JORDAN. "Maine's pioneer
automobile men." Down East, 13 (March, 1967),
52-55.

327 DIXON, JOSEPH H. "The Aroostook War." Old
Eliot, 8 (1908), 192-195.

328 DOCUMENTARY history of the Maine Law: comprising the original Maine Law, the New-York
Prohibitory Liquor Law, legislative debates,
arguments, judicial decisions, statistics,
important correspondence; "inquisition" and
prohibition versus "freedom" and anti-
prohibition.... N.Y.: Hall & Brother, 1855.
Pp. vi, 126.

329 DODD, MARION E. "Along New England's book
trails: I. Maine." Yankee, 4 (October,
1938), 19-21, 32-34.
Sketches of several Maine authors.

330 DODGE, STANLEY D. "Depopulation of Maine from
1840-1890." Association of American Geographers. Annals, 30 (1943), 86-87.

331 DOLE, NATHAN HASKELL and IRWIN LESLIE GORDON.
Maine of the sea and pines; a description of
its scenic beauty, its rugged coastline, its
mountains, lakes and rivers; an account of
its settlement, its Indians and their legends,
and its appeal to the sportsman and vacationist; a survey of its commercial resources and
industries, and its possibilities for water
power development. Boston: L. C. Page,
1928. Pp. x, 375.

332 DOLE, RICHARD F. "Mother Hubbards, Mallet
Compounds and Hudsons, a history of Maine Cen-
tral steam power." Railroad Enthusiast, 9
(Winter and Spring, 1972), 20-32.

333 DOLE, SAMUEL THOMAS. "The Cumberland and Oxford Canal." MeHSC, 2 Ser., 9 (1898), 264-
271.

334 DONOVAN, MICHAEL C. The St. Croix boundary
question.... [Nashville, Tenn., 19--].
Pp. 15.

335 DOOLITTLE, DUANE, comp. Only in Maine: selections from Down East Magazine. Barre,
Mass.: Barre Publishers, 1969. Pp. ix, 274.

336 DORSETT, E. LEE. "The Maine whalers." Down
East, 2 (April, 1956), 14-15, 38-39.

337 DOW, FRED M. "History of prohibition in
Maine." Americana, 23 (1929), 182-189.

338 DOW, ROBERT L. "Commercial fisheries of
Maine." Maine Townsman, 16 (February, 1954),
8-9, 16, 18.

339 _____. The Maine blackback flounder: resource and fishery, 1925-1965. Augusta:
Maine Department of Sea and Shore Fisheries,
1967. 4 leaves. MeU.

340 ____. "Some characteristics of Maine coastal kitchen middens." MeArchSocB, 11 (Summer, 1971), 6-13.

341 DOW, STERLING THAYER. Maine postal history and postmarks. (1943) Lawrence, Mass.: Quarterman Publications, 1976. Pp. 235. MeHi.

342 DOWNEAST politics: the government of the State of Maine. James F. Horan, comp. Dubuque, Iowa: Kendall/Hunt, 1975. Pp. x, 189.

343 DRAKE, SAMUEL ADAMS. The Pine-tree coast. Boston: Estes & Lauriat, 1891. Pp. 393.

344 DRUILLETTES, GABRIEL. "Journal of an embassy from Canada to the United Colonies of New England, in 1650." New-York Historical Society. Collections, 2 Ser., 3 Pt. 1, (1857), 303-328.
Translated, with notes, by John Gilmary Shea.

345 DRUMMOND, JOSIAH HAYDEN. "Bibliographic memorandum of the laws of Maine." MeHSC, 2 Ser., 2 (1891), 391-402.

346 ____. The Maine Central Railroad system, an uncompleted historical sketch. n.p., 1902. Pp. 84.

347 DUBROS times: selected depositions of Maine Revolutionary War veterans. Sylvia J. Sherman, ed. Augusta: Maine State Archives, 1975. Pp. viii, 20.

348 DUNNACK, HENRY ERNEST. The Maine book. Augusta, 1920. Pp. xiii, 338.

349 ____. Rural life in Maine. Augusta: C. E. Nash & Son, 1928. Pp. 165.

350 DUREN, ELNATHAN FREEMAN. General Conference of the Congregational Churches in Maine; churches and ministers from 1672 to 1867, with the minutes of the forty-first annual meeting ... June 25, 26, 27, 1867. Portland: Brown Thurston, 1867. Pp. 157. MBC.
A continuation for the period 1867 to 1876 appears in the "Minutes" of the Conference for 1876 on pp. 147-184. A further continuation for the period 1877 to 1886 appears in the "Minutes" for 1886 on pp. 169-208.

351 DURIN, DEA. "Statistics of the Maine General Conference of Churches, from its organization." CongQ, 8 (1866), 309-310.

352 DURNIN, RICHARD GERRY. "For piety, virtue and useful knowledge: Maine's eighteenth-century academies." MeHSN, 11 (1971-1972), 43-50, 54-63.

353 DUROST, LILLIAN MILLS and GRACE E. FITZ. History, Federation of Business and Professional Women's Clubs of Maine. n.p. [1944?]. Pp. 87. MeHi.

354 DYER, ISAAC WATSON. "The Cumberland and Oxford Canal." SJMH, 12 (1924), 94-113.

355 DYER, RICHARD NYE. "253 years of Maine art." Down East, 9 (May, 1963), 20-25.

356 DYER, WALTER A. "Historical and documented antiques from Maine." The Antiquarian, 14 (1930), 60-62, 80, 88.
Furniture.

357 "EARLY Indian tribes in Maine and Nova Scotia." MeHistMag, 8 (1893), 89.

358 "EARLY mills on Penobscot River." BHistMag, 5 (1889-1890), 82-86.

359 "EARLY post offices in eastern Maine." BHistMag, 1 (1885-1886), 12-13.

360 "EARTHQUAKE history of Maine." Earthquake Information Bulletin, 5 (May-June, 1973), 26-29.

361 EATON, LOUIS WOODBURY. Pork, molasses, and timber; stories of bygone days in the logging camps of Maine. N.Y.: Exposition Pr., [1954]. Pp. 75.

362 ECKSTORM, FANNIE HARDY. "Champlain's visit to the Penobscot." SJMH, 1 (1913-1914), 56-65.

363 ____. The handicrafts of the modern Indians of Maine. Bar Harbor, 1932. Pp. 72.

364 ____. "History of the Chadwick Survey from Fort Pownal in the District of Maine to the province of Quebec in Canada in 1764." SJMH, 14 (1926), 63-89.
Survey of a feasible route for a highway from the Penobscot River to Canada.

365 ____. Indian place-names of the Penobscot Valley and the Maine coast. Orono: Univ. Pr., 1941. Pp. xxix, 272.

366 ____ and MARY WINSLOW SMYTH. Minstrelsy of Maine: folk-songs and ballads of the woods and the coast. Boston: Houghton Mifflin, 1927. Pp. xvi, 390.

367 ECKSTORM, FANNIE HARDY. Old John Neptune and other Maine Indian shamans. Portland: Southworth-Anthoensen Pr., 1945. Pp. xii, 209.

368 "EDUCATIONAL legislation in Maine." Maine Journal of Education, 6 (1872), 218-223, 253-257.
Signed: Theta.

369 MAINE

369 EDWARDS, GEORGE THORNTON. Music and musicians of Maine, being a history of the progress of music in the territory which has come to be known as the State of Maine, from 1604 to 1928. Portland: Southworth Pr., 1928. Pp. xxv, 542.

370 EDWARDS, LLEWELLYN NATHANIEL. The evolution of early American bridges ... with a brief discussion of the geology of Maine rivers and streams and a history of six early Maine bridges. Orono, 1934. Pp. 30.

371 ELKINS, L. WHITNEY. "Maine's lime industry." Sun Up, 2 (October, 1925), 7, 56.

372 _____. The story of Maine: coastal Maine. Bangor: Hillsborough Company, 1924. Pp. 392.

373 ELWELL, EDWARD HENRY. "The newspaper press in Maine." MPAP, 22 (1885), 14-32.

374 EMERSON, WALTER CRANE. The latchstring [to] Maine woods and waters. Boston: Houghton Mifflin, 1916. Pp. xi, 228.

375 _____. When north winds blow. Lewiston: Journal Printshop and Bindery, 1922. Pp. 229.

376 EMERY, GEORGE FREEMAN. "Our state christening: its name." MeHSC, 2 Ser., 4 (1893), 337-350.

377 _____. "Reminiscences of bench and bar." MeHSC, 2 Ser., 8 (1897), 113-143.

378 _____. "The voice of Maine as heard in the genesis of our nationality." MeHSC, 2 Ser., 2 (1891), 51-82.
Delegates to the Philadelphia Constitutional Convention.

379 EMERY, LUCILIUS ALONZO. "Changes in equity procedure in Maine." Maine Law Review, 9 (1915-1916), 29-34.
1820-1915.

380 _____. "Changes in the judicial system of Maine." Maine Law Review, 9 (1915-1916), 89-97.

381 _____. "The growth of equity powers of the Maine courts." Maine Law Review, 9 (1915-1916), 1-7.
1821-1891.

382 _____. "Maine and the federal Constitution." SJMH, 5 (1917-1918), 32-33.
Maine's part in the Constitutional Convention of 1788.

383 _____. "Some changes in the procedure in actions at law in Maine." Maine Law Review, 9 (1915-1916), 219-224.
1821-1879.

384 ENGLISH, THOMAS DUNN. Prohibition in Maine, a scathing exposure of the result of thirty years' effort.... Newark, N.J., 1882. Pp. 12. MeHi.

385 ENO, JOEL N. "The expansion of Maine--chronological--based on official records." Americana, 25 (1931), 380-410.

386 EVERSON, JENNIE G. Tidewater ice of the Kennebec River. Freeport: Published for the Maine State Museum, by Bond Wheelwright, 1970. Pp. xiii, 241.

387 THE EXCITER Magazine, electric railroad edition. Augusta: Central Maine Power Co., 1960. Pp. 28. Me.
Street railroads.

388 EXPLORATIONS in Maine history: miscellaneous papers. Proceedings of the sesquicentennial colloquium of the University of Maine, Orono, March 30, 1970. Orono: Univ. of Maine, 1970. Pp. 64. MeHi.

389 EXPRESSIONS from Maine, 1976. Hobe Sound, Fla.: Hobe Sound Gallery, [1976]. Unpaged. MeU.
A catalog of works by Maine artists with accompanying biographical sketches.

390 FAIRFIELD, JOHN. The letters of John Fairfield; a representative in Congress from 1835 to 1837; a member of the Senate of the United States from 1843 to 1847, and a governor of Maine in 1839, 1840, 1842 and a part of 1843. Arthur G. Staples, ed. Lewiston: Lewiston Journal, 1922. Pp. xxxiv, 475.

391 FARNHAM, MARY FRANCES, comp. The Farnham papers.... Portland: Thurston Print, 1901-1902. 2v.
Documents relating to the territorial history of Maine, 1603-1871; volume two has the imprint Portland: Lefavor-Tower, 1902.

392 FARRER, HIRAM P. "Maine historical anecdotes." SJMH, 13 (1925), 242-244.

393 FARRINGTON, INEZ. Maine is forever. Manchester: Falmouth Publishing House, 1954. Pp. 164.
Social life and customs.

394 _____. My Maine folks. Portland: Bond Wheelwright, 1956. Pp. 96.
Social life and customs.

395 FASSETT, FREDERICK GARDINER. A history of newspapers in the District of Maine, 1785-1820. Orono: Univ. Pr., 1932. Pp. 242.

396 FAVOUR, EDITH. Indian games, toys, and pastimes of Maine and the Maritimes. Bar Harbor: Robert Abbe Museum, 1974. Pp. 21.

397 FEDERAL WRITERS' PROJECT. MAINE. Maine: a guide to the Vacation State. Ray Bearse, ed. 2d ed. rev. Boston: Houghton Mifflin, 1969. Pp. xii, 460.
First edition of 1937 has the title: Maine, a guide 'Down East.'

398 FELLOWS, DANA WILLIS. History of dentistry in Maine; being a history of the Maine Dental Society.... Portland: Maine Dental Society, 1924. Pp. 126. MeBa.

399 FELT, JOSEPH BARLOW. Statistics of towns, Maine territory. American Statistical Association. Collections, 1 (1847), 57-99.

400 FENN, WILLIAM HENRY. The hope of Maine, a discourse delivered Thanksgiving Day, Nov. 26, 1868. Portland: Hoyt & Fogg, 1868. Pp. 23.

401 FEWKES, JESSE WALTER. "A contribution to Passamaquoddy folk-lore." Journal of American Folklore, 3 (1890), 257-280.

402 "THE FIRST English settlements in that part of Acadia now eastern Maine." MeHistMag, 8 (1893), 1-4.

403 "THE FIRST European settlement in New England." BHistMag, 2 (1886-1887), 225-228.
Pierre du Gast, Sieur de Mont, 1604.

404 FISHER, CHARLES E. "Locomotives of the Maine Central R.R." RLHSB, No. 55 (1941), 64-72; No. 56 (1941), 87-97.

405 FISHER, ELIJAH. Elijah Fisher's journal while in the War for Independence, and continued two years after he came to Maine, 1775-1784. William Berry Lapham, ed. Augusta: Badger & Manley, 1880. Pp. 29.

406 FISHER, J. ALVIN. "Maine coast Christmas." Down East, 8 (January, 1962), 33-34, 42-43.

407 "FISHERIES on the coast of Maine and Acadia." MeHistMag, 9 (1894-1895), 210-211.

408 FLETCHER, LUCILLE. "Indian legends of Maine's magnificent mountains." Sun Up, 3 (November, 1926), 12, 18-20.

409 ____. "Romance and history in Maine trees." Sun Up, 5 (February, 1928), 5, 21, 23, 26.

410 FOBES, CHARLES BARTLETT. "Historic forest fires in Maine." Economic Geography, 24 (1948), 269-273.

411 ____. "The ice clearing dates of the Maine lakes." American Meteorological Society. Bulletin, 26 (1945), 331-333.
1880-1944.

412 ____. "Indian names for Maine mountains." Appalachia, 34 (1962-1963), 521-529.

413 ____. "Lightning fires in the forests of northern Maine, 1926-1940." Journal of Forestry, 42 (1944), 291-293.

414 ____. "Maine winters--are they getting warmer or colder?" Down East, 22 (January, 1976), 28-33, 63.

415 ____. "Path of the settlement and distribution of population of Maine." Economic Geography, 20 (1944), 65-69.

416 ____. "Snowfall in Maine." GeogRev, 32 (1942), 245-251.
1895-1935.

417 FOGG, W. FRED P. The Republican Party in American politics, with a brief account of the movements to which the present great organization can trace its origin, together with the history of its formation in Maine on the recurrence of the thirtieth anniversary. Lewiston, 1884. Pp. 57.

418 FOLSOM, GEORGE. A catalogue of original documents in the English archives, relating to the early history of the State of Maine.... N.Y.: G. B. Teubner, 1858. Pp. iv, 135.

419 ____. "Discourse before the [Maine Historical] Society at its annual meeting, Sept. 6, 1846." MeHSC, 2 (1847), 3-79.
Discovery and settlement.

420 FOSTER, BENJAMIN BROWNE. Down East diary. Charles H. Foster, ed. [Orono]: Univ. of Maine at Orono Pr., 1975. Pp. 377.

421 FOSTER, ELIZABETH. The islanders. Boston: Houghton Mifflin, 1946. Pp. 348.
Rangeley Lakes.

422 FRANKLIN, LYNN. Profiles of Maine. Waldoboro: Maine Antique Digest, 1976. Pp. 160. MeU.
Biographies.

423 FREDYMA, JAMES P. A directory of Maine silversmiths and watch and clockmakers. Hanover, N.H., 1972. Pp. v, 26.
1636-1904.

424 FREEMAN, CHARLES. "Historical sketch of Presbyterianism in the State of Maine, with some account of Presbyterianism in New England." New Hampshire Repository, 1 (1846), 253-263.

425 ____. "History of the General Conference of Maine." American Quarterly Register, 10 (1837), 154-158.
Includes list of Congregational ministers by county.

426 FREEMASONS. MAINE. GRAND LODGE. Exercises at the seventy-fifth anniversary of the Grand Lodge of Maine, Free and Accepted Masons,

May 8, 1895. Portland: Stephen Berry, 1895. Pp. 44.
Includes historical address by Edward P. Burnham.

427 _____. Proceedings at the centennial celebration of the Grand Lodge of Maine, Ancient Free and Accepted Masons, held at Masonic Temple. Portland, Maine, Wednesday, May 5, 1920. Charles B. Davis, comp. Portland: Tucker, 1920. Pp. 194.

428 FROST, JOHN ELDRIDGE. Maine genealogy: a bibliographical guide. Portland: Maine Historical Society, 1977. Pp. 46.

429 FULLER, HENRY MORRILL. Sir Ferdinando Gorges, 1566-1647, naval and military commander, father of English colonization in America. N.Y., Newcomen Society in North America, 1952. Pp. 24.

430 FULLER, NATHAN. "Maine Christmas, 1655." Down East, 2 (November, 1955-January, 1956), 34-35.

431 FURBUSH, MRS. C. G. "Baker family." MHGR, 8 (1895), 154-167.

432 GALLATIN, ALBERT. "A memoir on the North Eastern Boundary." New-York Historical Society. Proceedings, (1843), Appendix.

433 GANONG, WILLIAM FRANCIS. "The Ashburton Treaty." New Brunswick Magazine, 1 (1898), 297-305.

434 _____. "A monograph of the evolution of the boundaries of the Province of New Brunswick." Royal Society of Canada. Proceedings and Transactions, 2 Ser., 7 Pt. 2 (1901), 139-449.

435 _____. "The St. Croix of the Northeastern Boundary." MagAmHist, 26 (1891), 261-265.
Treaty of 1873.

436 GARDINER, HENRY. New England's vindication. Charles Edward Banks, ed. Portland: The Gorges Society, 1884. Pp. 83.
The editor believed the author to be Edward Godfrey.

437 GARDINER, ROBERT HALLOWELL, 1782-1864. Early recollections of Robert Hallowell Gardiner, 1782-1864. Hallowell: White & Horne, 1936. Pp. 226.

438 _____. "History of the Kennebec Purchase." MeHSC, 2 (1847), 269-294.

439 _____. "Observations on the opening and closing of the Kennebec River, Maine." Smithsonian Institution. Annual Report, (1858), 434-436.
1785-1803.

440 GARNISS, GEORGE W. Historical beginnings. [Yarmouth: Yarmouth Historical Society], 1970. Unpaged. Me.

441 GAUVIN, MARIE ANNE. Linguistic and cultural heritage of the Acadians of Maine and New Brunswick. Madawaska: Priv. Print, 1969. Pp. 56.

442 GEAGAN, BILL. The good trail. N.Y.: Coward-McCann, 1954. Pp. 237.

443 "GENERAL Knox and the Bingham Purchase, 1791." BHistMag, 5 (1889-1890), 164-165.

444 GETCHELL, IRA E. Tables showing the magnetic declination in the State of Maine from 1609 to 1880, with notes on the variation of the compass; the secular, the annual and the diurnal change. North Vassalboro, 1880. Unpaged.

445 GILL, GEORGE J. "Edward Everett and the Northeastern Boundary controversy." NEQ, 42 (1969), 201-213.

446 GILLETT, ELIPHALET. "Complete list of the Congregational ministers, pastors of churches, in the State of Maine, from the settlement of the country to the present time, (September, 1841)." American Quarterly Register, 13 (1840-1841), 144-162, 253-269; 14 (1841-1842), 269-284.

447 GILMAN, STANWOOD CUSHING and MARGARET COOK GILMAN. Land of the Kennebec; 'ye great and beneficial river,' 1604-1965. Boston: Branden Pr., 1966. Pp. 173.

448 GIVEN, CHARLES S. "Early locomotive[s] of the Maine Central Railroad." RLHSB, No. 12 (1926), 34-38.

449 _____. "The first locomotives in the State of Maine." RLHSB, No. 15 (1927), 34-37.

450 _____. "The Maine Central Railroad and its leased lines." RLHSB, No. 3 (1922), 45-53.

451 GODFREY, JOHN EDWARDS. "The ancient Penobscot." MeHSC, 7 (1876), 1-22, 103-105.
River.

452 _____. "The ancient Penobscot, or Panawanskek." HistMag, 3 Ser., 1 (1872), 84-92.
River.

453 _____. Bashaba and the Tarratines. MeHSC, 7 (1876), 93-102.
Indians.

454 _____. "Castine the younger." HistMag, 3 Ser., 2 (1873), 121-127.
Baron Anselm de Saint Castin.

455 _____. "Norambega." MeHSC, 8 (1881), 317-332.

456 GOLDEN era of logging on the Penobscot. [Bangor]: Penobscot Heritage, 1970. Pp. 12. MeBa.

457 GOODWIN, EMMA R. "Old school days on the Maine coast." NEM, 48 (1912-1913), 474-480.

458 GOODWIN, WILLIAM FREDERIC, ed. "Thatcher Papers." HistMag, 2 Ser., 6 (1869), 257-271. George Thatcher.

459 GOOLD, WILLIAM. "Governor Christopher Gore and his visit to Maine." MeHSC, 2 Ser., 5 (1894), 71-80. In 1809; Governor of Massachusetts.

460 GORDON, ADELBERT W. "Schooling in unorganized territory in Maine." SJMH, 12 (1924), 173-175.

461 GORDON, HUGH TAYLOR. The Treaty of Washington, concluded August 9, 1842, by Daniel Webster and Lord Ashburton. Berkeley, Calif: Univ. Pr., 1908. Pp. 85. Also paged [173]-257.

462 GORGES, RAYMOND. The story of a family through eleven centuries, illustrated by portraits and pedigrees, being a history of the family of Gorges. Boston: Merrymount Pr., 1944. Pp. xxiv, 289.

463 GORHAM STATE COLLEGE. A manual of Maine history; a guide for the teaching of Maine history ... by the class of 1933 in history methods. [Gorham, 1933?]. Variously leaved. Me.

464 GOSS, LEROY E. Afterglow: a Maine narrative of Penobscot Bay islanders. Portland: House of Falmouth, 1966. Pp. 158. Social life and customs.

465 GOULD, EDWARD KALLOCH. British and Tory marauders on the Penobscot. Rockland, 1932. Pp. 41.

466 GOULD, JOHN. And one to grow on: recollections of a Maine boyhood. N.Y.: William Morrow, 1949. Pp. 253.

467 _____. The Jonesport raffle, and numerous other Maine veracities. Boston: Little, Brown, 1969. Pp. 191.

468 _____ and LILLIAN ROSS. Maine lingo: boiled owls, billdads & wazzats. Camden: Down East Magazine, 1975. Pp. xiv, 342.

469 GOULD, JOHN. "Railroading the Maine mail." Down East, 16 (November, 1969), 24-27.

470 _____. "Who owns off-shore Maine?" Yankee, 34 (March, 1970), 64-69, 102-107.

471 GOULD, RALPH ERNEST. Yankee drummer. N.Y.: Whittlesey House, 1947. Pp. 236. Commercial travelers.

472 _____. Yankee storekeeper. N.Y.: Whittlesey House, 1946. Pp. vi, 195.

473 GOVE, WILLIAM G. "Rough logging on the Wild River Railroad." Down East, 17 (November, 1970), 30-33, 64-65, 68, 73-75, 77-79, 81-82.

474 "GOVERNORS of Maine, 1820 to 1892." MeHistMag, 7 (1891-1892), 121-130. Biographical sketches.

475 GOWER, CALVIN W. "The CCC: the forest service and politics in Maine, 1933-1936." New England Social Studies Bulletin, 30 (Spring, 1973), 15-21. Civilian Conservation Corps.

476 GRACE, PATRICK W. "The octagonals." Down East, 23 (October, 1976), 40-43. Houses.

477 GRAHAM, ELINOR MISH. Maine charm string. N.Y.: Macmillan, 1946. Pp. 231. Social life and customs.

478 _____. My window looks Down East. N.Y.: Macmillan, 1951. Pp. 218. Social life and customs.

479 _____. Our way Down East. N.Y.: Macmillan, 1943. Pp. 173. Social life and customs.

480 GRAHAM, FRANK. Where the place called morning lies. N.Y.: Viking Pr., 1973. Pp. xvi, 238. Petroleum industry and the environment.

481 GRAND ARMY OF THE REPUBLIC. DEPARTMENT OF MAINE. Historical journal, 1867-1948.... Portland, 1948. Pp. 69. Me.

482 GRANT, PHILIP A., JR. "The campaign of 1834 and the bank question." MeHSN, 12 (1972-1973), 72-83.

483 GRAY, ROLAND PALMER, ed. Songs and ballads of the Maine lumberjacks, with other songs from Maine. Cambridge: Harvard Univ. Pr., 1924. Pp. xxi, 191.

484 GREAT NORTHERN PAPER COMPANY. A greater Great Northern. Wood, water, power, and people, making paper in a completely integrated operation, from forest to consumer. Bangor, [1953?]. Pp. 52.

485 GREEN, SAMUEL M. "Maine's architectural heritage." Colby Alumnus, 35 (October, 1945), 7-9.

486 [GREENE, CHARLES WARREN]. Maine. Philadelphia: J. B. Lippincott, 1890. Pp. 7.

487 GREENE, MARC T. "The old home ship." Ships and the Sea, 7 (Fall, 1957), 38-39. 'Kennebec'; sidewheeler steamer operating between Bath and Boston.

488   GREENING, W. E. "The historic Kennebec
       Road." Canadian Geographical Journal, 75
       (1967), 162-167.

489   GREENLEAF, JONATHAN. Sketches of the eccle-
       siastical history of the State of Maine,
       from the earliest settlement to the present
       time. Portsmouth, N.H.: Harrison Gray,
       1821. Pp. vi, 293.
         Copy at the Maine Historical Society con-
       tains manuscript additions and corrections
       by the author.

490   GREENLEAF, MOSES. A statistical view of the
       District of Maine; more especially with
       reference to the value and importance of its
       interior. Boston: Cummings and Hilliard,
       1816. Pp. viii, 154.

491   _____. A survey of the State of Maine, in
       reference to its geographical features,
       statistics and political economy; illustrated
       by maps. Portland: Shirley and Hyde, 1829.
       Pp. viii, 468.

492   GRIFFIN, JOSEPH. History of the press of
       Maine. Brunswick: The Press, [1872].
       Pp. 284 [i.e. 276].
         Includes a "Bibliography of Maine," on
       pp. [215]-272.

493   _____. Supplement to the history of the
       press of Maine, with complete indexes....
       Brunswick, [1874]. Pp. 289-320.
         Pagination continued from previous entry.

494   GRIFFIN, RALPH H., comp. Letters of a New
       England coaster, 1868-1872. n.p., [1968].
       Pp. 284.
         Seafaring life.

495   GRIFFITH, FRANK CARLOS, comp. Maine's hall
       of fame; Griffith's list of men and women
       born in Maine who have risen to distinction.
       [South Poland?], 1905. Pp. 12.

496   GRIFFITH, GEORGE BANCROFT, comp. The poets
       of Maine; a collection of specimen poems
       from over four hundred verse-makers of the
       Pine-Tree State, with biographical sketches.
       Portland: Elwell, Pickard, 1888. Pp. viii,
       856.

497   GRIFFITHS, THOMAS MORGAN. Maine sources in
       'The house of the seven gables.' Waterville,
       1945. Pp. viii, 49.

498   _____ and ARTHUR MORGAN GRIFFITHS, eds. A
       pictorial history of the State of Maine on
       the occasion of its 150th birthday, 1970.
       Lewiston: Twin City Printery, 1970. Un-
       paged.

499   GRINDLE, ROGER LEE. Quarry and kiln: the
       story of Maine's lime industry. Rockland:
       Courier-Gazette, 1971. Pp. 331.

500   GROVER, ARCHER LEWIS. Historical graph show-
       ing senators and representatives from the
       State of Maine to the United States Congress,
       1820-1946. Hallowell, 1946. Broadside,
       22 1/2 x 15 1/4 inches. MeU.

501   GRUENING, ERNEST. "Maine as a political
       barometer." Current History, 37 (1932-1933),
       420-424.
         Elections.

502   GUIGNARD, MICHAEL. "Maine's Corporation Sole
       controversy." MeHSN, 12 (1972-1973), 111-
       130.
         An 1887 law which made the Bishop of Port-
       land sole owner of all parish property in
       his diocese.

503   GYLES, JOHN. Memoirs of odd adventures,
       strange deliverances, &c. in the captivity of
       John Gyles, Esq; commander of the garrison on
       St. George's River. Boston: S. Kneeland &
       T. Green, 1736. Pp. 40.
         Manuscript note on flyleaf of a copy in the
       Boston Public Library states that this work
       was actually written by Joseph Seccombe.

504   HAAG, JAMES J. A study of plantation govern-
       ment in Maine. Orono: Bureau of Public Ad-
       ministration, Univ. of Maine, 1973. Pp. 20.

505   HADLOCK, WENDELL STANWOOD and ERNEST STANLEY
       DODGE. "A canoe from the Penobscot River."
       AmNep, 8 (1948), 289-301.

506   HADLOCK, WENDELL STANWOOD. "Indian relics in
       the Maine woods." In the Maine Woods, (1941),
       55-59.

507   _____. "Observations concerning the 'Red
       Paint culture.'" American Antiquity, 7
       (1941), 156-161.

508   HAGGERTY, MICHAEL. "Maine's big ditch: the
       Cumberland-Oxford Canal." Down East, 19
       (August, 1972), 66-69, 101, 104.

509   [HAIG, GEORGE CANTERBURY]. Land of enchant-
       ment: the Penobscot Bay, Mount Desert region
       of Maine. Concord, N.H.: Sugar Ball Pr.,
       1945. Pp. 181.

510   HALE, CLARENCE. "A century of the Federal
       courts in Maine." Maine Bar Association.
       Proceedings, 22 (1920-1921), 72-108.

511   _____. "The State of Maine." SJMH, 9 (1921),
       3-8.

512   HALE, HORATIO EMMONS. Remarks on the lan-
       guage of the St. John's or Wlastukweek Indi-
       ans, with a Penobscot vocabulary. Boston,
       1834. Pp. 8.

513   HALE, NATHAN. "North Eastern and Northern
       Boundary." North American Review, 33 (1831),
       261-286.

514 ____. "The North Eastern Boundary." North American Review, 26 (1828), 421-444.

515 HALE, RICHARD WALDEN, JR. "The forgotten Maine Boundary Commission." MHSP, 71 (1953-1957), 147-155.
Northeast Boundary.

516 HALE, ROBERT. Early days of church and state in Maine. Brunswick: [Bowdoin] College, 1910. Pp. 52.

517 HALL, CHARLES B. "The National Guard of the State of Maine." Outing, 29 (1896-1897), 77-80, 181-184, 285-288, 388-391, 493-496, 597-600; 30 (1897), 77-80, 182-184, 281-284.
History to 1895.

518 HALL, DREW BERT. "Reference list on Maine local history." New York State Library. Bibliography Bulletin, No. 28 (June, 1901), 775-917.
Supplemented by entry 933.

519 HALL, EDWARD WINSLOW. History of higher education in Maine. Washington: Govt. Print. Off., 1903. Pp. 241.

520 HALL, ROBERT E. "Maine's admission to the Union." SJMH, 8 (1920), 8-18.

521 HALLET, RICHARD. "All finished with the engines." Down East, 8 (June, 1962), 44-47.
Steamboats.

522 ____. "When prohibiton came to Maine." Yankee, 25 (February, 1961), 38-41.

523 HALLOCK, LEAVITT HOMAN. Discourse delivered at the 75th anniversary of the Bible Society of Maine at Williston Church, Portland, Maine, May 24, 1885. Portland: William M. Marks, 1885. Pp. 16. MeB.

524 HAMLIN, CHARLES. "The Supreme Court of Maine." Green Bag, 7 (1895), 457-475, 504-523, 553-576; 8 (1896), 14-27, 61-82, 111-127.

525 HAMLIN, HELEN. Nine mile bridge: three years in the Maine woods. N.Y.: W. W. Norton, 1945. Pp. 233.

526 HAMM, MARGHERITA ARLINA. "The last settlement of a race." Peterson Magazine, New Ser., 7 (1897), 640-647.
Penobscot Indians.

527 HANCE, HELEN R. "The discovery of Maine: Vinland-Norumbega." Maine Dig, 2 (Spring, 1968), 69-73.

528 A HANDFUL of spice: a miscellany of Maine literature and history. Richard S. Sprague, ed. Orono: Univ. of Maine Pr., 1968. Pp. v, 205.

529 HARDING, ANNE BORDEN. "The 'eastern lands' of New Plymouth and Massachusetts Bay." NEHGR, 119 (1965), 15-22.

530 HARDING, R. BREWSTER. Greetings from Maine: celebrating America's bicentennial, 1975-1976. Portland: Old Port Publishing, 1975. Pp. 80.
Postal cards.

531 HARKNESS, O. A. "Log haulers twenty years ago." The Northern, 7 (December, 1927), 5, 15.

532 HARRINGTON, JOHN M. "Orono--Catholic Indian chief." SJMH, 5 (1917-1918), 9-16.

533 HARRIS, MAY PASHLEY. Twenty-five years of progress, a pageant of the Argicultural Extension Service. Orono: Univ. Pr., [1938?]. Pp. 31. MeU.

534 HASELTON, WALLACE M. Busy building Maine: the story of Depositors Corporation. N.Y.: Newcomen Society in North America, 1971. Pp. 24.

535 HASENFUS, NATHANIEL JOHN. More vacation days in Maine. West Roxbury, Mass.: Sagadahoc Publishing, 1949. Pp. 245.
Social life and customs; sequel to the following entry.

536 ____. We summer in Maine. West Roxbury, Mass.: Sagadahoc Publishing, 1946. Pp. 165.
Social life and customs.

537 HASENFUS, ROBERT. Maine Driver Education Association, history, 1955-1965. n.p., 1965. Pp. 30. Me.

538 HASKELL, CALEB. Caleb Haskell's diary, May 5, 1775-May 30, 1776, a Revolutionary soldier's record before Boston and with Arnold's Quebec Expedition. Lothrop Withington, ed. Newburyport, Mass.: W. H. Huse, 1881. Pp. 23.

539 HASKELL, JESSICA J. "State arms of Maine." DARMag, 50 (1917), 14-16.

540 HASKELL, LOREN E. "The great fore and afters." Yankee, 22 (February, 1958), 28-31.
Sailing ships built in Maine.

541 HASKELL, WILLIAM EDWIN. The International Paper Company, 1898-1924, its origin and growth in a quarter of a century, with a brief description of the manufacture of paper from the harvesting of pulpwood to the finished roll. N.Y.: International Paper Company, [1924]. Pp. 41.

542 MAINE

542 HASKINS, DAVID GREENE, JR. Biographical sketches of Captain Ebenezer Davis, and his son, the Hon. Charles Stewart Daveis, of Portland, Maine, members of the Massachusetts Society of the Cincinnati. Cambridge, Mass.: J. Wilson and Son, 1873. Pp. 17.

543 HASSE, ADELAIDE ROSALIA. Index of economic material in documents of the states of the United States: Maine, 1820-1904. [Washington]: Carnegie Institution of Washington, 1907. Pp. 95.

544 _____. "The North Eastern Boundary." Bulletin of the New York Public Library, 4 (1900), 391-411.
A bibliography, 1609-1871.

545 HATCH, BENTON LE ROY. "Lucius Lee Hubbard's map of northern Maine, 1879-1929, a checklist." Appalachia, 28 (1950-1951), 453-464.
History of the map with a descriptive bibliography of all editions.

546 HATCH, LOUIS CLINTON. Maine: a history: a facsimile of the 1919 edition ... with a new introduction and bibliography by William B. Jordan, Jr. Somersworth, N.H.: New Hampshire Publishing, 1974. Pp. 946.

547 HAVEN, HERBERT M. W. Tales of a homemade naturalist: the Maine diaries of Herbert M. W. Haven. Philip Morrill, ed. Winthrop: Winthrop Mineral Shop, 1966. Pp. 153.

548 HAWES, HILDRETH GILMAN. Early Maine cabinetmakers. [Augusta]: Maine State Museum, 1971. Variously leaved. Me.

549 HAY, DONALD GORDON, et al. Rural organization in three Maine towns. [Orono]: Agricultural Extension Service, 1949. Pp. 56. MeU.
Addison, Easton, and Turner.

550 HAYDEN, RALPH HENRY. "How the Church came to Maine." The Northeast, 85 (October, 1958), 8-9.
Episcopal Church.

551 HAYFORD, ELBERT D. "The District of Maine in Congress, 1789-1820." SJMH, 12 (1924), 34-38.

552 HAYNES, GEORGE HENRY. The State of Maine, in 1893. N.Y.: Moss Engraving, 1893. Pp. 98.

553 HAYWARD, JOHN. A gazetteer of the United States, comprising a series of gazetters of the several states and territories. Maine. Portland: S. H. Colesworthy, 1843. Pp. 92.

554 HAZELTON, LOUISE. Special subject resources in Maine, 1972. Augusta: Maine State Library, 1972. Pp. 63. MeP.

555 HEALY, RICHARD WYMAN. The history of secondary education in Androscoggin and Franklin counties in Maine. Orono: Univ. Pr., 1949. Pp. vii, 165.

556 HEBERT, RICHARD A. "The making of Maine: Bates Manufacturing Company." Pine Cone, 2 (Summer, 1946), 31-36.
In Augusta, Lewiston, and Saco; textiles.

557 _____. Modern Maine: its historic background, people, and resources. N.Y.: Lewis Historical, 1951. 4v.

558 HECHT, ARTHUR and PAUL HANNEMANN. The post-offices of the District of Maine; a historical and geographical arrangement of the early Main [sic] offices. Jamaica, N.Y.: F. Billig, 1960. Pp. 22. MeBa.

559 HECHT, ARTHUR. "Postal history of the District of Maine in 1795." Collectors Club Philatelist, 36 (November, 1957), 305-308.

560 HEFFERNAN, JOHN PAUL. "A Maine family of Smiths." Down East, 21 (April, 1975), 36-41, 66-68, 70.

561 _____. "War clouds over Maine." NEG, 10 (Fall, 1968), 3-8.
Gubernatorial election of 1879.

562 HELMREICH, ERNST CHRISTIAN. Religion and the Maine schools, an historical approach. Brunswick: Bureau for Research in Municipal Government, 1960. Pp. 83.

563 HEMPSTEAD, ALFRED GEER. "Getting Penobscot logs into Kennebec waters." The Northern, 7 (January, 1928), 5-6.
1839-1893.

564 _____. The Penobscot boom and the development of the west branch of the Penobscot river for log driving. Orono: Univ. Pr., 1931. Pp. 187.

565 HENDERSON, KENNETH A., ed. "Penobscot East Branch in 1861: from the diary and letters of Alpheus Spring Packard." Appalachia, 28 (1950-1951), 414-426.

566 HENRY, JOHN JOSEPH. Campaign against Quebec: being an accurate and interesting account of the hardships and sufferings of that band of heroes who traversed the wilderness, by the route of the Kennebec, and Chaudiere River, to Quebec in 1775. (1812) Rev. ed. with corrections and alterations. Watertown, N.Y.: Knowlton & Rice, 1844.
First edition has the title: "An accurate and interesting account..."; an 1877 printing has the title: "Account of Arnold's campaign against Quebec...."

567 HERRICK, ROBERT. "The State of Maine--'Down East.'" Nation, 115 (August 23, 1922), 182-183.

568 HESELTINE, CHARLES DANA. "Maine narrow gauge railroads." Narrow Gauge Society Newsletter, 2, No. 1 (1972), entire issue.

569 HILL, WINFIELD SCOTT. "Early Kennebec taverns." SJMH, 9 (1921), 21-23.
    At points along the river.

570 HILTON, CECIL MAX. Rough pulpwood operating in northwestern Maine, 1935-1940. Orono: Univ. Pr., 1942. Pp. viii, 197.

571 HILTON, SEAVERNS W. Arnold's march to Quebec: an account in pictures. [Augusta?, 1968]. Unpaged.

572 HINCKS, FRANCIS. The boundaries formerly in dispute between Great Britain and the United States, a lecture ... 9th June, 1885. Montreal: John Lovell & Son, 1885. Pp. 29.

573 HISTORIC AMERICAN BUILDINGS SURVEY. Maine catalog: a list of measured drawings, photographs, and written documentation in the survey, 1974. Denys Peter Myers, comp. [Augusta]: Maine State Museum, 1974. Pp. vii, 254.

574 "HISTORIC forest fires of Maine." The Northern, 7 (May, 1927), 3-5.

575 HISTORIC Maine and Indian mythology. N.Y.: Consolidated Steamship Lines, [1906?]. Unpaged. Me.

576 "AN HISTORICAL note on the Association's early growth." New England Townsman, 1 (January, 1939), 9.
    Maine Municipal Association.

577 HISTORICAL RECORDS SURVEY. MAINE. Counties, cities, towns and plantations of Maine: a handbook of incorporations, dissolutions and boundary changes. Portland, 1940. 165 leaves.

578 _____. Directory of churches and religious organizations in Maine. Portland, 1940. iii, 166 leaves.

579 _____. Inventory of federal archives in the states ... series IX, Department of Agriculture, No. 18, Maine. Rockland: National Archives Project, 1938. 86 leaves.

580 _____. Inventory of the town and city archives of Maine. Portland, 1938-1940. 7v.

581 _____. Town government in Maine. (Preliminary ed.) Portland, 1940. Pp. ii, 206.
    No other edition appeared.

582 "HISTORICAL sketch of the Baptist denomination in Maine." Baptist Memorial and Chronicle, 3 (1843), 353-363.

583 "HISTORICAL sketch of the Maine Educational Association." Maine Pedagogical Society. Proceedings, (1880-1881), 1-44.

584 "HISTORY of state general relief." Maine Townsman, 13 (January, 1951), 11-12.

585 HOLMES, HERBERT EDGAR. The makers of Maine: essays and tales of early Maine history, from the first explorations to the fall of Louisberg, including the story of the Norse expeditions. Lewiston: Haswell Pr., 1912. Pp. 251.

586 HOOPES, DONELSON F. "Regional accent: Maine, a faith in nature." Art in America, 51, No. 3 (1963), 70-79.
    American artists' reliance on Maine subject matter.

587 HOPKINS, JAMES DEAN. "Members of the bar in the District, now State, of Maine, from its first settlement to the year 1760, during which period it constituted only one county, viz. York." American Quarterly Register, 12 (1839-1840), 274-284.
    Includes Cumberland County 1700-1838.

588 HORMELL, ORREN CHALMER. Maine towns. Brunswick: Bowdoin College, 1932. Pp. 101.

589 HOUGHTON, LLOYD E. "Arnold's march through Maine." The Northern, 4 (March, 1925), 3-5, 14-15; 5 (April, 1925), 6-7.

590 HOUGHTON, MRS. WILLIAM ADDISON. Maine's colonial claims. n.p.: National Society of Colonial Dames of America in Maine, [1900?]. Unpaged. MeHi.

591 HOWARD, PRESCOTT L. "The era of the Lombard log hauler." Forest History, 6 (1962-1963), 2-8.
    Half-track log hauler invented by Alvin O. Lombard and used by Taylor Brothers Lumber Company of Maine in 1908.

592 HUBBARD, LUCIUS LEE. Woods and lakes of Maine: a trip from Moosehead Lake to New Brunswick in a birch-bark canoe, to which are added some Indian place-names and their meanings, now first published. Boston: J. R. Osgood, 1884. Pp. xvi, 223.

593 HUESTON, ETHEL POWELSON. Coasting Down East. N.Y.: Dodd, Mead, 1924. Pp. 304.

594 HUMISTON, FRED S. Blue water men--and women. Portland: G. Gannett, 1965. Pp. 172.
    Seafaring life.

595 MAINE

595 _____. Windjammers and walking beams. Portland: Blue Water Books, 1968. Pp. 199.

596 NO ENTRY.

597 HUNT, HARMON C. "Keep Maine's village clocks running." Down East, 21 (November, 1974), 40-43.

598 HUSSEY, ARTHUR M., II. Bibliography of Maine geology, 1672-1972. Augusta: Department of Conservation, 1974. Pp. v, 269. MeU.

599 HUSTON, A. J., BOOKSELLER, PORTLAND. A check list of Maine local histories.... [Portland], 1915. Pp. 44.

600 HUSTON, JAMES A. "The logistics of Arnold's march to Quebec." Military Affairs, 32 (1968-1969), 110-124.

601 HUTCHINS, ARTHUR E. and DANA A. LITTLE. Progress in Maine municipal planning, 1956-1966; a report of municipal planning activity in the state. [Augusta]: Maine Dept. of Economic Development, Division of Research and Planning, 1967. Pp. iv, 24.

602 HYLAN, JOHN COFFEY. The history of secondary education in York and Oxford counties in Maine. Orono: Univ. Pr., 1933. Pp. 78.

603 ILLUSTRATED souvenir 1908. [Lewiston]: R. J. Lawton, 1908. Pp. 62. MeU.

604 "INDEX to Maine public documents, 1834-1867." Maine State Library, 32d Biennial Report, (1905-1906), 26-90.

605 "THE INDIAN Bashaba." SJMH, 1 (1913-1914), 47-52.

606 "INDIAN names in Maine." Journal of American Folklore, 18 (1905), 316-317.

607 "INDIANS of Maine in the American Revolution." MeCathHM, 4 (April, 1915), 16-24.

608 INTERNATIONAL BOUNDARY COMMISSION (U.S., ALASKA AND CANADA). Joint report upon the survey and demarcation of the boundary between the United States and Canada from the source of the St. Croix River to the Atlantic Ocean, in accordance with the provisions of articles I and II of the treaty signed at Washington, April 11, 1908, articles I and II of the treaty signed at Washington, May 21, 1910, and article III of the treaty signed at Washington, February 24, 1925.... Washington: Govt. Print. Off., 1934. Pp. xiv, 318.

609 _____. Joint report upon the survey and demarcation of the boundary between the United States and Canada from the source of the St. Croix River to the St. Lawrence River, in accordance with the provisions of article III of the treaty signed at Washington, April 11, 1908.... Washington: Govt. Print. Off., 1925. Pp. xv, 512.

610 IRISH, MARIA M. "The Northeastern Boundary of Maine." JAmHist, 16 (1922), 311-322.

611 "ISLANDS and Gulf of Maine." Oceans, 7 (May-June, 1974), 8-47.
Social life and customs.

612 JEWELL, MARGARET H. "Country life in Maine a century ago." OTNE, 23 (1932-1933), 28-38.

613 _____. "Notes on Maine potteries." OTNE, 22 (1931-1932), 184-187.

614 JEWETT, FRED EUGENE. A financial history of Maine. N.Y.: Columbia Univ. Pr., 1937. Pp. 235.

615 JOHNSON, ALLEN. "Report on the archives of the State of Maine." American Historical Association. Annual Report, (1908), I, 257-318.

616 JOHNSON, THEODORE ELLIOT. Hands to work and hearts to God: the Shaker tradition in Maine. [Brunswick]: Bowdoin College Museum of Art, 1969. Unpaged.

617 JOHNSTON, JOHN. "Abraham Shurt and John Earthy: two interesting characters in the early history of the State of Maine." NEHGR, 25 (1871), 131-137,

618 JONES, CARMITA DE SOLMS. "Acadia in Maine." American Catholic Historical Society of Philadelphia. Records, 36 (1925), 359-371.
Catholics.

619 _____. "The blackgowns among the Abnakis." American Catholic Historical Society of Philadelphia. Records, 33 (1922), 275-299.
Capuchins and Jesuits.

620 JONES, HERBERT GRANVILLE. I discover Maine: little-known stories about a well-known state. Portland: Machigonne Pr., 1937. Pp. vii, 99.
A two-volume braille edition was published by the WPA Braille Project in Portland in 1940.

621 _____. The King's Highway from Portland to Kittery: stagecoach & tavern days on the old post road. Portland: Longfellow Pr., 1953. Pp. 226.

622 _____. Maine memories: little-known stories about a well-known state. Portland: Harmon Publishing, 1940. Pp. 223.

623 JONES, HOWARD. "Anglophobia and the Aroostook War." NEQ, 48 (1975), 519-539.

624 JONES, WILBUR DEVEREUX. "The influence of slavery on the Webster-Ashburton negotiations." Journal of Southern History, 22 (1956), 48-58.

625 _____. "Lord Ashburton and the Maine boundary negotiations." MVHR, 40 (1953), 477-490.

626 JORDAN, NELLIE WOODBURY. "The Cumberland and Oxford Canal." SJMH, 10 (1922), 23-26.

627 JORDAN, WILLIAM BARNES, JR., comp. A bibliography of Maine bibliography. n.p., 1952.
4 leaves.

628 _____. Episodes from the Unitarian Universalist experience in Maine. Norway: Oxford
Hills Pr., 1974. Pp. 12. MeHi.

629 _____. Maine in the Civil War: a bibliographical guide. Portland: Maine Historical
Society, 1976. Pp. 74.

630 _____. Maine in the War of the Rebellion,
1861-1865: check list and bibliography.
Portland: Bosworth Memorial Civil War Museum, 1962. 35 leaves.

631 JORGENSEN, FREDERICK E. 25 years a game
warden. Brattleboro, Vt.: Stephen Daye Pr.,
1937. Pp. 161.

632 JULIAN, GEORGE WASHINGTON. "Webster and
Blaine: historic justice." Magazine of
Western History, 8 (1888), 466-472.

633 KAHN, RICHARD. "An historical sketch of
medical education in Maine." Maine Medical
Association. Journal, 62 (1971), 212-216.

634 [KALER, JAMES OTIS]. Geography of Maine.
Portland: The Eagle Pr., 1910. Pp. 23.

635 KEARNEY, W. D. The open hand: an epic poem
dealing with the early settlement of Maine
and New Brunswick, founded on tradition.
Hartland, N.B.: Observer, Ltd., 1926.
Pp. 58.

636 KEENE, CARTER B. "The evolution of the American postal service: something about its
history in Maine." SJMH, 7 (1919-1920),
123-131.

637 NO ENTRY.

638 KELLIHER, JOHN T. "The Red Paint Indian
culture of Maine." Maine Naturalist, 10
(1930), 45-48.

639 KENDE, BERTHOLD. "History of life insurance
in Maine." BTJ, 17 (1904-1905), 535-542.

640 KENNEBEC AND WISCASSET RAILROAD COMPANY.
Narrow gauge railroads: their history and
progress, the Kennebec and Wiscasset rail-
road, the first narrow gauge enterprise in
Maine. Augusta: Sprague, Owen & Nash, 1872.
Pp. 31.

641 KERSHAW, GORDON E. "John Wentworth vs. Kennebeck proprietors: the formation of Royal
mast policy 1769-1778." AmNep, 33 (1973),
95-119.

642 _____. The Kennebeck proprietors, 1749-1775:
"gentlemen of large property & judicious men."
Somersworth, N.H.: New Hampshire Publishing,
1975. Pp. xvi, 343.

643 _____. "A question of orthodoxy: religious
controversy in a speculative land company:
1759-1775." NEQ, 46 (1973), 205-235.
Kennebec Purchase Company.

644 KEUNE, RUSSELL V. and JAMES REPLOGLE. "Two
Maine farmhouses." SocArchHistJ, 20 (1961),
38-39.
Miles Cobb Farm in Hinckley's Corner and
Perkins Homestead in Newcastle.

645 KIDDER, FREDERIC. "Colonel John Allan and
his operations in Maine and Nova Scotia, in
the Revolution." HistMag, 2 Ser., 4 (1868),
263-264.

646 _____. Military operations in eastern Maine
and Nova Scotia during the Revolution,
chiefly comp. from the journals and letters
of Col. John Allan, with notes and a memoir
of Col. John Allan. Albany: J. Munsell,
1867. Pp. x, 336.

647 KILBY, CYRUS HAMLIN. Binding of the links:
a story of forty years in Odd Fellowship.
Portland, [1889]. Pp. 125.

648 KILBY, WILLIAM HENRY. "Benedict Arnold on
the eastern frontier." BHistMag, 2 (1886-
1887), 188-190.

649 KING, MARQUIS FAYETTE, comp. Changes in
names by special acts of the Legislature of
Maine, 1820-1895. [Portland?, Priv. Print.],
1901. Pp. 67.

650 KIRTLEY, BASIL F. "On the origin of the
Maine-Maritimes legend of the plucked gorbey."
Journal of American Folklore, 87 (1974), 364-
365.

651 KLEIN, ELSA. The story of the State of Maine
Division of the American Association of University Women in its first five years.
n.p., [1952?]. Pp. 19. MeBa.

652 KNIGHT, ENOCH. The new story of the State of
Maine. Portland: Dresser, McLellan, 1876.
Pp. 26.

653 KNOWLTON, CLARENCE H. "History of the Josselyn Botanical Society of Maine." Josselyn
Botanical Society of Maine. Bulletin, No. 10
(1975), 21-24.

654 KNOWLTON, NEWELL R. A history of Odd Fellowship in the tenth district of Maine. Farmington: Knowlton & McLeary, 1898. Pp. 236.
MeU.

655 KNOWLTON, WILLIAM SMITH. The old schoolmas-
ter; or forty-five years with the girls and
boys. Augusta: Burleigh & Flynt, 1905.
Pp. 269.

656 KOHL, JOHANN GEORG. A history of the discovery of Maine. With an appendix on the voyages of the Cabots, by M. d'Avezac.... Portland: Bailey and Noyes, 1869. Pp. viii, 535.
See also entry 306.

657 KURT, FRANKLIN T. "The little white steamers of Penobscot Bay." Down East, 18 (June, 1972), 56-59, 92, 97-98, 105.
Eastern Steamship Company.

658 KYPER, FRANK. "Maine Central perspective." Railroad Enthusiast, 9 (Winter and Spring, 1972), 3-6.

659 LACOGNATA, ANGELO A. We the Italians of Maine. [Portland?], 1975. Pp. 20. MeHi.

660 LADD, VAUGHN. "Adaptation of diesel locomotives by the Bangor & Aroostook Railroad." Maine Association of Engineers. Journal, No. 21 (April, 1950), 47-52.

661 LAMB, FRANCES A. "Shipwrecked shoppers." DARMag, 93 (February, 1959), 88.
Wreck of the 'Trial' at mouth of Kennebec in November, 1820.

662 LANCASTER, LANE W. "The Democratic Party in Maine." National Municipal Review, 18 (1929), 744-749.

663 LAPHAM, WILLIAM BERRY. "Notes on the Skillings family." MHGR, 2 (1885), 45-49.

664 LARSON, EDWIN VAN HORN. The forest wealth of Maine. Portland: Maine Forest Service, 1961. Pp. 29.
Includes history.

665 LAWRANCE, WILLIAM A. A twenty-five year review of Androscoggin River pollution control activities. Lewiston, 1967. Pp. 28. MeU.

666 LAWTON, R. J., comp. Franco-Americans of the State of Maine, U.S.A., and their achievements; historical, descriptive and biographical. J. H. Burgess, ed. Lewiston: H. F. Roy, 1915. Pp. 211.

667 "LEADING events in the colonial history of Maine." SJMH, 3 (1915-1916), 32-34.

668 LEAMON, JAMES S. "Maine's Swedish pioneers." Swedish Pioneer Historical Quarterly, 26 (1975), 73-91.

669 _____. "The Revolution comes to Maine." The Bates College Bulletin, 73 (April, 1976), 2-5.

670 LEAVITT, HAROLD WALTER. "Some interesting phases of the development of transportation in Maine." Maine Association of Engineers. Journal, No. 16 Pt. 2 (April, 1940), entire issue.

671 LE BLANT, ROBERT. Une figure légendaire de l'histoire acadienne: le baron de St-Castin. Dax, France: Editions P. Pradeu, [1934]. Pp. 175.

672 LE DUC, THOMAS HAROLD ANDRÉ. "The Maine frontier and the Northeastern Boundary controversy." AHR, 53 (1947-1948), 30-41.

673 LEE, RICHARD H. "Old railroad days on the Newport line." Down East, 18 (November, 1971), 42-45.

674 LEE, WILLIAM STORRS, comp. Maine: a literary chronicle. N.Y.: Funk & Wagnalls, 1968. Pp. xv, 487.

675 _____. "Maine, a literary chronicle." Maine Dig, 3 (Winter, 1969), 92-111.

676 LEGER, MARY CELESTE. The Catholic Indian missions in Maine (1611-1820). Washington: The Catholic Univ. of America, 1929. Pp. x, 184.

677 LEGER, PAUL A. "Hasey's Maine stages." Bus History, 1 (Fall, 1974), 3-6.
Buses.

678 LELAND, CHARLES GODFREY. The Algonquin legends of New England, or myths and folk lore of the Micmac, Passamaquoddy, and Penobscot tribes. (1884) 2d ed. Boston: Houghton, Mifflin, 1885. Pp. xv, 379.

679 _____. "Legends of the Passamaquoddy." Century, 28 (1884), 668-677.

680 LENHART, JOHN M. The Capuchins in Acadia and northern Maine (1632-1638). American Catholic Historical Society. Records, 27 (1916), 191-229, 300-327; 28 (1917), 47-63.

681 LERMOND, NORMAN WALLACE and ARTHUR HERBERT NORTON. Bibliography of mollusca of Maine, 1605-1930. Maine Naturalist, 10 (1930), 49-73, 100-121.

682 LEWIS, GERALD E. Up here in Maine. Garland: Lewis, 1974. Pp. 134.

683 LIBBY, RICHARD J. "A decade in elementary education in Maine." Maine Teachers' Digest, 1 (1940-1941), 141, 174-175.
1931-1940.

684 LIBBY, STEVE. "Nothing like the trolleys." Down East, 12 (January, 1966), 35-38.

685 LINCOLN, J. J. "The Revere bells of Maine." Down East, 17 (January, 1971), 34-37, 63-64, 66.
Bells made by Paul Revere.

686 LINSCOTT, EDWARD LYON. The history of secondary education in Washington and Hancock counties in Maine. Orono: Univ. Pr., 1937. Pp. viii, 171.

687 "LIST of books and documents in the State Library relating to the discovery, settlement, and growth of Maine." Maine State Library. Annual Report, (1891-1892), 19-33.

688 LITOFF, JUDY BARRETT and HAL LITOFF. "Working women in Maine: a note on sources." LabHist, 17 (1976), 88-95.

689 LITTLE, GEORGE BARKER. The kingdom of God not in externals: sermon delivered at Bath, June 24, 1857, before the Maine Missionary Society, at its fiftieth anniversary. Augusta: Elias G. Hodge, 1857. Pp. 64.
Includes a history of the Society.

690 LITTLE, GEORGE THOMAS, ed. Genealogical and family history of the State of Maine ... and including among other local contributors Rev. Henry S. Burrage ... and Albert Roscoe Stubbs.... N.Y.: Lewis Historical Publishing, 1909. 4v.
Paged continuously.

691 "LOCAL rimes and quatrains of the northeast." Folksong Society of the Northeast. Bulletin, No. 3 (1931), 17-20.

692 LOCKE, HERBERT E. "Right of access to great ponds by the Colonial Ordinance." Maine Law Review, 12 (1918-1919), 148-164.

693 LOHNES, BARRY J. "A new look at the invasion of eastern Maine, 1814." MeHSQ, 15 (1975-1976), 5-25.
War of 1812; a comment by Ronald F. Banks follows on pages 26-29.

694 LOMBARD, LUCINA HAYNES. "The antiquarians: a sketch of the history of antique collecting in Maine." Maine's Own Magazine, 8 (April, 1930), 11-16, 29.

695 _____. "The covered bridges of Maine." Maine's Own Magazine, 7 (October, 1929), 11, 26.

696 _____. "The growth of Maine's granite industry." Sun Up, 9 (April, 1931), 4-5, 12, 26.

697 _____. "How springs helped make Maine history." Sun Up, 8 (July, 1930), 17, 44.

698 _____. "John Greenleaf Whittier and Lucy Larcom in Maine." Sun Up, 9 (June, 1931), 4-5, 28, 30.

699 _____. "The latchstring of Maine: some interesting facts about the history of commerce in the Pine Tree State. Sun Up, 9 (January, 1931), 7, 28-29, 31.

700 _____. "The lure of historic Maine houses." Sun Up, 2 (April, 1926), 10, 25, 31.

701 _____. "Maine roads are rich in romantic legend and history." Maine's Own Magazine, 7 (January, 1929), 4, 27.

702 _____. "Maine sea captains and their homes." Sun Up, 3 (February, 1927), 7, 27.

703 _____. "Maine's Paul Revere bells." Sun Up, 9 (July, 1931), 18, 29-31.

704 _____. "Mystic Indian water trails." Sun Up, 5 (August, 1928), 4-5, 24-25.

705 _____. "Post roads and taverns of old Maine." Sun Up, 3 (January, 1927), 12, 14, 37.

706 LOOMIS, ALFRED FULLERTON. Ranging the Maine coast. N.Y.: W. W. Norton, 1939. Pp. 274.

707 LOOMIS, CHARLES DANA. An architectural monograph on port towns of Penobscot Bay. St. Paul: White Pine Bureau, 1922. Pp. 16.
Belfast, Camden, and Castine.

708 LORD, ARTHUR. "The sale of Matchebiguatus, 1644." MHSP, 49 (1915-1916), 357-360.
Trading settlement at mouth of Penobscot River.

709 LORING, PHILIP QUINCY. "Outline history of Maine." Sun Up, 2 (October, 1925), 12, 25, 49-50, 52.

710 LOVEJOY, SCOTT K. "Small stream bridges of Maine." Down East, 4 (September, 1957), 18-20.

711 LOVERING, FRANK W. "The railroad that survived on chicken feed." Railroad Enthusiast, 4 (Winter and Spring, 1967), 3-7.
Belfast & Moosehead Lake Railroad.

712 _____. "Watering places of the gay nineties." Down East, 6 (September, 1959), 16-19.
Resorts.

713 LOWENTHAL, DAVID. "The Maine press and the Aroostook War." CanHistRev, 32 (1951), 315-336.

714 LUBBOCK, ALFRED BASIL. The Down Easters, American deep-water sailing ships, 1869-1929. Boston: C. E. Lauriat, 1929. Pp. xvi, 285.

715 LUCEY, WILLIAM LEO. The Catholic Church in Maine. Francestown, N.H.: M. Jones, 1957. Pp. 372.

716 _____. "Some correspondence of the Maine commissioners regarding the Webster-Ashburton Treaty." NEQ, 15 (1942), 332-348.
Northeast Boundary dispute.

717 MAINE

717 LUND, MORTEN. Cruising the Maine coast. N.Y.: Walker, 1967. Pp. 224.

718 LUNT, DUDLEY CAMMETT. The woods and the sea: wilderness and seacoast adventures in the State of Maine. N.Y.: Knopf, 1965. Pp. ix, 304.

719 LYFORD, ELMORE B. "By way of the Kennebec." Yankee, 33 (November, 1969), 46-50, 52-54, 57-58, 63.
     Arnold's Expedition.

720 McALEER, NEIL. "Maine's meteorites." Down East, 21 (November, 1974), 61-63.

721 McCARTHY, MARCIA. "Maine breeds the best." Pine Cone, 3 (Spring, 1947), 22-28.
     Trotting horses.

722 MacDONALD, WILLIAM. "French Canadians in Maine." Nation, 63 (October 15, 1896), 285-286.

723 _____. The government of Maine: its history and administration. N.Y.: Macmillan, 1902. Pp. ix, 263.

724 MacDOUGALL, WALTER M. "Arnold's Expediton to Quebec, 1775." Down East, 22 (September, 1975), 36-41, 74, 77.

725 _____. "Lombard's iron monster." Yankee, 29 (March, 1965), 72, 77, 132, 135, 137.
     Steam powered log hauler.

726 _____. "The lower lakes." Down East, 13 (April, 1966), 22-26, 59.

727 _____. "Seboomook and Northeast Carry." Down East, 11 (April, 1965), 26-29, 38-41, 44.
     Overland transportation connecting two waterways.

728 MacDUFFIE, MALCOLM. "The old Vinal, gone but not forgotten." Steamboat Bill, 27 (1970), 214-216.
     Steamer 'Vinal Haven,' 1892-1945.

729 McKEEN, JOHN. "Remarks on the voyage of George Waymouth, to the coast of Maine, 1605." MeHSC, 5 (1857), 309-338.

730 McKENNEY, LEWIS TIMOTHY. Memories of Maine. Boston: Meador Publishing, 1934. Pp. 210.

731 MacKENZIE, GERTRUDE. My love affair with the State of Maine. N.Y.: Simon and Schuster, 1955. Pp. 311.
     Social life and customs.

732 McKUSICK, VINCENT L. [History of the Maine Supreme Judicial Court.] Maine State Bar Association. Report, 57 (1968), 142-153.

733 McLEAN, JAMES A. "Thumbnail sketch of militia history." MeLAB, 28 (February, 1967), 3-4.

734 McLIN, WILLIAM HELLEN. "The Maine Central and the 'off-beat' gauges." Railroad Enthusiast, 9 (Winter and Spring, 1972), 7-11.

735 McMURTRIE, DOUGLAS CRAWFORD. Maine imprints, 1792-1820; an open letter to R. Webb Noyes. Chicago: Priv. Print., 1935. 12 leaves.

736 _____. "Pioneer printing in Maine." National Printer Journalist, 50 (March, 1932), 18-19, 94-95.

737 MacWILLIAMS, JAMES DONALD. Yours in sports, a history: baseball, basketball, boxing, and bowling in Maine. Volume one. [Monmouth]: Monmouth Pr., 1969. Pp. 301A. MeHi.
     No more published.

738 MAINE (COLONY). Province and court records of Maine. Portland: Maine Historical Society, 1928-.
     Six volumes published as of 1977 covering 1636-1727.

739 MAINE (DISTRICT). CONSTITUTIONAL CONVENTION, 1819. The debates and journal of the Constitutional Convention of the State of Maine 1819-'20, and amendments subsequently made to the Constitution. Charles E. Nash, ed. Augusta: Maine Farmers' Almanac Press, 1894. Various pagings.

740 _____. The debates, resolutions, and other proceedings, of the convention of delegates, assembled at Portland on the 11th, and continued until the 29th day of October, 1819, for the purpose of forming a constitution for the State of Maine, to which is prefixed the constitution taken in convention. Jeremiah Perley, ed. Portland: A. Shirley, 1820. Pp. iv, 300.

741 MAINE. ADJUTANT GENERAL'S OFFICE. History, Maine State Guard, from its inception to 30 June 1946. [Augusta, 1946?]. Pp. 126. MeBa.

742 _____. Roster of Maine in the military service of the United States and allies in the World War, 1917-1919.... Augusta, 1929. 2v.

743 MAINE. AGRICULTURAL EXPERIMENT STATION, ORONO. Teamwork in the blueberry industry by the growers, processors, research and extension personnel, a 10-year history, 1945-1954. Orono, 1954. 36 leaves. MeU.

744 MAINE. ATTORNEY GENERAL. Index to the private and special laws enacted by the legislatures of the State of Maine from 1820-1944, inclusive. Augusta, 1944. Pp. 557. Me.

745 _____. Index to the private and special laws enacted by the legislatures of the State of Maine from 1944 to 1957. [Augusta, 1958]. Pp. 58. Me.

746 MAINE. BUREAU OF LABOR AND INDUSTRY. History of the Bureau of Labor and Industry. (1965) 2d revision. C. Wilder Smith and Madge E. Ames, comps. [Augusta]: Maine Dept. of Manpower Affairs, 1974. 119 leaves.
First edition has title: History of the Department of Labor and Industry.

747 MAINE. CENTENNIAL COMMITTEE. One hundredth anniversary of Maine's entrance into the Union; official program of state celebration, Portland, June 26th to July 5th, 1920, including list of towns to hold local observances and all other information regarding the event.... Augusta: C. E. Nash & Son, 1920. Pp. 36.

748 MAINE. CIVILIAN DEFENSE CORPS. The official history of the Maine Civilian Defense Corps. ... [Augusta, 1945?]. Pp. 218.

749 MAINE. COUNCIL. Aroostook War: historical sketch and roster of commissioned officers and enlisted men called into service for the protection of the northeastern frontier of Maine, from February to May, 1839. Augusta: Kennebec Journal Print, 1904. Pp. 95.

750 MAINE. DEPARTMENT OF EDUCATION. 150 years of education in Maine: sesqui-centennial history of Maine's educational system and the growth and development of the Maine State Department of Education. Kermit S. Nickerson, comp. Augusta, 1970. Pp. 58.

751 _____. A study of the history of education in Maine and the evolution of our present school system. [Augusta, 1901?]. Pp. 104.

752 _____. Through Maine on printed paths: a list of Maine books for teachers and pupils. Augusta, 1956. Pp. 58.

753 MAINE. DEPARTMENT OF EDUCATION AND CULTURAL SERVICES. History of Maine vocational rehabilitation program, 1921-1972. [Augusta?, 1973?]. 43 leaves. Me.

754 MAINE. DEPARTMENT OF HEALTH AND WELFARE. Condensed history of the State of Maine Department of Health and Welfare. [Augusta, 1961?]. 3 leaves. Me.

755 MAINE. DEPARTMENT OF SEA AND SHORE FISHERIES. Commercial fisheries of Maine.... (1957) George H. Taylor, ed. Rev. ed. [Augusta], 1963. Pp. 43.

756 MAINE. DEVELOPMENT COMMISSION. AGRICULTURAL SURVEY COMMITTEE. Report of the Agricultural Survey Committee of the Maine Development Commission on progress in Maine agriculture 1850 to 1920. [Augusta, 1929?]. Pp. 24.

757 MAINE. FOREST COMMISSIONER. Brief history and present organization. [Augusta?], 1929. Pp. 23.

758 _____. Report on public reserved lots: chapter 76, Resolves of 1961. [Augusta], 1963. Pp. 75.
History of public lands.

759 MAINE. FORESTRY DEPARTMENT. Maine forest fire record, 1903-1970. [Augusta, 1971?]. Broadside. 11 x 8 3/8 inches. MeU.

760 MAINE. GEOLOGICAL SURVEY. Bibliography on Maine geology, 1836-1957. Augusta: Department of Economic Development, 1958. Pp. 143.

761 MAINE. GOVERNOR, 1967-1974 (KENNETH M. CURTIS). The Curtis years: 1967-1974. Allen G. Pease ed. Augusta: Office of the Governor/New England Regional Commission, 1974. Pp. 203. MeBa.

762 MAINE. HYDROGRAPHIC SURVEY. The water-power of Maine. Augusta: Sprague, Owen & Nash, 1869. Pp. vii, 526.

763 MAINE. LAWS, STATUTES, ETC. Digest of the resolves of Maine, having the force of law, from 1820 to 1862 inclusive. Joseph B. Hall, comp. Augusta: Stevens and Sayward, 1862. Pp. xiii, 175, xii.

764 MAINE. NATIONAL GUARD. A brief history of the National Guard and the Maine National Guard. 2d. ed. Augusta, 1963. Pp. 12. Me.

765 _____. Historical and pictorial review, National Guard of the State of Maine. Baton Rouge, La.: Army and Navy Publishing, 1939. Pp. xxxvi, 152.

766 MAINE. OFFICE OF STATE COMMISSIONER OF EDUCATION. One hundred years of statehood, centennial studies, celebrations in the public schools of Maine, 1920, one hundred leading facts. Augusta, 1920. Pp. 38.

767 _____. The work of a decade in the schools of Maine. [Augusta, 1906?]. Pp. 14.

768 MAINE. STATE ARCHIVES. Agencies of government, State of Maine, 1820-1971. Augusta, [1972]. Pp. viii, 235.

769 _____. Microfilm list: Maine town records and Maine census records. Augusta, 1976. Pp. 32. MeP.

770 MAINE. STATE CHAMBER OF COMMERCE AND AGRICULTURAL LEAGUE. History of the public or school lots. Portland, [1923]. Unpaged. MeHi.

771 _____. History of the wild lands of Maine. Portland, [1923]. Pp. 11. MeHi.

772   MAINE. STATE HIGHWAY COMMISSION. A history
       of Maine roads, 1600-1970. Augusta, 1970.
       Pp. 39.

773   MAINE. STATE LIBRARY, AUGUSTA. Bibliography
       on Maine history. [Augusta], 1931. 7
       leaves. Me.

774   _____. Maine forts. Augusta: Charles E.
       Nash & Son, 1924. Pp. 252.

775   _____. Maine in the Civil War: a list of
       material in the Maine State Library. [Augus-
       ta], 1961. Pp. 13.

776   MAINE. STATE MUSEUM. Artists listed in city
       directories in Maine, 1850-1899. [Augusta,
       1976]. Unpaged. MeU.

777   _____. Maine furniture makers. [Augusta,
       1976]. Unpaged. MeU.
       From colonial to the early Victorian
       period.

778   MAINE. STATE PLANNING OFFICE. Maine popula-
       tion trends, 1960-1970. [Augusta], 1972.
       Pp. 25.

779   MAINE. STATE POLICE. History and functions
       of Maine State Police. (1968) 3d. revision.
       [Augusta], 1974. 28 leaves. Me.

780   MAINE. STATE WATER STORAGE COMMISSION.
       Gazetteer of the rivers and lakes of Maine.
       Waterville: Sentinel Publishing, 1914.
       Pp. 323.
       Arranged alphabetically by drainage basins.

781   MAINE. UNIVERSITY. Survey of higher educa-
       tion in Maine, by the University of Maine,
       in cooperation with Bates, Bowdoin and Colby
       Colleges. [Orono?, 1932?]. Pp. x, 430.

782   MAINE. UNIVERSITY. COLLEGE OF AGRICULTURE.
       DEPARTMENT OF ANIMAL PATHOLOGY. Forty years
       of pullorum disease eradication in poultry for
       the State of Maine. Orono, [1962?]. Pp. 19.

783   MAINE. UNIVERSITY. COLLEGE OF AGRICULTURE.
       EXTENSION DEPARTMENT. Fifty years of dairy
       extension work in Maine. Ralph Corbett, ed.
       Orono, 1962. Pp. 19. Me.

784   MAINE. UNIVERSITY. DEPARTMENT OF HISTORY
       AND GOVERNMENT. A reference list of manu-
       scripts relating to the history of Maine.
       Elizabeth Ring, comp. Orono: Univ. Pr.,
       1938-1941. 3v.

785   MAINE. UNIVERSITY. FORESTRY DEPARTMENT.
       Golden anniversary, 1903-1953. Orono, 1954.
       Pp. 92.

786   ["MAINE."] Holiday, 2 (August, 1947), 43-57,
       97-100.

787   "MAINE artists." MeLB, 16 (1930-1931), 29-
       30.

788   "THE MAINE boundary controversy." The North-
       ern, 5 (July, 1925), 3-6, (August, 1925),
       3-5.

789   MAINE BROADCASTING SYSTEM. The first 40 years,
       1925-1965. n.p., [1965]. Unpaged.

790   MAINE CENTRAL RAILROAD COMPANY. A century of
       service to the State of Maine, 1862-1962....
       [Waterville?, 1963?]. Pp. 20.

791   _____. An historical account of the Maine
       Central Railroad Company.... [Portland?],
       1879. Pp. 16. MeHi.

792   _____. History of the capitalization of the
       Maine Central Railroad Company during the
       period June 30, 1911, to June 30, 1914. n.p.,
       [1915]. Pp. 31.

793   "THE MAINE Central Railroad Company and its
       system." BHistMag, 1 (1885-1886), 192-194.

794   "MAINE churches are historical landmarks."
       Sun Up, 5 (December, 1927), 9, 21-23.

795   "MAINE covered bridges." MeLB, 17 (1931-
       1932), 86-90.

796   MAINE FEDERATION OF MUSIC CLUBS. 25th anni-
       versary [of the] Maine Federation of Music
       Clubs, Lewiston-Auburn, May 13-14, 1948.
       [Lewiston?, 1948]. Unpaged.

797   MAINE FEDERATION OF WOMEN'S CLUBS. Histori-
       cal sketches, 1892-1924. Georgia Pulsifer
       Porter, comp. Lewiston: Lewiston Journal
       Printshop, 1925. Pp. 165.

798   _____. History of the Maine Federation of
       Women's Clubs.... Lewiston, 1898. Pp. 52.

799   _____. Maine in history and romance. Lewis-
       ton: Lewiston Journal, 1915. Pp. 242.

800   _____. Prominent personalities in the Maine
       Federation of Women's Clubs. West Boothbay
       Harbor: James F. Waugh, 1962. Pp. iv, 217.

801   _____. The trail of the Maine pioneer.
       Lewiston: Lewiston Journal, 1916. Pp. 340.

802   MAINE HISTORIC PRESERVATION COMMISSION. His-
       toric preservation plan: the historic back-
       ground. [Portland], 1973. Pp. 64. MeHi.

803   MAINE historical memorials.... [Augusta?]:
       Printed for the State, 1922. Pp. xi, 199.

804   MAINE HISTORICAL SOCIETY. Indians of Maine:
       a preliminary inventory of material on the
       history of the Indians of Maine in the Soci-
       ety Library. Roger B. Ray, ed. Portland,
       1969. Pp. ii, 11.

805 _____. Tercentenary of Martin Pring's first voyage to the coast of Maine, 1603-1903. Portland, [1905?]. Pp. 73.
Includes a bibliography.

806 _____. Waymouth tercentenary: an account of the celebration of the landing of George Waymouth on the coast of Maine. Portland, [1905?]. Pp. 53.

807 MAINE HISTORICAL SOCIETY. LIBRARY. The Indians of Maine: a bibliographical guide, being largely a selected inventory of material on the subject in the Society's library. Roger B. Ray, comp. Portland, 1972. Unpaged.

808 "MAINE history day by day--December." Sun Up, 2 (December, 1925), 16, 20.

809 "MAINE history day by day--February." Sun Up, 2 (February, 1926), 17.

810 "MAINE history day by day--January." Sun Up, 2 (January, 1926), 13, 45.

811 "MAINE history day by day--June." Sun Up, 3 (June, 1926), 36.

812 "MAINE history day by day--July." Sun Up, 3 (July, 1926), 55.

813 "MAINE history day by day--March." Sun Up, 2 (April, 1926), 25.

814 "MAINE history day by day--May." Sun Up, 2 (May, 1926), 31.

815 MAINE in review, 1776-1876. [Brunswick], 1976. Pp. 96. MeHi.

816 "MAINE: its early history--physical aspect--agricultural and mineral resources--commerce--manufactures--government--finances--population--schools, colleges, &c., &c." De Bow's Review, 12 (1852), 603-610.

817 "MAINE, its No. 1 industry--shoes." Leather and Shoes, 130 (December 3, 1955), 11-12, 14-16, 24.

818 "THE MAINE law, its history and results." Tait's Edinburgh Magazine, New Ser., 20 (1853), 666-670.
Prohibition; signed: S. P.

819 MAINE LEAGUE OF HISTORICAL SOCIETIES AND MUSEUMS. Maine, a guide "Down East." (1937) 2d ed. Dorris A. Isaacson, ed. Rockland: Courier-Gazette, 1970. Pp. xxiv, 510.
First edition written by the staff of the Federal Writers' Project.

820 "MAINE libraries." MeLAB, 2 (July, 1941), 2.

821 MAINE LIBRARY ASSOCIATION. BICENTENNIAL COMMITTEE. Bibliography of Maine, 1960-1975. Eric S. Flower, comp. Orono, 1976. 109 leaves.

822 MAINE OSTEOPATHIC ASSOCIATION. Golden Jubilee, 1904-1954. n.p., [1954]. Pp. 30. Me.

823 MAINE PEDAGOGICAL SOCIETY. Proceedings of the Maine Pedagogical Society for 1880-81, with a historical sketch of the Maine Educational Association, and journal of proceedings of the Maine Teachers' Association, 1875-80. Farmington: Knowlton, McLeary, 1883. Pp. 159.

824 "MAINE savings banks." Sun Up, 2 (November, 1925), 32-33, 38.

825 MAINE STATE BAR ASSOCIATION. Report ... for 1920 and 1921. Augusta: Charles E. Nash & Son, 1921. Pp. 328.
Includes celebration of the first century of jurisprudence in the state which was held in Augusta, January 12, 1921.

826 MAINE STATE BICENTENNIAL COMMISSION. Maine bicentennial atlas: an historical survey. Gerald E. Morris and Richard D. Kelly, Jr., eds. Portland: Maine Historical Society, 1976. Pp. 20.
Sixty-nine plates and accompanying historical notes.

827 MAINE STATE FEDERATED LABOR COUNCIL, AFL-CIO. Six decades of history, 1904-1963. [Augusta? 1964]. Pp. 15.

828 MAINE through the eyes of her artists. Portland: Hem Publishing, 1965. Unpaged.
Includes biographies of the artists.

829 "MAINE Turnpike story." The Maine Trail, (December, 1955), entire issue.
Includes a history of the turnpike by Lucius D. Barrows.

830 MAINE WRITERS RESEARCH CLUB. Historic churches and homes of Maine. Portland: Falmouth Book House, 1937. Pp. x, 289.

831 _____. Just Maine folks. Lewiston: Journal Printshop, 1924. Pp. 331.
Biographies.

832 _____. Maine Indians in history and legends. Portland: Severn-Wylie-Jewett, [1952]. Pp. 180.

833 _____. Maine, my state. Lewiston: Journal Printshop, 1919. Pp. 350.

834 _____. Maine, past & present. Boston: D. C. Heath, 1929. Pp. x, 321.

835 MAINE

835 _____. Maine writers of fiction for juveniles. Orono: Univ. of Maine, 1965. Pp. v, 69.

836 "MAINE'S early history." BTJ, 4 (1891-1892), 331.

837 "MAINE'S early Irish colonists." MeCathHM, 2 (February, 1914), 17-21, (March, 1914), 48-51.

838 "MAINE'S library background." MeLAB, 2 (April, 1941), 4-5.

839 "MAINE's railroad covered bridges." Down East, 14 (August, 1967), 60-63.

840 "MALECITE and Passamaquoddy tales." Northeast Folklore, 6 (1964), entire issue.

841 MANTOR, AGNES P. Our State of Maine: its story briefly told. Farmington: Knowlton & McLeary, 1933. Pp. 43.

842 MARBLE, ALBERT PRESCOTT. "Geography and history of Maine." Worcester HSProc, 6 (1883), 29-47.

843 _____. Geography of Maine. Cincinnati: Van Antwerp, Bragg, 1880. Pp. 10.

844 "THE MARCH of Benedict Arnold through the District of Maine." SJMH, 11 (1923), 144-150, 195-208.

845 MARKS, ARTHUR E. "Indian relics in Maine." MHGR, 8 (1895), 183-184.

846 MARRINER, ERNEST CUMMINGS. "Maine doctors of long ago." Maine Medical Association. Journal, 32 (1941), 161-167.

847 _____. "The Maine economy: before 1820." Thomas Business Review, 3 (Fall, 1975), 2-5.

848 _____. Remembered Maine. Waterville: Colby College Pr., 1957. Pp. 149.

849 MARSHALL, ROBERT BRADFORD. Spirit leveling in Maine, 1899-1915. Washington: Govt. Print. Off., 1916. Pp. 64.

850 MARTIN, FREDERIC THURMAN. The first fifty years of the Maine Section of the American Chemical Society. [Orono]: Univ. Pr., [1962?]. Pp. 7. MeU.

851 MARTIN, GEORGE CASTOR. "Indian burial in New Jersey, Maine and Maryland." Archaeological Bulletin, 2 (March, 1910), 33-38.

852 MARTIN, KENNETH R. "The folk art of Maine's whalemen." The Quarterdeck, 2 (Spring-Summer, 1972), 10-11.

853 MASSACHUSETTS. GENERAL COURT. Documents relating to the North Eastern Boundary of Maine. Boston: Dutton & Wentworth, 1828. Pp. 275.

854 MASSACHUSETTS BAR ASSOCIATION. Some accounts of early Maine history, presented at the regional meeting of the American Bar Association.... n.p., [1957]. Pp. 31.

855 MASTA, HENRY LORNE. Abenaki Indian legends, grammar and place names. Victoriaville, P.Q.: La Voix des bois-francs, 1932. Pp. 110.

856 MATTHEWS, ALBERT. "Edward Goddard's journal of the peace commission to the eastern Indians." CSMP, 20 (1917-1919), 129-147.

857 _____. "Origin of the name of Maine." CSMP, 12 (1908-1909), 366-382.

858 MAUNDER, ELWOOD R. and AMELIA FRY. "Samuel Trask Dana, the early years." Forest History, 10 (July, 1966), 2-13.
Maine Forest Commissioner.

859 MAURAULT, JOSEPH PIERRE ANSELME. Histoire des Abenakis, depuis 1605 jusqu' à nos jours. [Sorel, Quebec]: Imprimé à l'atelier typographique de la "Gazette de Sorel," 1866. Pp. iii, x, 631.

860 MAXFIELD, EZRA KEMPTON. "Maine dialect." American Speech, 2 (1927), 76-83.

861 _____. "Maine list." Dialect Notes, 5 (1926), 385-390.

862 MEAD, EDGAR THORN, JR. "Bridgton and Saco River R.R.: riding the narrow gauge to Bridgton." Down East, 15 (October, 1968), 30-33.

863 "MEANING of the Indian names Penobscot and Kennebec." Ladies' Repository, 24 (1864), 631.
Signed: H. Y. W.

864 MEIGS, RETURN JONATHAN. Journal of the expedition against Quebec under command of Col. Benedict Arnold in the year 1775. Charles Ira Bushnell, ed. N.Y.: Priv. Print., 1864. Pp. vi, 57.

865 MELLON, GERTRUD A. and ELIZABETH F. WILDER, eds. Maine and its role in American art, 1740-1963. N.Y.: Viking Pr., 1963. Pp. 178.

866 MELVIN, JAMES. The journal of James Melvin, private soldier in Arnold's Expedition against Quebec in the year 1775. Andrew A. Melvin, ed. Portland: H. W. Bryant, 1902. Pp. 90.

867 MEN of progress: biographical sketches and portraits of leaders in business and professional life in and of the State of Maine. Richard Herndon, comp. Boston: New England Magazine, 1897. Pp. 626.

868 MENDENHALL, THOMAS CORWIN. "Twenty unsettled mules in the Northeast Boundary." AASP, New Ser., 11 (1896-1897), 188-210.

869 MERCHANT, CHARLES HENRY. "Changes in the apple industry in Maine." Maine Agricultural Experiment Station. Report, 62 (1945-1946), 35-63.
　　1924-1944.

870 _____. "Maine farm prices during world war periods." Maine Agricultural Experiment Station. Report, 61 (1944-1945), 293-399.

871 _____. Prices on farm products in Maine. Orono: Maine Agricultural Experiment Station, 1933. Pp. 179. MH-BA.
　　1852-1932.

872 MERK, FREDERICK. Fruits of propaganda in the Tyler administration. Cambridge: Harvard Univ. Pr., 1971. Pp. x, 259.
　　Northeast Boundary.

873 MERRILL, DAPHNE WINSLOW. The lakes of Maine: a compilation of fact and legend. Rockland: Courier-Gazette, 1973. Pp. 263.

874 METZGER, HOMER B. and VANCE E. DEARBORN. Commercial farming in Maine, 1960-70: income, production, location, prices. Orono: Maine Cooperative Extension Service, 1971. Pp. 32. MeU.

875 MILIKEN, HENRY. "Old-time logging camp clerk." Down East, 19 (March, 1973), 48-51.

876 MILITARY ORDER OF THE LOYAL LEGION OF THE UNITED STATES. MAINE COMMANDERY. Historical address at the fiftieth anniversary of the Maine Commandery, December 7, 1916, by Henry S. Burrage. Portland: Fred. L. Tower, 1917. Pp. 20. Me.

876A MILLER, ALAN R. "America's first political satirist, Seba Smith of Maine." Journalism Quarterly, 47 (1970), 488-492.

877 MILLER, C. S. S. "The story of the states No. 6: Maine." Pearson's Magazine, 12 (August, 1901), 216.

878 MILLET, JOSHUA. A history of the Baptists in Maine; together with brief notices of societies and institutions, and a dictionary of the labors of each minister. Portland: C. Day, 1845. Pp. xii, 472.

879 MILLIKEN, PHILIP I. Notes on the Cumberland and Oxford Canal and the origin of the Canal Bank. Portland: Bradford Pr., 1935. Pp. 40.

880 MILLS, DUDLEY A. "British diplomacy in Canada: the Ashburton Treaty." United Empire, New Ser., 2 (1911), 683-712.

881 MILLS, HIRAM FRANCIS. Natural resources and their development. Memorial ... to the Governor and Council of Maine.... Augusta: Stevens & Sayward, 1867. Pp. 23.

882 MILLS, WILLIAM HOWARD. "Benedict Arnold's march to Canada." MagAmHist, 13 (1885), 143-154.

883 "MILLS at the eastward prior to 1800." BHist Mag, 6 (1890-1891), 18-21.
　　East of the Penobscot River.

884 ["MINERALS of Maine."] Rocks and Minerals, 5 (June, 1932), entire issue.

885 MINOT, JOHN CLAIR. "Maine's contribution to literature." MeLB, 8 (1918-1919), 104-106; 9 (1919-1920), 6-8, 31-34, 57-61.

886 "MISSIONS in Maine from 1603 to 1854." Catholic World, 22 (1875-1876), 666-677.

887 MITCHELL, DOROTHY. Along the Maine coast. N.Y.: McGraw-Hill, 1947. Pp. 97.

888 MITCHELL, EDWIN VALENTINE. Anchor to windward. N.Y.: Coward-McCann, 1949. Pp. 270.

889 _____. It's an old State of Maine custom. N.Y.: Vanguard Pr., 1949. Pp. 248.

890 _____. Maine summer. N.Y.: Coward-McCann, 1939. Pp. 210.

891 MOFFETT, ROSS. "Some samples of red ochre." MASB, 15 (1953-1954), 58.
　　Red Paint People.

892 MONTAGUE, HENRY BURT. "Some legal incidents in the separation of Maine from Massachusetts." Maine Law Review, 3 (1909-1910), 126-138.

893 MONTGOMERY, JOB HERRICK. "The judiciary of Maine." Maine Law Review, 7 (1913-1914), 222-235.

894 MOODY, LINWOOD W. The Maine two-footers: the story of the two-foot gauge railroads of Maine. Berkeley, Calif.: Howell-North, 1959. Pp. xv, 203.

895 _____. "Two foot gage." Railroad Magazine, 67 (December, 1955), 22-33.
　　Ten two-foot lines in Maine.

896 MOODY, RALPH. The fields of home. N.Y.: Norton, 1953. Pp. 335.
Country life.

897 MOODY, ROBERT EARLE. "A letter from Thomas Gorges' letterbook." MeHSN, 12 (1972-1973), 45-50.

898 _____. A proprietary experiment in early New England history: Thomas Gorges and the Province of Maine. [Boston]: Boston University Pr., 1963. Pp. 33.

899 MOORE, GLOVER. The Missouri controversy 1819-1821. Lexington: Univ. of Kentucky Pr., 1953. Pp. vii, 383.

900 MOORE, MARJORIE ANN. Literary landmarks of Maine. Veazie, 1969. Unpaged. Me.
Homes of Maine authors.

901 MOOREHEAD, WARREN KING. "The Red-Paint People of Maine." American Anthropologist, New Ser., 15 (1913), 33-47.
A comment on this article by D. I. Bushnell, Jr. in American Anthropologist, New Ser., 15 (1913), 707 was answered by Moorehead in his "'The Red-Paint People'--a reply." American Anthropologist, New Ser., 16 (1914), 358-361.

902 _____. A report on the archaeology of Maine; being a narrative of explorations in that state, 1912-1920, together with work at Lake Champlain, 1917. Andover, Mass.: Andover Pr., 1922. Pp. 272.

903 MORISON, SAMUEL ELIOT. "Notes from Maine." American Speech, 4 (1929), 356.

904 MORRELL, JENNIE MAY. Reminiscences of early meetings of the Josselyn Botanical Society. Josselyn Botanical Society of Maine. Bulletin, No. 10 (1955), 18-19.

905 MORRIS, EDWARD PARMELEE. "Along the Maine coast." Yale Review, New Ser., 5 (1916), 843-855.
Social life and customs.

906 MORRIS, GERALD E. ["Maine state seal."] MeHSN, 10 (1970-1971), 35-42, 70.

907 MORSE, FRANK LEANDER STAPLES. The history of secondary education in Knox and Lincoln counties in Maine. Orono: Univ. Pr., 1939. Pp. vii, 86.

908 MOSELEY, EMMA. "Maine's prima donnas." Sun Up, 3 (June, 1927), 7, 47-48.
Singers.

909 MOULTON, AUGUSTUS FREEDOM. Maine historical sketches. Lewiston: Lewiston Journal Printshop, 1929. Pp. 293.

910 _____, ed. Memorials of Maine: a life record of men and women of the past, whose sterling character and energy and industry have made them preeminent in their own and many other states. N.Y.: American Historical Society, 1916. Pp. 415.

911 _____. Sir Fernando Gorges and his palatinate of Maine: an address delivered before the Society of the Colonial Dames of America resident in the State of Maine, November 2, 1903. Portland: Printed for the Society, 1903. Pp. 28.

912 MUNSON, GORHAM BERT. "First Penobscot cruise: Champlain in 1604." Down East, 5 (April, 1959), 26-28, 33, 38-39.

913 _____. "Maine's first vacationist." Down East, 5 (January, 1959), 27-35.
Henry David Thoreau.

914 _____. Penobscot: Down East paradise. Philadelphia: Lippincott, 1959. Pp. 399.
Penobscot Valley.

915 MYERS, EDWARD A. "The law of the lobster." NEG, 4 (Spring, 1963), 13-20.

916 "NARRATIVE of the sufferings of Robert Forbes & family: their journey in 1784 from Canada to the Kennebec River." Down East, 3 (April, 1957), 20-23, 36-37.
A variation of an earlier account by Arthur Bradman; see entry 134.

917 NASON, EMMA HUNTINGTON. Old colonial houses in Maine built prior to 1776. Augusta: Kennebec Journal, 1908. Pp. x, 106.

918 _____. "The Pilgrim Fathers on the Kennebec." NEM, New Ser., 30 (1904), 309-320.
Kennebec Patent.

919 "NATIVE poets of Maine." MeLB, 13 (1927-1928), 101-114.

920 "NEGRO folk-songs from Maine." Folksong Society of the Northeast. Bulletin, No. 8 (1934), 13-16; No. 9 (1935), 10-15; No. 10 (1935), 21-24.

921 NETT, BRUCE OWEN. "44 miles of memories." Down East, 7 (April, 1961), 36-40.
Wiscasset, Waterville and Farmington Railroad.

922 NO ENTRY.

923 NEWELL, WILLIAM STARK. Shipbuilding in Maine: a brief history. Princeton, N.J.: Princeton Univ. Pr., 1938. Pp. 24.

924 NICHOLS, CHARLES JOSEPH. "Completion of Arnold's march through Maine." SJMH, 13 (1925), 69-78.

925 NICHOLS, GEORGE E. "Raised bogs in eastern Maine." GeogRev, 7 (1919), 159-167.
     Peat moss for surgical dressings.

926 NICHOLS, L. NELSON. "Studies in early American title pages--Maine." American Printer, 80 (March 20, 1925), 44-45.

927 NITKIN, NATHANIEL. "The lumberers." NEG, 11 (Winter, 1970), 28-36.

928 NIXON, MILTON A. "Supreme court of judicature." Maine Law Review, 14 (1962), 58-65.
     Supreme Judicial Court.

929 NOBLE, JOHN. "Land controversies in Maine--1736-1770." CSMP, 8 (1902-1904), 104-117.

930 "NORTH Eastern Boundary of the U. States." Boston Monthly Magazine, 1 (1825), 571-584.

931 NORWOOD, LESLIE E. "Colony Ordinance of 1641-47 and its effect on Maine law." Peabody Law Review, 3 (1939), 77-83.

932 NOYES, REGINALD WEBB. A bibliography of Maine imprints to 1820. Stonington, 1930. Pp. ix, 22.
     Supplemented by entry 934.

933 _____. A guide to the study of Maine local history. [Ann Arbor? Mich.], 1936. v, 87 leaves.
     Supplement to entry 518.

934 _____. Supplement to "A bibliography of Maine imprints to 1820." Stonington, 1934. Pp. 11. MeBa.
     See entry 932.

935 NUTTING, WALLACE. Maine beautiful: a pictorial record covering all the counties of Maine, with text between. Framingham, Mass.: Old America, 1924. Pp. 302.

936 O'BRIEN, FRANCIS MASSEY. "Selected readings in Maine history: local history." MeHSN, 5 (May, 1966), 5-9.

937 O'BRIEN, MICHAEL J. "The early Irish in Maine." AIrHSJ, 10 (1911), 162-170.

938 NO ENTRY.

939 ODD FELLOWS. INDEPENDENT ORDER OF. MAINE. GRAND LODGE. I.O.O.F., history of Odd Fellowship in Maine. Portland: F. G. Rich, 1878. Pp. iv, 356.

940 O'DWYER, GEORGE FRANCIS. "Captain James Howard, Col. William Lithgow, Col. Arthur Noble, and other Irish pioneers of Maine." AIrHSJ, 19 (1920), 71-88.

941 OGDEN, MARGUERITE. "How our church came to Maine." Spirit of Missions, 83 (1918), 135-142.
     Episcopal Church.

942 OLIVER, VELMA K. A history, State of Maine Division, American Association of University Women, 1946-1974. n.p., [1974?]. Pp. 36. MeBa.

943 OLMSTED, CAROLYN and MARGARET OLMSTED. Penobscot Bay treasures. Portland: Falmouth Publishing, 1950. Pp. 118.

944 ORCHARD, WILLIAM C. "Notes on Penobscot houses." American Anthropologist, New Ser., 11 (1909), 601-606.
     Penobscot Indian tepees.

945 "ORIGIN of the name of some of our Maine towns." MeLB, 13 (1927-1928), 25-27.

946 OSBORN, WILLIAM C. The paper plantation: Ralph Nader's study group report on the pulp and paper industry in Maine. N.Y.: Grossman Publishers, 1974. Pp. xx, 300.

947 O'TOOLE, FRANCIS J. and THOMAS N. TUREEN. "State power and the Passamaquoddy tribe: 'a gross national hypocrisy.'" Maine Law Review, 23 (1971), 1-39.

948 OWEN, HOWARD, comp. Biographical sketches of the members of the Senate and House of Representatives of Maine.... Augusta, 1872-1967. 53v.

949 OWEN, M. B. Story of Benedict Arnold's march on Quebec. n.p., [197-?]. Pp. 12. MeP.

950 PACKARD, ALPHEUS SPRING. "Discourse of Rev. Prof. Alpheus S. Packard, D.D., of Bowdoin College, at the semi-centennial anniversary of the General Conference of Congregational Churches in Maine, delivered in Portland, June 28, 1876." General Conference of Congregational Churches in Maine. Minutes, (1875), 111-133.

951 PACKARD, LEONARD O. "The decrease of population along the Maine coast." GeogRev, 2 (1916), 334-341.

952 PARK, FRANCIS E. "Eastward with No. 71." Down East, 9 (September, 1962), 34-36, 52.
     Maine Central Railroad.

953 PARKER, LESTER WARD. "Diary of a young man, 1807-1808." NEG, 7 (Summer, 1965), 31-42.
     Everett Howard, silhouette maker.

954 PARKER, WILLIAM J. "The Seguin: the little tugboat that has served Maine shipping since 1884." Down East, 6 (November, 1959), 38-40.

955 MAINE

955 PARSONS, USHER. "Memoir of Charles Frost."
NEHGR, 3 (1849), 249-262.
Seventeenth-century Maine.

956 PARSONS, VESTA M. "Thoreau's 'The Maine
Woods'; an essay in appreciation." Husson
Review, 1 (1967-1968), 17-27.

957 PATRONS OF HUSBANDRY. MAINE STATE GRANGE.
Golden jubilee, Maine State Grange, 1873-
1923. n.p., [1923?]. Pp. 64. MeU.
Includes history by E. H. Libby.

958 PATTANGALL, WILLIAM ROBINSON. The Meddybemps
letters, reproduced from the Machias Union of
1903-1904; Maine's hall of fame, reproduced
from the Maine Democrat of 1909-1910; memorial addresses. Lewiston: Lewiston Journal,
1924. Pp. 359.

959 PATTERSHALL, MARGARET S. "One hundred books
about Maine." Maine Teacher, 13 (December,
1952), 103-105.

960 PATTERSON, WILLIAM DAVIS. "Dunning family of
Maine." BHistMag, 6 (1890-1891), 35-42.

961 PAYNE, WILLIAM ELISHA. "History of homeopathy
in Maine." North American Journal of Homeopathy, 16 (1867-1868), 210-226.

962 PEABODY, HENRY GREENWOOD, comp. The coast of
Maine, Campobello to the Isles of Shoals.
Boston, 1889. Pp. 71.

963 PEAKS, JOSEPH B. "Maine's railroad growth."
BTJ, 16 (1903-1904), 14-15.

964 PEARL, CYRIL. "Maine, as a field for moral
and religious enterprise." American Quarterly
Register, 10 (1837), 185-192.

965 PECK, HENRY AUSTIN. Seaports in Maine: an
economic study. Orono: Univ. Pr., 1955.
Pp. v, 70.

966 PEIRCE, CHARLES. The unmasked nabob of Hancock County; or, the scales dropt from the
eyes of the people. Portsmouth, N.H., 1796.
Pp. 24.
A satire referring to the Kennebec Patent.

967 PÉLADEAU, MARIUS B. "Maine: preservation
Yankee style." Historic Preservation, 25
(October-December, 1973), 4-11.
Architecture.

968 PELLETIER, LAWRENCE LEE. The initiative and
referendum in Maine. Brunswick, 1951.
Pp. 35.

969 "PENOBSCOT Bay in 1556." BHistMag, 5 (1889-
1890), 61.

970 PERHAM, HAROLD C., ed. The Maine book on
Universalism. Norway: Advertiser-Democrat,
1953. Pp. 220.

971 PERKINS, ANNE E. "More notes on Maine dialect." American Speech, 5 (1929), 118-131.

972 _____. "Vanishing expressions of the Maine
coast." American Speech, 3 (1927), 134-141.

973 PERKINS, EDWARD H. "The evolution of Maine
scenery." Maine Naturalist, 9 (1929), 47-52.

974 PERKINS, VIRGINIA CHASE. "A mining boom in
Maine." NEQ, 14 (1941), 437-456.
1870s.

975 PERRY, TRUEMAN SUMMERFIELD. A sermon delivered before the Union Conference, at the
semi-centennial session, South Bridgton,
Maine, June 14, 1886. Portland: B. Thurston, 1886. Pp. 23. MB.
Formed from Congregational churches in Cumberland and Oxford counties.

976 PETERS, BRADLEY L. Maine Central Railroad
Company, a story of success and independence.
[Portland]: Maine Central Railroad Company,
1976. Pp. 16. MeHi.

977 PHILOON, JAMES E. The Maine Universalist
Convention: a brief history. Boston: Universalist Publishing, [1929]. Pp. 62.

978 PIERCE, WILLIAM C. "The rise and fall of the
York and Cumberland Rail Road." MeHSQ, 15
(1975-1976), 106-128.

979 PILSBURY, CHARLES ALBERT. "Some early Maine
journalists." SJMH, 3 (1915-1916), 41-43.

980 POLLARD, J. A. Polluted paradise: the story
of the Maine rape. Lewiston: Twin City
Printing, 1973. Pp. 328. MeP.
Environmental policy.

981 POLLARD, RALPH J. Freemasonry in Maine,
1762-1945. Portland: Tucker, [1945?].
Pp. 310. MeBa.

982 POOR, JOHN ALFRED. English colonization in
America: a vindication of Sir Ferdinando
Gorges, as the father of English colonization
in America. (Delivered before the Historical
Societies of Maine, and New York.) N.Y.:
D. Appleton, 1862. Pp. 144.

983 _____. The first international railway and
the colonization of New England. Laura E.
Poor, ed. N.Y.: G. P. Putnam's Sons, 1892.
Pp. 400.

984 _____. "Railroads in Maine." American Railroad Journal, 2 Ser., 4 (November 18, 1848),
737-738.

985 _____. The railway: remarks at Belfast,
Maine, July 4, 1867. Boston: Little, Brown,
1867. Pp. 61.

986 PORTER, FLORENCE COLLINS and HELEN BROWN
TRASK, eds. Maine men and women in southern
California: a volume regarding the lives of
Maine men and women of note and substantial
achievement, as well as those of a younger
generation whose careers are certain, yet
still in the making. Los Angeles: Kingsley,
Mason & Collins, 1913. Pp. 144.

987 PORTER, FREDERIC HUTCHINSON. A survey of
existing colonial architecture in Maine.
Architectural Review, 7 (1918), 29-32, 47-51,
94-96; 11 (1920), 13-15, 45-48, 83-88, 119-
120, 155-156, 183-186; 12 (1921), 41-46, 64,
73-76, 179-184. American Architect, 120
(1921), 149-151.

988 [PORTER, JOSEPH WHITCOMB.] "The Aroostook
War." SJMH, 1 (1913-1914), 142-143.
Author attribution by the editor.

989 [_____.] "Notes on the early history of the
Catholic Church in eastern Maine." SJMH, 1
(1913-1914), 66-68.
Author attribution by the editor.

990 [_____.] "Owners of Maine lands when Maine
became a state." SJMH, 2 (1914-1915), 16-25.
Author attribution by the editor.

991 _____. "Porter families in Maine." Maine
Genealogist and Biographer, 1 (1875-1867),
45-49.

992 POTTLE, GEORGE. "The growth of Maine in the
last decade." BTJ, 16 (1903-1904), 44-46.

993 POWERS, W. A. "Maine." Town and Country, 108
(June, 1954), 42-45, 89-90, 93.
Social life and customs.

994 PREHISTORIC peoples of Maine: a Maine State
Museum teacher's resource unit. (1970) Rev.
William H. Soule, ed. Augusta: Maine State
Museum, 1975. Pp. 55. Me.

995 PRENTISS, THOMAS MELLEN. The Maine spelling
book: containing rules and examples for
spelling and pronouncing the English language ... to which is annexed a concise geographical description of Maine, its boundaries, bays, islands, counties, capital towns,
mountains, rivers, character, etc; designed
for the use of schools in the District of
Maine. Leominster, Mass.: Charles & John
Prentiss, 1799. Pp. vii, 123.

996 "PRESBYTERIANISM in Maine, prior to 1870."
BHistMag, 3 (1887-1888), 205-207.

997 "PRESIDENTIAL electors in the District of
Maine when it was part of Massachusetts."
BHistMag, 4 (1888-1889), 127-128.
1789-1816.

998 PRINCE, GEORGE. "The voyage of Capt. Geo.
Weymouth to the coast of Maine in 1605."
MeHSC, 6 (1859), 291-306.

999 PRINCE, J. DYNELEY. "Notes on Passamaquoddy
literature." New York Academy of Sciences.
Annals, 13 (1900-1901), 381-386.

1000 _____. "A Passamaquoddy tobacco famine."
International Journal of American Linguistics,
1 (1917), 58-63.

1001 _____. "The Passamaquoddy wampum records."
American Philosophical Society. Proceedings,
36 (1897), 479-495.

1002 _____. "The Penobscot language of Maine."
American Anthropologist, 12 (1910), 183-208.

1003 _____. "Some Passamaquoddy witchcraft tales."
American Philosophical Society. Proceedings,
38 (1899), 181-189.

1004 PROMINENT men of Maine: individual biographic studies with character portraits. N.Y.:
Historical Records, 1940. Unpaged.
Morrill Goddard and Charles William Goddard;
no more published.

1005 PROSSER, ALBERT L. "History of the Josselyn
Botanical Society." Josselyn Botanical Society of Maine. Bulletin, No. 10 (1975), 6-17.

1006 PROTESTANT EPISCOPAL CHURCH IN THE U.S.A.
MAINE (DIOCESE). One hundredth anniversary
of the Diocese of Maine, 1820-1920, Christ
Church, Gardiner, Maine, May thirtieth to
June third. Gardiner, 1920. Pp. xi, 159.

1007 PROVOST, HONORIUS. "Un chapitre d'histoire
religieuse dans le Maine." La Revue de
l'Université Laval, 2 (June, 1948), 853-860.
Services of l'Abbé Moyse Fortier to Canadian immigrants in Maine, 1838-1845.

1008 "PUBLISHERS and journalists of Maine." MeLB,
14 (1928-1929), 55-75.

1009 PULLEN, JOHN J. A shower of stars: the
Medal of Honor and the 27th Maine. Philadelphia: Lippincott, 1966. Pp. 269.
An historical mystery of the disappearance
of a barrelful of medals and the showering of
medals on members of the 27th Maine Regiment,
less than half of whom were qualified to re-
ceive them.

1010 PURCELL, RICHARD J. "Maine: early schools
and Irish teachers." Catholic Educational
Review, 33 (1935), 211-225.

1011 PUTNAM, FRANK ARTHUR. "Maine: a study in
land-grabbing, tax-dodging, and isolation."
NEM, New Ser., 36 (1907), 515-540.

1012 MAINE

1012 PUTNAM, FREDERICK WARD. "The kitchen-middings of Maine." Kansas City Review, 6 (1882-1883), 523-526."

1013 [RADCLIFFE, JANE E.] 150 years of Maine governors. Augusta: Maine State Museum, 1972. Unpaged. Me.

1014 RAHILL, PETER JAMES. "A new trail is blazed in Maine." Social Justice Review, 51 (December, 1958), 264-267.
Catholics in Maine since 1780.

1015 RAND, EDWIN HOLMES. "Maine privateers in the Revolution." NEQ, 11 (1938), 826-834.

1016 RANDALL, DANIEL BOODY. A statistical history of the Maine Conference of the M. E. Church from 1793 to 1893. Portland: Lakeside Pr., 1893. Pp. 233.

1017 RANLETT, CHARLES EVERETT. Master mariner of Maine, being the reminiscences of Charles Everett Ranlett, 1816-1917, as told to his son Frederick Jordan Ranlett, with additional chapters by his daughter Susan Alice Ranlett; an introduction and notes by his grandson L. Felix Ranlett and notes by Lincoln Colcord. Portland: Southworth-Anthoensen Pr., 1942. Pp. xi, 145.

1018 [RATTERMANN, HEINRICH ARMIN.] "Geschichte des deutschen Elements in Staate Maine: dessen Ursprung, Entwickelung und Verfall, vom Jahre 1739 bis Gegenwart." Der Deutsche Pionier, 14 (1882-1883), 7-13, 53-62, 90-98, 141-150, 174-188, 217-233, 266-276, 292-303, 338-361, 425-434, 464-468; 15 (1883-1884), 74-82, 104-114, 201-210, 226-235, 267-283, 358-375; 16 (1884-1885), 11-18, 71-77, 98-102, 195-204, 227-238, 276-281, 302-311, 349-359.

1019 RAWLINGS, CHARLES. "The secret of Maine cider." Saturday Evening Post, 231 (October 25, 1958), 44-15, 106-108.
Social life and customs.

1020 RAY, ROGER BRAY. "Maine Indians' concept of land tenure." MeHSQ, 13 (1973-1974), 28-51, 178-179.

1021 _____. "The Norsemen and the Indians of Maine." MeHSN, 9 (1969-1970), 61-62.

1022 READE, JOHN. "Some Wabanaki songs." Royal Society of Canada. Proceedings and Transactions, 5 Pt. 2 (1887), 1-8.

1023 "RECORD of big game shipments, 1895-1908." In the Maine Woods, (1909), 83.

1024 REDDEN, JOHN. "The beginnings of Catholic education in Maine." Catholic Educational Review, 37 (1939), 509-516.
1612-1864.

1025 REDDINGTON, ASA. "Complete list of attorneys at law in the counties of Franklin and Somerset, Maine." American Quarterly Register, 13 (1840-1841), 293-295.

1026 REED, DONALD WINSLOW. Tax trends in Maine towns.... Orono: Maine Agricultural Experiment Station, 1939. Pp. 12. MeBa.

1027 REED, PARKER McCOBB. History of the lower Kennebec, 1602-1889. Bath: Sentinel & Times Print, 1889. Pp. 72.

1028 "REGARDING soldiers of the American Revolution: Maine Indians in the Revolution." SJMH, 6 (1918-1919), 105-111.

1029 REID, JOHN G. "Styles of colonisation and social disorders in early Acadia and Maine: a comparative approach." Société Historique Acadienne. Cahiers, 7 (1976), 105-117.

1030 "REMARKS on the Indian languages." MeHSC, 1 (1831), 310-323.
Abenaqui and Norridgewock Indians.

1031 REYHER, REBECCA. "Maine ship carvings of the nineteenth century." Down East, 21 (November, 1974), 44-47.

1032 REYNOLDS, HORACE. "Down East dialects." Yankee, 19 (January, 1955), 68-69.

1033 RICE, MARSHALL. "Indian history." MeArch SocB, No. 7 (October, 1967), 14-17.

1034 RICE, W. A. and ISAAC R. CLARK. Objects and history of United Fellowship in Maine. Bangor: O. F. Knowles, 1883. Pp. 32. MeHi.
Fraternal organization.

1035 RICE, WILLIAM B. "Sidewheelers and propellers, 1823-1860." The Quarterdeck, 1 (Summer, 1971), 6-7, 14-15; 2 (Winter, 1972), 12-14.
Steamships.

1036 RICH, LOUISE DICKINSON. The coast of Maine, an informal history. (1956) Updated ed. N.Y.: Crowell, 1975. Pp. xiv, 385.

1037 _____. Happy the land. Philadelphia: J. B. Lippincott, 1946. Pp. 259.

1038 _____. The natural world of Louise Dickinson Rich. N.Y.: Dodd, Mead, 1962. Pp. xxvi, 195.

1039 _____. State o' Maine. N.Y.: Harper & Row, 1964. Pp. xvi, 302.

1040 _____. We took to the woods. Philadelphia: J. B. Lippincott, 1942. Pp. 322.

1041 RICHARDS, JOSEPHINE. "The descendants of Rev. John Lovejoy in Maine, and reminiscences of early Maine times." SJMH, 3 (1915-1916), 112-114.

1042 RICHARDSON, HOBART WOOD. "The Pemaquid country under the Stuarts." MeHSC, 8 (1881), 183-195.
Land given to the Duke of York by his brother, King Charles II, in 1664.

1043 RICHARDSON, JOHN MITCHELL. Steamboat lore of the Penobscot: an informal story of steamboating in Maine's Penobscot region. (1941) 5th ed. Rockland: Courier Gazette, 1971. Pp. 207. MeP.

1044 RICKER, JOSEPH. Personal recollections: a contribution to Baptist history and biography. Augusta: Burleigh & Flynt, 1894. Pp. x, 434.

1045 RIDLON, GIDEON TIBBETTS. Saco Valley settlements and families: historical, biographical, genealogical, traditional and legendary.... Portland, 1895. Pp. xiv, 1250.

1046 RINEHART, JONATHAN. "Down East." USA *1, 1 (June, 1962), 76-84.

1047 RING, ELIZABETH. Maine bibliographies: a bibliographical guide. Portland: Maine Historical Society, 1973. Pp. 34.

1048 _____. The progressive movement of 1912 and third party movements of 1924 in Maine. Orono: Univ. Pr., 1933. Pp. 68.

1049 _____. A unit of study in Maine history and government based on the "Maine Register." Portland: Fred L. Tower, 1945. Pp. 24. MeBa.

1050 ROBERTS, KENNETH LEWIS. "Don't say that about Maine." Saturday Evening Post, 221 (November 6, 1948), 30-31, 126, 130, 132, 135-136.
Social life and customs; a reply to uncomplimentary remarks in Arnold J. Toynbee's "Study of History."

1051 _____, ed. March to Quebec: journals of the members of Arnold's Expedition. N.Y.: Doubleday, Doran, 1938. Pp. xiv, 657.

1052 _____. Trending into Maine. (1938) Rev. ed. N.Y.: Doubleday, Doran, 1944. Pp. 421.

1053 ROBINSON, CLARENCE CROMWELL. A study of the background and work experience of war production trainees in Maine, 1940-1943. Augusta: Vocational Training for War Production Workers, 1943. 25 leaves.

1054 ROBINSON, CLAUDE E. "Maine--political barometer." PolSciQ, 47 (1932), 161-184.

1055 ROBINSON, WILLIAM A. "Maine's century of statehood." Granite Mo, 52 (1920), 170-171.

1056 RODGER, WILLIAM. "Maine's folk art." Down East, 22 (November, 1974), 44-47.

1057 ROGERS, DONALD. "Capture of the rumrunner 'Grey Ghost.'" Down East, 18 (June, 1972), 60-61, 113-114, 119-120.
1920s.

1058 ROGERS, LORE ALFRED and CALEB WARREN SCRIBNER. "The log haulers." The Northern Logger and Timber Processer, 16 (August, 1967), 8-9, 34-38.

1059 ROGERS, LORE ALFRED. "The old pine days." Down East, 8 (March, 1962), 28-32, 44-45.
Logging and log drives.

1060 _____ and CALEB WARREN SCRIBNER. "The peavey cant-dog." CEAIA, 20 (June, 1967), 17-21.
Lumbering tools.

1061 ROSIER, JAMES. Rosier's relation of Waymouth's voyage to the coast of Maine, 1605. Henry S. Burrage, ed. Portland: Gorges Society, 1887. Pp. xi, 176.

1062 ROSS, LINWOOD. "The adoption of an archival program for Maine." American Archivist, 29 (1966), 395-402.
History of archival legislation.

1063 ROUNDY, CHARLES G. "Some geographic aspects of civilian defense during World War II." Maine Geographer, No. 4 (November, 1969), 1-7.

1064 ROUNDY, RODNEY W. Cooperation, a record of Christian service, the Interdenominational Commission of Maine. n.p., 1950. Pp. 35. MBC.

1065 _____. "Sesquicentennial." MeCP, 44 (February 15, 1957), 8-9, (March 15, 1957), 3-4.
Maine Missionary Society.

1066 ROWE, JOHN HOWLAND. "Archaeology and history in eastern Maine." MASB, 2 (July, 1941), 7-13.

1067 ROWE, WILLIAM HUTCHINSON. The maritime history of Maine, three centuries of shipbuilding and seafaring. N.Y.: W. W. Norton, 1948. Pp. 333.

1068 RUSH, NIXON ORWIN. The history of college libraries in Maine. Worcester, Mass.: Clark Univ. Library, 1946. Pp. 53.

1069 RUSSELL, WALTER E. "Evolution of the Maine Teachers' Association." Maine Teachers' Digest, 3 (1942-1943), 9-10.

1070 RUTHERFORD, PHILLIP R. The dictionary of Maine place-names. Freeport: Bond Wheelwright, 1971. Pp. xx, 283.

1071 MAINE

1071 RYAN, ALLIE. Penobscot Bay, Mount Desert and Eastport steamboat album. Camden: Down East Enterprise, 1972. Pp. 72.

1072 SABINE, LORENZO. "Forest lands and timber trade of Maine." North American Review, 58 (1844), 299-335.

1073 _____. "Indian tribes of New England." Christian Examiner, 52 (1852), 96-117; 62 (1857), 27-54, 210-237.

1074 SALTONSTALL, RICHARD. Maine pilgrimage: the search for an American way of life. Boston: Little, Brown, 1974. Pp. x, 353.

1075 SANBORN, V. C. "Stephen Bachiler and the Plough Company of 1630." MeHSC, 3 Ser., 2 (1906), 342-369.

1076 SANDS, DONALD B. "The nature of the generics in island, ledge, and rock names of the Maine coast." Names, 7 (December, 1959), 193-202.

1077 SANGER, DAVID and ROBERT G. MacKAY. Maine prehistory: a selection of short papers. Orono: Univ. of Maine, 1973. Variously leaved. Me.

1078 SANGER, DAVID. "Who were the Red Paints?" MeArchSocB, 13 (Spring, 1973), 3-12.

1079 SARGENT, PAUL. "Maine highways and their history...." Sun Up, 3 (January, 1927), 10-11, 18, 20, 22, 39.

1080 SARGENT, WILLIAM MITCHELL. "Bearing of Captain John Mason's titles upon Maine history." MeHSC, 2 Ser., 8 (1897), 53-66, 175-193.
Land titles.

1081 _____. Maine wills, 1640-1760. Portland: Brown, Thurston, 1887. Pp. xii, 953.

1082 SAVAGE, ALBERT RUSSELL. An index-digest of the reports of cases decided by the Supreme Judicial Court of Maine, volumes 1 to 88, Maine Reports, inclusive. 1820-1896. Portland: Loring, Short & Harmon, 1897. Pp. 1180.

1083 _____. A supplemental index-digest of the reports of cases decided by the Supreme Judicial Court of Maine, volumes 89 to 103, Maine Reports, inclusive. 1896-1908. Portland: Loring, Short & Harmon, 1909. Pp. 404.

1084 SAVAGE, RICHARD A. "Maine steamboating, 1818-1868." Steamboat Bill, 27 (1970), 196-203.

1085 SAWTELLE, WILLIAM OTIS. Historic trails and waterways of Maine. Augusta: Maine Development Commission, 1932. Pp. 108.

1086 SAWYER, ALDEN H. History of trust business in Maine. New Brunswick, N.J.: Rutgers Univ., 1949. 92 leaves. MeP.

1087 SCAMMON, E. PARKER. "An interesting chapter of the early history of Maine." Catholic World, 56 (1892-1893), 181-190.

1088 _____. "Maine of a later day." Catholic World, 56 (1892-1893), 549-559.
Father Rasles and Maine in the Revolution.

1089 _____. "The settlement of Maine." Catholic World, 56 (1892-1893), 365-375.

1090 SCAMMON, JONATHAN YOUNG. An address delivered before the Society of the Sons of the State of Maine in Illinois, at its second annual meeting, at the Palmer House, Chicago, March 15, 1882; together with a sketch of its organization and proceedings, constitution, by-laws, list of officers, and roll of members. Chicago: Fergus Printing, 1882. Pp. 39.

1091 SCHMECKEBIER, L. F. "How Maine became a state." MeHSC, 2 Ser., 9 (1898), 146-171.

1092 SCHRIVER, EDWARD OSWALD. "Abolitionists organize: the Maine Antislavery Society." MeHSN, 9 (1969-1970), 33-38, 73-78.

1093 _____. "Antislavery: the Free Soil and Free Democratic parties in Maine." NEQ, 42 (1969), 82-94.

1094 _____. "Black politics without blacks: Maine 1841-1848." Phylon, 31 (1970), 194-201.

1095 _____. Go free: the antislavery impulse in Maine, 1833-1855. Orono: Univ. of Maine Pr., 1970. Pp. xvi, 154.

1096 _____. "Maine: a bibliographical review." Acadiensis, 5 (Spring, 1976), 154-162.

1097 _____. Maine newspapers in the smaller Maine public libraries. Orono, n.d. 17 leaves. MeU.

1098 _____. "Select list of unpublished master's theses from the University of Maine." MeHSN, 8 (May, 1969), 8-15; 9 (1969-1970), 17-19.
All on Maine subjects.

1099 SCOFIELD, JOHN. "Character marks the coast of Maine." National Geographic Magazine, 133 (1968), 799-843.

1100 SCONTRAS, CHARLES ANDREW. Two decades of labor politics in Maine, 1880-1900. Orono: Bureau of Labor Education, Univ. of Maine, 1969. Pp. 202.
A shorter version of this work was published in 1966 with the title "Organized labor and labor politics in Maine 1880-1890."

1101 SCULL, GIDEON DELAPLAINE, ed. "The Montrésor Journals." New-York Historical Society. Collections, 14 (1881), xi-xiv, 3-578.
Includes expedition across Maine from Canada, 1760.

1102 "THE SEAL of the State of Maine." MeLB, 15 (1929-1930), 114-116.

1103 SEWALL, RUFUS KING. Ancient dominions of Maine, embracing the earliest facts, the recent discoveries of the remains of aboriginal towns, the voyages, settlements, battle scenes, and incidents of Indian warfare, and other incidents of history, together with the religious developments of society within the ancient Sagadahoc, Sheepscot and Pemaquid precincts and dependencies. Bath: E. Clark, 1859. Pp. x, 366.

1104 _____. Ancient voyages to the western continent: three phases of history on the coast of Maine. N.Y.: Knickerbocker Pr., 1895. Pp. ix, 79.

1105 SHAILER, WILLIAM HOSMER. A historical discourse delivered in Winthrop, June 16, 1874 before the Maine Baptist Missionary Convention. Portland: B. Thurston, 1874. Pp. 68. MeHi.
Baptists; Pages [37]-67 have a separate title page: A memorial paper read at the semi-centennial meeting of the Maine Baptist Missionary Convention, held at East Winthrop, June 16, 17, 18, 1874. By Charles Greenleaf Porter. Portland: B. Thurston, 1874.

1106 SHARF, FREDERIC ALAN. "Fitz Hugh Lane: visits to the Maine coast, 1848-1855." EIHC, 98 (1962), 111-120.

1107 SHAUGHNESSY, JIM. "Ghost train in the Maine woods." Down East, 13 (July, 1966), 40-43, 79.
Transportation routes in northern Maine.

1108 SHAY, FLORENCE NICOLA. History of the Penobscot tribe of Indians. n.p., Priv. Print., 1941. Pp. 15. Me.

1109 SHEA, JOHN GILMARY. "Early missions in Acadia." Catholic World, 12 (1870-1871), 629-643, 826-837.

1110 SHELDON, EDWARD STEVENS. "Some specimens of Canadian French dialect spoken in Maine." Modern Language Association of America. Transactions and Proceedings, 3 (1887), 210-218.

1111 SHENTON, EDWARD H. Historical review of oil spills along the Maine coast, 1953-1973. [Portland?]: Research Institute of the Gulf of Maine, 1973. v.p. MeU.

1112 SHERWOOD, MARY P. "Thoreau's Penobscot Indians." Thoreau Journal, 1 (January 15, 1969), 1-13.

1113 SHERWOOD, R. H. "Missions in Maine from 1613 to 1854." Catholic World, 22 (1876), 666-678.

1114 SHETTLEWORTH, EARLE G., JR. Maine historic resources inventory. Augusta: Maine Historic Preservation Commission, 1975. 128 leaves.

1115 SHORT, VINCENT. Sail and steam along the Maine coast. Portland: Bond Wheelwright, 1955. Pp. 203.

1116 SHUTE, ALBERTA VAN HORN. "Or ever the silver cord." n.p., 1957. Pp. 71.
Social life and customs.

1117 SIEBERT, WILBUR HENRY. "The exodus of the loyalists from Penobscot and the loyalist settlements at Passamaquoddy." New Brunswick Historical Society. Collections, 3 (1914), 485-529.

1118 SIEUR de Monts commission. De Monts and Acadia, an appreciation. George B. Dorr, ed. Bar Harbor: Wild Gardens of Acadia, [1917?] Pp. 12.

1119 SILBER, MARK, comp. The family album: photographs of the 1890s & 1900s, by Gilbert Wight Tilton and Fred W. Record. Boston: D. R. Godine, 1973. Pp. 93.

1120 NO ENTRY.

1121 SILSBY, HERBERT T., II. "A secret emissary from Down East." MeHSN, 11 (1971-1972), 106-126.
George Herbert in the War of 1812.

1122 SILSBY, SAMUEL SCHOPPEE. History of statutory law in the State of Maine. [St. Paul, Minn.: West, 1964.] Pp. 225. Me.
Reprinted from volume one of Maine Revised Statutes Annotated.

1123 _____. Materials in collected public documents of Maine on state constitutional amendments, 1833-1963. Augusta, 1963. 58 leaves. Me.

1124 SIMMONS, MILDRED. "They're off ... harness racing past and present." Down East, 2 (September, 1955), 16-20.

1125 SIMPSON, DOROTHY. The Maine islands, in story and legend. Philadelphia: Lippincott, 1960. Pp. 256.

1126 SIMPSON, SUELLEN, ed. ["Bicentennial Maine."] Salt, 3 (June, 1976), entire issue.

1127 MAINE

1127 SINCOCK, W. E. "In Maine, looking back 50 years." Maine Medical Association. Journal, 33 (1942), 31-33.

1128 "SKETCH of the life of General Lafayette, with an account of his visit to Maine." MeHSC, 2 Ser., 3 (1892), 57-78.
Visited in 1825.

1129 SLAFTER, EDMUND FARWELL. "The discovery of America by Northmen in the early part of the eleventh century." BHistMag, 5 (1889-1890), 78-80.

1130 SMALL, ALBION KEITH PARRIS. Memorial sermon ... East Brunswick Baptist Church ... 75th anniversary of the Cumberland Association.... Portland: B. Thurston, 1885. Pp. 14. MeHi.

1131 SMALL, CARLETON POTTER. "Unitarianism in Maine." UHSP, 8 Pt. 2 (1950), 18-33.

1132 SMALL, EDWIN SUMNER. A centennial review of the Bowdoinham Association of Baptist Churches in Maine delivered at the one hundredth anniversary meeting, at Bowdoinham, September 13, 1887. Portland: B. Thurston & Co., 1887. Pp. 54. Me.

1133 SMALL, WILLIAM A. "Schooling in the unorganized territory of Maine." Elementary School Journal, 56 (November, 1956), 117-120.
1895-1945.

1134 SMILLIE, WILSON GEORGE and JEAN ALONZO CURRAN. Medical care in the State of Maine, 1956-1962. Bethel: Bingham Associates Fund, [1962]. Pp. 156.

1135 SMITH, BENJAMIN L. "An analysis of the Maine cemetery complex." MASB, 9 (1947-1948), 21-71.
Notes on forty-four cemeteries in Maine.

1136 _____. "Some aspects of the use of red ochre in prehistoric burials." MASB, 11 (1949-1950), 22-28.

1137 SMITH, CHARLES W. A history of clockmaking in Maine. National Association of Watch and Clock Collectors. Bulletin, 15 (April, 1973).

1138 SMITH, DAVID CLAYTON. A history of lumbering in Maine, 1861-1960. Orono: Univ. of Maine Pr., 1972. Pp. xvi, 468.

1139 _____. "The logging frontier." Forest History, 18 (1974), 96-106.

1140 _____. Lumbering and the Maine woods: a bibliographical guide. Portland: Maine Historical Society, 1971. Pp. 34.

1141 _____. "Wood pulp paper comes to the northeast, 1865-1900." Forest History, 10 (April, 1966), 12-25.

1142 SMITH, DOROTHY, ed. Union list of serials in Maine libraries. Orono: Univ. Pr., 1937. Pp. x, 257.

1143 SMITH, EDGAR CROSBY. "Maine map-makers and their maps: Osgood Carleton." SJMH, 2 (1914-1915), 3-9.

1144 _____. Maps of the State of Maine: a bibliography of the maps of the State of Maine. Bangor, 1903. Pp. 29.

1145 _____. Moses Greenleaf, Maine's first map-maker; a biography, with letters, unpublished manuscripts and a reprint of Mr. Greenleaf's rare paper on Indian place-names; also a bibliography of the maps of Maine. Bangor: C. H. Glass, 1902. Pp. xviii, 165.

1146 _____. "Short biographies of the members of the first Maine Senate." SJMH, 8 (1920), 22-26.

1147 SMITH, ELIZABETH OAKES PRINCE. "Maine: an historical sketch." Potter's AmMo, 13 (1879), 198-202.

1148 SMITH, GEORGE OTIS. "Maine, the outpost state: some forgotten incidents in the life of an old stout-hearted commonwealth." National Geographic Magazine, 67 (1935), 533-592.

1149 SMITH, JOSEPH COBURN. "The life of the Maine woodsmen in 1926." CEAIA, 26 (1973), 45-48.

1150 _____. "Maine and her trees." Maine Naturalist, 7 (1927), 3-14.
Forest history.

1151 _____. "The tools of the Maine woodsmen in 1926." CEAIA, 25 (1972), 49-54.

1152 _____. "The work of the woodsmen in the Maine woods." CEAIA, 26 (1973), 28-29.

1153 SMITH, JOSEPH S. "How two Maine parishes started." The North East, 35 (December, 1907), 8-10.
Grace Church, Bath and the first Episcopal service in Wiscasset.

1154 SMITH, JUSTIN HARVEY. Arnold's march from Cambridge to Quebec: a critical study, together with a reprint from Arnold's journal. N.Y.: G. P. Putnam's Sons, 1903. Pp. xix, 498.

1155 _____. Our struggle for the fourteenth colony: Canada and the American Revolution. N.Y.: G. P. Putnam's Sons, 1907. 2v.
Arnold's Expedition.

1156 SMITH, LINCOLN. "The Great Pond Ordinance--collectivism in northern New England." BULRev, 30 (1950), 178-190.
1641.

1157 ____. "Maine's power embargo--how it may
be terminated." Cornell Law Quarterly, 36
(1951), 342-354.
   Fernald Law (1909), prohibiting export of
electrical power from Maine.

1158 ____. The power policy of Maine. Berkeley:
Univ. of California Pr., 1951. Pp. vi, 344.

1159 SMITH, MARION JAQUES. A history of Maine,
from wilderness to statehood. Portland:
Falmouth Publishing, 1949. Pp. 348.

1160 SMITH, MARION WHITNEY. Algonquian and Abenaki Indian myths and legends. Lewiston:
Central Maine Pr., 1962. Unpaged.

1161 ____. Strange tales of Abenaki shamanism.
Lewiston: Central Maine Pr., 1963. Pp. 47.

1162 SMITH, NICHOLAS N. "The challenge of Maine
archaeology." MeArchSocB, No. 1, (Spring,
1964), [3-4].

1163 ____. Penobscot traditions: Penobscot life
in prehistoric times. n.p., n.d. Unpaged.
MeHi.

1164 ____. "Smoking habits of the Wabanaki."
MASB, 18 (1956-1957), 76-77.
   Indians.

1165 ____. "The survival of the Red Paint complex in Maine." MASB, 17 (1955-1956), 4-6.

1166 SMITH, OSCAR S. The lumber industry on
Penobscot waters. The Northern, 4 (April,
1924), 5-10, (May, 1924), 2-3, 5-10, (June,
1924), 2-4, 13-15, (July, 1924), 2-9, (August, 1924), 3-4, 14, (September, 1924),
5-6, 9, 15.

1167 SMITH, ROLAND. "Maine beginnings." Sun Up,
9 (June, 1931), 1.

1168 SMITH, WALTER BROWN. "Aboriginal axes of
the Penobscot." Bangor Historical Society.
Proceedings, (1914-1915), 34-41.

1169 ____. Indian remains of the Penobscot Valley and their significance. Orono: Univ.
Pr., 1926. Pp. 90.

1170 ____. The lost Red Paint People of Maine,
a few things we think we know about them
and more that we know we don't. Bar Harbor,
1930. Pp. 43.

1171 SMITH, WILLIAM H. "The King family of
Maine." MHGR, 1 (1884), 1-8, 33-40.

1172 ____. "Reminiscences of the Grand Lodge of
Maine." FR, 13 (1883-1884), 381-382.
   Freemasons.

1173 "SMUGGLING in Maine during the War of 1812."
BHistMag, 3 (1887-1888), 201-203.

1174 "SMUGGLING in Maine in 1813." BHistMag, 3
(1887-1888), 105-108.

1175 SMYTH, LAWRENCE T. "The lumber industry in
Maine." NEM, New Ser., 25 (1901-1902), 629-
648.

1176 SNOW, CHARLES AUGUSTUS. The history of the
development of public school supervision in
the State of Maine. Orono: Univ. Pr.,
1939. Pp. vii, 99.

1177 SNOW, DEAN R. "A century of Maine archaeology." MeArchSocB, No. 8 (1968), 8-25.

1178 ____. "The changing prey of Maine's early
hunters." Natural History, 83 (November,
1974), 15-16, 18, 22, 24.

1179 ____. The Penobscot Indians in Thoreau's
time." Thoreau Journal, 2 (January 15, 1970),
7-11.

1180 ____. "Rising sea level and prehistoric
cultural ecology in northern New England."
American Antiquity, 37 (1972), 211-221; 39
(1974), 136-137.
   Second part is a comment by Walter S. Newman.

1181 ____. A summary of prehistoric sites in the
State of Maine. [Orono]: Department of
Anthropology, Univ. of Maine, 1969. Pp. v,
142.

1182 ____. "Wabanaki family hunting territories."
American Anthropologist, 70 (1968), 1143,
1151.

1183 SOCIETY OF COLONIAL WARS. MAINE. History
of Society of Colonial Wars in the State of
Maine, 1898-1946, and roll of members.
Charles J. Nichols, comp. [Portland?], 1947.
Pp. x, 81.

1184 ____. Register of the officers and members
of the Society of Colonial Wars in the State
of Maine; also history, roster and record of
Colonel Jedidiah Preble's regiment, campaign
of 1758; together with Capt. Samuel Cobb's
journal. Portland: Marks Printing, 1905.
Pp. 180.

1185 "SOLON Chase and 'them steers' back in Maine
days in 1878." Sun Up, 3 (February, 1927),
26.
   Greenback Party and the election of 1878.

1186 "SOME account of the Catholic missions in
Maine." MeHSC, 1 (1831), 323-340.
   Seventeenth century.

1187 "SOME representative Maine men of yesterday and today." SJMH, 8 (1920), 50-78, 117-118.

1188 SONS OF THE AMERICAN REVOLUTION. MAINE SOCIETY. What the Society in Maine has done, organization and officers of the Society, constitution of the Society, roll of members, officers of National Society, constitution of the National Society. Portland: LeFavor-Tower, 1903. Pp. 259.

1189 SOULE, ALFRED MORTON GILMORE. "The Maine Department of Agriculture." Maine. Commissioner of Agriculture. Biennial Report, (1948-1950), 79-92.
      A departmental history.

1190 SOULE, PHELPS. "The Hampton Boat." AmNep, 3 (1943), 141-147.
      Shipbuilding.

1191 SOULE, WILLIAM H., ed. European exploration, discovery, and early settlement of Maine. Augusta: Maine State Museum, 1975. Pp. v, 113. Me.

1192 "SOURCES for a maritime history of Maine." MeLB, 17 (1931-1932), 34-40.
      Bibliography.

1193 SOUTHARD, EUGENIA M. and CHARLES E. CAMPBELL. "Books by Maine authors and books about Maine, 1950-1951." Pine Cone, 7 (Spring, 1951), 30-33.

1194 SPALDING, JAMES ALFRED. "Lowell vs. Faxon and Hawkes, a celebrated malpractice suit in Maine." American Academy of Medicine. Bulletin, 11 (1910), 4-31.
      1821-1826.

1195 _____. Maine physicians of 1820: a record of the members of the Massachusetts Medical Society practicing in the District of Maine at the date of separation. Lewiston: Lewiston Journal Printshop, 1928. Pp. 179.

1196 SPANOGLE, JOHN A., JR. "Changes in the present Maine law created by the Maine Consumer Credit Code." Maine Law Review, 26 (1974), 173-215.
      Legislative history of the code.

1197 SPECK, FRANK GOULDSMITH. Penobscot man: the life history of a forest tribe in Maine. Philadelphia: Univ. of Pennsylvania Pr., 1940. Pp. xx, 325.

1198 _____. "Penobscot shamanism." American Anthropological Association. Memoirs, 6 (1919), 239-288.

1199 _____. "Penobscot tales and religious beliefs." Journal of American Folklore, 48 (1935), 1-107.

1200 _____. "Penobscot transformer tales." International Journal of American Linguistics, 1 (1918), 187-244.

1201 _____. "Symbolism in Penobscot Art." American Museum of Natural History. Anthropological Papers, 29 Pt. 2 (1927), 25-80.

1202 _____. "A visit to the Penobscot Indians." University of Pennsylvania Museum Journal, 2 (1911), 21-26.

1203 _____. Wawenock myth texts from Maine. U.S. Bureau of American Ethnology. Annual Report, 43 (1925-1926), 165-197.

1204 SPENCER, WILBUR DANIEL. Maine immortals, including many unique characters in early Maine history. Augusta: Northeastern Pr., 1932. Pp. viii, 316.

1205 _____. The Maine Spencers: a history and genealogy, with mention of many associated families, 1596-1898. Concord, N.H.: Rumford Pr., 1898. Pp. 247.

1206 _____. Pioneers on Maine rivers, with lists to 1651, compiled from the original sources. ... Portland: Lakeside Printing, 1930. Pp. 414.

1207 SPERRY, WILLARD LEAROYD. Summer yesterdays in Maine: memories of boyhood vacation days. N.Y.: Harper & Bros., 1941. Pp. xi, 263.

1208 SPRAGUE, JOHN FRANCIS. "Aroostook War documents." SJMH, 2 (1914-1915), 31-34.

1209 _____. Backwoods sketches. Augusta: Kennebec Journal Shop, 1912. Pp. 154.

1210 _____. "Brief notes on ancient Kennebec." SJMH, 3 (1915-1916), 83-88.
      Kennebec Valley.

1211 _____. "Canadian refugees in Maine and New England during the Revolution." SJMH, 12 (1924), 16-20.

1212 _____. "A century of the bar in Maine." Maine State Bar Association. Proceedings, 22 (1920-1921), 21-68.

1213 _____. "The counties of Maine--town government in Maine." SJMH, 8 (1920), 205-207.

1214 _____. "Indian treaties in Maine." SJMH, 8 (1920), 183-195.

1215 _____. "Maine." SJMH, 8 (1920), 3-7.

1216 _____. "Maine as a district and as a state has had two successful immigration enterprises." SJMH, 8 (1920), 38-41.
      Attempts at promoting foreign immigration; Germans to Waldoboro and Swedes to New Sweden.

1217 _____. "Making history in the Maine woods--culture for the lumberjack." SJMH, 9 (1921), 126-130.

1218 _____. "A Massachusetts colonial ordnance that is the law of Maine." SJMH, 1 (1913-1914), 201-205.
Great Pond Ordnance, 1641.

1219 _____. "The Millerites in Maine." SJMH, 10 (1922), 3-6.

1220 _____. The North Eastern Boundary controversy and the Aroostook War. Dover: Observer Pr., 1910. Pp. 116.

1221 _____. Three men from Maine: Sir William Pepperrell, Sir William Phips, James Sullivan; and, A bit of old England in New England, by Bertram E. Packard. Dover-Foxcroft: Sprague's Journal of Maine History, 1924. Pp. 89.

1222 _____. "William Bingham and the million acre tract." PCHSC, 1 (1910), 434-441.
Bingham Purchase.

1223 _____. "Your river in history." Good Will Record, 29 (November, 1916), 292-298.
Kennebec.

1224 SPRAGUE, RICHARD. "Carl Sprinchorn in the Maine woods." Forest History, 14 (1970), 6-15.
Art.

1225 SPRINGER, JOHN S. Forest life and forest trees; comprising winter camp-life among the loggers, and wild-wood adventure; with descriptions of lumbering operations on the various rivers of Maine, and New Brunswick. N.Y.: Harper and Bros., 1851. Pp. xii, 259.
Includes lumbering statistics.

1226 STAACK, F. "A journey into Maine, 1786." Down East, 6 (January, 1960), 22-25, 41, 43-46.
Luigi Castiglioni's trip from Portsmouth, N.H. to Old Town, Me. to study plants and trees for the Italian government.

1227 STACKPOLE, EVERETT BIRNEY. "State banking in Maine." Sound Currency, 7 (May, 1900), 57-88.

1228 STACKPOLE, EVERETT SCHERMERHORN, ed. "An old journal." MeHSC, 3 Ser., 2 (1906), 241-244.
Lieut. John Stackpole.

1229 STANLEY, GEORGE FRANCIS GILMAN. "British operations on the Penobscot in 1814." Society for Army Historical Research Journal, 19 (1940), 168-178.
War of 1812.

1230 _____. Canada invaded, 1775-1776. Toronto: Hakkert, 1973. Pp. xiv, 186.
Arnold's Expedition.

1231 STANLEY, RUEL H. and GEORGE O. HALL. Eastern Maine and the rebellion; being an account of the principal local events in eastern Maine during the war, and brief histories of eastern Maine regiments; contains accounts of mobs, riots, destruction of newspapers, war meetings, drafts, Confederate raids, peace meetings, celebrations, soldiers' letters, and scenes and incidents at the front, never before in print. Bangor, 1887. Pp. 392.

1232 STANTON, DON C. A history of the white-tailed deer in Maine. Augusta, 1963. Pp. viii, 75.

1233 STANWOOD, EDWARD. "The separation of Maine from Massachusetts." MHSP, 3 Ser., 1 (1907-1908), 125-164.

1234 STAPLES, ARTHUR GRAY. "Conservation problems of central Maine." SJMH, 12 (1924), 128-135, 191-197.
Water power.

1235 _____. The inner man; or, some contemporary portraits of prominent men of Maine. Lewiston: Lewiston Journal, 1923. Pp. 248.

1236 _____. The passing age: a collection of familiar essays as published in the newspaper of which the writer is editor-in-chief. Augusta: Katahdin Publishing, 1924. Pp. 416.
Social life and customs.

1237 STAPLES, FRANKLIN. "Reminiscences of Maine medical schools and physicians." JMS, 3 (1896-1897), 86-89.

1238 STARBIRD, CHARLES MILLARD. The Indians of the Androscoggin Valley: tribal history, and their relations with the early English settlers of Maine. [Lewiston]: Lewiston Journal Printshop, 1928. Pp. 108.

1239 STARKEY, GLENN WENDELL. Maine, its history, resources, and government. (1920) 4th ed. N.Y.: Silver Burdett, 1947. Pp. x, 263.

1240 STARR, JOHN T. My Maine islands. American Forests, 73 (February, 1967), 38-41, 60.

1241 START, EDWIN A. "Penobscot Bay." NEM, New Ser., 14 (1896), 579-600.

1242 "THE STATE of Maine, now with us more than 100 years." Literary Digest, 65 (May 8, 1920), 69-70.

1243 STERLING, ROBERT THAYER. Lighthouses of the Maine coast and the men who keep them. Brattleboro, Vt.: Stephen Daye Pr., 1935. Pp. 223.

1244 STETSON, WILLIAM WALLACE. History and civil government of Maine ... and, The government of the United States by B. A. Hinsdale. Chicago: Werner, 1898. Pp. 340.

1245 ____. "History of education and the evolu-
tion of the present school system in Maine."
Maine. State Superintendent of Public
Schools. Report, (1900), 56-156.

1246 STEVENS, SUSAN MacCULLOCH. Passamaquoddy
economic development in cultural and historical perspective. Mount Vernon, 1973.
Pp. 162. Me.
Passamaquoddy Indians.

1247 STEWART, ALICE ROSE. "The State of Maine
and Canadian Confederation." CanHistRev, 33
(1952), 148-164.

1247A ____. "Suggested readings in Maine history:
the Northeastern Boundary dispute." MeHSN, 2
(May, 1963), 8.

1248 STEWART, JOHN C. "Biographical sketches of
natives of Maine who have served in the
Congress of the United States." SJMH, 10
(1922), 85-96, 140-154, 196-208; 11 (1923),
35-42, 61-71, 150-160.

1249 STOKESBURY, JAMES L. "Jonathan Eddy and the
fourteenth colony." Down East, 22 (April,
1976), 18-22, 25, 27.

1250 STOLLE, JOHN WILLIAM. Maine stories. Bang-
or: H. P. Snowman, 1953. Pp. 148. MB.
Social life and customs.

1251 STORMS, ROGER C. A history of three corners.
Lee: Lee Academy, 1971. 168 leaves.
Twenty-four towns in the vicinity of the
adjacent corners of Aroostook, Penobscot and
Washington counties.

1252 A STRANGE account of the rising and breaking
of a great bubble. [Boston], 1767. Pp. 22.
An attack on the Kennebec proprietors.

1253 STUART, RICHARD KENNETH. Financing public
improvements by the State of Maine. Orono:
Univ. Pr., 1957. Pp. viii, 188.
1820-1957.

1254 "A STUDY of the schools of northeastern
Maine." Maine. State Superintendent of
Public Schools. Report, (1897), 45-78.

1255 STUIVER, MINZE and HAROLD W. BORNS, JR.
"Late quarternary marine invasion in Maine:
its chronology and associated crustal movement." Geological Society of America. Bulletin, 86 (1975), 99-104.

1256 NO ENTRY.

1257 SULLIVAN, JAMES. The history of the District
of Maine. Boston: I. Thomas and E. T. Andrews, 1795. Pp. vii, 421.

1258 ____. "The history of the Penobscot Indians." MHSC, 9 (1804), 207-232.

1259 ____. Index of names and places in Sullivan's District of Maine; the manuscript of
this index was found in a copy of the above
work formerly the property of John Wingate
Thornton. Portland: A. J. Huston, [1914?].
Unpaged.

1260 SWEETSER, MOSES FOSTER. Summer days Down
East. Portland: Chisholm Bros., 1883
Pp. 160. MeU.

1261 SWETT, CLYDE W. and MARY L. HASKELL. All
about Maine: print and film materials to en-
rich the study of Maine history in grade
eight. Augusta: Maine State Department of
Education, 1969. Pp. 90. Me.

1262 SWETT, SOPHIA MIRIAM. Stories of Maine.
N.Y.: American Book Co., 1899. Pp. 278.

1263 SWITZER, DAVID C. "Down-East ships of the
Union navy." United States Naval Institute.
Proceedings, 90 (November, 1964), 82-88.

1264 SYLVESTER, HERBERT MILTON. The land of St.
Castin. Boston: W. B. Clarke, 1909.
Pp. 380.
Also published the same year as volume five
of the author's "Maine pioneer settlements."

1265 ____. The Sokoki trail. Boston: Stanhope
Pr., 1907. Pp. 465.
Also published in 1909 as volume three of
the author's "Maine pioneer settlements."

1266 TALBOT, ARCHIE LEE. "A new Plymouth Colony
at Kennebeck": John Carver, the first governor of Plymouth Colony, the Moses of the
Pilgrims, a symbol of America; an earnest
appeal for the erection of a Pilgrim memorial
monument, in Maine, by the State, and a statue of John Carver at Plymouth, by the Commonwealth of Massachusetts; Hubbard Hall, Bowdoin College, Brunswick, Maine, Thursday,
January 9, 1930.... [Brunswick?, 1930].
Pp. 14.

1267 TALLMAN, RONALD D. and JULIE I. TALLMAN.
"The diplomatic search for the St. Croix
River, 1796-1798." Acadiensis, 1 (Spring,
1972), 59-71.

1268 TAYLOR, CLYDE C. A review of lobster rearing
in Maine. Augusta: Maine Department of Sea
and Shore Fisheries, 1950. Pp. 16. Me.

1269 TEBBETTS, LEON HAROLD. The amazing story of
Maine. Portland: Falmouth Book House,
1935. Pp. ix, 104.

1270 "TEN years of bookmobile service in Maine."
MeLAB, 24 (November, 1963), 3-5.

1271 THAYER, HENRY OTIS. "Early ministry on the
Kennebec." MeHSC, 2 Ser., 8 (1897), 289-312;
9 (1888), 113-123.
Robert Gutch and Ichabod Wiswall.

1272   ____. "The Lithgow immigrants." SJMH, 10
(1922), 70-85.

1273   ____. "Loyalists of the Kennebec and one of
them--John Carleton." SJMH, 5 (1917-1918),
241-262.

1274   ____. "Ministry on the Kennebec: period of
the Indian Wars." MeHSC, 2 Ser., 10 (1899),
263-281.

1275   ____. "The problem of Hammond's Fort:
Richard Hammond, his home and death." MeHSC,
2 Ser., 1 (1890), 261-294.

1276   THAYER, SIMEON. The invasion of Canada: including the journal of Captain Simeon Thayer,
describing the perils and sufferings of the
army under Colonel Benedict Arnold, in its
march ... to Quebec. Edwin Martin Stone, ed.
Providence: Knowles, Anthony, 1867.
Pp. xxiv, 104.

1277   THIELEN, BENEDICT. "The wild and beautiful
coast of Maine." Holiday, 32 (July, 1962),
45-57.

1278   THOMAS, ELMER ERWIN. In the north woods of
Maine: the story of a winter in the wilder-
ness fifty years ago. Yonkers-on-Hudson,
N.Y.: World Book, 1923. Pp. vii, 109.

1279   THOMAS, MIRIAM STOVER. Come hell or high
water. n.p., 1970. Pp. 138. MeU.
Essays.

1280   ____. Flotsam and jetsam. n.p., 1973.
Pp. 121.

1281   THOMPSON, DEBORAH, ed. Maine forms of American architecture. Waterville: Colby Museum
of Art, 1976. Pp. xxxii, 362. Me.

1282   THOMPSON, GARRETT W. "The Germans in Maine."
The Pennsylvania German, 12 (1911), 595-602,
684-691, 724-735. Penn Germania, New Ser., 1
(1912), 36-44, 106-113, 161-169.

1283   THOMPSON, JOHN WALLACE. Sketches, historical
and descriptive, of noted Maine horses, past
and present, their ancestors and descendants;
with an alphabetical index, a list of Maine
2.30 horses, alphabetically arranged....
Portland: Hoyt & Fogg, 1874-1877. 2v.

1284   THURLOW, CLINTON F. Over the rails by steam:
a railroad scrapbook. Weeks Mills, 1965.
Pp. 104.

1285   ____. The W W & F two footer, hail and fare-
well. (1964) 2d ed. Weeks Mills, 1965.
Pp. 116.
Wiscasset, Waterville & Farmington Railroad.

1286   THURSTON, BROWN. "The mechanical condition
and improvements in the art of printing in
Maine for the past one hundred years." MPAP,
22 (1885), 32-41.

1287   TITUS, ANSON. "Reminiscences of early American Universalism: Universalism in Maine
prior to 1820." The Universalist Quarterly,
42 (1885), 430-453.

1288   TITUS, EDWARD KIRK. "Prehistoric Maine--a
glimpse of aboriginal life." MagHist, 12
(1910), 105-108.

1289   TOD, GILES M. S. The last sail Down East.
Barre, Mass.: Barre Publishers, 1965.
Pp. xii, 281.

1290   TODD, ALAN. "Memories of Maine." Railroad
Magazine, 50 (1949), 80-95.
Reminiscences of an engineer on the Bangor
and Aroostook Railroad.

1291   TRASK, WILLIAM BLAKE, ed. Letters of Colonel
Thomas Westbrook and others relating to Indian
affairs in Maine 1722-1726. Boston: G. E.
Littlefield, 1901. Pp. 196.
Indexed.

1292   TRAVIS, HAROLD G. "Maine's pre-1850 law offices." Maine History News, 9 (April, 1974),
4-5, 10, (October, 1974), 10; 10 (January,
1975), 14, 16.

1293   TRUE, NATHANIEL TUCKERMAN. "Indian names on
the Androscoggin." HistMag, 8 (1864), 237-
238.

1294   ____. "The Indians." Old Times, 3 (1879),
351-354.

1295   ____. "Mineralogy among the aborigines of
Maine." Portland Society of Natural History.
Proceedings, 1 Pt. 2 (1869), 165-168.

1296   ____. "Names and location of the tribes on
the Androscoggin." HistMag, 8 (1864), 150-
151.

1297   TRUEMAN, STUART. The ordeal of John Gyles;
being an account of his odd adventures,
strange deliverances, etc., as a slave of the
Maliseets. Toronto: McClelland and Stewart,
1966. Pp. ix, 155.

1298   TUNLEY, ROUL. "Maine and her artists." Woman's Day, (August, 1964), 62-66, 68.

1299   THE TWO banner prohibition states; being a
careful review of conditions in Maine and Kansas under prohibition legislation. Prohibition at its best in Maine, by Cyrus W. Davis
.... Facts about Kansas "on the water wagon,"
by Hon. Royal E. Cabell.... Cincinnati: National Home Rule Association, 1914. Pp. 31.

1300   TYZZER, E. E. "Animal tooth implements from
shell heaps of Maine." American Antiquity, 8
(1943), 354-360.

1301 MAINE

1301 UNITED STATES. COMMISSION ON CIVIL RIGHTS. MAINE ADVISORY COMMITTEE. Federal and state services and the Maine Indian: a report. Washington, 1974. Pp. ix, 108.

1302 U. S. DISTRICT COURT. MAINE. Reports of cases argued and determined in the District Court of the United States for the District of Maine; 1822-[1866].... Portland: Colman & Chisholm, 1839-1874. 3v.

1303 U. S. LIBRARY OF CONGRESS. Maine: the sesquicentennial of statehood; an exhibition in the Library of Congress, Washington, D.C., December 21, 1970 to September 6, 1971. Washington: Govt. Print. Off., 1970 [i.e. 1971]. Pp. 86.

1304 VARNEY, GEORGE JONES. A brief history of Maine. (1880) 2d ed. Portland: McLellan, Mosher, 1890. Pp. 336. MeHi.

1305 _____. A gazetteer of the State of Maine. Boston: B. B. Russell, 1881. Pp. 611.
A typescript index by Genevieve R. Ireland is at the Maine Historical Society.

1306 _____. The young people's history of Maine; from its earliest discovery to the final settlement of its boundaries in 1842. (1873) 3d ed., rev. Portland: Dresser, McLellan, 1877. Pp. xviii, 289. MeHi.

1307 VEAZIE, CARL E. "The Maine economy, 1940-1975." Thomas Business Review, 3 (Fall, 1975), 32-42.

1308 VERRILL, ALPHEUS HYATT. Romantic and historic Maine. N.Y.: Dodd, Mead, 1933. Pp. xx, 277.

1309 VETROMILE, EUGENE. "The Abnaki Indians." MeHSC, 6 (1859), 203-244.

1310 _____. The Abnakis and their history; or, historical notices of the aborigines of Acadia. N.Y.: J. B. Kirker, 1866. Pp. xi, 171.

1311 VICKERY, JAMES BERRY, III. "A bibliography of local history--the town registers of Maine." MeHSN, 5 (November, 1965), 7-11.

1312 _____. "Some magazines of Maine." MeLAB, 29 (November, 1968), 3-14; 30 (February, 1969), 3-11, 14-21.

1313 "VIEW of the history and present condition of the Commonwealth of Maine." American Quarterly Register, 5 (1832-1833), 105-121.

1314 VIGNERAS, LOUIS-ANDRÉ. "Letters of an Acadian trader, 1674-1676." NEQ, 13 (1940), 98-110.
Henri Brunet.

1315 VINTON, JOHN ADAMS. "Thomas Gyles, and his neighbors." NEHGR, 21 (1867), 352-363.

1316 VIRGIN, WILLIAM WIRT. Digest of the decisions of the Supreme Judicial Court, of the State of Maine, contained in volumes twenty-seven to forty-three, (both inclusive), of the Maine Reports, [1847-1857]. Hallowell: Masters, Smith, 1859. Pp. lxxx, 604.

1317 VOSE, CLEMENT E. Political party platforms, State of Maine, 1952-1958. Brunswick: Bowdoin College, 1958. Variously leaved. MeU.

1318 "THE VOYAGE of Captain George Waymouth to the coast of Maine in 1605." BHistMag, 2 (1886-1887), 205-208.

1319 VROOM, JAMES. "Penobscot loyalists." Acadiensis, 3 (1903), 172-182.

1320 WADSWORTH, R. C. "The men in medicine in eastern Maine during the early days." Maine Medical Association. Journal, 44 (1953), 150-155.

1321 WALDRON, C. W. "The Northeastern Boundary." Pine Tree Magazine, 5 (1906), 557-560.

1322 WALKER, CHARLES HOWARD. "Some old houses on the southern coast of Maine." WPSAM, 4 (April, 1918), 3-14.
Wiscasset, York, Kennebunk, South Berwick, and Wells.

1323 WALKER, DAVID BRADSTREET. A Maine profile: some conditioners of her political system. Brunswick: Bowdoin College, Bureau for Research in Municipal Government, 1964. Pp. 55.

1324 _____. Politics and ethnocentrism: the case of the Franco-Americans. Brunswick: Bowdoin College, Bureau for Research in Municipal Government, 1961. Pp. 48.

1325 WALKER, ELINOR STEVENS. More about Maine. Rumford: Rumford Publishing, 1974. Pp. 199.

1326 WALKER, WILLARD. The Indians of Maine. n.p., [196-]. v.p. MeBa.

1327 _____. The pre-history of the Maine-Maritime area. [Middletown, Conn.?], 1970. 42 leaves. MeU.

1328 WALSH, LOUIS SEBASTIAN. "Sermon on the tercentenary of [the] Catholic Church in Maine." MeCathHM, 1 (August, 1913), 10-23.

1329 WARE, JOSEPH. "Expedition against Quebec." NEHGR, 6 (1852), 129-145.
An edited journal with notes by Justin Winsor; Arnold's Expedition.

1330 WARNER, MAURICE J. Civil War memorials erected in the State of Maine. [Augusta]: Maine Civil War Centennial Commission, 1965. Pp. 79.

1331 WARREN, JULIET MARION STANLEY. Maine centennial, 1820-1920, historical souvenir poem. Portland, 1920. Pp. 7.

1332 WASHBURN, FREMONT E. Flinches and other strange birds: the history and humor of Maine trapshooting since 1874. South Berwick: Chronicle Print Shop, 1971. Pp. 58. MeU.

1333 WASHBURN, ISRAEL, 1813-1883. "The North-Eastern Boundary." MeHSC, 8 (1881), 1-106.

1334 WASSON, GEORGE SAVARY. Sailing days on the Penobscot: the story of the river and the bay in the old days. (1932) New ed. N.Y.: W. W. Norton, 1949. Pp. 246.

1335 WATERMAN, CHARLES ELMER. "Shaker communities of Maine." SJMH, 6 (1918-1919), 139-146.

1336 _____. "Some knights of the road." SJMH, 6 (1918-1919), 10-17.
      Postal delivery and the development of roads and other forms of transportation.

1337 WATTS, GEORGE B. "Catholic missionaries in Maine, the Middle West, Louisiana: colonial days." French Review, 37 (1963), 11-35.

1338 WAYNE, JOHN LAKMORD. "Odd names of early Down East periodicals." Hobbies, 47 (November, 1942), 103.

1339 WEBBER, SAMUEL R. "Early days in Maine surgery." NEJMed, 260 (January, 1959), 167-169.

1340 WEBSTER, DANIEL. Mr. Webster's vindication of the Treaty of Washington of 1842; in a speech delivered in the Senate of the United States, on the 6th and 7th of April, 1846. Washington: J. & G. S. Gideon, 1846. Pp. 88.
      Two other printings of 1846 contain 64 and 85 pages respectively.

1341 WEBSTER, DONALD B., JR. "The Penobscot Expedition of 1814." Tradition, 4 (January, 1961), 45-58.

1342 WEBSTER, HENRY SEWALL. History of Maine Commandery, No. 1, of Knights Templar, from its organization as King Darius's Council of Knights of the Red Cross, May 29, 1806, to December 1, 1893. Gardiner: Reporter-Journal Pr., 1893. Pp. 110. MeBa.

1343 WELSH, DAVID. "The Passamaquoddy Indians." Ramparts, 5 (March, 1967), 40-45.

1344 WENTWORTH, BERTRAND HEBRON. A chart of Maine winters--1785 to 1913--from Kennebec River records, and daily observations at Gardiner, Maine. Portland: Southworth Print, 1914. Broadside, 14 1/2 x 11 1/2 inches.

1345 WESTON, ISAAC. "Law and lawyers." Northern Monthly, 1 (1864), 173-176.

1346 WETHERBE, R. L. "The Acadian boundary disputes and the Ashburton Treaty." Nova Scotia Historical Society. Collections, 6 (1887-1888), 17-51.

1347 WETHERELL, ALICE M. "Two pioneers from Maine." MeLAB, 13 (May, 1952), 14-16.
      Alice M. Jordan and Anne Carroll Moore; librarians.

1348 WHEATLAND, STEPHEN. "History of Pingree heir timberland ownership." Maine. Biennial Report of the Forest Commissioner, 38 (1969-1970), 119-121.

1349 WHILE Maine grew. By the pen of a Maine writer. n.p., 1971. Pp. 34. MeU.

1350 WHIPPLE, JOSEPH. The history of Acadie, Penobscot Bay and River, with a more particular geographical and statistical view of the District of Maine than has ever before been published, also, statistical tables, shewing at one view the comparative progress of the population of Maine with each other individual state in the Union, with an alphabetical list of all the towns with their date of incorporation, census in 1810, polls and valuation in 1812, counties, and distances from Boston. Bangor: Peter Edes, 1816. Pp. 102.
      Pub. also at Bangor, 1816, under title: A geographical view of the District of Maine ... including the history of Acadie, Penobscot Bay....

1351 WHITE, JOHN W. "The Burleigh scheme: an idea that became a railroad." New England Social Studies Bulletin, 15 (March, 1958), 5-11.
      Albert A. Burleigh and the Bangor and Aroostook Railroad.

1352 WHITESIDE, WILLIAM B. "The Maine economy: 1860-1900." Thomas Business Review, 3 (Fall, 1975), 11-20.

1353 WHITIN, ERNEST STAGG. Factory legislation in Maine. N.Y.: Columbia Univ., 1908. Pp. 145.

1354 WHITMAN, WILLIAM EDWARD SEAVER and CHARLES HENRY TRUE. Maine in the war for the Union: a history of the part borne by Maine troops in the suppression of the American rebellion. Lewiston: N. Dingley, Jr., 1865. Pp. viii, 637.

1355 WHITNEY, CLINTON. "Bangor and Aroostook Railroad." Railroad Enthusiast, 3 (March-August, 1966), 10-14.

1356 _____ and DICK MURRAY. "The Maine Central Railroad." Railroad Enthusiast, 2 (March-August, 1965), 14-16.

1357 WHITNEY, SETH HARDING. The Kennebec Valley: this work is devoted to the early history of the valley; also relating many incidents and adventures of the early settlers, including a brief sketch of the Kennebec Indians. Augusta: Sprague, Burleigh & Flynt, 1887. Pp. 122.

1358 _____. New Somersetshire or a sketch of Kennebec and Somerset counties. Waterville: W. M. Ladd, 1900. Pp. 23. MeHi.

1359 WHO'S who in Maine. Lewiston: Twin City Printery, [1947]. Pp. 147. MeBa.

1360 WIGGIN, FRANCES TURGEON. Maine composers and their music: a biographical dictionary. [Rockland?]: Maine Federation of Music Clubs, 1959-1976. 2v.
    Volume two was published by the Maine Historical Society.

1361 WIGGIN, RUBY CROSBY. Big dreams and little wheels. Clinton, 1971. Pp. 103.
    Wiscasset, Waterville & Farmington Railroad.

1362 WILKINS, AUSTIN HORATIO. The forests of Maine, their extent, character, ownership, and products. Augusta: Maine Forest Service, 1932. Pp. 107.

1363 _____. [History of Maine forests and forestry. Augusta: Maine Forest Service, 1969?]. 26 unnumbered leaves. MeU.

1364 WILKINS, RAYMOND S. "The state appelate court now and forty years ago." Maine State Bar Association. Proceedings, 41 (1952), 75-83.

1365 WILLEY, AUSTIN. The history of the antislavery cause in state and nation. Portland: B. Thurston, 1886. Pp. xii, 503.

1366 WILLIAMSON, JOSEPH. A bibliography of the State of Maine from the earliest period to 1891. Portland: Thurston Print, 1896. 2v.

1367 _____. "Capital trials in Maine before the separation." MeHSC, 2 Ser., 1 (1890), 159-172.

1368 _____. "Condition of the religious denominations of Maine, at the close of the Revolution." MeHSC, 7 (1876), 217-229.

1369 _____. "Daniel Webster's visit to Maine, in 1835." HistMag, 2 Ser., 9 (1871), 11-13.

1369A _____. "Historical review of literature in Maine." MeHSC, 2 Ser., 2 (1891), 113-127. Intellectual life.

1370 _____. "The Northmen in Maine." HistMag, 2 Ser., 5 (1869), 30-31.

1371 _____. "Presidential visits to Maine." Hist Mag, 22 (1873), 340-345.
    John Adams, James Monroe, James K. Polk, Ulysses S. Grant.

1372 _____. "The professional tours of John Adams in Maine." MeHSC, 2 Ser., 1 (1890), 301-308. 1765-1774.

1373 _____. "Slavery in Maine." MeHSC, 7 (1876), 207-216.

1374 _____. "Smuggling on the Penobscot, 1814." BHistMag, 3 (1887-1888), 167.

1375 WILLIAMSON, ROBERT B. "The convention of 1819." MeHSN, 9 (1969-1970), 64-72.
    Held to consider separation from Massachusetts.

1376 WILLIAMSON, WILLIAM DURKEE. The history of the State of Maine; from its first discovery, A.D. 1602, to the separation, A.D. 1820, inclusive; with an appendix and general index. (1832) A new impression.... Hallowell: Glazier, Masters & Smith, 1839. 2v.

1377 _____. "Sketches of the lives of early Maine ministers." MeHSC, 2 Ser., 3 (1892), 41-55, 191-208, 293-315; 4 (1893), 62-82, 186-208, 320-327, 410-424; 5 (1894), 99-103, 211-214, 320-328, 427-434; 6 (1895), 85-93, 184-196, 306-320, 441-445; 7 (1896), 45-52, 204-212, 313-326.

1378 WILLIS, JOHN LEMUEL MURRAY. "Early history of medicine in Maine." Old Eliot, 6 (1903), 109-119.

1379 _____. "Submission of Maine to Massachusetts." Old Eliot, 7 (1906), 53-64. 1652.

1380 _____. "The submission of Maine to Massachusetts." Old Eliot, 9 (1909), 123-150. Differs from above entry.

1381 WILLIS, WILLIAM. A business directory of the subscribers to the new map of Maine, with a brief history and description of the state; also valuable statistics and advertisements. Portland: J. Chace, Jr., 1862. Pp. 344.

1382   _____. "A descriptive catalogue of books and pamphlets relating to the history and statistics of Maine, or portions of it." HistMag, 17 (1870), 145-182.

1383   _____. A history of the law, the courts, and the lawyers of Maine, from its first colonization to the early part of the present century. Portland: Bailey & Noyes, 1863. Pp. viii, 712.

1384   _____. "Inaugural address containing biographical notices of former presidents [of the Maine Historical Society."] MeHSC, 5 (1857), xvii-lxviii.
        Also published the same year as a book with title: "An address delivered before the Maine Historical Society, at Augusta, March 5, 1857...."

1385   [_____.] "Judicial changes in Maine." Monthly Law Reporter, 11 (1848), 429-431.
        Changes in the Maine Supreme Judicial Court: author attribution by Joseph Williamson.

1386   _____. "Language of the Abnaquies." MeHSC, 4 (1856), 95-117.
        Brief history of tribe and excerpts from Father Rasles' dictionary.

1387   [_____.] "Notes on the early jurisprudence of Maine." Law Reporter, 3 (1840-1841), 31-35, 41-51, 121-127.
        Signed "W"; author attribution by Joseph Williamson.

1388   _____. "The Scotch-Irish immigration to Maine, and Presbyterianism in New England." MeHSC, 6 (1859), 1-37.

1389   WILLOUGHBY, CHARLES CLARK. Prehistoric burial places in Maine. Cambridge, Mass.: Peabody Museum, 1898. Pp. 52.

1390   WILSON, CHARLES MORROW. "Gateway to the north." Railroad Magazine, 69 (December, 1957), 19-26.
        Bangor and Aroostook Railroad since 1892.

1391   WILSON, JAMES and ROBERT WATKINS CROWE. Managers in Maine. Brunswick: Bowdoin College, Bureau for Research in Municipal Government, 1962. Pp. 40.
        City managers.

1392   WING, HENRY A. Maine's war upon the liquor traffic: a series of historical articles, ... published in the Portland Evening Express. [Portland, 1909?] Pp. 89.

1393   WINSOR, JUSTIN. "The settlement of the Northeastern Boundary." MHSP, 2 Ser., 3 (1886-1887), 349-368.

1394   WISCASSET AND QUEBEC RAILROAD. Wiscasset and Quebec Railroad. Wiscasset: Charles E. Emerson, 1877. Pp. 15. MH.
        Includes brief history of the railroad.

1395   "WITCHCRAFT in Maine." NEHGR, 13 (1859), 193-196.

1396   WOHLFARTH, J. B. "Evolution of Maine water powers." SJMH, 12 (1924), 64-65.

1397   "WOMEN fiction writers of Maine." MeLB, 14 (1928-1929), 8-24.
        Biobibliographies.

1398   WOOD, CHARLES DAYTON and E. R. MANSFIELD. Studies of the food of Maine lumberman. Washington: Govt. Print. Off., 1904. Pp. 60. MeBa.

1399   WOOD, ETHEL M. "The Maine Indians, and their relations with the white settlers." SJMH, 9 (1921), 61-69, 120-125, 170-174; 10 (1922), 6-17.

1400   WOOD, RICHARD GEORGE. "A bibliography of travel in Maine, 1783-1861." NEQ, 6 (1933), 426-439.

1401   _____. A history of lumbering in Maine, 1820-1861. Orono: Univ. Pr., 1935. Pp. 267.

1402   WOODBURY, KENNETH B., JR. "An incident between the French Canadians and the Irish in the Diocese of Maine in 1906." NEQ, 40 (1967), 260-269.
        Opposition of French Canadians to assimilation into American culture.

1403   WOODBURY, NATHAN FRANKLIN. Prohibition in Maine: history of its origin, results, political nullification and final ratification, from 1837 to 1920. Lewiston: Journal Printshop and Bindery, 1920. Pp. 30.

1404   _____, comp. The prohibition law of Maine, from the revised statutes of 1883, with amendments of 1885 and 1887, revised to 1888; also some decisions thereon by the Supreme Judicial Court; the prohibitory constitutional amendment, adopted in 1884; brief history of the law; amendments desired, etc.; important decision on prohibition by United States Supreme Court. Auburn: Prohibition Club, 1888. Pp. 36.

1405   WOODS, JOHN B. "The forests of Maine." American Forests, 54 (June, 1948), 266-268, 285, 287.

1406   WOODSIDE, CHARLES L. and LURA WOODSIDE WATKINS. "Three Maine pewterers." Antiques, 22 (1932), 8-10.
        Allen Porter, Freeman Porter, and Rufus Dunham.

1407   WOOLLEY, DION E. "Amateur journalism in Maine." Sun Up, 9 (May, 1931), 4-5, 25, 29-30.

1408   MAINE

1408   WORTHEY, MARY G. Liquor sales in Maine, 1936-1960. Waterville: Civic League Publications, [1962?]. Unpaged. MeU.
    Statistical tables.

1409   WRAY, RUTH ARLINE. The history of secondary education in Cumberland and Sagadahoc counties in Maine. Orono: Univ. Pr., 1940. Pp. vii, 158.

1410   WRIGHT, HAROLD W. "Designating our wild land townships." The Northern, 5 (December, 1925), 3-4, 14.

1410A WYMAN, MARY ALICE. Two American pioneers, Seba Smith and Elizabeth Oakes Smith. N.Y.: Columbia Univ. Pr., 1927. Pp. viii, 249.

1411   YEARBOOK and church directory with historical sketches; churches of Saco Valley and vicinity, 1932-1933. n.p., [1933?]. Pp. 33. MeHi.

1412   YERXA, DONALD A. "The State of Maine and the new navy, 1889-1893." MeHSQ, 14 (1974-1975), 183-205.

1413   YORK, DICK. "The man who brough music to Maine." Down East, 21 (January, 1975), 54-56, 61.
    William Rogers Chapman and the Maine Music Festival.

1414   YORK, ROBERT M. "Down-East Yankees in national politics." New England Social Studies Bulletin, 10 (December, 1952), 3-10.

1415   _____. "The Maine economy: 1900-1940." Thomas Business Review, 3 (Fall, 1975), 21-31.

1416   _____. "A quick trip through historical Maine." Maine Alumnus, 38 (February, 1957), 14-16.

1417   _____. "Suggested reading in Maine history: a bibliography of religious history." MeHSN, 4 (February, 1965), 7-10.

1418   _____. "The three R's in early Maine." The Bates College Bulletin, 73 (April, 1976), 13-15.

1419   YORK, VINCENT. The Sandy River & its valley. Farmington: Knowlton & McLeary, 1976. Pp. 251. MeHi.

1420   YORKE, DANE. "The Florida of the north." American Mercury, 20 (1930), 275-280.
    Maine tourist trade.

1421   YOUNG, HAROLD H. "Trolley days in central Maine." Down East, 21 (October, 1974), 49-53.

Counties

ANDROSCOGGIN COUNTY

1422 BATEMAN, LUTHER C. "The industrial heart of Maine." National Magazine, 25 (1906-1907), [113-119].
Lewiston and Auburn.

1423 DINGLEY, NELSON, JR. ["History of the press in Androscoggin County."] MPAP, 24 (1887), 25-27.

1424 KIWANIS CLUB, AUBURN-LEWISTON, ME. 25th anniversary history, Auburn-Lewiston Kiwanis Club ... 1922-1947. n.p., [1947?]. Unpaged. MeU.

1425 LADD, WILLIAM. "Annals of Bakerstown, Poland, and Minot." MeHSC, 2 (1847), 111-130.
Poland and Minot were formerly a tract known as Barkerstown.

1426 THE LEWISTON and Auburn directory, containing the names of the inhabitants, their occupation and place of business, etc., the officers of the various societies, together with a history of Lewiston and Auburn. Lewiston: W. F. Stanwood, 1864. Pp. 179.

1427 LOMBARD, LUCINA HAYNES. "Lewiston and Auburn: historical and industrial centers." Sun Up, 5 (February, 1928), 12-15, 18-19.

1428 MERRILL, GEORGIA DREW, ed. History of Androscoggin County, Maine. Boston: W. A. Fergusson, 1891. Pp. xiv, 879.
Pages 432a-432f follow page 432 and pages 690a-690b follow page 690.

1429 OWEN, HOWARD. ["History of the press in Androscoggin County."] MPAP, 26 (1889), 34.

1430 PIDGIN, WILLIAM ABNER. ["History of the press in Androscoggin County."] MPAP, 43 (1906), 25.

1431 RAND, JOHN A. The peoples Lewiston-Auburn, Maine, 1875-1975. Freeport: Bond Wheelwright, 1975. Pp. xi, 116.
Introduction in English and French.

1432 ST. JOHN, FREDERIC. "Lewiston-Auburn." Sun Up, 8 (October, 1930), 15, 27.
Author's name is a pseudonym.

1433 SANFORD, EVERTS & CO. Atlas and history of Androscoggin County, Maine.... Philadelphia, 1873. Pp. 120. MeHi.

1434 SKINNER, RALPH BURGESS. Historically speaking on Lewiston-Auburn, Maine, churches: an historical study of the origin and development of religious organizations in a two-city community from its date of settlement to and including the ecumenical year 1964. Lewiston: Twin City Printery, 1965. Pp. v, 176.

1435 SMITH, EDGAR CROSBY. "Androscoggin notes." SJMH, 3 (1915-1916), 39-40.

1436 WATERMAN, CHARLES ELMER. ["History of the press in Androscoggin County."] MPAP, 31 (1894), 20-22; 32 (1895), 27-28; 33 (1896), 35-36; 34 (1897), 27; 35 (1898), 19-20; 36 (1899), 33-34; 37 (1900), 33-34; 38 (1901), 34; 39 (1902), 36-37; 40 (1903), 36-37; 44 (1907), 47; 46 (1909), 28-29; 47 (1910), 10-11; 48 (1911), 29; 49 (1913), 24-26; 50 (1913), 24-25; 51 (1914), 27-28.

SEE ALSO entry 555.

AROOSTOOK COUNTY

1437 ALBERT, JULIE A. "The Madawaska and Fort Kent centennials." Down East, 15 (July, 1969), 66-67.

1438 ART work of Aroostook County, Maine. Chicago: W. H. Parish, 1895. Unpaged. MeHi.
Includes an historical sketch of the county.

1439 BAILEY, JACOB WHITMAN. The St. John River in Maine, Quebec, and New Brunswick. Cambridge, Mass.: Riverside Pr., 1894. Pp. iv, 178.

1439A BANGOR AND AROOSTOOK RAILROAD COMPANY. Inside northern Maine. [Bangor?, 1949]. Pp. 45.

1440 AROOSTOOK COUNTY

1440 BARNES, ANNA. The pageant of Aroostook and Major Dickey, the Duke of Fort Kent, by Beulah Sylvester Oxton. [Lewiston]: Lewiston Journal Co., 1916. Pp. 40. [MeHoC.]

1441 BRASSARD, FRANCIS. The origin of certain public schools in the St. John River Valley of Aroostook County, Maine. Cassadaga, N.Y., 1967. 174 leaves. MeU.

1442 CARY, THEODORE. "Record of newspapers in Aroostook County." MPAP, [5] (1868), 31-35; 31 (1894), 22; 32 (1895), 27-28.

1443 CHOUINARD, EVA. Notre heritage vivant. n.p., 1973. Pp. 66. [MeMaHi.]

1444 DAY, CLARENCE ALBERT. A history of the M P G, Inc., 1932-1952. n.p., [1952?]. Pp. 88, 4. [MePriT.]
Maine Potato Growers.

1445 DAY, RICHARD L. Aroostook Valley Railroad Company. Chicago: Central Electric Railfans' Association, 1946. Pp. 11. MeBa.

1446 DIETZ, LEW. The Allagash. N.Y.: Holt, Rinehart, Winston, 1968. Pp. xxiv, 264.
Allagash River.

1447 _____. "The Allagash." Down East, 13 (October, 1966), 20-23, 50-52.

1448 ELWELL, EDWARD HENRY. Aroostook: with some accounts of the excursions thither of the editors of Maine, in the years 1858 and 1878, and of the colony of Swedes, settled in the town of New Sweden. Portland: Transcript Printing, 1878. Pp. 50.

1449 FACES of Aroostook: a bicentennial portrait of Aroostook County. Presque Isle: Polar Star Associates, [1976]. Pp. 72. MeU.

1450 FOGG, CHARLES H. ["History of the press in Aroostook County."] MPAP, 47 (1910), 11; 49 (1912), 26-27; 50 (1913), 25-26.

1451 GILMAN, GEORGE H. ["History of the press in Aroostook County."] MPAP, 24 (1887), 25; 26 (1889), 34-35; 30 (1893), 29-30; 35 (1898), 20-21; 36 (1899), 34-35; 38 (1901), 34-35; 39 (1902), 37.

1452 GILMAN, WILLIAM S. ["History of the press in Aroostook County."] MPAP, 17 (1880), 11; 19 (1882), 25.

1453 GRANT, RENA V. Three men from Aroostook: the story of the Hardison family. Berkeley, Calif.: Brazelton-Hanscom, 1963. Pp. 172.

1454 HAMLIN, HELEN. Pine, potatoes and people: the story of Aroostook. N.Y.: W. W. Norton, 1948. Pp. 238.

1455 HANNAN, ANNE. "Aroostook yesterdays." Down East, 3 (November, 1956-January, 1957), 18-20.

1456 HEDE, RICHARD, comp. and ed. Centennial history of Maine's Swedish colony: New Sweden, Westmanland, Stockholm, and adjoining areas, 1870-1970. [Stockholm?]: Thayer's, [1970?]. v.p. Me.

1457 HUFF, JEAN KEIRSTEAD. The history of secondary education in Aroostook County in Maine. Orono: Univ. Pr., 1946. Pp. vii, 138.

1458 JACKSON, ANNETTE. My life in the Maine woods: a game warden's wife in the Allagash country. N.Y.: W. W. Norton, 1954. Pp. 236.

1459 KIDNEY, DOROTHY BOONE. Away from it all. South Brunswick, N.J.: A. S. Barnes, 1969. Pp. 200.
Allagash River.

1460 MICHAUD, A. J. An Acadian heritage: from the Saint John River Valley. Madawaska: Valley Publishing, [1972]. Pp. 87.

1461 "THE POTATO industry in Aroostook County." The Northern, 3 (February, 1924), 8-13.

1462 PULLEN, CLARENCE. In fair Aroostook, where Acadia and Scandinavia's subtle touch turned a wilderness into a land of plenty. Bangor: Bangor & Aroostook Railroad, 1902. Pp. 94.

1463 PUTNAM, BEECHER. "History of Aroostook County probate office and records." SJMH, 4 (1916-1917), 255-259.

1464 RAYMOND, WILLIAM ODBER. The river St. John, its physical features, legends and history, from 1604 to 1784. St. John, N.B.: J. A. Bowes, 1910. Pp. 552.

1465 ROGERS, MARY ELIZABETH BARKER. "Aroostook pioneers." Down East, 12 (April, 1966), 32-36, 49-50, 53, 56, 58, 60.

1466 RULE, GLENN K. "Aroostook--its people and hospitality." In the Maine Woods, (1934), 117-120.
Social life and customs.

1467 SPRAGUE, RICHARD W. "The face of Aroostook." Down East, 4 (October, 1957), 14-17.

1468 _____. "Potato, king of Aroostook." Down East, 2 (October, 1955), 22-25.

1469 STICKNEY, DANIEL. ["History of the press in Aroostook County."] MPAP, 13 (1876), 23-24; 15 (1878), 23-30.

1470 VALLEAU, STEVEN L. Lumbering history of the Allagash. [Orono]: Univ. of Maine Environmental Studies Center, [1975]. Pp. 187. MeBa.

1471 VIOLETTE, LAWRENCE A. How the Acadians came to Maine. n.p., 1951. Pp. 79. Me.

1472 WALKER, HOWELL. "Aroostook County, Maine, source of potatoes." National Geographic, 94 (1948), 459-478.

1473 WALKER, RAYMOND J. "Early newspapers in Aroostook County." Hobbies, 60 (December, 1955), 119, 125.
      1857-1872.

1474 WATSON, ANDREW ELWELL. "A study of land use in thirty-one towns in Aroostook County, Maine." Maine Agricultural Experiment Station. Report, 59 (1942-1943), 53-106.

1475 WHITE, JOHN W. "Early transportation in northernmost New England, 1820-1870." New England Social Studies Bulletin, 12 (March, 1955), 18-24.

1476 WIGGIN, EDWARD. Aroostook: extracts from address ... delivered before the Farmer's Club, at Boothbay, Dec. 14, 1885; also, opinions of others with reference to that county. Portland: Tucker Printing, 1887. Pp. 26.

1477 _____. History of Aroostook. Vol. 1. Presque Isle: Star-Herald Pr., 1922. 2 pts. in 1 v.
      Part two is by George H. Collins; Part one was also issued separately; no more published.

1478 WILSON, CHARLES MORROW. Aroostook: our last frontier; Maine's picturesque potato empire. Brattleboro, Vt.: Stephen Daye Pr., 1937. Pp. 240.

1479 WILSON, ELLA M. "The Aroostook Valley: a study in potatoes." GeogRev, 16 (1926), 196-205.

      SEE ALSO entries 108, 207, 1251, and 2673.

CUMBERLAND COUNTY

1480 BACHELDER, PETER DOW. Lighthouses of Casco Bay. Portland: Breakwater Pr., 1975. Pp. x, 88.

1481 BAXTER, JAMES PHINNEY. George Cleeve of Casco Bay, 1630-1667, with collateral documents.... Portland: Gorges Society, 1885. Pp. 339.

1482 BIOGRAPHICAL review: this volume contains biographical sketches of leading citizens of Cumberland County, Maine.... Boston: Biographical Review Publishing, 1896. Pp. 706.

1483 CHAPMAN, LEONARD BOND. "Block and garrison houses of ancient Falmouth." MeHSC, 2 Ser., 6 (1895), 37-53.
      Ancient Falmouth included Falmouth, Cape Elizabeth, Portland, Deering, and Westbrook.

1484 CHASE, ALBRO ELMORE. ["History of the press in Cumberland County."] MPAP, 21 (1884), 23.

1485 CLAYTON, W. WOODFORD. History of Cumberland Co., Maine; with illustrations and biographical sketches of its prominent men and pioneers.... Philadelphia: Everts & Peck, 1880. Pp. 456.

1486 COLESWORTHY, DANIEL CLEMENT. Chronicles of Casco Bay. Portland: Sanborn and Carter, 1850. Pp. 56.

1487 COUNCIL OF SOCIAL AGENCIES, PORTLAND, ME. Greater Portland's, Portland, South Portland, Cape Elizabeth, Falmouth, provisions for health, education, safety, welfare. Margaret B. Hodges, ed. Portland, 1941. Pp. 284.

1488 CRITTENDEN, HENRY TEMPLE. "Bridgton & Harrison Railway." RLHSB, No. 57 (1942), 73-86.

1489 CUMBERLAND ASSOCIATION OF CONGREGATIONAL MINISTERS. The centennial of the Cumberland Association of Congregational Ministers, at the Second Parish Church in Portland, Maine ... May 28 and 29, 1888. Portland: B. Thurston, 1888. Pp. 75.
      Historical address by Abiel H. Wright.

1490 CUMBERLAND COUNTY, ME. 200TH ANNIVERSARY COMMITTEE. Cumberland County, 1760, bicentennial, 1960. [Portland?], 1960. Pp. 132. Me.

1491 DINGLEY, ROBERT JORDAN. "Songo River steamers." Down East, 21 (July, 1975), 82-85, 94.

1492 DIRECTORY of the city of Portland, and of the towns of Cape Elizabeth, Deering, Westbrook and Falmouth, for A.D. 1882, being the 250th anniversary of the settlement of those towns which comprised the territory of "Ancient Falmouth," containing the names, occupations, and residence of each adult inhabitant of the city; a street directory, showing the occupant of each building in the city, designated by street and number; a business directory; lists of copartnerships with the members comprising them; corporations with their officers; societies, institutions, etc., historical and statistical matters relating thereto. John T. Hull, comp. Portland: Dresser, McLellan, 1882. Pp. 720, 150.

1493 DOLE, SAMUEL THOMAS. "Gambo, old and new." MeHSC, 2 Ser., 8 (1897), 255-262.
      Gunpowder manufacture at Gambo Falls on the Presumpscot River between Gorham and Windham.

1494 CUMBERLAND COUNTY

1494 _____. "White's Bridge." MeHSC, 2 Ser., 6 (1895), 252-255.
      Between towns of Windham and Standish.

1495 DUNN, WILLIAM WARREN. Casco Bay steamboat album. Camden: Down East Enterprise, 1969. Pp. 42. MeHi.

1496 ELDEN, ALFRED OWEN. "Beacons that shine in Casco Bay." Pine Tree Magazine, 6 (1906-1907), 38-44.

1497 ELWELL, EDWARD HENRY. "History of the press in Cumberland County." MPAP, 12 (1875), 4-7; 13 (1876), 25-27; 14 (1877), 22-31; 15 (1878), 31.

1498 FOBES, CHARLES S. "The story of the Presumpscot." MeHSC, 2 Ser., 5 (1894), 360-386.
      River.

1499 GARDNER, FRANK A. "Colonel Edmund Phinney's 26th Regiment." MassMag, 11 (1918), 12-36.

1500 GILBERT, FRANK Y. "Hospitals in Cumberland County." Sun Up, 3 (September, 1926), 52-53.

1501 GOOLD, NATHAN. Col. Edmund Phinney's 18th Continental Regiment; one year's service, commencing January 1, 1776. MeHSC, 2 Ser., 9 (1898), 45-106.

1502 _____. "History of Col. Edmund Phinney's 31st Regiment of Foot." MeHSC, 2 Ser., 7 (1896), 85-102, 151-185.
      Raised in Cumberland County.

1503 HAYNES, WILLIAMS. Casco Bay yarns. N.Y.: D. O. Haynes, 1916. Pp. 189.

1504 HOLDEN, CHARLES. "The origin and history of the newspaper press of Cumberland County." MPAP, [6] (1869), 29-56.

1505 HOLDEN, THEODORE L. and RUSSELL W. KNIGHT. "The Songo River steamboats." AmNep, 24 (1964), 233-246.
      1847-1930.

1506 HOPKINS, JAMES DEAN. An address to the members of the Cumberland bar, delivered during the sitting of the Court of Common Pleas, at Portland, June term, 1833. Portland: C. Day, 1833. Pp. 79.

1507 "A HUNDRED years ago Sebago Lake was connected with the sea: the history of an old canal." Sun Up, 2 (May, 1926), 15, 36.
      Sebago Lake to Portland.

1508 JEPSON, ADA F. "Presumpscot Union Parish 20th anniversary." MeCP, 145 (January, 1949), 27-29.

1509 JOHNSON, THEODORE ELLIOT, ed. "Elder Otis Sawyer's 'A complete register of all the deaths that have occurred in the United Societies of Gorham and New Gloucester, Maine.'" Shaker Quarterly, 1 (1961), 32-42.

1510 JONES, HERBERT GRANVILLE. The isles of Casco Bay in fact & fancy. Portland: Jones Book Shop, 1946. Pp. 141.

1511 _____. Sebago Lake land in history, legend and romance. Portland: Bowker Pr., 1949. Pp. 130.

1512 [KALER, JAMES OTIS]. The story of old Falmouth. By James Otis, pseud. N.Y.: Thomas Y. Crowell, 1901. Pp. 127.

1513 KENNEDY, BEN F. Buried treasure of Casco Bay, Maine: a guide to locations for the modern hunter. Falmouth: Grace Pr., 1963. Pp. 79.

1514 LOWRY, LOIS. "The Maine boyhoods of Longfellow and Hawthorne." Down East, 22 (March, 1976), 32-35, 58.
      In Portland and Raymond respectively.

1515 [McLAUGHLIN, PETER J.] Casco Bay Islands, Casco Bay, Maine. By Carthwheel Baxtree, pseud. Portland: Casco Bay Line, [1964?]. Pp. 10. MeP.

1516 MEAD, EDGAR THORN, JR. "In behalf of a railroad." Yankee, 6 (July, 1940), 25-26.
      Bridgton & Harrison Railway.

1517 MUNN, HENRY. "The shell heaps of Casco Bay." Maine Field Naturalist, 12 (April, 1956), 34-40.

1518 OLIPHANT, DUNCAN. Maine's Cumberland County. [Portland]: Maine Printing, [1961?]. Pp. 56. Me.

1519 "PAPERS in Mass. archives relating to settlements in Casco Bay." Putnam's HM, 2 (1893-1894), 227-228.

1520 PICKARD, SAMUEL THOMAS. ["History of the press in Cumberland County."] MPAP, 20 (1883), 18.

1521 ROWE, WILLIAM HUTCHINSON. Ancient North Yarmouth and Yarmouth, Maine, 1636-1936: a history. Yarmouth, 1937. Pp. xiii, 427.

1522 _____. Shipbuilding days and tales of the sea, in old North Yarmouth and Yarmouth, Maine. Portland: Marks Printing, 1924. Pp. 145.

1523 _____. Shipbuilding days in Casco Bay, 1727-1890; being footnotes to the maritime history of Maine. Yarmouth, 1929. Pp. xii, 222.

1524 _____. Yarmouth personages, an introduction: an attempt to revive the memory of individuals whose names were once household words in old North Yarmouth and Yarmouth. [Yarmouth?, 1916]. Unpaged.

1525 SALE, THOMAS D. ["History of the press in Cumberland County."] MPAP, 49 (1903), 37-38; 41 (1904), 45; 42 (1905), 32-33; 43 (1906), 25; 44 (1907), 47-48; 45 (1908), 30-31; 46 (1909), 29; 47 (1910), 11-12; 48 (1911), 29-30; 52 (1915), 13.

1526 SCHNEIDER, STEWART P. "Casco Bay steamboats." Down East, 12 (June, 1966), 30-33, 64-66, 68-70.

1527 SHOREY, HENRY A. ["History of the press in Cumberland County."] MPAP, 34 (1897), 27-30.

1528 SNOW, EDWARD ROWE. The romance of Casco Bay. N.Y.: Dodd, Mead, 1975. Pp. x, 228.

1529 SYLVESTER, HERBERT MILTON. Ye romance of Casco Bay. Boston: Stanhope Pr., 1904. Pp. 348.
   Also published in 1909 as volume one of the author's "Maine pioneer settlements."

1530 _____. "Ye romance of Casco Bay." NEM, New Ser., 6 (1892), 379-390, 500-512, 756-766; 7 (1892-1893), 728-735; 8 (1893), 62-70.

1531 THURSTON, BROWN. ["History of the press in Cumberland County."] MPAP, 16 (1879), 29; 17 (1880), 12-15; 18 (1881), 27-28; 19 (1882), 25-27; 23 (1886), 19-20; 24 (1887), 27-28; 25 (1888), 27; 27 (1890), 29; 28 (1891), 28-29; 29 (1892), 23-24; 30 (1893), 30-32.

1532 WALDRON, HOLMAN DOUGLAS. "Casco Bay." NEM, New Ser., 14 (1896), 355-374.

1533 WESTON, ISAAC. "History of the Association of Ministers of Cumberland County, Maine, from 1788 to 1867." CongQ, 9 (1867), 334-347.

1534 WILLIS, WILLIAM. "Remarks on coins found at Portland in 1849, and Richmond's Island in 1855, with a general notice of coins and coinage." MeHSC, 6 (1859), 127-151.

1535 WISH, OSCAR R. ["History of the press in Cumberland County."] MPAP, 39 (1902), 38.

1536 WYMAN, DREW T. A brief sketch of the history of the Cumberland Association, 1811-1892. Portland: Brown Thurston, 1892. Pp. 16. Me.
   Baptists.

SEE ALSO entries 228, 333, 354, 508, 587, 626, 879, 975, 978, 1045, 1409, 2709, and 4386.

FRANKLIN COUNTY

1537 AUSTIN, HARRY B. "The Sandy River and Rangeley Lakes Railroad." Sun Up, 5 (June, 1928), 13-15.

1538 BRACKETT, LUCY B. ["History of the press in Franklin County."] MPAP, 50 (1913), 26-28.

1539 CORNWALL, L. PETER and JACK W. FARRELL. Ride the Sandy River: a trip into the past on what was America's largest two-foot gauge railroad. Edmonds, Wash.: Pacific Fast Mail, 1973. Pp. 248.

1540 CRITTENDEN, HENRY TEMPLE. The Maine scenic route: a history of the Sandy River & Rangeley Lakes Railroad. Parsons, W. Va.: McClain Printing, 1966. Pp. 229.

1541 _____. "The Sandy River & Rangeley Lakes Railroad." RLHSB, No. 57 (1942), 15-72.

1542 _____. "Sandy River & Rangeley Lakes R.R. System." RLHSB, No. 37 (1935), 15-32.

1543 _____. Supplement--the Maine scenic route. n.p., 1966. Pp. 8, 16. MeHi.
   Sandy River & Rangeley Lakes Railroad.

1544 DURRELL, JANICE. Franklin County, Maine. Portland: Gross & Allen, [1973?]. Pp. 72. MeU.

1545 FRANKLIN COUNTY AGRICULTURAL SOCIETY. Historical sketch, by-laws, and list of members of the Franklin County Agricultural Society, incorporated March 13, 1840. Farmington: Knowlton, McLeary, 1888. Pp. 26. MeHi.
   Historical sketch is by Edward A. Hall.

1546 HOAR, JAY S. Small-town motion pictures, and other sketches of Franklin County, Maine. Farmington: Knowlton & McLeary, 1969. Pp. 92.

1547 HUNTER, JOHN M. S. ["History of the press in Franklin County."] MPAP, 31 (1894), 22-23; 32 (1895), 28; 33 (1897), 30.

1548 KEYES, CHARLES WESLEY. ["History of the press in Franklin County."] MPAP, 14 (1877), 31-37; 16 (1879), 29-30; 18 (1881), 29; 19 (1882), 27-28; 20 (1883), 18-19; 21 (1884), 23-26; 22 (1885), 43; 23 (1886), 20-21; 24 (1887), 28-29.

1549 KNOWLTON, DAVID HUNTER. ["History of the press in Franklin County."] MPAP, 25 (1888), 27-29; 35 (1898), 21-23; 36 (1899), 35; 37 (1900), 34; 38 (1901), 35; 39 (1902), 38-39; 40 (1903), 38-39; 43 (1906), 26; 44 (1907), 48-49; 46 (1909), 29-30.

1550 MOODY, LINWOOD W. "Mighty midgets of the old F & M." Down East, 11 (March, 1965), 28-32.
   Franklin and Megantic Railroad.

1551 _____. "Shadow of the Sandy River." Trains, (August, 1946), 10-16.
    Sandy River and Rangeley Lakes Railroad.

1551A NETT, BRUCE OWEN. "The old narrow gauge." Down East, 1 (October, 1954), 19-22.
    Sandy River and Rangeley Lakes Railroad.

1552 WILSON, CHARLES G. "Rolling into Kingfield on the Sandy River line." Down East, 9 (January, 1963), 8-21.
    Sandy River and Rangeley Lakes Railroad.

    SEE ALSO entries 109, 555, and 1025.

HANCOCK COUNTY

1553 BARTER, J. MALCOLM. "Deer Isle and Stonington." Down East, 22 (April, 1976), 54-60.

1554 BROOKES, GEORGE S. These hundred years: history of the Hancock Association of Congregational Churches and Ministers, 1825-1925. n.p., [1923?]. Pp. 56. MeHi.

1555 BROWN, LENARD E. Acadia National Park, Maine: history basic data. Washington: Office of History and Historic Architecture, Eastern Service Center, 1971. Pp. iii, 191.

1556 _____. Significance of St. Sauveur Mission, established 1613, Mount Desert Island. Washington: Office of History and Historic Architecture, Eastern Service Center, 1970. iv, 57 leaves.

1557 BURT, FRANK H. "Mount Desert's mountain railway." Appalachia, 24 (1942-1943), 435-440.
    Green Mountain Railway.

1558 BUTCHER, RUSSELL D. Maine paradise: Mount Desert Island and Acadia National Park. N.Y.: Viking Pr., 1973. Pp. 94.

1559 CHADWICK, JOSEPH. "Journal through part of Mount Desart, 1768." MeHistMag, 9 (1894-1895), 123-129.
    Edited.

1560 CHAPMAN, CARLETON ABRAMSON. The geology of Acadia National Park. [Chatham, Mass.]: Chatham Pr., 1970. Pp. 128.

1561 CHATTO, CLARENCE I. and CLAIR E. TURNER. Register of the towns of Sedgwick, Brooklin, Deer Isle, Stonington, and Isle au Haut, 1910. Brooklin: Friend Memorial Public Library, 1972. Pp. 243.
    Includes historical sketches of the towns.

1562 CHILCOTT, JAMES C. ["History of the press in Hancock County."] MPAP, 26 (1889), 35; 27 (1890), 29-30; 28 (1891), 29; 29 (1892), 24; 30 (1893), 32.

1563 COLLIER, SARGENT F. Acadia National Park: George B. Dorr's triumph, with map and the illustrated story of "Mt. Desert, the most beautiful island in the world." Farmington: Knowlton & McLeary, 1965. Pp. 96.

1564 _____ and THOMAS PATRICK HORGAN. Mount Desert, the most beautiful island in the world. Boston: Houghton Miflin, 1952. Pp. ii, 106.

1565 CUMMINGS, EPHRAIM CHAMBERLAIN. "Father Biard's relation of 1616 and Saint Sauveur." MeHSC, 2 Ser., 5 (1894), 81-99.
    Saint Sauveur was Biard's early settlement on Mount Desert Island.

1566 DE COSTA, BENJAMIN FRANKLIN. The hand-book of Mount Desert, coast of Maine, with all the routes thither, descriptions of the scenery and topography, sketches of the history, with illustrations and a map of Mount Desert, and Penobscot and Frenchman's Bay, from the United States Coast Survey.... (1868) Boston: A. Williams, 1878. Pp. xiii, 161.
    First edition, 1868, has title: Scenes in the isle of Mount Desert.

1567 _____. "Mount Desert." National Repository, 4 (1878), 97-110.

1568 _____. Rambles in Mount Desert; with sketches of travel on the New England coast, from Isles of Shoals to Grand Menan. N.Y.: A. D. F. Randolph, 1871. Pp. 280.

1569 "THE DE GREGOIRE Grant of Mount Desert Island and what is now Ellsworth, Hancock, Trenton and Lamoine." BHistMag, 2 (1886-1887), 81-83.

1570 DODGE, E. H. Mount Desert Island, and the Cranberry Isles.... Ellsworth: N. K. Sawyer, 1871. Pp. 64.

1571 DORR, GEORGE BUCKNAM. Acadia National Park. Bangor: Burr Print, 1942-1948. 2v.

1572 _____. "Acadia National Park." Nature Magazine, 13 (1929), 315-318, 345-348.

1573 _____. The Sieur de Monts National Monument as commemorating Acadia and early French influences of race and settlement in the United States. Bar Harbor: Wild Gardens of Acadia, [1917?]. Pp. 15.

1574 _____, ERNEST HOWE FORBUSH and MERRITT CALDWELL FERNALD. "The unique island of Mount Desert." National Geographic, 26 (1914), 75-89.

1575 EDWARDS, HERBERT. "Mt. Desert writers." Down East, 11 (August, 1964), 42-45, 72-74, 76.

1576 ELIOT, CHARLES WILLIAM. "The forgotten millions: a study of the common American mode of life." Century, 40 (1890), 556-564.
Economic conditions on Mt. Desert Island, 1880s.

1577 ELIOT, SAMUEL ATKINS. "The romance of Mount Desert." NEM, New Ser., 20 (1899), 682-697.
French exploration.

1578 FISHER, JONATHAN. "Origin of the name of Union River between Surry and Ellsworth." BHistMag, 6 (1890-1891), 48.
Written in 1827 and contributed by Joseph Williamson.

1579 FOSS, THOMAS. A brief account of the early settlements along the shores of Skilling's River, including West Sullivan, West Gouldsborough, Trenton Point and North Hancock; also reminescences [sic] and anecdotes of old times and old folks. [Ellsworth]: N. K. Sawyer, 1870. Pp. 25.

1580 GRAZIER, JOHN S. "Prologue." NEG, 9 (Spring, 1968), 31-39.
A confrontation in Frenchman's Bay in 1613 between the French vessel "Jonas" from Nova Scotia and English vessel "Treasurer" from Jamestown, which was the prologue to Anglo-French rivalry.

1581 GREEN, SAMUEL M. "Thomas Lord, joiner and housewright." Magazine of Art, 40 (1947), 230-235.

1582 HADLOCK, WENDELL STANWOOD. "Bone implements from shell heaps around Frenchman's Bay." American Antiquity, 8 (1943), 341-353.

1583 _____. The three shell heaps on Frenchman's Bay. [Bar Harbor], 1941. Pp. 23.

1584 "HANCOCK County lawyers." BHistMag, 2 (1886-1887), 173-176.
Brief biographies.

1585 HIGGINS, ALBERT L. Notes from the early history of Mt. Desert Island. [Bar Harbor?], 1929. Unpaged. MeBa.

1586 HILTON, FLORA A. "Historical sketch of Old Point." American Monthly Magazine, 36 (1910), 398-404.
Hancock and Lamoine.

1587 THE ISLAND of Mount Desert register, with the Cranberry Isles, 1909-1910. Auburn: Lawton-Jordan, 1910. Pp. 334.
Includes history of Mount Desert, Bar Harbor, Tremont, Southwest Harbor, and Cranberry Isles.

1588 JOHNSON, LELIA ARDELL CLARK. Sullivan and Sorrento since 1760. Ellsworth: Hancock County Publishing, 1953. Pp. 410.

1589 LAPHAM, WILLIAM BERRY. Bar Harbor and Mount Desert Island.... (1886) 3d ed., rev. and enl. Augusta: Maine Farmer Job Print, 1888. Pp. 72.

1590 MAINE. STATE PLANNING OFFICE. A bibliography of Mount Desert Island. Augusta, 1974. 20 leaves. MeU.

1591 MARTIN, CLARA BARNES. Mount Desert, on the coast of Maine ... (1867) 6th ed. Portland: Loring, Short & Harmon, 1885. Pp. 115.

1592 MORISON, SAMUEL ELIOT. The story of Mount Desert Island, Maine. Boston: Little, Brown, 1960. Pp. 81.

1593 "MOUNT Desert." MeHistMag, 8 (1893), 19-23.

1594 "MOUNT Desert Island." BHistMag, 1 (1885-1886), 179-192.

1595 THE MOUNT Desert Larger Parish, historic and descriptive manual of the first seven years of the organization, 1925-1932. n.p., [1932]. Pp. 32. Me.

1596 "MOUNT Desert Rock: Maine's outermost light." Down East, 8 (October, 1961), 38-41.

1597 "PENOBSCOT, Castine and Brooksville." MeHist Mag, 8 (1893), 6-12.
Biographies of early settlers.

1598 PERRY, ADELAIDE E. This is Maine's Hancock County. Portland: Gross and Allen, [1971?]. Pp. 100. MeU.

1599 POHL, FREDERICK J. "The adventure of the hasty grave." American-Scandinavian Review, 40 (March, 1952), 15-24.
Alleged battle between Leif Ericsson and Indians on Mt. Desert Island.

1600 RAISZ, ERWIN JOSEPHUS. "The scenery of Mt. Desert Island: its origin and development." New York Academy of Sciences. Annals, 31 (1929), 121-186.

1601 "REPRESENTATIVES to General Court, from what is now Hancock County, prior to 1820." BHistMag, 3 (1887-1888), 138.
Chronological within each locale.

1602 [ROBINSON, BERNICE NELKE]. Our island lighthouse. By Bernice Richmond, pseud. N.Y.: Random House, 1947. Pp. 275.

1603 ROLLINS, FRANK W. ["History of the press in Hancock County."] MPAP, 44 (1907), 49.

1604 SAVAGE, RICHARD A. "The collectors of old Frenchman's Bay." NEG, 14 (1973), 21-29.
Collectors of customs, 19th century.

1605 SAWTELLE, WILLIAM OTIS. Acadia National Park: random notes of the significance of the name. [Bar Harbor?], 1929. Unpaged. MeBa.

1606 _____. "Father Pierre Biard, superior of the Mount Desert Jesuit Mission of Saint Sauveur." SJMH, 10 (1922), 179-191.

1607 _____. "The island of Mount Desert: the romantic story of Charles Maurice de Talleyrand-Perigord, one of the world's most famous diplomats, and its connection with Maine's early history." SJMH, 11 (1923), 127-143.

1608 _____. "Mount Desert: Champlain to Bernard." SJMH, 13 (1925), 131-186.
Samuel de Champlain and John Bernard.

1609 _____. "Mount Desert: the story of Saint Sauveur." SJMH, 9 (1921), 101-120.

1610 _____. "Pioneers of Mount Desert, 1763." SJMH, 14 (1926), 179-187.

1611 _____. "Sir Francis Bernard and his grant of Mount Desert." CSMP, 24 (1920-1922), 197-238.

1612 SAWYER, NATHANIEL KNIGHT. "Record of newspapers in Hancock County." MPAP, 3 (1866), 5-10.

1613 SCHAUFFLER, ROBERT HAVEN. "Unique Mount Desert." Century, 82 (1911), 477-490.
Mount Desert Island.

1614 "THE SECOND settlement in Acadia, now Maine, 1611-13." BHistMag, 6 (1890-1891), 1-3.
Saint Sauveur.

1615 SELIGMANN, HERBERT J. "Acadia National Park: mountain playground by the sea." Down East, 6 (August, 1959), 36-41, 60.

1616 STREET, GEORGE EDWARD. Mount Desert: a history. (1905) Samuel A. Eliot, ed. New ed. Boston: Houghton, Mifflin, 1926. Pp. x, 339.

1617 THORNTON, NELLIE C. Traditions and records of Southwest Harbor and Somesville, Mount Desert Island, Maine. Auburn: Merrill & Webber, 1938. Pp. vi, 346.

1618 TRUAX, C. V. "The pink granite of Somes Sound." Down East, 19 (October, 1972), 34-37, 67-69, 71.

1619 WASSON, SAMUEL. A survey of Hancock County, Maine. Augusta: Sprague, Owen & Nash, 1878. Pp. 91.

1620 WEBSTER, ARTHUR GORDON. "Evolution of Mount Desert." Nation, 99 (September 17, 1914), 347-348.

1621 WHEELER, GEORGE AUGUSTUS. History of Castine, Penobscot, and Brooksville, Maine; including the ancient settlement of Pentagöet. Bangor: Burr & Robinson, 1875. Pp. x, 401.

1622 WOOD, JOSEPH. ["History of the press in Hancock County."] MPAP, 22 (1885), 45-47; 23 (1886), 21-22; 24 (1887), 29; 25 (1888), 29; 33 (1896), 36-37; 34 (1897), 30-31; 35 (1898), 23; 37 (1900), 34; 39 (1902), 39; 41 (1904), 45-46; 42 (1905), 33-34; 43 (1906), 26-27.

SEE ALSO entries 108, 686, and 966.

KENNEBEC COUNTY

1623 ADAMS, SARAH B. Reminiscences of the churches and pastors of Kennebec County, read at the Kennebec Conference in Waterville, Oct. 17, 1894. Hallowell: Register Job Print, 1894. Pp. 24. MBC.
Limited to Congregational churches and pastors.

1624 ANDREWS, RICHARD L. "From Randolph to Togus on the Kennebec Central." Trains, 11 (September, 1951), 24-26.
Kennebec Central Railroad Company, 1889-1929.

1625 BOARDMAN, SAMUEL LANE. The agriculture and industry of the county of Kennebec, Maine, with notes upon its history and natural history. Augusta: Kennebec Journal, 1867. Pp. 199. MH.

1626 _____. History of the agriculture of Kennebec County, Maine. N.Y.: Blake, 1892. Pp. 40.

1627 BOWDITCH, HORACE E. ["History of the press in Kennebec County."] MPAP, 48 (1911), 30; 49 (1912), 27.

1628 BRANIN, M. LELYN. "The early stoneware potteries in Gardiner-Farmingdale, Maine." National Antiques Review, 4 (January, 1973), 24-26.

1629 CRITTENDEN, HENRY TEMPLE. "The Kennebec Central Railroad." RLHSB, No. 57 (1942), 103-111.
Randolph to Togus.

1630 DUNBAR, KENDALL M. ["History of the press in Kennebec County."] MPAP, 27 (1890), 30-31.

1631 FINLEY, RAYMOND STEVENS. The history of secondary education in Kennebec County in Maine. Orono: Univ. Pr., 1941. Pp. vii, 119.

1632 FLYNT, CHARLES F. ["History of the press in Kennebec County."] MPAP, 36 (1899), 36.

1633 HANSON, JOHN WESLEY. History of Gardiner, Pittston and West Gardiner, with a sketch of the Kennebec Indians; and New Plymouth purchase, comprising historical matter from 1602 to 1852; with genealogical sketches of many families. Gardiner: W. Palmer, 1852. Pp. xi, 343.

1634 KINGSBURY, HENRY D. and SIMEON L. DEYO, eds. Illustrated history of Kennebec County, Maine: 1625-1799-1892. N.Y.: H. W. Blake, 1892. 2v.

1635 LAPHAM, WILLIAM BERRY. ["History of the press in Kennebec County."] MPAP, 15 (1878), 31-32; 24 (1887) 30; 25 (1888), 30; 26 (1889), 35-36; 30 (1893), 32.

1636 MARRINER, ERNEST CUMMINGS. Kennebec yesterdays. Waterville: Colby College Pr., 1954. Pp. 320.

1637 "NEW England manufacturing towns." New England Magazine of Industry and Trade, 1 (1859), 72-75.
     Gardiner, Hallowell, and Augusta.

1638 OWEN, HOWARD. "History of the press in Kennebec County." MPAP, 12 (1875), 7.

1639 POPE, ALTON S. and RAYMOND S. PATTERSON. "M. Appleton, 1800, chronicler of colonial medicine." Harvard Medical Alumni Bulletin, 36 (Spring, 1962), 17-23.
     His journal in Waterville and Winslow in early 1800s.

1640 QUINBY, GEORGE WASHINGTON. ["History of the press in Kennebec County."] MPAP, 18 (1881), 29-32; 19 (1882), 28.

1641 REDDINGTON, ASA. "Attorneys at law in Kennebec County, Maine." American Quarterly Register, 15 (1842-1843), 501.

1642 RICHARDS, ROSALIND. A northern countryside. N.Y.: Henry Holt, 1916. Pp. vi, 210.

1643 SANBORN, FRED W. ["History of the press in Kennebec County."] MPAP, 49 (1912), 27.

1644 SHAILER, WILLIAM HOSMER. A discourse delivered at the fiftieth anniversary of the Kennebec Association, at Norridgewock, September 2, 1879. Portland: B. Thurston, 1879. Pp. 24. MB.
     Baptists.

1645 SIDNEY, ME. The town register: Sidney, Vassalboro, China, Albion. Augusta: Mitchell-Cony, 1908. Pp. 160, 216, 51. MB.
     Includes histories of the four towns.

1646 SMITH, CAROLYN B. Union list of periodicals in the libraries of the Kennebec Valley region. Waterville: Kennebec Valley Library Service Area Council, 1972. Pp. 33. MeP.

1647 SPRAGUE, CHARLES A. ["History of the press in Kennebec County.]" MPAP, 20 (1883), 19.

1648 THURLOW, CLINTON F. "The Kennebec Central Railroad." Down East, 15 (May, 1969), 50-55.

1649 WEBSTER, HENRY SEWALL. Land titles in old Pittston. Gardiner: Reporter-Journal Pr., 1912. Pp. 55.
     By "Old Pittston" is here meant the town as it existed at the time of its incorporation. It comprised the territory now lying in Pittston, Randolph, Gardiner, most of West Gardiner, and part of Farmingdale.

1650 WRITERS' PROGRAM. MAINE. Augusta-Hallowell on the Kennebec. [Augusta]: Kennebec Journal Print Shop, 1940. Pp. 123.

SEE ALSO entries 16 and 1358.

KNOX COUNTY

1651 ART work of Knox County, Maine.... [Chicago]: W. H. Parish Publishing, 1895. 15 leaves.
     Includes an historical sketch of the county by True P. Pierce.

1652 BEVERIDGE, NORWOOD P. "Yankees from Finland." Down East, 3 (February-March, 1957), 20-21, 28.

1653 CAMDEN HERALD PUBLISHING COMPANY. Camden-Rockport bicentennial 1769-1969: commemorative book. Camden, 1969. Pp. 68.

1654 CHRONICLES of Cushing and Friendship, containing historical, statistical, and miscellaneous information of the two towns.... Rockland: Maine Home Journal, 1892. Pp. 80.

1655 CILLEY, JONATHAN PRINCE. ["History of the press in Knox County."] MPAP, 34 (1897), 31-34; 35 (1898), 23-24; 37 (1900), 34-35; 38 (1901), 35.

1656 CRONE, ALTON H. The Fox Islands, Vinalhaven-North Haven, sesquicentennial celebration, 1789-1939. Camden: Megunticook Pr., [1939]. Pp. 64.

1657 CUMMINGS, OSMOND RICHARD. "Rockland, Thomaston and Camden Street Railroad." Transportation, 6 (January, 1952), 1-18.
     1892-1931.

1658 _____. "Rockland, Thomaston & Camden Street Railway." Down East, 18 (October, 1971), 46-49, 87-88, 91-92.

1659 DIETZ, LEW. "A special place--the Oyster River Bog." Down East, 22 (November, 1975), 24-27, 58.
     Rockland, Rockport, Warren, and Thomaston.

1660 KNOX COUNTY

1660   EATON, CYRUS. History of Thomaston, Rock-
        land, and South Thomaston, Maine, from their
        first exploration, A.D. 1605; with family
        genealogies. Hallowell: Masters, Smith,
        1865. 2v.

1661   FILLMORE, ROBERT B., comp. Chronicles of
        Knox County. [Rockland?], 1922. Pp. 106.

1662   ____. Chronicles of Knox County. n.p.,
        1923. Pp. 20.

1663   GOULD, ALBERT TROWBRIDGE. The St. George's
        River. [Beverly Farms?, Mass.], 1950.
        Pp. xii, 188.

1664   HESELTINE, CHARLES DANA. "Maine's 'Tooner-
        ville Trolley.'" Down East, 20 (October,
        1973), 64-65.
            Rockland, South Thomaston & St. George
        Railway.

1665   JONES, ARNOLD H. ["History of the press in
        Knox County."] MPAP, 50 (1913), 28.

1666   THE MAINE magazine. Special ed. Rockland,
        Camden and environs, 1907. n.p., [1907?].
        Pp. 56.
            Camden, Rockland, Rockport, Thomaston, and
        Warren.

1667   MOODY, LINWOOD W. "The doodlebug railroad."
        Down East, 15 (January, 1969), 50-53, 60, 63-
        64, 66.
            George's Valley Railroad.

1668   ____. "The Rockport Railroad." Down East,
        14 (July, 1968), 44-45, 81-82, 85, 88.

1669   OGIER, JESSE H. ["History of the press in
        Knox County."] MPAP, 41 (1904), 56; 46
        (1909), 30.

1670   PERRY, WILDER WASHINGTON. ["History of the
        press in Knox County."] MPAP, 20 (1883),
        19-20.

1671   ROBINSON, REUEL. History of Camden and Rock-
        port, Maine. Camden: Camden Publishing,
        1907. Pp. xiii, 644.

1672   SPRAGUE, EDWIN. "Record of newspapers in
        Knox County." MPAP, 3 (1866), 10-13; 15
        (1878), 32-34.

1673   STIMPSON, MARY STOYELL. "Rockland, Rockport
        and Camden." NEM, New Ser., 31 (1904-1905),
        3-15.

1674   TENNEY, HELEN. Ship's Timbers: a cottage on
        the coast of Maine. N.Y.: Exposition Pr.,
        1971. Pp. 71.
            Social life and customs.

1675   VOSE, Z. POPE. ["History of the press in
        Knox County."] MPAP, 16 (1879), 30-31; 18
        (1881), 32.

1676   WALKER, HAROLD S. "Knox Railroad, formerly
        Georges Valley R.R." RLHSB, No. 41 (1936),
        44-46.

        SEE ALSO entries 107 and 907.

LINCOLN COUNTY

1677   ALLEN, CHARLES EDWIN. "Ancient Pownalboro
        and her daughters." NEM, New Ser., 24 (1901),
        516-534.
            Pownalboro, Wiscasset, Dresden, Alna and
        Perkins.

1678   CASTNER, HAROLD WEBBER. The story of the
        Great Salt Bay and Vaughn's Pond. (1950)
        2d ed. Boothbay Harbor: Boothbay Register,
        1956. Pp. 34.

1679   ____. A story of the mystifying, prehistor-
        ic oyster shell heaps of the Damariscotta
        River; containing records of explorations by
        scientists and all known data on this man-
        made wonder of antiquity, together with pic-
        tures of the excavation, 1886. (1930) 3rd
        ed. Boothbay Harbor, 1956. Pp. 20.

1680   CHRISTIAN, SHELDON. "How the Enterprise beat
        the Boxer." Down East, 10 (September, 1963),
        29-31, 50.
            War of 1812.

1681   "THE CHRONOLOGICAL history of the Boothbay
        region." Sun Up, 3 (September, 1926), 60-62.
            1000-1926.

1682   CLIFFORD, HAROLD BURTON. The Boothbay region,
        1906 to 1960. Freeport: Bond Wheelwright,
        1961. Pp. 354.

1683   CUSHMAN, DAVID QUIMBY. The history of ancient
        Sheepscot and Newcastle including early Pema-
        quid, Damariscotta, and other contiguous
        places, from earliest discovery to the present
        time, together with the genealogy of more than
        four hundred families. Bath: E. Upton & Son,
        1882. Pp. xvii, 458.

1684   DAMARISCOTTA, ME. Centennial celebration at
        Damariscotta and Newcastle, July 4th, 1876,
        together with the historical address delivered
        by Gen. James A. Hall. Waldoboro: Miller &
        Atwood, 1876. Pp. 18.

1685   DUNBAR, KENDALL M. ["History of the press in
        Lincoln County."] MPAP, 27 (1890), 31-32;
        29 (1892), 25.

1686   FERTIG, ILONKA. Eighteenth-century meeting
        houses, Lincoln County, Maine. [Pemaquid]:
        Pemaquid Historical Association, 1970. Pp. 11.
        MeHi.

1687 FILLMORE, ROBERT B., comp. Chronicles of Lincoln County. Augusta: Kennebec Journal Print Shop, 1924. Pp. 152.

1688 FREDERICKS, KATHERINE M. E. Bar-bits from old court records in Lincoln County, Maine. [Wiscasset], County Commissioners of Lincoln County, 1970. Pp. 74. Me.

1689 GREENE, FRANCIS BYRON. History of Boothbay, Southport and Boothbay Harbor, Maine, 1623-1905; with family genealogies. Portland: Loring, Short & Harmon, 1906. Pp. vi, 693.

1690 HALLET, RICHARD. Boothbay region story, 1764-1964, 200th anniversary. n.p., 1964. Pp. 47. Me.
    Boothbay, Boothbay Harbor, and Southport.

1691 HANKS, CARLOS C. "Gun brigs off Pemaquid." United States Naval Institute. Proceedings, 62 (1936), 371-372.
    'Enterprise' and 'Boxer' in War of 1812.

1692 HOLMAN, W. O. Centennial of the Lincoln Baptist Association: historical discourse at the hundredth anniversary held in the First Baptist Church, St. George, September 5 and 6, 1904. n.p., [1904]. Pp. 18.

1693 JOHNSTON, JOHN. A history of the towns of Bristol and Bremen in the State of Maine, including the Pemaquid settlement. Albany, N.Y.: Joel Munsell, 1873. Pp. v, 524.

1694 JONES, CARMITA DE SOLMS. "Missions in Lincoln County, Maine." American Catholic Historical Society of Philadelphia. Records, 36 (1925), 396-400.

1695 LANG, CONSTANCE ROWE. Kennebec, Boothbay Harbor steamboat album, including Monhegan Island, Sheepscot and Damariscotta Rivers. Camden: Down East Enterprise, 1971. Pp. 51.

1696 LINCOLN COUNTY BICENTENARY COMMITTEE. The Lincoln County pilgrimage. n.p., [1960]. Unpaged. MeHi.
    Historic houses.

1697 MARPLE, HOWARD A., ed. Lincoln County, Maine, 1760-1960. Rockland: Seth Low Pr., [1960]. Unpaged. MeHi.

1698 MILLER, SAMUEL LLEWELLYN. ["History of the press in Lincoln County."] MPAP, 18 (1881), 32-33; 19 (1882), 29; 20 (1883), 20; 21 (1884), 26; 23 (1886), 22; 24 (1887), 30-31; 26 (1889), 36; 44 (1907), 49; 45 (1908), 31.

1699 MOUNTFORT, JULIA ANN DYKE. Drogeo land. Damariscotta: Lincoln County News, [1936?]. Pp. 18.

1700 OGIER, JESSE H. ["History of the press in Lincoln County."] MPAP, 32 (1895), 28; 34 (1897), 34-35; 35 (1898), 24.

1701 PATTERSON, WILLIAM DAVIS. "Old mansion houses in Lincoln County." BHistMag, 5 (1889-1890), 231.

1702 ____, ed. The probate records of Lincoln County, Maine, 1760 to 1800; compiled and edited for the Maine Genealogical Society. Portland: Printed for the Society, 1895. Pp. xxi, 368.
    Index of names and places.

1703 PICKING, SHERWOOD. Sea fight off Monhegan: Enterprise and Boxer. Portland: Machigonne Pr., 1941. Pp. x, 195.

1704 "POWNALBOROUGH and Lincoln County." BHistMag, 3 (1887-1888), 121-125.

1705 PREBLE, GEORGE HENRY. "Three historic flags and three September victories." NEHGR, 28 (1874), 17-41.
    Bon Homme Richard, 1779; Enterprise (Boxer vs. Enterprise), and Fort McHenry.

1706 SAWYER, EDITH A. "Three old meeting-houses in Maine." NEM, New Ser., 24 (1901), 594-604.
    Alna, Waldoborough, and Walpole.

1707 SEWALL, RUFUS KING. Memorials of the bar of Lincoln County, Maine, 1760-1900. [2d ed.] Wiscasset: Sheepscot Echo Print, 1900. Pp. 40.

1708 SIDELINGER, LOWELL H. List of vessels built in Newcastle, Damariscotta, Nobleboro and Bristol ... with historical sketches of some of the old vessels and builders. n.p., [1896?]. Pp. 25. MeHi.

1709 STURGES, FLORENCE M. High points in the history of the Newcastle-Damariscotta area. [Damariscotta?]: Newcastle-Damariscotta Woman's Club, 1976. Pp. 46. Me.

1710 THAYER, HENRY OTIS. "Centenary of [the] War [of] 1812-15: naval combat of Enterprise and Boxer, September 5, 1813." SJMH, 2 (1914-1915), 63-73.

1711 WOOD, JOSEPH. "History of the press in Lincoln County." MPAP, 12 (1875), 10-11; 14 (1877), 37-39; 15 (1878), 34-35; 17 (1886), 15; 18 (1881), 39.

1712 WOODBURY, CHARLES LEVI. "Pemaquid and Monhegan." HPHR, 1 (1891-1892), 5-8, 20-26, 46-50, 61-64.

SEE ALSO entries 16, 107, 907, and 966.

OXFORD COUNTY

1713 BARKER, FRED COSHIN and JOHN S. DANFORTH. Hunting and trapping on the Upper Magalloway

1714 OXFORD COUNTY

River and Parmachenee Lake: a winter in the wilderness. (1882) Rev. ed. Boston: Lothrop, Lee & Shepard, 1929. Pp. 238.
1876.

1714 BOWLER, ERNEST C. ["History of the press in Oxford County."] MPAP, 41 (1904), 56-57.

1715 CLEPPER, HENRY EDWARD. "The Parmachenee Belle." American Forests, 62 (March, 1956), 12-13, 56-57.
Fishing in Parmachenee Lake, 1876-1956.

1716 CROCKETT, GEORGE B., comp. Consolidated history of the churches of the Oxford Baptist Association, State of Maine; and a historical sketch of the Association. Bryant's Pond: A. M. Chase, 1905. Pp. 138.

1717 FORBES, ARTHUR ELBRIDGE. ["History of the press in Oxford County."] MPAP, 24 (1887), 31; 25 (1888), 30-31; 26 (1889), 36; 27 (1890), 32-33; 28 (1891), 30; 29 (1892), 25; 30 (1893), 33; 31 (1894), 23; 33 (1896), 38; 34 (1897), 35; 35 (1898), 24; 36 (1899), 36; 37 (1900), 36; 38 (1901), 36; 40 (1903), 39.

1718 HEBERT, RICHARD A. "Norway and South Paris." Pine Cone, 1 (Winter, 1945-1946), 25-28.

1719 MOULTON, AUGUSTUS FREEDOM. "The county of Lincoln." SJMH, 13 (1925), 3-28.

1720 SANBORN, FRED W. ["History of the press in Oxford County."] MPAP, 50 (1913), 28.

1721 STEVENS, JANE PERHAM. Maine's treasure chest: gems and minerals of Oxford County. West Paris: Perham's Maine Mineral Store, 1972. Pp. 216.

1722 STONE, THOMAS TREADWELL. Sketches of Oxford County. Portland: Shirley and Hyde, 1830. Pp. 111.

1723 TIDD, MARSHALL, M. "Up the Magalloway River in 1861." Appalachia, 31 (1956-1957), 457-471; 32 (1955-1959), 45-65.
Edited by Benton L. Hatch and Louis Felix Ranlett from Tidd's manuscript journal in the Bangor Public Library.

1724 WATERMAN, CHARLES ELMER. The Oxford Hills and other papers. Auburn: Merrill & Webber, [1929?]. Pp. 90.

1725 WATKINS, GEORGE HENRY. ["History of the press in Oxford County."] MPAP, 14 (1877), 39; 16 (1879), 31-32; 18 (1881), 33; 21 (1884), 29-30; 22 (1885), 47; 23 (1886), 23.

1726 WIGHT, DENHAM BARTLETT. The Androscoggin River Valley, a gateway to the White Mountains. Rutland, Vt.: Charles E. Tuttle, 1967. Pp. 561.

1727 WOOD, JACOB. A sermon delivered at the dedication of the New Universalist Meeting House in Norway Village, September 30, 1829, to which is added an appendix containing a short sketch of the history of the Universalist Society and Church in Norway and Paris. Norway: Goodnow & Phelps, 1829. Pp. 20. MeHi.

SEE ALSO entries 109, 228, 333, 354, 508, 602, 626, 879, 975, and 1045.

PENOBSCOT COUNTY

1728 "ANCIENT Norumbega." BHistMag, 2 (1886-1887), 134-135.
Supposedly the Penobscot River.

1729 BAKER, RICHARD W. Penobscot County, Maine. Portland: Gross and Allen, 1973. Pp. 75.

1730 BARTLETT, CHARLES H. "Reminiscences of the Penobscot Bar." SJMH, 13 (1925), 30-34.

1731 BARTLETT, EDMUND HOBART. Local government in Penobscot County. Orono: Univ. Pr., 1932. Pp. 82.

1732 DOLE, RICHARD F. "Maine's first steam railroad--Bangor to Old Town." Down East, 18 (May, 1972), 52-54, 59, 62, 64.
Bangor and Piscataquis Canal and Railroad Company.

1733 "EARLY settlements on Penobscot River, now Orono, Milford, Argyle, [and] Bradford." BHistMag, 1 (1885-1886), 206-210.

1734 "THE FIRST steam railroad built in Maine and probably New England." MeHistMag, 7 (1891-1892), 29-30.
Bangor and Piscataquis Canal and Railroad Company.

1735 FISHER, CHARLES E. "The Bangor and Piscataquis R.R." RLHSB, No. 55 (1941), 73-75.

1736 FLOOD, ERNEST CECIL. History of Methodism in Bangor and Brewer, 1814-1964. n.p., 1964. Pp. 17.

1737 GANONG, WILLIAM FRANCIS. "The origin and place-names Acadia and Norumbega." Royal Society of Canada. Proceedings and Transactions, 3 Ser., 11 Pt. 2 (1917), 105-111.
Norumbega as the Penobscot River.

1738 HAYNES, AARON. "Reminiscences of [the] Penobscot River." BHistMag, 2 (1886-1887), 100-102.

1739 HEMPSTEAD, ALFRED GEER. "Improvements on the West Branch of the Penobscot River: the Penobscot Log Driving Company, 1856-1903." The Northern, 8 (May, 1928), 3-4.

1740 ____. "The Penobscot boom." The Northern, 8 (June, 1928), 5-6.
Lumbering.

1741 HISTORY of Penobscot County, Maine, with illustrations and biographical sketches. Cleveland: Williams, Chase, 1882. Pp. 922.
Williamson's "Bibliography of the State of Maine" states that "the putative author or compiler of the work was Henry A. Ford of Detroit;" chapter seventeen is a bibliography.

1742 "JAILS of Penobscot County." BHistMag, 5 (1889-1890), 112.

1743 KEITH, PHILIP EDWARD. The history of secondary education in Penobscot County in Maine. Orono: Univ. Pr., 1948. Pp. v, 249.

1744 KIMBALL, MARION REED. "Steamboating on the upper Penobscot." Down East, 20 (April, 1974), 58-59, 77-78.

1745 "LAWYERS admitted to practice in courts of Penobscot County." BHistMag, 3 (1887-1888), 228-229.
Chronological listing for the period 1824-1847.

1746 "THE LUMBERMAN." Eastern Magazine, 1 (1835-1836), 33-43.

1747 LYNN, JOHN A. "Samuel de Champlain in the Penobscot wilderness." Down East, 23 (March, 1975), 40-42.

1748 MASON, WILLIAM CASTEIN, JERRIE K. PHILLIPS and THOMAS U. COE. History of the Penobscot County Medical Association.... Bangor, 1898. Pp. 79. MeBa.

1749 NILE, LE ROY. Tales of the Rangeley Lakes. Farmington: Knowlton & McLeary, 1948. Pp. 128. Me.

1750 NORTON, DAVID. "Sketches of Old Town and Orono." MHGR, 9 (1898), 183-191.

1751 PAINE, ALBERT WARE. "The territorial history of Bangor and vicinity." MeHSC, 9 (1887), 223-234.

1752 PERHAM, DAVID. "Early history of Orrington and Brewer." BHistMag, 1 (1885-1886), 17-20.

1753 "ROADS on the Penobscot River above Bangor." BHistMag, 5 (1889-1890), 77-78.

1754 ROBBINS, CHESTER W. ["History of the press in Penobscot County."] MPAP, 29 (1892), 26; 30 (1893), 33; 35 (1898), 24-25.

1755 ROWE, HERBERT W. ["History of the press in Penobscot County."] MPAP, 44 (1907), 49-50.

1756 "SENATORS from Penobscot County from 1820 to the incorporation of Piscataquis County, March 23, 1838." BHistMag, 5 (1889-1890), 21-23.
Senators and representatives arranged chronologically.

1757 SMITH, FRANK K. ["History of the press in Penobscot County."] MPAP, 13 (1876), 28-32.

1758 "SOME pioneer settlers on upper Penobscot River." BHistMag, 6 (1890-1891), 28-34.

1759 SPRAGUE, JOHN FRANCIS. "Norombega." SJMH, 8 (1920), 91-96.

1760 "THE STORY OF the Penobscot bar." BHistMag, 6 (1890-1891), 25-26.

1761 THAYER, MILDRED N. "The Bon Ton ferries." Down East, 13 (March, 1967), 49, 72.
Bangor to Brewer.

1762 ____ and AGNES H. AMES. Brewer, Orrington, Holden, Eddington, history and families. [Brewer?], 1962. Pp. 285, ccvii.

1763 WALKER, HAROLD S. "The Bangor, Oldtown & Milford Railroad, 1836-1869." RLHSB, No. 106 (1962), 40-48.

1764 WARD, KENT. Penobscot County, Maine. Portland: Gross & Allen, [1971?]. Pp. 96. MeU.

1765 WILLIAMSON, WILLIAM DURKEE. "Sketches of early lawyers in Penobscot County." BHistMag, 4 (1888-1889), 24-25.
Pelatiah Hitchcock, Samuel Upham, Andrew Morton, and Peleg Chandler.

SEE ALSO entry 1251.

PISCATAQUIS COUNTY

1766 "ALONG the old Savage Road." SJMH, 1 (1913-1914), 145-147.

1767 NO ENTRY.

1768 AVERY, MYRON HALBURTON. "The story of the Wassataquoik, a Maine epic." Maine Naturalist, 9 (1929), 83-96.
Lumbering.

1769 BEARD, GEORGE MILLER. "Experiments with the 'Jumper of Maine.'" Popular Science Monthly, 18 (1880-1881), 170-178.
"Jumping" is a disease similar to epilepsy; experiments conducted in the Moosehead Lake region.

1770 BOARDMAN, SAMUEL LANE. "Moosehead Lake." In the Maine Woods, (1907), 115-121.

1771   NO ENTRY.

1772   EARLE, A. GERTRUDE. "Universalism in Piscataquis County." PCHSC, 1 (1910), 86-99.

1773   ECKSTORM, FANNIE HARDY. "Is Kokadjo Indian?" SJMH, 13 (1925), 95-97.
        Indian names for lakes and mountains in Moosehead Lake region.

1774   EVANS, LISTON P. ["History of the press in Piscataquis County."] MPAP, 36 (1899), 37; 37 (1900), 36; 29 (1902), 39; 40 (1903, 39; 43 (1906), 27; 44 (1907), 50; 45 (1908), 31; 46 (1909), 30; 47 (1910), 13; 48 (1911), 30; 51 (1914), 28; 52 (1915), 14.

1775   GAGNON, LANA. Chesuncook memories. Greenville: Oscar Gagnon, 1974. Pp. 67. MeU.
        Chesuncook Lake region.

1776   HASKELL, CHARLES B. ["History of the press in Piscataquis County."] MPAP, 31 (1894), 23.

1777   HAYES, CHARLES WELLS. "Early navigation on Sebec Lake." PCHSC, 1 (1910), 127-137.

1778   HEMPSTEAD, ALFRED GEER. "The Sourdnahunk Dam and Improvement Company, 1878-1900." The Northern, 7 (June, 1927), 3-4, 8-9.
        Sourdnahunk Stream.

1779   _____. "Sourdnahunk Dam and Improvement Company, 1900-1927." The Northern, 7 (August, 1927), 5-6.
        Sourdnahunk Stream.

1780   HERRING, CHARLES MACOMBER. Historical discourse at the semi-centennial of the Piscataquis Baptist Association at Dexter, August 27, 1889. Portland: B. Thurston, 1889. Pp. 15.

1781   JACKSON, HERBERT G., JR. "Boat rides, blueberries, and band concerts: steamboat days on Sebec Lake." Down East, 21 (September, 1974), 60-63, 96.

1782   KENISTON, FRANK WALTER. Biographies of Guilford, Sangerville, Abbot, and Parkman, Maine. Auburn: Merrill & Webber, 1942. Pp. 109.

1783   LORING, AMASA. History of Piscataquis County, Maine, from its earliest settlement to 1880. Portland: Hoyt, Fogg & Donham, 1880. Pp. 304.

1784   MacDOUGALL, WALTER M. "Moosehead Lake steamboats." Down East, 9 (May, 1963), 40-43, 45.

1785   McGUIRE, JOSEPH DEAKINS. "Ethnological and archeological notes on Moosehead Lake, Maine." American Anthropologist, New Ser., 10 (1908), 549-557.

1786   MOOSEHEAD souvenir booklet, a collection of articles, 1776, 1836, 1976. n.p., [1976]. Unpaged. MeU.

1787   "NAVIGATION on Moosehead Lake: a brief account of the activities of the Coburn Steamboat Company activities and its predecessors." The Northern, 6 (May, 1926), 3-4, 15.

1788   PARSONS, WILLIS E. "Odd Fellowship in Piscataquis County." SJMH, 1 (1913-1914), 85-117.

1789   PISCATAQUIS COUNTY HISTORICAL SOCIETY, DOVER, ME. Piscataquis County Historical Society, its by-laws and membership, etc., and a bibliography of Piscataquis County. Dover: Observer Publishing, 1916.

1790   PRATT, F. H. "History of the Baptist churches in Piscataquis County." PCHSC, 1 (1910), 66-85.

1791   RED EAGLE, HENRY. "Historic Moosehead Lake, early explorers and pioneers." In the Maine Woods, (1936), 37-42.

1792   ROGERS, LORE ALFRED. "The Telos Cut." Northern Logger, 14 (May, 1966), 26-27, 40-45.
        Lumbering.

1793   "RONCO'S Camp and Mud Pond carry." The Northern, 6 (November, 1926), 6-7, (January, 1927), 5.

1794   SMITH, EDGAR CROSBY. "Sketches of some revolutionary soldiers of Piscataquis County." PCHSC, 1 (1910), 154-203.

1795   SMITH, FRANK K. ["History of the press in Piscataquis County."] MPAP, 13 (1876), 32-33.

1796   SPRAGUE, JOHN FRANCIS. Address delivered before the Piscataquis County Historical Society,... July 23, 1908. n.p., 1908. Pp. 9. Me.

1797   _____. Piscataquis biography and fragments. Bangor: C. H. Glass, 1899. Pp. 102.

1798   STEELE, THOMAS SEDGWICK. Canoe and camera: a two hundred mile tour through the Maine forests. N.Y.: O. Judd, 1880. Pp. 139.

1799   THOMPSON, WINFIELD MARTIN. Debsconeag. Boston: Barta Pr., 1902. Pp. 16.
        Debsconeag Lakes.

1800   THOREAU, HENRY DAVID. The Maine woods. (1864) Joseph J. Moldenhauer, ed. Princeton: Princeton Univ. Pr., 1972. Pp. 485.

1801   WARD, JULIUS HAMMOND. "Moosehead Lake." Harper's New Monthly Magazine, 51 (1875), 350-365.

SEE ALSO entries 30 and 108.

SAGADAHOC COUNTY

1802 BALLARD, EDWARD. "Location of Sasanoa's
River, in Maine." HistMag, 2 Ser., 3 (1868),
164-166.

1803 BARKER, FEN. G. "History of the press in
Sagadahoc County." MPAP, 15 (1878), 36.

1804 DUNBAR, KENDALL M. ["History of the press in
Sagadahoc County."] MPAP, 26 (1889), 37.

1805 GARDINER, ROBERT HALLOWELL, 1782-1864.
"Jones's Eddy." MeHSC, 4 (1856), 45-48.
    On Kennebec River below Bath; established
to rival Wiscasset but never attracted trade.

1806 LEMONT, LEVI P. 1400 historical dates of the
town and city of Bath, and town of Georgetown, from 1604 to 1874, together with the
address of Francis Winter delivered at Bath
... July 4, 1825. Bath: E. Upton & Son,
1874. Pp. 104.

1807 MAYERS, CLAYTON W. "Duck hunting on Merry-
meeting Bay 60 years ago." Down East, 7
(October, 1960), 31-33, 40-41.

1807A O'BRIEN, MICHAEL J. "The lost town of Cork,
Maine: an early attempt by Robert Temple and
emigrants from Ireland to establish a settlement in the Kennebec wilderness." AIrHSJ, 12
(1913), 175-184.
    Controversy as to location.

1808 PURINGTON, WILLIAM C. "The Bath and Woolwich
railroad ferries." Down East, 22 (April,
1976), 61-64.

1809 THAYER, HENRY OTIS. "The transient town of
Cork." MeHSC, 2 Ser., 4 (1893), 240-265.

1810 UPTON, JOSHUA FOY. ["History of the press in
Sagadahoc County."] MPAP, 18 (1881), 34-38;
37 (1900), 36-39; 43 (1906), 27-29.

    SEE ALSO entries 107 and 1409.

SOMERSET COUNTY

1811 BOWEN, HOWARD LANCASTER. The history of secondary education in Somerset County in Maine.
Orono: Univ. Pr., 1935. Pp. 85.

1812 CHATTO, CLARENCE I. East Somerset County
register, 1911-12. Auburn: Chatto and Turner, [1911?]. Pp. 539. Me.

1813 DANFORTH, FLORENCE WAUGH. Somerset County in
the World War. Lewiston: Journal Printshop,
[1920?]. Pp. 330.

1814 DOLE, RICHARD F. Sebasticook and Moosehead
Railroad Company. n.p., 1961. 5 leaves.
MeU.
    1886-1911.

1815 GOVE, WILLIAM G. "The railroad that went no-
where." Down East, 19 (May, 1973), 21-22, 25-
26, 29-32, 34, 36.
    Seboomook Lake and St. John Railroad; car-
ried pulpwood to paper mills at Millinocket.

1816 HANSON, JOHN WESLEY. History of the old
towns, Norridgewock and Canaan, comprising
Norridgewock, Canaan, Starks, Skowhegan, and
Bloomfield, from their early settlement to
the year 1849; including a sketch of the Abnakis Indians. Boston, 1849. Pp. 371.
    Williamson's "Bibliography of the State of
Maine" notes that the first part, comprising
120 pages, was issued with a separate title
page as "Historical sketch of the Norridgewock Indians," perhaps without the author's
knowledge.

1817 HASKELL, CHARLES B. ["History of the press
in Somerset County."] MPAP, 33 (1896), 38-
39; 36 (1899), 37; 37 (1900), 39.

1818 HASKELL, LOUIS O. ["History of the press in
Somerset County."] MPAP, 50 (1913), 28-29.

1819 NO ENTRY.

1820 KILBY, CYRUS HAMLIN. ["History of the press
in Somerset County."] MPAP, 13 (1876), 34;
14 (1877), 40; 15 (1878), 36-37; 16 (1879),
32-33; 17 (1880), 15-16.

1821 MacDONALD, THOMAS L. Scenes of Flagstaff and
Dead River. Flagstaff: Flagstaff Cemetery
Association, 1974. Pp. 76.

1822 MacDOUGALL, WALTER M. "Gulf Stream trestle."
Down East, 22 (November, 1975), 36-39, 61.
    Somerset Railroad.

1823 _____. "The old Somerset Railroad." Down
East, 8 (November, 1961), 32-37.

1824 _____. "Wooden spans of the Somerset Railroad." Down East, 16 (June, 1970), 66, 87,
90, 94-95, 99-100, 102.

1825 MERRIMAN, EDWARD A. ["The story of the press
in Somerset County."] MPAP, 43 (1906), 30.

1826 PORTER, ALBERT O. "When all was not harmony
on the Harmony line." Down East, 14 (January,
1968), 32-33, 48-49.
    Sebasticook and Moosehead Railroad.

1827 PRINCE, HENRY C. ["History of the press in
Somerset County."] MPAP, 44 (1907), 50-51;
48 (1911), 30-31.

1828 SMITH, JOSEPH OTIS. ["History of the press
in Somerset County."] MPAP, 23 (1886), 23-24;
24 (1887), 31; 25 (1888), 31; 26 (1889), 38;
28 (1891), 30; 30 (1893), 34; 31 (1894), 23-
24.

1829 SOMERSET COUNTY FARM BUREAU. Ten years of extension and farm bureau work in Somerset County, 1918-1928. n.p., [1929?]. Unpaged. Me.

1830 SOMERSET County, Maine. Portland: Gross & Morris, [1962]. Pp. 88. MeHi.

1831 WOOD, JOSEPH. ["History of the press in Somerset County."] MPAP, 19 (1882), 29-30.

SEE ALSO entries 108, 1025, and 1358.

WALDO COUNTY

1832 BRACKETT, GEORGE EMERSON. ["History of the press in Waldo County."] MPAP, 29 (1892), 26-27; 31 (1894), 24.

1833 DAKIN, MOSES. Monterey, or the mountain city: containing a description of the boundaries, situation, mountains, lakes, rivers, soil and climate ... of the southern part of the county of Waldo, Maine; to which is added an appendix, giving a brief account of some of the islands of Penobscot Bay. Boston: Mead's Pr., 1847. Pp. 26.
Camden, Hope, Lincolnville, and Northport.

1834 LANG, JOHN WILSON. A survey of Waldo County, Maine: historical, physical, agricultural. Augusta: Sprague, Owen & Nash, 1873. Pp. 131. MeHi.

1835 MURCH, LUCIUS H. ["History of the press in Waldo County."] MPAP, 32 (1895), 28-29; 33 (1896), 39; 34 (1897), 35; 35 (1898), 25-26; 36 (1899), 37-38; 37 (1900), 39-40.

1836 PILSBURY, CHARLES ALBERT. ["History of the press in Waldo County."] MPAP, 21 (1884), 26-28; 23 (1886), 24; 24 (1887), 31; 26 (1889), 37-39.

1837 "REPRESENTATIVES to General Court, prior to 1820, from what is now Waldo County." BHist Mag, 3 (1887-1888), 155.
Arranged chronologically within each locale.

1838 WATSON, ANDREW ELWELL. Land classification in Waldo County, Maine. Orono: Maine Agricultural Experiment Station, 1943. Pp. 313. MeP.
Includes brief agricultural history.

SEE ALSO entries 30 and 107.

WASHINGTON COUNTY

1839 "ANCIENT Machias Bay and River." BHistMag, 6 (1890-1891), 75.

1840 BACON, GEORGE FOX. Calais, Eastport and vicinity, their representative business men, and points of interest, embracing Calais, Eastport, Machias, Machiasport, Milltown, Jonesport, Princeton, Millbridge, Cherryfield and Lubec. Newark, N.J.: Glenwood Publishing, 1892. Pp. 119.

1841 BORDER cities souvenir. [Lewiston]: R. J. Lawton, 1908. Pp. 77. MeHi.
Includes Calais and Eastport.

1842 BOYD, CHARLES H. "An incident on the coast of Maine in 1861." MagHist, 15 (1912), 38-41.
First Confederate flag captured by U.S. forces in Passamaquoddy Bay.

1843 COMAN, DALE REX. Pleasant River. N.Y.: W. W. Norton, 1966. Pp. 169.

1844 DAVIS, HAROLD ARTHUR. "The Fenian raid on New Brunswick." CanHistRev, 36 (1955), 316-334.
Launched from Calais/Eastport region.

1845 _____. An international community on the St. Croix, 1604-1930. Orono: Univ. Pr., 1950. Pp. 412.

1846 _____. "Shipbuilding on the St. Croix. Am Nep, 15 (1955), 173-190.
1784-1870s.

1847 DAY, CLARENCE ALBERT. A history of the blueberry industry in Washington County. Orono, [1954?]. 22 leaves. MeU.

1848 _____. Title deeds to land in the Pleasant River Valley. n.p., n.d. 7 leaves. MBNEH.

1849 "'DOWN East' fifty years ago." BTJ, 1 (1888-1889), 271.

1850 DRISKO, GEORGE WASHINGTON. "Record of newspapers in Washington County." MPAP, [4] (1867), 27-35; 21 (1884), 28; 24 (1887), 32-33; 27 (1890), 33; 34 (1897), 36; 36 (1899), 38; 38 (1901), 36; 40 (1903), 40; 42 (1905), 39-40.

1851 _____. The revolution: life of Hannah Weston, with a brief history of her ancestry, also a condensed history of the first settlement of Jonesborough, Machias and other neighboring towns. (1857) 2d ed. Machias: G. A. Parlin, 1902. Pp. 140.

1852 DU WORS, RICHARD E. "Persistence and change in local values of two New England communities." Rural Sociology, 17 (September, 1952), 207-217.
Eastport and Lubec; based on historical data for 1798-1924 and interviews during 1938-1949.

1853   GATSCHET, ALBERT SAMUEL. "All around the
       Bay of Passamaquoddy." National Geographic
       Magazine, 8 (1897), 16-24.
           Includes origin of Indian place names;
       supplemented by an article in the "Eastport
       Sentinel," September 15, 1897.

1854   GLUEK, ALVIN C., JR. "The Passamaquoddy Bay
       Treaty, 1910: a diplomatic sideshow in Cana-
       dian-American relations." CanHistRev, 47
       (1966), 1-21.

1855   GREENAN, JOHN THOMAS, ed. Way Down East in
       Maine: the story of a pioneer family, as
       told by themselves. Morristown, N.J.: Comp-
       ton Pr., 1958. Pp. 210.

1856   GREENE, NANCY H. and CLARENCE H. DRISKO. A
       history of Columbia and Columbia Falls in
       honor of the American bicentennial, 1776-
       1976. Cherryfield: Narraguagus Printing,
       [1976]. Pp. 65. MeHi.

1857   GRINNELL, ART. "Quoddy power." Down East,
       22 (May, 1976), 70-73, 99-100, 103.

1858   HAMMOND, ROBERT B. An era to remember: a
       historical sketch of the shipbuilding indus-
       try in West Washington County. [Harring-
       ton?], 1972. Pp. 102. Me.

1859   HEBERT, RICHARD A. "Eastport and Lubec."
       Pine Cone, 2 (Spring, 1946), 15-18.

1860   KEELER, SETH HARRISON. A semi-centennial
       discourse delivered in Calais, Maine, June 3,
       1879, in memory of the organization of the
       Washington County Conference of Congrega-
       tional Churches organized at Eastport, Feb-
       ruary 13, 1829. Calais: J. A. Sears,
       [1879]. Pp. 24. MeHi.

1861   KILBY, CYRUS HAMLIN. "Incidents at the set-
       tlement of Dennysville and Edmunds in Wash-
       ington County." MHGR, 8 (1895), 218-223;
       9 (1898), 11-18.

1862   THE LOGGERS: or six months in the forests of
       Maine. Boston: H. B. Fuller, 1870. Pp. 75.

1863   MACHIASPORT HISTORICAL SOCIETY. The Whitney-
       ville and Machiasport Railroad. [Machias-
       port, 1976?]. Pp. 20. MeHi.

1864   MILLIKEN, JAMES ALPHONSO. The Narraguagus
       Valley: some account of its early settle-
       ment and settlers. Machias: C. O. Furbush,
       [1886]. Pp. 24.

1865   MITCHELL, HARRY EDWARD and EDWARD MELVIN
       CAMPBELL, comps. The Addison and Harrington
       register, 1905. Brunswick: H. E. Mitchell,
       1905. Pp. 126.
           Contains sketches of the early history of
       both towns.

1866   MURCHIE, GUY. Saint Croix, the sentinel
       river: historical sketches of its discovery,
       early conflicts and final occupation by Eng-
       lish and American settlers, with some com-
       ments on Indian life. N.Y.: Duell, Sloan
       and Pearce, 1947. Pp. 281.

1867   NEAL, BEN. "Early days in the wildcat dis-
       trict." Down East, 18 (November, 1971),
       13-14, 17-20.
           Hunting.

1868   "REPRESENTATIVES from Washington County,
       1820-1851." BHistMag, 4 (1888-1889), 105-
       109.
           A chronological listing.

1869   SAYLOR, JOHN P. "Passamaquoddy boondoggle."
       Public Utilities Fortnightly, 74 (January 17,
       1963), 15-22.

1870   "SENATORS from Washington County, 1820-1852."
       BHistMag, 4 (1888-1889), 16.
           A chronological listing.

1871   "SETTLEMENT of the Maine border." Americana,
       6 (1911), 27-31.

1872   SMITH, LINCOLN. "Tidal power in Maine."
       Land Economics, 24 (1948), 239-252.
           Passamaquoddy Tidal Project, 1920-1947.

1873   TODD, WILLIAM. Todds of the St. Croix valley.
       Mount Carmel, Conn., 1943. Pp. 24.

1874   VROOM, JAMES. "The Fenians on the St. Croix."
       Canadian Magazine, 10 (1897-1898), 411-413.
           In vicinity of Eastport and Calais.

1875   WILLEY, A. S. Historical sketch of Cherry-
       field and Harrington.... Machias: C. O.
       Furbush, 1893. Pp. 49. Me.

1876   WINTER, CARL GEORGE. "A note on the Passama-
       quoddy boundary affair." CanHistRev, 34
       (1953), 46-53.
           Line through the Bay, 1908-1910.

       SEE ALSO entries 108, 686, and 1251.

YORK COUNTY

1877   ANDREWS, RALPH. Index to the probate records
       of the county of York, Maine, from January 1,
       1917 to January 1, 1949. Saco: Reny Bros.,
       1950. Pp. 497.
           A copy is in the York County Probate Office,
       Alfred, Maine.

1878   BAER, ANNIE WENTWORTH. "Early farming." Old
       Eliot, 8 (1908), 33-42.

1879 BARTLETT, RALPH SYLVESTER. The history of York County, Maine, and a rambling narrative about the town of Eliot and its mother-town old Kittery, with personal reminiscences: an address delivered by Ralph Sylvester Bartlett at exercised held in Eliot, Maine, August 29, 1936, in commemoration of the 300th anniversary of the founding of York County in the Province of Maine. Boston: Jerome Pr., 1938. Pp. 21.

1880 BECKFORD, WILLIAM HALE. Leading business men of Kennebunkport, Kennebunk and Old Orchard Beach, with an historical sketch of each place. Boston: Mercantile Publishing, 1888. Pp. 62.

1881 "BIDDEFORD and Saco." Sun Up, 19 (March, 1931), 10-13.

1882 BIOGRAPHICAL review: this volume contains biographical sketches of leading citizens of York County, Maine.... Boston: Biographical Review Publishing, 1896. Pp. 619.

1883 BOURNE, EDWARD EMERSON, 1797-1873. "Garrison houses, York County." MeHSC, 7 (1876), 107-120.

1884 _____. The history of Wells and Kennebunk from the earliest settlement to the year 1820, at which time Kennebunk was set off, and and incorporated; with biographical sketches. Edward E. Bourne, Jr., ed. Portland: B. Thurston, 1875. Pp. xxiii, 797.

1885 BUTLER, JOYCE. "Canoes on the Kennebec." Down East, 20 (July, 1974), 72-75.

1886 CLAYTON, W. WOODFORD. History of York County, Maine: with illustrations and biographical sketches of its prominent men and pioneers.... Philadelphia: Everts & Peck, 1880. Pp. 442.
    Includes a roster of Civil War soldiers from York County.

1887 CONGREGATIONAL CHURCHES IN MAINE. YORK COUNTY CONFERENCE. Semi-centennial of York County Conference, Buxton, Maine, June 4 and 5, 1872; papers there read, and sketches of the Congregational churches in the county, with notes appended down to the present time, June, 1876. John D. Emerson and Benjamin P. Snow, eds. Portland: Hoyt, Fogg & Donham, 1876. Pp. 119.

1888 COOK, JULIA ANNA. "Black Thursday." Yankee, 31 (October, 1967), 102-103, 128-130, 133-137.
    Forest fire of October 23, 1947.

1889 CREDIFORD, ANNIE JOYCE. ["History of the press in York County."] MPAP, 47 (1910), 13; 48 (1911), 31; 49 (1912), 27-28; 50 (1913) 29-30; 51 (1914), 28; 52 (1915), 14-15.

1890 CUMMINGS, OSMOND RICHARD. The Biddeford and Saco Railroad. Chicago: Electric Railway Historical Society, 1956. Pp. 35. MeBa.

1891 DEXTER, FRANK HENRY ["History of the press in York County."] MPAP, 27 (1890), 34; 28 (1891), 30-31; 29 (1892), 27; 30 (1893), 34; 31 (1894), 24-25; 33 (1896), 39-40; 34 (1897), 36-37; 35 (1898), 26; 37 (1900), 40; 39 (1902), 39-40; 40 (1903), 40-41.

1892 ELWELL, EDWARD HENRY. ["History of the press in York County."] MPAP, 25 (1888), 31-33; 26 (1889), 39.

1893 FOLSOM, GEORGE. History of Saco and Biddeford.... (1830) Somersworth, N.H.: New Hampshire Publishing, 1975. Pp. 331.
    This reprint contains a new foreword by Robert E. Moody and an index prepared in 1922 by Frank C. Deering.

1894 GOULD, NATHAN. "Col. James Scamman's 30th Regiment of foot, 1775." MeHSC, 2 Ser., 10 (1899), 337-402.

1895 "HOSPITALS in York County." Sun Up, 3 (August, 1927), 68.

1896 JOY, KENNETH. The Kennebunks: out of the past. Freeport: Bond Wheelwright, 1967. Pp. xvi, 135.
    Kennebunk and Kennebunkport.

1897 KEEFE, FRANCIS. "Some of the earlier dwellers on the long reach of the Piscataqua River." Old Eliot, 1 (1897), 45-61.

1898 MORANG, BRUCE. Journal of the Kennebunks. [Kennebunk]: Kennebunk Journal, [1952?]. Unpaged. Me.
    Kennebunk and Kennebunkport.

1898A MORGAN, CHARLES S. Shipbuilding on the Kennebunk, the closing chapter; adapted from an address ... to the [Historical] Society [of Kennebunkport] on the occasion of its first public meeting, February 15, 1952. Kennebunkport, [1952]. Pp. 40.

1899 MOUNTFORT, JULIA ANN DYKE and KATHERINE EASTMAN MARSHALL. Witch trot land; being a bit about the mother of Maine, York County, or Yorkshire, or New Somersetshire, from which all Maine counties came, of her hopes and dreams and heartbreaks, and of the first incorporated English city in America.... Damariscotta: Lincoln County News, 1937. Pp. 43.

1900 MURRAY, JOHN CHICK. History of the Grange in York County.... Sanford: Averill Pr., 1922. Pp. 154.

1901 PEPPERELL MANUFACTURING COMPANY. The romance of Pepperell, being a brief account of the career of Sir William Pepperrell, soldier, pioneer, American merchant and developer of New England industry, for whom the Pepperell Manufacturing Company was named, and of the towns of Saco and Biddeford in the State of Maine, wherein the first manufacturing unit of the Pepperell Company was established. Boston, 1943. Pp. 48.

1902 PERKINS, ESSELYN GILMAN. Billowing sails. Portland: House of Falmouth, 1947. Pp. 90.
Shipbuilding.

1903 PERRY, ADELAIDE E. York County. Portland: Gross and Allen, [1971]. Pp. 72. MeU.

1904 PEVERLY, ELAINE M. and WILLIAM H. McLIN. "The Old Orchard 'dummy line.'" Down East, 19 (September, 1972), 74-75.
Orchard Beach Railroad; Old Orchard to Camp Ellis.

1905 RANDEL, WILLIAM PEIRCE. "Town names of York County, Maine." NEQ, 11 (1938), 565-575.

1906 REMICK, OLIVER PHILBRICK. "Piscataqua Pioneers." Old Eliot, 9 (1909), 1-8.
An historical society.

1907 _____. A record of the services of the commissioned officers and enlisted men of Kittery and Eliot, Maine, who served their country on land and sea in the American Revolution, from 1775 to 1783. Boston: A. Mudge & Son, 1901. Pp. 223.

1908 SAMUELS, HARRIET BROCKMAN. A Maine county, rich in beauty and historic lore. [Princeton?, N.J.], 1961. Pp. 39.

1909 SHAPLEIGH, CHARLES A. "Glances at people and localities." Old Eliot, 9 (1909), 30-33.

1910 TAYLOR, HELEN V. A time to recall: the delights of a Maine childhood. N.Y.: Norton, 1963. Pp. 224.

1911 THOMPSON, RALPH E. and MATTHEW R. THOMPSON. Pascataway: de facto capital of New England, 1623-1630. Monmouth, Oregon, 1973. Pp. 58.
Berwick, Eliot, Kittery, and South Berwick.

1912 TITCOMB, EDWARD S. Index to the probate records of the county of York, Maine, from January 1, 1901, to January 1, 1917. [Biddeford]: Biddeford Journal, 1918. Pp. 220.
A copy is in the York County Probate Office, Alfred, Maine.

1913 YORK CO., ME. REGISTER OF DEEDS. York deeds. Portland: John T. Hull, 1887-1896; Bethel, 1903-1910. 18 v. in 19.
Covers 1642-1737; detailed indexes of grantors, grantees, and other persons; imprint varies.

SEE ALSO entries 602, 978, and 1045.

Cities, Towns, and Other Civil Divisions

ABBOT (PISCATAQUIS CO.)

1914   "THE MOOSE horn sign in Abbot, Maine." SJMH,
2 (1914-1913), 194-201.
Town history.

SEE ALSO entry 1782.

ACTON (YORK CO.)

1915   BRACKETT, MURIEL. Pine cones and forget me
nots. n.p., [1951?]. 4v. MeHi.

1916   FULLONTON, JOSEPH. The history of Acton,
Me. Dover, N.H.: William Burr, 1847.
Pp. iv, 36.

ADAMSTOWN TOWNSHIP (OXFORD CO.)

1917   No items located.

ADDISON (WASHINGTON CO.)

1918   SEE entries 549 and 1865.

ALBANY TOWNSHIP (OXFORD CO.)

1919   BALL, WILBUR I. "The Albany sesquicentennial." MeCP, 40 (October 15, 1953), 8.
Congregational church.

1920   PERRY, TRUEMAN SUMMERFIELD. A hundred years:
historical address delivered at the centennial of the Congregational Church in Albany,
Maine. Bethel: E. C. Bowler, 1903. Pp. 14.
MBC.

ALBION (KENNEBEC CO.)

1921   WIGGIN, RUBY CROSBY. Albion on the Narrow
Gauge. [Clinton?], 1964. Pp. 282.
Wiscasset, Waterville & Farmington Railroad.

SEE ALSO entry 1645.

ALDER BROOK TOWNSHIP (SOMERSET CO.)

1922   No items located.

ALDER STREAM TOWNSHIP (FRANKLIN CO.)

1923   No items located.

ALEXANDER (WASHINGTON CO.)

1924   No items located.

ALFRED (YORK CO.)

1925   "THE ALFRED Shakers." MeLB, 16 (1930-1931),
111-112 [i.e. 17 (1931-1932), 3-4].

1926   BARKER, R. MILDRED. "A history of 'Holy
Land'--Alfred, Maine." Shaker Quarterly, 3
(1963), 75-95, 107-127.

1927   BRADLEE, CHARLES W. Historical sermon, delivered at the semi-centennial celebration of
Methodism at Alfred, Maine, December 14th,
1879. Bridgton: H. S. Shorey, 1880. Pp. 16.
MeBa.

1928   DANE, MARY ELIZABETH. Alfred. n.p., [191-?].
Pp. 7.

1929   JOHNSON, THEODORE ELLIOT, comp. "A complete
register of deaths which have occurred in the
United Society of Believers, Alfred, Maine
1790-1931." Shaker Quarterly, 1 (1961), 168-
178.

1930   KELLEY, MARY CARPENTER. "When the Shaker
sisters made soap." Down East, 11 (May, 1965),
26-29.

1931   PARSONS, USHER. A centennial history of Alfred, York County, Maine, with a supplement by
Samuel M. Came. Philadelphia: Sanford, Everts, 1872. Pp. 36.

1932 PARSONS MEMORIAL LIBRARY, ALFRED, ME. Parsons Memorial Library, Alfred, Maine. [Al-
fred, 1905?]. Pp. 46.

1933 PERKINS, LUCIUS M. "How the town of Alfred
disposed of its share of the U.S. revenue
surplus, 1836-7." SJMH, 6 (1918-1919), 72-
73.

1934 ST. JOHN, FREDERIC. "Alfred." Maine's Own
Magazine 8 (May and June, 1930), 16, 29.
Author's name is a pseudonym.

ALLAGASH PLANTATION (AROOSTOOK CO.)

1935 DIETZ, LEW. "The 'lost' settlement of the
Allagash." Down East, 14 (October, 1967),
26-29, 56, 58.

1935A KELLEY, EDITH. Bits and pieces of Allagash
history. Madawaska: St. John Valley Printers, 1976. Pp. 28. [MeMaHi.]

ALNA (LINCOLN CO.)

1936 BROWN, FRANK CHOUTEAU. "The Congregational
Church at Head Tide, Maine." OTNE, 30 (1939-
1940), 95-100.

1937 CUMMINGS, RANDALL FREDERICK. Elementary
school history of Alna, Dresden, Edgecomb,
Pittston, Wiscasset, State of Maine. [North
Edgecomb, 1933]. Pp. 86.

1938 MERRY, EDWIN D. "Captain Jote Jones--scowman
out of Puddle Dock." Down East, 21 (June,
1975), 60-61, 79-81.

1939 SEWALL, RUFUS KING. Centennial memorial services of old Alna meetinghouse, Alna, Maine,
September 11, 1889. Wiscasset: Emerson,
1896. Pp. 24.

SEE ALSO entries 1677, 1704, and 1706.

ALTON (PENOBSCOT CO.)

1940 No items located.

AMHERSET (HANCOCK CO.)

1941 JELLISON, CONSTANCE HANSCOM. Amherst, Maine,
her settlement and her people, 1790-1975.
[Bar Harbor]: Bar Harbor Times, 1975.
Pp. 116. Me.

AMITY (AROOSTOOK CO.)

1942 No items located.

ANDOVER (OXFORD CO.)

1943 No items located.

ANDOVER NORTH SURPLUS (OXFORD CO.)

1944 No items located.

ANDOVER WEST SURPLUS (OXFORD CO.)

1945 No items located.

ANSON (SOMERSET CO.)

1946 ANSON ACADEMY. Anson Academy centennial,
1823-1923. Lewiston: Journal Printshop
and Bindery, [1923]. Pp. 72. MeHi.

1947 MOORE, ALBERT. History of Northern Star
Lodge, No. 28, of Free and Accepted Masons,
North Anson, Me. North Anson, 1875. Pp. 35.
MeBa.

SEE ALSO entry 3362.

APPLETON (KNOX CO.)

1948 No items located.

APPLETON TOWNSHIP (SOMERSET CO.)

1949 No items located.

ARGYLE TOWNSHIP (PENOBSCOT CO.)

1950 SEE entry 1733.

ARROWSIC (SAGADAHOC CO.)

1951 "ARROWSIC Island." BHistMag, 3 (1887-1888),
41-44.

ARUNDEL (YORK CO.)

1952 No items located.

ASHLAND (AROOSTOOK CO.)

1953 No items located.

ATHENS (SOMERSET CO.)

1954   ATHENS VICTORY CLUB. A historical sketch of Athens, Maine commemorative of its sesquicentennial, July 2-5, 1804-1954. Skowhegan: Skowhegan Pr., 1954. Pp. 44. Me.

1955   JONES, MRS. C. H. Brief historical sketch of Athens, Maine, commemorative of its centennial observance on Wednesday, June 22nd, 1904. Skowhegan: J. O. Smith, [1904]. Pp. 19. MBNEH.

1956   SOMERSET ACADEMY, ATHENS, ME. Somerset Academy, a brief statement of its history, condition and need. n.p., [1933]. Pp. 11. MeHi.

ATKINSON (PISCATAQUIS CO.)

1957   CROSBY, S. P. "Notes on the Crosby family and a sketch of the life of Josiah Crosby." PCHSC, 1 (1910), 204-215.

ATTEAN TOWNSHIP (SOMERSET CO.)

1958   No items located.

AUBURN (ANDROSCOGGIN CO.)

1959   AUBURN, ME. ELM STREET UNIVERSALIST PARISH. Semi-centennial exercises of the Elm Street Universalist Parish, Auburn, Maine, February 11th, 12th and 13th, 1879, historical address by Rev. William R. French, poem by Mrs. Mary Salina Read. Lewiston: Geo. A. Callahan, 1879. Pp. 14.

1960   "AUBURN, the shire town of Androscoggin County." BTJ, 25 (1912-1913), 523, 525, 527.

1961   BANKS, ELIAS. "Historical sketch of Danville, Me." MHGR, 5 (1888), 12-16.

1962   BARRON, EARL T. "St. Michael's Church, Auburn." The Northeast, 71 (Pentecost, 1944), 2-4.

1963   BLOUNT, EDWARD F. Historical notes on the construction of the First Universalist Church, Auburn, Maine, one hundred years ago. Auburn: First Universalist Church, 1976. Pp. 23. MeHi.

1964   KELLY, FRANCIS R. "Seventy-fifth anniversary of [the] Sixth Street Congregational Church." MeCP, 146 (October, 1950), 28.

1965   LEPAGE, REGIS A. Seventy years of quality: the F. R. Lepage Bakery, Inc. N.Y.: Newcomen Society in North America, 1973. Pp. 20.

1966   MARTIN, ROBERT. History of Tranquil Lodge, No. 29, F. & A. M., Auburn, Maine. Lewiston: Geo. A. Callahan, 1876. Pp. 40.

1967   MORRILL, JOHN ADAMS. Historical address on the occasion of the one hundredth anniversary of the High Street Congregational Church, Auburn, Maine, Sunday, June 13, 1926. n.p., [1926]. Pp. 57. MeHi.

1968   [NORRIS, JANE P.] Mechanic Savings Bank, one hundred years of growth, 1875-1975. n.p., [1975]. Unpaged. MeHi.
       Author attribution by the Maine Historical Society.

1969   SKINNER, RALPH BURGESS, JOHN E. LIBBY and DAPHNE WINSLOW MERRILL. 1869--Auburn--1969: 100 years a city; a study in community growth. Lewiston: Twin City Printery, 1968. Pp. 410.

1970   WING, GEORGE CURTIS. Auburn, Maine, "Fifty years a city," address delivered ... September 12, 1919. [Auburn]: Auburn Chamber of Commerce, [1919]. Unpaged. MB.

       SEE ALSO entries 1422, 1424, 1426-1427, 1431-1432, 1434, and 3532.

AUGUSTA (KENNEBEC CO.)

1971   ALLEN, JOSHUA. "Mortality in Augusta, Maine, 1852-1855." MeHSC, 5 (1857), 431-435.

1972   AUGUSTA, ME. ALL SOULS CHURCH (UNITARIAN). Centennial services, 1826-1926, combined with "The first seventy-five years," by Hon. Leslie C. Cornish, Augusta, Maine, January 10, 1926. Augusta, [1926]. Pp. 30.

1973   AUGUSTA, ME. SESQUICENTENNIAL COMMITTEE. The romance of Augusta, 1797-1947. [Augusta]: Augusta Pr., [1947]. Unpaged. Me.

1974   AUGUSTA, ME. SOUTH PARISH CONGREGATIONAL CHURCH. The articles of faith and covenant of the South Congregational Church in Augusta, adopted January, 1874, with a list of the members from 1794 to 1874. Augusta: Sprague, Owen & Nash, 1874. Pp. 72.
       Includes a brief historical sketch.

1975   _____. Dedicatory exercises of the chapel and church home of the Congregational Church and Society, Dec. 17, 1890. Augusta: Maine Farmers' Almanac, 1891. Pp. 48.
       Includes history by Charles E. Nash.

1976   AUGUSTA SAVINGS BANK. 1848. 1898. Fiftieth anniversary of the Augusta Savings Bank, September 29, 1898.... Augusta: Maine Farmer Publishing, 1898. Pp. 30.

1977   _____. Seventy-fifth anniversary 1848-1923 ... September 29, 1923. [Augusta, 1923]. Unpaged.

1978   "THE AWAKENING of an old parish." MeCathHM, 3 (November, 1914), 37-42.
        St. Mary's Church.

1979   BALLARD, EDWARD. "Augusta: at Small Point Harbor." Northern Monthly, 1 (1864), 475-478.

1980   BASSETT, NORMAN L. "History of the Blaine Mansion." SJMH, 8 (1920), 196-201.

1981   BECK, JOSEPH T. Historical notes on Augusta, Maine. Farmington: Knowlton & McLeary, 1962-1963. 2v.

1982   "BLAINE House." MeLB, 15 (1929-1930), 79-82.

1983   BOARDMAN, SAMUEL LANE. "A chapter in the history of ancient Cushnoc--now Augusta." MeHSC, 3 Ser., 2 (1906), 310-330.

1984   BOWLES, ELLA SHANNON. "Augusta, city of personalities." Yankee, 2 (January, 1936), 19-23.

1985   BUTLER, BENJAMIN and NATALIE STURGES BUTLER. "Pilgrim traders on the Kennebec." Mayflower Quarterly, 41 (1975), 117-120.

1986   CHURCHILL, EDWIN A. "Fort Western: a reading bibliography." Friends of Fort Western Newsletter, 2 (May, 1976), 1.

1987   LE CLUB CALUMET, INC. Semicentennial celebration history, 1922-1972, fifty years of progress. Augusta: K. J. Litho, 1972. Pp. 70. Me.

1988   CUMMINGS, OSMOND RICHARD. "Trolleys to Augusta, Maine." Transportation Bulletin, No. 76 (January-August, 1969), 1-52.

1989   CURTIS, SILAS. Sermon preached at the dedication of the Free Will Baptist Meeting House, Augusta, Maine, Thursday, November 3, 1853. Augusta: Russell Eaton, 1853. Pp. 46.
        Includes a brief history of the Free Will Baptists in Augusta.

1990   DEMERS, MABEL GOULD. "Doorways and beyond." Pine Cone, 3 (Autumn, 1947), 33-37.
        Reuel Williams House.

1991   DOW, GEORGE FRANCIS. Fort Western on the Kennebec: the story of its construction in 1754 and what has happened there. Augusta: Gannett, 1922. Pp. 59.

1992   DOW, STERLING THAYER. "Hallowell Court House post office--Maine." Mekeel's Weekly Stamp News, 67 (July 15, 1946), 51.

1993   DROWN, EDWARD S. "There was war in heaven." NEQ, 4 (1931), 30-53.
        1840, South Parish Congregational Church.

1994   FEDERAL WRITERS' PROJECT. MAINE. Maine's capitol. Augusta: Kennebec Journal Print Shop, 1939. Pp. 60.

1995   FISH, JOHN L. "Side-light on ancient local history and modern spiritualism in the Kennebec region." SJMH, 14 (1926), 146-151.
        Execution of Joseph Sanger, convicted of murdering his wife Phoebe, 1836.

1996   "FORT Western." Down East, 7 (September, 1960), 42-45.

1997   HAMLEN, EWING W. "Augusta, the capital of Maine." NEM, New Ser., 14 (1896), 195-213.

1998   HAWES, HILDRETH GILMAN. "Augusta--past and present." Maine's Own Magazine, 7 (July, 1929), 9.

1999   HENDERSON, RUTH. "Augusta--Maine's executive city and a beautifully located community." Sun Up, 3 (June, 1927), 11-27.

2000   HILL, HENRY FRANCIS, JR. Augusta's city hall and city government, 1797-1968. Augusta, 1968. 6 leaves. Me.

2001   _____. Remembrances, etc., of Gannett's Woods, Augusta, Maine. Augusta, 1966. 14 leaves. Me.

2002   "HISTORY of the State House." MeLB, 6 (1916-1917), 115.

2003   HUNT, HARRY DRAPER. The Blaine House: home of Maine's governors. Somersworth, N.H.: New Hampshire Publishing, 1974. Pp. 136.

2004   HUNT, ISAAC H. Astounding disclosures! Three years in a mad house. By a victim. Written by himself. A true account of the barbarous, inhuman and cruel treatment of Isaac H. Hunt, in the Maine Insane Hospital, in the years 1844, '45, '46, and '47, by Drs. Isaac Ray, James Bates, and their assistants and attendants.... Skowhegan: Amos Angier Mann, 1851. Pp. 84.

2005   JONES, HERBERT GRANVILLE. Koussinoc, the Indian trading post, address given for Daughters of Colonial Wars, Portland, Maine, August, 1928. [Portland, 1938.] Pp. 12.

2006   KENNEBEC JOURNAL. Augusta centennial souvenir, June 9, 1897. [Augusta, 1897.] Pp. 63. Me.

2007   "LIBRARY service in Maine." Sun Up, 3 (February, 1927), 4, 28, 30.
        Maine State Library.

2008   LITHGOW LIBRARY AND READING ROOM, AUGUSTA, ME. The Lithgow Library and Reading Room, Augusta, Maine. Augusta: Maine Farmers' Almanac Pr., 1897. Pp. 174.

2009 LOVETT, ROBERT WOODBERRY. "Publisher and advertiser extraordinary: the E. C. Allen Collection." BBHS, 24 (1950), 210-215.
E. C. Allen Co., 1871-1895; collection is at Baker Library, Harvard University.

2010 McLANATHAN, RICHARD B. K. "Bulfinch's drawings for the Maine State House." SocArch HistJ, 14 (May, 1955), 12-17.

2011 MAINE. STATE HOSPITAL, AUGUSTA. Augusta State Hospital, established October 14, 1840. [Augusta?, 1965]. Pp. 55.

2012 _____. With the years. Thorndike: Hutchins Bros., [1938?]. Pp. 77. MeHi.
History of the hospital, nursing school, and Nurses' Alumni Association.

2013 "THE MAINE State Library, 1839/1970." Maine. State Library. Biennial Report, 60 (1968-1970), entire issue.

2014 MASON, EDWARD G. "The presidential campaign of 1884 in Mr. Blaine's home city." NEM, New Ser., 24 (1901), 248-257.

2015 MOORE, KATRINA. "Blaine House." Down East, 5 (May, 1959), 24-25, 36, 39.

2016 NASH, CHARLES ELVENTON. The history of Augusta: first settlements and early days as a town, including the diary of Mrs. Martha Moore Ballard, 1785 to 1812. Augusta: Charles E. Nash & Son, 1904 [i.e. 1961]. Pp. vii, 612.
Signatures printed in 1904, first published in 1961.

2017 NEWBERT, E. E. "Outline history of the Unitarian Church of Augusta." The Church Exchange, 4 (1896-1897), 34-35.

2018 NORTH, JAMES WILLIAM. The history of Augusta, from the earliest settlement to the present time; with notices of the Plymouth Company, and settlements on the Kennebec; together with biographical sketches and genealogical register. Augusta: Clapp and North, 1870. Pp. xii, 990.

2019 PARTRIDGE, CORA PRESSON. "Maine state capitol." DARMag, 69 (1935), 390.

2020 PÉLADEAU, MARIUS B. "Guardian of the northern frontier: the Kennebec Arsenal." Down East, 23 (September, 1976), 60-63, 82.

2021 [PIERCE, HARRY H.] A short history of Augusta. Augusta: J. Frank Pierce Store, [1931]. Pp. 20. Me.

2022 ST. JOHN, FREDERIC. "Fort Western." Sun Up, 8 (December, 1930), 18.
Author's name is a pseudonym.

2023 SANFORD, LEWIS W. "Brief history of the All Souls Church (Unitarian) of Augusta." The Maine Church Exchange, No. 20 (September, 1944), Inside of front cover and page 1.

2024 SAYWARD, DOROTHY STEWARD. Comfort Magazine, 1888-1942: a history and critical study. Orono: Univ. of Maine, 1960. Pp. 108.

2025 SHUTE, ALBERTA VAN HORN. A year and a day along Bond Brook. South Windham: Living Word Pr., 1954. Pp. 80.

2026 _____. A year and a day in the park. Litchfield: Living Word Pr., 1956. Pp. 40. MeP.

2027 SMITH, EDGAR CROSBY. "The State of Maine burying ground." SJMH, 8 (1920), 30-33.

2028 "THE SOUTH Parish Congregational Church of Augusta." MeCP, 52 (April, 1965), 3.

2029 "THE STATE House, Augusta." BHistMag, 2 (1886-1887), 145-150.

2030 STUBBS, MARION BRAINERD. Centennial anniversary program and historical sketch of Green Street Methodist Episcopal Church, Augusta, Maine, November 11-14, 1928. n.p., 1928. Pp. 12. Me.

2031 TRUE, MRS. HILTON W. Quarto-centenary history, Unity Club, Augusta, Maine. Augusta: Journal Print, [1905]. Unpaged. Me.

2032 UPJOHN, SAMUEL. A sermon preached in St. Mark's Church, Augusta, Me., on the Sunday Next Before Advent, November 25, 1883. Augusta: Sprague & Son, 1883. Pp. 15. Me.
Relates to the church.

2033 WESTON, NATHAN. Oration at the centennial celebration of the erection of Fort Western, on the anniversary of American independence, July 4, 1854. Augusta: William H. Simpson, 1854. Pp. 23.

2034 WILLIAMSON, JOSEPH. "The first Democratic State Convention in Maine during the Rebellion." MeHSC, 3 Ser., 2 (1906), 279-284.
1861.

2035 "YACHTING on the Kennebec." BTJ, 24 (1911-1912), 574-575.
Augusta Yacht Club.

SEE ALSO entries 143, 556, 1637, 1650, and 3532.

AURORA (HANCOCK CO.)

2036 SILSBY, HERBERT T., II. A history of Aurora, Maine.... Ellsworth: Hancock Publishing, 1958. Pp. 159.

AVON (FRANKLIN CO.)

2037　SEE entry 1419.

BAILEYVILLE (WASHINGTON CO.)

2038　BAILEY, ALBERT W. History: early Baileyville, Maine, and its pioneers.... Calais: Calais Advertiser Pr., 1972. Pp. 100.

2039　BRUMMITT, HOWARD. "Love and labor serve the Lord: thirty-five years in Eastern Maine." The Northeast, 78 (May, 1951), 5-7.
　　　St. Luke's Church.

2040　OBER, GRACE M. Some history of Woodland: the village in Baileyville. Calais: Advertiser Publishing, 1975. Pp. 108. MeU.

BALD MOUNTAIN TOWNSHIP (SOMERSET CO.)

2041　No items located; there are two unorganized townships by this name in Somerset County.

BALDWIN (CUMBERLAND CO.)

2042　BALDWIN, ME. Souvenir of Baldwin, Maine, 1912. Brunswick: Maine Map & Register, 1912. Pp. 39. Me.
　　　Includes historical sketch.

BANCROFT (AROOSTOOK CO.)

2043　No items located.

BANGOR (PENOBSCOT CO.)

2044　ADAMS, WILLIAM CUSHING. "Memories and appreciations of Bangor Theological Seminary professors, 1886-1936." The Alumni Bulletin of Bangor Theological Seminary, 11 (January, 1937), 1-3, 7-8.

2045　"ANCIENT Norombega." BHistMag, 6 (1890-1891), 49.
　　　Supposedly Bangor.

2046　ART work of Bangor, Maine. Chicago: W. H. Parish, 1895. Unpaged. MeU.

2047　BACON, GEORGE FOX. Bangor: its points of interest and its representative business men; including an historical sketch of Brewer. Newark, N.J.: Glenwood Publishing, 1891. Pp. 95.

2048　BANGOR, ME. The centennial celebration of the settlement of Bangor, September 30, 1869. Bangor: Benjamin A. Burr, 1870. Pp. 182.
　　　Historical address by John Edwards Godfrey.

2049　_____. City councils and mayors, from incorporation of the city, in 1834 to 1881.... Bangor: B. A. Burr, 1881. Pp. 50. MeBa.

2050　BANGOR, ME. BOARD OF TRADE. The city of Bangor, "Queen City of the East," a condensed historical and descriptive review, together with a brief statement of facts relating to her commercial and manufacturing advantage ... for the year 1882. Bangor, 1883. Pp. 36.

2051　BANGOR, ME. CENTRAL CONGREGATIONAL CHURCH. Central Congregational Church, Bangor, Maine, 1847-1912: historical address delivered January 24, 1912, by Edward Mitchell Blanding.... Bangor, 1912. Pp. 31. MeBa.

2052　BANGOR, ME. CHAMBER OF COMMERCE. Historic Bangor.... Bangor, 1940. Pp. 13. MeBa.

2053　BANGOR, ME. CONGREGATION BETH ISRAEL. Diamond jubilee, 1888-1963. Henry H. Segal, ed. Bangor: Furbush-Roberts, [1963]. Pp. 163.

2054　BANGOR, ME. FIRST BAPTIST CHURCH. Semicentennial anniversary of the First Baptist Church, Bangor, January 25, 1868. Bangor: Wheeler & Lynde, 1868. Pp. 34. MeBa.
　　　Historical discourse by Albion K. P. Small.

2055　BANGOR, ME. FIRST CONGREGATIONAL CHURCH. Historical sketch of the First Congregational Church, Bangor, Maine, 1811-1911. Bangor: Ira H. Joy, 1911. Pp. 46.

2056　BANGOR, ME. FIRST METHODIST EPISCOPAL CHURCH. Centennial anniversary, First Methodist Episcopal Church, Bangor, Maine, 1837-1937.... n.p., [1937]. Pp. 28. MeBa.

2057　BANGOR, ME. FIRST UNIVERSALIST CHURCH. Highlights of the history of the First Universalist Church and Society. n.p., 1961. Unpaged.

2058　BANGOR, ME. HAMMOND STREET CONGREGATIONAL CHURCH. Seventy-fifth anniversary, December 6, 8, 9, 1908. n.p., 1908. Unpaged.

2059　NO ENTRY.

2060　BANGOR, ME. ST. GEORGE GREEK ORTHODOX CHURCH. Fortieth anniversary and history. n.p., 1967. Unpaged.

2061　BANGOR, ME. ST. JOHN'S CATHOLIC CHURCH. The story of St. John's, 1856-1906. [Bangor, 1906]. Unpaged. MeBa.

2062 BANGOR, ME. ST. MARY'S CATHOLIC CHURCH. The bells of St. Mary's.... n.p., 1967. Unpaged.

2063 _____. St. Mary's Church, Bangor, Me., 1872-1972, 100 years of faith. n.p., 1972. Unpaged. MeBa.

2064 BANGOR, ME. SECOND BAPTIST CHURCH. Jubilee of the Second Baptist Church, of Bangor; historical discourse by the pastor, George B. Ilsley and poem by Ellen Hamlin Butler, Thursday eve, Sept. 12, at the First Baptist's house of worship. Bangor, 1895. Pp. 12. MeBa.

2065 BANGOR, ME. WATER DEPARTMENT. History of the Bangor Water Works, from its commencement, while under the charge of the first board of water commissioners. Bangor: Burr & Robinson, 1877. Pp. 64. MeBa.

2066 NO ENTRY.

2067 NO ENTRY.

2068 NO ENTRY.

2069 BANGOR CHILDREN'S HOME. Historical sketch of the Bangor Female Orphan Asylum, 1868. Bangor: Smith & Hill, 1868. Pp. 23. MeBa.

2070 BANGOR DAILY NEWS. A bicentennial look at bygone Bangor. Bangor, 1976. Pp. 52. Me.

2071 BANGOR HEBREW COMMUNITY CENTER. Dedication of the Bangor Hebrew Community Center at the Liss Memorial Building, September 18, 1938. Bangor, [1938]. Pp. 24. MeBa.
    Includes a history of the settlement of the Jews in Bangor by Catherine Epstein and Lucille Epstein.

2072 BANGOR HEBREW SCHOOL. Fortieth anniversary, 1907-1947.... n.p., [1947]. Pp. 36. MeBa.
    Includes history by Mrs. Lawrence Cutler.

2073 BANGOR HISTORICAL SOCIETY. Fiftieth anniversary of the Bangor Historical Society: proceedings at the Bangor Public Library, Wednesday, April 8th, 1914. Bangor, 1914. Pp. 88.
    Historical address by Edward Mitchell Blanding.

2074 "THE BANGOR House." BTJ, 25 (1912-1913), 253.
    Hotel.

2075 BANGOR, Maine, a city of progress. Bangor: C. H. Glass, [1912?]. Pp. 32.

2076 BANGOR MECHANIC ASSOCIATION. [Historical sketch]. n.p., 1929. Unpaged. MeBa.

2077 BANGOR SAVINGS BANK. Rounding out a century, 1852-1952. Bangor, [1952?]. Pp. 32. MeBa.

2078 "BANGOR: the lumber trade." Merchant's Magazine and Commercial Review, 18 (1848), 517-520.
    Includes chronological table of output.

2079 BANGOR THEOLOGICAL SEMINARY. Historical catalogue of Bangor Theological Seminary.... [Bangor], 1928. 2 v. in 1.

2080 NO ENTRY.

2081 BARWISE, MARK A. "Sources of land title in Bangor." Maine Law Review, 10 (1916-1917), 201-209.

2082 BECKFORD, WILLIAM HALE and GEORGE W. RICHARDSON. Leading business men of Bangor, Rockland and vicinity; embracing Ellsworth, Bucksport, Belfast, Camden, Rockport, Thomaston, Old Town, Orono, Brewer.... Boston: Mercantile Publishing, 1888. Pp. 260.

2083 BLANCHARD, DOUGLAS. "Great days at the Bangor salmon pool." Down East, 13 (April, 1966), 36-38.

2084 BLANDING, EDWARD MITCHELL. "Bangor, Maine." National Magazine, 17 (1902-1903), 800-805.

2085 _____. "Bangor, Maine." NEM, New Ser., 16 (1897), 225-244.
    Differs from above article.

2086 _____. Central Congregational Church, Bangor, Maine, 1847-1912: historical address delivered January 24, 1912. Bangor, 1912. Pp. 31.

2087 _____, comp. The city of Bangor: the industries, resources, attractions and business life of Bangor and its environs.... Bangor: Industrial Journal, 1899. Pp. 256.

2088 BLANDING, INA POTTER, comp. History of the Bangor District Nursing Association, Inc.... 1913-1941, inclusive. [Bangor, 1941]. 19 leaves. MeBa.

2089 BOARDMAN, SAMUEL LANE. Descriptive sketches of six private libraries of Bangor, Maine. Bangor, 1900. Pp. 161.

2090 BOSTON AND BANGOR STEAMSHIP COMPANY. History of the Boston and Bangor Steamship Company, formerly known as Sanford's Independent Line, (1823-1882). Boston: T. R. Marvin & Son, 1882. Pp. 26.

2091 CHAPMAN, HARRY J. "The first Bangor city hall." Bangor Historical Society. Proceedings, (1914-1915), 51-56.

2092 CLARK, CALVIN MONTAGUE. History of Bangor Theological Seminary. Boston: Pilgrim Pr., 1916. Pp. xix, 408.

2093 CLIFFORD, ANGELA GODFREY. Cliff Cottage, 1847-1947. Bangor, 1947. Pp. 37. MeBa.
Clifford and Godfrey families.

2094 COFFIN, HAROLD WILHELM. A brief history of Dow Field. n.p., [1946?]. 15 leaves. MeU.

2095 COLLAMORE, CHARLES I. "History of Rising Virtue Lodge of F. & A. M. of Bangor, and of other lodges growing out of it." MeHistMag, 7 (1891-1892), 1-13.

2096 COOK, WALTER LEONARD. Bangor Theological Seminary: a sesquicentennial history. Orono: Univ. of Maine Pr., 1971. Pp. x, 217.

2097 CROSBY, JAMES HENRY. "A bell." Bangor Historical Society. Proceedings, (1914-1915), 42-44.
A Paul Revere bell.

2098 DOUCETTE, EARL. "Something special about fly rods." Yankee, 6 (April, 1940), 16-17.
Thomas Rod Company.

2099 "EARLY settlement of Bangor." BHistMag, 1 (1885-1886), 2-4.

2100 FELLOWS, RAYMOND. "Daniel Webster and Maine." Portland University Law Review, 4 (1955-1956), 28-34.
Visits in 1804 and 1835.

2101 FIELD, GEORGE WARREN. Fiftieth anniversary of the Central Congregational Church: historical address ... delivered April 1, 1897. [Bangor], 1897. Unpaged.

2102 "THE FIRST Congregational Church and Society in Bangor, Me." BHistMag, 3 (1887-1888), 101-103.

2103 "THE FIRST printer in Bangor." BHistMag, 4 (1888-1889), 235-236.
Peter Edes.

2104 "FIRST settlers in Bangor, and their lots." BHistMag, 1 (1885-1886), 119-124."

2105 FLAGG, CHARLES ALLCOTT. "The Bangor Public Library." CCJM, 28 (1915-1916), 203-204.

2106 GILMAN, CHARLES. "Bangor." American Magazine of Useful and Entertaining Knowledge, 3 (1837), 329-332.

2107 GODFREY, GEORGE FREDERICK. A sketch of Bangor .... Boston: James R. Osgood, 1882. Pp. 68.

2108 GRAHAM, EDWARD MONTROSE. John R. Graham (1847-1915) and the Bangor Railway & Electric Co. N.Y.: Newcomen Society in North America, 1950. Pp. 24.

2109 HEBERT, RICHARD A. "Bangor." Pine Cone, 2 (Winter, 1946-1947), 13-17.

2110 HENNESSEY, WILFRID A. "Peter Edes and the De Burians." Bangor Historical Society. Proceedings, (1914-1915), 45-50.
The De Burians was a club of bibliophiles founded in 1900.

2111 HESELTINE, CHARLES DANA. "Bangor Street Railway." Transportation Bulletin, No. 81 (1974), entire issue.

2112 "HISTORY of postal affairs in Bangor." Bangor Local Postal Guide, 1 (September, 1899), 1-12.

2113 ["HISTORY of the Girls' High School, Bangor."] Burr's Fifty Cent Monthly, (October, 1873), 1-3.

2114 HOLBROOK, STEWART H. "Bangor, Maine." American Forests, 44 (1938), 69-71, 94.
Lumbering.

2115 _____. "The flowering of a lumbertown." Down East, 21 (January, 1975), 36-39, 64-65, 67-69.

2116 HUTCHINS, CURTIS MARSHALL and RUSSELL H. PETERS. Dead River Co.: a history, 1907-1972. Farmington: Knowlton & McLeary, [1973?]. Unpaged. MeU.
Lumber.

2117 NO ENTRY.

2118 JOHNSTON, DONALD P. "History and problems of the Bangor Water Department." New England Water Works Association. Journal, 67 (1953), 212-229.
1875-1952.

2119 KNICKERBOCKER, FRANCES WENTWORTH CUTLER. The minister's daughter: a time-exposure photograph of the years 1903-1904. Charles H. Knickerbocker, ed. Philadelphia: Dorrance, 1974. Pp. 148.

2120 KNOWLES' Bangor business almanac for 1875, with historical sketches of Bangor, and its business enterprises. Charles Phelps Roberts, ed. Bangor: O. F. Knowles, 1875. Pp. 84. MeBa.
Includes biographies of business men.

2121 LEAGUE OF WOMEN VOTERS OF BANGOR. Bangor, Maine. (1960) Rev. ed. Bangor, 1968. Pp. 24.

2122 LINDQUIST, VERNON R. "Emerson in Bangor: the disenchantment of a Transcendental intruder." The Alumni Bulletin [of Bangor Theological Seminary], 44 (Winter, 1969), 3-12.
Visits of 1834 and 1846.

2123 NO ENTRY.

2124 McGOVERN, JAMES R. Yankee family. New Orleans: Polyanthos, 1975. Pp. iv, 191.
Poor and Pierce families.

2125 MELITA CLUB, BANGOR, ME. Annals of Melita from 1884 to 1900. Bangor, [1900?]. Pp. 40. MeU.

2126 MOULTON, WARREN J. "What the Hammond Street Church has meant to Maine." MeCP, 31 (May, 1944), 5-7.

2127 "MUNICIPAL history of Bangor." BHistMag, 1 (1885-1886), 4-8.

2128 NEW ENGLAND TELEPHONE AND TELEGRAPH COMPANY. The story of the telephone in Bangor. n.p., [1954]. Unpaged. MeBa.

2129 PAINE, ALBERT WARE. "The graveyards of Bangor." BHistMag, 4 (1888-1889), 84-86.

2130 _____. History of Mt. Hope Cemetery, Bangor, Maine. Bangor: O. F. Knowles, 1907. Pp. iv, 103.

2131 _____. "Residences of early settlers and prominent citizens of Bangor." BHistMag, 3 (1887-1888), 169-174, 233-235.

2132 _____. "The streets of Bangor." BHistMag, 3 (1887-1888), 213-216.

2133 PENOBSCOT SAVINGS BANK. 100 years, Penobscot Savings Bank, Bangor, and the world, 1869-1969. L. Felix Ranlett, ed. Bangor, [1969]. Pp. 23.

2134 PERRY, GEORGE SESSIONS. "The cities of America: Bangor, Maine." Saturday Evening Post, 223 (March 10, 1951), 24, 89-90, 92, 94, 97.

2135 PHILIPS, DAVID E. "Bangor--Queen City." Down East, 4 (April, 1958), 16-20, 35-37.

2136 POND, ENOCH. "Bangor Theological Seminary." CongQ, 12 (1870), 484-497.

2137 _____. An historical address delivered at the semi-centennial anniversary of the Theological Seminary at Bangor, July 27th, 1870.... Cambridge, Mass.: Welch, Bigelow, 1870. Pp. 16.

2138 _____. "Historical sketch of the Theological Seminary at Bangor." American Quarterly Register, 14 (1842), 27-33.

2139 PORTER, J. B. "Early history of Bangor, Maine." MNEH, 1 (1891), 1-7.

2140 [PORTER, JOSEPH WHITCOMB.] "The Bangor Theological Seminary." SJMH, 1 (1913-1914), 68-72, 136-140, 185-187.
    Author attribution by the editor.

2141 POTTER, EDWARD WESLEY. "Bangor, the consequences of industrial change." Talos, 2 (Summer, 1970), 31-39.

2142 POTTER, MARK L. "First saw mill on the Kenduskeag in Bangor, and Joseph Potter." Me HistMag, 8 (1893), 44-45.

2143 RANLETT, LOUIS FELIX. All Souls Congregational Church (United Church of Christ), Bangor, Maine. [Bangor]: Furbush-Roberts, 1962. Pp. 69.
    Fiftieth anniversary.

2144 _____. The Samuel Hersey Fund and the Bangor Public Library. Bangor, 1956. Unpaged.

2145 REYNOLDS, HARRIS WALTER. The beginnings of St. John's Church, Bangor, Maine. Brookline, Mass.: Priv. Print., 1934. Pp. 24. MBNEH.

2146 ROBERTS, CHARLOTTE. The first forty years of the Shakespeare Club of Bangor, 1896-1936. Mary-Louise Rowe, ed. n.p., [1936]. Pp. 32. MeBa.

2147 ROBINSON, D. A. "The schools of Bangor." BTJ, 25 (1912-1913), 243, 245, 247, 249.

2148 ROTARY INTERNATIONAL, BANGOR, ME. Twenty-fifth anniversary of the Rotary Club, Bangor, Maine. n.p., [1942]. Unpaged. MeBa.
    Includes brief history.

2149 ROWE, HERBERT W. ["The earliest Bangor newspaper."] MPAP, 41 (1904), 57-61; 42 (1905), 34-39.

2150 [ROWE, JAMES SWETT.] Fire service of Bangor. [Bangor]: Firemen's Relief Association, 1890. Pp. 62. MeHi.
    Author attribution by Maine Historical Society.

2151 "ST. JOHN'S Church, Bangor, 1835-1945." The Northeast, 72 (Christmas, 1945), 1-4.
    Signed: J. A. F.

2152 [SANDFORD, WILLIAM.] Historical sketch, articles of faith, covenant and catalogue of the First Congregational Church, Bangor, Me., from 1811 to 1856. Bangor: Samuel S. Smith, 1856. Pp. 55. MeBa.
    Author attribution by Joseph Williamson.

2153 SHETTLEWORTH, EARLE G., JR. Bangor historical resources inventory, 1975. Augusta: Maine Historic Preservation Commission, 1975. 94 leaves. Me.

2154 SIMPSON, CORELLI C. W. Leaflets of artists. Bangor: John H. Bacon, 1893. Pp. 59.
    Biographical sketches of Bangor artists.

2155 "SKETCH of Bangor." Maine Monthly Magazine, 1 (1836-1837), 529-533.

2156 SMITH, EDGAR CROSBY. "Brief notes on the early settlement of Bangor." SJMH, 1 (1913-1914), 33-36.

2157 SNIDER, ROSE. "Oscar Wilde's progress Down East." NEQ, 13 (1940), 7-23.
    Visit in 1882.

2158 SPRAGUE, JOHN FRANCIS. "An old Maine news-paper." SJMH, 14 (1926), 17-18.
Bangor Jeffersonian.

2159 TROWBRIDGE, MASON, JR., CARL E. BLAISDELL and GEORGE R. WALKER. "125 years of Bangor medicine." Maine Medical Association. Journal, 50 (1959), 441, 444-446.

2160 VETERANS OF FOREIGN WARS OF THE UNITED STATES. MAINE. NORMAN N. DOW POST, BANGOR. Comrades of all wars: Bangor--its people and history. [Bangor]: Hugh V. Knox, 1936. Unpaged.

2161 VICKERY, JAMES BERRY, III. An illustrated history of the city of Bangor, Maine. (1969) Rev. ed. Bangor: Bangor Bicentennial Committee, 1976. Pp. 118. MeBa.

2162 WHITTAKER, FREDERICK W. "Sesquicentennial perspective." The Alumni Bulletin of Bangor Theological Seminary, 41 (October, 1966), 1-7.
Bangor Theological Seminary.

2163 WILLIAMSON, WILLIAM DURKEE. "Annals of the city of Bangor, Maine." MeHistMag, 9 (1894-1895), 1-16.

2164 WOMAN'S CHRISTIAN TEMPERANCE CRUSADE. A partial history of the Woman's Christian Temperance Crusade of Bangor, Maine. Mrs. L. B. Wheelden, comp. Bangor: Industrial Journal, [1897]. Pp. 28. MeBa.
1874-1897.

SEE ALSO entries 171, 1736, 1751, 1761, and 4510.

BAR HARBOR (HANCOCK CO.)

2165 "BAR Harbor." The New Englander, No. 400 (July, 1957), 19, 38-40.

2166 BAR HARBOR VILLAGE LIBRARY. [History of the Library], 1875-1905. n.p., [1905]. Pp. 12.

2167 BLANK, JOHN S., III. "Bar Harbor." Ships and the Sea, 2 (August, 1952), 42-45.
Shipping since 1900.

2168 BUETTELL, ROGER B. "The Bar Harbor Express." Yankee, 31 (August, 1967), 138-147.

2169 CHILMAN, C. WILLIAM. "'Baymeath' and the Bar Harbor that was." NEG, 14 (Summer, 1972), 10-20.
Home of Mrs. Joseph T. Bowen.

2170 _____. "I'm sorry, Miss Lona...." Yankee, 37 (January, 1973), 150-156.
Hull's Cove Grammar School.

2171 "THE CHURCH of Our Father, Hull's Cove." The Northeast, 75 (May, 1948), 3-6.

2172 CLAYTON, CATHLEEN SHERMAN. "Memories of old Bar Harbor." Down East, 22 (July, 1976), 68-73.

2173 COLE, NAN. "A native's memories of old Bar Harbor." Down East, 17 (September, 1970), 60-62, 67, 90, 95-98.

2174 _____. "Personal glimpses of Bar Harbor's lush era." Down East, 15 (July, 1969), 42-47, 81-83, 87-89, 92.
1890s-1900s.

2175 COLLIER, SARGENT F. Green grows Bar Harbor: reflections from Kebo Valley, including profiles of the town that refused to die. [Bar Harbor?], 1964. Pp. 107.

2176 "EARLY settlements on Mount Desert at Town Hill, now West Eden." MeHistMag, 7 (1891-1892), 57-58.

2177 FREEMASONS. BAR HARBOR, ME. BAR HARBOR LODGE NO. 185. History of Bar Harbor Lodge, No. 185, Free and Accepted Masons, at Bar Harbor, Maine, from date of precedence, April 19th, 1882, to January 1st, 1890. Benjamin L. Hadley, comp. Bar Harbor: Bar Harbor Pr., 1890. Pp. 27.

2178 [GRANT, A. J.]. Directory of Bar Harbor ... also a historical sketch and guide.... Ellsworth: W. F. Stanwood & W. H. Perry, 1886. Pp. 62.

2179 GRANT, ROBERT. "A plea for Bar Harbor." Outing, 6 (1885), 515-524.
Social life and customs.

2180 HALE, RICHARD WALDEN, JR. "Cadillac's old Green Mountain Railway." Down East, 3 (July, 1957), 40-43.

2181 _____. The story of Bar Harbor: an informal history recording one hundred and fifty years in the life of a community. N.Y.: I. Washburn, 1949. Pp. 259.

2182 HAMMEL, MARGARET F. "Bar Harbor's great cottages." Down East, 19 (June, 1973), 58-63.

2183 HAMOR, H. E. "First meeting house at Hull's Cove, Eden, Me." BHistMag, 6 (1890-1891), 50.

2184 HARRISON, CONSTANCE CARY. "Bar Harbor." Independent, 55 (June 4, 1903), 1308-1313.

2185 HAYDEN, RALPH HENRY. "'I want these things to endure': an historical sketch of St. Saviour's, Bar Harbor." The Northeast, 81 (May, 1954), 12-19.

2186 OPDYCKE, LEONARD. Naval visits to Bar Harbor. Bar Harbor: Bar Harbor Times, 1952. Pp. 31.

2187 PEABODY, MARIAN L. "Old Bar Harbor days." Down East, 11 (July, 1965), 34-35, 64, 67-68, 72, 74-76.

2188 RINEHART, MARY ROBERTS. "Phoenix in New England: Bar Harbor, yesterday and tomorrow." Town and Country, 103 (July, 1949), 32-33, 90-92.

2189 SAVAGE, RICHARD A. "The Bar Harbor auto war." Down East, 22 (August, 1975), 66-69, 84, 87.
     1903-1913.

2190 _____. "Bar Harbor: the hotel era, 1868-1880." MeHSN, 10 (1970-1971), 101-121.

2191 SELIGMANN, HERBERT J. "Bar Harbor--from Eden to tourism." Down East, 4 (August, 1957), 24-29, 45-46.

2192 SPIKER, LA RUE. "Equestrian extravaganza." Down East, 14 (August, 1967), 40-43.
     Horse racing.

2193 _____. "Maine's sea coast mission." Down East, 20 (January, 1974), 40-45, 64-66.
     Maine Seacoast Missionary Society.

2194 WILLIAMS, ANSON R. and MARGARET WILLIAMS. "The big fire: thousands flee as raging blaze sweeps Bar Harbor, October, 1947." Down East, 9 (October, 1962), 14-19, 40-41.
     As told to Mary Wilkes Haley.

     SEE ALSO entries 20, 171, 603, 1587, and 1589.

BARING PLANTATION (WASHINGTON CO.)

2195 CHASE, CLIFFORD G. A history of Baring, compiled for the centenary celebration, July 4, 1925, and revised to July 1, 1950. n.p., [1950?]. Pp. 28. Me.

BARNARD PLANTATION (PISCATAQUIS CO.)

2196 TRUE, MABEL L. "Some early settlers of Barnard, Maine." SJMH, 13 (1915-1916), 220.

BATCHELDERS GRANT (OXFORD CO.)

2197 "THE MOST unique village in Maine." BTJ, 18 (1905-1906), 207-208.
     Hastings.

BATH (SAGADAHOC CO.)

2198 APPLEBEE, ROBERT B. "Notes on the Palmer schooners." AmNep, 5 (1945), 79-81.
     Palmer family.

2199 BAILEY, LOUISE C. "The little brick town of Bath." Yankee, 35 (May, 1971), 102-107, 166-169.
     Domestic architecture.

2200 BAKER, WILLIAM AVERY. A maritime history of Bath, Maine, and the Kennebec River region. Bath: Marine Research Society of Bath, 1973. 2v.

2201 BARTLET, WILLIAM STOODLEY. "A contribution to the history of Bath." MeHSC, 3 (1853), 273-277.

2202 BATH, ME. CENTENNIAL COMMITTEE. Bath, Maine, centennial, 1847-1947. Bath, 1947. Pp. 52. Me.

2203 BATH, ME. CENTRAL CONGREGATIONAL CHURCH. The 125th anniversary of Central Congregational Church, Bath, Maine. [Bath?, 1960?]. Pp. 8. MBC.
     Historical sketch is by Jane Stevens.

2204 BATH, ME. WINTER STREET CONGREGATIONAL CHURCH. A century of church history: celebration of the one hundredth anniversary of the Winter Street Congregational Church at Bath, Maine, Sunday and Monday, December 8 and 9, 1895. Bath: Times Company Print, 1896. Pp. 72.

2205 _____. Manual of the Winter Street Church, of Bath, Maine, containing its articles of faith, covenant, standing rules, list of members, and history. [Bath]: Geo. E. Newman, 1888. Pp. 25. MeHi.

2206 BATH HISTORY CLUB OF 1935. Brief history of early Bath. [Bath?, 1936?]. 59 leaves. Me.

2207 BATH IRON WORKS. Bath Iron Works Corporation: condensed history. Bath, 1971. Pp. 23. MeU.
     Shipbuilding.

2208 BATH NATIONAL BANK. Our first hundred years: the story of the Bath National Bank, 1855-1955. Bath, 1955. Pp. 89.

2209 "BATH, past and present." Maine Magazine, 1 (November, 1906), 81-120.

2210 BRAGDON, ROGER. "Last of the Bath-built square riggers." Down East, 22 (March, 1976), 44-45.
     "Astral," "Acme," and "Atlas."

2211 DOUGLAS, ALICE MAY. "Bath's oldest schoolhouse." SJMH, 10 (1922), 26-28.

2212 BATH

2212 ESKEW, GARNETT LAIDLAW. Cradle of ships.
N.Y.: Putnam, 1958. Pp. 279.
Bath Iron Works.

2213 NO ENTRY.

2214 GAULD, JOSEPH W. The courage to grow.
[Bath?, 1974?]. Pp. 91. MeU.
Hyde School.

2215 GLIDDEN, WALTER S. A history of Montgomery
and St. Bernard Royal Arch Chapter No. 2,
Bath, Maine. Bath: Times Co., 1912.
Pp. 48. MeB.

2216 GRANT, MANLEY. "Boy, I'd love to have a big
yacht." Yankee, 37 (September, 1973), 76-
82, 174-178, 180-181.
Yachts built at the Bath Iron Works.

2217 GREENE, MARC T. "Bath, Maine." Yankee, 20
(August, 1956), 27-35.

2218 HEFFERNAN, JOHN PAUL. "Charles W. Morse:
Bath's king of ice and steam." Down East,
22 (January, 1976), 38-43.

2219 HENNESSY, MARK WILLIAM. The Sewall ships of
steel. Augusta: Kennebec Journal Pr.,
1937. Pp. xxx, 686.
Arthur Sewall & Co.

2220 HUNTER, MICHAEL REED. "Maine's largest family." New Hampshire Profiles, 5 (June, 1959),
40-43.
State Military and Naval Children's Home,
1866-1959.

2221 JONES, CLIF. "The Bath-built Down Easter
'Challenger.'" Down East, 21 (March, 1975),
23-24, 26-28, 30.

2222 KING, WILLIAM and MARK LANGDON HILL. Remarks
upon a pamphlet published at Bath, Me., relating to alleged infractions of the laws
during the embargo, non-intercourse and war.
Bath: T. Eaton, 1825. Pp. 25.

2223 LYMAN, JOHN, ed. "Maine shipbuilding."
Nautical Research Journal, 3 (February, 1951),
15-16, 21.
Methods employed by William Rogers, 1847-
1902.

2224 MAINE. STATE MILITARY AND NAVAL CHILDREN'S
HOME. State Military and Naval Children's
Home, 1868-1946. n.p., [1946?]. Unpaged.
Me.

2225 OWEN, HENRY WILSON. "Bath, Maine." National
Magazine, 24 (1906), [668-673].

2226 _____. The Edward Clarence Plummer history
of Bath, Maine. Bath: Times Co., 1936.
Pp. 547, xxviii.

2227 PATTEN FREE LIBRARY, BATH, ME. Historical
sketch, deed of gift, by-laws and corporate
members. Bath, 1907. Unpaged. MeB.

2228 _____. Patten Free Library, 1889-1930. Bath,
[1930]. Pp. 20. MeBa.

2229 _____. Patten Free Library, 1847-1952: a
handbook containing brief historical data....
[Bath, 1952]. Pp. 24. MeBa.

2230 "PATTEN Library Association of Bath started
in 1847." SJMH, 9 (1921), 76-77.

2231 PLUMMER, EDWARD CLARENCE. "Bath, the city of
ships." NEM, New Ser., 15 (1896-1897), 353-
374.

2232 PORTER, JOSEPH WHITCOMB. "A famous lawsuit
relating to Bath and the Kennebec River."
SJMH, 3 (1915-1916), 15-18, 98-100.
David Jeffries vs. Joseph Sergeant, 1765.

2233 PREBLE, GEORGE A. and F. S. PARTRIDGE, comps.
Complete schedule of vessels built and regis-
tered in the District of Bath, Maine, commencing at 1783.... Bath: Fen. G. Barker,
1878. Pp. 48. MeHi.
See also entry 2235.

2234 QUINN, WILLIAM P. "The 90 year wonder--
Seguin." Steamboat Bill, 31 (1974), 221-222.
Tugboat.

2235 RAYMOND, JOHN H. Complete schedule of ves-
sels built and enrolled in the District of
Bath, Maine commencing at 1781. Bath: Fen.
G. Barker, 1878. Pp. 49-75. MeHi.
Paging continued from 1878 work by Preble
and Partridge; see entry 2233.

2236 REED, PARKER McCOBB. History of Bath and environs, Sagadahoc County, Maine, 1607-1894....
Portland: Lakeside Pr., 1894. Pp. 526.

2237 ROSS, FRANK D. A personal memento of destroy-
ers built for victory in World War II. Lewiston: Twin City Printers, 1946. Unpaged.
MeHi.
Bath Iron Works.

2238 ST. JOHN, FREDERIC. "Old landmarks of Bath."
Maine's Own Magazine, 8 (March, 1930), 15.
Author's name is a pseudonym.

2239 SEWALL, FRANK. "Beginnings and founders of
the New Church in America--the Church in Bath,
Maine." New-Church Messenger, 86 (May 11,
1904), 270-273, (May 18, 1904), 287-289,
(May 25, 1904), 299-301.
New Jerusalem Church.

2240 SEWALL, JOSEPH. "History of Bath." MeHSC, 2 (1847), 189-228.

2241 "SHIPBUILDING in Bath, Maine." Maine's Own Magazine, 8 (March, 1930), 12, 14.
   Bath Iron Works.

2242 SMITH, MARION JAQUES. Brief history of education in Bath, Maine. Bath: Adams Pr., [1957]. Pp. 20. Me.

2243 SNOW, RALPH L. "Percy and Small shipyard." Maine History News, 9 (April, 1974), 11.

2244 SOUVENIR of the three hundredth anniversary of American shipbuilding, Bath, Maine, August 5-9, 1907. Bath: Times Co., 1907. Unpaged. MeHi.
   Shipbuilding in Bath.

2245 TANNER, VIRGINIA. A pageant of the State of Maine in celebration of the official dedication of the Carlton Bridge, Bath, Maine ... June 30, July 2, 3, 4 ... 1928. [Augusta], 1928. Pp. 136.

2246 THAYER, HENRY OTIS. "The last tragedy of the Indian Wars: the Preble Massacre at the Kennebec." MeHSC, 3 Ser., 1 (1904), 406-420.
   June 9, 1758.

2247 TROTT, RAYMOND H. "A Down East merchant fleet." AmNep, 4 (1944), 45-52.
   Built, owned, and operated by the Houghton family.

2248 TURNER, WALTER FRYE. Illustrated historical souvenir of the city of Bath, Maine, containing half-tone engravings of the mayors, ship-builders, business and professional men of 1800-1899. [Bath], 1899. Pp. 320.

2249 WESLEY METHODIST-EPISCOPAL CHURCH, BATH, ME. Wesley Methodist-Episcopal Church, Bath, Maine, 1884-85. Bath: H. W. Howard, [1885?]. Pp. 24. MeU.
   Includes historical sketch.

2250 "WINTER Street Church, Bath." MeCP, 39 (April 15, 1952), 15.

   SEE ALSO entries 259, 286, 923, 1153, 1806, 1808, and 3532.

BEALS (WASHINGTON CO.)

2251 CURRIER, ISABEL. "Beals--Maine's 'tight little island.'" Down East, 15 (September, 1968), 40-43, 72-77, 80, 83.

2252 JONESPORT-BEALS HIGH SCHOOL. AMERICAN HISTORY DEPARTMENT. Pictorial history of the town of Beals, Maine. Jonesport, [1975?]. Pp. iii, 140. MeU.

BEATTIE TOWNSHIP (FRANKLIN CO.)

2253 No items located.

BEDDINGTON (WASHINGTON CO.)

2254 "JEFF Davis on Mt. Humpback." Yankee, 17 (November, 1953), 20-24.
   1858.

BELFAST (WALDO CO.)

2255 ABBOT, HERMAN. History of Belfast, Maine, to 1825. Belfast: Grace E. Burgess, 1900. Pp. 18.

2256 BELFAST, ME. City of Belfast, Maine, 1853-1953. n.p., [1953]. Unpaged. MeHi.

2257 BELFAST, ME. CONGREGATIONAL CHURCH. LADIES' CIRCLE. Footnotes of Belfast history. [Belfast]: Waldo County Herald Job Print, 1913. Pp. 26. MeU.

2258 BELFAST, ME. NORTH CHURCH. Celebration of the one hundredth anniversary of the organization of the First Congregational Church (now called the North Church) at Belfast, Maine, Tuesday ... December 29, 1896. Belfast: Belfast Age Publishing, 1897. Pp. 68.

2259 NO ENTRY.

2260 "THE BELFAST Free Library, an historical sketch." LJ, 13 (1888), 250-251.

2261 "BELFAST, Maine." BTJ, 3 (1890-1891), 297-300.
   Signed: Winkle.

2262 BENNETT, WELLS. "Doric interlude." Journal of the American Institute of Architects, 11 (1949), 33-39, 69-75.
   Historic houses.

2263 "THE CATHOLIC church in Belfast." MeCathHM, 7 (1916-1917), 222-237.
   St. Francis of Assisi Church.

2264 [CLARK, CORNELIUS EDWARDS]. "Sesquicentennial in Belfast." MeCP, 143 (February, 1947), 26-27.
   First Congregational Church; author attribution by the editor.

2265 DURHAM, MRS. J. C. Old houses of Belfast. [Belfast]: Waldo County Herald Job Printing Department, 1911. Pp. 11. MBNEH.

2266 DYER, RUSSELL GLOVER. History of Corinthian Chapter, No. 7, of Royal Arch Masons, Belfast, Maine, from 1848 to 1880. Belfast: G. W. Burgess, 1880. Pp. 80. MeHi.

2267 BELFAST

2267 [_____]. "Masonic temple, Belfast, Maine."
FR, 15 (1885-1886), 253-256.
Author attribution by the editor; signed
R. G. D.

2268 KUHNERT, DALE WILLIAM. "The Belfast fire of
1873." Down East, 20 (August, 1973), 52-55.

2269 LOCKE, JOHN LYMBURNER. History of Phoenix
Lodge, No. 24, of Belfast, Maine. Belfast:
Belfast Printing, 1900. Pp. 112. MeHi.
Freemasons, 1817-1900.

2270 WALSH, LOUIS SEBASTIAN. "St. Francis of
Assisi, Belfast, silver jubilee sermon."
MeCathHM, 7 (1916-1917), 245-253.

2271 WHITE, WILLIAM. A history of Belfast, with
introductory remarks on Acadia. Belfast:
E. Fellowes, 1827. Pp. 119.

2272 WILLIAMSON, JOSEPH. Belfast Academy fifty
years ago. Belfast: Geo. W. Burgess, 1888.
Pp. 7. MeBa.

2273 _____. History of the city of Belfast in the
State of Maine.... Portland: Loring, Short
and Harmon, 1877-1913. 2v.
Includes a bibliography, 1875-1900; volume
two, completed and edited by Alfred Johnson,
was published in Boston by Houghton Mifflin.

SEE ALSO entries 707, 2082, and 4589.

BELGRADE (KENNEBEC CO.)

2274 "BELGRADE, Maine." Sun Up, 3 (June, 1926),
42-44, 46-47, 49.

2275 GUPTILL, ROBERT A., CAROL F. NYE, and H.
PAULINE PLOURDE. Past & present pictures and
people of Belgrade, Maine, 1774-1976. [Bel-
grade]: Heritage Committee of Belgrade Bicentennial Observance, [1976]. Pp. 64. MeU.
Includes errata slip.

2276 PENNEY, WILL and MINNIE PENNEY. Eighty-eight
years on a Maine farm. Lawrence M. Sturtevant, ed. Farmington: Knowlton & McLeary,
1970. Pp. 144. MeHi.

BELMONT (WALDO CO.)

2277 No items located.

BENEDICTA (AROOSTOOK CO.)

2278 BENEDICTA, ME. Souvenir program of the cen-
tenary of Benedicta, 1834-1934. n.p., [1934?].
Pp. 16.
A copy is at the Aroostook Historical and
Art Museum, Houlton.

BENTON (KENNEBEC CO.)

2279 BENTON, ME. 100TH YEAR HISTORICAL SURVEY
COMMITTEE. Town of Sebasticook-Benton,
Maine, 1842-1942. Chester E. Basford, ed.
Fairfield: Galahad Pr., 1942. Pp. 54.

SEE ALSO entry 1421.

BERWICK (YORK CO.)

2280 BERWICK, ME. The story of Berwick, published
on the occasion of the town of Berwick's
250th anniversary, June 30-July, 1963. J.
Wilfrid Albert, comp. Berwick, 1963.
Pp. 166.

2281 DAVIS, ANDREW McFARLAND. "The case of Frost
vs. Leighton." AHR, 2 (1897), 229-240.
1739.

2282 JEWETT, SARAH ORNE. "The old town of Berwick." NEM, New Ser., 10 (1894), 585-609.

2283 SPENCER, WILBUR DANIEL, comp. A list of
Revolutionary soldiers of Berwick, compiled
from the records of the town. [Berwick],
1898. Pp. 18.

2284 WEBSTER, MILLARD D. Highlights of Berwick
history. Berwick, 1939. Unpaged. MeU.

SEE ALSO entry 1911.

BETHEL (OXFORD CO.)

2285 BEAN, EVA MARION. East Bethel Road. Bethel:
Citizen Print Shop, 1959. Pp. 452.

2286 BETHEL, ME. Report of the centennial cele-
bration at Bethel, August 26, 1874. Portland:
B. Thurston, 1874. Pp. 78.
Historical address by Nathaniel Tuckerman
True.

2287 BETHEL SAVINGS BANK. Bethel Savings Bank,
1872-1972. n.p., [1972]. Unpaged. Me.

2288 CROSBY, RUTH. I was a summer boarder. Boston: Christopher Publishing, 1966. Pp. 142.
Social life and customs.

2289 LAPHAM, WILLIAM BERRY. History of Bethel,
formerly Sudbury, Canada, Oxford County,
Maine, 1768-1890; with a brief sketch of
Hanover and family statistics. Augusta:
Maine Farmer, 1891. Pp. xv, 688.

2290 PARKMAN, FRANCIS. The Gould Academy story,
1836-1976. Bethel: Gould Academy, 1976.
Pp. x, 226. MeHi.

2291 TIBBETTS, MRS. RAYMOND R. "A brief history of the West Parish Congregational Church of Bethel." MeCP, 143 (October, 1947), 38-39.

BIDDEFORD (YORK CO.)

2292 ABENAKEE CLUB, BIDDEFORD, ME. The Abenakee Club of Biddeford Pool, Maine. [Biddeford, 1911]. Pp. 18.

2293 BIDDEFORD, ME. FIRST UNIVERSALIST CHURCH. First Universalist Church, Saco and Biddeford, Maine. n.p. [1898?]. Pp. 23. MeHi.
   Includes a history of the church.

2294 BIDDEFORD, ME. PAROISSE ST. JOSEPH. Paroisse St. Joseph, 75e anniversaire, programme-souvenir, 6-7 Mai, 1945. [Saco]: Reny Frères, 1945. Pp. 89. MBC.

2295 BIDDEFORD, ME. PUBLIC LIBRARY. An introduction to Biddeford's history and a chronological outline of events. [Biddeford], 1944. 57 leaves.

2296 _____. Stories and legends of old Biddeford. Biddeford, 1945-1946. 2v. Me.
   1600-1800.

2297 BIDDEFORD, ME. SECOND CONGREGATIONAL CHURCH. Order of exercises for the celebration of the one hundredth anniversary of the organization, 1805-1905, with historical notes. Biddeford: Biddeford Journal Print, 1905. Pp. 16.

2298 DAY, BENJAMIN F. and NAHUM S. DROWN. History of Dunlap Lodge No. 47, F. and A. M., commencing with organization of Buxton Lodge in 1826, located at Buxton, and continuing its history after its removal to Biddeford in 1854, and reorganization as Dunlap Lodge, up to A.D. 1890. Biddeford: Standard Publishing, 1890. Pp. 99. [MePGLM].

2299 EMERY, GEORGE ADDISON. "The old Thornton Academy." MeHSC, 2 Ser., 10 (1899), 1-51.

2300 "FORT St. George, or the ancient dominion of New England." Knickerbocker Magazine, 16 (1840), 308-316.
   Signed: P. S.

2301 GUIGNARD, MICHAEL. "Maine's Franco-Americans: Biddeford." Maine History News, 7 (July, 1972), 8-9, 12, 14.

2302 HALEY, ADELAIDE. "The Haley House and Farm, 763 Pool Road, Biddeford, Maine." OTNE, 35 (1944-1945), 3-9.

2303 HERRICK, MARY DARRAH. "The oldest public library in Maine." MeLAB, 3 (February, 1942), 8-9.
   Established in 1863; McArthur Public Library.

2304 LAWRENCE, CHARLES K. C. "A sketch of Christ Church, Biddeford, Maine." The Northeast, 73 (May, 1946), 8-9.

2305 MEEDS, MELVIL F. "Fort Mary." SJMH, 14 (1926), 7-8.

2306 PEPPERELL MANUFACTURING COMPANY. Biddeford, the home of Pepperell. Biddeford, [1937?]. Unpaged. MeHi.

2307 "RAVAGES of fire erased in summer community; S. Philip's by the Sea, Fortune's Rocks rebuilt." The Northeast, 78 (July, 1951), 12-14.
   Includes history.

2308 "THE SECOND Church, Biddeford, Maine." CongQ, 11 (1869), 241-248.

2309 TATTERSON, ESTELLE MORRIS. Three centuries of Biddeford: an historical sketch. n.p., [1916]. Unpaged. MeBa.

2310 WEYMOUTH, GORHAM N. and CORA BELLE BICKFORD. The city of Biddeford and vicinity [and] local landmarks. Biddeford: Riverside Pr., 1900. Pp. 38. MeHi.

2311 YORKE, DANE. The men and times of Pepperell, an account of the first one hundred years of the Pepperell Manufacturing Company, incorporated February 16, 1844. Boston, 1945. Pp. 107.

SEE ALSO entries 799, 1265, 1881, 1890, 1893, 1901, 4181, and 4465.

BIG SIX TOWNSHIP (SOMERSET CO.)

2312 No items located.

BIG SQUAW TOWNSHIP (PISCATAQUIS CO.)

2313 No items located.

BIG TEN TOWNSHIP (SOMERSET CO.)

2314 No items located.

BIG TWENTY TOWNSHIP (AROOSTOOK CO.)

2315 No items located.

BIG W TOWNSHIP (SOMERSET CO.)

2316 No items located.

BIGELOW TOWNSHIP (SOMERSET CO.)

2317 No items located.

BINGHAM (SOMERSET CO.)

2318 ELDEN, ALFRED OWEN. "Bingham's first banquet." The Northern, 8 (June, 1928), 14.
    Following the presidential election of
1828.

2319 HISTORY COMMITTEE OF THE BINGHAM SESQUICEN-
TENNIAL. Bingham sesquicentennial history,
1812-1962. Skowhegan: Skowhegan Pr., 1962.
Pp. 110.

BLAINE (AROOSTOOK CO.)

2320 No items located.

BLAKE GORE (SOMERSET CO.)

2321 No items located.

BLANCHARD PLANTATION (PISCATAQUIS CO.)

2322 BLANCHARD, EDWARD P. "The Blanchard family
of Blanchard." PCHSC, 1 (1910), 442-445.

2323 _____. "Charles Blanchard, proprietor of
the town of Blanchard, Maine." SJMH, 2
(1914-1915), 89-91.

BLUE HILL (HANCOCK CO.)

2324 THE ACADEMIES of Blue Hill, Maine, 1802-
1952. Blue Hill, 1952. Pp. 19. MeU.
    Blue Hill Academy and George Stevens
Academy.

2325 BLUE HILL, ME. CONGREGATIONAL CHURCH. Cen-
tennial, Congregational Church, Blue Hill,
Maine. Bangor: Samuel S. Smith & Son, 1874.
Pp. 34. MeBa.
    Historical address by Stephen Thurston.

2326 "BLUE Hill and settlers." MeHistMag, 8
(1893), 17-19.
    Includes ecclesiastical history of the town.

2327 BLUE HILL TROUPE, NEW YORK. The Blue Hill
Troupe, 25th anniversary. N.Y., 1949.
Pp. 95.
    Community theater.

2328 CANDAGE, RUFUS GEORGE FREDERICK. The centennial of Blue Hill Academy: a paper ... read
at the meeting of the [Brookline Historical]
Society, December 23, 1903. [Brookline,
Mass.]: The [Brookline Historical] Society,
1904. Pp. 15.

2329 _____. Dedication of bowlders and tablets
to John Roundy and James Candage, a founder
and an early settler of Bluehill, Maine, with
memorial addresses ... at Blue Hill Neck,
August 22, 1905. Ellsworth: Hancock County
Publishing, 1905. Pp. 21.

2330 _____. Historical sketches of Bluehill,
Maine. Ellsworth: Hancock County Publishing, 1905. Pp. 83.

2331 _____. Settlement and progress of the town
of Bluehill, Maine, an historical address ...
at Bluehill Falls, September 7, 1886. Blue
Hill: Ladies' Social Library, 1886. Pp. 43.

2332 _____. "Sketches of the representatives to
the [General] Court of Massachusetts from
Blue Hill, Me., prior to 1820." BHistMag, 3
(1887-1888), 191-193.

2333 CLOUGH, ANNIE L. Head of the bay: sketch and
pictures of Blue Hill, Maine, 1762-1952....
Blue Hill: Shoreacre Pr., 1953. Pp. 52.
MeBa.

2334 CUMMINGS, ABBOTT LOWELL. "The house the parson built." OTNE, 56 (1955-1956), 91-107.
    Jonathan Fisher House.

2335 DODGE, REUBEN GEORGE WASHINGTON. "The Congregational Church at Bluehill." BHistMag,
2 (1886-1887), 113-117.
    From notes prepared by Jonathan Fisher in
1810 with additions by Dodge.

2336 FISHER, JONATHAN. "Sketches of Bluehill."
BHistMag, 1 (1885-1886), 148-153.

2337 FOBES, CHARLES BARTLETT. "Blue Hill in
Maine." Appalachia, 29 (1952-1953), 531-533.

2338 LITTLEFIELD, OTIS. History of Ira Berry
Lodge, No. 187, Free and Accepted Masons,
Blue Hill, Me., from its organization, Nov.
12, 1883, to Jan. 1, 1902. Portland: Stephen Berry, 1902. Pp. 30. MeBa.

2339 NEVIN, DORIS. "Summer days in old Blue Hill."
Down East, 21 (September, 1974), 54-57, 83-84.
    Social life and customs.

2340 STANWOOD, CORDELIA J. "Glimpses of old Bluehill." House Beautiful, 45 (April, 1919),
222-223.

2341 WINCHESTER, ALICE. "Rediscovery: Parson
Jonathan Fisher." Art in America, 58 (November-December, 1970), 92-99.
    Fisher as an artist.

2342 WOOD, ESTHER E. "Blue Hill rusticators." Down East, 2 (September, 1955), 35-36, 39. Social life and customs.

2343 _____. Country fare. Somersworth, N.H.: New Hampshire Publishing, 1976. Pp. ix, x, 157.

2344 _____. "Historic Maine parsonage--the Jonathan Fisher House, Blue Hill, Maine." DARMag, 95 (1961), 537-538, 540, 572.

2345 _____. "The Jonathan Fisher House." Down East, 13 (August, 1966), 40-43.

SEE ALSO entries 207 and 1581.

BOOTHBAY (LINCOLN CO.)

2346 COAN, LEANDER SAMUEL. A century in one of the early New England churches: a sermon delivered in the First Congregational Church, Boothbay, Maine, September 23, 1866. Boston: T. R. Marvin & Son, 1866. Pp. 26.

2347 DIETZ, LEW. The story of Boothbay. n.p., 1937. Unpaged. MBNEH.

2348 RICE, GEORGE WHARTON. The shipping days of old Boothbay from the Revolution to the World War, with mention of adjacent towns. Boothbay Harbor, 1938. Pp. xv, 419.

2349 STEVENS, JAMES P., JR. "Boothbay schooners." Down East, 15 (September, 1968), 34-39, 68-70.

2350 THOMPSON, WINFIELD MARTIN. "Damariscove." NEM, New Ser., 11 (1894-1895), 34-41.

SEE ALSO entries 1681-1682 and 1689-1690.

BOOTHBAY HARBOR (LINCOLN CO.)

2351 BALDWIN, SIDNEY. Casting off from Boothbay Harbor, Maine. Boothbay Harbor: George M. Lowden, 1948. Pp. 127. Me.

2352 HALLET, RICHARD. "The deep roots of Boothbay Harbor." Down East, 5 (August, 1958), 36-41, 55.

2353 KYNETT, HAROLD HAVELOCK. Maine harbor, adventures in relaxation. [Philadelphia], 1940. Pp. 132.

2354 LARKIN, ALICE T. Our growing years. Boothbay Harbor: Harbor Print Shop, 1975. Pp. 63. MeU.

SEE ALSO entries 1681-1682 and 1689-1690.

BOWDOIN (SAGADAHOC CO.)

2355 No items located.

BOWDOIN COLLEGE GRANT EAST (PISCATAQUIS CO.)

2356 No items located.

BOWDOIN COLLEGE GRANT WEST (PISCATAQUIS CO.)

2357 No items located.

BOWDOINHAM (SAGADAHOC CO.)

2358 ADAMS, SILAS. The history of the town of Bowdoinham, 1762-1912. Fairfield: Fairfield Publishing, 1912. Pp. 295.

2359 AMES, JOHN WALLACE. Bowdoinham was my home. Kennebunk: Star Pr., 1975. Pp. 167. MeBa.

2360 BOWDOINHAM, ME. BICENTENNIAL HISTORICAL BOOKLET COMMITTEE. Bowdoinham: the seventeenth town in Maine, 1762-1962, bicentennial. Brunswick: Brunswick Publishing, 1962. Pp. 61. Me.

2361 CUMMINS, ROBERT. "Vessels built in Bowdoinham." MeHSN, 6 (November, 1966), an unpaged supplement at end of the issue. 1768-1877.

BOWERBANK (PISCATAQUIS CO.)

2362 No items located.

BOWMANTOWN TOWNSHIP (OXFORD CO.)

2363 No items located.

BOWTOWN TOWNSHIP (SOMERSET CO.)

2364 No items located.

BRADFORD (PENOBSCOT CO.)

2365 SEE entry 1733.

BRADLEY (PENOBSCOT CO.)

2366 "THE TOWN of Bradley, Maine." BHistMag, 3 (1887-1888), 79.

BRADSTREET TOWNSHIP (SOMERSET CO.)

2367   No items located.

BRASSUA TOWNSHIP (SOMERSET CO.)

2368   No items located.

BREMEN (LINCOLN CO.)

2369   BINGHAM, MILLICENT TODD. "Rescuing an is-
        land." Natural History, 39 (1937), 318-328.
          Hog Island.

2370   GIBBS, IRIS and ALONZO GIBBS. Bremen by-
        gones: 1876-1976. Bremen: Bremen Bicenten-
        nial Committee, 1976. Pp. 80. MeU.

        SEE ALSO entry 1693.

BREWER (PENOBSCOT CO.)

2371   BREWER, ME. FIRST CONGREGATIONAL CHURCH.
        Historical sketch of the First Congregational
        Church, Brewer, Maine, 1800-1928. Basil C.
        Gleason, comp. n.p., [1928?]. Pp. 36.
        MeU.

2372   "THE FIRST Congregational church and minis-
        ters on the Penobscot River." BHistMag, 1
        (1885-1886), 139-144.
          Brewer Church, formerly the Orrington
        Church.

2373   GARDINER, HARRY NORMAN. "Investigation of
        clairvoyance in a drowning accident at Brew-
        er, Maine." American Society for Psychical
        Research. Journal, 4 (1910), 447-464.
          Accident occurred in 1906; investigated
        for the author by Fannie H. Eckstorm.

2374   "150TH anniversary of [the] First Congrega-
        tional Church in Brewer." MeCP, 146 (June,
        1950), 20.

2375   VICKERY, JAMES BERRY, III. A pictorial his-
        tory of Brewer, Maine. [Brewer]: Brewer
        Bicentennial Committee, 1976. Pp. 59. Me.

        SEE ALSO entries 1736, 1752, 1761-1762, 2047,
        and 2082.

BRIDGEWATER (AROOSTOOK CO.)

2376   RIDEOUT, ANNIE E. History of Bridgewater,
        Maine. Manchester: Falmouth Publishing,
        1953. Pp. 153.

BRIDGTON (CUMBERLAND CO.)

2377   BRIDGTON, ME. FIRST CONGREGATIONAL CHURCH.
        Manual and history of the First Congregational
        Church, Bridgton, Maine. Minnie Gertrude
        Lewis, comp. n.p., 1929. Pp. 24. MBC.

2378   ____. Rules and regulations of the First
        Congregational Church, Bridgton, Me., togeth-
        er with the confession of faith, covenant,
        and a brief history of the church. Bridgton:
        Bridgton News Print, 1876. Pp. 16. MeHi.

2379   BRIDGTON ACADEMY, NORTH BRIDGTON, ME. Pro-
        ceedings at the re-union of the alumni of
        Bridgton Academy held at North Bridgton, Me.,
        on July 12th, 1882. Bridgton: Bridgton News
        Print, 1883. Pp. 69.
          History by A. S. Kimball.

2380   BRIDGTON, Maine 1768-1968. Eula M. Shorey
        and Cara Cook, eds. Bridgton: Bridgton
        Historical Society, 1968. Pp. 627. Me.

2381   CORLISS, LEWIS H. History of Oriental Lodge,
        No. 13, Free and Accepted Masons, Bridgton,
        Me., 1804-1894. [Bridgton]: Bridgton News
        Print, 1895. Pp. 111. MeU.

2382   CRAM, MARSHALL. An address delivered ... at
        the dedication of the town house in Bridgton,
        January 8, 1852. Portland: Brown Thurston,
        1852. Pp. 44.
          Town history.

2383   DAVIS, BLYNN EDWIN. Moody Bridges, Pondi-
        cherry, and the beginnings of Bridgton.
        Bridgton, 1959. Pp. 70.

2384   ____. The Ridge. Bridgton, 1971. 95
        leaves.

2385   McINTYRE, PHILIP WILLIS. An account of the
        ceremonies at the dedication of the soldiers'
        monument, Bridgton, Maine, July 21, 1910,
        containing also the addresses delivered on
        that occasion and biographical sketches.
        [Bridgton?, 1910]. Pp. 48.

2386   McLIN, WILLIAM HELLEN, ROBERT JORDAN DINGLEY,
        and EDGAR THORN MEAD, JR. The twenty-four-
        inch gauge railroad at Bridgton, Maine.
        Bridgton: Bridgton News, 1941. Pp. 36.
          Bridgton & Harrison Railway.

2387   MEAD, EDGAR THORN, JR. "Busted and still
        running:" the famous two-foot gauge railroad
        of Bridgton, Maine. Brattleboro, Vt.:
        Stephen Greene Pr., 1968. Pp. vi, 58.
          Bridgton and Saco River Railroad Company.

2388   MONK, GUY MAXWELL. The story of North Bridg-
        ton, Maine, 1761-1958: a little history, a
        little legend, and some recollections. [North
        Bridgton?], 1958. Pp. 70.

2389 ODD FELLOWS, INDEPENDENT ORDER OF. BRIDGTON, ME., CUMBERLAND LODGE NO. 30. Anniversary address ... Sunday afternoon, April 21, '07. Bridgton: News Print, 1907. Pp. 31. MeHi.
Address is by Henry A. Shorey.

2390 STEVENS, ERNEST N. A brief history of Bridgton Academy, 1808-1957. Cambridge, Mass.: Cuneo Pr., 1958. Pp. 194.

2391 WOOD, SOLOMON. "Journal of a survey of Bridgeton, Me., in 1776." NEHGR, 28 (1874), 63-67.
Edited by Isaac B. Choate.

BRIGHTON PLANTATION (SOMERSET CO.)

2392 No items located.

BRISTOL (LINCOLN CO.)

2393 "ANCIENT Pemaquid, Maine--occupied by whites before Plymouth." BTJ, 13 (1900-1901), 271-272.

2394 BANKS, CHARLES EDWARD. "The pirate of Pemaquid." MHGR, 1 (1884), 57-61.
Dixey Bull.

2395 BRISTOL HIGH SCHOOL. Inside Bristol. Damariscotta: Twin Village Printing, [1951]. Pp. 68. Me.

2396 BURRAGE, HENRY SWEETSER. "The first mention of Pemaquid in history." MeHSC, 2 Ser., 6 (1895), 53-62.

2397 _____. "Military operations at Pemaquid, in the second war with Great Britain." MeHSC, 2 Ser., 3 (1892), 187-190.
War of 1812.

2398 CAMP, HELEN B. Archaeological excavations at Pemaquid, Maine, 1965-1974. Augusta: Maine State Museum, 1975. Pp. xx, 89. Me.

2399 _____. Pemaquid lost and found. Arlington, Mass.: Ancient Pemaquid Restoration, 1967. Pp. 44.

2400 CARTLAND, JOHN HENRY. Ancient pavings of Pemaquid. Pemaquid Beach, 1899. Pp. 11.

2401 _____. Ten years at Pemaquid: sketches of its history and its ruins. Pemaquid Beach, 1899. Pp. vi, 196.

2402 _____. Twenty years at Pemaquid: sketches of its history and its remains, ancient and modern. Pemaquid Beach, 1914. Pp. 224.

2403 CASTNER, HAROLD WEBBER. The story of ancient Pemaquid, "Metropolis of the New World." (1950) 3d ed. Boothbay Harbor, 1956. Pp. 23.

2404 DANFORTH POINT TRUST. A brief description of Danforth Point, New Harbor, Maine, with an account of the Danforth Point Trust. Exeter, N.H.: Academy Pr., 1924. Unpaged.

2405 DUNBAR, ROBERT E. "The fort that wouldn't stay built." Down East, 23 (August, 1976), 82-85.
Fort William Henry.

2406 FOGG, CLARA NEWHALL. "Maine's most historic spot." DARMag, 64 (1931), 91-92.
Pemaquid.

2407 FULLER, G. SPENCER. "The old fort at Pemaquid." PVMA, 5 (1905-1911), 432-447.
Fort William Henry.

2408 HACKELTON, MARIA W. Jamestown of Pemaquid: a poem, read on the site of Fort Frederic, on the reception of the committee of the Maine Historical Society by the citizens of Bristol, August 26, 1869. N.Y.: Hurd and Houghton, 1869. Pp. 40.

2409 HAWES, HILDRETH GILMAN. "Maine's first pirate sacked Fort Pemaquid." Sun Up, 10 (May, 1932), 27, 32.
Dixey Bull, 1632.

2410 HOUGH, FRANKLIN BENJAMIN. Papers relating to Pemaquid and parts adjacent in the present State of Maine, known as Cornwall County, when under the colony of New-York, compiled from official records in the office of the Secretary of State at Albany, N.Y. Albany: Weed, Parsons, 1856. Pp. vii, 136.

2411 _____. "Pemaquid in its relation to our colonial history." MeHSC, 7 (1876), 127-164.

2412 JOHN, TIMOTHY. "Restoration of the Harrington Meeting House." Down East, 22 (April, 1976), 48-51.

2413 JOHNSON, ALFRED. "Some recent impressions of the forts and other evidences of early occupancy at Pemaquid, and elsewhere, in Maine." CSMP, 25 (1922-1924), 427-430.

2414 [KALER, JAMES OTIS]. The story of Pemaquid. By James Otis, pseud. N.Y.: T. Y. Crowell, 1902. Pp. 181.

2415 LABRIE, ROSE CUSHING. The story of Pemaquid Light. Hampton, N.H.: Hampton Publishing, 1961. Pp. 19. Me.

2416 LIBBY, HILDA. The story of the Pemaquid Point lighthouse. n.p., [1975?]. Pp. 27. Me.

2417 LOWELL, W. L. "Historical Pemaquid." BTJ, 9 (1896-1897), 17.

2418 McCRILLIS, HERBERT O. "Ancient Pemaquid: Jamestown of New England." NEM, New Ser., 34 (1906), 278-288.

2419 _____ and JOHN HENRY CARTLAND. A brief sketch of Pemaquid. Boothbay Harbor: Register Book and Job Print, 1917. Pp. 38.

2420 McCRILLIS, HERBERT O. "Pemaquid, the Jamestown of the North." Pine Tree Magazine, 7 (1907), 311-326.

2421 MOOREHEAD, WARREN KING. "The ancient remains at Pemaquid, Maine: some observations." OTNE, 14 (1923-1924), 133-141.
   Discusses possibility of pre-Plymouth settlement at Pemaquid.

2422 NELSON, G. J. "Historic Pemaquid." BTJ, 15 (1902-1903), 143-144.

2423 NOBLE, JOHN. "Land controversies in Maine--1769-1772." CSMP, 6 (1899-1900), 11-57.
   Pemaquid Patent.

2424 PALTSITS, VICTOR HUGO. "The depredation at Pemaquid in August, 1698." MeHSC, 3 Ser., 2 (1906), 261-274.

2425 PARKER, ARLITA DODGE. A history of Pemaquid, with sketches of Monhegan, Popham and Castine. Boston: MacDonald & Evans, 1925. Pp. 226.

2426 _____. "Traces of probable Norse relics--and mysterious stone pavements uncovered at historic Pemaquid." Sun Up, 3 (August, 1927), 30-32.

2427 ROBINSON, GRACE LOUISE. "St. George's at Popham: forerunner of all American forts." JAmHist, 14 (1920), 233-235.

2428 SEWALL, RUFUS KING. Pemaquid, its genesis, discovery, name and colonial relations to New England. Read before the Lincoln County Historical Society, May 22, 1896. [Wiscasset]: The [Lincoln County Historical] Society, 1896. Pp. 21.

2429 SYLVESTER, HERBERT MILTON. Ye romance of olde Pemaquid. Boston: Stanhope Pr., 1908. Pp. 431.
   Also published in 1909 as volume four of the author's "Maine pioneer settlements."

2430 TAFT, LEWIS A. "The republic of Muscongus." Yankee, 28 (September, 1964), 64-69, 138.
   Election of 1860.

2431 THAYER, HENRY OTIS. "Ancient Pemaquid." MeHSC, 3 Ser., 2 (1906), 374-388.

2432 _____. "Beginnings at Pemaquid." MeHSC, 2 Ser., 6 (1895), 62-84.

2433 THOMPSON, ERNEST. "Louds Island." Down East, 8 (April, 1962), 20-24.

2434 THORNTON, JOHN WINGATE. "Ancient Pemaquid: an historical review." MeHSC, 5 (1857), 141-299.

2435 VINTON, JOHN ADAMS. The Giles memorial ... with a history of Pemaquid, ancient and modern; some account of early settlements in Maine, and some details of Indian warfare.... Boston: H. W. Dutton & Son, 1864. Pp. viii, 600.

2436 VONDEL, JOSEPH LEMAN. "The restoration of Pemaquid." MagHist, 11 (1909), 139-144.

2437 YOUNG, ARTHUR H. "The big dig at Pemaquid." Yankee, 31 (September, 1967), 82-85, 170, 173.

2438 _____. Pemaquid, New England's first city.... n.p., 1969. Pp. 22.

SEE ALSO entries 286, 799, 1683, 1693, 1708, 1712, and 4100.

BROOKLIN (HANCOCK CO.)

2439 BROOKLIN CENTENNIAL COMMITTEE. Centennial celebration, Brooklin, Me., July 29-31, 1949. George M. Murray, ed. [Brooklin?, 1949]. Pp. 51. Me.

2440 FISH, E. S. History of Brooklin: an address delivered at Brooklin, Maine, July 4, 1876. Bangor: Burr & Robinson, 1876. Pp. 32.

2441 FREEMASONS. BROOKLIN, ME. NASKEAG LODGE, NO. 171. History of Naskeag Lodge, No. 171, of F. and A. Masons, June, 1873 to 1890. Portland: Stephen Berry, 1890. Pp. 27. MeBa.

SEE ALSO entries 1561 and 1589.

BROOKS (WALDO CO.)

2442 NORWOOD, SETH WADEMERE, comp. Sketches of Brooks history. Dover, N.H.: J. B. Page, 1935. Pp. 454.
   Includes short biographies and genealogies.

BROOKSVILLE (HANCOCK CO.)

2443 BROOKSVILLE HISTORICAL SOCIETY. Traditions and records of Brooksville, Maine, collected by the Brooksville Historical Society, 1935-1936. Grace Limeburner, et al., eds. Auburn: Merrill & Webber, 1936. Pp. 152.

2444 CARBERG, WARREN C. "The amazing Tapley brothers." Yankee, 33 (January, 1969), 122-123, 125.

2445 LIMEBURNER, GRACE M. GRINDLE. Stories of Brooksville. Bangor: Seely, 1924. Pp. 81.
   History, not literature.

2446 SNOW, WALTER A., comp. Brooksville, Maine, "A town of the Bagaduce." Blue Hill: Blue Hill Packet, 1967. Pp. 136.

2447 _____. Brooksville, Maine, a town in the Revolution. [Brooksville: Brooksville] Bicentennial Committee, 1976. Pp. iii, 75. MeU.

   SEE ALSO entries 1581, 1597, and 1621.

BROOKTON TOWNSHIP (WASHINGTON CO.)

2448 No items located.

BROWNFIELD (OXFORD CO.)

2449 BROWNFIELD, ME. CONGREGATIONAL CHURCH. Service at the Congregational Church ..., sermon by Rev. Samuel Tyler; Brownfield centennial, 1802-1902, commemorative service, Sunday, August 24, 1902. Brownfield, 1902. Pp. 24.

2450 STICKNEY, ELIZA ANN GIBSON. Reminiscences of Brownfield: short sketches from the history of the town. East Brownfield, 1901. Pp. 69.

2451 TEG, WILLIAM. History of Brownfield, Maine. Cornish: Carbrook Pr., 1966. Pp. 202.
   Includes errata slip.

BROWNVILLE (PISCATAQUIS CO.)

2452 BROWNVILLE, ME. A handbook of Brownville history, with records of its centennial celebration.... Susan M. Lewis, comp. Bangor: Jordan-Frost, 1935. Pp. 122. MeBa.

2453 "THE CALLIOPEAN baseball team." The Pioneer, 1 (February, 1912), [3-5].

2454 "COMING of the Welch people and the slate quarries." The Pioneer, 1 (July, 1911), [1-2].

2455 GERRISH, JUDSON C. and HENRY GERRISH. History of Brownville, 1824-1924. Dover-Foxcroft: F. D. Barrows, 1924. Pp. 59.

2456 JENKINS, SUE PERRIGO. Memories of Ebeeme: the delights of nature and living at a summer camp in Maine. N.Y.: Exposition Pr., 1959. Pp. 43.

2457 JENKS, E. A. "The lotting of Brownville." The Pioneer, 1 (July, 1911), [5].
   Land.

2458 MacDOUGALL, WALTER M. "Brownville slate and slaters." Down East, 15 (September, 1968), 58-61, 90.

2459 "REMINISCENCES." The Pioneer, 1 (June, 1911), [5-6].

2460 RUSSELL, CARRIE PAGE. "In the early days." The Pioneer, 1 (April, 1912), [4].

2461 TIBBETTS, R. G. "Brick-making in North Brownville." The Pioneer, 1 ([August], 1911), [4].

2462 _____. "Sketch of some of the early settlers of Brownville." The Pioneer, 1 (May, 1911), [1-3].

BRUNSWICK (CUMBERLAND CO.)

2463 ACHORN, EDGAR OAKES, ed. Bowdoin in the World War: the story of the cooperation of the college with the government and the record of Bowdoin men who served with the colors. [Brunswick: Bowdoin] College, 1929. Pp. xv, 225.

2464 ALLEN, WILLIAM, 1780-1873. "Brunswick Convention of 1816." MeHSC, 2 Ser., 2 (1891), 129-142.
   Convention to count votes cast by Maine towns regarding separation from Massachusetts.

2465 ASHBY, THOMPSON ELDRIDGE. A history of the First Parish Church in Brunswick, Maine. Louise R. Helmreich, ed. Brunswick: J. H. French, 1969. Pp. xv, 414.

2466 _____. "'Uncle Tom's Cabin' and the Brunswick Church." MeCP, 28 (February, 1941), 3-6.

2467 BEREAN BAPTIST CHURCH, BRUNSWICK, ME. Centennial anniversary of the Berean Baptist Church, October 28, 1940. n.p., [1940?]. Pp. 12. MeU.
   Includes history by Evelyn E. Langford.

2468 "BIRTHPLACE of a national industry." Sun Up, 9 (October, 1931), 14, 48.
   Dennison paper boxes.

2469 BLISS, FRANCIS R. "The rise of music at Bowdoin." BA, 14 (1939-1940), 107-111.

2470 BOWDOIN COLLEGE. Addresses and poem on the occasion of the one hundredth anniversary of the incorporation of Bowdoin College, June 27 and 28, 1894. Brunswick, 1894. Pp. 86.
  This work and entry 2477 were also bound together and published in the same year with the title: Memorial of the one hundredth anniversary of the incorporation of Bowdoin College.

2471 _____. Addresses at the centennial exercises of the Bowdoin Medical School, June 23, 1920. Brunswick, 1920. Pp. 18.
  Addresses by Kenneth Charles Morton Sills and Addison Sanford Thayer.

2472 _____. Bowdoin College, 1802-1952: the commemoration of the opening of the college. Brunswick, 1952. Pp. 79.
  Includes historical address by Herbert Ross Brown.

2473 _____. Bowdoin College, 1794-1944: exercises of the sesquicentennial of the college charter. June 24: the convocation, the sesquicentennial dinner. June 25: the service of thanksgiving and remembrance. Brunswick, 1944. Pp. v, 87.

2474 _____. Bowdoin College, 1794-1949: an historical sketch. [Brunswick], 1950. Pp. 46. MeHi.

2475 _____. A decade of progress, 1952-1962. Brunswick, 1962. Pp. 35. Me.

2476 _____. General catalogue of Bowdoin College and the Medical School of Maine: a biographical record of alumni and officers, 1794-1950. Brunswick, 1950. Pp. xv, 670.

2477 _____. General catalogue of Bowdoin College and the Medical School of Maine 1794-1894; including a historical sketch of the institution during its first century prepared by George Thomas Little. Brunswick, 1894. Pp. cxii, 216.
  This work and entry 2470 were also bound together and published in the same year with the title: Memorial of the one hundredth anniversary of the incorporation of Bowdoin College.

2478 _____. Named professorships at Bowdoin College. Brunswick, 1976. Pp. vi, 99. MeHi.

2479 BOWDOIN COLLEGE. ATHENAEAN SOCIETY. Catalogue of the Athenaean Society, Bowdoin College. [Brunswick: J. Griffin], 1856. Pp. 68. MH.
  Prefaced by an historical sketch of the society.

2480 BOWDOIN COLLEGE. BOWDOIN ALUMNI ASSOCIATION OF BOSTON. History of the Bowdoin Alumni Association of Boston and vicinity, 1868-1887. Frank V. Wright, Arthur T. Parker, and Frank R. Kimball, comps. Salem, Mass.: Salem Pr., 1888. Pp. 128.

2481 BOWDOIN COLLEGE. MASQUE AND GOWN. The Masque and Gown of Bowdoin College presents. Brunswick, 1939. Pp. 20. Me.
  A history with a list of plays produced from 1903/04-1939/40.

2482 BOWDOIN COLLEGE. MUSIC DEPARTMENT. Ten years of music at Bowdoin, 1936-1946. Brunswick: Bowdoin College, [1946]. Pp. 16.

2483 "BOWDOIN College." Old and New, 4 (1871), 112-115.

2484 "A BOWDOIN journal of 1850." BA, 3 (1928-1929), 35-36.
  Kept by John Glidden Stetson.

2485 "BOWDOIN'S intercollegiate track beginnings." BA, 8 (1933-1934), 63-64.

2486 BOYER, KENNETH J. "The college library--past, present, future." BA, 15 (1940-1941), 73-76.
  Bowdoin College.

2487 _____. "Library facilities at Bowdoin College 1802-1960." BA, 34 (December, 1959), 2-7.

2488 BRAULT, GÉRARD J. "The earliest painting of the Bowdoin College campus." OTNE, 51 (1960-1961), 101-103.

2489 _____. "On the name 'Bowdoin.'" BA, 34 (June, 1960), 6-7.

2490 BRUNEAU, CHARLES G. E. M. "A Frenchman looks at Brunswick." BA, 6 (1931-1932), 33-37.
  In French.

2491 BRUNSWICK, ME. Brunswick, 200 years a town, 1739-1939. Brunswick: The Town, 1939. Pp. 80. MBNEH.

2492 _____. Celebration of the one hundred and fiftieth anniversary of the incorporation of the town of Brunswick, June 13, 1899. Brunswick: Pejepscot Historical Society, 1889. Pp. 92.
  Oration by Charles Carroll Everett.

2493 BRUNSWICK, ME. BICENTENNIAL COMMITTEE. Bicentennial commemoration of American independence, Brunswick, Maine, July 3rd, 4th, & 5th, 1976. Brunswick: Brunswick Publishing, 1976. Unpaged. MeHi.
  Includes historical sketch of Brunswick by Philip S. Wilder.

2494 BRUNSWICK, ME. CHURCH OF ST. JOHN THE BAP-
TIST. Souvenir of the 50th anniversary of
St. John the Baptist Parish, Brunswick, Maine.
Brunswick: Brunswick Publishing, 1927.
Pp. 80.
In French and English.

2495 BRUNSWICK, ME. FIRST PARISH CONGREGATIONAL
CHURCH. First Congregational Church in Brunswick, Me.; historical sketch, confession of
faith, covenant rules of the church, and catalogue of members, to January 15, 1872. Brunswick: Joseph Griffin, 1872. Pp. 72.

2496 _____. The First Parish in Brunswick, Maine.
n.p., [1953?]. Unpaged. MBC.

2497 _____. Manual of the First Parish Congregational Church, Brunswick, Maine, June 15,
1909. Brunswick: Record Pr., 1909. Pp. 52.
MBNEH.
Includes chronology by George T. Little.

2498 "THE BRUNSWICK bicentennial." MeCP, 25
(April, 1938), 8-9, 16-17.
First Parish Church.

2499 BURNHAM, PHILIP E. "Hawthorne's 'Fanshawe'
and Bowdoin College." EIHC, 80 (1944), 131-
138.

2500 BURTON, ALFRED E. "The engineering school at
Bowdoin." BA, 4 (1929-1930), 33-35.
1871-1881.

2501 CAMPBELL, HELEN A. "Housed in historic
Brunswick mansion." Sun Up, 10 (February,
1932), 12, 32.
Gilman Mansion.

2502 CHAPMAN, HENRY LELAND. "Early movements to
separate the District of Maine from Massachusetts; and the Brunswick Convention of 1816."
PejHSC, 1 Pt. 1 (1889), 1-20.

2503 _____. "History of Bowdoin College." BTJ,
17 (1904-1905), 344-347.

2504 CHASE, F. HALCYON. Brunswick, a brief history
of the growth and development of the town....
Brunswick: Brunswick Record, 1903. Pp. 32.
Me.

2505 CHRISTIAN, SHELDON. One hundred and twenty-
five years of religious pioneering; being the
history of the First Universalist Church in
Brunswick, Maine. [Brunswick?], 1937.
Pp. 18.

2506 CLEAVELAND, NEHEMIAH. History of Bowdoin College; with biographical sketches of its graduates, from 1806 to 1879, inclusive. Boston:
J. R. Osgood, 1882. Pp. iv, 905.
Edited and completed by Alpheus Spring Packard; for additions and corrections see entry
2526.

2507 CLEAVELAND, PARKER. Results of meteorological
observations made at Brunswick, Maine, between
1807 and 1859. Reduced and discussed at the
expense of the Smithsonian Institution by
Charles A. Schott.... Washington: Smithsonian Institution, 1867. Pp. v, 53.

2508 CUMMINGS, OSMOND RICHARD. "Trolleys to Brunswick, Maine, 1896-1937." Transportation Bulletin, No. 73 (1966), 1-42.

2509 DAGGETT, ATHERN P. "The Chapel." BA, 20
(November, 1945), 3-4.
Bowdoin College Chapel, built in 1845.

2510 DOLE, FREDERICK HOWARD, ed. A history of the
Alpha-Rho Chapter of Kappa Sigma, Bowdoin Col-
lege, March 22, 1895-1945. n.p., [1945].
Pp. 126.

2511 EATON, THOMAS H. "Memories of Chi Phi." BA,
5 (1930-1931), 78-79.
Bowdoin College.

2512 ELLIOTT, VAN COURTLANDT. "Hellenism in the
20th century at Bowdoin." BA, 10 (1935-1936),
81-83.
Teaching of Greek.

2513 FLETCHER, EDWARD GARLAND. Bowdoin, 1794-1944:
occasional stanzas. Portland: Machigonne Pr.,
1944. Pp. 11.

2514 FURBISH, JOHN. Facts about Brunswick, Maine.
[Brunswick: Pejepscot Historical Society],
1976. Pp. 62. Me.
1862-1879.

2515 HAMMOND, ANNE W. "Skolfield: shipbuilders &
seafarers." Down East, 21 (April, 1975), 52-
55, 71.

2516 HASTINGS, CHARLES H. "The eight-oared crews
of fifty years ago." BA, 15 (1940-1941), 107-
111.
Bowdoin College.

2517 HATCH, LOUIS CLINTON. The history of Bowdoin
College. Portland: Loring, Short & Harmon,
1927. Pp. xii, 500.

2518 HAWES, CHARLES T. "The first twenty years of
football at Bowdoin." BA, 13 (1938-1939),
9-12, 56-60.

2519 "HAWTHORNE'S 'Pot-8-0 Club' at Bowdoin College." EIHC, 67 (1931), 225-232.

2520 HELMREICH, LOUISE ROBERTS, ed. Our town:
reminiscences and historical studies of Brunswick, Maine. Brunswick, 1967. Pp. 93. Me.

2521 HERRING, CHARLES MACOMBER. Historical discourse at the semi-centennial of the Berean
Baptist Church of Brunswick, at Brunswick,
September 2, 1890.... Brunswick: H. C. Upton, 1890. Pp. 15.

2522 BRUNSWICK

2522 KIRKLAND, EDWARD CHASE. Brunswick's golden age. Lewiston: C. P. Loring, 1941. Pp. 45.

2523 LADD, HORATIO O. "Life at Bowdoin, 1855-1859." BA, 5 (1930-1931), 110-114.

2524 LINCOLN, CHARLES STUART FESSENDEN. "Close bond between St. Paul's Church and Bowdoin faculty and students." The Northeast, 71 (October, 1944), 8-14.
Includes history of the parish.

2525 _____. The story of the first hundred years of St. Paul's Episcopal Church in Brunswick, Maine, 1844-1944. [Brunswick]: The Church, 1944. Pp. 45.

2526 [LITTLE, GEORGE THOMAS]. Additions and corrections to [the] history of Bowdoin College. n.p., 1887. Pp. [909]-933. MH.
Pagination continued from Nehemiah Cleaveland's history of the college, entry 2506; authorship attributed by Joseph Williamson.

2527 LOCKE, WILLIAM NASH. "The French colony at Brunswick, Maine, a historical sketch." Archives de Folklore, 1 (1946), 97-111.

2528 _____. "Notes on the vocabulary of the French Canadian dialect spoken in Brunswick, Maine." French Review, 19 (1945-1946), 416-422.

2529 _____. Pronunciation of the French spoken at Brunswick, Maine. Greensboro, N.C.: American Dialect Society, 1949. Pp. 201.

2530 LUNT, ROBERT H. "Bowdoin's Graeco-Roman war." BA, 16 (1941-1942), 14-15.
Literary societies.

2531 McINTIRE, GLENN R. "Chi Psi centennial." BA, 19 (November, 1944), 7-8.
Bowdoin College.

2532 "THE MAKING of Maine: H. C. Baxter & Bro." Pine Cone, 2 (Autumn, 1946), 32-38.
Canners.

2533 MALLETT, RICHARD PURINGTON. "Bowdoin leisure, 1840-1846." BA, 21 (May, 1947), 2-3.

2534 MEANS, EDGAR L. "Some baseball recollections of the eighties." BA, 10 (1935-1936), 76-78.
Bowdoin College.

2535 MEDEIROS, JOHN. "'The Orient': the early years." BA, 45 (March, 1971), 6-9.
Student newspaper at Bowdoin College.

2536 MICHENER, ROGER. "Rivals and partners: early literary societies at Bowdoin College." JLibHist, 10 (1975), 215-230.
Philomathian Society (became Peucinian Society in 1807) and the Athenaean Society.

2537 MINOT, JOHN CLAIR and DONALD FRANCIS SNOW, eds. Tales of Bowdoin: some gathered fragments and fancies of undergraduate life in the past and present told by Bowdoin men. Augusta: Kennebec Journal, 1901. Pp. 377.

2538 MINOT, JOHN CLAIR. Theta of Delta Kappa Epsilon: the story of sixty years, 1844-1904; being a historical sketch of ΔKE Fraternity at Bowdoin College, and brief biographies of its members, from its establishment to date. Augusta: Kennebec Journal Print, 1904. Pp. 272.

2539 _____, ed. Under the Bowdoin pines: a second collection of short stories of the life at Bowdoin College written by Bowdoin men. Augusta: Kennebec Journal Print, 1907. Pp. vi, 157.

2540 MITCHELL, WILMOT BROOKINGS. A remarkable Bowdoin decade, 1820-1830: a paper read at a meeting of the Town and College Club, Brunswick, Maine, December, 1950. Brunswick: Bowdoin College, 1952. Pp. 34.

2541 _____. Three score and ten: the Town and College Club, 1884-1954, and historical essay. Brunswick: [Bowdoin College], 1954. Unpaged.

2542 NIXON, PAUL. "Phi Beta Kappa at Bowdoin, 1910-1939." BA, 14 (1939-1940), 74-75.

2543 NORTH, JAMES WILLIAM. "The establishment of a college in the District of Maine." Maine Genealogist and Biographer, 1 (1875-1876), 113-116.
Bowdoin College.

2544 [PACKARD, ALPHEUS SPRING]. "Historical sketch of Bowdoin College." American Quarterly Register, 8 (1835-1836), 105-117.
Author attribution by Joseph Williamson in his "Bibliography of the State of Maine."

2545 _____. Our alma mater: an address delivered before the association of the alumni of Bowdoin College. Brunswick: J. Griffin, 1858. Pp. 49.

2546 PACKARD, CHARLOTTE MELLEN. "A New England college town." American Home Magazine, (1896), 191-199.

2547 PACKARD, GEORGE THOMAS. "Sketch of Bowdoin College." Scribner's Monthly Magazine, 12 (1876), 47-61.

2548 PARSONS, LOUIS A. "St. Paul's Parish, Brunswick, fifty years ago." The North East, 39 (December, 1911), 6-10.

2549 PHI BETA KAPPA. MAINE ALPHA, BOWDOIN COL-
LEGE. Catalogue of the fraternity of Phi
Beta Kappa, Alpha of Maine, Bowdoin College,
Brunswick. Lewiston: Journal Office, 1888.
Pp. 77. MeB.
Prefaced by an historical sketch by Henry
Leland Chapman.

2550 PRINCE, KATHERINE H. "Bowdoin and medicine
since 1921." BA, 8 (1933-1934), 42-43.

2551 [PUTNAM, HENRY]. A description of Brunswick,
Me. in letters, by a Gentleman from South
Carolina, to a friend in that state. (1820)
2d ed. Brunswick, 1823. Pp. 39. MB.

2552 REED, THOMAS BRACKETT. "May training." University Quarterly, 1 (1860), 264-268.
Military display at Bowdoin College in
1836.

2553 RICHARDS, HELEN M. "The 'bad book' which
made good." Yankee, 20 (March, 1956), 41-46.
Harriet Beecher Stowe in Brunswick.

2554 SCHUYLER, MONTGOMERY. "Bowdoin, 1794." Architectural Record, 29 (1911), 151-156.

2555 SEARS, GEORGE B. "The beginning of football
at Bowdoin." BA, 9 (1934-1935), 39-40.

2556 SHIPMAN, WILLIAM D. The early architecture
of Bowdoin College and Brunswick, Maine.
[Brunswick]: Brunswick Publishing, 1973.
Pp. 65.

2557 NO ENTRY.

2558 SILLS, KENNETH CHARLES MORTON. "Bowdoin College." Pine Cone, 3 (Spring, 1947), 18-21.

2559 _____. Joseph McKeen (1757-1807) and the beginnings of Bowdoin College, 1802. N.Y.:
Newcomen Society, 1945. Pp. 28.

2560 "SKETCH of Bowdoin College." HistMag, 2 Ser.,
8 (1870), 371-373.
From the Salem Gazette under the signature
of "Gris."

2561 SLATTERY, CHARLES LEWIS. "Brunswick and Bowdoin College." NEM, New Ser., 5 (1891-1892),
449-469.

2562 SMITH, LINCOLN. "Political leadership in a
New England community." Review of Politics,
17 (1955), 392-409.
1902-1954.

2563 _____. "Power politics in Brunswick: a case
study." Human Organization, 22 (Summer,
1963), 152-158.

2564 _____. "This may happen in Brunswick, Maine."
Social Science, 38 (June, 1963), 140-144.
Town meeting.

2565 _____. "Town manager government--a case
study." Social Science, 33 (January, 1958),
27-35.
1929-1957.

2566 _____. "Town meeting government." Social
Science, 30 (June, 1955), 174-185.

2567 _____. "Unrequited quest for city status--
a case study of 100 years." Rural Sociology,
26 (1961), 170-186.

2568 SMYTH, EGBERT COFFIN. Three discourses upon
the religious history of Bowdoin College,
during the administrations of presidents
M'Keen, Appleton and Allen. Brunswick: J.
Griffin, 1858. Pp. 80.

2569 TILLSON, GEORGE W. "Freshman recollections
of the seventies." BA, 14 (1939-1940), 77-
80.
Bowdoin College.

2570 TITCOMB, JOSEPH, JOHN MARSHALL BROWN and
JOTHAM BRADBURY SEWALL. The Memorial Hall of
Bowdoin College: its history and present
advancement. n.p., [1873]. Pp. 3. MeB.

2571 TOBIE, WALTER E. "Old-fashioned medical
school." Maine Medical Association. Journal,
33 (August, 1942), 175-179.
Bowdoin College.

2572 WEED, ERNEST H. "The river." Down East, 16
(April, 1970), 53-55.
Androscoggin River; reminiscences of a paper
mill worker.

2573 WHEELER, GEORGE AUGUSTUS and HENRY WARREN
WHEELER. History of Brunswick, Topsham and
Harpswell, Maine, including the ancient ter-
ritory known as Pejepscot. Boston: Alfred
Mudge & Son, 1878. Pp. viii, 959.

2574 WHEELER, HENRY WARREN. "Brunswick at the
time of its incorporation." PejHSC, 1 Pt. 1
(1889), 21-45.

2575 _____. "Brunswick wharf." PejHSC, 1 Pt. 1
(1889), 65-66.

2576 WHEELER, WILLIAM A. Brunswick yesterdays, a
boy's eye view of the old town in the early
'80s. Gorham, 1944. Pp. 30. Me.

2577 WHITE, BRUCE H. M. "Delta Kappa Epsilon centennial." BA, 19 (February, 1945), 3-4.
Bowdoin College.

2578 WHITTIER, ISABEL MARY SKOLFIELD. Captain Alfred Skolfield's home, a Victorian mansion.
Brunswick: Brunswick Publishing, 1956. Unpaged. MeHi.

2579 WILDER, GERALD G. "Twenty-five years in Hubbard Hall." BA, 2 (1927-1928), 104-105.
Bowdoin College Library.

2580 WILDER, PHILIP S. "The beginnings of hockey at Bowdoin." BA, 8 (1933-1934), 33-34.

2581 _____. "Bowdoin College." Maine's Own Magazine, 7 (April, 1929), 7, 28, 36.

2582 _____. "The President's House." BA, 27 (February, 1953), 2-3.
Bowdoin College.

SEE ALSO entries 259, 516, and 3532.

BUCKFIELD (OXFORD CO.)

2583 BUCKFIELD, ME. A pictorial history of Buckfield, Maine, 1776-1976. Dixfield: Coburn Farm Pr., 1976. Pp. 55. MeU.

2584 COLE, ALFRED and CHARLES FOSTER WHITMAN. A history of Buckfield, Oxford County, Maine, from the earliest explorations to the close of the year 1900. Buckfield, 1915. Pp. 758.

2585 LONG, ZADOC. From the journal of Zadoc Long, 1800-73. Peirce Long, ed. Caldwell, Id.: Caxton Printers, 1943. Pp. 316.

SEE ALSO entry 3532.

BUCKSPORT (HANCOCK CO.)

2586 BUCK, RUFUS. "Buck family of Bucksport." BHistMag, 2 (1886-1887), 19-22.

2587 _____. "A history of Bucksport, up to 1857." BHistMag, 1 (1885-1886), 65-72, 85-89, 103-108.

2588 BUCKSPORT, ME. The 150th anniversary of Bucksport, Maine, June 25, 1942. Bucksport: Bucksport Free Pr., 1942. Pp. 51. Me.

2589 BUCKSPORT, ME. ELM STREET CONGREGATIONAL CHURCH. 150th anniversary booklet ... 1803-1953. n.p., [1953]. Pp. 13. MBC.

2590 "BUCKSPORT is out on a limb." Yankee, 17 (August, 1953), 14-17.
Monument to Jonathan Buck.

2591 BUCKSPORT, past and present. n.p., 1951. Pp. 54.

2592 BUXTON, PHILIP W. "The Jed Prouty Tavern." Down East, 1 (Winter, 1955), 41-44.

2593 HATCH, FRANCIS WHITING. "Down East western." Yankee, 22 (October, 1958), 30-31.
An 1898 fracas.

2594 _____. "From Bucksport to Broadway: Dustin and William Farnum." Down East, 19 (July, 1973), 72-75, 91-93.

2595 LITTLE, HENRY. "An account of Bucksport in 1827." BHistMag, 6 (1890-1891), 42-45.

2596 MITCHELL, GEORGE O. History of Felicity Lodge, No. 19, Free and Accepted Masons, Bucksport, Maine, from March 14, 1809 to Dec. 1, 1890. Portland: Stephen Berry, 1892. Pp. 118. MeBa.

2597 WEBB, NATHAN B. East Maine Conference Seminary war record. Boston: Albert J. Wright, 1877. Pp. 54.

2598 WHITTEMORE, JAMES O. "The witch's curse, a legend of an old Maine town." NEM, New Ser., 27 (1902-1903), 111-113.

SEE ALSO entries 2082 and 4589.

BURLINGTON (PENOBSCOT CO.)

2599 No items located.

BURNHAM (WALDO CO.)

2600 No items located.

BUXTON (YORK CO.)

2601 BUXTON, ME. Bicentennial, 1772-1972, historical souvenir book, Buxton, Maine, August 10, 11, 12, and 13, 1972. n.p., 1972. Pp. 96. Me.

2602 _____. The one hundred and fiftieth anniversary of the incorporation of the town of Buxton, Maine, held at Buxton Lower Corner, August 16, 1922; with additional history. Portland: Southworth Pr., 1926. Pp. 200.

2603 _____. A report of the proceedings at the celebration of the first centennial anniversary of the incorporation of the town of Buxton, Maine, held at Buxton, August 14, 1872; being a full account of the exercise of the day--historical address ... and a list of the Revolutionary soldiers from Buxton.... Joel M. Marshall, ed. Portland: Dresser, McLellan, 1874. Pp. 288.

2604 BUXTON, ME. PROPRIETORS. Records of the proprietors of Narraganset Township, No. 1, now the town of Buxton, York County, Maine, from August 1, 1733 to January 4, 1811. William F. Goodwin, ed. Concord, N.H.: Priv. Print., 1871. Pp. xx, 400.

2605 COFFIN, CHARLES. "Narraganset Number One, now the town of Buxton, Maine." HistMag, 2 Ser., 4 (1868), 202-204.

2606 COUSENS, ALICE C. and OLIVE W. HANNAFORD. Recollections of Old Buxton, Maine. Farmington: Knowlton & McLeary, 1972. Pp. 173.

2607 LOMBARD, LUCINA HAYNES. "The Garland Tavern." Pine Tree Magazine, 7 (1907), 266-271.

2608 SARGENT, CHARLES F. Pastoral reminiscences. East Brookfield, Mass.: Sargent Holm Pr., [1918?]. Pp. 27. Me.
Buxton Congregational Church.

2609 WILLIAMS, NATHANIEL WEST. An address, delivered at Buxton, Maine, in the Congregational meeting-house, being the first centennial celebration of the settlement of this town ... 1850. Portland: Thurston, 1850. Pp. 34.

2610 WOODMAN, CYRUS. A sermon by Rev. Paul Coffin, D.D. preached August 15, 1762 in Narraganset No. 1, now Buxton, Maine and an address delivered there August 15, 1886 by Cyrus Woodman. Cambridge, Mass.: J. Wilson and Son, 1888. Pp. 95.
Woodman's address is historical; includes a bibliography of works relating to the town.

SEE ALSO entry 2298.

BYRON (OXFORD CO.)

2611 No items located.

C SURPLUS (OXFORD CO.)

2612 No items located.

CALAIS (WASHINGTON CO.)

2613 BOONE, FLORENCE E. Calais schools yesterday and today. Calais: Calais Advertiser, 1948. Pp. 46. Me.

2614 BRUMMITT, HOWARD. "An Episcopalian outpost in northeastern Maine: St. Anne's Church, Calais." The Northeast, 74 (September, 1947), 15-17.

2615 CALAIS, ME. FIRST CONGREGATIONAL CHURCH. A brief history of the First Congregational Church, Calais, Maine; their articles of faith, church covenant, standing rules, questions for self-examination and catalogue of church members. Boston: Printed for the Church, 1855. Pp. 19. MBC.

2616 _____. Historical sketch of the First Congregational Church, Calais, Maine, with confession of faith, rules, and catalogue of members to May, 1877. Boston: Thomas Todd, 1877. Pp. 35. MeHi.

2617 CALAIS, ME. ORDINANCES, ETC. The charter, ordinances, and a brief history of the city of Calais, Maine, together with other matter relating to city affairs. William J. Fowler, comp. Calais: Advertiser Publishing, 1901. Pp. 165.

2618 "THE CENTENARY of St. Anne's." The Northeast, 80 (July, 1953), 2-3.
St. Anne's Church.

2619 CHURCHILL, LAURIE. "The Gregory House." Roots, 1 (Spring, 1975), 26-31.

2620 COLE, SHARON. "Memories of Calais." Roots, 1 (Spring, 1975), 39-42.

2621 GANONG, WILLIAM FRANCIS. Ste. Croix (Dochet) Island. (1902) Susan Brittain Ganong, ed. [2d ed.]. Saint John, N.B., 1945. Pp. xix, 125.

2622 GARDNER, OLIVE. "Retrospective glances." Pine Tree Magazine, 6 (1906-1907), 426-432.

2623 HADLOCK, WENDELL STANWOOD. "Recent excavations at De Monts' Colony, St. Croix Island, Maine." OTNE, 44 (1953-1954), 93-99.

2624 KNOWLTON, ISAAC CASE. Annals of Calais, Maine, and St. Stephen, New Brunswick; including the village of Milltown, Me., and the present town of Milltown, N.B. Calais: J. A. Sears, 1875. Pp. 208.

2625 MAINE HISTORICAL SOCIETY. Tercentenary of De Mont's settlement at St. Croix Island, June 25, 1904. Portland, 1905. Pp. 78.
Includes address by Joshua Lawrence Chamberlain.

2626 MILLIGAN, D. WINFIELD. History of the First Methodist Episcopal Church of Calais, Maine. ... [Calais]: Calais Advertiser Pr., [1935?]. Pp. 19. MBNEH.

2627 PARKER, BARRETT. Saint Croix Island, 1604-1942. Cambridge, Mass.: Crimson Printing, 1942. Pp. 19.

2628 ROGERS, C. TALBOT. "America's first Christmas." Yankee, 25 (December, 1961), 32-33, 100, 102.

2629 SHAW, DONALD E. "Calais Street Railway." Transportation, 3 (January, 1949), 1-4.

2630 SMITH, MASON PHILIP. "Confederate raid on Calais." Down East, 13 (October, 1966), 30-33, 43-45, 48-49.
1864.

SEE ALSO entries 1840-1841, 1844, and 1874.

CAMBRIDGE (SOMERSET CO.)

2631   No items located.

CAMDEN (KNOX CO.)

2632   "A BRIEF historical sketch of the Camden Public Library." MeLB, 16 (1930-1931), 99-100.

2633   CAMDEN, ME. CHESTNUT STREET BAPTIST CHURCH.
The 150th anniversary of the Chestnut Street
Baptist Church, Camden, Maine, 1808-1958.
n.p., [1958]. Pp. 8. MeHi.

2634   CAMDEN, ME. FIRST CONGREGATIONAL CHURCH.
Services in celebration of the 100th anni-
versary of the First Congregational Church,
Camden, Maine, Sept. 10-11-12, 1905. Camden:
Camden Publishing, 1905. Pp. 80. MBC.

2635   ["CAMDEN, Maine."] BTJ, 22 (1909-1910),
321-364.

2636   CAMPBELL, LEROY A. History of the Chestnut
Street Baptist Church of Camden, Me. [Cam-
den]: Camden Pub., 1934. Pp. 28. MeHi.

2637   CHASE, BENJAMIN CHAPMAN. An address ... delivered at Camden, Maine, September 11, 1855,
at the expiration of half a century, from
the organization of the First Congregational
Church in that town; also a brief sketch of
the revival there in the year 1836, names of
church members.... Boston: T. R. Marvin,
1855. Pp. 28.

2638   CROCKETT, FRED E. "The yachts 'Robador' of
Camden." Down East, 22 (September, 1975),
42-45, 70-71.
   Several vessels of the same name owned by
members of the Law family.

2639   CULLER, R. D. Skiffs and schooners. Camden:
International Marine Publishing, 1974.
Pp. 199.

2640   CUMMINGS, MILDRED H. "The golden turrets of
Norumbega." Down East, 21 (August, 1974),
56-59, 88, 92.
   A stone castle built in the 1880s by Joseph
B. Stearns.

2641   DIETZ, LEW. Camden Hills: an informal history of the Camden-Rockport region. Camden:
Camden Herald Pr., 1947. Pp. 93.

2642   LOCKE, JOHN LYMBURNER. Sketches of the history of the town of Camden, Maine; including
incidental references to the neighboring
places and adjacent waters. Hallowell:
Masters, Smith, 1859. Pp. xii, 267.

2643   "A LOVELY English church on the green in
Camden town." The Northeast, 73 (September,
1946), 10-12.
   St. Thomas' Church.

2644   MALCOLM, JOHN. "Maine's historic Conway
House." Down East, 12 (August, 1965), 39-41.

2645   MUNSON, GORHAM BERT. "Parnassus on Penobscot." NEQ, 41 (1968), 264-273.

2646   ROBINSON, REUEL. History of Amity Lodge,
No. 6, Free and Accepted Masons, Camden,
Maine. Camden: Camden Publishing, 1897.
Pp. 103.

2647   "THE SACRIFICE, a tale of the War of 1814."
Eastern Magazine, 1 (1835-1836), 1-13.

2648   "SAINT Thomas' Church, Camden, 1855-1955."
The Northeast, 82 (July, 1955), 10-19.

2649   TEWKSBURY, JOHN LESLIE. History of Camden
Commandery, No. 23, Knights Templar, Camden,
Maine, chartered February 10, 1905. Camden:
Camden Herald Print, 1930. Pp. 95. Me.

2650   WEBBER, JOHN W. "The high mountains of Penobscot: notes on the Camden Hills." Appalachia, 27 (1948-1949), 131-148.

SEE ALSO entries 707, 1653, 1666, 1671, 1673,
1833, 2082, 4589, and 4612.

CANAAN (SOMERSET CO.)

2651   JOHNSON, GEORGE W. History of Carrabasett
Lodge, No. 161, Free and Accepted Masons,
Canaan, Me., from March 2, 1871 to October,
1891. Portland: Stephen Berry, 1892.
Pp. 27. MeBa.

2652   LEWIS, JULIA TUTTLE. "Canaan, Maine." SJMH,
10 (1922), 33-34.

2653   SMITH, LILLIAN CLAYTON. Old Canaan during
the Revolution, by Lillian Clayton Smith;
Grandmother's grandmother, by Louise Helen
Coburn. Skowhegan: Independent Reporter,
1910. Unpaged.

SEE ALSO entry 1816.

CANTON (OXFORD CO.)

2654   FREEMASONS. CANTON, ME. WHITNEY LODGE.
No. 167. History of Whitney Lodge, Canton,
from March 21, A.D. 1872, to December 31,
A.D. 1880. Canton: J. W. Bicknell, 1880.
Pp. 23. [MePGLM].
   Signed by committee of W. H. H. Washburn,
Dana Bradford, and T. C. Wright.

SEE ALSO entry 3532.

CAPE ELIZABETH (CUMBERLAND CO.)

2655 BAXTER, JAMES PHINNEY. "Richmond's Island." MeHSC, 3 Ser., 1 (1904), 66-87.

2656 CAPE ELIZABETH, ME. FIRST CHURCH OF CHRIST. Address and poem delivered at Cape Elizabeth, Maine, September 10, 1884, at the 150th anniversary of the First Church of Christ (North Congregational). Portland: Southworth Bros., 1884. Pp. 27. MeHi.
    Address by Edwin A. Harlow; poem by Louisa E. Harris.

2657 DELANO PARK AND ANNEX ASSOCIATION, CAPE ELIZABETH, ME. History and by-laws of the Delano Park and Annex Association, 1885-1965. n.p., [1965?]. Pp. 21. MeHi.

2658 NO ENTRY.

2659 JORDAN, WILLIAM BARNES, JR. A history of Cape Elizabeth, Maine. Portland: House of Falmouth, 1965. Pp. 385.

2660 NORWOOD, LESLIE E. "The port of Richmond's Island." SJMH, 13 (1925), 100-101.

2661 OGDEN, MARGUERITE. "A visit to an historical island." SJMH, 7 (1919-1920), 154-155.
    Richmond's Island.

2662 RAY, ROGER BRAY. Cape Elizabeth and the American Revolution. Cape Elizabeth, 1975. Unpaged.

2663 REYNOLDS, EDWARD CLAYTON, comp. The Cape Elizabeth High School, a history. Portland: Stevens & Jones, 1892. Pp. 76.

2664 ROERDEN, HAROLD H. Collections from Cape Elizabeth, Maine. Cape Elizabeth: Published by the Town, 1965. Pp. 144.

2665 TRYON, SYLVIA. "Maine's leading light-house." Maine's Own Magazine, 8 (April, 1930), 6.
    Cape Elizabeth Light.

2666 WILLIS, WILLIAM. "Treasure trove in Maine." Bankers Magazine, 10 (1855), 9-12.

    SEE ALSO entries 1265, 1483, 1487, 1492, 1512, 1534, 4202, 4287, and 4820.

CARATUNK PLANTATION (SOMERSET CO.)

2667 CARATUNK, ME. CONGREGATIONAL CHURCH OF CHRIST. The seventy-fifth anniversary service ... August 12, 1962. n.p., [1962]. Pp. 4. MBC.
    Includes a history of the church.

CARIBOU (AROOSTOOK CO.)

2668 CARIBOU, ME. Caribou centennial 1859-1959, week of July 19-25, historical program. [Caribou]: Caribou Publishing, 1959. Pp. 56. Me.

2669 CARIBOU, ME. FIRST UNIVERSALIST CHURCH. Addresses delivered Sunday, January 19, 1975 celebrating the Society's 80th anniversary. n.p., 1975. Unpaged. MeHi.
    Historical addresses by Clara C. Piper, Marjorie A. Crockett, and Earle T. McKinney.

2670 CARTER, GEORGE M. "Caribou--the potato town." Sun Up, 5 (October, 1927), 14-17.

2671 COLLINS, (S. W.) CO., CARIBOU, ME. Lumber than and now: S. W. Collins Co., 1844-1959. Caribou, 1960. Unpaged. MeU.

2672 COLLINS, SAMUEL WILSON, JR. 100 years of lumbering by the Collins family of Caribou, Maine. [Caribou], 1944. Unpaged. Me.

2673 HARDISON, GROVER M. and FRANK W. LOVERING. Romance of the Eaton Grant--part of Caribou Township and early land surveys in Aroostook County. Caribou, 1947. Pp. 22. MeHi.

2674 SINCOCK, LORA K. A history of the First Universalist Church of Caribou, Maine, 1895-1935. n.p., [1935?]. Unpaged. MBC.

2675 WHITE, STELLA KING. Early history of Caribou, Maine, 1843-1895. [Houlton?], 1945. Pp. 147.

    SEE ALSO entry 50.

CARMEL (PENOBSCOT CO.)

2676 No items located.

CARRABASSETT VALLEY (FRANKLIN CO.)

2677 No items located.

CARROLL PLANTATION (PENOBSCOT CO.)

2678 No items located.

CARRYING PLACE TOWN TOWNSHIP (SOMERSET CO.)

2679 No items located.

CARRYING PLACE TOWNSHIP (SOMERSET CO.)

2680   No items located.

CARTHAGE (FRANKLIN CO.)

2681   No items located.

CARY PLANTATION (AROOSTOOK CO.)

2682   No items located.

CASCO (CUMBERLAND CO.)

2683   HOLDEN, WILLIAM CROSS. The story and history of Casco, Maine. Casco, 1941. Pp. 60. Me.

2684   "RATTLESNAKE Mountain has moved." Yankee, 17 (June, 1953), 19-21.

CASTINE (HANCOCK CO.)

2685   ADAMS, GEORGE MOULTON. Castine sixty years ago, a historical address delivered in connection with old home week in Castine, Maine, Sunday evening, August 12, 1900. Boston: Samuel Usher, 1900. Pp. 17.

2686   BALLARD, WILLIAM. "Castine, October 1, 1815 [i.e. 1814]." BHistMag, 2 (1886-1887), 45-51.

2687   BATCHELDER, SAMUEL FRANCIS. "Adventures of John Nutting, Cambridge loyalist." Cambridge [Massachusetts] Historical Society. Publications, 5 (1910), 56-98.

2688   BOURNE, MIRIAM ANNE and RUSSELL BOURNE. "A man for Castine." Yankee, 33 (October, 1969), 76-81, 126-127, 129-131.
        John Perkins.

2689   BOURNE, RUSSELL. "The Penobscot fiasco." Am Heritage, 25 (October, 1974), 28-33.
        Ill-starred attempt to eject British in 1779.

2690   BROOKS, NOAH. "An old town with a history." Century, 24 (1882), 695-708.

2691   [CALEF, JOHN]. The siege of Penobscot by the rebels; containing a journal of the proceedings of His Majesty's forces, detached from the 74th and 82d regiments, consisting of about 700 rank and file, under the command of Captain Brigadier General Francis M'Lean, and of three of His Majesty's sloops of war, of 16 guns each, under the command of Captain Henry Mowat, senior officer; when besieged by three thousand three hundred (rebels) land forces, under the command of Brigadier-General Solomon Lovell, and seventeen rebel ships and vessels of war, under the command of G. Saltonstall, commodore; to which is annexed a Proclamation issued June 15, 1779, by General M'Lean and Captain Barclay to the inhabitants; also Brigadier-General Lovell's proclamation to the inhabitants; and his letter to Commodore Saltonstall, found on board the rebel ship Hunter; together with the names, force, and commanders, of the rebel ships destroyed in Penobscot Bay and River, August 14 and 15, 1779. With a chart of the peninsula of Majabigwaduce, and of Penobscot River. To which is subjoined a postscript, wherein a short account of the country of Penobscot is given. Nathan Goold, ed. N.Y.: W. Abbatt, 1910. Pp. 55.
        Originally published in London in 1781.

2692   CAMPBELL, THOMAS JOSEPH. "A link with the past." CathHistRev, New Ser., 2 (1922), 283-284.
        Early Catholic mission.

2693   CASTINE, ME. The centennial of Castine: an account of the exercises at the celebration of the one hundredth anniversary of the incorporation of the town, July 9, 1896. Castine, 1896. Pp. 67.

2694   "THE CASTINE centennial." The Church Exchange, 6 (1898-1899), 17-21.
        Unitarian Society.

2695   "CASTINE-1814." Wilson Museum Bulletin, 1 (Winter, 1972-73), [1-3].

2696   "A CASTINE summer, 1779." Wilson Museum Bulletin, 2 (Fall, 1975), [1-3].

2697   CAYFORD, JOHN E. The Penobscot Expedition, being an account of the largest American naval engagement of the Revolutionary War. Orrington: C & H Publishing, 1976. Pp. xi, 132. Me.

2698   CLARK, GEORGE FABER. "Military operations at Castine, Maine." Worcester HSProc, 9 (1889), 18-38.
        1525 through the Civil War.

2699   CLAYTON, TOM. "Maine Maritime Academy." Down East, 5 (October, 1958), 16-18.

2700   CUMMINGS, EPHRAIM CHAMBERLAIN. "Capuchin and Jesuit Fathers at Pentagoët." MeHSC, 2 Ser., 5 (1894), 161-188.

2701   DEVEREUX, CHARLENE. Castine then's and now's. n.p., [1966?]. Pp. 24. MeHi.

2702   DRAKE, SAMUEL ADAMS. "The Plymouth trading-house at Penobscot: where was it?" MeHSC, 2 Ser., 3 (1892), 409-418.
        Drake claims it was at Castine.

2703 "EASTERN State Normal School." Maine Teachers' Digest, 1 (1940-1941), 64-65, 75.

2704 EVANS, ELIZABETH EDSON GIBSON. "A new watering place." Harper's New Monthly Magazine, 55 (1877), 345-356.

2705 FELLOWS, RAYMOND. "The trial of Ebenezer Ball." Peabody Law Review, 2 (1937-1938), 43-46, 70-75.
　　Murder of John Tileston Downes in Robbinston in 1811.

2706 FREEMASONS. CASTINE, ME. HANCOCK LODGE, NO. 4. History of Hancock Lodge, No. 4, Free and Accepted Masons, Castine. Portland: S. Berry, 1872-1911. 5v.
　　Volume 5 has imprint: Ellsworth: Hancock County Publishing Company.

2707 GODFREY, JOHN EDWARDS. "Pilgrims at Penobscot." American Historical Record, 3 (1874), 366-371.

2708 "'THE GOOD old days,' a hundred years ago in Castine." Wilson Museum Bulletin, 1 (Summer, 1969), [1-2].

2709 GOOLD, NATHAN. "Colonel Jonathan Mitchell's Cumberland County Regiment: Bagaduce Expedition, 1779." MeHSC, 2 Ser., 10 (1899), 52-80, 143-174.

2710 GOULD, EDWARD KALLOCH. Storming of the heights: Maine's embattled farmers at Castine in the Revolution. Rockland: Courier-Gazette Pr., 1932. Pp. 59.

2711 GREENBIE, SYDNEY and MARJORIE LATTA BARSTOW GREENBIE. Castine, a dramatized biography of a town, in three parts. n.p., Traversity Pr., 1948. Pp. 95.

2712 HARVEY, D. C. "The Halifax-Castine Expedition." Dalhousie Review, 18 (1938), 207-213.
　　War of 1812.

2713 HATCH, FRANCIS WHITING. "Castine--historic gem of Penobscot Bay." Down East, 17 (July, 1971), 66-69, 88, 91.

2714 _____. "Dennett's Wharf." Yankee, 24 (April, 1960), 52-53, 100-102.

2715 _____. "Seagoing bank notes with denominational masts." AmNep, 15 (1955), 213-216.

2716 HATCH, FRIEDA. "Facts of interest concerning Fort George." SJMH, 12 (1924), 47-52.

2717 "HISTORICAL geology of Maine." Wilson Museum Bulletin, 1 (Winter, 1968), [1].

2718 "IN old Castine." MeCathHM, 5 (July, 1915), 38-53.

2719 JACK, EDWARD. "Loyalists at Penobscot." BHistMag, 1 (1885-1886), 97-101.

2720 MUNSON, GORHAM BERT. "St. Castin: a legend revised." Dalhousie Review, 45 (1965), 339-360.

2721 NASH, GILBERT. The original journal of General Solomon Lovell, kept during the Penobscot Expedition, 1779; with a sketch of his life, together with the proceedings of the [Weymouth Historical] Society for 1879-1880. [Weymouth, Mass.]: Weymouth Historical Society, 1881. Pp. 127.

2722 NOE, SYDNEY PHILIP. The Castine deposit: an American hoard. N.Y.: American Numismatic Society, 1942. Pp. 37.

2723 "NOTES on colonial Penobscot." SJMH, 1 (1913-1914), 17-21.

2724 "ONCE upon a time on Perkins Street." Wilson Museum Bulletin, 1 (Winter, 1968), [2-3].

2725 "'QUALITY avenue'--Upper Main Street, Castine." Wilson Museum Bulletin, 1 (Summer, 1974), entire issue.

2726 ROY, LUCIENNE C. "Castine." Women's Canadian Historical Society of Ottawa. Transactions, 9 (1925), 48-54.
　　Castine as an outpost of New France.

2727 "ROYALISTS at Penobscot, Fort George now Castine, 1777, 1782." BHistMag, 5 (1889-1890), 89-91.

2728 SCOTT, KENNETH. "New Hampshire's part in the Penobscot Expedition." AmNep, 7 (1947), 200-212.

2729 SEWALL, RUFUS KING. "Field day of the Maine Historical Society at Castine, Sept. 21, 1880." MeHistMag, 8 (1893), 60-64.
　　Relates to Castine.

2730 SHAW, HENRY I., JR. "Penobscot assault--1779." Military Affairs, 17 (Summer, 1953), 83-94.

2731 SPRAGUE, JOHN FRANCIS. "The proposed province of New Ireland." SJMH, 2 (1914-1915), 219-220.
　　A new British province to be colonized by American loyalists, 1780.

2732 STANWOOD, CORDELIA J. "Castine, a village by the sea." House Beautiful, 48 (1920), 92-94, 126, 128.
　　Historic houses.

2733 STEVENSON, EDWARD IRENAEUS. "The story of Castine, Maine." MagAmHist, 29 (1893), 21-31.

2734 STORM, COLTON. "The relief of Fort George." ColbLibQ, 1 (1943), 60-64.
 Penobscot Expedition, 1779.

2735 SYLVESTER, TORREY A. "Down East naval defeat." Down East, 12 (September, 1965), 32-33, 46-49, 51, 53, 55.
 Penobscot Expedition, 1779.

2736 UPHAM, FRANK KIDDER. Genealogy and family history of the Uphams, of Castine, Maine, and Dixon, Illinois.... Newark, N.J.: Advertiser Printing, 1887. Pp. iv, 68.

2737 WALSH, LOUIS SEBASTIAN. "Old mission site regained by Church." MeCathHM, 8 (1919-1928), 206-211.

2738 WHEELER, GEORGE AUGUSTUS. Castine past and present: the ancient settlement of Pentagöet and the modern town. Boston: Rockwell and Churchill, 1896. Pp. ix, 112.

2739 _____. "Fort Pentagöet and the French occupation of Castine." MeHSC, 2 Ser., 4 (1893), 113-123.

2740 WILLIAMSON, JOSEPH. "The British occupation of Penobscot during the Revolution." MeHSC, 2 Ser., 1 (1890), 389-400.

2741 _____. "Castine, and the old coins found there." MeHSC, 6 (1859), 105-126.

2742 _____. "The conduct of Paul Revere in the Penobscot Expedition." MeHSC, 2 Ser., 3 (1892), 379-392.

2743 _____. "The proposed province of New Ireland." MeHSC, 7 (1876), 199-206.
 A new British province to be colonized by American loyalists, 1780.

2744 _____. "The proposed province of New Ireland." MeHSC, 3 Ser., 1 (1904), 147-157.
 Differs from earlier article above.

2745 _____. "The trial of Ebenezer Ball, at Castine, 1811." BHistMag, 3 (1887-1888), 61-65.
 Accused of killing John Tileston Downes in Robbinston in 1811.

2746 WILSON MUSEUM, CASTINE, ME. Castine. Castine, 1958. Unpaged.

2747 "THE WILSON Museum--on its 50th birthday." Wilson Museum Bulletin, 1 (Spring, 1971), entire issue.

2748 "WINTERS in old Castine." Wilson Museum Bulletin, 1 (Winter, 1973-1974), [1-2].

 SEE ALSO entries 707, 962, 1264, 1597, 1621, 2425, and 4587.

CASTLE HILL (AROOSTOOK CO.)

2749 No items located.

CASWELL PLANTATION (AROOSTOOK CO.)

2750 No items located.

CENTERVILLE (WASHINGTON CO.)

2751 No items located.

CHAIN OF PONDS TOWNSHIP (FRANKLIN CO.)

2752 No items located.

CHAPMAN (AROOSTOOK CO.)

2753 No items located.

CHARLESTON (PENOBSCOT CO.)

2754 SMITH, OSCAR L. History of Olive Branch Lodge, No. 124, of Free and Accepted Masons, Charleston, Me., from A.D. 1864 to A.D. 1881. Portland: Stephen Berry, 1881. Pp. 24. MeBa.

CHARLOTTE (WASHINGTON CO.)

2755 CHARLOTTE, ME. SESQUICENTENNIAL COMMITTEE. Charlotte, Maine, sesquicentennial, 1825-1975, historical souvenir book. n.p., 1975. Pp. 80. Me.

2756 FISHER, LEWIS BEALS. The story of a Down East plantation: facts and fancies about the Pine Tree State. Chicago, 1914. Pp. 219.

CHASE STREAM TOWNSHIP (SOMERSET CO.)

2757 No items located.

CHELSEA (KENNEBEC CO.)

2758 BARTER, J. MALCOLM. "A century at Togus, 1866-1966." Down East, 12 (June, 1966), 34-35, 54-55, 60-61.
 National Home for Disabled Volunteer Soldiers.

2759 WHITMAN, WILLIAM EDWARD SEAVER. History and description of the eastern branch of the National Home for Disabled Volunteer Soldiers, near Augusta, Maine: a complete guide book for visitors. Augusta: Sprague, Owen & Nash, 1879. Pp. viii, 79.

SEE ALSO entries 1624, 1629, and 1648.

CHERRYFIELD (WASHINGTON CO.)

2760 MILLIKEN, JAMES ALPHONSO. "Ancient Narraguagus." MeHistMag, 7 (1891-1892), 162-164.

2761 "125TH anniversary at Cherryfield." MeCP, 45 (December 15, 1958), 10.
First Congregational Church.

SEE ALSO entries 1840, 1864, and 1875.

CHESTER (PENOBSCOT CO.)

2762 BOOKER, MABEL LIBBY. History and genealogy of Chester, Maine.... n.p., [1949?]. Pp. 180.

CHESTERVILLE (FRANKLIN CO.)

2763 BUTLER, BENJAMIN and NATALIE STURGES BUTLER. Father Sewall and his Zion's Hill neighborhood, Chester (Chesterville), Maine, c. 1800. [Chester], 1967. Pp. 65.

2764 SEWALL, OLIVER. History of Chesterville, Maine. Farmington: J. S. Swift, 1875. Pp. 96.

SEE ALSO entry 1419.

CHESUNCOOK TOWNSHIP (PISCATAQUIS CO.)

2765 GETCHELL, DAVID R. "Ghost town--Chesuncook." Down East, 4 (June, 1958), 32-34.

CHINA (KENNEBEC CO.)

2766 CHINA, Maine: a bicentennial history. Weeks Mills: Marion T. Van Strien, 1975. Pp. xi, 290, iii, 121.

2767 JONES, RUFUS M. Reminiscences of South China. [South China]: South China Library Association, 1955. 46 leaves. MeU.

2768 THURLOW, CLINTON F. The Weeks Mills "Y" of the two-footer. [Weeks Mills?], 1964. Pp. 63.
Railroad.

SEE ALSO entry 1645.

CLIFTON (PENOBSCOT CO.)

2769 No items located.

CLINTON (KENNEBEC CO.)

2770 DODGE, A. D. History of Sebasticook Lodge, No. 146, of Free and Accepted Masons, Clinton, Maine, from A.D. 1881 to A.D. 1891. Clinton: B. T. Foster, [1891?]. Pp. 23. MeHi.

2771 FISHER, CARLETON EDWARD. History of Clinton, Maine. Augusta: K. J. Printing, 1970. Pp. x, 409.

2772 HAMMONS, EVERETT. History of Sebasticook Lodge, No. 146, of Free and Accepted Masons, Clinton, Maine, from 1874 to 1881. Clinton: B. T. Foster, 1881. MeHi.

2773 HATCH, M. P. History of Sebasticook Lodge, No. 146, of Free and Accepted Masons, Clinton, Maine, from A.D. 1868, to A.D. 1874. Portland: Stephen Berry, 1875. Pp. 19. MeBa.

SEE ALSO entry 799.

COBURN GORE (FRANKLIN CO.)

2774 No items located.

CODYVILLE PLANTATION (WASHINGTON CO.)

2775 No items located.

COLUMBIA (WASHINGTON CO.)

2776 DAY, CLARENCE ALBERT. Leighton's Store at Epping Lower Corner. n.p., n.d. 6 leaves. MBNEH.

2777 _____. Town affairs in old Columbia. n.p., n.d. 10 leaves. MBNEH.

2778 HARRIS, HERBERT. History of the Tuscan Lodge, Free and Accepted Masons, Columbia, Maine, from its organization in 1798, to its close in 1817. Portland: The Grand Lodge, 1894. Pp. 36.

2779 LEIGHTON, LEVI. Centennial historical sketch of the town of Columbia as gathered from the town records, family records and traditional history from the memory of its aged citizens; from 1796 to 1896. Machias: The Republican, 1896. Pp. 31.

2780 _____. "Sketches in Columbia, Maine." MHGR, 9 (1898), 84-94.
Biographies.

SEE ALSO entry 1856.

COLUMBIA FALLS (WASHINGTON CO.)

2781 BUCKNAM, SAMUEL. "The town of Columbia Falls." BHistMag, 1 (1885-1886), 136-137.

2782 CHAMBERLAIN, SAMUEL. "The Thomas Ruggles House in Columbia Falls, Maine." Antiques, 101 (1972), 367-373.

2783 CRANE, J. R. "Priceless example of a lost art." Yankee, 18 (January, 1954), 60-63.
Woodcarving in the Ruggles House.

2784 DONWORTH, C. B. "The Thomas Ruggles House at Columbia Falls, Maine." SJMH, 10 (1922), 138-139.

2785 GOLDSMITH, MARGARET O. "The Ruggles House at Columbia Falls, Maine." OTNE, 15 (1924-1925), 68-76.

2786 SELIGMANN, HERBERT J. "First flower of the wilderness, the Ruggles House." Down East, 6 (June, 1960), 47-50.

SEE ALSO entry 1856.

COMSTOCK TOWNSHIP (SOMERSET CO.)

2787 No items located.

CONCORD TOWNSHIP (SOMERSET CO.)

2788 No items located.

CONNOR TOWNSHIP (AROOSTOOK CO.)

2789 No items located.

COOPER (WASHINGTON CO.)

2790 No items located.

COPLIN PLANTATION (FRANKLIN CO.)

2791 No items located.

CORINNA (PENOBSCOT CO.)

2792 WOOD, LILLA EVA. A brief history of Corinna, Maine, from its purchase in 1804 to 1916. Bangor: J. P. Bass, 1916. Pp. 55.

CORINTH (PENOBSCOT CO.)

2793 PALMER, MASON SKINNER. Early gleamings and random recollections of the town of Corinth, Maine, from 1792 to 1883. Bangor: B. A. Burr, 1883. Pp. 34.

CORNISH (YORK CO.)

2794 ELLIS, LEOLA CHAPLIN and KERA C. MILLARD. Early Cornish, 1616-1916. n.p., [1972?]. Pp. 135. MBNEH.

2795 _____. More about early Cornish. [Cornish?, 1975]. Pp. 217. MeHi.

2796 FREEMASONS. CORNISH, ME. GREENLEAF LODGE, NO. 117. History of Greenleaf Lodge, No. 117, Cornish, Maine, instituted May 4, A. L. 6863. Portland: Stephen Berry, 1873. Pp. 14. MeBa.

2797 HILLSIDE CONGREGATIONAL CHURCH, CORNISH, ME. Hillside Congregational Church, sixty-fifth anniversary in memory of the Reverend Albert Cole, M.A. ... record of exercises and historical address.... Portland: Southworth, 1905. Pp. 51. MeHi.

2798 SMALL, LAURISTON WARD. The old Baptist Church in Cornish, Maine. Kezar Falls: R. Fult: Wormwood, 1887. Pp. 55. MeHi.

CORNVILLE (SOMERSET CO.)

2799 FOLSOM, EMMA B. "Cornville's old church." Sun Up, 10 (March, 1932), 17, 56.
Built in 1825.

COVE POINT TOWNSHIP (PISCATAQUIS CO.)

2800   No items located.

COX PATENT (AROOSTOOK CO.)

2801   No items located.

CRANBERRY ISLES (HANCOCK CO.)

2802   "THE CRANBERRY Islands." BHistMag, 4 (1888-1889), 22-23.

2803   GROSSINGER, RICHARD. Book of the Cranberry Islands. Los Angeles: Black Sparrow Pr., 1974. Pp. ix, 308.

2804   SPIKER, LA RUE. "The Cranberry Islands." Down East, 13 (May, 1966), 30-35.

        SEE ALSO entries 1570, 1587, and 1617.

CRAWFORD (WASHINGTON CO.)

2805   McKEOWN, JUDY. "The common school." Roots, 1 (Spring, 1975), 52-54.

CRYSTAL (AROOSTOOK CO.)

2806   No items located.

CUMBERLAND (CUMBERLAND CO.)

2807   CHEBEAGUE ISLAND METHODIST HISTORICAL SOCIETY. The church on Chebeague, 1802-1960. n.p., [1960]. Pp. 54. MeHi.

2808   CUMBERLAND CENTRE, ME. CONGREGATIONAL CHURCH. One hundredth anniversary of the Congregational Church, Cumberland Centre, Me., September 21, 1893. Portland: Southworth Bros., 1893. Pp. 64.
        Includes historical addresses by Trueman Summerfield Perry and B. B. Merrill.

2809   HAUK, ZARAH WILLIAM. The stone sloops of Chebeauge and the men who sailed them; also some Chebeague miscellany. (1949) 2d ed. rev. Boston: Alden-Hauk, 1953. Pp. 167. MeHi.

2810   PERRY, TRUEMAN SUMMERFIELD. A sermon, preached on the eighty-fifth anniversary of the Congregational Church, at Cumberland, Maine, September 1, 1878. Portland: Globe Publishing, 1879. Pp. 20.

2811   SWEETSER, MARY E. History of the town of Cumberland, Maine for the centennial celebration, July 2-4, 1921. Yarmouth: A. F. Tilton, [1921?]. Pp. 36. Me.

2812   SWEETSER, PHYLLIS STURDIVANT. Cumberland, Maine in four centuries. Cumberland, 1976. Pp. viii, 351. Me.

2813   WESTON, ISAAC. A history of the Congregational Church and Society in Cumberland, Me. Portland: Brown Thurston, 1861. Pp. 55. MeBa.

CUSHING (KNOX CO.)

2814   SEE entries 1654 and 4660.

CUTLER (WASHINGTON CO.)

2815   CUTLER, Maine. Boston: E. H. Pierce, n.d. Pp. 15. MeHi.

        SEE ALSO entry 962.

CYR PLANTATION (AROOSTOOK CO.)

2816   CYR Plantation centennial, 1870-1970. n.p., [1970?]. Pp. 312.

DALLAS PLANTATION (FRANKLIN CO.)

2817   No items located.

DAMARISCOTTA (LINCOLN CO.)

2818   BERRY, GEORGE STILLMAN. "The great shell mounds of Damariscotta." NEM, New Ser., 19 (1898-1899), 178-188.

2819   CHADBOURNE, PAUL ANSEL. "Oyster shell deposit in Damariscotta." MeHSC, 6 (1859), 347-351.

2820   DUNBAR, ROBERT E. "Lord of the mills: the James Kavanagh House, 1803." Down East, 23 (September, 1976), 40-43, 79.

2821   GOLDTHWAIT, RICHARD P. "The Damariscotta shell heaps and coastal stability." American Journal of Science, 5 Ser., 30 (1935), 1-13.

2822   HILTON, WILLIAM H. History of Alna Lodge, No. 43, Damariscotta, from its institution to April, 1874. Portland: Stephen Berry, 1874. Pp. 24.
        Freemasons; continued by entries 2824 and 2825.

2823 LINCOLN, EDWARD JOSHUA. The Blackstones and
their Indian's paradise (old Damariscotta).
Damariscotta: News Print Shop, 1952.
Pp. 52.
Blackstone family.

2824 MERRY, CHARLES GLIDDEN. History of Alna
Lodge, No. 43, Free and Accepted Masons,
Damariscotta, Me., from April, 1874 to December, 1880. Portland: Stephen Berry,
1883. Pp. 25-40. MeBa.
Pagination continued from a history covering 1823 to April, 1874 by William H. Hilton;
entry 2822.

2825 _____. History of Alna Lodge, No. 43, Free
and Accepted Masons, Damariscotta, Maine,
from 1880 to 1881 ... Part III. Portland:
Stephen Berry, 1891. Pp. 41-68. MeBa.
Pagination continued from previous entry.

2826 WEYGANDT, CORNELIUS. "Red swarms." Yankee,
1 (December, 1935), 28-30.
Shell heaps.

SEE ALSO entries 1678, 1683-1684, 1708-1709,
and 4589.

DANFORTH (WASHINGTON CO.)

2827 LOVE, WILBUR J. A history of Danforth, Maine.
n.p., [1936]. Pp. 64. Me.

SEE ALSO entry 50.

DAVIS TOWNSHIP (FRANKLIN CO.)

2828 NILE, LE ROY. Kennebago summer. Farmington:
Knowlton & McLeary, 1947. Pp. 107.
Social life and customs; Kennebago Lake.

DAYS ACADEMY GRANT (PISCATAQUIS CO.)

2829 No items located.

DAYTON (YORK CO.)

2830 DAYTON, ME. HISTORICAL COMMITTEE. 100th anniversary, Dayton, Maine, 1854-1954. Gorham:
H. F. Brent, [1954]. Unpaged. Me.

DEAD RIVER TOWNSHIP (SOMERSET CO.)

2831 SEE entry 1821.

DEBLOIS (WASHINGTON CO.)

2832 No items located.

DEDHAM (HANCOCK CO.)

2833 EMERY, MARTHA. History of Dedham, Maine.
[Dedham]: Dedham Bicentennial Committee,
[1976]. Pp. 69. MeU.

DEER ISLE (HANCOCK CO.)

2834 ALLEN, MILDRED SELLERS. Deer Isle's history,
comprising that territory now the towns of
Deer Isle, Stonington and Isle au Haut.
Rockland: Courier-Gazette, 1934. Pp. 44.

2835 ALLISON, ROLAND. "Shell heaps around Deer
Isle." MeArchSocB, No. 2 ([October, 1964]),
[3-5, 7].

2836 DEER ISLE, ME. Bicentennial, 1762-1962.
[Deer Isle]: Deer Isle-Stonington Historical
Society, [1962]. Unpaged. Me.
Includes a brief history of the town.

2837 "DEER Isle and settlers." MeHistMag, 8 (1893),
13-16.

2838 ENK, JOHN C. A family island in Penobscot
Bay: the story of Eagle Island. Rockland:
Courier-Gazette, 1973. Pp. vii, 350.

2839 HOSMER, GEORGE LAWRENCE. An historical sketch
of the town of Deer Isle, Maine; with notices
of its settlers and early inhabitants. Boston: Fort Hill Pr., 1905. Pp. 289.

2840 HUTCHINSON, VERNAL R. Deer Isle in the Revolution. Ellsworth: Hancock County Publishing, 1949. Unpaged.

2841 _____. A Maine town in the Civil War: a
chronicle of the vanished town of Old Deer
Isle, Maine, during the crucial years 1861-
1865, as found in town, state and national
records, and as retained in the memories of
the last survivors of that generation. Freeport: Bond Wheelwright, 1967. Pp. 114.
First published in 1957 with title: A
Yankee town in the Civil War.

2842 _____. When revolution came: the story of
Old Deer Isle in the Province of Maine during
the War for American Independence. Ellsworth:
Ellsworth American, 1972. Pp. x, 186.

2843 NOYES, BENJAMIN LAKE. Deer Isle pioneers
(including Stonington) Maine, plus an appendix, Caleb Haskell's war diary. Stonington,
1901 [i.e. 1928]. 104, xxi leaves.

2844 SMALL, HERMAN WESLEY. History of Marine Lodge, No. 122, Free and Accepted Masons, Deer Isle, Me. from its institution March 29, 1864, to January 5, 1914. Portland: Stephen Berry, 1914. Pp. 191. MeHi.

SEE ALSO entries 1553 and 1561.

DENMARK (OXFORD CO.)

2845 DENMARK CONGREGATIONAL CHURCH. The Denmark Congregational Church, Denmark, Maine, centennial anniversary, 1829-1929. n.p., [1929]. Unpaged. Me.

2846 McMULLAN, JEAN G. "Fifty years in Maine." Pine Cone, 7 (Spring, 1951), 3-6.
Camp Wyonegonic.

2847 SANBORN, EVELYN. This way to Denmark: a vignette (somewhat enlarged) of a Maine town. ... Denmark: Cardinal Printing, 1957. Unpaged.

2848 SCRIBNER, FRED C., JR. Remarks by Under Secretary of the Treasury Fred C. Scribner, Jr., on the occasion of the 150th anniversary of the founding of the town of Denmark, Maine, August 10, 1957, 2:30 p.m. n.p., [1957?]. 6 leaves. MeU.

DENNISTOWN PLANTATION (SOMERSET CO.)

2849 SEE entry 3377A.

DENNYSVILLE (WASHINGTON CO.)

2850 DENNYSVILLE, ME. Memorial of the 100th anniversary of the settlement of Dennysville, Maine, 1886. Portland: B. Thurston, 1886. Pp. 115.

2851 DENNYSVILLE, ME. CONGREGATIONAL CHURCH. Exercises in commemoration of the one hundredth anniversary of the Congregational Church, Dennysville, Maine, October 25, 1905. Bangor: O. F. Knowles, [1905]. Pp. 42.
Historical address by Charles Whittier.

2852 DRAPER, RUTH L. W. "Old days--old ways." Down East, 19 (March, 1973), 40-41.
Reminiscences.

2853 _____. "Through the stereoscope." Down East, 15 (June, 1969), 44-47.
Lincoln family and their home.

2854 "HISTORY of Dennysville and vicinity with an account of some of the first settlers there." BHistMag, 6 (1890-1891), 269-272.

SEE ALSO entry 1861.

DETRIOT (SOMERSET CO.)

2855 No items located.

DEVEREAUX TOWNSHIP (WASHINGTON CO.)

2856 No items located.

DEXTER (PENOBSCOT CO.)

2857 BARRON MEMORIAL CONGREGATIONAL CHURCH, DEXTER, ME. Manual of the Barron Memorial Congregational Church, Dexter, Maine. Dexter: Eastern State Publishing, 1889. Pp. 23. MeHi.
Includes an historical sketch.

2858 BRADFORD, E. ALICE. Interesting bits of local history. n.p., [1929]. Pp. 20. Me.

2859 CHASE, HALCYON. The early history of the town of Dexter. Dexter, 1904. Pp. 32.

2860 DEXTER, ME. HIGH SCHOOL. CLASS OF 1916. Brief history of Dexter, prepared by members of the Class of 1916, Dexter High School, as a part of their graduation exercises on the one hundredth anniversary of the incorporation of the town, 1816-1916. Dexter: Eastern Gazette, 1916. Pp. 19.

2861 DEXTER, ME. UNIVERSALIST CHURCH. Souvenir booklet and history of the one hundredth anniversary of the Universalist Church of Dexter, Maine, September 20, 21, 22, 1929. n.p., [1929]. Unpaged. Me.

2862 DEXTER GRAMMAR SCHOOL. CLASS of 1937. Facts and incidents about our town. [Dexter?], 1937. Unpaged. Me.

2863 EASTERN GAZETTE, DEXTER, ME. Dexter, Maine, our town for 150 years, 1801-1951. [Dexter], 1951. Pp. 52. Me.

2864 HAYNES, GEORGE HENRY. The scenic beauties, industries, and resources of Dexter, Maine. Dexter: W. S. Ladd, [189-]. Unpaged. MeHi.

2865 KEENE, HIRAM A. History of the Methodist Episcopal Church, Dexter, Maine, 1822-1900. Dexter: Eastern Gazette, 1900. Unpaged. MeU.

2866 MOWER, ELLA J., comp. History of Dexter. Dexter: Gazette Book and Job Print, 1908. Pp. 14.

2867 ROSS, LELAND A. and FRANK B. ARNOLD. One hundred years of Masonry, history of Penobscot Lodge, No. 39. Dexter: Eastern Gazette, 1922. Pp. 111. Me.

SEE ALSO entry 3532.

DIXFIELD (OXFORD CO.)

2868　DIXFIELD BICENTENNIAL COMMITTEE. The early history of Dixfield, Maine including the section of Mexico near Webb's River. Dixfield: Coburn Farm Pr., 1976. Pp. 92. MeHi.

DIXMONT (PENOBSCOT CO.)

2869　CHADBOURNE, SUMNER J. Recollections of the old meeting house and history of the new Union Church. n.p., [1900?]. Pp. 33. MeBa.

2870　KIMBALL, AMOS. 100th anniversary history of Archon Lodge, A.F. and A.M., East Dixmont, Me., 1866-1966. n.p., [1966]. Pp. 52. MeU.

2871　TOOTHAKER, LLEWELLYN P. and ELEANOR A. TOOTHAKER. The history of Dixmont, Maine. [Dixmont]: Bi-centennial Committee, [1976]. Pp. 77. MeU.
　　Latter portion, by Eleanor Toothaker, updates original work which was delivered as a speech in 1907.

DOLE BROOK TOWNSHIP (SOMERSET CO.)

2872　No items located.

DOVER-FOXCROFT (PISCATAQUIS CO.)

2873　BEASLEY, KATHERINE A. and THOMPSON L. GUERNSEY. Thompson Free Library, fiftieth anniversary, 1898-1948, Dover-Foxcroft, Maine. n.p., 1948. Unpaged.

2874　DAVIS, B. H. "Reminiscences of the old towns of Dover and Foxcroft." SJMH, 11 (1923), 163-166.

2875　"DOVER, Maine." MeHistMag, 9 (1894-1895), 208-210."

2876　EVANS, LISTON P. and ORA L. EVANS. History of Dover-Foxcroft Congregational Church (United Church of Christ), 150th anniversary observance, December 31, 1972. Farmington: Knowlton, McLeary, 1972. Pp. 34. MBC.
　　History for 1822 through 1922 was written in the latter year by Liston P. Evans.

2877　"FAVOR Tavern, Dover." SJMH, 8 (1920), 47-49.

2878　"FOXCROFT centennial." SJMH, 5 (1917-1918), 51-134.

2879　HAYES, CHARLES WELLS. "Joseph Ellery Foxcroft, the original proprietor of the town of Foxcroft, Maine." SJMH, 1 (1913-1914), 150-156.

2880　KENISTON, FRANK WALTER. Biographies of Dover-Foxcroft. Bangor: Furbush-Roberts, 1948. Pp. 154.

2881　KOHN, CLYDE FREDERICK. The history of land use in old Foxcroft, Maine. Orono: University of Maine Pr., 1944. Pp. 32.

2882　LOWELL, MARY CHANDLER, comp. Old Foxcroft, Maine: traditions and memories, with family records. Concord, N.H.: Rumford Pr., 1935. Pp. x, 262.

2883　PARSONS, WILLIS E. "Foxcroft Academy." PCHSC, 1 (1910), 100-117.

2884　PISCATAQUIS OBSERVER, DOVER, ME. The Piscataquis Observer, sixty-fifth anniversary, October, 1902, Dover, Maine. [Dover, 1902]. Pp. 59.

DRESDEN (LINCOLN CO.)

2885　ALLEN, CHARLES EDWIN. History of Dresden, Maine, formerly part of the old town of Pownalborough, from its earliest settlement to the year 1900.... Augusta: Kennebec Journal Print Shop, 1931. Pp. 894.

2886　_____. "Leaves from the early history of Dresden." MeHSC, 2 Ser., 1 (1890), 313-320.

2887　_____. "The old Gardiner Mills now standing at Dresden, Maine." SJMH, 11 (1923), 18-19. Grist and saw mills.

2888　_____. "Rev. Freeman Parker and the church in Dresden." MeHSC, 3 Ser., 1 (1904), 212-220.

2889　_____. "Some Huguenot and other early settlers on the Kennebec in the present town of Dresden." MeHSC, 2 Ser., 3 (1892), 351-379.

2890　BOLTÉ, MARY. "1761 courthouse on the Kennebec." Down East, 22 (July, 1976), 63-67, 90. Pownalborough Court House.

2891　"DEDICATION exercises, memorial boulder and tablet, Dresden, Maine, July 19, 1925." SJMH, 13 (1925), 209-227.

2892　DRESDEN FREE HIGH SCHOOL. A history of Dresden Free High School or Dresden Academy. Wiscasset: Chas. E. Emerson, [1889]. Pp. 40. MeBa.

2893 GARDINER, ROBERT HALLOWELL, b. 1882. "An early settlement on the Kennebec." SJMH, 9 (1921), 83-85.

2894 HALLET, RICHARD. "A frontier courthouse." Down East, 1 (November-December, 1954), 17-19.
Pownalborough Court House.

2895 KERSHAW, GORDON E. "Settling in the district called Frankfort." MeHSN, 10 (1970-1971), 73-83.

2896 MAYERS, CLAYTON W. "The oddest ship ever built in Maine." Down East, 9 (March, 1963), 45, 67-68.
'Experiment' built by James Tupper.

2897 WEST, ALBERT. "A frontier of Massachusetts justice." MassLQ, 42 (July, 1957), 70-74.
Pownalborough Court House.

SEE ALSO entries 1677, 1704, and 1937.

DREW PLANTATION (PENOBSCOT CO.)

2898 No items located.

DUDLEY TOWNSHIP (AROOSTOOK CO.)

2899 No items located.

DURHAM (ANDROSCOGGIN CO.)

2900 ST. JOHN, FREDERIC. "The church on the hill." Maine's Own Magazine, 8 (February, 1930), 16.
South Durham Friends' Meeting House; author's name is a pseudonym.

2901 STACKPOLE, EVERETT SCHERMERHORN. History of Durham, Maine; with genealogical notes. Lewiston: Lewiston Journal, 1899. Pp. vii, 314.

DYER BROOK (AROOSTOOK CO.)

2902 No items located.

DYER TOWNSHIP (WASHINGTON CO.)

2903 No items located.

E PLANTATION (AROOSTOOK CO.)

2904 No items located.

EAGLE LAKE (AROOSTOOK CO.)

2905 No items located.

EAGLE LAKE TOWNSHIP (PISCATAQUIS CO.)

2906 No items located.

EAST MACHIAS (WASHINGTON CO.)

2907 FREEMASONS. EAST MACHIAS, ME. WARREN LODGE, NO. 2. History of Warren Lodge, No. 2, Free and Accepted Masons, East Machias, Me., from its organization to June, 1896. By Herbert Harris.... Machias: The Republican, 1898. Pp. 245.

2908 _____. A history of Warren Lodge, No. 2, Free and Accepted Masons, East Machias, Maine, from September, 1778 to July, 1886. Machias: C. O. Furbish, 1886. Pp. 22.

2909 WASHINGTON ACADEMY, EAST MACHIAS, .ME. Memorial of the centennial celebration, at East Machias, Me., August 7th, 8th and 9th, 1892, commemorative of the founding of Washington Academy. n.p., [1892]. Pp. viii, 149.
Historical address by George F. Talbot.

2910 _____. Washington Academy alumni book; containing brief biographies of the students attending Washington Academy between the years 1823 and 1906. May Pierce, Emily F. Sanborn, Maud Elma Kingsley, comps. [East Machias, 1906?]. Pp. 126.

2911 WHITTIER, HENRY SMITH. East Machias, 1765-1926. Machias: Univ. of Maine, 1975. 2v. MeU.

SEE ALSO entry 603.

EAST MIDDLESEX CANAL GRANT (PISCATAQUIS CO.)

2912 No items located.

EAST MILLINOCKET (PENOBSCOT CO.)

2913 EAST MILLINOCKET, ME. FIRST CONGREGATIONAL CHURCH. The First Congregational Church of East Millinocket, Me. In observance of its fiftieth anniversary, June 17, 1959. n.p., [1959]. Unpaged. MBC.
Includes a history of the church.

2914 MACK, JAMES H. Early history of East Millinocket. n.p., [1951?]. 6 leaves. Me.

2915 TURNER, DANIEL. "Ten years of dramatics in a small high school." The High School Thespian, 9 (January-February, 1938), 8-9.
Schenck High School.

EAST MOXIE TOWNSHIP (SOMERSET CO.)

2916 No items located.

EASTBROOK (HANCOCK CO.)

2917 No items located.

EASTON (AROOSTOOK CO.)

2918 EASTON, ME. Centennial celebration, town of Easton, County of Aroostook, State of Maine, July 9 and 10, 1965. n.p., [1965?]. Unpaged. [MePriT].

SEE ALSO entry 549.

EASTPORT (WASHINGTON CO.)

2919 BROWN, C. DONALD. "Eastport: a maritime history." AmNep, 28 (1968), 113-127.

2920 BUTTERFIELD, CHESTER F. "One hundred years of Methodism in Eastport, Maine." Zion's Herald, (September 4, 1940), 857.

2921 BUTWIN, DAVID. "Portrait of a declining town." Saturday Review, 51 (October 5, 1968), 17-19, 40, 42.

2922 DONNELL, ALBERT. Historical address delivered at the seventieth anniversary of the formation of the Central Congregational Church, of Eastport, Friday, February 8, 1899. Eastport: Sentinel Office, 1889. Pp. 20.

2923 "EASTPORT, farthest east parish in U.S.; has history linked with sea and pearls." The Northeast, 84 (June, 1957), 12-14.
Christ Church.

2924 KILBY, WILLIAM HENRY, comp. Eastport and Passamaquoddy: a collection of historical and biographical sketches. Eastport: Edward E. Shead, 1888. Pp. 505.

2925 _____. The Eastport Sentinel: a historical sketch, 1818-1893. Eastport: Sentinel Pr., 1893. 20 leaves.
Newspaper.

2926 _____. "A New England town under foreign martial law." NEM, New Ser., 14 (1896), 685-698.
British military rule, 1814-1818.

2927 KINGSBURY, ISAAC W. and WENDELL S. HADLOCK. "An early occupation site, Eastport, Maine." MASB, 12 (1950-1951), 22-26.
Shell heap.

2928 LOWRY, LOIS. "Eastport, Maine: the same salty whiff." Yankee, 39 (May, 1975), 66-71.

2929 McINNIS, A. E. "Thunder on Middle Street." Down East, 14 (May, 1968), 36-38, 43, 55-56.
Fire department.

2930 MILLIKEN, FRED G. "Eastport, Maine." Pine Tree Magazine, 6 (1906-1907), 359-366.

2931 "THE PASSING of Fort Sullivan." BTJ, 14 (1901-1902), 75.

2932 SABINE, LORENZO. "Early settlers of Eastport." BHistMag, 1 (1885-1886), 115-118.

2933 _____. "Moose Island and its dependencies, four years under martial law." HistMag, 2 Ser., 7 (1870), 220-229, 317-324.
War of 1812.

2934 TAKACH, STEVE. "Birth of a Maine newspaper: 'The Quoddy Times.'" Down East, 17 (May, 1971), 44-45, 68-74.

2935 VARNEY, MARIANNE. "The easternmost parish in America: the story of Christ Church, Eastport." The Northeast, 74 (July, 1947), 5-6, 9.

2936 VESEY, MAXWELL. "A strange interlude in border history." Dalhousie Review, 30 (1941), 417-424.
British occupation, 1814-1818.

2937 WESTON, JONATHAN DELESDERNIER. The history of Eastport, and vicinity: a lecture, delivered April, 1834, before the Eastport Lyceum. Boston: Marsh, Capen and Lyon, 1834. Pp. 61.

2938 YOUNG, NORMA. "Eastport--the Sunrise City." Down East, 9 (June, 1963), 30-35, 67-69.

SEE ALSO entries 1071, 1840-1841, 1844, 1852, 1859, and 1874.

EDDINGTON (PENOBSCOT CO.)

2939 [HARRISON, O. M.]. Historical sketch of East Eddington area: a review of the early settlement from Meadow Brook to Clifton and the Holden lines. By Burdock Rube, pseud. [Bangor]: Morse-Norris Press, 1942. Pp. 40. Me.

2940 PORTER, JOSEPH WHITCOMB. Memoir of Col. Jonathan Eddy of Eddington, Me.; with some account of the Eddy family, and of the early settlers on Penobscot River. Augusta: Sprague, Owen & Nash, 1877. Pp. 72.

SEE ALSO entry 1762.

EDGECOMB (LINCOLN CO.)

2941 AVERILL, ESTHER C. "Furnished in days gone by for a long dead queen: The Marie Antoinette House in Edgecomb, Maine." Sun Up, 5 (November, 1927), 6, 27, 32.

2942 CHASE, VIRGINIA. "Fanny Stone." Down East, 5 (April, 1959), 22-25.
    Her general store and tenure as postmistress.

2943 _____. "Fort Edgecomb on the Sheepscot." Down East, 4 (July, 1958), 36-39.

2944 _____. "Village library." Down East, 5 (March, 1959), 28, 53-56.

2945 _____. "Village school." Down East, 5 (September, 1958), 30-31, 40-41.

2946 DOGGETT, MARGARET F. "Doggett Castle." Down East, 20 (May, 1974), 13-14, 17-18, 21-22, 24, 28.

2947 LOWELL, W. L. "Fort Edgecomb." MHGR, 8 (1895), 33-34.

2947A PATTERSON, WILLIAM DAVIS. "Old Fort Edgecomb." SJMH, 14 (1926), 165-179.

2948 PITCHER, DONALD T. "A queen's asylum at Wiscasset." Down East, 19 (May, 1973), 66-69.
    Clough House; it was moved to Edgecomb in 1838.

2949 ST. JOHN, FREDERIC. "The house that was built for a queen." Maine's Own Magazine, 8 (January, 1930), 11.
    Marie Antoinette House; author's name is a pseudonym.

2950 SEWALL, RUFUS. History of the Congregational Church, Edgecomb, embracing articles of faith and covenant and a full schedule of members. Portland: Stephen Berry, 1871. Pp. 20. MBNEH.

2951 SEWALL, RUFUS KING. "A refuge for Marie Antoinette in Maine." MeHSC, 2 Ser., 5 (1894), 284-305.
    Clough House.

SEE ALSO entry 1937.

EDINBURG (PENOBSCOT CO.)

2952 No items located.

EDMUNDS TOWNSHIP (WASHINGTON CO.)

2953 HOBART, ISAAC. "A sketch of No. 10, now Edmunds, Washington County, Maine." BHistMag, 1 (1885-1886), 49-52.
    Edited by Peter E. Vose.

SEE ALSO entry 1861.

ELIOT (YORK CO.)

2954 "ALL aboard for Eliot! The history of a depot." Shoreliner, 3 (November, 1952), 43-45.

2955 BUTLER, MARY A. "East Eliot M. E. Church." Old Eliot, 9 (1909), 105-107.

2956 CALDWELL, AUGUSTINE. "The first minister of the First Church, Eliot, Maine, the Rev. John Rogers, and Mrs. Susannah (Whipple) Rogers, his wife." Old Eliot, 7 (1906), 1-14.

2957 CHASE, A. L. "The Eliot Meeting House of 1715 and early religious customs." Old Eliot, 3 (1899), 97-103.

2958 CHASE, EDITH F. "The growth of a grange." Shoreliner, 3 (October, 1952), 41-47.
    John F. Hill Grange.

2959 COLE, AARON BURR and JOHN LEMUEL MURRAY WILLIS, eds. History of the centennial of the incorporation of the town of Eliot, Maine, August 7th-13th, 1910. Eliot: A. Caldwell, 1912. Pp. 133.

2960 COLE, ICHABOD. "Shipbuilders and shipbuilding in Eliot." Old Eliot, 2 (1898), 9-11.

2961 DIXON, JOSEPH H. "Eliot in the Rebellion." Old Eliot, 7 (1906), 157-175.

2962 _____. "Town meetings and current events: Eliot, 1810-1880." Old Eliot, 2 (1898), 109-117.

2963 ELIOT, ME. CONGREGATIONAL CHURCH. Twenty-fifth anniversary of the dedication of the meeting house of the Congregational Church and Society, Eliot, Maine; commemorative services. Eliot: J. A. Coleman, 1906. Pp. 40.

2964 ELIOT HISTORICAL SOCIETY. Twice told tales of old Eliot. Eliot, [1968]. Pp. 42. Me.

2965 ELIOT miscellany: bits of forgotten history. [Eliot?, 1876?]. Pp. 10.

2966 "THE ELIOT Second Advent Church." Old Eliot, 9 (1909), 41-43.

2967 FERNALD, FRANK L. "The naval constructors of Eliot." Old Eliot, 8 (1908), 167-179.
      Biographies.

2968 FERNALD, WILLIAM LINWOOD. "The Hanscoms: a family of shipbuilders." Old Eliot, 2 (1898), 1-9.

2969 FROSST, GEORGE W. "The old Fields Meeting Houses." Old Eliot, 2 (1898), 103-108.

2970 GOOLD, NATHAN. "The Furbush or Furbish family." Old Eliot, 3 (1899), 1-4.

2971 _____. "The old Shapleigh House." Old Eliot, 3 (1899), 13-14.

2972 HAYES, ADA. "A church of their own." Shoreliner, 2 (October, 1951), 61-63.
      East Eliot Methodist Episcopal Church.

2973 "INDIAN mound near the Eliot B. and M. station." Old Eliot, 9 (1909), 39-40.

2974 INGERSOLL, ANNA JOSEPHINE. Greenacre on the Piscataqua. N.Y.: Alliance Publishing, 1900. Pp. 22.

2975 KEEFE, FRANCIS. "The early Hills of Eliot." Old Eliot, 5 (1902), 62-76.
      Hill family.

2976 _____. "Eliot incorporation papers." Old Eliot, 1 (1897), 127-164.

2977 _____. "Eliot Social Library." Old Eliot, 1 (1897), 189-197.

2978 "'THE OLD road.'" Old Eliot, 9 (1909), 28-30.

2979 REEVE, SAMUEL H. "South Eliot M. E. Church." Old Eliot, 9 (1909), 109-111.

2980 "THE SCHOOL house of 1804, school district no. V, Eliot." Old Eliot, 7 (1906), 46-52.

2981 SHAPLEIGH, CHARLES A. "Items of Eliot history." Old Eliot, 7 (1906), 29-33.
      Eliot Academy, the Town House, and the Third Congregational Church.

2982 "SOME facts in the ministry of John Rogers and in the early history of the Congregational Church of Eliot." Old Eliot, 3 (1899), 81-95.

2983 "SOME well known men of the past generation." Old Eliot, 8 (1908), 179-191; 9 (1909), 217-220.

2984 SPINNEY, MARY L. "Witch days in long ago Eliot." Old Eliot, 8 (1908), 139-140.

2985 STACKPOLE, EVERETT SCHERMERHORN. "Josselyn's Point." Old Eliot, 5 (1902), 30-34.

2986 STAPLES, CHARLES J. "The Staples family." Old Eliot, 6 (1903), 37-43.

2987 WILLIS, JOHN LEMUEL MURRAY. "Eliot in the olden time." Old Eliot, 6 (1903), 145-147.

2988 _____. "Eliot in the Revolution." Old Eliot, 7 (1906), 101-156.

2989 _____. "Notes on Eliot." Old Eliot, 1 (1897), 1-6, 9-13.

2990 _____. "The old houses of Eliot." Old Eliot, 1 (1897), 33-34.
      "To be continued," but no more published.

2991 _____. "The physicians of Eliot." Old Eliot, 7 (1906), 176-196.

2992 _____. "Story of Eliot Academy." Old Eliot, 6 (1903), 125-133.

      SEE ALSO entries 987, 1879, 1907, and 1911.

ELLIOTTSVILLE PLANTATION (PISCATAQUIS CO.)

2993 MacDOUGALL, WALTER M. "The Onawa wreck." Down East, 19 (November, 1972), 36-39, 63-65, 68.
      A train wreck on December 20, 1919.

ELLESWORTH (HANCOCK CO.)

2994 BLACK Mansion, Ellsworth, Maine. n.p., n.d. Pp. 24. MeU.

2995 CHILCOTT, JAMES C. and JAMES E. PARSONS. History of Lygonia Lodge, No. 40, Free and Accepted Masons, Ellsworth, Maine, from January 1, 1874 to January 1, 1890. Ellsworth: Hancock County Publishing, 1891. Pp. 45.

2996 CUNNINGHAM, AGNES H. History of Ellsworth, 1763 to 1910. n.p., [1936?]. Unpaged. Me.

2997 DAVIS, ALBERT H. "Early history of Ellsworth, Maine." SJMH, 13 (1925), 228-234.

2998 _____. History of Ellsworth, Maine. Lewiston: Lewiston Journal Printshop, 1927. Pp. 244.

2999 DEANE, JOSEPH AUGUSTUS. History of Lygonia Lodge, No. 40, Free and Accepted Masons, at Ellsworth, Maine, from 1822 to 1874. Revised by John B. Redman. Ellsworth: Hancock County Publishing, 1874. Pp. 57. MeBa.

3000 DEMERS, MABEL GOULD. "Doorways and beyond." Pine Cone, 3 (Summer, 1947), 29-32.
    Black Mansion.

3001 DURNBAUGH, JERRY L. "The Black House." Down East, 2 (July, 1956), 28-31.

3002 ELLSWORTH, ME. Historical record and program, bicentennial celebration, July 20-27, 1963. Bangor: Furbush-Roberts, 1963. Unpaged. Me.
    Includes history by Herbert T. Silsby, II.

3003 _____. Souvenir program, historical sketches, of Ellsworth, Me. n.p., [1925?]. Pp. 44. MeU.
    Includes history by Albert H. Davis.

3004 ELLSWORTH, ME. FIRST CONGREGATIONAL CHURCH. Centennial exercises of the founding of the First Congregational Church and Society in Ellsworth, Maine, September 12, 1912. Ellsworth: Hancock County Publishing, 1913. Pp. 61. Me.

3005 "ELLSWORTH, one of the most pleasant spots on the coast of Maine." Sun Up, 3 (April, 1927), 51-55.

3006 GREEN, FRED C. "Last of the Ellsworth fleet." Down East, 2 (August, 1955), 22-25.
    Schooner "Lavolta."

3007 HADLOCK, WENDELL STANWOOD and DOUGLAS S. BYERS. "Radio carbon dates from Ellsworth Falls, Maine." American Antiquity, 21 (1956), 419-420.

3008 HALE, CLARENCE. "An address delivered by the honorable Clarence Hale at the centennial celebration of the First Congregational Church at Ellsworth, Maine, September 12, 1912." SJMH, 1 (1913-1914), 3-13.

3009 LORD, TRUEMAN C. History of Esoteric Lodge, No. 159, of Free and Accepted Masons, at Ellsworth, Maine, from its organization, Sept. 3, 1870 to Jan. 1, 1891. Ellsworth: Hancock County Publishing, 1891. Pp. 37. [MePGLM].

3010 "MATERIALS for a history of Ellsworth, Me." MeHistMag, 8 (1893), 181-218.

3011 MILES, CARLTON E. "Ellsworth's treasure from historic days." Sun Up, 10 (April, 1932), 12-13, 20.
    Black Mansion.

3012 MILLER, ALICE M. "Back to yesterday: old Black House, Ellsworth, Maine." National Historical Magazine, 72 (1938), 28-29.

3013 MOOR, JOHN LOUDER. "An account of the first settlement of what is now Ellsworth--Union River." BHistMag, 3 (1887-1888), 125-127.

3014 PECK, CALVIN. "History of Ellsworth." BHist Mag, 5 (1889-1890), 106-108.

3015 SILSBY, HERBERT T., II. A church has been gathered: history of the First Congregational Church in Ellsworth, Maine. Ellsworth: Hancock County Publishing, 1962. Pp. 97. MBC.

3016 _____. "Maine river town: Ellsworth." Maine Dig, 2 (Spring, 1968), 74-76, 78.

3017 STANWOOD, CORDELIA J. "The story of Ellsworth, Maine." House Beautiful, 46 (1919), 373-375.
    Historic houses.

3018 STURGES, WALTER KNIGHT. "The Black House, Ellsworth--an Asher Benjamin house in Maine." Antiques, 65 (1954), 398-400.

3019 TREACY, GERALD C. "Father John Bapst, S.J., and the Ellsworth outrage." U.S. Catholic Historical Society. Records and Studies, 14 (1920), 7-19.
    Anti-Catholic sentiment in 1850s and 1860s.

3020 UNION TRUST COMPANY, ELLSWORTH, ME. Seventy-five years of service, 1887-1962. n.p., [1962]. Unpaged.

3021 WASSON, MILDRED. "Up the road to yesterday." Country Life in America, 58 (May, 1930), 65-66, 96, 108.
    Black Mansion.

3021A WHITMORE, ALLAN R. "Portrait of a Maine "Know-Nothing": William H. Chaney (1821-1903); his early years and his role in the Ellsworth nativist controversy, 1853-1854." MeHSQ, 14 (1974-1975), 1-57.

3022 YALLALEE, BUD. "The doll house." Down East, 18 (April, 1972), 42-43, 81, 86-87.
    Doll museum.

    SEE ALSO entries 603, 1569, 1578, 2082, and 4589.

ELM STREAM TOWNSHIP (SOMERSET CO.)

3023 No items located.

EMBDEN (SOMERSET CO.)

3024 WALKER, ERNEST GEORGE. Embden town of yore: olden times and families there and in adjacent towns. Skowhegan: Independent-Reporter, 1929. Pp. xiv, 760.

ENFIELD (PENOBSCOT CO.)

3025 No items located.

ETNA (PENOBSCOT CO.)

3026   CARTER, BERTHA WHEELER. Etna sesquicentennial program, June 13-14, 1970. [Etna?], 1970.
Pp. 15. Me.

EUSTIS (FRANKLIN CO.)

3027   No items located.

EXETER (PENOBSCOT CO.)

3028   No items located.

FAIRFIELD (SOMERSET CO.)

3029   DUREN, GLADYS, RAY TOBEY and CLIFTON HORNE.
Gleanings of the past and present of Fairfield, Maine. n.p., [1963?]. Pp. 46. MeU.
Cover title: 175th anniversary and history of the town of Fairfield, 1788-1963.

3030   "GOOD Will." Sun Up, 5 (November, 1927), 8,
25-27.
Charity.

3031   "GOOD Will Home Association." SJMH, 9
(1921), 196-197.

3032   HINCKLEY, GEORGE WALTER. Fifty years with
the Good Will Record. Hinckley: Good Will
Publishing, 1937. Pp. 149.
Newspaper.

3033   _____. The Good Will idea. Hinckley:
Good Will Publishing, 1929. Pp. 105.

3034   MARTIN, ELEANOR DUTTON. "A living monument."
Pine Cone, 3 (Winter, 1947-1948), 7-13.
Good Will Home Association.

3035   SHETTLEWORTH, EARLE G., JR. "A mark upon the
land: the life and work of Charles D. Lawrence, a mid-nineteenth-century Fairfield,
Maine builder." OTNE, 58 (1967-1968), 31-48.

3036   WINSLOW, WILL P. Early history of Larone.
n.p., 1918. Pp. 26. MeP.

SEE ALSO entries 1421, 3532, and 5041.

FALMOUTH (CUMBERLAND CO.)

3037   NO ENTRY.

3038   BROWN, DAVID A. and EDGAR P. LUND. "Old Falmouth is modern." Maine Townsman, 18 (August, 1956), 14-15, 25-26, (September, 1956),
12-13, 25, (October, 1956), 10-11.

3039   DOW, STERLING THAYER. "Pennyweights and
grains." Mekeel's Weekly Stamp News, 66
(February 25, 1946), 163-164.
Eighteenth-century postal rates.

3040   FALMOUTH, ME. Falmouth, Maine, 250th anniversary, 1718-1968. [Falmouth: Grace Pr.,
1968?]. Pp. 32.

3041   HOLT, ANNE CARROLL PAYSON. "A memorial to the
dead for the benefit of the living: Church of
Saint Mary the Virgin, Falmouth Foreside."
The Northeast, 75 (January, 1948), 17-20.

3042   WALLACE, CHARLOTTE and DONALD WALLACE. E
Pluribus Unum, a story of Falmouth, Maine.
[Falmouth]: Falmouth Historical Society,
1976. Pp. 56. MeHi.

3043   WINSLOW, HOWARD L. A history of Congregation-
alism in Falmouth, 1754-1954.... Portland:
Grace Pr., 1954. Unpaged. MBC.
A history of the Falmouth Congregational
Church.

SEE ALSO entries 1483, 1487, 1492, and 1512.

FARMINGDALE (KENNEBEC CO.)

3044   [WHITE, JESSIE WING], ed. History of town of
Farmingdale, Maine ... 1852-1952. n.p.,
[1952?]. Pp. 85. Me.

SEE ALSO entries 1628 and 1649.

FARMINGTON (FRANKLIN CO.)

3045   ABBOTT, MORETON. "Farmington's August 17th."
Yankee, 31 (August, 1967), 76-77, 118-123.
Concert by Lillian Nordica, August 17, 1911.

3046   ABBOTT SCHOOL, FARMINGTON, ME. The Abbott
School: the Little Blue School founded by
Rev. Samuel Abbot [in] 1844 on [the] estate
of Jacob Abbott. [Farmington?], 1926.
Pp. 48. MeU.

3047   BUTLER, BENJAMIN and NATALIE STURGES BUTLER.
"Early meeting-houses in Farmington, Maine."
Pioneer America, 1 (January, 1969), 27-32.

3048   _____. The Falls: where Farmington, Maine
began in 1776. Farmington: Knowlton &
McLeary, 1976. Pp. 131. Me.

3049   _____. Farmington's musical heritage from
Belcher to 'TDX.' Farmington: Knowlton &
McLeary, 1975. Pp. 48. MeU.

3050   _____. History of the Old South Church,
United Church of Christ, Farmington, Maine,
1814-1965. Farmington: Knowlton & McLeary,
1966. Pp. 258.

3051 _____. Porter and Russell lived on a hill (Farmington, Maine) c. 1800. [Farmington?: Farmington Historical Society?], 1969. Pp. 83.

3052 _____. The Red Schoolhouse neighborhood (Farmington, Maine). Farmington: Farmington Historical Society, 1973. Pp. 79.
Historic houses.

3053 _____. Thomas Wendell moves to Fairbanks (Farmington, Maine) c. 1794. n.p., 1966. Pp. 89.

3054 BUTLER, FRANCIS GOULD. A history of Farmington, Franklin County, Maine, from the earliest explorations to the present time, 1776-1885. Farmington: Knowlton, McLeary, 1885. Pp. 683.

3055 "A CHAPTER of biography, the Solomon Adams family." Franklin Historical Magazine, 1 (April, 1881), 9-26.

3056 DEMERS, MABEL GOULD. "Doorways and beyond." Pine Cone, 4 (Autumn, 1948), 19-21.
Lillian Nordica's birthplace.

3057 FARMINGTON, ME. FIRST CONGREGATIONAL CHURCH. Historical sketch and principles and regulations.... Farmington: Knowlton & McLeary, 1915. Pp. 67. MBC.

3058 _____. Manual of the First Congregational Church in Farmington, Maine, containing a brief sketch of its history, a list of those formerly connected with it, the creed, covenant, and rules, and a list of its officers. Farmington: Knowlton, McLeary, 1884. Pp. 31. [MeFarP].

3059 "FARMINGTON." Pine Cone, 2 (Summer, 1946), 9-13.

3060 FARMINGTON HISTORICAL SOCIETY. Pilgrimage, October 3, 1965, to some homes of "William Allen's new world." Sandy River Township (Farmington) c. 1792. Benjamin and Natalie Sturges Butler, comps. n.p., [1965]. Pp. 23.

3061 "FARMINGTON State Normal School." Maine Teachers' Digest, 1 (1940-1941), 96-97, 110.

3062 "THE FIRST Unitarian Society of Farmington, Maine." The Church Exchange, 4 (1896-1897), 49-50.

3063 FLINT, J. P. "Farmington's banking institutions." BTJ, 23 (1910-1911), 685, 687.

3064 "HISTORICAL notes about Farmington, Maine." SJMH, 14 (1926), 97-99.

3065 MALLETT, RICHARD PURINGTON. University of Maine at Farmington: a study in educational change, 1864-1974. Freeport: Bond Wheelwright, 1974. Pp. xiv, 288.

3066 MALLETT, WILBERT GRANT. "Farmington, a school town." BTJ, 23 (1910-1911), 674-677.

3067 MARCH, HELEN SEARLES. "Let's go back to the farm." OTNE, 25 (1934-1935), 141-144.
Social life and customs.

3068 PARKER, THOMAS. History of Farmington, Maine, from its settlement to the year 1846. (1846) 2d ed. Farmington: J. S. Swift, 1875. Pp. 120.

3069 PURINGTON, GEORGE COLBY. History of the State Normal School, Farmington, Maine; with sketches of the teachers and graduates. Farmington: Knowlton, McLeary, 1899. Pp. v, 204.

3070 STIMPSON, MARY STOYELL. "Farmington, Maine." NEM, New Ser., 30 (1904), 387-403.

3071 YEATON, POLLY. War paint: a historical and pictorial revue of the Old Crow Indian Band. Farmington: Heritage Printing, 1975. Pp. 120. MeU.

SEE ALSO entries 1419 and 3532.

FAYETTE (KENNEBEC CO.)

3072 STURTEVANT, REGINALD H. The Fayette Baptist Church, 1792-1967. [Livermore Falls?, 1967?]. Pp. 64. MeHi.

3073 UNDERWOOD, JOSEPH H. History of Fayette; Russell C. Tuck, ed. Augusta: C. E. Nash, 1956. Pp. 174.
The manuscript of this work is in the Maine State Library.

FLAGSTAFF TOWNSHIP (SOMERSET CO.)

3074 ROUNDY, RODNEY W. "Our Flagstaff Church." MeCP, 39 (January 15, 1952), 8-9.

SEE ALSO entry 1821.

FOREST CITY TOWNSHIP (WASHINGTON CO.)

3075 No items located.

FOREST TOWNSHIP (WASHINGTON CO.)

3076 No items located.

THE FORKS PLANTATION (SOMERSET CO.)

3077   No items located.

FORKSTOWN TOWNSHIP (AROOSTOOK CO.)

3078   No items located.

FORSYTH TOWNSHIP (SOMERSET CO.)

3079   No items located.

FORT FAIRFIELD (AROOSTOOK CO.)

3080   "CHRISTIAN pioneers establish the Apostolic Church: the story of Saint Paul's, Fort Fairfield." The Northeast, 74 (March, 1947), 10-11.

3081   ELLIS, CALEB HOLT. History of Fort Fairfield and biographical sketches. Fort Fairfield: Fort Fairfield Printing, 1894. Pp. 382.

3082   FORT FAIRFIELD, ME. Sesquicentennial observance of the first settlement of Fort Fairfield, Maine, July 22, 23, 24, 1966. n.p., [1966?]. Unpaged. [MeForF].
     Includes brief history by Mrs. Roger L. Durepo.

3083   THE HISTORIC pageant of Fort Fairfield and the Aroostook Valley, produced at the celebration of the centennial of the first settlement of Fort Fairfield, Maine, August 8, 9, and 10, 1916; Eva Winnifred Scates, director.... Fort Fairfield: "Review" Pr., 1916. Pp. 55.

3084   HOPKINS, RUTH. "Fort Fairfield." Sun Up, 5 (October, 1927), 20-21, 23.

3085   TRAFTON, JOHN B. and BENONI T. DURGIN. History of Eastern Frontier Lodge, No. 112, of Free and Accepted Masons, Fort Fairfield, Maine, from A.D. 1862 to 1871. Portland: Stephen Berry, 1871. Pp. 18. MeBa.

SEE ALSO entry 50.

FORT KENT (AROOSTOOK CO.)

3086   DUBAY, GUY. With justice for all. n.p., 1976. Pp. iii, 73. [MeForK].
     Egery et al. vs. Berube, land title case, 1876.

3087   FIRST NATIONAL BANK, FORT KENT, ME. Fort Kent, 1829-1929. Fort Kent, 1930. Pp. 55. Me.

3088   FORT KENT, ME. CENTENNIAL BOOK COMMITTEE. Fort Kent centennial, 1869-1969. n.p., n.d. Pp. 159.

3089   "MADAWASKA Training School--Fort Kent." Maine Teachers' Digest, 2 (1941-1942), 14-15, 49.
     Now the University of Maine at Fort Kent.

SEE ALSO entry 1437.

FOWLER TOWNSHIP (WASHINGTON CO.)

3090   No items located.

FRANKFORT (WALDO CO.)

3091   JONES, ERASMUS ARCHIBALD. History of the town of Frankfort. Winterport: Advertiser Job Print, 1897. Pp. 57.
     Includes the early history of Winterport.

SEE ALSO entry 1282.

FRANKLIN (HANCOCK CO.)

3092   OBERMANN, HENRY B. Franklin, Maine, a history. Franklin: Franklin Historical Society, 1975. Pp. 103.

FREEDOM (WALDO CO.)

3093   No items located.

FREEMAN TOWNSHIP (FRANKLIN CO.)

3094   "OLDEST house in Franklin County." SJMH, 11 (1923), 33-35.
     Dodge Farm.

3095   SEDGLEY, GEORGE BURBANK. The Wellcome family of Freeman, Maine. Israel Riggs Bray, 1808-1890. Henry Solomon Wellcome, 1853-1936. Phillips: Phillips Print Shop, 1939. Pp. 26.

FREEPORT (CUMBERLAND CO.)

3096   "BAPTIST Church in Freeport, Me." American Baptist Memorial, 13 (1854), 335-336.

3097 BARTLETT, ARTHUR. "The discovery of L. L. Bean." Saturday Evening Post, 219 (December 14, 1946), 30-31, 92, 95-97, 99.

3098 BEAN, LEON LEONWOOD. My story: the autobiography of a Down-East merchant. Freeport, 1960. Pp. 163.
    L. L. Bean, sporting goods.

3099 BENSEN, RICHARD A. "Where students go at daybreak's glow." BA, 47 (November, 1973), 24-25.
    L. L. Bean, sporting goods.

3100 DIETZ, LEW. "Bean, Maine, U.S.A." Down East, 16 (March, 1970), 38-41.
    L. L. Bean, sporting goods.

3101 FREEPORT, ME. FIRST PARISH CHURCH, CONGREGATIONAL. A history of the First Parish Church, Congregational, Freeport, Maine, 1774-1959. [Portland]: Fred. L. Tower, 1959. Pp. 29. MeHi.

3102 FREEPORT HISTORICAL SOCIETY AND FREEPORT SESQUICENTENNIAL COMMITTEE. Freeport yesterdays. Freeport, 1970. Unpaged. Me.

3103 "FREEPORT, Maine, past and present." BTJ, 17 (1904-1905), 237-244.

3104 GOULD, JOHN. "Let's go to the old sand farm." Yankee, 32 (October, 1968), 84-85, 152, 155-156.
    "The Desert of Maine."

3105 HAYNES, GEORGE HENRY. Wolf's Neck, the gem of Casco Bay, the charming suburb of Freeport, Maine, with its many important industries, and superior granite productions. Portland, 1890. Pp. 31.

3106 HENDERSON, RUTH. "Casco Castle." Down East, 10 (July, 1964), 42-43.
    A hotel destroyed by fire in 1914.

3107 HOSMER, MIRIAM. "Old days on Bustins Island." Down East, 15 (June, 1969), 60-61.

3108 "L. L. Bean's bonanza: how a Maine man improved the hunting boot and founded the firm that made Freeport famous." Down East, 1 (April, 1955), 38-40.

3109 NASON, REUBEN. "A topographical and historical sketch of Freeport, county of Cumberland, and District of Maine." MHSC, 2 Ser., 4 (1816), 176-184.

3110 RICHARDSON, MRS. EDWIN A. "The birthplace of the State of Maine." SJMH, 3 (1915-1916), 169-171.
    Papers separating Maine from Massachusetts were signed in Jameson's Tavern, March 15, 1820.

3111 RICHARDSON, GEORGE B. History of Bustins Island, Casco Bay, 1660-1960. Bustins Island, 1960. Pp. 84.

3112 TALBOT, LOUISA. South Freeport notes. n.p., [1972?]. Unpaged. Me.

3113 THURSTON, FLORENCE G. and HARMON S. CROSS. Three centuries of Freeport, Maine. Freeport, 1940. Pp. x, 254.

SEE ALSO entry 3532.

FRENCHTOWN TOWNSHIP (PISCATAQUIS CO.)

3114 No items located.

FRENCHVILLE (AROOSTOOK CO.)

3115 FRENCHVILLE, ME. ST. LUCE PARISH. Livre d'or de la Paroisse Ste. Luce, 1843-1943. n.p., [1943?]. Unpaged.

FRIENDSHIP (KNOX CO.)

3116 ENDURING friendships, by Roger F. Duncan et al. Al Roberts, ed. Camden: International Marine Publishing, 1970. Pp. 74.
    Friendship sloops.

3117 JONES, HERALD A., ed. It's a Friendship. Friendship: Friendship Sloop Society, 1965. Pp. 95.

3118 MORSE, IVAN. Friendship Long Island. Middletown, N.Y.: Whitlock Pr., 1974. Pp. v, 140. MeU.

3119 VOGEL, C. WILLIAM. Friendship: 150 years. Orono, 1957. 12 leaves. Me.

SEE ALSO entry 1654.

FRYEBURG (OXFORD CO.)

3120 AMES, NATHANIEL P. Story of Lovewell's fight. [Medford, Mass., 190-?]. Pp. 14.

3121 BARROWS, JOHN STUART. "Fryeburg." NEM, New Ser., 9 (1893-1894), 33-45.

3122 _____. Fryeburg, Maine, an historical sketch. Fryeburg: Pequawket Pr., 1938. Pp. 309.

3123 BEEBE, RICHARD W. The first 200 years: the history of the First Congregational Church, Fryeburg, Maine. Center Conway, N.H.: Walker's Pond Pr., 1975. Pp. 118.

3124 BICKFORD, GAIL H. "Lovewell's fight, 1725-1958." AmQ, 10 (1958), 358-366.

3125 _____. "Lovewell's fight, 1725-1975." Down East, 21 (April, 1975), 50-51, 72.

3126 CHAMBERLAIN, GEORGE WALTER. "John Chamberlain, the Indian fighter at Pigwacket." MeHSC, 2 Ser., 9 (1898), 1-14.
    1725.

3127 DAVEIS, CHARLES STEWART. An address delivered on the commemoration at Fryeburg, May 19, 1825. Portland: James Adams, Jr., 1825. Pp. 64.
    Centennial of the Pigwacket fight.

3128 ECKSTORM, FANNIE HARDY. "Pigwacket and Parson Symmes." NEQ, 9 (1936), 378-402.
    New evidence to refute Thomas Symmes, chronicler of the Pigwacket fight.

3129 ENGLISH, J. S. "Captain Lovewell's fight with Paugus." Pine Tree Magazine, 5 (1906), 456-458.
    Pigwacket fight.

3130 EVANS, GEORGE HILL. Pigwacket: Part I, old Indian days in the valley of the Saco. [Conway, N.H.:], Conway, N.H. Historical Society, 1939. Pp. 135.
    No more published.

3131 FRYEBURG, ME. The centennial celebration of the settlement of Fryeburg, Me., with the historical address, by Rev. Samuel Souther. ... Worcester, Mass.: Tyler & Seagrave, [1864]. Pp. 79.

3132 FRYEBURG Webster centennial, celebrating the coming of Daniel Webster to Fryeburg, 100 years ago, to take the principalship of Fryeburg Academy; Fryeburg, January 1st, 1902. Fryeburg: A. F. Lewis, 1902. Pp. 83.

3133 HARVEY, GEORGE A. The First Congregational Church, Fryeburg, Maine, a brief history, 1775-1963. [Fryeburg?], 1963. Pp. 22. MBC.

3134 THE ILLUSTRATED Fryeburg Webster memorial. Fryeburg: A. F. & C. W. Lewis, 1882. Pp. 39.

3135 KIDDER, FREDERIC. The expeditions of Capt. John Lovewell, and his encounters with the Indians; including a particular account of the Pequauket battle, with a history of that tribe, and a reprint of Rev. Thomas Symmes's sermon. Boston: Bartlett & Halliday, 1865. Pp. 138.

3136 LEWIS, ALONZO FREEMAN. Festival of the Fryeburg septuagenarians born in 1834; held at Fryeburg, Maine, August 9th, 1904. Fryeburg, 1904. Pp. 143.

3137 [LINCOLN, ENOCH]. The village: a poem. Portland: Edward Little, 1816. Pp. 180.

3138 LOVEJOY, DAVID SHERMAN. "Lovewell's fight and Hawthorne's 'Roger Malvin's Burial.'" NEQ, 27 (1954), 527-531.
    Pigwacket fight as the source for a Hawthorne tale.

3139 "LOVEWELL'S fight." WMHJ, 1 (1825-1826), 20-26.

3140 McCLINTOCK, JOHN NORRIS. "Lovewell's War." BSM, 1 (1884), 80-83.

3141 "175TH anniversary of [the] Fryeburg Church." MeCP, 146 (June, 1950), 18.

3142 RIEDEL, WESLEY U. "Fryeburg Academy." MeCP, 29 (May, 1942), 5-6, 46.

3143 "THE SEVEN covered bridges of Fryeburg." Down East, 13 (August, 1966), 52-55.

3144 SMITH, SEBA. "Lovewell's fight." The Ladies' Companion, 13 (1840), 199-201.

3145 SYMMES, THOMAS. The original account of Capt. John Lovewell's "great fight" with the Indians, at Pequawket, May 8, 1725. (1725) A new edition with notes by Nathaniel Bouton. Concord, N.H.: P. B. Cogswell, 1861. Pp. vi, 48.
    First edition has title: Lovewell lamented.

3146 WHITE, JOHN. Scout journals, 1725: journal of Capt. John White, one of the scouts during Lovewell's War in northern New England. G. Waldo Browne, ed. Manchester, N.H.: Priv. Print., 1907. Pp. 11.

3147 WINSOR, JUSTIN. "Lovewell's fight with the Indians." MHSP, 2 Ser., 3 (1886-1887), 259-260.

GARDINER (KENNEBEC CO.)

3148 BARSTOW, JAMES S. My Tilbury town. [N.Y.?], 1939. Pp. 11.
    Author's memories of Gardiner during his youth and that of Edwin Arlington Robinson.

3149 BEANE, C. H. Souvenir of the flood of March 2, 1896 with an historical sketch of Gardiner. n.p., [1896]. Unpaged. Me.

3150 "THE CATHOLIC Church in Gardiner: notes on her early history." MeCathHM, 6 (1916), 45-48.

3151 CHADWICK, EDMUND ALEXANDER and J. N. STODDARD. History of Hermon Lodge, No. 32, of Free and Accepted Masons, Gardiner, Maine, from January 23, 1820, to January, 1870. Gardiner: G. O. Bailey, 1870. Pp. 58. [MePGLM].

3152 CLASON, O. B. "Wide awake Gardiner." BTJ, 20 (1907-1908), 561-568.

3153 COOPER, JOHN H. "An account of the Gardiner Lyceum, the first trade school established in the United States." Journal of the Franklin Institute, 140 (1895), 275-287.

3154 DUNN, CHARLES, JR. "Oaklands." Pine Tree Magazine, 7 (1907), 158-166.
Home of the Gardiner family.

3155 DUNN, GERALD C. and WILLIAM S. FOWLER. "An Indian campsite on Cobbosecontee Stream." MASB, 12 (1950-1951), 1-8.

3156 ERSKINE, ROBERT J., LAUREN M. SANBORN and ELMER D. COLCORD. The Gardiner story, 1849-1949: historical sketches of the plantation, town, city, and noted people. Gardiner: The City, 1949. Unpaged.

3157 FOSSETT, MILDRED B. "For over 125 years, a sentinel of the Episcopal Church: Christ Parish, Gardiner, Maine." The Northeast, 74 (May, 1947), 3-6.

3158 GARDINER, ME. The centennial of Gardiner: an account of the exercises at the celebration of the one hundredth anniversary of the incorporation of the town, June 25, 1903. Gardiner, 1903. Pp. 79.
Includes a sketch of Gardiner's early history by Josiah S. Maxcy.

3159 GARDINER, ME. BOARD OF TRADE. The city of Gardiner, Maine, U.S.A.; its water power, industries, water front, picturesque avenues, attractions and surroundings.... [Gardiner], 1896. Pp. 112.

3160 _____. Gardiner and Bostonians: 55 years of progress. [Gardiner, 1951?]. Unpaged. MB.
Commonwealth Shoe and Leather Company; Bostonian shoes.

3161 GARDINER, ME. FIRST CONGREGATIONAL CHURCH. Semi-centennial of the Congregational Church in Gardiner, July 28, 1885; historical address by Rev. Richard W. Jenkins. Gardiner: E. W. Morrell, 1885. Pp. 29. MBC.

3162 GARDINER, ME. FIRST UNIVERSALIST CHURCH. One hundredth anniversary of the First Universalist Church of Gardiner, Maine, observed on Sunday, February 7, 1943, celebration on Tuesday, May 18, 1943. n.p., [1943]. Unpaged. Me.

3163 GARDINER SAVINGS INSTITUTION. Seventy-fifth anniversary of the Gardiner Savings Institution, June 26th, 1909. [Gardiner], 1909. Pp. 48. MeHi.

3164 GILMORE, EVELYN LANGDON. Christ Church, Gardiner, Maine: antecedents and history. Gardiner: Reporter-Journal Pr., 1893. Pp. 157.
A 1962 reprint published by the Kennebec Journal includes "A continuation of the story of Christ Church," by John Richards (70 pp.).

3165 HALE, ENOCH. History and description of an epidemic fever, commonly called spotted fever, which prevailed at Gardiner, Maine, in the spring of 1814. Boston: Wells and Lilly, 1818. Pp. xvi, 246.

3166 HATHAWAY, GEORGE E. "Gardiner post-offices past and present." SJMH, 10 (1922), 100-101.

3167 LEANE, JOHN J. "When mummies made paper in Maine." Yankee, 35 (February, 1971), 64-65, 112, 115.
Importation of rags from Egypt by I. Augustus Stanwood.

3168 MAXCY, JOSIAH SMITH. Centenary of Christ Church, Gardiner, Maine; historical address, May 31, 1920. n.p., [1920?]. Unpaged.

3169 MORRELL, HIRAM KELLY. "The newspapers and serials of Gardiner, with sketches of men connected with them." MPAP, 41 (1904), 46-56.

3170 "REMINISCENCES of Gardiner." MeCathHM, 6 (1916), 37-41.
Catholics.

3171 RICHARDS, LAURA ELIZABETH HOWE. Laura E. Richards and Gardiner. Augusta: Gannett Publishing, 1940. Pp. 152.

3172 ROBBINS, LINVILLE W. Annals of the people called Methodists in the city of Gardiner, Me. Augusta: Kennebec Journal, 1900. Pp. 93. MeHi.

3173 SMITH, DAVID CLAYTON. "Coastal shipping trade on the eve of the railroad: Gardiner, Maine in the early 1830's." MeHSQ, 13 (1974-1975), 148-177.

3174 STEVENS, NEIL E. "America's first agricultural school." The Scientific Monthly, 13 (1921), 531-540.
Gardiner Lyceum.

3175 WEBSTER, HENRY SEWALL. History of Hermon Lodge, No. 32, of Free and Accepted Masons, Gardiner, Maine, from January 1st, 1870 to April 1st, 1880. Gardiner: R. B. Caldwell, 1880. Pp. 35. Me.

SEE ALSO entries 1221, 1628, 1633, 1637, 1642, 1649, and 3532.

GARFIELD PLANTATION (AROOSTOOK CO.)

3176　No items located.

GARLAND (PENOBSCOT CO.)

3177　GARLAND, ME. CONGREGATIONAL CHURCH. One hundredth anniversary of the Congregational Church, Garland, Maine, June 13, 1911. Dexter: Gazette Book and Job Print, 1912. Pp. 20. MeBa.

3178　OAK, LYNDON. History of Garland, Maine. Dover: Observer Publishing, 1912. Pp. xii, 401.

GEORGETOWN (SAGADAHOC CO.)

3179　ALLEN, CHARLES EDWIN. "Light-keeper of old Seguin, a footnote to history." NEM, New Ser., 36 (1907), 700-702.
　　　John Polereczky; served 1796-1802.

3180　CRANSHAW, FLORENCE F. A history of the first one hundred years of the Island Home Club of Five Islands, Maine. [Georgetown]: Island Home Club, 1972. Pp. 90, 7. Me.

3181　ETNIER, ELIZABETH. On Gilbert Head: Maine days. Boston: Little, Brown, 1937. Pp. 272.

3182　GILMAN, STANWOOD CUSHING and MARGARET COOK GILMAN. Georgetown on Arrowsic: the ancient dominions of Maine on the Kennebec, 1716-1966; 250th anniversary celebration. [Georgetown?, 1966]. Pp. 26.

3183　THAYER, HENRY OTIS. "Georgetown, Maine: the ancient and the modern." SJMH, 3 (1915-1916), 91-92.

　　　SEE ALSO entry 1806.

GILEAD (OXFORD CO.)

3183A　CHAPMAN, GEORGE WHITEFIELD. Brief history of Gilead, and prose and poetic writings. 3rd ed., with additions. Portland, 1867. Pp. 139.

3184　"GILEAD and gold." BTJ, 18 (1905-1906), 313-314.

GLENBURN (PENOBSCOT CO.)

3185　BERRY, CLYDE G. and NAIDA J. GALLANT. The story of a town: Glenburn, 1822-1972. n.p., [1972]. Pp. 109.

GLENWOOD PLANTATION (AROOSTOOK CO.)

3186　No items located.

GORE A2 (PISCATAQUIS CO.)

3187　No items located.

GORHAM (CUMBERLAND CO.)

3188　BARKER, R. MILDRED. "History of Union Branch, Gorham, Maine, 1784-1819." Shaker Quarterly, 7 (1967), 64-82.
　　　Shakers.

3189　COTTON, FRANCES MESERVE. "The old Hugh McLellan House." SJMH, 4 (1916-1917), 17-19.

3190　DOLE, SAMUEL THOMAS. "Little Falls, a chapter of local history." MeHSC, 2 Ser., 9 (1898), 197-206.

3191　EMERY, DANIEL C. History of Harmony Lodge, to which is added some notice of the Morgan excitement. Portland: Stephen Berry, 1870. Pp. 48.
　　　Freemasons and antimasonry.

3192　FERRIS, LEONARD ZENAS. Sermon delivered before the society of the First Congregational Church ... at Gorham, Maine, September 24, 1877. Portland: Stephen Berry, 1877. Pp. 26. MBC.
　　　A history of the church.

3193　GORHAM, ME. Bicentennial commemoration of the incorporation of the town of Gorham, Maine, 1764-1964. Portland: Bryant Pr., 1964. Pp. 18. Me.

3194　_____. Celebration of the one hundred and fiftieth anniversary of Gorham, Maine, May 26, 1886. Portland: B. Thurston, 1886. Pp. 133.
　　　Addresses by Elijah Kellogg, John A. Waterman, George B. Emery, Edward Robie, C. W. Deering, and George L. Prentiss.

3195　"GORHAM, Maine." BTJ, 15 (1902-1903), 41-54.

3196　GORHAM SAVINGS BANK. Heritage one hundred, Gorham Savings Bank, Gorham, Maine, 1868-1968. [Gorham, 1968?]. Pp. 23. MeHi.

3197　"GORHAM State Normal School." Maine Teachers' Digest, 1 (1940-1941), 144-145, 162-163.
　　　Now the University of Maine at Portland-Gorham.

3198　HUNTINGTON, HENRY STRONG. A farewell sermon; preached in the Congregational Church, Gorham, Maine, June 12, 1887. Portland: Brown Thurston, 1887. Pp. 21.
　　　Includes an historical appendix.

3199 JOHNSON, WALTER H., comp. Bi-centennial history of Gorham, Maine, 1736-1936: an account of the anniversary celebration of the town. Westbrook: Henry S. Cobb, 1936. Pp. 171.

3200 LOMBARD, LUCINA HAYNES. "The Codman House." Pine Tree Magazine, 7 (1907), 338-339.

3201 _____. "Gorham, Maine, in the days of Gorham's first school teacher." SJMH, 7 (1919-1920), 29-34.

3202 _____. "Longfellow's vacations at Gorham." Pine Tree Magazine, 7 (1907), 21-27.

3203 McLELLAN, HUGH DAVIS. History of Gorham, Me. Katharine B. Lewis, comp. and ed. Portland: Smith & Sale, 1903. Pp. 860.

3204 MAINE. STATE TEACHERS COLLEGE, GORHAM. An account of the establishment of the State Normal School and of the exercises at the dedication of the new school building, Dec. 26, 1878. Portland: Daily Pr., 1879. Pp. 36.
Now the University of Maine at Portland-Gorham.

3205 NASON, REUBEN. A valedictory address on relinquishing the charge of Gorham Academy, August 19, 1834. Portland: Mirror Office, 1834. Pp. 14.
Includes a brief history of the academy.

3206 OAK, LYNDON. A sketch of the life of General James Irish of Gorham, Me., 1776-1863. Boston: Lee & Shepard, 1898. Pp. 70.

3207 PIERCE, JOSIAH. The centennial anniversary of the settlement of Gorham: an address delivered on May 26, 1836. Portland: Charles Day, 1836. Pp. 36.

3208 _____. A history of the town of Gorham, Maine. Portland: Foster & Cushing, 1862. Pp. iv, 239.

3209 ROMAINE, LAWRENCE B. "A country doctor's finances." CEAIA, 2 (1937-1944), 129-130.
Joseph S. G. Hitchcock.

3210 SOCIETY OF COLONIAL WARS. MAINE. The fort at Gorhamtown, 1744-1764. n.p., 1930. Pp. 24. MBNEH.
Historical address by Isaac W. Dyer.

SEE ALSO entries 799, 1493, and 1508-1509.

GORHAM GORE (FRANKLIN CO.)

3211 No items located.

GOULDSBORO (HANCOCK CO.)

3212 "AN ACCOUNT of Gouldsborough, Maine." MeHist Mag, 7 (1891-1892), 67-71.

3213 BRAZER, ESTHER STEVENS. "The tinsmiths of Stevens Plains." Antiques, 35 (1939), 294-296; 36 (1939), 134-136.

3214 COLE, ERNEST H. "Last of its kind." Yankee, 30 (November, 1966), 76-78.
Hunting match in 1900.

3215 DAUGHTERS OF LIBERTY. GOULDSBORO, ME. Historical researches of Gouldsboro, Maine. Gouldsboro, 1904. Pp. 108.

3216 HADLOCK, WENDELL STANWOOD. The Taft's Point shell mound at West Gouldsboro, Maine. [Bar Harbor: Robert Abbe Museum], 1939. Pp. 30.

3217 McKINNEY, STEPHEN N. "Don't give up the bell." Yankee, 37 (May, 1973), 84-87, 123-125.

3218 MERRIAM, ANN VAN NESS. Glimpses into other days of Prospect Harbor. [Prospect Harbor?]: Woman's Club of Prospect Harbor, [1964?]. Unpaged.

3219 RICH, LOUISE DICKINSON. The peninsula. (1958) Riverside, Conn.: Chatham Pr., 1971. Pp. 285.
A republication of the 1958 edition with the addition of one new chapter.

3220 SMITH, WALTER BROWN. The Jones Cove shell heap at West Gouldsboro, Maine. Bar Harbor: Sherman Publishing, 1929. Pp. 28.

SEE ALSO entry 1579.

GRAFTON TOWNSHIP (OXFORD CO.)

3221 FOBES, CHARLES BARTLETT. Grafton, Maine: a human and geographical study. Orono: Univ. Pr., 1951. Pp. v, 29.

3222 WOOD, RICHARD GEORGE. "Obituary for a township." Appalachia, 28 (1950-1951), 465-466.

GRAND FALLS PLANTATION (PENOBSCOT CO.)

3223 No items located.

GRAND ISLE (AROOSTOOK CO.)

3224 No items located.

GRAND LAKE STREAM PLANTATION (WASHINGTON CO.)

3225 ATKINSON, MINNIE. Hinckley Township: or, Grand Lake Stream Plantation, a sketch. Newburyport, Mass.: Newburyport Herald Pr., 1920. Pp. 122.

GRAY (CUMBERLAND CO.)

3226 BUTLER, BENJAMIN and NATALIE STURGES BUTLER. "The Mayall Woolen Mill: first in the United States." Down East, 17 (September, 1970), 29, 31-32, 35, 71, 74, 77.

3227 ST. JOHN, FREDERIC. "The birth of an industry." Maine's Own Magazine, 8 (April, 1930), 18.
Woolen industry; author's name is a pseudonym.

3228 _____. "Gray, once New Boston." Sun Up, 8 (November, 1930), 18.
Author's name is a pseudonym.

GREAT POND PLANTATION (HANCOCK CO.)

3229 No items located.

GREENBUSH (PENOBSCOT CO.)

3230 No items located.

GREENE (ANDROSCOGGIN CO.)

3231 MOWER, WALTER LINDLEY. History of the Old Baptist Church of Greene and read at the 140th anniversary. n.p., 1934. Pp. 7. Me.

3232 _____. Sesquicentennial history of the town of Greene, Androscoggin County, Maine, 1775 to 1900, with some matter extending to a later date. Auburn: Merrill & Webber, 1938. Pp. xiv, 578.

GREENFIELD (PENOBSCOT CO.)

3233 No items located.

GREENVILLE (PISCATAQUIS CO.)

3234 DIETZ, LEW. "100 years at the same old stand: D. T. Sanders & Son, a famous Maine store, celebrates its centennial." Down East, 4 (September, 1957), 32-34.

3235 "THE ELIZABETH House." The Northern, 6 (May, 1926), 7.
Hotel.

3236 LANDER, DONNA and CATHERINE SKINNER. A brief history of Greenville, Maine and Mountain View Farm. n.p., [1971?]. Unpaged. MeBa.

3237 LORING, AMASA. "Early history of Greenville." The Northern, 6 (October, 1926), 3-5.

3238 SHAW, CHARLES D. "History of the Shaw family with a sketch of Milton G. Shaw of Greenville." PCHSC, 1 (1910), 424-433.

3239 _____. "Some facts relating to the early history of Greenville and Moosehead Lake." PCHSC, 1 (1910), 52-65.

3240 SMITH, EDMUND WARE. "Greenville, Maine." Pine Cone, 9 (Summer, 1953), 18-21.

3241 TRUE, EMMA J. History of Greenville, 1836-1936. Augusta: Augusta Pr., [1936]. Pp. 36. Me.

GREENWOOD (OXFORD CO.)

3242 No items located.

GRINDSTONE TOWNSHIP (PENOBSCOT CO.)

3243 No items located.

GUILFORD (PISCATAQUIS CO.)

3244 GUILFORD, ME. Guilford, Maine sesquicentennial. Milo: Milo Printing, 1966. Pp. 112. MBNEH.

3245 "GUILFORD centennial, 1816-1916." SJMH, 4 (1915-1916), 67-190.

3246 HUDSON, HENRY. "Some facts in regard to the early history of the town of Guilford." PCHSC, 1 (1910), 35-51.

3247 WADE, ABNER TURNER, L. H. WHITTIER, and W. L. BATES. History of Mount Kineo Lodge, No. 109, Free and Accepted Masons, Guilford, Maine, from its organization in 1861 to June, 1946. Guilford: Guilford Recorder Print, 1946. Pp. 185. Me.

SEE ALSO entry 1782.

HALLOWELL (KENNEBEC CO.)

3248 ALLEN, WILLIAM, 1780-1873. "Now and then." MeHSC, 7 (1876), 267-287.

3249 BAKER, HENRY KNOX. The Hallowell book. Hallowell: Register Pr., 1902. Pp. 51.

3250 BOARDMAN, SAMUEL LANE. "Hallowell and its library." NEHGR, 34 (1880), 293-297.
 Hubbard Free Library.

3251 CRANDALL, CHRISTINE. "Old Hallowell ... on the Kennebec." Down East, 9 (August, 1962), 32-35, 60-62, 64, 70.

3252 FREEMASONS. HALLOWELL, ME. ROYAL ARCH MASONS. History of Jerusalem Royal Arch Chapter, Hallowell, Maine. Hallowell: Masters & Livermore, 1876. Pp. 80

3253 FULLER, GEORGE. "Hallowell, the granite city of Maine." BTJ, 20 (1907-1908), 521-523, 525-526.

3254 "GOLDEN jubilee celebration at St. Matthew's Church, Hallowell." The North East, 38 (December, 1910), 3-4.

3255 GOLDSMITH, MARGARET O. "Two early homes in Hallowell, Maine." House Beautiful, 55 (1924), 361-364, 410, 412.
 Vaughan House and Merrick House.

3256 HALLOWELL, ME. City Hall dedication and Hallowell reunion, with oration, poem, letters and register of visitors, Wednesday, July 12, 1899. Hallowell: Register Pr., 1899. Pp. 43.

3257 HALLOWELL SAVINGS INSTITUTION. The record of fifty years: Hallowell Savings Institution, 1854-1904. Portland: Lakeside Pr., [1904]. Pp. 32. Me.

3258 HUBBARD FREE LIBRARY, HALLOWELL, ME. Address and poem at the dedication of the Hallowell Public Library, March 9, 1880, with historical sketch. Portland: Hoyt, Foss & Donham, [1880]. Pp. 66.
 Address is by Henry Vaughan Emmons; poem is by Emma Huntington Nason.

3259 HUNT, FITZ HERBERT L. A walking tour through Hallowell, Maine, in the late 1800's with "Bert" Hunt. Augusta: KJ Printing, 1966. Pp. 31.

3260 MAINE. INDUSTRIAL SCHOOL FOR GIRLS, HALLOWELL. By-laws and statutes ... of the Maine Industrial School for Girls at Hallowell [and] a historical sketch of its establishment.... Augusta: Sprague, Owen & Nash, 1875. Pp. 27. MeHi.

3261 MARSTON, DOROTHEA M. Old Hallowell on the Kennebec: the first ninety years, 1762 to 1852. [Hallowell?], 1962. 58 leaves. Me.

3262 NASON, EMMA HUNTINGTON. Old Hallowell on the Kennebec. Augusta: Burleigh & Flynt, 1909. Pp. 359.

3263 NORTON, EDWARD PREBLE. Legends and otherwise of Hallowell and Loudon Hill.... Augusta: Charles E. Nash & Son, 1923. Pp. 77. MeBa.

3264 PAGE, ANNIE FRAZIETTE. Historical sketch of the South Congregational Church of Hallowell. ... Hallowell: Register Pr., 1900. Pp. 43. MeBa.

3265 RIGBY, HAZEN F. "The Church in Maine's smallest city: the story of Saint Matthew's Parish, Hallowell." The Northeast, 75 (March, 1948), 14-17.

3266 SNELL, KATHERINE H. and VINCENT P. LEDEW. Historic Hallowell. [Augusta]: Kennebec Journal Print Shop, 1962. Pp. 112.

3267 VAUGHAN, WILLIAM WARREN. Hallowell memories. Hallowell: Priv. Print., 1913. Pp. 187.
 Vaughan family.

3268 WATKINS, MALCOLM. "A regional collection of glass lamps." Antiques, 39 (1941), 249-250.

3269 WIGHT, CHARLES A. Doorways of Hallowell, with historical sketches. Augusta: Kennebec Journal, [1907]. Pp. 37. Me.

 SEE ALSO entries 1637, 1650, and 3532.

HAMLIN PLANTATION (AROOSTOOK CO.)

3270 No items located.

HAMMOND PLANTATION (AROOSTOOK CO.)

3271 No items located.

HAMMOND TOWNSHIP (SOMERSET CO.)

3272 No items located.

HAMPDEN (PENOBSCOT CO.)

3273 CHAPMAN, HARRY J. "The Battle of Hampden." SJMH, 2 (1914-1915), 185-193.
 September 3, 1814.

3274 COTTLE, LAURA BICKFORD. "My one-room schoolhouse." Down East, 18 (April, 1972), 24, 27-28, 30.

3275   HAMPDEN, ME. FIRST CONGREGATIONAL CHURCH.
Manual of the First Congregational Church in
Hampden, Maine. Bangor: C. H. Glass, 1910.
MBNEH.
    Includes historical sketch.

3276   HAMPDEN HISTORICAL SOCIETY. Historical
sketches, Hampden, Maine, 1767-1976. Ellsworth: Ellsworth American, 1976. Pp. 172.
MeBa.

3277   HOLT, GEORGE D. "The Lawrence Silver Mining
Co., of Hampden, Penobscot County, Maine."
Maine Mining Journal, 2 (September 17, 1880),
183.

3278   MATHEWS, SAMUEL WORCESTER. History of Mystic
Lodge, No. 65, of Free and Accepted Masons,
Hampden, Maine, from March 1st, 1857 to
March 1st, 1875. Bangor: G. O. Bailey, 1875.
Pp. 27. [MePGLM].

3279   "TOWN of Hampden." BHistMag, 2 (1886-1887),
25-32.

HANCOCK (HANCOCK CO.)

3280   CRABTREE, ALFRED B. and HATTIE B. MARTIN.
Hancock, 1828-1928. Augusta: Kennebec
Journal, 1928. Pp. 90.

3281   CURRIER, ISABEL. "A castle in Maine." Down
East, 16 (October, 1969), 42-44, 49, 69, 72.
    Cuniculocus Castle, home of Altea and Neva
Austin.

3282   "THE FABULOUS 'cat castle.'" Yankee, 18
(March, 1954), 18-21.
    Home of Altea and Neva Austin.

    SEE ALSO entries 1569, 1579, and 1586.

HANOVER (OXFORD CO.)

3283   SEE entry 2289.

HARFORDS POINT TOWNSHIP (PISCATAQUIS CO.)

3284   No items located.

HARMONY (SOMERSET CO.)

3285   McLAUGHLIN, CHARLES CARROLL. Harmony's history, happenings, habits and humor ... to
1962. Skowhegan: Skowhegan Press, [1962?].
Pp. 96. Me.

HARPSWELL (CUMBERLAND CO.)

3286   ALEXANDER, WILLIAM T. Harpswell on Casco Bay:
its early history and shipbuilding. Portland: Print Shop, 1973. Pp. iii, 251.

3287   BAILEY, FRANK LINWOOD. Home folks of Harpswell and other poems. Plymouth, Mass.:
Rogers Print, 1961. Unpaged. MeHi.

3288   BAILEY ISLAND CHURCH. Bailey Island Church,
Bailey Island, Maine, 1885-1935. n.p. [1935].
Unpaged. MeHi.

3289   DOUGHTY, WILLIAM H. Historical sketch of
Orr's Island, with landscape descriptions.
Portland: Six Towns Times Print, 1899.
Pp. 53.

3290   HARPSWELL, ME. CONGREGATIONAL CHURCH. Sou-
venir of Elijah Kellogg Church. Franklin,
Mass.: Franklin Job Print, 1911. Unpaged.
MBC.

3291   JUST a peek at Orr's & Bailey Island, Maine.
Orr's Island: Orr's and Bailey Island Sports-
men's Club, [not before 1949]. Unpaged.
MeHi.

3292   LORING, AMASA. "A venerable tabernacle."
MHGR, 1 (1884), 85-86.
    Elijah Kellogg Church.

3293   MAGILL, ROBERT N. A short history of Damariscove Island. Walpole: Ira C. Darling Center,
1975. Pp. 5. MeP.

3294   MERRIAM, MRS. PELEG. "Historic old church at
Harpswell Center." Congregationalism in
Maine, 13 (1926), 27.
    Elijah Kellogg Church.

3295   MURPHY, THOMAS E. "Elijah's church: ye call
me chief and they still do." NEG, 9 (Spring,
1968), 12-22.
    Elijah Kellogg Church.

3296   O'CONNOR, THOMAS P. "Memento of Merryconeag."
Steamboat Bill, 27 (1970), 204-205.
    Fire aboard the Merryconeag at Orr's Island,
November 29, 1918.

3297   ROLLINS, RUTH. "One-of-a-kind: the cribstone
bridge." Down East, 22 (May, 1976), 58-59,
79.

3298   ROUX, WILLAN C. "Admiral Peary's quarter."
Yankee, 30 (August, 1966), 77-79, 102, 105-
106, 109.

3299   _____. "The bridge that divided a town."
Yankee, 30 (March, 1966), 68-69, 137-141.

3300 SINNETT, CHARLES NELSON. Historic Harpswell, Harpswell, Maine, its historic Congregational Church and famous ministers, 1758-1903. Haverhill, Mass.: C. C. Morse & Son, 1903. Pp. 19.

3301 THOMAS, MIRIAM STOVER. Harpswell in the American Revolution. n.p., [1976]. 18 leaves. MeU.

3302 _____. "South Harpswell's old tide mill." Down East, 19 (September, 1972), 21-23.

3303 THWING, ANNIE HAVEN. The story of Orr's Island, Maine. Boston: Geo. H. Ellis, 1925. Pp. 18.

3304 TODD, MARGARET and CHARLES TODD. Beautiful Harpswell: the Neck and its 45 island jewels. [Orr's Island?, 1967]. Pp. 58.

3305 WAUGAMAN, CHARLES A. "Harpswell's club for all seasons." Down East, 17 (June, 1971), 54-55, 77, 79-81.
        Harpswell Garden Club.

3306 WEST HARPSWELL BAPTIST CHURCH. One hundred years, 1836-1936, West Harpswell Baptist Church, West Harpswell, Maine. n.p., [1936]. Unpaged.
        Historical sketch by Mrs. Charles K. Durgan.

3307 WILL, RICHARD T. Digging up pre-history in southern coastal Maine. Tuscon, Ariz.: Alphagraphics, 1976. Pp. iv, 41. MeU.

        SEE ALSO entry 2573.

HARRINGTON (WASHINGTON CO.)

3308 SEE entries 603, 1864-1865, and 1875.

HARRISON (CUMBERLAND CO.)

3309 MOULTON, ALPHONSO, HOWARD L. SAMPSON, and GRANVILLE FERNALD. Centennial history of Harrison, Maine, containing the centennial celebration of 1905, and historical and biographical matter. Portland: Southworth Printing, 1909. Pp. xii, 727.

3310 RIDLON, GIDEON TIBBETTS. Early settlers of Harrison, Maine, with an historical sketch of the settlement, progress and present condition of the town. Skowhegan: Kilby & Woodbury, 1877. Pp. 138.

3311 WARD, ERNEST E. My first sixty years in Harrison, Maine. Denmark: Cardinal Printing, 1967. Pp. 92.

HARTFORD (OXFORD CO.)

3312 No items located.

HARTLAND (SOMERSET CO.)

3313 HARTLAND, ME. 1820, Hartland, Maine, 1970. n.p., [1970]. Pp. 83. Me.
        Historical sketch by F. Wayne Libby.

HAYNESVILLE (AROOSTOOK CO.)

3314 "HISTORY of Haynesville." Liberty Bell, 1 (1934), 5-16.
        A publication of the Haynesville Junior High School; a copy is in the Maine State Library.

HEBRON (OXFORD CO.)

3315 BEARCE, ROGER M. and HAROLD E. HALL. A history of the Hebron Church, 1791-1966, the first 175 years. Hebron, 1966. Pp. 67. MWA.

3316 BONNEY, PERCIVAL. "William Barrows--John Tripp." MeHSC, 2 Ser., 3 (1892), 149-186.

3317 HEBRON, ME. BAPTIST CHURCH. Manual of the Baptist Church in Hebron, Maine, including its history, covenant, articles of faith, standing rules, and list of members' names, August, 1854. Portland: Brown Thurston, 1854. Pp. 24. MeBa.

3318 HEBRON ACADEMY. Hebron Academy: some thoughts on its history and its accomplishments, 1804-1954. [Hebron]: Record Pr., 1954. Unpaged.

3319 _____. Semi-centennial celebration of Hebron Academy, at Hebron, Maine, September 5, 1855. Paris: W. A. Pidgin, 1855. Pp. 39.

        SEE ALSO entry 4049.

HERMON (PENOBSCOT CO.)

3320 HERMON, ME. Sesquicentennial souvenir and history of Hermon, Penobscot County, Maine, 1814-1964. n.p., [1964]. Pp. 36.

3321 HERMON, ME. HISTORICAL COMMITTEE. Centennial souvenir and history of Hermon, Penobscot County, Maine, 1814-1914. Frank A. Bishop, Roscoe W. Snow, and Annie Mayhew, comps. Carmel: Carmel Print, [1914]. Pp. 33.

HERSEY (AROOSTOOK CO.)

3322   No items located.

HERSEYTOWN TOWNSHIP (PENOBSCOT CO.)

3323   DINGLEY, THEDA C. "Summit Farms of Maine."
        Sun Up, 2 (May, 1926), 11, 36-37.
            Dairy farm in the village of Davidson.

HIBBERTS GORE (LINCOLN CO.)

3324   No items located.

HIGHLAND PLANTATION (SOMERSET CO.)

3325   No items located.

HIRAM (OXFORD CO.)

3326   DUNN, CHARLES, JR. "Wadsworth Hall." Pine
        Tree Magazine, 7 (1907), 33-44.
            Estate of Peleg Wadsworth, Longfellow's
        grandfather.

3327   "EARLY history--Hiram, Maine." Maine Idler,
        1 (August, 1950), 7.

3328   HIRAM, ME. Official program ... one hun-
        dredth anniversary.... Cornish: Webb-Smith,
        [1914]. Pp. 34. MeHi.
            Includes history by Llewellyn Andrew Wads-
        worth.

3329   TEG, WILLIAM. History of Hiram. (1941)
        Sesquicentennial [i.e. rev. and enl.] ed.
        Cornish: Carbrook Pr., 1964. Pp. 137.

3330   WADSWORTH, LLEWELLYN ANDREW. "First settle-
        ment of Hiram, Me." Maine Genealogist and
        Biographer, 2 (1876-1877), 94-96.

        SEE ALSO entry 168.

HOBBSTOWN TOWNSHIP (SOMERSET CO.)

3331   No items located.

HODGDON (AROOSTOOK CO.)

3332   SCOTT, G. M. "W. H. Harding, potato barrel
        king of Aroostook." Down East, 22 (October,
        1975), 58-61.

HOLDEN (PENOBSCOT CO.)

3333   SEE entry 1762.

HOLEB TOWNSHIP (SOMERSET CO.)

3334   SEE entry 3377A.

HOLLIS (YORK CO.)

3335   LOMBARD, LUCINA HAYNES. "The first Baptist
        church in Maine." SJMH, 8 (1920), 34-35.

HOPE (KNOX CO.)

3336   HOPE, ME. Hope chronicle, census, history,
        statistics, business directory, etc. Union:
        Union Publishing, 1888. Pp. 32. MeHi.

        SEE ALSO entry 1833.

HOPKINS ACADEMY GRANT (PENOBSCOT CO.)

3337   No items located.

HOULTON (AROOSTOOK CO.)

3338   "AN ACCOUNT of Houlton, Me." BHistMag, 3
        (1887-1888), 14-15.

3339   BARNES, ANNA. "History of postal affairs in
        Houlton." Houlton Local Postal Guide, 1
        (January, 1901), 1-9.

3340   [BARNES, FRANCIS]. The story of Houlton from
        the public records, and from the experiences
        of its founders, their descendants, and asso-
        ciates to the present time.... Houlton:
        Will H. Smith, 1899. Unpaged.

3341   COTTON, PERCY G. "The faithful shepherding
        of God's flock: the record of the Church of
        the Good Shepherd, Houlton." The Northeast,
        74 (November, 1947), 4-6.

3342   HOULTON, ME. Houlton has its 150th birthday:
        souvenir program, sesquicentennial celebra-
        tion, August 17-24, 1957. Roland Atchison,
        comp. Houlton: Aroostook Print Shop, [1957].
        Unpaged.

3343   "HOULTON, the Aroostook capital." New North-
        east, 1 (1894), 35-49.

3344   "HOULTON--the gateway city to the garden of
        Maine." Sun Up, 3 (June, 1927), 27-30.

3345 [KENDALL, JOSEPH and GEORGE H. GILMAN].
History of the town of Houlton, (Maine),
from 1804 to 1883. By an old pioneer.
Haverhill, Mass.: C. C. Morse & Son, 1884.
Pp. 60.

3346 PUTNAM, AMOS. A history of Monument Lodge,
No. 96, 1858-1939. Houlton, [1939?].
Pp. 83. [MeHoC].
Freemasons.

3347 PUTNAM, CORA M. CARPENTER. The story of
Houlton. Portland: House of Falmouth,
1958. Pp. 423.

3348 [_____]. Supplement to [the] story of Houlton. n.p., [1969?]. Unpaged. [MeHoC].

3349 RICH, GEORGE B. "Ricker still pioneers."
Pine Cone, 7 (Spring, 1951), 7-11.
Ricker College.

3350 "RICKER Classical Institute and Junior College." Sun Up, 8 (October, 1930), 13, 31.
Now Ricker College.

3351 RICKER COLLEGE, HOULTON, ME. The RCI story,
Ricker Classical Institute, Houlton, Maine.
[Houlton, 1961?]. Pp. 8. [MeHoR].

3352 SALVATION ARMY, HOULTON, ME. 62nd anniversary, 1888-1950, Salvation Army Corps, Houlton, Maine. n.p., [1950?]. Unpaged.
[MeHoR].

3353 SHIRETOWN saga. [Houlton?, 1957?]. 38
leaves. [MeHoC].
Bicentennial pageant, August, 1957.

3354 SPAULDING, ROYAL CRAFTS. Autobiographical
sketch of Rev. Royal Crafts Spaulding, and
extracts from letters of himself, and of his
wife, Jerusha Bryant Spaulding. Francis
Barnes, ed. Houlton: W. H. Smith, 1891.
Pp. 53.

3355 THIBADEAU, WILLIAM JARVIS. The Irishman, a
factor in the development of Houlton; a
history of the Parish of St. Mary's; a word
about the Acadians of Madawaska. Augusta:
Kennebec Journal, [1910?]. Pp. 109. MBNEH.

SEE ALSO entries 50 and 1463.

HOWLAND (PENOBSCOT CO.)

3356 No items located.

HUDSON (PENOBSCOT CO.)

3357 No items located.

INDIAN ISLAND PENOBSCOT INDIAN RESERVATION (PENOBSCOT CO.)

3358 No items located.

INDIAN STREAM TOWNSHIP (SOMERSET CO.)

3359 No items located.

INDIAN TOWNSHIP STATE INDIAN RESERVATION (WASHINGTON CO.)

3360 No items located.

INDUSTRY (FRANKLIN CO.)

3361 ALLEN, WILLIAM, 1780-1873. History of Industry, Maine, from the first settlement in
1791. (1854) 2d ed., improved and enl.
Skowhegan: Smith & Emery, 1869. Pp. 48.

3362 HATCH, WILLIAM COLLINS. A history of the
town of Industry, Franklin County, Maine,
from the earliest settlement in 1787 down to
the present time, embracing the cessions of
New Sharon, New Vineyard, Anson and Stark; in
two parts, including the history and genealogy
of many of the leading families of the town.
Farmington: Knowlton & McLeary, 1893.
Pp. xiv, 862.

ISLAND FALLS (AROOSTOOK CO.)

3363 SAWYER, NINA G., comp. A history of Island
Falls, Maine, from its settlement in 1843 to
its centennial year 1972, and a collection of
historical sketches. [Island Falls, 1972].
Pp. 154.

ISLE AU HAUT (KNOX CO.)

3364 BATES, ARLO. "Isle au Haut." Outing, 6
(1885), 649-656.

3365 EUSTIS, ELIZABETH B. "Acadia's Isle au Haut
area." National Parks Magazine, 26 (January-
March, 1952), 14-17, 37-40.

3366 ISLE AU HAUT, ME. UNION CONGREGATIONAL
CHURCH. Union Congregational Church of Isle
au Haut, Maine, 1857-1957. Cambridge, Mass.:
Riverside Pr., 1957. Pp. 20.
The copy at the Maine State Library is
signed "Mary Hubbard French, author."

3367 ISLE AU HAUT

3367 "ISLE au Haute papers." BHistMag, 3 (1887-
1888), 1-5.
Origin of the name.

3368 PRATT, CHARLES. Here on the island; being
an account of a way of life several miles
off the Maine coast. N.Y.: Harper & Row,
1974. Pp. 178.

SEE ALSO entries 611, 1561, 2834, 2836, and
2840-2842.

ISLESBORO (WALDO CO.)

3369 COOK, JOEL. An Islesboro sketch. [Boston]:
Boston Photogravure, 1890. Pp. 36.

3370 DANIELS, CAROLINE T. LE FAVOR. Facts and
fancies and repetitions about Dark Harbor,
by one of the very oldest cottagers. Cambridge, Mass.: Cosmos Pr., 1935. Pp. 58.

3371 FARROW, JOHN PENDLETON. History of Isles-
borough, Maine. Bangor: T. W. Burr, 1893.
Pp. xii, 313.

3372 HATCH, MARGARET TODD. "Islesboro's nabobs
and neighbors." Down East, 10 (August, 1963),
32-36, 62, 65.
Social life and customs.

3373 HATCH, W. H. "Islesboro net makers." Down
East, 15 (March, 1969), 42-43.
Fishing nets.

3374 KELLOGG, FREDERICK C. "God's rustic house at
Islesboro: the chapel at Dark Harbor." The
Northeast, 77 (July, 1950), 8.
Christ Chapel.

3375 "LONG Island--Islesboro." BHistMag, 1 (1885-
1886), 167-172.

3376 ROGERS, DONALD. "The wreck of the 'Alice E.
Clark.'" Down East, 21 (September, 1974),
23-24.
1909.

3377 ROLERSON, DARRELL A. "When Islesboro said
'whoa' to the horseless carriage." Down East,
14 (April, 1968), 44-47.

JACKMAN (SOMERSET CO.)

3377A JACKMAN BICENTENNIAL BOOK COMMITTEE. The
history of the Moosehead Valley: Jackman,
Moose River, Dennistown, Long Pond, Parlin
Pond, Holeb, Skinner and Lowelltown. [Augus-
ta]: KJ Printing, [1976]. Pp. 169. MeU.

3378 SPRAGUE, JOHN FRANCIS. "Jackman and the
Moose River region." SJMH, 3 (1915-1916),
55-74.

JACKSON (WALDO CO.)

3379 MORTON, EVERETT E. Historical address of the
town of Jackson, given at the one hundredth
anniversary of Jackson as a plantation and of
the Congregational Church, October 5-6, 1912.
Waterville: Mail Publishing, 1912. Pp. 15.
Me.

JAY (FRANKLIN CO.)

3380 CUSHMAN, HELEN CALDWELL. Horizons unlimited:
a history of Jay. Livermore Falls: Livermore Falls Trust Company, 1967. Pp. 39.

3381 FOURNIER, PAUL J. "Little planes--big business." Flying, 65 (August, 1959), 46-47, 64-
66.
Use of aircraft by Maine Woodlands Department of the International Paper Company,
1946-1959.

3382 LAWRENCE, BENJAMIN F. History of Jay, Franklin County, Maine. Boston: Griffith-Still-
ings Pr., 1912. Pp. vi, 93.

JEFFERSON (LINCOLN CO.)

3383 FREEMASONS. JEFFERSON, ME. RIVERSIDE LODGE.
NO. 135. History of Riverside Lodge, Free
and Accepted Masons, Jefferson, Maine. Waldoboro: Miller & Atwood, 1874. Pp. 15.
[MePGLM].

3384 JEFFERSON, ME. Centennial celebration of the
town of Jefferson, Lincoln County, Maine,
U.S.A., August 21, 1907. Alberto A. Bennett,
comp. Lewiston: Journal Printing, 1908.
Pp. 61.

3385 RICHARDSON, CHARLES ALBERT, comp. Richardson
letters: letters written to Albert Richardson from 1832 to 1881, with biographical
sketches and a partial genealogy of the Richardson family. Jefferson, 1954 [i.e. 1955].
Pp. xii, 318.
Social life and customs.

JIM POND TOWNSHIP (FRANKLIN CO.)

3386 No items located.

JOHNSON MOUNTAIN TOWNSHIP (SOMERSET CO.)

3387 No items located.

JONESBORO (WASHINGTON CO.)

3388   SEE entry 1851.

JONESPORT (WASHINGTON CO.)

3389   BENSON, EARL M. "The promised land." Down
        East, 2 (September, 1955), 21-23, 40-41.
            George Jones Adams, founder of the Church
        of the Messiah, led a group of Maine colonists
        to the Holy Land in 1866 and started a colony
        at Jaffa.

3390   DAVIS, HAROLD ARTHUR. "The Jaffa colonists
        from Downeast." AmQ, 3 (1951), 344-356.

3391   DORSON, RICHARD M. "Collecting folklore in
        Jonesport, Maine." American Philosophical
        Society. Proceedings, 101 (1957), 270-289.

3392   EIDELBERG, SHLOMO. "The Adams colony in Jaf-
        fa (1866-1868)." Midstream, 3 (Summer, 1957),
        52-61.

3393   GARDNER, GEORGE PEABODY. "Roque Island--home
        anchorage." Down East, 6 (September, 1959),
        20-24, 38-39.

3393A   JONESPORT: a group of historical sketches
        written in honor of the centennial. Machias:
        Teague Publishing, [1932?]. Pp. 52. MeU.

3394   MONKS, JOHN PEABODY. "The history of Roque
        Island, Maine." CSMP, 42 (1952-1956), 423-
        472.

3395   _____. Roque Island, Maine. Diana Whitehill
        Laing, ed. Boston: Colonial Society of Mas-
        sachusetts, 1964. Pp. 51.

3395A   NORTON, ALTON ACKLEY. Moosabec manavelins.
        [Swarthmore?, Pa.], 1950. Pp. 140.

3396   PEARCE, GRACE NASH. "Bathed in light from
        three lighthouses." Nautical Research Jour-
        nal, 3 (June, 1951), 83-84.
            Shipbuilding and the migration of George
        Jones Adams and his followers to Palestine in
        1866.

3396A   SHAW, DAVID E. "Maine's Holy Land colonists."
        Down East, 23 (January, 1977), 40-43.
            Jaffa Colony.

        SEE ALSO entries 467, 603, and 1840.

KATAHDIN IRON WORKS TOWNSHIP (PISCATAQUIS CO.)

3397   BROCKWAY, MARJORIE. "Katahdin Iron Works."
        Down East, 8 (October, 1961), 20-25.

3398   EASTMAN, JOEL WEBB. "David Pingree's iron
        works." EIHC, 103 (1967), 189-198.
            Katahdin Iron Works Company.

3399   KOHN, CLYDE FREDERICK. "Katahdin Iron Works,
        Maine: a study in population distribution."
        Michigan Academy of Science, Arts, and Let-
        ters. Papers, 25 (1939), 397-405.

3400   SAWYER, RALPH S. "Katahdin Iron Works." Sun
        Up, 4 (September, 1927), 9, 52, 55.

3401   WORTHINGTON, J. W. "Katahdin Iron Works."
        Appalachia, 22 (1938-1939), 346-355.

KENDUSKEAG (PENOBSCOT CO.)

3402   WINTERS, ERMA. A history of Kenduskeag,
        Maine. Kenduskeag, 1966 [i.e. 1973]. Pp. 85.

KENNEBUNK (YORK CO.)

3403   BARRY, WILLIAM EDWARD. Chronicles of Kenne-
        bunk, being scenes and episodes in an old
        Maine village and vicinity. N.Y.: Redfield,
        Kendrick, Odell, 1923. Pp. 86.

3404   _____. A stroll by a familiar river, compris-
        ing the colloquy of saunterers by its lower
        course, and household words pertaining to its
        early history. Kennebunk: Enterprise Pr.,
        1911. 99 leaves.
            Mousum River.

3405   _____. A stroll thro' the past, accompanied
        by an invisible associate, and using an 18th-
        century stage-route and river road, preceded
        by a summary of the early ownerships and pro-
        vincial governments of Maine, together with a
        collection of historical data gathered in and
        around Kennebunk village and sketches of
        buildings which have long since disappeared.
        Portland: Southworth Pr., 1933. Pp. vi, 93.

3406   BOURNE, EDWARD EMERSON, 1797-1873. Ancient
        history of Kennebunk written in 1831. Kenne-
        bunk: Star Print, [1970]. Pp. 122. MeHi.

3407   BOURNE, EDWARD EMERSON, III and HARTLEY LORD,
        II. Kennebunk folks. [Kennebunk]: Brick
        Store Museum, 1967. Pp. 62.

3408   _____. Kennebunk in the nineties, and bio-
        graphical sketches. Kennebunk: Brick Store
        Museum, 1965. Pp. 80.

3409   BRYANT, SETH EMERY, comp. District of Kenne-
        bunk: a list of vessels built, from 1800 to
        1873. Kennebunk, 1874. Pp. 12.

3410   DRAKE, J. H. "You are not invited." Yankee,
        33 (June, 1969), 30-34.
            The Wedding Cake House.

3411 FREEMAN, MELVILLE CHASE. "History of the First Congregational Parish Unitarian of Kennebunk." UHSP, 9 Pt. 2 (1952), 25-37.

3412 GILPATRIC, GEORGE A. and ALBERT W. MESERVE. History of York Lodge, No. 22, F. & A. M., from 1813 to 1913. Kennebunk: W. L. Watson, 1913. Pp. 183. MeHi.

3413 GILPATRIC, GEORGE A. Kennebunk history, not a history of Kennebunk but a few items in addition to and a sequel to "The Village of Kennebunk, Maine." Kennebunk: Star Print, 1939. Pp. 148. Me.

3414 _____. The village of Kennebunk, Maine: interesting facts from old documents and maps, and observations by the author. Kennebunk: Star Print, 1935. Pp. 79.

3415 KENNEBUNK, ME. BRICK STORE MUSEUM. In commemoration of the founding of the Brick Store Museum, twenty-fifth year, 1936-1961. [Kennebunk, 1961?]. Unpaged. MeHi.

3416 _____. Old family portraits of Kennebunk. Kennebunk, 1944. Unpaged.

3417 _____. Old houses of Kennebunk. Kennebunk, 1939. Unpaged.

3418 LEFFINGWELL, B. H. "Ye Olde Stagecoach Homestead, Kennebunk, Maine." Hobbies, 65 (June, 1960), 88-89.
Originally called Barnard's Inn; later known as Towles' Tavern and Frost Tavern.

3419 MESERVE, ALBERT W. A history of Murray Royal Arch Chapter, No. 33, holden at Kennebunk, Maine, 1869 to 1909. Portland: Stephen Berry, 1909. Pp. 87. MeBa.
Freemasons.

3420 POWERS, JESSIE D. O. "First Parish Church, Kennebunk, Maine." The Church Exchange, 6 (1898-1899), 69.

3421 REMICH, DANIEL. History of Kennebunk from its earliest settlement to 1890, including biographical sketches. Carrie E. Remich, ed. Portland: Lakeside Pr., 1911. Pp. viii, 542, xxxvi.

3422 SCHMIDT, HENRIETTA. Through the years. Thomas E. Bradbury, ed. Kennebunk: Star Pr., 1975. Pp. 94.

3423 THOMPSON, MARGARET JEFFERDS. Captain Nathaniel Lord Thompson of Kennebunk, Maine, and the ships he built, 1811-1889. Boston: Charles E. Lauriat, 1937. Pp. xix, 140.

3424 WALKER, ANDREW. Military and naval history of residents of Kennebunk, who enlisted during the late Civil War. Kennebunk, 1868. Pp. 24.

3425 WEST KENNEBUNK, ME. METHODIST CHURCH. One hundredth anniversary, 1868-1968. n.p., [1968?]. Unpaged. MeHi.

SEE ALSO entries 987, 1322, 1880, 1884, 1896, and 1898.

KENNEBUNKPORT (YORK CO.)

3426 ADAMS, ELEANOR. "Kennebunkport's little green man." Down East, 8 (September, 1961), 49.
Discovery of a copy of a Renaissance statue in Kennebunkport in 1924 and the theory of its origin.

3427 ADAMS, FRANK FORRESTAL. "A one time old Maine inn." Sun Up, 4 (September, 1927), 11, 54-55.
Luques House.

3428 BRADBURY, CHARLES. History of Kennebunk Port, from its first discovery by Bartholomew Gosnold, May 14, 1602 to 1837. (1837) Kennebunkport: Durrell Publications, 1967. Pp. 338.
This reprint edition contains indexes.

3429 BRADBURY, THOMAS E. "Arundel and the Revolution." Down East, 22 (September, 1975), 68.

3430 BROOKS, ANNIE PEABODY. Ropes' ends: traditions, legends and sketches of old Kennebunkport and vicinity. Kennebunkport, 1901. Pp. 236.

3431 BUTLER, JOYCE. "Abbott Graves, artist and citizen of Kennebunkport." Down East, 21 (January, 1975), 44-47.

3432 _____. The South Congregational Church, Kennebunkport, Maine: an architectural history. [Kennebunkport]: South Congregational Church, 1973. Pp. 8. MeHi.

3433 DOW, JOY WHEELER. Old-time dwellings in Kennebunk Port. Kennebunk: Star Print, 1926. Pp. 82.

3434 FREEMAN, MELVILLE CHASE. History of Cape Porpoise. Cape Porpoise, 1955. Pp. 107.

3435 FREEMASONS. KENNEBUNKPORT, ME. ARUNDEL LODGE, NO. 76. History of Arundel Lodge, No. 76, F. & A. M., Kennebunkport, Me., from 1854 to 1870. Portland: Stephen Berry, 1870. Pp. 28.

3436 _____. Supplementary history of Arundel Lodge, No. 76, Free and Accepted Masons, Kennebunkport, Me., from 1870 to 1890. Portland: Stephen Berry, 1894. Pp. 43. MeHi.

3437 HISTORICAL RECORDS SURVEY. MAINE. An inventory of the town archives of Kennebunkport. Portland, 1937. 8 leaves. Me.

3438 KENNEBUNKPORT, ME. ST. ANN'S CHURCH. St. Ann's Church, Kennebunkport, Maine, 1912. [Kennebunkport?, 1912]. Pp. 16.

3439 KENNEBUNKPORT, ME. 300TH ANNIVERSARY COMMITTEE. 300th anniversary Cape Porpoise, Arundel, Kennebunkport, 1653-1953. Kennebunkport: Star Print, [1953?]. Pp. 64.

3440 KNIGHT, HENRY F. "Cape Porpoise, old and new." MeHSC, 2 Ser., 6 (1895), 153-175.

3441 LOMBARD, LUCINA HAYNES. "Cape Porpoise days." Pine Tree Magazine, 7 (1907), 509-514.

3442 LOWRY, LOIS. "New life for the house Captain Lord built." Down East, 23 (November, 1976), 32-37.
       Nathaniel Lord.

3443 MacALISTER, LORIMER W. Chronicles of Cape Porpoise and Kennebunkport. Cape Porpoise: Atlantic Firemen's Educational Association, 1949. Unpaged. MeHi.

3444 MOWER, IRVING B. History of the Baptist Church, Kennebunkport. Biddeford: Times Book and Job Print, 1890. Pp. 17.

3445 WASHBURN, JENNIE M. "Kennebunkport--old and new." Pine Tree Magazine, 8 (1907), 21-30.

3446 WILLARD, LAWRENCE F. "The clock that D.S.T. begins." Yankee, 30 (April, 1966), 70-71, 155.
       Emmons Clock Farm.

       SEE ALSO entries 1880, 1896, and 1898.

KIBBY TOWNSHIP (FRANKLIN CO.)

3447 No items located.

KINEO TOWNSHIP (PISCATAQUIS CO.)

3448 FOBES, CHARLES BARTLETT. "Mt. Kineo, Maine." Appalachia, 36 (1966-1967), 521-527.

3449 MacDOUGALL, WALTER M. "Kineo." Down East, 22 (May, 1976), 62-67, 85-86, 89.

3450 SPRAGUE, JOHN FRANCIS. "Mount Kineo and the Maine summer resort industry." SJMH, 2 (1914-1915), 10-16.

KING & BARTLETT TOWNSHIP (SOMERSET CO.)

3451 No items located.

KINGFIELD (FRANKLIN CO.)

3452 ERICKSON, HAZEL CUSHMAN. I grew up on the narrow gauge. N.Y.: Carlton Pr., 1971. Pp. 48. [MeHoC].

3453 KINGFIELD, ME. Souvenir of historic Kingfield, 1816-1916. n.p., 1916. Pp. 20. MeHi.

3454 KINGFIELD, ME. SESQUICENTENNIAL COMMITTEE. Salute to Kingfield's past: Kingfield, Maine sesquicentennial, 1816-1966. n.p., [1966]. Pp. 80. Me.

3455 VOSE, JOSEPHINE. "The Kingfield rebellion." Down East, 9 (June, 1963), 77.
       Draft riot during the Civil War.

       SEE ALSO entry 1552.

KINGMAN TOWNSHIP (PENOBSCOT CO.)

3456 SEE entry 50.

KINGSBURY PLANTATION (PISCATAQUIS CO.)

3457 No items located.

KITTERY (YORK CO.)

3458 ALDEN, JOHN. "Portsmouth Naval Shipyard." United States Naval Institute. Proceedings, 90 (November, 1964), 89-105.
       Includes a list of vessels built there.

3459 ALLEN, NEAL WOODSIDE, JR. "A Maine witch." OTNE, 61 (1970-1971), 75-81.
       Sarah Keene.

3460 BAXTER, JAMES PHINNEY. "Piscataqua and the Pepperells." MeHSC, 2 Ser., 4 (1893), 426-430.

3460A BENNETT, JACOB. "George Savary Wasson and the dialect of Kittery Point, Maine." American Speech, 49 (1974), 54-66.

3461 BONAR, JAMES CHARLES. Canada greets Kittery. Kittery: Piscataqua Pr., 1947. Pp. 24.

3462 BROWN, JOHN HERBERT. Portsmouth Navy Yard, 1800, and her early commandants. N.Y.: Newcomen Society, 1974. Pp. 40.

3463 BURRAGE, HENRY SWEETSER. "The Baptist church in Kittery." MeHSC, 2 Ser., 9 (1898), 382-391.

3464 COLBY, FRED M. "A day at old Kittery." Granite Mo, 2 (1879), 68-71.

3465 DENNETT, MARK. "Kittery in the olden time." Old Eliot, 8 (1908), 49-62.

3466 DRAKE, SAMUEL ADAMS. "The Pepperells of Kittery Point, Maine." Appleton's Journal, 11 (1874), 65-66.

3467 DUNN, CHARLES, JR. "Pepperell House." Pine Tree Magazine, 6 (1906-1907), 231-240.

3468 DUNNACK, HENRY ERNEST. A history of Fort McClary Memorial. Augusta: State Park Commission, [1955?]. Pp. 27. Me.

3469 DUTTON, JOHN G. History of the Second Christian Church of Kittery, Maine, organized May 25th, 1843. n.p., [1891?]. Pp. 8. MeB.

3470 FAIRCHILD, BYRON. Messrs. William Pepperell: merchants at Piscataqua. Ithaca: Cornell Univ. Pr., 1954. Pp. xi, 223.

3471 FENTRESS, WALTER E. H. 1775. 1875. Centennial history of the United States Navy Yard, at Portsmouth, N.H. Portsmouth, N.H.: O. M. Knight, 1876. Pp. 84.

3472 FROSST, GEORGE W. "Old Kittery." Old Eliot, 2 (1898), 21-23.
Origin of its name.

3473 FROST, JOHN ELDRIDGE. Colonial village. Kittery Point: Gundalow Club, [1948?]. Pp. 82.
Historic houses.

3474 FROST, JOSEPH WILLIAM PEPPERELL. "Pepperell Mansion, Kittery Point, Maine." Antiques, 89 (1966), 368-373.

3475 _____. Sir William Pepperrell, Bart., 1696-1759, His Britannic Majesty's obedient servant of Piscataqua. N.Y.: Newcomen Society in North America, 1951. Pp. 40.

3476 GEORGES, JUSTINE FLINT. "The house of the month." Shoreliner, 2 (December, 1951), 15-24.
Dennett House.

3477 HIGGINS, ROLAND W. "The Portsmouth Navy Yard." Shoreliner, 3 (July, 1952), 39-44.

3478 HILDRETH, HORACE A. The Pine Tree State salutes Kittery. Kittery: Piscataqua Pr., 1948. Pp. 16.

3479 KITTERY, ME. FIRST BAPTIST CHURCH. The First Baptist Church of Kittery Point, Maine. South Berwick: Chronicle Print Shop, 1973. Pp. 51. MeHi.
Includes a history of the church.

3480 KITTERY, ME. 300TH ANNIVERSARY PUBLICATION COMMITTEE. Old Kittery, 1647-1947; 300th anniversary. Kittery, 1947. Pp. 36.

3481 KITTERY BICENTENNIAL COMMITTEE. Kittery kaleidoscope. Somersworth, N.H.: New Hampshire Publishing, 1976. Pp. 76. MeHi.

3482 KITTERY COMMUNITY SERVICE ASSOCIATION. Kittery, ancient and modern. Kittery, 1925. Pp. 40.

3483 LIBBY, CHARLES THORNTON. "Naming of Kittery, Me." NEHGR, 71 (1917), 89-91.

3484 MERROW, JAMES. "Frisbee's Market." Yankee, 39 (August, 1975), 56-59, 100-102.

3485 MITCHELL, HORACE. "Eagles with feeling." Yankee, 29 (September, 1965), 28-30, 33.
Wooden eagles carved by John Haley Bellamy (1836-1914).

3486 _____. "Maine's oldest church." Down East, 10 (July, 1964), 36-37.
First Congregational Church.

3487 MITCHELL, JEANETTE GORDON. Kittery men & women in World War II. Kittery: Kittery Pr., 1947. Unpaged. MeHi.

3488 NEAGLE, MARJORIE SPILLER. "Appledore--Maine's house of entertainment." Down East, 9 (July, 1963), 34-37, 60.
Appledore Hotel on Appledore Island.

3489 "THE OLD Kittery Burying-Ground." MHGR, 8 (1895), 233-237.

3490 "THE OLD mill--Kittery." Old Eliot, 3 (1899), 104-107.
A grist mill built in 1706.

3491 PENROSE, CHARLES. Old Kittery, land of adventure, 1647, and Captain Francis Champernowne (1614-1687). N.Y.: Newcomen Society of England, American Branch, 1947. Pp. 40.

3492 PREBLE, GEORGE HENRY. History of the United States Navy Yard, Portsmouth, N.H. Washington: Govt. Print. Off., 1892. Pp. 219.

3493 REMICK, OLIVER PHILBRICK. "The gift of land for the first and only Episcopal Church in the towns of Kittery and Eliot." Old Eliot, 2 (1898), 141-145.
Granted by Jacob Remick, Jr.

3494 ROBIE, VIRGINIA. "Colonial pilgrimage, No. 3--Sir William Pepperell and his staircase." House Beautiful, 15 (1903-1904), 315-317.
Sparhawk House.

3495 RICHARDSON, HARRIET T. "John Bray House in Kittery, Maine." House Beautiful, 65 (1929), 704, 706, 708, 710, 712.

3496 ROLDE, NEIL. "The William Pepperell Mansion." Down East, 22 (May, 1976), 42-47.

3497 SAFFORD, MOSES A. "Historic homes of Kittery." MeHSC, 2 Ser., 5 (1894), 113-128, 387-407.

3498 _____. "Physicians of Kittery." Old Eliot, 7 (1906), 196-202.

3499 SAFFORD, VICTORIA. "John Haley Bellamy, the woodcarver of Kittery Point." Antiques, 27 (1935), 102-106.

3500 "A SKETCH of Kittery." MHGR, 9 (1898), 252-256.

3501 STACKPOLE, EVERETT SCHERMERHORN. Old Kittery and her families. Lewiston: Lewiston Journal, 1903. Pp. 822.

3502 SWEETSER, MARY CHISHOLM. "The legend of Appledore." NEG, 7 (Spring, 1966), 22-28.
      Celia Thaxter, poetess.

3503 TRANI, EUGENE P. The Treaty of Portsmouth: an adventure in American diplomacy. Lexington: Univ. of Kentucky Pr., 1969. Pp. 194.

3504 VAUGHAN, DOROTHY M. "An afternoon at the Lady Pepperell Mansion." OTNE, 40 (1949-1950), 157-158.

3505 "WHEN Washington came to Maine." Sun Up, 10 (February, 1932), 52-53.
      1789.

3506 WILSON, FRED ALLAN. The early history of the Wilson family of Kittery, Maine. Lynn, Mass.: J. Macfarlane, 1898. Pp. 98.

      SEE ALSO entries 987, 1879, 1907, and 1911.

KNOX (WALDO CO.)

3507 No items located.

KOSSUTH TOWNSHIP (WASHINGTON CO.)

3508 No items located.

LAGRANGE (PENOBSCOT CO.)

3509 No items located.

LAKE VIEW PLANTATION (PISCATAQUIS CO.)

3510 No items located.

LAKEVILLE PLANTATION (PENOBSCOT CO.)

3511 No items located.

LAMBERT LAKE TOWNSHIP (WASHINGTON CO.)

3512 No items located.

LAMOINE (HANCOCK CO.)

3513 CHILDS, FRANCES SERGEANT. "Fontaine Leval, a French settlement on the Maine coast, 1791." AASP, New Ser., 51 (1941), 187-222.

3514 DOUGLAS, JOHN SHERMAN. The First Baptist Church, Lamoine, Maine.... n.p., [1932]. Pp. 22.

3515 "A FRENCH description of Frenchman's Bay, 1792." NEQ, 1 (1928), 396-410.
      Unsuccessful settlement of Fontaine Leval, the present town of Lamoine.

3516 TALLMAN, RICHARD S. "James A. Herne and Lamoine, Maine." NEQ, 46 (1973), 94-105.
      Playwright.

      SEE ALSO entries 1569 and 1586.

LANG TOWNSHIP (FRANKLIN CO.)

3517 No items located.

LEBANON (YORK CO.)

3518 CHAMBERLAIN, GEORGE WALTER. The beginnings of Lebanon, Maine; for the York County tercentenary, West Lebanon, Maine, August 29, 1936. [West Lebanon, 1936]. Pp. 13.

3519 _____. Soldiers of the American Revolution, of Lebanon, Maine. Weymouth, Mass.: Weymouth & Braintree Publishing, 1897. Pp. 48.
      Biographies.

3520 _____. "Studies on families surnamed Cowell, Door (Dore or Dorr) and Chamberlain of Lebanon, Maine." MeHSC, 2 Ser., 5 (1894), 306-311.

3521 LEBANON, ME. Town of Lebanon, York County, Maine, bicentennial observance, July 1-2-3-4. n.p., [1967]. Pp. 31. MBNEH.

3522 LEBANON HISTORICAL SOCIETY. This is Lebanon, Maine, 1765 to 1965. East Lebanon: Winifred Van Houten, [1965]. Pp. 20. MeHi.

3523   SINNETT, CHARLES NELSON. Historic Lebanon: Lebanon, Maine, and the grand work of its Congregational Church in one hundred and thirty-eight years. Haverhill, Mass.: C. C. Morse & Son, 1903. Pp. 16.

LEE (PENOBSCOT CO.)

3524   HOUGHTON, VINAL A. The story of an old New England town: history of Lee, Maine. Wilton: Nelson Print, 1926. Pp. 248.

3525   HOUSE, C. J. "Soldiers from Lee, Penobscot County, in the War of the Rebellion." Maine Bugle, 1 (1894), 263-266.

LEEDS (ANDROSCOGGIN CO.)

3526   STINCHFIELD, JOHN CLARK. History of the town of Leeds, Androscoggin County, Maine, from its settlement June 10, 1780. Lewiston: Lewiston Journal, 1901. Pp. viii, 419.

LEVANT (PENOBSCOT CO.)

3527   LEVANT, ME. Levant, Maine, sesquicentennial celebration, August 3, 1963. n.p., [1963]. Pp. 63. MeBa.

LEWISTON (ANDROSCOGGIN CO.)

3528   "ANGLICANS coming to America want their Church: the story of Trinity Parish, Lewiston, Maine." The Northeast, 76 (March, 1949), 14-16.

3529   ANNETT, JOHN B. "Chemistry at Bates." Bates College Bulletin, 46 (May 1, 1949), 2-3.

3530   ANTHONY, ALFRED WILLIAMS. Bates College and its background: a review of origins and causes. Philadelphia: Judson Pr., 1936. Pp. 284.

3531   BARBER, WILLIAM H. "Bates College in the eighties." Bates Alumnus, 19 (March, 1939), 11-14, (June, 1939), 3-4.

3532   BECKFORD, WILLIAM HALE. Leading business men of Lewiston, Augusta and vicinity, embracing, also, Auburn, Gardiner, Waterville, Oakland, Dexter, Fairfield, Skowhegan, Hallowell, Richmond, Bath, Brunswick, Freeport, Canton, Buckfield, Mechanic Falls, South Paris, Norway, Farmington and Winthrop, with an historical sketch of each place. Boston: Mercantile Publishing, 1889. Pp. 360.

3533   BISCHOFF, CARL H. "Lewiston, a changing city." Sun Up, 8 (September, 1930), 6-8, 28.

3534   BUKER, MARGARET. "The Irish in Lewiston, Maine: a search for security on the urban frontier, 1850-1880." MeHSQ, 13 (Special, 1973), 3-25.

3535   CALLAHAN, GEORGE A. History of King Hiram's Chapter, No. 9, of Royal Arch Masons, Lewiston, Maine, date of precedence, Nov. 28, 1854. Lewiston, 1885. Pp. 61. MeHi.

3536   CHASE, CLARENCE AUGUSTINE. "Lewiston and Bates College." NEM, New Ser., 13 (1895-1896), 513-532.

3537   DAVIES, WALLACE EVANS. "A collectivist experiment Down East: Bradford Peck and the Coöperative Association of America." NEQ, 20 (1947), 471-491.
        1899-1912.

3538   EATON, MABEL. "Bates College Library." MeLAB, 7 (June, 1946), 1.

3539   EATON, MIRIAM. "Oh tempora, oh mores." Bates College Bulletin, 54 (May, 1957), 6-8. Bates College.

3540   EMERSON, R. E. "Distinct[ive]ly different." Sun Up, 2 (December, 1925), 50-51. Bates Street Shirts.

3541   GOULD, SAMUEL B. "The lighter side." Bates Alumnus, 16 (November, 1935), 3-8, 13. Social life at Bates College.

3542   HALLOCK, LEAVITT HOMAN. Manual of Pine Street Congregational Church, Lewiston, Maine, with historical sketch.... Lewiston: Journal Print Shop, 1909. Pp. 20. Me.

3543   JAKEMAN, ADELBERT M. "Athletics at Bates in history and story: football from Briggs to Morey." Bates Alumnus, 15 (November, 1934), 2-7.

3544   _____. "Hockey and winter sports at Bates." Bates Alumnus, 16 (February, 1936), 3-8.

3545   _____. "Men's Athletic Association." Bates Alumnus, 17 (February, 1937), 3-6. Bates College.

3546   _____. "Sixty-five years of baseball." Bates Alumnus, 15 (May, 1935), 2-11. Bates College.

3547   _____. "Sixty years of track and field sports." Bates Alumnus, 15 (February, 1935), 3-11. Bates College.

3548   _____. "Tennis at Bates." Bates Alumnus, 16 (May, 1936), 11-14, 18.

3549 KENDALL, RAYMOND. "Twenty-one years of summer school at Bates." Bates Alumnus, 20 (June, 1940), 10, 22.

3550 KIRK, GENEVA. "The story of Lewiston." Maine Townsman, 37 (September, 1975), 10-12.

3551 LEAMON, JAMES S. Historic Lewiston: a textile city in transition. [Lewiston]: Lewiston Historical Commission, 1976. Pp. vii, 60. MeHi.

3552 LEWISTON, ME. BOARD OF TRADE. Official manual of the Lewiston Board of Trade, containing portraits of officers, constitution, list of members, history, views, etc. [Lewiston], 1912. Pp. 91. MeBa.

3553 LEWISTON, ME. MANUFACTURERS AND MECHANICS LIBRARY ASSOCIATION. A brief history of the Manufacturers and Mechanics Library Association of Lewiston, Me.; with constitution and by-laws. Lewiston: Journal Office, 1897. Pp. 15.

3554 LEWISTON, ME. PAROISSE SAINT-PIERRE ET SAINT-PAUL. Album souvenir du 75e anniversaire de la Paroisse Saint-Pierre et Saint-Paul de Lewiston, Maine. n.p., [1946?]. Pp. 88. Me.

3555 _____. Paroisse Canadienne-Française de Lewiston (Maine), album historique. [Lewiston]: Les Pères Dominicains, 1899. Pp. 107. MBC.

3556 LEWISTON, ME. SAINTE MARIE. Vingt-cinquième anniversaire de la Paroisse Sainte-Marie, 1907-1932. Lewiston, 1932. Pp. 48.

3557 LEWISTON, ME. TRINITY CHURCH. A brief history of Trinity Parish, Lewiston, Maine, 1854-1903; to which are appended list of communicants, baptisms, confirmations, marriages and burials since the organization of the parish.... Lewiston: Haswell Pr., 1902. Pp. 89. MeBa.

3558 LEWISTON HISTORICAL COMMISSION. Lewiston school names. [Lewiston], 1971. 26 leaves. MeHi.
Biographies of persons after whom the schools were named.

3559 LEWISTON WEEKLY JOURNAL. A historical sketch of the Lewiston Weekly Journal and Daily Evening Journal.... Lewiston, 1887. Pp. 11. MeU.

3560 "MANUFACTURERS National Bank, Lewiston, Me." Bankers Magazine, 93 (1916), 449-453.

3561 MICHAUD, CHARLOTTE, ADELARD JANELLE, and JAMES S. LEAMON. Historic Lewiston: Franco-American origins. [Lewiston]: Lewiston Historical Commission, 1974. Pp. 47. MeU.

3562 MICHAUD, CHARLOTTE. "Maine's Franco-Americans: Lewiston." Maine History News, 7 (July, 1972), 8-9, 12, 14-16.

3563 PACKARD, BERTRAM EVERETT. History of the Polymnian Society of Bates College. Auburn: Merrill & Webber, 1899. Pp. 46. MeHi.

3564 PECK, BRADFORD. The world a department store: a story of life under a coöperative system. Lewiston, 1900. Pp. xv, 311. Coöperative Association of America.

3565 PHILLIPS, CHARLES FRANKLIN. Bates College in Maine: enduring strength and scholarship. N.Y.: Newcomen Society, 1952. Pp. 24.

3566 RAMSDELL, HARRIET J. "In the beginning, Hathorn was the College." Bates College Bulletin, 70 (Winter, 1973), 1-6. Hathorn Hall, Bates College.

3567 READE, JOHN L. "The Bates Alumni Association." Bates Alumnus, 6 (May, 1926), 17-18.

3568 RICKER, GEORGE S. "College sports in the sixties." Bates Alumnus, 11 (May, 1931), 17. Bates College.

3569 ROUNDY, RODNEY W. "Pine Street's one hundred years." MeCP, 41 (November 15, 1954), 10. Pine Street Congregational Church.

3570 ROWE, HARRY W. "The College Club, 1891-1932." Bates Alumnus, 12 (May, 1932), 13-15. Bates College.

3571 SAWYER, WILLIAM H. "Biology at Bates." Bates College Bulletin, 54 (January 15, 1957), 6-7, 33.

3572 _____. "Our campus trees." Bates Alumnus, 14 (November, 1933), 1-7.

3573 STANTON BIRD CLUB, LEWISTON, ME. Fifty years with the Stanton Bird Club, 1919-1969, anniversary booklet. Dorothy P. Webber and Shirley Clifford Hoy, eds. n.p. [1969?]. Unpaged. MeU.

3574 STONE, ELEANOR BAILEY. "Bates College--her past, present, and future." Sun Up, 3 (February, 1927), 9, 12, 22.

3575 _____. "Bates College, pioneer in international debating." Sun Up, 5 (February, 1928), 10-11, 20-21.

3576 THOMAS, HOWARD E. "Forty years of intercollegiate debating." Bates Alumnus, 16 (May, 1936), 9-10. Bates College.

3577 TURNER, AUGUSTUS R. Souvenir program of the
one hundredth anniversary of the city of
Lewiston, giving an historical sketch with
incidents relating to the growth of the city,
its principal business firms, scenery, etc.
... July fourth, 1895. Auburn: Merrill &
Webber, 1895. Pp. 120.

SEE ALSO entries 556, 1422, 1424, 1426-1427,
1431-1432, 1434, and 4561.

LEXINGTON TOWNSHIP (SOMERSET CO.)

3578 No items located.

LIBERTY (WALDO CO.)

3579 FREEMASONS. LIBERTY, ME. LIBERTY LODGE, NO.
111. History of Liberty Lodge, No. 111,
Montville, Maine, originally, now Liberty,
Maine, from Nov. 8, 1861, to Jan. 1, 1890,
with by-laws of lodge and appendix. Belfast:
George W. Burgess, 1891. Pp. 40. [MePGLM].

3580 FREEMASONS. LIBERTY, ME. ST. GEORGES CHAP-
TER, NO. 45. History of St. Georges Chapter,
No. 45, Liberty, Maine, from March 10th,
1881, to Jan. 1st, 1890, with by-laws of chap-
ter and appendix. Belfast: George W. Bur-
gess, 1892. Pp. 30. [MePGLM].
   Signed: George W. Berry, Edwin A. Porter,
A. P. Cargill, Committee on History.

3581 HURWITZ, ALFRED. The history of Liberty,
Maine, 1827-1975. Liberty: Liberty Historical Society, 1975. Pp. 93. Me.

3582 LIBERTY, ME. HISTORICAL COMMITTEE. The town
of Liberty: its history and geography.
Thorndike: Newell White, 1927. Pp. 120.

LILY BAY TOWNSHIP (PISCATAQUIS CO.)

3583 No items located.

LIMERICK (YORK CO.)

3584 FREEMAN, CHARLES. "An account of Limerick."
MeHSC, 1 (1831), 245-253.

3585 ILSLEY, GEORGE BOARDMAN. 1796-1896. Histori-
cal sermon and centennial poem at the one
hundredth anniversary of the Limerick Baptist
Church. Portland: Thurston Print, 1896.
Pp. 11.
   Poem is by Mrs. S. E. Ilsley.

3586 LAMPREY, LOUISE. History of Limerick. Cornish: Chester V. Small, [1927?]. Pp. 20.

3587 TAYLOR, LINDA MAULE. Limerick historical
notes. Limerick: The Town, 1975. Pp. 127.
Me.

LIMESTONE (AROOSTOOK CO.)

3588 GIBBS, GEORGE C. "The diamond jubilee of the
Advent, Limestone." The Northeast, 74 (Novem-
ber, 1947), 7.
   Church of the Advent.

3589 LIMESTONE, ME. Limestone centennial, 100th
celebration, 1869-1969: the review of a century. n.p., [1970]. Unpaged. Me.

LIMINGTON (YORK CO.)

3590 CHICK, OLIVE M. A history of Limington Academy, 1848-1948. Cornish: Webb-Smith, 1948.
Pp. 47. MeHi.

3591 LIMINGTON, ME. Limington sesquicentennial,
1798-1948. n.p., [1948]. Pp. 24. MeHi.

3592 LIMINGTON, ME. CONGREGATIONAL CHURCH. Manual
of the Congregational Church, Limington, York
County, Maine, containing history.... Portland: Southworth Bros., 1893. Pp. 32.
MBNEH.

3593 TAYLOR, ROBERT L. History of Limington,
Maine, 1668-1900. Norway: Oxford Hills Pr.,
1975. Pp. ii, 211. Me.

LINCOLN (PENOBSCOT CO.)

3594 BAILEY, MAY MURRAY EDWARDS. The history of
Methodism in Lincoln, including a sketch of
all the ministers who have been sent here to
labor for their Lord, 1836-1954. Old Town:
Penobscot Times, [1954]. Pp. 44.

3595 _____. History of Trans Alpine, the southern-
most part of the town of Lincoln, Maine, beyond the Alps. Lincoln, 1950. Pp. 109.

3596 FELLOWS, DANA WILLIS. History of the town of
Lincoln, Penobscot County, Maine, 1822-1928.
Lewiston: Dingley Pr., 1929. Pp. 436.

3597 GOODWIN, KATHRYN. Personal glimpses of the
early settlers of Lincoln, Maine. n.p., 1970.
Pp. 79. MeU.
   Biographies.

3598 NELSON, JEREMY. "Notes on Lincoln, Maine." BHistMag, 1 (1885-1886), 89-91.

SEE ALSO entry 50.

LINCOLN PLANTATION (OXFORD CO.)

3599 WILSONS MILLS, ME. SESQUICENTENNIAL BOOKLET COMMITTEE. History of Wilsons Mills, Maine and the Magalloway settlements. Wilsons Mills: The Town, 1975. Pp. 285. Me.

LINCOLNVILLE (WALDO CO.)

3600 DAVIS, WILL R. Village Down East: sketches of village life on the northeast coast of New England, before "gas-buggies" came, by John Wallace, from conversations with Zackary Adams, Duck Trap Cove, Maine. Brattleboro, Vt.: Stephen Daye Pr., 1943. Pp. 184.

3601 MEARA, EMMETT and NANCY MEARA. "Lincolnville Volunteer Fire Department." Down East, 18 (May, 1972), 60-61.

SEE ALSO entries 1833 and 4612.

LINNEUS (AROOSTOOK CO.)

3602 No items located.

LISBON (ANDROSCOGGIN CO.)

3603 GOULD, RALPH ERNEST. Yankee boyhood: my adventures on a Maine farm seventy years ago. N.Y.: Norton, 1950. Pp. 251.

3604 HUDSON, MRS. D. E. "Lisbon annals: reminiscences of the Catholic history of Lisbon, Me., from the beginning in 1874." MeCathHM, 3 (September, 1914), 40-42.

3605 PLUMMER, FRANCIS W. Lisbon: the history of a small Maine town. Charles W. Plummer, ed. Lewiston: Twin City Printery, 1970. Pp. 225.

3606 "SAINT Matthew's celebrates its fortieth anniversary." The Northeast, 73 (November, 1946), 6-7, 12.

LITCHFIELD (KENNEBEC CO.)

3607 LITCHFIELD, ME. History of Litchfield and an account of its centennial celebration, 1895. Augusta: Kennebec Journal Print, 1897. Pp. 548.

3608 LITCHFIELD, ME. BICENTENNIAL COMMITTEE. Litchfield yesterdays. Litchfield, 1976. Pp. 61. MeU.

3609 SMITH, ASA P. History of the Congregational Church of Litchfield, Maine, written for its centennial celebration, June 15, 1911. n.p., [1911?]. Unpaged. MeHi.

3610 SPRINGER, ISAAC W., CYRUS KENDRICK, and J. E. CHASE. History of Morning Star Lodge No. 41, Free and Accepted Masons, Litchfield Corners, Me. Gardiner: H. K. Morrell and Son, 1884. Pp. 21. [MePGLM].

3611 THURSTON, DAVID. "Sketch of the half century history of the Congregational Church in Litchfield, Maine." CongQ, 4 (1862), 253-258.

LITTLE SQUAW TOWNSHIP (PISCATAQUIS CO.)

3612 No items located.

LITTLE W TOWNSHIP (SOMERSET CO.)

3613 No items located.

LITTLETON (AROOSTOOK CO.)

3614 No items located.

LIVERMORE (ANDROSCOGGIN CO.)

3615 FREEMASONS. LIVERMORE, ME. ORIENTAL STAR LODGE, NO. 21. History of Oriental Star Lodge, Livermore, Maine, from February 21, 1871 to January 1, 1881. Lewiston: Geo. A. Callahan, 1882. Pp. 20. MeHi.

3616 _____. History of Oriental Star Lodge, No. 21, Livermore, Me. Lewiston: Geo. A. Callahan, 1873. Pp. 34. MeHi.

3617 _____. History of Oriental Star Lodge, No. 21, Livermore, Me., from September, 1881 to January 15, 1892. Lewiston: Geo. A. Callahan, 1892. Pp. 13. MeHi.

3618 HUNT, GAILLARD, comp. Israel, Elihu and Cadwallader Washburn: a chapter in American biography. N.Y.: Macmillan, 1925. Pp. vi, 397.

3619 MONROE, IRA THOMPSON. History of the town of Livermore, Androscoggin County, Maine, from its inception in 1735 and its grant of land in 1772 to its organization and incorporation in 1795 up to the present time, 1928. Lewiston: Lewiston Journal Printshop, 1928. Pp. 275.

3620 LIVERMORE

3620 STURTEVANT, REGINALD H. A history of Livermore, Maine. Lewiston: Twin City Printery,
1970. Pp. 256.

3621 _____. "Seven sons." Down East, 2 (June,
1956), 20-24, 38-39.
Algernon, Elihu, Cadwallader, Israel,
Charles, William D. and Samuel Washburn; sons
of Israel and Martha Washburn.

3622 WASHBURN, ISRAEL, 1813-1883. Notes, historical, descriptive, and personal, of Livermore,
in Androscoggin (formerly in Oxford) County,
Maine.... Portland: Bailey & Noyes, 1874.
Pp. 169.

3623 WASHBURN, LILIAN. My seven sons: the true
and amazing story of the seven famous Washburn
brothers, as told by the old grandsire, Israel, Sr., and transcribed by his granddaugh-
ter, Lilian Washburn. Portland: Falmouth
Publishing, 1940. Pp. 143.

3624 WASHBURN, REUEL. History of Oriental Star
Lodge, No. 21, Livermore, Maine. Portland:
Ira Berry & Son, 1862. Pp. 12. MH.

LIVERMORE FALLS (ANDROSCOGGIN CO.)

3625 LIVERMORE FALLS, ME. FIRST BAPTIST CHURCH.
First Baptist Church, Livermore Falls, Maine,
1811-1911, centenary exercise, November 19-
23, 1911. Livermore Falls: Advertiser,
[1911?]. Pp. 33. MeHi.
Includes history by Charlotte H. Sturtevant.

3626 LIVERMORE FALLS TRUST COMPANY. Fiftieth anniversary, Livermore Falls Trust Company,
1895-1945. n.p., [1945?]. Unpaged. MeHi.

3627 STURTEVANT, REGINALD H. "Livermore Falls--
Maine's boom town." Down East, 12 (March,
1966), 6-10, 56-57, 60, 62.

LOBSTER TOWNSHIP (PISCATAQUIS CO.)

3628 No items located.

LONG A TOWNSHIP (PENOBSCOT CO.)

3629 No items located.

LONG ISLAND PLANTATION (HANCOCK CO.)

3630 No items located.

LONG POND TOWNSHIP (SOMERSET CO.)

3631 SEE entry 3377A.

LOVELL (OXFORD CO.)

3632 LE BARON, WILLIAM B. Historical record of
West Lovell. Arthur P. Stone, ed. n.p.,
[1946?]. 30 leaves. MBNEH.
Originally written in 1899.

3633 MOORE, PAULINE WINCHELL. Blueberries and
pusley weed, the story of Lovell, Maine.
Kennebunk: Star Press, 1970. Pp. 260, vii,
ix. Me.

3634 PAISLEY, EVA COCHRAN WILSON. Sanctuary: a
finding of life. N.Y.: E. P. Dutton, 1940.
Pp. 253.

LOWELL (PENOBSCOT CO.)

3635 No items located.

LOWELLTOWN TOWNSHIP (OXFORD CO.)

3636 SEE entry 3377A.

LOWER CUPSUPTIC TOWNSHIP (OXFORD CO.)

3637 No items located.

LOWER ENCHANTED TOWNSHIP (SOMERSET CO.)

3638 No items located.

LUBEC (WASHINGTON CO.)

3639 ADAMS, FRANKLIN P., SR. "Notes on the maritime history of Lubec, Maine." AmNep, 24
(1964), 38-60.

3640 DRUMMOND, R. R. "The centennial of Lubec,
Maine." Penn Germania, New Ser., 2 (1913),
215-216.

3641 GREET, WILLIAM CABELL. "A record from Lubec,
Maine and remarks on the coastal type."
American Speech, 6 (1931), 397-403.

3642 HALLET, RICHARD. "The great Quoddy gold hoax:
one of the greatest swindles of the age."
Down East, 1 (Winter, 1955), 18-20.
Perpetrated by Prescott Ford Jernegan and
Charles Fisher in 1898.

3643 JOHNSON, RYERSON. 200 years of Lubec history, 1776-1976. [Lubec]: Lubec Historical Society, [1976]. Pp. 145. MeU.

3644 LYFORD, ELMORE B. "There is such a place as Baileys Mistake!" Yankee, 32 (March, 1968), 162-163.

3645 McGREGOR, JAMES. History of Washington Lodge, No. 37, Free and Accepted Masons, Lubec, Maine, 1822, 1890. Portland: E. W. Brown and J. B. Neagle, 1892. Pp. 99.
        Includes a brief sketch of the history of the town.

3646 MASON, JOHN. "The great sea-water swindle." Yankee, 29 (February, 1965), 56-59, 110-112.
        Prescott Ford Jernegan and the Electrolytic Marine Salts Co., 1897.

3647 SMYTH, LAWRENCE T. "When the Cambridge was lost." Steamboat Bill, 16 (1959), 15-16.
        Shipwreck on Old Man Ledge off Allen's Island, February 9, 1886.

        SEE ALSO entries 603, 1840, 1852 and 1859.

LUDLOW (AROOSTOOK CO.)

3648 No items located.

LYMAN (YORK CO.)

3649 LYMAN, ME. FIRST CONGREGATIONAL CHURCH. Programme of the dedication services of the Congregational Church, Lyman, Dec. 2, 1882. n.p., 1882. Pp. 8. MBC.

LYNCHTOWN TOWNSHIP (OXFORD CO.)

3650 HEYWOOD, DANIEL E. Diary of Daniel E. Heywood, a Parmachenee guide at Camp Caribou, Parmachenee Lake, Oxford County, Maine, fall of 1890. Bristol, N.H.: R. W. Musgrove, 1891. Pp. 101.

3651 MOSES, GEORGE H. "John Danforth and Camp Caribou." Granite Mo, 19 (1895), 315-320.
        Sportsmen's camp, established in 1870s on Parmachenee Lake.

MACHIAS (WASHINGTON CO.)

3652 BEAM, LURA ELLA. A Maine hamlet. N.Y.: W. Funk, 1957. Pp. 236.

3653 CHURCHILL, EDWIN A. "The historiography of the 'Margaretta' affair, or, how not to let the facts interfere with a good story." MeHSQ, 15 (1975-1976), 60-74.
        1775.

3654 COMAN, EDWIN TRUMAN and HELEN MARILLA GIBBS. Time, tide, and timber: a century of Pope & Talbot. Stanford, Calif.: Stanford Univ. Pr., 1949. Pp. xvi, 480.
        Lumber.

3655 DAUGHTERS OF THE AMERICAN REVOLUTION. MAINE. HANNAH WESTON CHAPTER, MACHIAS. Naval battle at Machias, June 12, 1775. Machias: Sanborn Publishing, [19--?]. Unpaged.

3656 _____. The story of Hannah Weston and her part in the first naval engagement of the Revolution, June 12, 1775. Machias, 1925. 12 leaves.

3657 DIETZ, LEW. "Long-log drive." Down East, 2 (April, 1956), 24-28.

3658 DONWORTH, GRACE. "Burnham Tavern, ancient hostelry at Machias." DARMag, 69 (1935), 35.

3659 DRISKO, GEORGE WASHINGTON. Narrative of the town of Machias, the old and the new, the early and the late. Machias: The Republican, 1904. Pp. 589.

3660 GARDNER, FRANK A. "State schooner Diligent." MassMag, 3 (1910), 40-46.

3661 HARDING, HENRY FISKE. Memorial address on the occasion of the centennial anniversary of the formation of Centre Street Congregational Church, at Machias, Me.; together with a brief history of the Congregational Sabbath School to September, 1884. Machias: C. O. Furbush, 1884. Pp. ix, 70.

3662 HARVEY, D. C. "Machias and the invasion of Nova Scotia." Canadian Historical Association. Report, (1932), 17-28.
        1776-1777.

3663 HAWES, HILDRETH GILMAN. The Bellamy treasure: the pirates of the Whydah in the Gulf of Maine. Augusta: Augusta Pr., 1940. Pp. 71.

3664 JONES, STEPHEN. "Historical account of Machias." MeHSQ, 15 (1975-1976), 44-56.
        Margaretta affair of 1775; written in 1822.

3665 LENHART, JOHN M. "Two Revolutionary chaplains in government employ (1780-1784)." CathHist Rev, 23 (1937-1938), 446-466.
        Father Frederick de Bourges and Father Juniper Berthiaume were sent to Maine by the Provincial Council of Massachusetts to give spiritual aid to Catholic Indians who sided with the Americans.

3666 MACHIAS, ME. Memorial of the centennial anniversary of the settlement of Machias. Machias: C. O. Furbush, 1863. Pp. 179
Joseph Williamson attributes authorship to William Bartlett Smith who is the author of the "historical sketch."

3667 "MACHIAS one hundred years ago." MeHistMag, 9 (1894-1895), 153-157.

3668 NATIONAL ARCHIVES PROJECT. Ship registers and enrollments of Machias, Maine, 1780-1930. Rockland, 1942. 2v.

3669 "NOTES about Machias with some account of its first settlers." MeHistMag, 8 (1893), 70-85.

3670 O'BRIEN, JOHN. "Exertions of the O'Brien family of Machias, Maine in the American Revolution." MeHSC, 2 (1847), 242-249.

3671 OXTON, BEULAH SYLVESTER. "The first naval battle of the American Revolution." Maine's Own Magazine, 8 (May and June, 1930), 12-13, 32.

3672 PAGEANT of Machias Valley ... the celebration of the one hundred and fiftieth anniversary of the founding of Machias.... Machias: Machias Republican Pr., 1913. Pp. 28. MeU.

3673 PARKER, FOXHALL ALEXANDER. "The first sea-fight of the Revolution." MagAmHist, 1 (1877), 209-221.

3674 POPE, CHARLES HENRY. "Machias in the Revolution." MeHSC, 2 Ser., 6 (1895), 121-138.

3675 POTTER, GAIL M. "The Lexington of the seas." NEG, 10 (Spring, 1969), 50-57.
First naval battle of the Revolution, June, 1775.

3676 SELIGMANN, HERBERT J. "From eastern Maine, 1823." Down East, 3 (June, 1957), 26-27, 48-49.
"Eastern Star," a newspaper.

3677 _____. "Washington County's capital—Machias." Down East, 4 (July, 1958), 26-32, 52-54.

3678 SHERMAN, ANDREW MAGOUN. The O'Briens of Machias, Me., patriots of the American Revolution: their services to the cause of liberty. A paper read before the American-Irish Historical Society at its annual gathering in New York City, January 12, 1904; together with a sketch of the clan O'Brien by Thomas Hamilton Murray. Boston: For the Society, 1904. Pp. 87.

3679 SMITH, M. E. C. "Machias in the Revolution and afterward." NEM, New Ser., 12 (1895), 673-688.

3680 SPRAGUE, JOHN FRANCIS. "The Lexington of the seas." SJMH, 1 (1913-1914), 157-164, 175-184.
Margaretta affair.

3681 TALBOT, GEORGE FOSTER. "The capture of the Margaretta: the first naval battle of the Revolution." MeHSC, 2 Ser., 2 (1891), 1-17.

3682 _____. "The first naval battle of the Revolution at Machias, Maine, June 11, 1775." BHistMag, 3 (1887-1888), 161-167.

3683 "WASHINGTON State Normal School." Maine Teachers' Digest, 2 (1941-1942), 124-125, 135-136.
Now the University of Maine at Machias.

SEE ALSO entries 603, 799, 1840, and 1851.

MACHIASPORT (WASHINGTON CO.)

3684 SEE entries 603, 1840, and 1863.

MACWAHOC PLANTATION (AROOSTOOK CO.)

3685 No items located.

MADAWASKA (AROOSTOOK CO.)

3686 ALBERT, JULIE D. Madawaska centennial, 1869-1969. n.p., [1969?]. Pp. 152.

3687 _____. St. David Parish: centennial, 1871-1971. Madawaska: St. John Valley Times, [1971]. Pp. 72.

3688 ALBERT, THOMAS. Histoire du Madawaska d'après les recherches historiques de Patrick Therriault et les notes manuscrites de Prudent L. Mercure. Quebec: Imprimerie franciscaine missionaire, 1920. Pp. xxiii, 448.
A photocopy of a typescript translation by Marie Antoinette Page is at the University of Maine at Orono.

3689 COLLINS, CHARLES W. The Acadians of Madawaska, Maine. Boston: Thomas A. Whalen, 1902. Pp. 66.

3690 DEANE, JOHN GILMORE and EDWARD KAVANAGH. "State of the Madawaska and Aroostook settlements in 1831." New Brunswick Historical Society. Collections, 3 (1907-1914), 344-484.
Edited by William O. Raymond.

3691 LUCEY, WILLIAM LEO. "Madawaska on the River St. John: New England's last frontier." American Catholic Historical Society of Philadelphia. Records, 60 (1949), 147-164.

3692 MELVIN, CHARLOTTE LENENTINE. Madawaska, a chapter in Maine-New Brunswick relations. Madawaska: St. John Valley Publishing, 1975. Pp. vii, 86, xxvi.

3693 STEWART, RONALD E. "Madawaska." Pine Cone, 6 (Winter, 1950-1951), 32-35.

SEE ALSO entries 1437 and 3355.

MADISON (SOMERSET CO.)

3694 CAIL, HAROLD L. "Lakewood--Maine's state theatre." Down East, 14 (July, 1968), 48-51.

3695 CLARK, EMMA FOLSOM, WILLIAM CASSIDY, and VIOLET CASSIDY. History of Madison. Madison, 1962. Pp. 370.

3696 OBLAK, JOHN BYRON. Bringing Broadway to Maine; the history of Lakewood, Lakewood, Maine. Terre Haute, Ind.: Moore-Langen, 1971. Pp. 213. MeHi.

MADRID (FRANKLIN CO.)

3697 SWIFT, JOSIAH SPOONER. "Saddleback in 1839, the account of an ascent." Appalachia, New Ser., 11, (December, 1945), 490-503. Edited by Benton L. Hatch.

SEE ALSO entry 1419.

MAGALLOWAY PLANTATION (OXFORD CO.)

3698 BENNETT, GERTRUDE ALLINSON. "A Magalloway schoolmarm never goes home." Down East, 12 (October, 1965), 35, 39-41, 44-45. Reminiscences of the author.

MANCHESTER (KENNEBEC CO.)

3699 MANCHESTER, ME. BICENTENNIAL COMMITTEE. Stories about the town of Manchester and its people. Augusta: J. S. McCarthy, 1975. Pp. ix, 152. Me. Includes two errata slips.

3700 SHUTE, ALBERTA VAN HORN. A year and a day on the farm. North Manchester: Balm O' Gilead Pr., 1972. Pp. 206. MeP. Social life and customs.

MAPLETON (AROOSTOOK CO.)

3701 No items located.

MARIAVILLE (HANCOCK CO.)

3702 No items located.

MARION TOWNSHIP (WASHINGTON CO.)

3703 No items located.

MARS HILL (AROOSTOOK CO.)

3704 MARS HILL, ME. CENTENNIAL BOOKLET COMMITTEE. Mars Hill, Maine, centennial, 1867-1967. n.p., [1967]. Unpaged. Me.

3705 TWEEDIE, GLADYS SYLVESTER. Mars Hill, typical Aroostook town. Presque Isle: Northern Printers, 1952. Pp. 74.

MARSHFIELD (WASHINGTON CO.)

3706 No items located.

MASARDIS (AROOSTOOK CO.)

3707 No items located.

MASON TOWNSHIP (OXFORD CO.)

3708 No items located.

MASSACHUSETTS GORE (FRANKLIN CO.)

3709 No items located.

MATINICUS ISLE PLANTATION (KNOX CO.)

3710 CONDON, VESTA. "An island store one hundred years ago." OTNE, 32 (1941-1942), 52-56.

3711 EMMONS, CELIA PHILBROOK. Highlights of life on Matinicus Island. Westbrook: H. S. Cobb, 1960. Pp. 32. Me.

3712 FILLMORE, ROBERT B., comp. Gems of the ocean. Rockland: Opinion Print, 1914. Pp. 38.

3713 LONG, CHARLES ALBERT EUGENE. Matinicus Isle: its story and its people. [Lewiston]: Lewiston Journal Printshop, 1926. Pp. 235.

3714 MATINICUS ISLE PLANTATION

3714   "THE STORY of Matinicus Isle." MeHistMag, 7 (1891-1892), 113-118.

3715   YOUNG, HAZEL. "Matinicus Island." Down East, 13 (August, 1966), 44-46.

MATTAMISCONTIS TOWNSHIP (PENOBSCOT CO.)

3716   No items located.

MATTAWAMKEAG (PENOBSCOT CO.)

3717   SMITH, GEORGE W., CHARLES F. PLUMLY, and JOHN E. CLARK. History of Mount Horeb Royal Arch Chapter, No. 49, Mattawamkeag, Maine from its organization to February, 1910. Portland: Stephen Berry, 1910. Pp. 89. MeHi.
    Freemasons.

3718   SMITH, GEORGE W. History of Pine Tree Lodge, No. 172, Free and Accepted Masons, Mattawamkeag, Penobscot County, Maine, from January 1, 1892 to January 1, 1908. Portland: Stephen Berry, 1908. Pp. 90. MeHi.

3719   _____. History of Pine Tree Lodge, No. 172, Free and Accepted Masons, Mattawamkeag, Penobscot County, Maine, from the date of its institution in 1873 to Jan. 1, 1892. Portland: Stephen Berry, 1892. Pp. 81. MeBa.

    SEE ALSO entry 50.

MAXFIELD (PENOBSCOT CO.)

3720   No items located.

MAYFIELD TOWNSHIP (SOMERSET CO.)

3721   No items located.

MECHANIC FALLS (ANDROSCOGGIN CO.)

3722   PENNEY, JOHN W. "Mechanic Falls, past and present." BTJ, 18 (1905-1906), 349-351.

3723   WATERMAN, CHARLES ELMER. Historical sketch of the town of Mechanic Falls. Mechanic Falls: Ledger Publishing, 1894. Pp. 55.

    SEE ALSO entry 3532.

MEDDYBEMPS (WASHINGTON CO.)

3724   No items located.

MEDFORD (PISCATAQUIS CO.)

3725   PATRONS OF HUSBANDRY. MAINE STATE GRANGE. COLD BROOK GRANGE, NO. 436. Medford notes, 1808-1958. Medford, [1958]. 78 leaves.

MEDWAY (PENOBSCOT CO.)

3726   BEATHEM, HAROLD C. History and genealogy of Medway Maine, compiled by the Medway Beathems for the centennial anniversary, 1875-1975. n.p., [1975]. Pp. 263. MeU.

MERCER (SOMERSET CO.)

3727   SEE entry 1419.

MERRILL (ARROSTOOK CO.)

3728   No items located.

MERRILL STRIP (FRANKLIN CO.)

3729   No items located.

MEXICO (OXFORD CO.)

3730   SEE entry 2868.

MILBRIDGE (WASHINGTON CO.)

3731   ANDERSON, MAIZIE FREEMAN. "Keeper of the light." Down East, 16 (August, 1969), 58-60.
    Petit Manan Light.

3732   BENSON, EARL M. "Down East emporium." Down East, 3 (October, 1956), 20-21, 34-35.
    General store and trading post owned by Joseph Wallace.

3733   "MILBRIDGE, Maine." MeHistMag, 9 (1894-1895), 223-226.

3734   SAWYER, FRANKLIN. History of Pleiades Lodge, No. 173, Free and Accepted Masons, Milbridge, Maine, from its organization, July, 1874 to July, 1892. Portland: Stephen Berry, 1892. Pp. 40. MeBa.

3735   SAWYER, PHILIP, et al. Milbridge, 1848-1948, centennial program. n.p., [1948]. Pp. 96. MeHi.

    SEE ALSO entries 1840 and 1864.

MILFORD (PENOBSCOT CO.)

3736   MILFORD BICENTENNIAL COMMITTEE. History of
        Milford, about its origin, growth and its
        people from 1800. [Milford], 1976. Pp. 90.
        MeU.

        SEE ALSO entry 1733.

MILLINOCKET (PENOBSCOT CO.)

3737   "THE DEVELOPMENT of Millinocket." Maine.
        Bureau of Industrial and Labor Statistics.
        Annual Report, 17 (1903), 150-174.

3738   EBERT, HERMAN. "Year by year at Millinocket:
        the record of Saint Andrew's Parish." The
        Northeast, 77 (November, 1950), 6-9.

3739   LAVERTY, DOROTHY BOWLER. Millinocket: magic
        city of Maine's wilderness. Freeport: Bond
        Wheelwright, 1973. Pp. xviii, 110.

3740   MILLINOCKET, ME. Millinocket, Maine, 50th
        anniversary, 1901-1951. n.p., [1951?].
        Pp. 32. Me.

3741   REILLY, M. W. "St. Martin of Tours, Milli-
        nocket." MeCathHM, 2 (January, 1914), 23-26.

MILO (PISCATAQUIS CO.)

3742   KENISTON, FRANK WALTER. Biographies of Milo,
        Maine. Auburn: Merrill & Webber, 1945.
        Pp. xiv, 148.

3743   WEST, RETHEL C. History of Milo, 1802-1923.
        ... Dover-Foxcroft: F. D. Barrows, 1923.
        Pp. 78. MeBa.

MILTON TOWNSHIP (OXFORD CO.)

3744   BENNETT, RANDY L. "Mount Zircon, noon tide
        spring." Down East, 20 (May, 1974), 40-43.
        Spring with curative powers.

MINOT (ANDROSCOGGIN CO.)

3745   MINOT, ME. Historical resumé of the town of
        Minot. n.p., [1962?]. Unpaged. Me.

3746   NOYES, CROSBY STUART. The crown of New Eng-
        land: the grand old town of Minot, Maine;
        an address delivered at the celebration of
        the centennial anniversary of the town of
        Minot, Maine, held at West Minot, August
        seventh, nineteen hundred and two. Washing-
        ton, D.C.: Judd & Detweiler, 1904. Pp. 32.

3747   SHAUB, BENJAMIN MARTIN. "Garnet locality of
        Minot." Rocks and Minerals, 32 (May-June,
        1957), 227-234.

3748   "WILLIAM Ladd." MeLB, 12 (1926-1927), 98-
        105.
            Includes a history of Minot and list of
        Ladd's writings.

        SEE ALSO entry 1425.

MISERY GORE (SOMERSET CO.)

3749   No items located.

MISERY TOWNSHIP (SOMERSET CO.)

3750   No items located.

MOLUNKUS TOWNSHIP (AROOSTOOK CO.)

3751   ATKINSON, MINNIE. "The Molunkus House."
        SJMH, 13 (1925), 82-90.
            Hotel.

MONHEGAN PLANTATION (LINCOLN CO.)

3752   ASHLEY, ALTA. The Monhegan ice pond. n.p.,
        [1969?]. Unpaged. Me.

3753   BURTON, CLARA R. "Monhegan shipwrecks."
        Down East, 13 (June, 1966), 52-57.

3754   ELLSWORTH, WOLCOTT WEBSTER. Monhegan Island
        Maine: brief description of the "Sentinel of
        New England." Hartford, Conn.: Case, Lock-
        wood & Brainard, 1912. Pp. 13.

3755   FULLER, ANNE. "Monhegan, the fortunate is-
        land." Down East, 7 (June, 1961), 30-34,
        64-65.

3756   GOSS, ELBRIDGE HENRY. "Something about Mon-
        hegan." MagAmHist, 12 (1884), 266-274.

3757   HAMLIN, AUGUSTUS CHOATE. "Supposed Runic in-
        scriptions." American Association for the
        Advancement of Science. Proceedings, 10 Pt. 2,
        (1856), 214-216.
            Manana Island.

3758   HOLMES, H. R. "Monhegan Island." Granite Mo,
        44 (1912), 147-149.

3759   "THE ISLAND of Monhegan." BHistMag, 3 (1887-
        1888), 141-145.

3760 JENKS, WILLIAM. "On an inscription on a rock in the island of Mananas." American Academy of Arts and Sciences. Proceedings, 2 (1848-1852), 267.

3761 JENNEY, CHARLES FRANCIS. The fortunate island of Monhegan: a historical monograph. (1922) 2d ed. with additions. New Bedford, Mass.: Reynolds Printing, 1927. Pp. 78.
    Originally appeared in AASP, New Ser., 31 (1922), 299-358.

3762 "A LEGEND of Monhegan." Maine Monthly Magazine, 1 (1836-1837), 202-204.

3763 "MONHEGAN Island, Maine." BTJ, 6 (1893-1894), 144.

3764 PETTENGILL, A. G. "Monhegan, historical and picturesque." NEM, New Ser., 19 (1898-1899), 65-81.

3765 PROPER, IDA SEDGWICK. Monhegan, the cradle of New England. Portland: Southworth Pr., 1930. Pp. xvii, 275.

3766 RAWLINGS, CHARLES. "Lobster town: Monhegan Island, Maine." Saturday Evening Post, 226 (August 15, 1953), 32-33, 74-77.

    SEE ALSO entries 611, 962, 1712, and 2425.

MONMOUTH (KENNEBEC CO.)

3767 BARTER, J. MALCOLM. "Maine business profile: Chick Orchards." Down East, 11 (March, 1965), 38.
    Includes history of the orchard.

3768 BRANIN, M. LELYN. "The Saffords: skilled earthenware potters of Monmouth, Maine." Spinning Wheel, 29 (January-February, 1973), 14-16.

3769 COCHRANE, HARRY HAYMAN. History of Monmouth and Wales. East Winthrop: Banner, 1894. 2v.

3770 HOOPER, EUNICE. "Beautiful Monmouth." Sun Up, 10 (August, 1932), 7, 22, 24.

3771 SOUTHARD, IRENE H. "The Custon Free Public Library." MeLAB, 16 (August, 1955), 10-11.

3772 TREAT, HARRY M. "Man failure!" Trains, 15 (March, 1955), 48-51.
    Collision on the Maine Central Railroad in 1906.

MONROE (WALDO CO.)

3773 No items located.

MONSON (PISCATAQUIS CO.)

3773A ANDREWS, RICHARD L. "Old 2 x 6." Trains & Travel, 13 (May, 1953), 28-30.
    Monson Railroad, 1883-1953.

3774 BUKER, H. W. "Mining slate in Maine." BTJ, 25 (1912-1913), 6-8.

3774A CRITTENDEN, HENRY TEMPLE. "The Monson Railroad." RLHSB, No. 57 (1942), 87-93.

3775 HAYNES, GEORGE HENRY. The Switzerland of Maine, short sketch of beautiful Monson, the discovery of slate and the use and growth of the Monson Maine Slate Company. Boston: Monson Maine Slate Co., 1889. Pp. 32. MeHi.

3776 HUSSEY, NELSON. "The 'two by six' railroad of Monson, Maine." Down East, 13 (March, 1967), 38-41.
    Monson Railroad Co.

3777 MONSON, ME. Semi-centennial address of Chas. Davison, poems by W. S. Knowlton and T. N. Lord, etc., Monson, April 22, 1872. Portland: Hoyt, Fogg & Breed, 1872. Pp. 36.

3778 REED, JEANNE BROWN, ALTHEA HAGGSTOM FRENCH, and ELIZABETH EMANUELSON DAVIS. Monson, Maine, history, 1822-1972. Monson, 1972. Pp. 219. MeU.

3779 SPRAGUE, JOHN FRANCIS. History of Doric Lodge, No. 149, of Free and Accepted Masons, Monson, Maine, from A.D. 1868 to A.D. 1901. ... Guilford: Recorder Publishing, 1902. Pp. 40, 26.
    "A continuation of the history of Doric Lodge from A.D. 1887 to A.D. 1901"; 26 pp. at end.

3780 _____. "Monson, Maine." BHistMag, 3 (1887-1888), 97-98.

MONTICELLO (AROOSTOOK CO.)

3781 No items located.

MONTVILLE (WALDO CO.)

3782 HALLDALE SCHOOL, MONTVILLE, ME. A brief history of the town of Montville. [Montville?, 1947]. Pp. 7. Me.

MOOSE RIVER (SOMERSET CO.)

3783 SEE entry 3377A.

MORO PLANTATION (AROOSTOOK CO.)

3784   No items located.

MORRILL (WALDO CO.)

3785   MORRILL MEETING HOUSE SOCIETY. An historical sketch of the "Meeting house at Morrill, Maine" 1848-1948. n.p., [1948?]. Unpaged. MBNEH.

3786   ROBINSON, TIMOTHY WEYMOUTH. History of the town of Morrill in the county of Waldo and State of Maine. Belfast: City Job Print, 1944-1957. 2v.
  Volume one was edited by Theoda Mears Morse; volume two, published by the Morrill Historical Society, is genealogical.

MOSCOW (SOMERSET CO.)

3787   MOSCOW HISTORY COMMITTEE. Makers of Moscow. Skowhegan: Independent-Reporter Pr., 1966. Pp. xii, 66.

MT. ABRAM TOWNSHIP (FRANKLIN CO.)

3788   No items located.

MOUNT CHASE PLANTATION (PENOBSCOT CO.)

3789   SEE entry 1833.

MOUNT DESERT (HANCOCK CO.)

3790   BUTCHER, RUSSELL D. "The Jordan Pond House." Down East, 16 (July, 1970), 52-55, 114-116.

3791   DAVISSON, JEAN. "Somesville summer party, 1855." Down East, 7 (August, 1960), 32-34, 58.

3792   HAMOR, EBEN M. History of Mt. Desert Lodge, No. 140, of Free and Accepted Masons, Mt. Desert, Maine, from February 14, 1867 to February 14, 1871. Portland: S. Berry, 1871. Pp. 14. MB.

3793   HAMOR, JAMES E. History of Mount Desert Lodge, No. 140, Free and Accepted Masons, at Mount Desert, Maine, from February 14, 1871 to February 14, 1892. Bar Harbor: Maine Coast Cottager Office, 1892. Pp. 16. MeHi.

3794   MEREDITH, IRVING. "Twenty-five years of Echo Lake Camp." Appalachia, 26 (1946-1947), 320-325.
  An Appalachian Mountain Club camp.

3795   NORTHEAST HARBOR, ME. UNION CHURCH. Fiftieth anniversary of the Union Church, Northeast Harbor, Me., ... July 16th, 1939. n.p., [1939]. Unpaged. MeBa.

3796   "A SUCCESSOR of the Apostles founds a parish." The Northeast, 75 (November, 1948), 14-18.
  St. Mary's-by-the-Sea, Northeast Harbor.

3797   [VAUGHAN, WILLIAM WARREN]. Northeast Harbor: reminiscences. By an old summer resident. [Hallowell]: White & Horn, 1930. Pp. 86.

3798   WILLISTON, BELVIN THOMAS. "Records of the First Church of Mount Desert, Maine, 1792-1867." NEHGR, 73 (1919), 279-291.

SEE ALSO entries 1587 and 1617.

MT. KATAHDIN TOWNSHIP (PISCATAQUIS CO.)

3799   AVERY, MYRON HALBURTON. "Forest fires at Mount Katahdin." The Northern, 8 (June, 1928), 3-4.
  1795-1923.

3800   _____. "Katahdin, its history." In the Maine Woods, (1939), 18-25.

3801   _____. "The Keep path and its successors: the history of Katahdin from the east and north." Appalachia, 17 (1928-1929), 132-147, 224-237.

3802   BAXTER, PERCIVAL PROCTOR. Greatest mountain: Katahdin's wilderness ... with a historical essay by Judith A. and John W. Hakola. San Francisco: Scrimshaw Pr., 1972. Pp. 21.

3803   BOWDITCH, HENRY INGERSOLL. "A trip to Katahdin in 1856." Appalachia, New Ser., 24 (1958-1959), 145-162, 331-348.

3804   DE LASKI, JOHN. "Glacial actions on Mount Katahdin." American Journal of Science, 103 (1872), 27-31.

3805   ECKSTORM, FANNIE HARDY. "The Katahdin legends." Appalachia, 16 (1924-1926), 39-52.

3806   LEAVITT, HAROLD WALTER. Katahdin skylines. Orono: Univ. of Maine Pr., 1970. Pp. xx, 99.

3807   MERRILL, LUCIUS H. "Ktaadn." Bangor Historical Society. Proceedings, (1914-1915), 19-30.

3808   NITKIN, NATHANIEL. "Wild, the mountain of Thoreau." NEG, 9 (Fall, 1967), 35-43.
  Mount Katahdin.

3809 SMITH, EDWARD STAPLES COUSENS and MYRON HAL-
BURTON AVERY. An annotated bibliography of
Katahdin, with corrigenda and 1937 supplement. Washington: Appalachian Trail Conference, 1950. Pp. iii, 75, 4. Me.

3810 SMITH, EDWARD STAPLES COUSENS. "Larrabee and
'the backwoods expedition.'" Appalachia, 19
(1926), 284-290.
William C. Larrabee at Mount Katahdin in
1837.

3811 _____ and PHILIP W. K. SWEET. "Rock Creep
on Mt. Ktaadn, Maine." GeogRev, 14 (1924),
388-393.

3812 SMITH, MARION WHITNEY. Katahdin fantasies:
stories based on old Indian legends. Millinocket: Millinocket Pr., 1953. Pp. 44.

3813 _____. "Katahdin legend." Down East, 2
(February-March, 1956), 15-16.
Legend of Pamola, evil spirit of Mount
Katahdin.

3814 SPRAGUE, JOHN FRANCIS. "Pamola." SJMH, 10
(1922), 215-220.
Evil spirit of Mount Katahdin in Indian
folklore.

3815 VOSE, PRESCOTT H. "Katahdin in '94." Appalachia, 27 (1948-1949), 334-339.

3816 WING, GEORGE CURTIS. "Mount Ktaadn sometimes
Mount Katahdin." SJMH, 10 (1922), 115-136.

3817 WITHERLE, GEORGE H. Explorations west and
northwest of Katahdin in the late nineteenth
century. 2d ed. [Augusta]: Reprinted by
Maine Appalachian Trail Club, 1950. ii, 57
leaves.

MOUNT VERNON (KENNEBEC CO.)

3818 BLAKE, GEORGE H. Echoes in the silence: the
memorials in the First Baptist Church of
Mount Vernon with essential references to
the history of town and church. n.p.,
[1967?]. Pp. 23. Me.

MOXIE GORE (SOMERSET CO.)

3819 No items located.

NAPLES (CUMBERLAND CO.)

3820 DINGLEY, ROBERT JORDAN. A mini-history of
Naples, Maine.... Naples: Naples Historical
Society, [1970?]. Unpaged. MeHi.

3821 NAPLES, ME. Souvenir program, Naples centennial, 1834-1934, August 10-11-12. n.p.,
[1934]. Unpaged. MeHi.
Includes a brief historical sketch.

3822 NAPLES, ME. CHURCH OF GOOD FELLOWSHIP.
Souvenir calendar, Church of Good Fellowship,
Naples, Maine, services of rededication,
August 12, 1934. n.p., [1934]. Unpaged.
MeHi.

NASHVILLE PLANTATION (AROOSTOOK CO.)

3823 No items located.

NESOURDNAHUNK TOWNSHIP (PISCATAQUIS CO.)

3824 No items located.

NEW CANADA PLANTATION (AROOSTOOK CO.)

3825 No items located.

NEW GLOUCESTER (CUMBERLAND CO.)

3826 CARR, FRANCES. "The New Gloucester Shaker
school and its teachers." Shaker Quarterly,
1 (1961), 16-20.

3827 _____. "The Tamar fruit compound: a Maine
Shaker industry." Shaker Quarterly, 2
(1962), 39-41.
The Shaker Tamar Laxative.

3828 DAY, DAVID. Born in a blockhouse: the re-
ligious heritage of New Gloucester, Maine.
Lewiston: Central Maine Pr., 1965. Pp. 88.
MBC.

3829 FERRANTI, FRANK T. "A Shaker experience."
New England Social Studies Bulletin, 32
(1974-1975), 17-23.

3830 GODING, GEORGE HENRY. History of Cumberland
Lodge, No. 12, F. & A. M., New Gloucester,
Me., from April 7, 1873 to December 31, 1900.
Lewiston: Lewiston Journal, 1901. Pp. [49]-
113. MeHi.
Pagination continued from Moses Plummer's
history for 1803 to 1873, entry 3846.

3831 HUTCHINSON, GLORIA. "The Shakers of Sabbathday Lake." Down East, 18 (October, 1971),
38-41, 66-67, 70, 75, 77.

3832 JOHNSON, THEODORE ELLIOT, ed. "The diary of
a Maine Shaker boy: Delmer Wilson--1887."
Shaker Quarterly, 8 (1968), 3-22.

3833 McCOOL, ELSIE A. "A brief history of the Central Dwelling, Sabbathday Lake." Shaker Quarterly, 1 (1961), 71-76.

3834 _____. "A brief history of the Shaker Mills, Sabbathday Lake, Maine." Shaker Quarterly, 3 (1963), 99-102.

3835 _____. "Gleanings from Sabbathday Lake church journals, 1872-1884." Shaker Quarterly, 6 (1966), 103-112, 124-134.

3836 _____. "Shaker woven poplar work." Shaker Quarterly, 2 (1962), 55-59.
      Baskets and boxes.

3837 MAYBERRY, STEPHEN PHINNEY. "Historical sketches in New Gloucester." MHGR, 1 (1884), 107-109.

3838 NEW GLOUCESTER, ME. The bicentennial of New Gloucester, being an account of the celebration of the two hundredth anniversary of the coming of the first settlers, 1739-1939. [New Gloucester]: New Gloucester, Maine, Historical Society, 1945. Pp. 38. MeHi.

3839 _____. The New Gloucester book, account of the 150th anniversary celebration of the incorporation of the town, with a comprehensive review of the history of the town by Florence Hunt Nelson. Auburn: Webber, 1925. Pp. 187. MBNEH.

3840 _____. The New Gloucester centennial, September 7, 1874. Thomas Hawes Haskell, comp. Portland: Hoyt, Fogg & Donham, 1875. Pp. 139.

3841 PARSONS, ISAAC. "An account of New Gloucester." MeHSC, 2 (1847), 151-164.

3842 PÉLADEAU, MARIUS B. "The Shakers of Maine." Antiques, 107 (1975), 1144-1153.
      Furniture.

3843 PENNEY, JOHN W. "Records of the proprietors of New Gloucester and reminiscences of some of the early settlers." MeHSC, 2 Ser., 8 (1897), 263-288.
      Eighteenth century.

3844 PHILBROOK, ELEANOR. "A brief history of the Shaker post office [in] Sabbathday Lake, Maine." Shaker Quarterly, 4 (1964), 38-40.

3845 _____. "Home thoughs from Sabbathday Lake." Shaker Quarterly, 1 (1961), 77-79.

3846 PLUMMER, MOSES. History of Cumberland Lodge, No. 12, of Free and Accepted Masons, of New Gloucester, Me., from 1803 to 1873. Portland: Stephen Berry, 1873. Pp. 48. MB.
      For continuation, see entry 3830.

3847 ROGERS, C. TALBOT. "The people called Shakers." Down East, 4 (October, 1957), 20-23.

3848 ROUNDS, JOHN. The Baptist Church in New Gloucester: an historical discourse preached at the re-opening of the Baptist meeting-house in New Gloucester, Sunday, August 16, 1857. Portland: J. B. Foster, 1857. Pp. 16. Me.

3849 SMITH, DAVID CLAYTON. "William A. Drew and the Maine Shakers." Shaker Quarterly, 7 (1967), 24-32.
      Newspaper promotion of Shaker grape crops.

3850 WILLIAMS, STEPHEN GUION. Chosen land: the Sabbathday Lake Shakers. Boston: Godine, 1975. Unpaged.

      SEE ALSO entry 1509.

NEW LIMERICK (AROOSTOOK CO.)

3851 No items located.

NEW PORTLAND (SOMERSET CO.)

3852 CURRIER, ALICE C. "Maine's oldest wire bridge." Yankee, 23 (September, 1959), 58.
      Completed in 1842.

3853 LIBBY, STEVE. "Maine's fool bridge still standing after 126 years." Maine Dig, 4 (Winter, 1970), 60-61.

3854 LUCE-WHEELER, JANICE. "Colonel Morse's 'fool bridge.'" Down East, 23 (November, 1976), 42-43, 64.
      F. B. Morse.

NEW SHARON (FRANKLIN CO.)

3855 PERRY, ANGELA H. "Maine's unique racquet factory." Down East, 13 (March, 1967), 42-44, 66-69.
      Tennis racquets; C. A. Thompson Company.

      SEE ALSO entries 1419 and 3362.

NEW SWEDEN (AROOSTOOK CO.)

3856 "ANNIVERSARY of the Congregational Church in New Sweden." MeCP, 24 (February, 1937), 8-9.

3857 MALMQUIST, MARIE. Lapptäcke. n.p., 1928-1929. 2v.
      In Swedish.

3858 MELVIN, CHARLOTTE LENENTINE. "The first hundred years in New Sweden." Swedish Pioneer Historical Quarterly, 21 (1970), 233-247.

3859 MILLGÅRD, PER-OLOF. "Letters from New Sweden, Maine." Swedish Pioneer Historical Quarterly, 26 (1975), 104-111.

3860 NEW SWEDEN, ME. Celebration of the decennial anniversary of the founding of New Sweden, Maine, July 23, 1880. Portland: B. Thurston, 1881. Pp. 87.
Historical oration by William W. Thomas, Jr.

3861 _____. Ninety years in New Sweden, 1870-1960. Caribou: Pride Printing, [1960?]. Unpaged. MeHi.

3862 _____. One hundred years in New Sweden. [Caribou: Pride Printing, 1970]. Unpaged. MeHi.

3863 _____. Souvenir of the 40th anniversary of the founding of New Sweden, Maine, June 25, 1910. n.p., 1910. Unpaged. MeHi.

3864 _____. The story of New Sweden as told at the quarter centennial celebration of the founding of the Swedish colony in the woods of Maine, June 25, 1895. Stanley J. Estes, ed. Portland: Loring, Short & Harmon, 1896. Pp. 134.
Oration by William W. Thomas, Jr.

3865 NORBERG, GARD E. "Stout-hearted Swedes took root in Maine." American Swedish Monthly, 42 (December, 1947), 22-23, 37-40.

3866 SETTERDAHL, LILLY. "A visit to New Sweden, Maine: reminiscences of an era." Swedish Pioneer Historical Quarterly, 26 (1975), 92-103.

3867 STAPLES, LINNEA STADIG. "New Sweden, Maine--its birth and settlement." National Historical Magazine, 73 (August, 1939), 77-79.

3868 SWANSON, EVADENE BURRIS. "Swedish colony in the Maine woods." Swedish Pioneer Historical Quarterly, 17 (1966), 3-21.

3869 THOMAS, WILLIAM WIDGERY, b. 1839. "The story of New Sweden." MeHSC, 2 Ser., 7 (1896), 53-85, 113-151.

3870 WIEDEN, CLIFFORD and MARGUERITE WIEDEN. "The beginnings of a New Sweden in Maine." American Swedish Historical Foundation. Yearbook, (1946), 85-96.

3871 WILSON, CHARLES G. "New Sweden." Down East, 5 (October, 1958), 31-33.

SEE ALSO entries 799, 1216, 1448, and 1456.

NEW VINEYARD (FRANKLIN CO.)

3872 BUTLER, BENJAMIN, NATALIE STURGES BUTLER, and DONALD W. McKEEN. Zephaniah builds a school-house--among other things. Farmington: Knowlton & McLeary, 1975. Pp. 101. MBNEH.

3873 ST. JOHN, FREDERIC. "The deserted village of Maine." Sun Up, 8 (July, 1930), 12.
Author's name is a pseudonym.

SEE ALSO entry 3362.

NEWBURGH (PENOBSCOT CO.)

3874 No items located.

NEWCASTLE (LINCOLN CO.)

3875 CUSHMAN, DAVID QUIMBY. "Ancient settlement of Sheepscott." MeHSC, 4 (1856), 209-233.

3876 FLYE, WILLIAM L. "A brief history of the First Congregational Parish in Newcastle." MeCP, 25 (March, 1938), 8-9, 20.

3877 GILDERSLEEVE, NELSON. "An active summer and winter ministry at lovely St. Andrew's Church at Newcastle." The Northeast, 76 (July, 1949), 13-16.

3878 JOHNSON, SAMUEL and WILLIAM WILLIS. "Account of an ancient settlement on Sheepscot River." MeHSC, 2 (1847), 229-237.

3879 LARRABEE, GEORGE H. A souvenir of Lincoln Academy, Newcastle, Maine. Portland: Lakeside Pr., [1898]. Pp. 46. MeHi.
Includes historical sketch.

3880 LUCEY, WILLIAM LEO. "Two Irish merchants of New England." NEQ, 14 (1941), 633-645.
James Kavanagh and Matthew Cottrill.

3881 NEWCASTLE, ME. Newcastle, Maine, program, committees, together with an historical sketch on the observance of the 200th anniversary of its incorporation, June 19-21, 1953. Damariscotta: News Print Shop, [1953]. Pp. 29. Me.

3882 NEWCASTLE, ME. SECOND CONGREGATIONAL CHURCH. Manual and history, together with a history of the First Congregational Church in Newcastle. ... Newcastle, 1917. Pp. 55. MeB.
History is by Oscar William Peterson.

SEE ALSO entries 644, 1678, 1683-1684, 1709, and 4589.

NEWFIELD (YORK CO.)

3883 BACHELER, GILBERT H. An historical sketch of the Congregational Church, West Newfield, Maine, presented at the centennial anniversary, September 29th, 1901. Norwich, Conn.: The Bulletin Company, 1901. Pp. 16.

NEWPORT (PENOBSCOT CO.)

3884 FRIEND, GILMAN N. Newport sesquicentennial, 1814-1964. [Newport, 1964]. Unpaged. Me.

3885 MITCHELL, WILLIAM H. A brief history of Newport, Maine, 1814-1914. Newport: A. W. Lander, 1914. Pp. 55.

3886 "THE NEWPORT centennial." MeCP, 1 (September, 1937), 8-9.
High Street Union Church.

NEWRY (OXFORD CO.)

3887 WIGHT, CARRIE. Newry, Maine, 1805-1955. Bethel: Oxford County Citizen, 1955. Pp. 37. Me.

NOBLEBORO (LINCOLN CO.)

3888 WHITTEMORE, EDWIN CAREY. History of the First Baptist Church of Nobleboro, Maine, 1793-1893. Portland: Brown Thurston, 1893. Pp. 19. Me.

SEE ALSO entries 1678 and 1708.

NORRIDGEWOCK (SOMERSET CO.)

3889 ALLEN, WILLIAM, 1780-1873. The history of Norridgewock: comprising memorials of the aboriginal inhabitants and Jesuit missionaries, hardships of the pioneers, biographical notices of the early settlers, and ecclesiastical sketches. Norridgewock: E. J. Peet, 1849. Pp. 252.

3890 _____. "Statistics of Norridgewock." MeHSC, 7 (1876), 288-289.
Mortality, 1849-1867.

3891 "THE ATTACK on Norridgewock." Down East, 11 (September, 1964), 25, 48.
British raiders destroyed village of Norridgewock and mission of Sebastian Rasles, 1724.

3892 CUMMINGS, EPHRAIM CHAMBERLAIN. "The mission of Father Rasles." MeHSC, 2 Ser., 4 (1893), 146-169, 265-301, 404-410.

3893 ECKSTORM, FANNIE HARDY. "The attack on Norridgewock." NEQ, 7 (1934), 541-578.
Jesuit missionary Sebastian Rasles killed by British raiders in 1724; see also entry 3896.

3894 GOYAU, GEORGES. "Le P. Sébastien Racle." Revue Histoire des Missions, 1 (September, 1924), 161-197.
Jesuit missionary among the Norridgewock Indians.

3895 HEFFERNAN, JOHN PAUL. "Silent bell." Down East, 11 (September, 1964), 24, 26-27.
Father Sebastian Rasles.

3896 MORRISON, KENNETH M. "Sebastian Racle and Norridgewock, 1724: the Eckstorm conspiracy thesis reconsidered." MeHSQ, 14 (1974-1975), 76-97.
See also entry 3893.

3897 O'DWYER, GEORGE FRANCIS. "Sebastian Râle and the Puritans." Catholic World, 112 (1920-1921), 45-51.

3898 SPRAGUE, JOHN FRANCIS. Sebastian Râlé: a Maine tragedy of the eighteenth century. Boston: Heintzemann Pr., 1906. Pp. 162.

3899 TRIPP, ALTA E. "Norrigewock's corn factories." Down East, 13 (October, 1966), 37.
Canning; Burnham and Morrill and the G. S. and F. E. Jewett Company.

3900 VARNEY, LLOYD H. "Epilogue at Old Point." MeArchSocB, No. 2 ([October, 1964]), 17.
Catholic mission.

3901 WILLIAMSON, JOSEPH. "A memorial of Father Rale." MeHSC, 2 Ser., 9 (1898), 137-141.

3902 WOOD, HENRIETTA DANFORTH. Early days of Norridgewock. Freeport: Freeport Pr., 1933. Pp. 124. MeHi.

SEE ALSO entries 171, 799, and 1816.

NORTH BERWICK (YORK CO.)

3903 BUFFAM, SAMUEL. Historical sketch of North Berwick. n.p., [1931?]. Pp. 35.

3904 HAYES, CHARLES F. Historical sketch of the Baptist Church at North Berwick, Me., 1768-1894. North Berwick: Journal Print, 1894. Pp. 12. MeHi.

3905 HUSSEY, PHILIP W., JR. The Hussey manufac-
turers, 1835-1960. North Berwick, 1960.
Pp. 72. MeHi.
Physical education facilities.

3906 NORTH BERWICK BICENTENNIAL COMMITTEE. A
pictoral [sic] history of North Berwick,
Maine. [North Berwick], 1976. Pp. 47. MeU.

3907 PERRY, JOSEPHA M. "Samuel Snow, tanner and
cordwainer." BBHS, 19 (1945), 183-193.

3908 ST. JOHN, FREDERIC. "The Morrills of Bonneg
Beg." Sun Up, 8 (September, 1930), 15, 22.
Author's name is a pseudonym.

3909 WEBBER, LAURANCE E. "From plowshares to
bleachers: the Hussey Manufacturing Company
of North Berwick, Maine." Down East, 17
(March, 1971), 62-65.
Agricultural equipment prior to 1915; gym-
nasium seating since that date.

3910 WORTH, EDMUND. Centennial discourse delivered on the one hundredth anniversary of the
organization of the Baptist Church of North
Berwick, Me., September 10th, 1868. Biddeford: J. E. Butler, 1868. Pp. 32. MB.

NORTH HAVEN (KNOX CO.)

3911 BEVERIDGE, NORWOOD P. The North Island:
early times to yesterday. North Haven, 1976.
Pp. 75. MeU.

3912 BOUSFIELD, LILLIE SNOWDEN, ed. Our island
town, by our townspeople and friends. Bar
Harbor: Bar Harbor Times Publishing, 1941.
Pp. 136.

3913 BREKKE, RAGNHILD. "Norminde: Norway comes
to Maine." Down East, 6 (September, 1959),
27-29, 45-46.

SEE ALSO entry 1656.

NORTH YARMOUTH (CUMBERLAND CO.)

3914 BANKS, CHARLES EDWARD. "The militia of North
Yarmouth in early times." Old Times, 7
(1883), 1064-1067.

3915 _____. "North Yarmouth ministers." Old
Times, 5 (1881), 649-653.

3916 _____. "The old planters of Westcustogo."
Old Times, 4 (1880), 437-443.

3917 BUXTON, PHEBE M. "N. Yarmouth & Falmouth
Social Library." Old Times, 3 (1879), 427-
429.

3918 DRINKWATER, NICHOLAS. "Corrections to article on the old church." Old Times, 3 (1879),
316-318.
See entry 3924.

3919 "FIRST Universalist Society of North Yarmouth,
Maine." Old Times, 1 (1877), 56-57.

3920 NO ENTRY.

3921 HUMPHREY, JAMES J. "Vessels [built at North
Yarmouth and Yarmouth, Maine, 1825-1879]."
Old Times, 5 (1881), 743-748.
Arranged chronologically.

3922 LORING, AMASA. "The four judges of North
Yarmouth." MeHSC, 2 Ser., 1 (1890), 57-77.
John Lewis, Jonas Mason, David Mitchell,
and Jeremiah Powell.

3923 _____. "Historical sketch of the Loring family; those who were early residents of North
Yarmouth, Maine." Old Times, 6 (1882), 875-
886, 924-937.

3924 MASON, ELLEN. "The old meeting-house of North
Yarmouth, Maine." Old Times, 2 (1878), 175-
191.
See also entry 3918.

3925 MERRILL, H. AUGUSTUS. "Hero of Westcustogo."
SJMH, 3 (1915-1916), 148-150.
Captain Walter Gendell; shot during skir-
mish with Indians.

3926 NORTH YARMOUTH, ME. FIRST CHURCH. Confes-
sion of faith and covenant, of the First
Church in North Yarmouth, Me. with a catalogue
of its members, and brief historical notices.
... Portland: Mirror Office, 1848. Pp. 64.
MeBa.

3927 "NORTH Yarmouth books." Old Times, 4 (1880),
447-448; 5 (1881), 638-640.

3928 "THE POST Office." Old Times, 1 (1877), 66-
67.

3929 RICH, MARSHALL NYE. "Early churches of
Maine." BTJ, 5 (1892-1893), 171-172.
Relates to the First Congregational Church
in North Yarmouth; a shorter version appeared
in "Old Times" in 1877.

3930 _____. "The North-west Religious Society of
North Yarmouth, Maine." Old Times, 1 (1877),
22-27, 86.

3931 _____. "Shipping interest of North Yarmouth,
Maine." Old Times, 1 (1877), 49-51.

3932 "THE RING Homestead." BTJ, 5 (1892-1893), 45.

3933 RUSSELL, EDWARD. "History of North Yarmouth."
MeHSC, 2 (1847), 165-188.

3934 SARGENT, WILLIAM MITCHELL. "The old church." Old Times, 4 (1880), 453-465.
First Congregational Church.

3935 SEABURY, SAMUEL DORRANCE. "North Yarmouth Academy." Old Times, 2 (1878), 271-274.

3936 STOCKBRIDGE, JOSEPH. "North Yarmouth." Old Times, 5 (1881), 607-611.

3937 TRUE, NATHANIEL TUCKERMAN. "North Yarmouth Academy." Old Times, 8 (1884), 1128-1130.

SEE ALSO entries 1521-1522 and 1524.

NORTH YARMOUTH ACADEMY GRANT (AROOSTOOK CO.)

3938 No items located.

NORTHEAST CARRY TOWNSHIP (PISCATAQUIS CO.)

3939 No items located.

NORTHFIELD (WASHINGTON CO.)

3940 No items located.

NORTHPORT (WALDO CO.)

3941 SEE entry 1833.

NORWAY (OXFORD CO.)

3942 BEAL, EZRA FLUENT. Journal of Ezra F. Beal: diary kept by a distinguished son of Norway; published serially in the Norway Advertiser, Norway, Maine. Don C. Seitz, ed. [N.Y.?], 1926. Pp. 50.

3943 KIMBALL, MERTON L. "Secret fraternities of Norway." BTJ, 17 (1904-1905), 285-287.

3944 LAPHAM, WILLIAM BERRY. Centennial history of Norway, Oxford County, Maine, 1786-1886, including an account of the early grants and purchases, sketches of the grantees, early settlers, and prominent residents, etc., with genealogical registers, and an appendix. Portland: Brown Thurston, 1886. Pp. xvi, 659.

3945 LYFORD, ELMORE B. "What a way to rob a bank!" Yankee, 31 (September, 1967), 92-93, 157-159.
Norway Savings Bank, September 22, 1867.

3946 NORWAY, ME. Norway, Maine, sesquicentennial, 1786-1936, a program of events and brief historical outline of the town. Norway: Advertiser-Democrat, [1936?]. Pp. 32. MeU.

3947 NORWAY HISTORICAL SOCIETY. Norway salutes our country's bicentennial celebration, 1776-1976. Norway, 1976. Pp. 24. Me.
A town history.

3948 NORWAY JUNIOR HIGH SCHOOL. Booklet of Norway past and present. [Norway, 1942]. Unpaged. Me.

3949 NOYES, DAVID. The history of Norway; comprising a minute account of its first settlement, town officers, the annual expenditures of the town, with other statistical matter; interspersed with historical sketches, narrative and anecdote, and occasional remarks by the author. Norway, 1852. Pp. v, 215.

3950 _____. "Norway settlers." MHGR, 9 (1898), 303-308, 328-333, 361-366.

3951 PACKARD, HARRY A. "Norway--a town of unparalleled beauty." Sun Up, 3 (March, 1927), 5-9.

3952 _____. "Something of Norway before the fire." BTJ, 17 (1904-1905), 281-282.

3953 PIKE, CLIFFORD L. Norway centennial poem, delivered on the occasion of the centennial celebration of the settlement of Norway, Maine, Sept. 8th, 1886.... Norway, 1886. Pp. 23.

3954 SMITH, HOWARD DANIEL. History of Oxford Lodge, No. 18, Free and Accepted Masons, Norway, Maine, from date of charter, September 14, 1807, to December, 1909. Norway: Advertiser Book and Job Print, 1910. Pp. 185.

3955 WHITMAN, CHARLES FOSTER. A history of Norway, Maine, from the earliest settlements to the close of the year 1922. Lewiston: Lewiston Journal Printshop, 1924. Pp. 581.

3956 _____. "Norway, Maine, Revolutionary soldiers." DARMag, 47 (1915), 37, 184-186.

3957 WHITMAN, VIC. "The Weary Club." Down East, 18 (August, 1971), 53, 124-130.
Men's club.

3958 WILLIAMS, MYRON R. "When life was young." NEG, 5 (Fall, 1963), 43-52.
Charles Asbury Stevens and glimpses of Norway, 1866-1870.

3959 WRIGHT, WALTER W. "Norway, Maine." Norwegian-American Studies and Records, 15 (1949), 219-222.
Origin of the name.

SEE ALSO entries 1718, 1729, and 3532.

NO. 14 PLANTATION (WASHINGTON CO.)

3960   No items located.

NO. 21 PLANTATION (WASHINGTON CO.)

3961   No items located.

OAKFIELD (AROOSTOOK CO.)

3962   OAKFIELD COMMUNITY HIGH SCHOOL. CLASS OF 1957. The story of Oakfield. Oakfield, [1957]. 2v. Me.
Text on rectos only.

OAKLAND (KENNEBEC CO.)

3963   BENSON, LOUISE M. "Oakland, Maine." Sun Up, 2 (April, 1926), 33-34, 36, 38, 41, 43-44, 46-47.

3964   BROWN, HAROLD F. "Music on Lake Messalonskee." Down East, 17 (September, 1970), 52-55.
New England Music Camp.

3965   GILMAN, JOHN WESLEY. History of Drummond R. A. Chapter, No. 27, West Waterville, Maine, from its organization to September, 1876. Portland: Stephen Berry, 1877. Pp. 38.
Freemasons.

3966   KEBABIAN, JOHN S. "A visit to the Peavey factory site, Oakland, Maine." CEAIA, 21 (1968), 62-63.
Peavey Manufacturing Co.; lumbering tools.

3967   "THE OLD axe shop in Oakland." Down East, 15 (June, 1969), 40-43.
Emerson & Stevens Manufacturing Co., Inc.

3968   SMALL, ABNER RANDALL. History of Messalonskee Lodge, West Waterville, from its organization to the year 1870. Portland: Stephen Berry, 1871. Pp. 48. MeBa.
Freemasons.

SEE ALSO entries 1421, 3532, and 5041.

OLD ORCHARD BEACH (YORK CO.)

3969   "THE CHURCH at work in the playground of two nations: a missionary enterprise at St. John's, Old Orchard Beach." The Northeast, 75 (July, 1948), 5-7, 9.

3970   FAIRFIELD, ROY P. "The Old Orchard 'set-off.'" NEQ, 27 (1954), 227-242.
Development of the ocean resort area.

3971   GARDNER, RALPH D. "By the beautiful sea: a tale of Old Orchard, 1886." NEG, 16 (Summer, 1974), 3-10.
Horatio Alger's visit in 1886.

3972   GRAVES, SARAH BRIDGE. "1800 feet of bad luck." Yankee, 21 (March, 1957), 34-37, 78-81.
Steel pier.

3973   JAKEMAN, ADELBERT M. The story of Ocean Park: an informal seventy-fifth anniversary history, 1881-1956. Ocean Park: Ocean Park Association, 1956. Pp. 121.

3974   LOCKE, JOHN STAPLES. Historical sketches of Old Orchard and the shores of Saco Bay: Biddeford Pool, Old Orchard Beach, Pine Point, Prout's Neck. (1880) Enl. ed. Boston: Chas. H. Woodman, 1884. Pp. 103.
Varies only slightly from first edition, which has the title "Shores of Saco Bay."

3975   _____. Old Orchard Beach, Maine. Portland: G. W. Morris, 1900. Pp. 81.

3976   _____. Old Orchard, Maine. Boston: Graves, Locke, 1879. Pp. 48.

3977   PEVERLY, ELAINE M. and WILLIAM HELLEN McLIN. The dummy. [Sanford]: Wilson's Printers, 1973. Pp. 48. MeP.
Old Orchard Beach branch of the Boston & Maine Railroad.

3978   ST. MARGARET'S CHURCH, OLD ORCHARD BEACH, ME. Golden anniversary souvenir brochure, 1926-1976. Biddeford: Atlantic Coastal Printing, [1976?]. Unpaged. MeU.

SEE ALSO entries 1880, 1904, 4232, and 4287.

OLD TOWN (PENOBSCOT CO.)

3979   GARY, HOBART JUDE. "In the ship mending their nets: an evaluation of Saint James, Old Town." The Northeast, 76 (November, 1949), 7-10.

3980   NORTON, DAVID. Sketches of the town of Old Town, Penobscot County, Maine, from its earliest settlement, to 1879; with biographical sketches. Bangor: S. G. Robinson, 1881. Pp. 152.

3981   OLD TOWN, ME. Old Town, Maine, the first 125 years, 1840-1965. n.p., [1965?]. Unpaged. MeU.

3982   PARENT-TEACHERS CLUB, STILLWATER, ME. A history of Stillwater, Maine. [Stillwater], 1952. Unpaged. Me.

3983 [PORTER, JOSEPH WHITCOMB]. "John Marsh, Jr., owner of the Orono island that bears his name." SJMH, 2 (1914-1915), 202-205.
Author attribution by the editor.

3984 ROTARY INTERNATIONAL, OLD TOWN, ME. Rotary Club of Old Town, Maine, a history, 1927-1944. n.p., [1944?]. Pp. 18. MeBa.

3985 SMITH, NICHOLAS N. The transition from wigwams to frame houses by the Old Town, Maine, Penobscot and Woodstock, New Brunswick, Malecite. n.p., 1971. 11 leaves. MeHi.

SEE ALSO entries 1750, 2082, and 4031.

ORIENT (AROOSTOOK CO.)

3986 No items located.

ORLAND (HANCOCK CO.)

3987 CHASE, FREEMAN HERSEY. History of Rising Sun Lodge, No. 71, of Free and Accepted Masons, Orland, Me., from A.D. 1852 to 1874. Portland: Stephen Berry, 1874. Pp. 35. MeBa.

3988 HARRIMAN, DANIEL. "Settlement of Orland." BHistMag, 1 (1885-1886), 54-55.

3989 MARDEN, GEORGE NATHANIEL. Sermon preached at the Congregational Church in Orland, October 28th, 1866. Ellsworth: N. K. Sawyer, 1867. Pp. 13. MB.
Includes an ecclesiastical history of the town.

ORNEVILLE TOWNSHIP (PISCATAQUIS CO.)

3990 SPRAGUE, JOHN FRANCIS. "General John Parker Boyd and Judge Henry Orne, the original proprietors of the town of Orneville." SJMH, 1 (1913-1914), 43-47, 131-136.

ORONO (PENOBSCOT CO.)

3991 ALPHA TAU OMEGA. BETA UPSILON CHAPTER. UNIVERSITY OF MAINE. Alpha Tau Omega: a history of Beta Upsilon Chapter, 1891-1971. [Orono?, 1971?]. 56 leaves. MeU.

3992 "ARREST and trial of Joseph Inman of Orono, for murder in 1801." BHistMag, 3 (1887-1888), 54-56.

3993 ASHMAN, ROBERT I. "Forestry at Maine." Maine Alumnus, 34 (February, 1953), 4-6, 12.

3994 BARKER, FLORENCE E. "A land boom in Maine one hundred years ago." Sun Up, 10 (June, 1932), 24.

3995 BOARDMAN, SAMUEL LANE. "Historical sketch of the State College." Maine. Board of Agriculture. Annual Report of the Secretary, 21 (1876), 208-220.

3996 "THE BOOKSTORE." Maine Alumnus, 30 (April, 1949), 7, 14.
University of Maine Bookstore.

3997 BURNHAM, JOHN. "The story of an outing club." Maine Alumnus, 47 (July, 1966), 22-25.
Maine Outing Club.

3998 CHAMBERLAIN, GEORGE WALTER. "The University of Maine." Americana, 5 (1910), 1-15.

3999 "THE 'COBURN Cadets'--a history of Maine's Military Department." Maine Alumnus, 19 (January, 1938), 5, 8.

4000 "CO-EDS of the seventies." Maine Alumnus, 26 (April, 1945), 5.
University of Maine.

4001 DAY, CLARENCE ALBERT. Historical sketch of Orono: the Orono sesquicentennial program celebrating the 150th anniversary of the incorporation of Orono, June 14, 15, 16, 1806-1956. n.p., [1956]. Pp. 108.

4002 _____. Twenty-five years of service. Orono: Univ. of Maine, 1937. Pp. 31. MeBa.
Agricultural Extension Service at the University of Maine.

4003 "THE DEPARTMENT of Mechanical Engineering." Maine Alumnus, 26 (April, 1945), 3-4.
University of Maine.

4004 ELLIOTT, LLOYD HARTMAN. Unique patterns in progress: the University of Maine and the pulp and paper industry. N.Y.: Newcomen Society in North America, 1964. Pp. 24.

4005 EVANS, WESTON S. "100 years at the U. of M." Down East, 11 (November, 1964), 24-28, 45-46.

4006 FERNALD, MERRITT CALDWELL. History of Maine State College and the University of Maine. Orono: Univ. of Maine, 1916. Pp. 450.

4007 _____. "The Maine State College of Agriculture and the Mechanic Arts." NEM, 5 (1886-1887), 546-557.

4008 "FIJI fiftieth." Maine Alumnus, 31 (December, 1949), 4.
Phi Gamma Delta Fraternity, University of Maine.

4009 "FOOTBALL in 1892." Maine Alumnus, 24 (November, 1942), 7.
University of Maine.

4010   HARVEY, KINGDON. "The development of Maine's
state university." Maine's Own Magazine, 8
(May and June, 1930), 4-5, 28-29.

4011   HASKELL, EDWIN J. "Recollections of the good
old days." Maine Alumnus, 47 (November,
1965), 5-6.
        University of Maine.

4012   HAUCK, ARTHUR ANDREW. Maine's university and
the land-grant tradition. N.Y.: Newcomen
Society in North America, 1954. Pp. 28.

4013   LAMBE, EMERSON P. "Memories of a student at
Maine during 1903-07." Maine Alumnus, 38
(February, 1957), 14.

4014   MAINE. AGRICULTURAL EXPERIMENT STATION,
ORONO. Exercises at the twenty-fifth anni-
versary of the Maine Agricultural Experiment
Station held at the University of Maine,
March 9, 1910; and a brief historical sketch
of the station. n.p., [1910]. Pp. 38.

4015   MAINE. UNIVERSITY. Commemorative exercises
for the seventy-fifth anniversary of the
founding of the University, February 25 and
26, 1940. [Orono?, 1940]. Pp. 49.

4016   _____. Dedication of Coburn Hall, June 26,
1888. Augusta: Burleigh & Flynt, 1888.
Pp. 71. MeBa.
        Historical address by Lyndon Oak.

4017   _____. Pride in the past, faith in the future, 1865-1965, University of Maine. Orono,
1965. Pp. 32.

4018   MAINE. UNIVERSITY. COLLEGE OF AGRICULTURE.
50th anniversary, Farm and Home Week ...
April 1-4, 1957. [Orono?], 1957. Pp. 20.
MeBa.

4019   MAINE. UNIVERSITY. COLLEGE OF AGRICULTURE.
EXTENSION DEPARTMENT. 50 years with the Cooperative Extension Service in Maine. Orono,
1962. Pp. 36.

4020   "MAINE Masque theatre enters second half century." Maine Alumnus, 37 (May, 1956), 10-11.
        University of Maine.

4021   ORONO, ME. Centennial celebration, and dedication of Town Hall, Orono, Maine, March 3,
1874.... Portland: Bailey & Noyes, 1874.
Pp. 168.

4022   ORONO, Maine: a bicentennial view. n.p.,
1976. Pp. 80. MeU.

4023   "THE PROPER study of mankind." Maine Alumnus,
20 (February, 1939), 5-12.
        The Department of Psychology at the Univer-
sity of Maine.

4024   SMITH, DAVID CLAYTON. "Forest history research and writing at the University of
Maine." Forest History, 12 (July, 1968),
27-31.
        1903-1968.

4025   STEVENS, JAMES STACY. "Librarians past and
present." Maine Alumnus, 20 (April, 1939),
8.
        University of Maine.

4026   _____. Meteorological conditions at Orono,
Maine. Orono, 1907. Pp. 52.
        Includes historical tables.

4027   _____. "The summer session, a historical
sketch." Maine Alumnus, 18 (April, 1937),
4.
        University of Maine.

4028   STEWART, ALICE ROSE. "A woman's place."
Maine Alumnus, 53 (April-May, 1972), 3-4.
        Women at the University of Maine.

4029   STEWART, PHYLLIS and CLARENCE ALBERT DAY. A
history of the Orono Methodist Church. n.p.,
[1960]. 15 leaves. MeU.

4030   "THREE quarters of a century." Maine Alumnus, 25 (January, 1944), 4-5.
        University of Maine.

4031   TURNER, PERCIE HOPKINS. The first forty
years of the Orono-Old Town Branch of the
American Association of University Women,
1924-1964. [Orono?, 1964?]. 12 leaves. MeU.

4032   _____. Phi Beta Kappa: the Delta of Maine,
1923-1973. Orono, 1972. Pp. 33. MeU.
        University of Maine.

4033   "WHERE quality is the watchword." Maine
Alumnus, 22 (March, 1941), 4-5.
        University Press.

4034   WHITE, THOMAS R. "Maine Masque: 60 years of
drama." Maine Alumnus, 47 (January, 1966),
6-9.
        University of Maine.

SEE ALSO entries 1733, 1750, and 2082.

ORRINGTON (PENOBSCOT CO.)

4035   PORTER, JOSEPH WHITCOMB. "An address delivered at the centennial celebration of the incorporation of the town of Orrington, June
28, 1888." MeHistMag, 7 (1891-1892), 183-
202.

SEE ALSO entries 1752 and 1762.

OSBORN PLANTATION (HANCOCK CO.)

4036   No items located.

OTIS (HANCOCK CO.)

4037   No items located.

OTISFIELD (CUMBERLAND CO.)

4038   HOLDEN, CHARLES F.   "A sketch of the life of David Ray, and the early history of the town of Otisfield, county of Cumberland." SJMH, 9 (1921), 14-19.

4039   LABBIE, EDITH. "One thing's certain: the world is flat." Yankee, 39 (February, 1975), 72-77.
   Joseph White Holden (1816-1900).

4040   ROBINSON, ERNEST W. "Old meeting house." Sun Up, 9 (December, 1931), 5, 37.
   Bell Hill Church.

4041   SPURR, WILLIAM SAMUEL. A history of Otisfield, Cumberland County, Maine from the original grant to the close of the year 1944. Oxford: W. S. Spurr, 1959. Pp. 661.

OWLS HEAD (KNOX CO.)

4042   BROOKS, ALFRED A.   "The boats of Ash Point, Maine." AmNep, 2 (1942), 307-323.
   Boat building.

4043   LEWIS, GRACE HEGGAR. "A summer cottage of long ago." Down East, 3 (September, 1956), 16-19.

4044   "OWL'S HEAD." Down East, 16 (April, 1970), 56-57.
   Owl's Head Light.

4045   SNOW, EDWARD ROWE. "The frozen couple of Owl's Head." Yankee, 20 (December, 1956), 32-35.
   Lydia Dyer and Richard Ingraham in a shipwreck on December 22, 1850.

OXBOW PLANTATION (AROOSTOOK CO.)

4046   No items located.

OXBOW TOWNSHIP (OXFORD CO.)

4047   No items located.

OXFORD (OXFORD CO.)

4048   ABBOTT, MORETON. "Biography of a house." Yankee, 28 (June, 1964), 78-79, 116-121.
   Oxford Spring House, a hotel.

4049   KING, MARQUIS FAYETTE, comp. Annals of Oxford, Maine, from its incorporation, February 27, 1829, to 1850; prefaced by a brief account of the settlement of Shepardsfield Plantation, now Hebron and Oxford, and supplemented with genealogical notes from the earliest records of both towns and other sources. Portland, 1903. Pp. xii, 298.

4050   WATERMAN, CHARLES ELMER. "Welchville and some of its early families." SJMH, 5 (1917-1918), 16-22, 147-154.

PALERMO (WALDO CO.)

4051   DOWE, MILTON E. History, town of Palermo, incorporated 1804. Palermo, 1954. Pp. 51.

4052   GOODWIN, ALLEN. A history of the early settlement of Palermo, Me. Belfast: Age Publishing, 1896. Pp. 34.

4053   HOWARD, MILLARD A. An introduction to the early history of Palermo, Maine. n.p., [1976]. Pp. 64. Me.

PALMYRA (SOMERSET CO.)

4054   PALMYRA, ME. Sesquicentennial, Palmyra, Maine, 1807-1957. [Pittsfield]: Pittsfield Advertiser, 1957. Pp. 20. Me.

PARIS (OXFORD CO.)

4055   HAMLIN, AUGUSTUS CHOATE. The history of Mount Mica of Maine, U. S. A. and its wonderful deposits of matchless tourmalines. Bangor: A. C. Hamlin, 1895. Pp. 72.

4056   KING, ABEL CHARLES THOMAS, GEORGE ADAM WILSON, and F. H. SKILLINGS. History of Paris Lodge, No. 94, of Free and Accepted Masons, situated at South Paris, Me. Portland: Berry, 1872. Pp. 26.

4057   KING, ABEL CHARLES THOMAS, ALBERT WARD WALKER, and HORATIO WOODBURY. History of Paris Lodge, No. 94, Free and Accepted Masons, situated at South Paris, Me. South Paris: Oxford Democrat, 1902. Pp. 55. Me.

4058   LABBIE, EDITH. Paris Hill, Olympus of Maine. Down East, 21 (July, 1975), 68-71.
   A village.

4059   LAPHAM, WILLIAM BERRY. After fifty years:
        semi-centennial of the Oxford Democrat; his-
        tory of the paper from the first issue, with
        sketches of its editors, publishers, etc.
        Paris: Oxford Democrat Office, 1886. Pp. 35.

4060   _____ and SILAS PACKARD MAXIM. History of
        Paris, Maine, from its settlement to 1880,
        with a history of the grants of 1736 & 1771,
        together with personal sketches, a copious
        genealogical register and an appendix. Paris,
        1884. Pp. 816.
            Historical address by Horatio King.

4061   MORTON, AGNES L. "South Paris, a well-known
        industrial center." Sun Up, 3 (March, 1927),
        11-13.

4062   PARIS, ME. FIRST BAPTIST CHURCH. Centennial
        of the First Baptist Church in Paris, Maine;
        observed October 1st, 1891. Paris: Oxford
        Democrat Office, 1892. Pp. 85.
            Historical discourse by Hiram C. Estes.

4063   SOUTH PARIS, ME. FIRST CONGREGATIONAL CHURCH.
        150 years, 1812-1962, First Congregational
        Church, South Paris, Maine. n.p., [1962].
        Pp. 28. MBC.
            Historical sketch by Earle R. Clifford.

4064   TUBBY, JOSIAH T. "Old granite gaol, South
        Paris, Maine, built in 1822." OTNE, 36
        (1945-1946), 12-13.

4065   WATERMAN, CHARLES ELMER. A city on a hill
        (Paris Hill) with high lights that hit it.
        Auburn: Merrill & Webber, 1931. Pp. 102.

4066   WILSON, GEORGE ADAM. "Paris, the shire town
        of Oxford County." BTJ, 18 (1905-1906),
        370-372.

        SEE ALSO entries 1718 and 1727.

PARKERTOWN TOWNSHIP (OXFORD CO.)

4067   No items located.

PARKMAN (PISCATAQUIS CO.)

4068   McKUSICK, VICTOR A. "Parkman, Maine, a fron-
        tier settlement." OTNE, 49 (1958-1959), 41-
        48.

4069   STORMS, ROGER C. History of Parkman: main-
        stream democracy in Parkman, Maine, 1794-
        1969. Freeport: Dingley Pr., 1969. Pp. 108.

        SEE ALSO entry 1782.

PARLIN POND TOWNSHIP (SOMERSET CO.)

4070   SEE entry 3377A.

PARMACHENEE TOWNSHIP (OXFORD CO.)

4071   No items located.

PARSONSFIELD (YORK CO.)

4072   DEARBORN, JEREMIAH WADLEIGH, ed. A history of
        the first century of the town of Parsonsfield,
        Maine; incorporated Aug. 29, 1785, and cele-
        brated with impressive ceremonies at North
        Parsonsfield, August 29, 1885. Portland:
        Brown Thurston, 1888. Pp. xiv, 499.

4073   KEZAR FALLS, ME. RIVERSIDE METHODIST EPISCO-
        PAL CHURCH. Centennial anniversary program
        and historical sketch ... September 6th and
        7th, 1933. Cornish: Webb-Smith, [1933].
        Pp. 31. MeHi.
            History by Ina Stanley Emery.

4074   PARSONSFIELD SEMINARY. Parsonsfield Seminary,
        first hundred years, 1832-1932. n.p.,
        [1932?]. Pp. 44. MBNEH.

PASSADUMKEAG (PENOBSCOT CO.)

4075   HADLOCK, WENDELL STANWOOD and THEODORE STERN.
        "Passadumkeag, a Red Paint cemetery, thirty
        five years after Moorehead." American Anti-
        quity, 14 (October, 1948), 98-103.
            For Moorehead's 1913 study, see entry 901.

4076   SNOW, DEAN R. A summary of excavation at the
        Hathaway site in Passadumkeag, Maine, 1912,
        1947, and 1968. [Orono]: Department of An-
        thropology, Univ. of Maine, 1969. Pp. v,
        106.

PATTEN (PENOBSCOT CO.)

4077   BENJAMIN, CHARLES H. A hill town in New Eng-
        land. Altadena, Calif., 1929. 45 leaves.
        MeU.

4078   OLSEN, IRENE A. The history of Patten Acad-
        emy, 1847-1947. Bangor: Furbush-Roberts,
        [1947?]. Pp. 157. MeU.

PEMBROKE (WASHINGTON CO.)

4079   CAMPBELL, B. A. History of Crescent Lodge, No. 78, Free and Accepted Masons, Pembroke, Me., from 1880 to December 31, 1890. Part III. Portland: Stephen Berry, 1893. Pp. 55. MeBa.
    A continuation of works by John E. Walker and John C. Campbell; see entries 4080 and 4082.

4080   CAMPBELL, JOHN C. History of Crescent Lodge, No. 78, Free and Accepted Masons, Pembroke, Maine, from 1870 to December 31, 1880. Portland: Stephen Berry, 1882. Pp. 21-40. MeBa.
    Pagination continued from a work by John E. Walker; see entry 4082.

4081   FREEMASONS. PEMBROKE, ME. CRESCENT ROYAL ARCH CHAPTER, NO. 26. History of Crescent Royal Arch Chapter, No. 26, Pembroke, Maine. Portland: Stephen Berry, 1876. Pp. 27. MeBa.

4082   WALKER, JOHN E. History of Crescent Lodge, No. 78, Free and Accepted Masons, Pembroke, Me., from 1854 to 1870. Portland: Stephen Berry, 1872. Pp. 20. MeBa.
    Continued by entries 4079 and 4080.

SEE ALSO entry 603.

PENOBSCOT (HANCOCK CO.)

4083   "AN ACCOUNT of the First Congregational Church and Parish in the town of Penobscot, Maine." BHistMag, 3 (1887-1888), 145-149.

4084   MONTGOMERY, JOB HERRICK. Address of J. H. Montgomery, Esq., at the centennial celebration of the town of Penobscot, Sept. 14, 1887. Camden: Herald Print, 1887. Unpaged. MeHi.

4085   MOORE, RILLA LEACH. Mill Creek, Penobscot, Maine. n.p., 1967. Pp. 54. MeU.
    Town history.

4086   WARDWELL, HOSEA B. "Early settlement of the town of Penobscot, Me." BHistMag, 5 (1889-1890), 96-100.

4087   _____. "The early settlers of the town of Penobscot." MeHistMag, 7 (1891-1892), 25-26.
    Banks family.

4088   _____. History of Rising Star Lodge, of Free and Accepted Masons, Penobscot, Maine, from August 4, 1875, to March 1, 1884. Portland: Stephen Berry, 1884. Pp. 12. MeBa.

4089   _____. History of Rising Star Lodge, of Free and Accepted Masons, Penobscot, Maine, from March 1, 1884, to December 31, 1890. Orland: R. P. Harriman, 1891. Pp. 15. MeHi.

SEE ALSO entries 1597 and 1621.

PERHAM (AROOSTOOK CO.)

4090   No items located.

PERKINS TOWNSHIP (FRANKLIN CO.)

4091   No items located.

PERKINS TOWNSHIP (SAGADAHOC CO.)

4092   BARROWS, JOHN STUART. "A legend of Swan Island." NEM, New Ser., 19 (1898-1899), 606-608.

SEE ALSO entry 1677.

PERRY (WASHINGTON CO.)

4093   COOKE, LE BARON P. "A picturesque tribe of New England Indians." National Magazine, 38 (1913), 437-438.
    Passamaquoddy.

4094   NO ENTRY.

4095   SESQUICENTENNIAL, 1818-1968; historical souvenir book, Perry, Maine. n.p., [1968]. Unpaged.

SEE ALSO entry 603.

PERU (OXFORD CO.)

4096   TURNER, HOLLIS. The history of Peru, in the county of Oxford and State of Maine, from 1789 to 1911: residents and genealogies of their families, also a part of Franklin plan. Augusta: Maine Farmer Publishing, 1912. Pp. 313.

4097   VAUGHN, MARY SEARLES. A history of the town of Peru, Maine. Rumford: Rumford Publishing, 1971. Pp. 124.

PHILLIPS (FRANKLIN CO.)

4098 PEASE, ALBERT. Sketches of the history of Phillips, Maine. Phillips: Phillips Historical Society, 1962. Pp. 56. MBNEH.

4099 WHITNEY, WENDELL. History of Phillips, history contest conducted by Phillips High School, 1933. n.p., [1933?]. 25, 9A leaves. MBNEH.

SEE ALSO entry 1419.

PHIPPSBURG (SAGADAHOC CO.)

4100 BALLARD, EDWARD, ed. Memorial volume of the Popham celebration, August 29, 1862; commemorative of the planting of the Popham Colony on the peninsula of Sabino, August 19, O.S., 1607, establishing the title of England to the continent. Portland: Bailey & Noyes, 1863. Pp. xiv, 368.

4101 BANKS, CHARLES EDWARD. "New documents relating to the Popham Expedition, 1607." AASP, New Ser., 39 (1929), 307-334.

4102 BAXTER, JAMES PHINNEY. The chief actors in the Sagadahoc drama: an address delivered at the tercentenary celebration of the landing of the Northern Virginia colony at the mouth of the Sagadahoc, August 29, 1907. n.p., 1907. Pp. 10.

4103 BOURNE, EDWARD EMERSON, 1797-1873. An address on the character of the colony founded by George Popham, at the mouth of the Kennebec River August 19th, (O.S.) 1607; delivered in Bath, on the two hundred and fifty-seventh anniversary of that event. Portland: B. Thurston, 1864. Pp. 60.

4104 _____. "First Christian worship in New England." HistMag, 2 Ser., 2 (1867), 1-3.
Popham Colony; answer to article in "Congregational Quarterly" by David Q. Cushman; see entry 4106.

4105 _____. "The Popham celebration." HistMag, 9 (1865), 358-361.

4106 CUSHMAN, DAVID QUIMBY. "First Christian worship in New England." CongQ, 9 (1867), 21-24.
Popham Colony; see also entries 4104 and 4111 for comments on this article.

4107 DAVIES, JAMES. A relation of a voyage to Sagadahoc; now first printed from the original manuscript in the Lambeth Palace Library. B. F. De Costa, ed. Cambridge, Mass.: John Wilson & Son, 1880. Pp. 43.

4108 DE COSTA, BENJAMIN FRANKLIN. "The Sagadahoc Colony." MHSP, 18 (1880-1881), 82-117.

4109 _____. "The two hundred and seventy-fifth anniversary of the landing at the Kennebec." MagAmHist, 8 (1882), 555-561.
Popham Colony.

4110 DUNNACK, HENRY ERNEST. A history of Fort Popham Memorial. Augusta: State Park Commission, [1955?]. Pp. 28. Me.

4111 "THE FIRST Christian worship in New England." CongQ, 9 (1867), 275-276.
Popham Colony; in answer to David Q. Cushman's article, entry 4106; signed "B."

4112 FOLSOM, GEORGE. Address delivered on the site of the Popham Colony, near the mouth of the Kennebec, in New England, before the Maine Historical Society, on the 28th August, 1863. Ventnor, Isle of Wight: Fletcher Moor, 1866. Pp. 34.

4113 GILMAN, STANWOOD CUSHING and MARGARET COOK GILMAN. Phippsburg on the Kennebec, 1606-1964. [Phippsburg?], 1964. Pp. 32.

4114 _____. Small Point: the Cape of Many Islands, 1667-1965. [Phippsburg?, 1965?]. Pp. 62.

4115 HILL, WINFIELD SCOTT. The site of Fort Saint George, erected by Captain George Popham, in 1607. Read before the [Kennebec Natural History and Antiquarian] Society, July 23, 1891. [Augusta, 1891?]. Pp. 4.

4116 LAPHAM, WILLIAM BERRY, comp. Popham Beach as a summer resort, with a sketch of Popham Colony and the ancient Province of Sabino. Augusta: Maine Farmer Job Print, 1888. Pp. 15.

4117 "A LETTER from George Popham, president of the Sagadahock Colony, to King James I, dated December 13, 1607." MeHSC, 5 (1857), 343-360.

4118 McKEEN, JOHN. "Some account of the early settlements at Sagadahock and on the Androscoggin River; with the suggestion that the exploration by Popham's Colony was up the Androscoggin River and not the Kennebec." MeHSC, 3 (1853), 311-324.

4119 MAINE HISTORICAL SOCIETY. Tercentenary of the landing of the Popham Colony at the mouth of the Kennebec River, August 29, 1907. Portland: Maine Historical Society, 1907. Pp. 58.

4120 PATTERSON, JAMES WILLIS. Responsibilities of the founders of republics: an address on the peninsula of Sabino, on the two-hundred and fifty-eighth anniversary of the planting of Popham Colony, Aug. 29, 1865. Boston: John K. Wiggin, 1865. Pp. 38.

4121   PERKINS, JAMES E. and JANE PERHAM STEVENS.
One man's world, Popham Beach, Maine.
Freeport: Bond Wheelwright, 1974. Pp. xii,
131.

4122   PHIPPSBURG CONGREGATIONAL CHURCH. 200th
anniversary of the organization of the
Phippsburg Congregational Church, 1765-1965.
[Phippsburg,?, 1965]. Unpaged. MBC.

4123   PHIPPSBURG HISTORICAL SOCIETY. Phippsburg,
fair to the wind. Lewiston: Twin City
Printery, 1964. Pp. 108, xvii.

4124   "THE PLYMOUTH Company and the settlement of
Maine in New England." Devon and Cornwall
Notes and Queries, 18 (1934-1935), 134-138.
Popham Colony.

4125   POOR, JOHN ALFRED. The first colonization
of New-England: an address, delivered at
the erection of a monumental stone in the
walls of Fort Popham, August 29th, 1862,
commemorative of the planting of the Popham
Colony on the peninsula of Sabino, August
19th, O.S. 1607, establishing the title of
England to the continent. N.Y.: A. D. F.
Randolph, 1863. Pp. iv, 58.

4126   THE POPHAM colony: a discussion of its historical claims, with a bibliography of the
subject. Boston: J. K. Wiggin and Lunt,
1866. Pp. 72.
A discussion between W. F. Poole, Edward
Ballard, and Frederic Kidder; reprinted from
the Boston Daily Advertiser, April 11-July
28, 1866.

4127   "POPHAM: first Christian worship in New
England." HistMag, 2 Ser., 5 (1869), 113-
115.

4127A   PRESTON, RICHARD ARTHUR. "Sir Ferdinando
Gorges--little-known colonizer." American
History Illustrated, 4 (June, 1969), 33-38.
Popham Colony.

4128   REED, PARKER McCOBB. "Reed family." MHGR,
5 (1888), 129-134.

4129   ROWSE, A. L. "New England in the earliest
days." Am Heritage, 10 (August, 1959), 23-
29.
Popham Colony.

4130   SEWALL, RUFUS KING. "Popham's town of Fort
St. George." MeHSC, 7 (1876), 291-322.

4131   THAYER, HENRY OTIS. "Notes concerning Ancient
Augusta at Small Point." MeHSC, 2 Ser., 3
(1892), 424-430.

4132   ____. "The Popham Colony once more." SJMH,
4 (1916-1917), 253-254.

4133   ____, ed. The Sagadahoc Colony: comprising
the relation of a voyage into New England
(Lambeth ms.). Portland: The Gorges Society, 1892. Pp. xi, 276.
Includes a bibliography.

4134   THORNTON, JOHN WINGATE. Colonial schemes of
Popham and Gorges: speech at the Fort Popham
celebration, August 29, 1862, under the aus-
pices of the Maine Historical Society. Boston: E. L. Balch, 1863. Pp. 20.

4135   VONDEL, JOSEPH LEMAN. "Sagadahoc Colony."
Pine Tree Magazine, 7 (1907), 535-544.

4136   WHEELER, HENRY WARREN. "Ancient Augusta."
MeHSC, 2 Ser., 3 (1892), 233-246.
A settlement which existed from 1716-1721.

4137   WILSON, JOSEPH KENNARD. "The door-step of
New England." NEM, New Ser., 27 (1902-1903),
3-14.

SEE ALSO entry 4613.

PIERCE POND TOWNSHIP (SOMERSET CO.)

4138   No items located.

PITTSFIELD (SOMERSET CO.)

4139   COOK, SANGER MILLS. Pittsfield on the Sebasticook. Bangor: Furbush-Roberts, 1966.
Pp. 191.

4140   MAINE CENTRAL INSTITUTE, PITTSFIELD, ME.
History of the alumni et alumnae ... 1869-
1877, by Blanche Robinson Getchell of '90;
1878-1886, by Flora Addie Boyd of '91; 1887-
1896 by Kate Wright Eldridge of '91. Portland: Lakeside Pr., 1897. Pp. 104.

4141   PITTSFIELD GRAMMAR SCHOOL. Pittsfield past
and present. Patricia Buxton and Lawrence
Hallee, eds. [Pittsfield], 1948. 51 leaves.
Me.

4142   WHITTEN, ALBION. History of Meridian Lodge,
No. 125, Free and Accepted Masons. Pittsfield, Maine, from its organization, 1864,
to 1878. Portland: Stephen Berry, 1878.
Pp. 31. MeBa.

PITTSTON (KENNEBEC CO.)

4143   PITTSTON, ME. Vital records of Pittston,
Maine, to the year 1892. Henry Sewall Web-
ster and Asbury Coke Stilphen, eds. Gardiner:
Reporter-Journal Pr., 1911. Pp. 387.

SEE ALSO entries 1633, 1649, and 1937.

PITTSTON ACADEMY GRANT (SOMERSET CO.)

4144   No items located.

PLEASANT POINT STATE INDIAN RESERVATION (WASHINGTON CO.)

4145   No items located.

PLEASANT RIDGE PLANTATION (SOMERSET CO.)

4146   No items located.

PLYMOUTH (PENOBSCOT CO.)

4147   No items located.

PLYMOUTH TOWNSHIP (SOMERSET CO.)

4148   No items located.

POLAND (ANDROSCOGGIN CO.)

4149   BENNETT, MARY E., ed. Poland: past and present, 1795-1970; published in commemoration of the 175th anniversary of Poland, Maine. Poland: Poland Anniversary Committee, 1970. Pp. 106.
  Errata slip inserted.

4150   GILLIS, CHARLES E. "Great Scott! What a hotel!" Yankee, 22 (October, 1958), 56-59, 102-103.
  Poland Spring House.

4151   LOVERING, FRANK W. "Poland water and the Ricker saga." Down East, 8 (July, 1962), 28-31.
  Resort at Poland Spring.

4152   POLAND, ME. Souvenir programme of Poland's centennial celebration held at Poland, Maine, Wednesday, September Eleventh, 1895. n.p., 1895. Unpaged. MeHi.
  Includes historical sketch by Charles E. Waterman.

4153   POLAND Spring centennial: a souvenir. N.Y.: A. H. Kellogg, 1895. Pp. 88.

4154   POOLE, HENRY A. and GEORGE W. POOLE. History of Poland ... embracing a period of over a century. Mechanic Falls: Poole Bros., 1890. Pp. vi, 145.

4155   RICKER, ALVAN BOLSTER. Poland centennial, September 11, 1895. N.Y.: A. H. Kellogg, 1896. Pp. 117.

4156   RICKER, HIRAM, & SONS, INC. Poland Mineral Spring Water, the story of its history and its marvellous curative properties. South Poland, 1891. Pp. 80. Me.

4157   ____. Poland Spring: the early history of this wonderful spring, its growth and development illustrated. South Poland, 1917. Unpaged.

4158   ROBBINS, MEL. Poland Spring: an informal history. [Poland Spring?], 1975. Pp. 24. MeU.
  Poland Spring House, hotel.

4159   VINCENT, PAL. The Moses bottle. Poland Spring: Palabra Shop, 1969. Pp. 58.
  Poland Spring Mineral Water.

  SEE ALSO entry 1425.

PORTAGE LAKE (AROOSTOOK CO.)

4160   No items located.

PORTER (OXFORD CO.)

4161   MOULTON, THOMAS. Porter, as a portion of Maine: its settlement, etc. Portland: Hoyt, Fogg & Donham, 1879. Pp. 96.

4162   TEG, WILLIAM. History of Porter. Kezar Falls: Parsonsfield-Porter Historical Society, 1957. Pp. xiv, 315.

PORTLAND (CUMBERLAND CO.)

4163   ACKERMAN, JOHN H. "Boynton's dream engine." Yankee, 31 (November, 1967), 170-173.
  E. Moody Boynton and his monorail locomotive.

4164   ALBION, ROBERT GREENHALGH. ["The port of Portland, Maine."] Ships and the Sea, 4 (August, 1954), 22, 44-48, 50.

4165   ANDERSON, ALBERT E. History of St. Alban Commandery, No. 8, Knights Templar. [Portland, 1942]. Pp. 39. MeHi.

4166   ANDREWS, DELMONT. "The people's hospital." Pine Cone, 3 (Autumn, 1947), 12-15.
  Maine General Hospital.

4167 ANTHOENSEN, FRED. Types and bookmaking, containing notes on the books printed at the Southworth-Anthoensen Press, and a bibliographical catalogue by Ruth A. Chaplin, with specimens of its work, types, borders, etc. Portland: Southworth-Anthoensen Pr., 1943. Pp. x, 170.

4168 ARMSTRONG, F. C. "Portland, Me., Longfellow's 'beautiful town.'" Chamber's Journal, 87 (February, 1910), 78-80.

4169 BACON, GEORGE FOX. Portland, its representative business men and its points of interest. Newark, N.J.: Glenwood Publishing, 1891. Pp. 200.

4170 BAKER, FLORENCE E. "Maine's first ice business." Sun Up, 10 (April, 1932), 17.
David Robinson, 1822.

4171 BAKER, RICHARD L. Historical synopsis of economic development in Portland, Maine. Portland, 1959. 100 leaves. MeP.

4172 BAKER, WILLIAM J. "Anglo-American relations in miniature: the Prince of Wales in Portland, Maine, 1860." NEQ, 45 (1972), 559-568.

4173 BAND, BENJAMIN. Portland Jewry, its growth and development. Portland: Jewish Historical Society, 1955. Pp. 117.

4174 _____ and JULES KREMS. Portland Jewry, supplement one. Portland: Jewish Historical Society, 1961. Pp. iii, 32. MeHi.

4175 BANGS, ELLA MATTHEWS. "An historic mansion." NEM, New Ser., 27 (1902-1903), 695-713.
Wadsworth-Longfellow House.

4176 _____. The story of the Woman's Literary Union of Portland, Maine. n.p., 1920. Unpaged. MeHi.

4177 BANKS, CHARLES EDWARD. "The destruction of Falmouth in 1775 and the responsibility therefor." MeHSC, 2 Ser., 5 (1894), 408-421.

4178 BASHFORD, JAMES WHITFORD. Outline history of Chestnut Street Methodist Episcopal Church, and directory of members. Portland: James S. Staples, 1887. Pp. 44. MeHi.

4178A BAXTER, JAMES PHINNEY. "New Casco Fort." MeHSC, 2 Ser., 9 (1898), 438-447.
Built in 1705.

4179 _____. The park system of Portland. Portland, 1905. Pp. 16.

4180 _____. "The story of Portland." NEM, New Ser., 13 (1895-1896), 349-370.

4181 BECKFORD, WILLIAM HALE and GEORGE W. RICHARDSON. Leading business men of Portland and vicinity; embracing Saco, Biddeford, Saccarappa and Deering. Boston: Mercantile Publishing, 1887. Pp. 228.

4182 "A 'BEETHOVEN Society' of 1819." MagHist, 7 (1908), 248-249.

4183 BENNETT, ERNEST NATHANIEL. "A temperance town." Nineteenth Century, 61 (1907), 87-96.

4184 BERRY, IRA. Sketch of the history of the Beethoven Musical Society, of Portland, Maine, 1819-1825. Portland: Stephen Berry, 1888. Pp. 48.

4185 BERRY, STEPHEN. History of Ancient Land-mark Lodge, No. 17, Free and Accepted Masons, Portland, Maine, from its organization in 1806 to 1880, inclusive. Portland, 1883. Pp. 204.

4186 _____. History of Mt. Vernon Chapter, No. 1, of Royal Arch Masons, Portland, Maine, from 1805 to 1878. Portland, 1879. Pp. 81. MeBa.

4187 _____. History of Portland Commandery, No. 2, of Knights Templar, including that of King Darius Council from 1805 to 1821, and of Maine Encampment No. 1, from 1821 till 1855, when its charter was given to Templars in the valley of the Kennebec. Portland, 1882. Pp. 139. MeBa.

4188 BIBLE SOCIETY OF MAINE. Act of incorporation and by-laws of the Bible Society of Maine with the by-laws of the trustees and a brief history of the society. Portland: Southworth Bros., 1896. Pp. 24. MeHi.

4189 BRANIN, M. LELYN. "The Dodge Pottery in Portland, Maine." OTNE, 59 (1968-1969), 75-84.

4190 _____. "The Lamson & Swasey Pottery in Portland, Maine." OTNE, 61 (1970-1971), 66-74.

4191 _____. "The Orcutt & Crafts Pottery in Portland, Maine." OTNE, 60 (1969-1970), 94-103.

4192 _____. "The Winslow Pottery in Portland." OTNE, 61 (1970-1971), 95-104.

4193 [BRINKLER, ALFRED]. "America's oldest music club celebrates golden jubilee; Rossini Club of Portland, Me., passes fiftieth anniversary." Musical America, 33 (February 5, 1921), 33.
Author attribution by the Bangor Public Library; signed with initials.

4194 _____. The Cathedral Church of Saint Luke, Portland, Maine: a history of its first century. Portland: House of Falmouth, 1967. Pp. 86.

4195 BURNHAM, EDITH. "Portland Observatory, or, the old brown tower." Americana, 4 (1909), 747-753.

4196 "THE BURNING of Falmouth, now Portland, Maine, Oct. 18, 1775." American Monthly Magazine, 11 (1838), 543-549.
   Signed: G. F.

4197 BURRAGE, THOMAS J. "The Portland Charitable Dispensary and the Portland tuberculosis class." Maine Medical Association. Journal, 34 (1943), 174-176, 188.

4198 BURTON, ALFRED M. History of Atlantic Lodge, No. 81, Free and Accepted Masons, Portland, Me., from May 3, 1855, to Dec. 21, 1870. Portland: S. Berry, 1871. Pp. 31.

4199 CAIL, HAROLD L. "Famous American theatres." Theatre Arts, 40 (September, 1956), 69.
   Jefferson Theatre.

4200 CALDERWOOD, CORNELIA L. The story of Victoria Mansion. [Portland]: Victoria Society of Maine Women, 1953. Pp. 15. MeHi.

4201 CAMMETT, STEPHEN. "The Longfellow town--Portland, Maine." Putnam's Monthly and the Critic, 1 (1906-1907), 648-657.

4202 CARNES, JOSHUA A. A trip to Portland, with a descriptive view of the harbor, islands and scenery from the observatory on Munjoy Hill, also a graphic description of a week's rambles at Cape Elizabeth, Casco Bay.... Boston: Hill & Libbey, 1858. Pp. vi, 134.

4203 CHAMBERLAIN, MARY L. "Thanksgiving Day, 1898." Down East, 10 (November, 1963), 38-41.

4204 CHAPLIN, RUTH A. "The Anthoensen Press and the 'Gentlemen of the peaceful apple orchard.'" Print, 8 (February-March, 1954), 17-24.

4205 CHAPMAN, LEONARD BOND. "Land titles in Monument Square, Portland." MeHSC, 2 Ser., 3 (1892), 281-291.

4206 _____. "The mast industry of old Falmouth." MeHSC, 2 Ser., 7 (1896), 390-404.

4207 CHEVERUS HIGH SCHOOL, PORTLAND, ME. Cheverus High School, 50th anniversary, 1917-1967. Andrew J. Sedénsky and James M. Keegan, eds. [Portland, 1967]. Pp. 40. MeHi.

4208 "THE CHILDREN'S Theatre of Portland, Maine." Maine Teachers' Digest, 4 (1943-1944), 12, 43.

4209 CHISHOLM, HUGH JOSEPH, b. 1886. A man in the paper industry, Hugh J. Chisholm (1847-1912). N.Y.: Newcomen Society in North America, 1952. Pp. 28.

4210 CHURCHILL, EDWIN A. "Merchants and commerce in Falmouth, (1740-1775)." MeHSN, 9 (1969-1970), 93-104.

4211 CLARK, CORNELIUS EDWARDS. "The building of the church," a sermon preached in the Woodfords Congregational Church, Portland, Maine, April 12, 1942. n.p., [1942?]. Unpaged. MeHi.

4212 "COMMERCIAL Portland, past and present." BTJ, 23 (1910-1911), 311-313, 315.

4213 CUMMINGS, GEORGE O. "Maine General Hospital: an historical sketch." Maine Medical Association. Journal, 51 (1960), 267-272, 279.

4214 CUMMINGS, OSMOND RICHARD. "Portland Railroad." Transportation, 11 (April, 1957), 1-42; 12 (January, 1959), 1-34.
   Street railroad.

4215 CURRIER, ISABEL. "Tate House--Portland's historic landmark." Down East, 18 (July, 1972), 60-63.

4216 DALTON, ASA. A sermon on the history and principles of St. Stephen's Parish, Portland, Maine; preached July 4th, 1886.... Portland: B. Thurston, 1886. Pp. 20.

4217 DANA, EDWARD F. A bibliographical catalog: twenty-one years of the Anthoensen Press, 1947-1967.... Portland: Anthoensen Press, 1971. Pp. 75. MeHi.

4218 DANA, ISRAEL THORNDIKE. History of the Portland School for Medical Instruction: an address at the dedication of the new school rooms, and the opening of the eighteenth annual course, 17th of June, 1874, with remarks of Israel Washburn [and others]. Portland: Stephen Berry, 1874. Pp. 33.

4219 [DAVIS, DANIEL]. "The proceedings of two conventions, held at Portland, to consider the expediency of a separate government in the District of Maine." MHSC, 4 (1795), 25-40.
   Both conventions held on September 6, 1786.

4220 DEANE, LLEWELLYN. Some reminiscences suggested by the semi-centennial celebration, October, 1881, of High Street Church, Portland, Maine.... [Washington, D.C., 1882]. Pp. 13.

4221 DEERING HIGH SCHOOL. Stroudwater sketches. n.p., 1938. Unpaged. MeHi.

4222 "THE DEERING Mansion in Portland, Maine." Sun Up, 2 (April, 1926), 11, 31.

4223 DIAMOND ISLAND ASSOCIATION. Great Diamond Island, Portland, Maine, 8000 B.C. to 1972 A.D. n.p., [1972]. Unpaged. MeHi.

4224 DORR, SUSAN ELVA. "Portland's oldest church." Cathedral Age, 23 (Summer, 1948), 26-27.
First Parish Church.

4225 DOW, EDWARD FRENCH and ORREN CHALMER HORMELL. City manager government in Portland, Maine. Orono: Univ. Pr., 1940. Pp. v, 119.

4226 DOW, STERLING THAYER. "The origin of the Portland, Maine Post Office." Mekeel's Weekly Stamp News, 67 (September 2, 1946), 191-192.

4227 DRISCOLL, JOSEPH A. and CARLETON POTTER SMALL. Preble Chapel in Portland, Maine, 1851-1951. n.p., [1951]. Unpaged. MBNEH.

4228 DRUMMOND, JOSIAH HAYDEN. History of Portland Lodge, No. 1, Free and Accepted Masons, Portland, Maine, from its organization (1769) to 1880. Portland: The Lodge, 1881. Pp. iv, 340.

4229 EDWARDS, GEORGE THORNTON. "'Highfield,' one of Longfellow's favorite haunts." Pine Tree Magazine, 7 (1907), 28-31.
Home of Alexander W. Longfellow.

4230 _____. The youthful haunts of Longfellow. Portland: G. T. Edwards, 1907. Pp. xxix, 205.

4231 ELDEN, ALFRED OWEN. "The Tate House, Stroudwater, Portland, Maine." OTNE, 26 (1935-1936), 138-140.

4232 ELWELL, EDWARD HENRY. Portland and vicinity, an illustrated souvenir and all-the-year-round guide to the city of Portland, with sketches of Old Orchard Beach, Cushing and Peak's Islands, and other famous resorts in the vicinity of Portland. (1876) [3d ed.]. Robert Grieve, ed. Portland: Loring, Short & Harmon, [1888?]. Pp. 162.

4233 _____. The schools of Portland, from the earliest times to the centennial year of the town, 1886. Portland: W. M. Marks, 1888. Pp. 37.

4234 EMERY, CARL S. Forest City (Portland, Maine). Portland, 1948. Pp. 149. MeP.

4235 FALES, MARTHA GANDY. "Benjamin Ilsley, cabinetmaker in federal Portland." Antiques, 105 (1974), 1066-1067.

4236 "FAREWELL to a birthplace." Yankee, 19 (November, 1955), 48.
Henry Wadsworth Longfellow; demolished in 1955.

4237 FEMALE ORPHAN ASYLUM OF PORTLAND. Semi-centennial report of the managers of the Female Orphan Asylum of Portland, October, 1878. Portland: Stephen Berry, 1878. Pp. 38. MeHi.
Includes historical sketch.

4238 FIRE service of Portland, a souvenir containing an account of the service from leather bucket times to the present fire department. Portland: Portland Firemen's Relief Association, 1888. Pp. 64. MB.

4239 "FIRST Baptist Church, Portland, Me." American Baptist Memorial, 13 (1854), 334-335.

4240 "THE FIRST printer in Maine." American Historical Record, 1 (1872), 331.
Benjamin Titcomb.

4241 FOBES, CHARLES BARTLETT. "The White Mountain Club of Portland, Maine, 1873-1884." Appalachia, 30 (1954-1955), 381-395.
Mountaineering society.

4242 FOBES, CHARLES S. "Changes in the commerce of Portland for half a century." BTJ, 16 (1903-1904), 314-316.

4243 "FORT McKinley and eleven years of C.M.T.C." Sun Up, 9 (May, 1931), 6-7.
Citizens' Military Training Camp.

4244 FRATERNITY CLUB, PORTLAND, ME. The book of the Fraternity Club, 1874-1924; issued in commemoration of the fiftieth anniversary of the organization of the club. Portland, 1925. Pp. 170.

4245 FREEMAN, FREDERIC WILLIAM. Mother Goose comes to Portland. Portland: Southworth Printing, 1918. Unpaged.
Caricatures and cartoons.

4246 FREEMASONS. PORTLAND, ME. ATLANTIC LODGE, NO. 81. 100th anniversary souvenir program and history of Atlantic Lodge, No. 81, A. F. and A. M., May 4 and 5, 1955. n.p., [1955?]. Pp. 45. MeP.

4247 FREEMASONS. PORTLAND, ME. PORTLAND LODGE, NO. 1. The one hundred and twenty fifth anniversary of Portland Lodge, No. 1, of Free and Accepted Masons, Portland, Maine, March 22, 1887. [Portland]: Published by the Committee, 1887. Pp. 33. MeBa.

4248 FREEMASONS. PORTLAND, ME. ROYAL AND SELECT MASTERS. PORTLAND COUNCIL. Historical sketch and by-laws of Portland Council of Royal and Select Masters. Portland: Stephen Berry, 1897. Pp. 48. MeHi.

4249 FRELLICK, ARLETTE F. Landmarks of Peaks Island, Maine. [Portland?], Temple V. Robinson, 1953. Unpaged. Me.

4250 FRENEAU, PETER. "When Longfellow was a Portland lad." CCJM, 27 (1914-1915), 439-443.

4251 THE GANNETTS: William Howard Gannett, Guy Patterson Gannett. Portland: Southworth-Anthoensen Pr., 1946. Pp. 16.
Newspaper publishers.

4252 GILLESPIE, CHARLES BANCROFT. Portland past and present. Portland: Evening Express, 1899. Pp. 236.

4253 GIVEN, CHARLES S. "The Portland Company." RLHSB, No. 9 (1925), 6-14.
Locomotive builders.

4254 GODFREY, EDWARDS. "Law and Maine." Maine Alumnus, 46 (February-March, 1965), 8-9.
University of Maine Law School.

4255 GOMME, LAWRENCE. "The 'Pirate of Portland'--Thomas Bird Mosher." Maine Dig, 1 (Summer, 1967), 105-106; 2 (Winter, 1968), 90-93.

4256 GOODBAR, OCTAVIA WALTON. "The canal that started a bank." Made in America Monthly, 12 (August, 1948), 8-9.
Cumberland and Oxford Canal and the Canal National Bank.

4257 GOODWIN, SHIRLEY B. 60th anniversary, Trinity Episcopal Church, 1891 to 1951. [Portland?, 1951]. Pp. 66. Me.

4258 GOOLD, NATHAN. "Falmouth Neck in the Revolution." MeHSC, 2 Ser., 8 (1897), 66-95, 143-169.

4259 _____. A history of Peaks Island and its people; also a short history of House Island, Portland, Maine. Portland: Lakeside Pr., 1897. Pp. 84.

4260 _____. The Wadsworth-Longfellow House, Portland, Maine. Portland, 1969. Pp. 43.
Revised by the Maine Historical Society from the original 1908 publication.

4261 GOOLD, WILLIAM. "The burning of Falmouth (now Portland), Maine, by a British squadron, in 1775." NEHGR, 27 (1873), 256-266.

4262 _____. "History of the Cumberland County buildings in Portland." MeHSC, 2 Ser., 9 (1898), 292-308.

4263 _____. "John Taber & Son of Portland, and their paper money." MeHSC, 2 Ser., 9 (1898), 128-132.
1804.

4264 _____. Portland in the past; with historical notes of old Falmouth. Portland: B. Thurston, 1886. Pp. 543.

4265 GOULD, WILLIAM EDWARD. "Portland banks." MeHSC, 2 Ser., 4 (1893), 89-108.

4266 GRAND ARMY OF THE REPUBLIC. DEPARTMENT OF MAINE. BOSWORTH POST, NO. 2, PORTLAND. Portland soldiers and sailors: a brief sketch of the part they took in the War of the Rebellion; published for sale at the fair held in Portland, June 2-7, 1884, in aid of the Soldiers and Sailors Monument. Portland: B. Thurston, 1884. Pp. 56.

4267 GRANT, GEORGE FREDERICK. History of Deering Lodge, No. 183, Free and Accepted Masons, Portland, Maine, from the organization of the lodge, April 2d, 1879, to February 11th, 1924. [Portland]: Smith and Sale, 1924. Pp. viii, 203.

4268 GREATER PORTLAND LANDMARKS, INCORPORATED. Portland. Architecture text, Patricia McGraw Pancoast. History text, Josephine H. Detmer. Portland, 1972. Pp. 236.

4269 GUIDE book for Portland and vicinity, to which is appended a summary history of Portland, by Hon. Wm. Willis, with maps and sixteen illustrations. Portland: B. Thurston and J. F. Richardson, 1859. Pp. 104.

4270 HALE, AGNES BURKE. "The poets sang of Portland, Maine." Holiday, 12 (November, 1952), 79-83, 85-86.

4271 HALE, ROBERT. "Cushing's Island: a memoir." Down East, 19 (September, 1972), 62-65, 80-82.

4272 _____ and AGNES BURKE HALE. Cushing's Island: two memoirs. n.p., [1971?]. Pp. 62. MeHi.

4273 HALPERT, HAROLD KARL, ed. Temple Beth El, dedication journal, 1950. 5711. Portland: Maine Printing, 1950. Unpaged. MeHi.
Includes a history of the temple.

4274 HAMBURGER, PHILIP PAUL. "Notes for a gazetteer: Portland, Maine." New Yorker, 36 (October 8, 1960), 177-179.
Social life and customs.

4275 HAMLEN, JAMES HOPKINSON. J. H. Hamlen & Son, Inc. 1846-1926. [Portland], 1926. Pp. iv, 14.
Lumber.

4276 HAMMEL, MARGARET F. "F. M. O'Brien, Portland's antiquarian bookseller." American Book Collector, 24 (October, 1973), 11-14.

4277 _____. "Victoriana." Down East, 20 (September, 1973), 55-59.
Victoria Mansion.

4278 HATCH, BENTON LE ROY. A check list of the publications of Thomas Bird Mosher of Portland, Maine, MDCCCXCI [to] MDCCCXXIII ... with a biographical essay by Ray Nash. [Northampton, Mass.]: Gehenna Pr. for the Univ. of Massachusetts Pr., 1966. Pp. 211.

4279 HATCH, FRANCIS WHITING. "The 'Rebs' invade Portland Harbor." Yankee, 18 (July, 1954), 38-39.
1863.

4280 HAYES, CHARLES WELLS. Twenty years of the second episcopate of Maine, an address in St. Luke's Cathedral, Portland, January 23, 1887. Westfield, N.Y.: Church Kalendar Pr., 1887. Pp. 25. MeHi.

4281 HEBERT, RICHARD A. "The making of Maine: the Burnham & Morrill Company." Pine Cone, 3 (Spring, 1947), 36-41.
Food production and canning.

4282 HILTON, JOHN J. "Portland Harbor's Fort Gorges." Down East, 19 (June, 1973), 68-71.
Built in 1864.

4283 "HISTORY of banking in Portland." CCJM, 29 (1916-1917), 303, 305, 307.

4284 HOLT, ERASTUS EUGENE. "The Portland Medical Club--1876 and 1902." JMS, 9 (1902-1903), 46-56.

4285 HOLVERSON, JOHN and WILLIAM DAVID BARRY. The McLellan-Sweat House, 1800: a brief guide. Portland: Portland Museum of Art, 1974. Pp. 12. MeHi.

4286 "THE HOUSE of a 'broad arrow' mast agent." Yankee, 29 (April, 1965), 72-73, 115-118.
Tate House.

4287 HULL, JOHN THOMAS. Hand-book of Portland, Old Orchard, Cape Elizabeth and Casco Bay.... Portland: Southworth Bros., 1888. Pp. 246.

4288 _____. The siege and capture of Fort Loyall, destruction of Falmouth, May 20, 1690 (O. S.): a paper read before the Maine Genealogical Society, June 2, 1885. Portland: Owen, Strout, 1885. Pp. 116.

4289 ILSLEY, CHARLES PARKER. Centennials of Portland. 1675, 1775, 1875 and 1975. Somerville, Mass.: George B. King, 1876. Pp. 56.

4290 "AN INTRODUCTION to the State Street Church in Portland, Maine." MeCP, 51 (April 15, 1964), 3, 26.

4291 JACKSON, CHARLES E. "Maine Charitable Mechanic Association." Pine Tree Magazine, 7 (1907), 515-523.

4292 JACKSON, GEORGE STUYVESANT. A Maine heritage: the history of the Union Mutual Life Insurance Company. Portland, 1964. Pp. 221.

4293 JOHNSON, ALMON L. History of Atlantic Lodge, No. 81, Free and Accepted Masons, Portland, Me., from its organization May 3, 1855, to December 20, 1911, inclusive. Portland: Stephen Berry, 1912. Pp. 189. MeHi.

4294 JOHNSON, ARTHUR MENZIES. "Confederate raid on Portland Harbor." Down East, 7 (July, 1961), 52-54, 62-64.
1863.

4295 JOHNSON, MARY KELLOGG. Longfellow's early home. Boston: H. H. Carter, 1905. Pp. 54.

4296 JOHNSON, THEODORE ELLIOT. "The great 'Portland meetings' of 1872." Shaker Quarterly, 12 (1972), 121-137.

4297 JONES, HERBERT GRANVILLE. Old Portland town. Portland: Machigonne Pr., 1938. Pp. 127.

4298 _____. When Dickens came to Portland. Portland: Machigonne Pr., 1938. Pp. 7. MeP.

4299 JONES, MARTHA YORK. "The Portland Glass Works." Antiques, 24 (1933), 56-57.

4300 KING, HENRY MELVILLE. Church of my boyhood: an address delivered at the seventy-fifth anniversary of the Free Street Baptist Church, Portland, Maine, Oct. 23, 1911. Providence, R.I.: F. H. Townsend, 1912. Pp. 16.

4301 LANE, CARLETON G. A Maine heritage: a brief history of Union Mutual Life Insurance Company, 1848-1968. N.Y.: Newcomen Society in North America, 1968. Pp. 28.

4302 "THE LAW of riot; the Portland riot." Monthly Law Report, New Ser., 8 (1855), 361-386.
The Maine Historical Society attributes authorship to Charles Stewart Daveis.

4303 LEARY, PETER, JR. "The ancient defenses of Portland." MeHSC, 2 Ser., 7 (1896), 1-22.
Fortifications.

4304 LEE, RUTH WEBB. "The tree of life and its sundry fruits." Antiques, 26 (1934), 141-143.
Portland Glass.

4305 LINK, EUGENE P., ed. "Papers of the Republican Society of Portland, 1794-1796." NEQ, 16 (1943), 299-316.

4306 LINNELL, WILLIAM SHEPHERD. Asa W. H. Clapp (1805-1891), John A. Poor (1808-1871), General Neal Dow (1804-1897) and others: a short history of the Portland Gas Light Company. N.Y.: Newcomen Society in North America, 1950. Pp. 32.

4307 LONGFELLOW, SAMUEL. "The old Portland Academy: Longfellow's 'fitting school.'" NEQ, 18 (1945), 247-251.

4308 LONGFELLOW STATUE ASSOCIATION, PORTLAND, ME. Exercises at the unveiling of the statue of Henry Wadsworth Longfellow, Portland, Maine, Sept. 29, 1888. Portland: Brown, Thurston, 1888. Pp. 41.
    Oration by Charles F. Libby.

4309 LORING, PRENTISS. "Portland, past and present." BTJ, 5 (1892-1893), 360-362.

4310 LOTHROP, HARRY WOODWARD. The boys of eighty-five. n.p., n.d. Unpaged. MeHi.
    Reminiscences.

4311 LOWELL, CARRIE THOMPSON, comp. Impressions in and about Portland, Maine. Portland: A. W. Lowell, 1910. Pp. 46.

4312 MacDOUGALL, WALTER M. "The Portland Company: wood burning locomotives to atomic reactors." Down East, 10 (March, 1964), 46-50, 52-53.

4313 McELWAIN, HAROLD A. "Effective ministry in Portland's East End." The Northeast, 76 (January, 1949), 14-18.
    Saint Paul's Church.

4314 MacKAY, CONSTANCE D'ARCY. The historical pageant of Portland, Maine, produced on the Eastern Promenade as a free civic celebration of the Fourth of July, 1913. Portland: Southworth Print, 1913. Pp. 47.

4315 "THE McLELLAN-Sweat House at the Portland Museum of Art." Down East, 20 (June, 1974), 62-64.

4316 MacMILLAN, DONALD BAXTER. Portland Observatory, rededication address, Portland, Maine, Flag Day, June the fourteenth, 1939. n.p., [1939?]. Pp. 15. MeHi.

4317 McPHARLIN, PAUL. "The Anthoensen Press: printing for its true purpose." Publishers' Weekly, 153 (March 6, 1948), 1249-1254, 1256, 1258.

4318 MacVANE, LOUIS. "Winds of Portland." Sun Up, 9 (March, 1931), 14.
    Windmills.

4319 MacWILLIAMS, JAMES DONALD. A time for men. Lewiston: Twin City Printery, 1967. Pp. 161.
    Portland in 1866.

4320 MAINE. DIRECTORS OF PORT OF PORTLAND. Port of Portland, State of Maine, and its hinterland; being an orderly listing of all port and terminal facilities, including wharfage, depth of water, width of channels, towing, bunkering, lighterage, stevedoring, storage, bulk and general cargo handling equipment, dry docks and ship repairs, port charges, administration and laws, etc. Clarence P. Day and William E. Meyer, eds. Portland, 1923. Pp. 89.

4321 "A MAINE boast." Sun Up, 2 (September, 1925), 12-13, 37, 40.
    Visits of famous musicians to Portland; signed "The Stroller," a local impresario.

4322 MAINE CHARITABLE MECHANIC ASSOCIATION. Constitution and history of the Maine Charitable Mechanic Association.... Portland: Bryant Pr., 1965. Pp. 101, 18. Me.

4323 ____. Constitution, instituted January 16, 1815, and incorporated June 14, 1815, with a historical sketch. Portland: Stephen Berry, 1896. Pp. 110.

4324 MAINE GENERAL HOSPITAL, PORTLAND. A sketch of the Maine General Hospital. Portland: Stephen Berry, 1872. Pp. 16.

4325 MAINE HISTORICAL SOCIETY. Centennial of the Maine Historical Society, April 11, 1922.... Portland, 1922. Pp. 51.

4326 MAINE SAVINGS BANK. 1859-1959. Portland, 1959. Pp. 32.

4327 [MANNING, PRENTICE CHENEY]. The semi-centennial anniversary of the Free Street Baptist Church, Portland, Me., September 26-27, 1886. Portland: Brown Thurston, 1887. Pp. viii, 88. MeHi.
    Author attribution by Joseph Williamson.

4328 MARSH, PHILIP M. "Maine's first newspaper editor: Thomas Wait." NEQ, 28 (1955), 519-534.
    Falmouth Gazette.

4329 MARSH, SCARBORO. "Cushing's Island." Pine Tree Magazine, 5 (1906), 564-571.

4330 "MEMORABLE events of the Catholic Church in Portland." MeCathHM, 8 (1919-1928), 9-11.
    1605-1869.

4331 MERRILL, PAUL E. Forty-six years a truckman: the story of Merrill Transport Company. N.Y.: Newcomen Society in North America, 1975. Pp. 26.

4332 MILLIKEN, TOMLINSON CO., PORTLAND. A history of the Milliken, Tomlinson Company, Portland, Maine. [Portland, 1965?]. Unpaged. MeHi.
    Grocers.

4333 MOLLOY, ANNE. "The Portland Stove Foundry." Down East, 13 (January, 1967), 28-29, 48-50.

4334 MORELAND, JAMES. "The theatre in Portland in the eighteenth century." NEQ, 11 (1938), 331-342.

4335 MORRILL, CHARLES S. "B & M," what two young Maine men founded 80 years ago! N.Y.: Newcomen Society in North America, 1950. Pp. 24.
Burnham and Morrill, food packagers.

4336 MOULTON, AUGUSTUS FREEDOM. Portland by the sea: an historical treatise. Augusta: Katahdin Publishing, 1926. Pp. 243.

4337 MOULTON, DAVID E. "History of the organization of the Portland Water District." New England Water Works Association. Journal, 43 (1929), 359-363.

4338 NEAL, JOHN. Account of the great conflagration in Portland, July 4th and 5th, 1866; and a new business guide giving removals, changes in business, etc. Portland: Starbird & Twitchell, 1866. Pp. 64, viii.

4339 _____. Portland illustrated. Portland: W. S. Jones, 1874. Pp. 160.

4340 NEALEY, ROBERT W. "Reminiscences of a Portland boyhood." Down East, 5 (May, 1959), 16-23.

4341 NELSON, BRUCE D. Portland: a collection of nineteenth-century engravings. Portland: Greater Portland Landmarks, 1976. 38 unnumbered leaves. MeU.

4342 NEW YORK INDUSTRIAL RECORDER. Portland, Maine, at the beginning of the 20th century, rapidly becoming the greatest mercantile centre in New England; showing its superior advantages on account of its shipping facilities and natural resources, with reviews of the leading business concerns who have helped to place it in its present proud position.... N.Y., 1900. Pp. 40.

4343 NEWTON, ROGER HALE. Victoria Mansion, Portland, Maine, an ante-bellum gem just rescued from wanton destruction. n.p., n.d. 3 leaves. MeBa.

4344 NICHOLS, ICHABOD. A discourse delivered at the dedication of the stone church, of the First Parish in Portland, February 9th, 1826; with an appendix containing a memoir of the parish. Portland: James Adams, Jr., 1826. Pp. 24.

4345 NICOLET, C. C. "Venture in independence." Outlook and Independent, 154 (April 16, 1930), 606-608, 636.
The Evening News.

4346 NOBLE, ROBERT E. "A glimpse of Portland, Maine, and its environs." Canadian Magazine, 5 (1895), 189-196.

4347 NORWOOD, LESLIE E. "Portland Head Light." SJMH, 11 (1923), 167-169.
First lighthouse on the Atlantic coast.

4348 _____. "Portland Observatory." SJMH, 12 (1924), 20-22.

4349 NOYES, EDWARD A. "History of banking in Portland." BTJ, 26 (1913-1914), 933, 935-937.

4350 "THE OLD church." Old Times, 2 (1878), 144-146.
Casco Street Baptist Church.

4351 "THE OLD Log Cabin Club of Portland." BTJ, 25 (1912-1913), 479.

4352 OLIPHANT, H. D. "Portland's finest eighty-two years ago." Sun Up, 9 (October, 1931), 20, 39.
Police department.

4353 "ONE HUNDRED years on Munjoy Hill." MeCP, 45 (March 15, 1958), 3.
St. Lawrence Congregational Church.

4354 OSGOOD, E. S. "Portland--its early romance and history." Sun Up, 3 (August, 1927), 7-10.

4355 OUR National Guard, historical sketch of Co's A.B.E.L., (2nd Battalion), 1st Reg. Inf., and Signal Corps, N.G.S.M. Portland: Southworth Bros, [1896?]. Unpaged. MeHi.

4356 "OVER one-hundred years in business." Maine's Own Magazine, 7 (January, 1929), 21, 31.
Byron Greenough and Company; men's clothing.

4357 OWEN, FRED K. "The Longfellows of Portland, Maine." SJMH, 10 (1922), 208-215.

4358 OWEN, MOSES. Ballads of Portland. Portland: W. S. Jones, 1874. Pp. 160.
Businessmen.

4359 PAIGE, EMELINE K. "Westbrook Junior College." Pine Cone, 6 (Winter, 1950-1951), 21-27.

4360 "A PARISH renaissance.' MeCathHM, 5 (December, 1915), 32-37.
St. Joseph's Church.

4361 "THE PASSING of a Portland industry." BTJ, 19 (1906-1907), 409-410.
Zenas Thompson & Brother, carriages.

4362 PAYSON, (H.M.) & CO. H. M. Payson & Co., partnership for 100 years, 1854-1954. n.p., [1954]. Pp. 24. MeHi.
Brokers.

4363 PEABODY, ELLEN ADAMS. Woolson School, home of the Girls' High School, Portland, Me., 1850-1863. n.p., 1903. Pp. 15. MeHi.

4364 PERKINS, DAVID PAGE. History of the Portland Society of the New Jerusalem, with a list of the secretaries, ministers, and members. Portland: Printed for the Society, 1883. Pp. 52. Me.

4365 PERKINS, JOHN CARROLL. "The First Parish in Portland." The Church Exchange, 4 (1896-1897), 66-67.
First Parish Church.

4366 _____. How the First Parish became Unitarian ... historical sermon ... May 7, 1899. Portland: Stephen Berry, 1900. Pp. 22. MBC.

4367 _____. "Rev. Thomas Smith, D.D., and his First Parish of Falmouth, now Portland." MeHSC, 3 Ser., 1 (1904), 288-315.

4368 _____. Some old papers recently found in the stone tower of the First Parish Church of Portland; read before the Maine Historical Society, January 25, 1894. [Portland, 1894]. Pp. 30.

4369 PERRY, GEORGE SESSIONS. "The cities of America: Portland, Maine." Saturday Evening Post, 219 (July 13, 1946), 14-15, 64, 67, 69, 71.

4370 PERRY, WILLIAM STEVENS. A century of episcopacy in Portland: a sketch of the history of the Episcopal Church in Portland, Maine, from the organization of St. Paul's Church, Falmouth, November 4, 1763, to the present time. Portland, 1863. Pp. 16.

4371 PETERSON, ROGER C. "Fire, fog, and storm." The Quarterdeck, 2 (Winter, 1972), 7-9.
Shipwrecks.

4372 PETTENGILL, BERTHA F. Sixty years with the Family Welfare Society. Portland: Portland Family Welfare Society, [1939]. Pp. 18. MeHi.

4373 PICTORIAL history, harbor defenses of Portland. Atlanta, Ga.: Army-Navy Publishers, 1941. Pp. 98. MeHi.

4374 PITMAN, LINWOOD T. One hundred years at Woodfords Congregational Church, United Church of Christ, Portland, Maine, 1872-1972. [Portland?], 1972. Pp. 61. MeHi.

4375 PORTER, CHARLES F. A brief history of works erected for the defense of Portland, Maine. Washington: Press of the [Army] Engineer School, 1904. Pp. 10.

4376 PORTLAND, ME. Centennial celebration: an account of the municipal celebration of the hundredth anniversary of the incorporation of the town of Portland, July 4th, 5th and 6th, 1886. John T. Hull, ed. Portland: Owen, Strout, 1886. Pp. 379.

4377 _____. City of Portland, Maine; the dedication of Lincoln Park being the public exercises held in the Payson Memorial Church and at Lincoln Park, February 12, 1909, in observance of the one hundredth anniversary of the birth of Abraham Lincoln. Portland: Smith & Sale, 1909. Pp. 35.
Includes a brief history of Portland.

4378 _____. Exercises at dedication of the new City Hall and Memorial Organ, Portland, Maine, August 22, 1912; full text of the addresses delivered on that occasion, and a brief review of municipal action following the burning of the old City Hall, January 24, 1908. Portland: Southworth Printing, 1912. Pp. 79.

4379 PORTLAND, ME. BOARD OF TRADE. History of the Board of Trade of Portland, Maine; what it has originated and accomplished since its organization, constitution and by-laws, original and present membership.... Portland: Ford & Rich, 1887. Pp. 104.

4380 PORTLAND, ME. CHESTNUT STREET METHODIST EPISCOPAL CHURCH. Sesquicentennial program of the Chestnut Street Methodist Church, Portland, Maine, November 11 to 18, 1945; historical data.... Portland: Forest City Printing, 1945. Pp. 76. MeHi.

4381 _____. 1795-1895. Centennial of Chestnut Street Methodist Episcopal Church, Portland, Maine, November 7 to 10, 1895; a complete report of all proceedings. Portland: Thurston Print, 1896. Pp. 146.

4382 PORTLAND, ME. CITY PLANNING BOARD. Historic places in Portland. Portland, 1964. ii, 15 leaves. Me.

4383 PORTLAND, ME. FIRST BAPTIST CHURCH. Directory of the occupants of the pews ... April 1st, 1871, with historical notes ... from its origin to the present time. Portland: Ford & Perry, 1871. Pp. 16. MeHi.

4384 _____. One hundred and fifty golden years for Jesus Christ, being a history of the First Baptist Church, Portland, Maine. Portland, 1951. Pp. 55. MeHi.

4385 _____. The one hundredth anniversary, First Baptist Church of Portland, Maine; organized July twenty-fourth, MDCCCI.... Portland: Lefavor-Tower, [1901?]. Pp. 81.

4386 PORTLAND, ME. FIRST PARISH CHURCH. Baptisms and admission from the records of First Church in Falmouth, now Portland, Maine; with appendix of historical notes. Marquis F. King, comp. Portland: Maine Genealogical Society, 1898. Pp. 219.
Appendix of historical notes concerns Portland and vicinity.

4387 _____. Bicentennial celebration commemorating the completion of two hundred years
of worship on the present site, 425 Congress
Street, July 20, 1941. n.p., 1941. Unpaged.
Me.

4388 _____. The fiftieth anniversary of the dedication of the meeting house of the First Parish, Portland, Maine, February 8, 1826.
[Portland]: Stephen Berry, 1876. Pp. 32.
Address by Thomas Hill.

4389 _____. Seventy-fifth anniversary of the
dedication of the stone meetinghouse, First
Parish, February 8, 1826--February 8, 1901.
Portland, 1901. Pp. 91.

4390 PORTLAND, ME. FIRST UNIVERSALIST SOCIETY.
Fiftieth anniversary of the First Universalist Society, Portland, Maine, Tuesday, April
18, 1871. Portland: Ford & Perry, 1871.
Pp. 47. MBNEH.

4391 _____. Twenty-fifth anniversary of the dedication of the church, Feb. 13, 1890. [Port-
land, 1890]. Pp. 24.

4392 PORTLAND, ME. FREE STREET BAPTIST CHURCH.
Catalogue of members of the Free Street Baptist Church, Portland, Me.; with historic
notes, covenant, and by-laws. Portland:
Thurston, 1886. Pp. 81.

4393 _____. Declaration of faith, with the church
covenant, and list of members of the Free
Street Baptist Church, Portland. Portland:
Charles Day, 1837. Pp. 16. MeHi.
Includes a brief history of the church.

4394 _____. Directory of the Free St. Baptist
Church, Portland, Maine. Portland: Brown
Thurston, 1889. Pp. 47. MeHi.
Includes history.

4395 _____. The semi-centennial anniversary of
the Free Street Baptist Church, Portland,
Me. September, 26, 27, 1886. Portland: B.
Thurston, 1887. Pp. 88. MeBa.

4396 PORTLAND, ME. HIGH STREET CONGREGATIONAL
CHURCH. Services at the semi-centennial of
High Street Church, Portland. Portland:
Brown Thurston, [1881?]. Pp. 87.

4397 PORTLAND, ME. HOLY TRINITY HELLENIC ORTHODOX
CHURCH. Golden jubilee, 1974; Holy Trinity
Hellenic Orthodox Church. Portland, 1975.
Pp. 138. MeP.

4398 PORTLAND, ME. HOUSING AUTHORITY. COMMISSION.
Sagamore Village, 1943-1963, twenty years of
progress. Portland, 1963. Unpaged. MeP.
Housing project.

4399 PORTLAND, ME. POLICE DEPARTMENT. The police
manual, a manual containing historical
sketches, aims and activities of the Portland Police Department, 1786 to 1925. Portland: Welch Printing, [1925]. Unpaged.
MeHi.
History by Lawrence C. Dame.

4400 PORTLAND, ME. PUBLIC LIBRARY. Dedicatory
exercises of the Baxter Building to the uses
of the Portland Public Library and Maine Historical Society, Thursday, Feb. 21, 1889.
Auburn: Lakeside Pr., 1889. Pp. 35.
Includes a history of the library by Edwin
A. Noyes.

4401 _____. Portland Public Library and its predecessors, 1763-1949. Grace Trappan, comp.
Portland, [1941?]. 15, 12 leaves. MeP.

4402 PORTLAND, ME. RENEWAL AUTHORITY. Portland
renewal: a decade of planning progress,
1951-1961. [Portland, 1962]. Unpaged.

4403 PORTLAND, ME. ST. DOMINIC'S PARISH. Souve-
nir history of St. Dominic's Parish: twenty-
fifth anniversary of the ordination of Rt.
Rev. Monsignor Edward F. Hurley, at Portland,
Maine, Nov. 1, 2, and 3, 1909. Portland:
Printwell Printing, 1909. Pp. 138.

4404 _____. Souvenir program of the one hundredth
anniversary of the founding of St. Dominic's
Parish, Portland, Maine, October 7-8-9, 1930.
Portland: Coughlin Pr., [1930?]. Unpaged.
MBC.

4405 PORTLAND, ME. SAINT STEPHEN'S CHURCH. A
book commemorating the one hundred and fiftieth anniversary of Saint Stephen's Church,
Portland, Maine; the first Episcopal parish
organized in the State of Maine. [Portland:
Printwell Printing, 1913?]. Unpaged.

4406 _____. 185th anniversary of old St. Stephens,
1763-1948. n.p., [1948?]. Unpaged. MeP.

4407 PORTLAND, ME. SECOND PARISH CHURCH. History
and manual of the Second Parish Church, Portland, Maine.... Portland: Smith & Sale,
1912. Pp. 42. MBC.

4408 _____. A history and manual of the Second
Parish Church of Portland, Me., with a list
of members. Portland: Smith & Sale, 1898.
Pp. 71.

4409 PORTLAND, ME. STAPLES SCHOOL. The reunion
of Master Franklin Staples' school boys,
April 19, 1901. Nathan Goold, ed. Portland:
Lakeside Pr., 1901. Pp. 70.

4410 PORTLAND, ME. STATE STREET CHURCH. Manual,
State Street Congregational Church, with a
brief historical sketch. Portland, 1904.
Pp. 74. Me.

4411 _____. State Street Church, Portland, Maine, 1852-1902: services in commemoration of the organization of the church, March seventeenth, 1852, and of the dedication of its house of worship on June second, 1852, held in the church June 1st and 2d, 1902. Boston: Thomas Todd, [1902]. Pp. 140.

4412 PORTLAND, ME. STEVENS AVENUE CONGREGATIONAL CHURCH. The seventy-fifth anniversary of the Stevens Avenue Congregational Church, (United Church of Christ), 1886-1961. n.p., [1961]. Pp. 24. MBC.

4413 PORTLAND, ME. WILLISTON CHURCH. Tenth anniversary memorial and directory of Williston Church, 1873-1883. Portland: B. Thurston, [1883]. Pp. 40.
Includes historical sermon by Frank E. Clark.

4414 _____. Twentieth anniversary of Williston Church, Portland, Me., 1873-1893. Portland, 1893. Pp. 53.

4415 PORTLAND, ME. WOODFORDS CONGREGATIONAL CHURCH. 50th anniversary, 1872-1922, Woodfords Congregational Church, Portland, Maine. n.p., [1922]. Unpaged. MeHi.

4416 _____. Manual of the Woodfords Congregational Church, Portland, Maine, with historical sketch. n.p., 1929. Pp. 17. MeHi.

4417 "PORTLAND." Maine Central, 3 (1895-1896), 58, 60, 62, 64, 66.

4418 PORTLAND BENEVOLENT SOCIETY. Portland Benevolent Society, 1803-1903; exercises in recognition of the Society's centennial, held in the First Parish Church, Portland, Maine, February 15, 1903. Portland: Stephen Berry, 1903. Pp. 36.

4419 PORTLAND CADETS. Portland Cadets' semicentennial, Congress Square Hotel, Portland, Maine, January 3, 1920. n.p., [1919?]. Unpaged. MeHi.
Includes a history by J. H. Dow.

4420 "PORTLAND Custom House and its collectors." BTJ, 12 (1899-1900), 38.

4421 PORTLAND MARINE SOCIETY. Exercises at the centennial celebration of the Portland Marine Society, February 27th, 1896. Portland: William M. Marks, 1896. Pp. 50. Me.

4422 PORTLAND MEDICAL CLUB. Anniversary exercises, 1876-1902. History and statistics by Erastus Eugene Holt. Portland: Marks Printing House, 1903. Pp. 15. MeP.

4423 "PORTLAND newspapers and printers of fifty years ago." BTJ, 14 (1901-1902), 232.

4424 "PORTLAND Observatory." BTJ, 12 (1899-1900), 82.

4425 "PORTLAND painters." Portland Magazine, 1 (1834-1835), 121-123, 147-149, 243-246.
Charles Codman, Frederic Mellen, and Joseph T. Harris.

4426 PORTLAND postal guide together with an historical sketch of postal affairs in Portland. ... [Portland]: Macdonald Bros., 1900. Pp. 38. MeHi.

4427 PORTLAND ROSSINI CLUB. Golden anniversary of the Portland Rossini Club, Portland, Frye Hall, January 21st, 1921. n.p., [1921?]. Pp. 32. MeHi.
Includes a history of the club.

4428 _____. 100th anniversary of the Portland Rossini Club, Portland, Maine, Frye Hall, 2:30 P.M., February fourteenth, 1971. n.p., [1971?]. Unpaged. MeHi.

4429 PORTLAND SAVINGS BANK. Portland Savings Bank: the first century, 1852-1952. Portland: Anthoensen Pr., 1952. Pp. 25. Me.

4430 _____. The story of fifty years of the Portland Savings Bank, 1852-1902. Portland, [1902]. Pp. 31.

4431 "THE PORTLAND Society of Natural History; from 1866 to 1869." Portland Society of Natural History. Proceedings, 1 Pt. 2 (1869), 193-203.

4432 "PORTLAND--the metropolis of Maine." CCJM, 28 (1915-1916), 95-99, 101-103, 105.

4433 PORTLAND WATER DISTRICT. Over a century of water service, 1869-1972. [Portland, 1972]. Pp. 24. MeP.

4434 _____. Portland Water Company, water supply, rates, rules, and regulations, with a sketch of its history, charter, &c., &c. Portland: William M. Marks, 1881. Pp. 55. MeHi.
History is by Dennis W. Clark.

4435 PORTLAND YACHT CLUB. Portland Yacht Club, 1869-1963. n.p., [1963?]. Pp. 124. Me.

4436 "THE PORTLAND Y.M.C.A. is fifty years old." BTJ, 16 (1903-1904), 232.

4437 POTTER, NELLIE. "The Longfellow Garden." Sun Up, 8 (July, 1930), 4-5.

4438 _____. The Longfellow Garden of yesterday and today. (1924) 3d ed. Portland: Longfellow Garden Club, 1926. Pp. 44.

4439 RAND, EMILY K. The Portland Rossini Club, Portland, Maine, 1871-1896. Portland: Stephen Berry, [1896?]. Pp. 41. MeHi.

4440 READ, JAMES N. and WILLIAM H. SMITH. A synopsis of the history of Eastern Star Encampment, No. 2, I.O.O.F., from its organization, April 10, 1844, up to July 1, 1875. Portland: Spaulding & Drinkwater, 1875. Pp. 21. MeHi.

4441 "RECORD of harbor work done here since 1836." BTJ, 15 (1902-1903), 142.

4442 [RICH, MARSHALL NYE]. "Collectors of customs at Portland, Maine." BTJ, 15 (1902-1903), 140.
Signed M. N. R.; attribution is by the editor.

4443 _____. "Portland, the metropolis of Maine." National Magazine, 15 (1901-1902), 712-717.

4444 "RISE and progress of the city of Portland." BTJ, 11 (1898-1899), 237-239.

4445 ROCKWOOD, CHARLES M. "Portland 1920." NEM, New Ser., 42 (1910), 531-544.

4446 ROLLINS, SARAH R. Early years at the Maine General Hospital. Portland, 1941. Pp. 23. MeHi.

4447 ROUNDY, RODNEY W. "State Street centennial." MeCP, 39 (April 15, 1952), 14-15.
State Street Congregational Church.

4448 ROWE, MARIAN BRADFORD. "History of the Maine Historical Society." New England Social Studies Bulletin, 11 (October, 1953), 20-27.
Also appeared in MeLAB, 14 (November, 1953), 3-7.

4449 _____. "Woodfords Congregational Church." MeCP, 50 (April 15, 1963), 31.

4450 ROWELL, GEORGE SMITH. "Maine's first newspaper." MeLB, 6 (1916-1917), 50-52.
Falmouth Gazette.

4451 ROWLAND, ELIZABETH McLELLAN GOULD. Story of the Girls' High School of Portland, Maine, 1850-1863. Lee, Mass.: Valley Gleaner, 1897. Pp. 46. MeHi.

4452 RUGG, HENRY W. "Ancient Land-Mark Lodge." FR, 12 (1882-1883), 273-274.
Freemasons.

4453 "ST. JOSEPH'S Academy." MeCathHM, 2 (April, 1914), 21-26.

4454 "ST. PAUL'S,--St. Stephen's,--St. Luke's: the background of Portland's oldest parishes." The Northeast, 76 (May, 1949), 9-12.

4455 SARGENT, RUTH. "Summer stock--where it all began." Down East, 22 (July, 1976), 86-87.
Greenwood Garden Theater, Peaks Island.

4456 SARGENT, WILLIAM MITCHELL. An historical sketch, guide book, and prospectus of Cushing's Island, Casco Bay, coast of Maine. N.Y.: American Photo-engraving, 1886. Pp. 100.

4457 SEARS, DONALD A. "Libraries and reading habits in early Portland (1763-1836)." MeHSN, 12 (1972-1973), 151-164.

4458 _____. "Portland's early experiments in adult education." MeHSN, 10 (1970-1971), 11-20.
1820s to 1840s.

4459 SHAILER, WILLIAM HOSMER. A discourse preached on the occasion of the seventy-fifth anniversary of the First Baptist Church in Portland, July 23, 1876. Portland: B. Thurston, 1876. Pp. 24. Me.

4460 SHARPE, PHILIP B. "The Portland Auto Show of 1907." Maine's Own Magazine, 8 (January, 1930), 8, 31-32.

4461 SHETTLEWORTH, EARLE G., JR. A history of the Heseltine School. Portland, 1966. 16 leaves. MeHi.
Demolished in 1962.

4462 _____ and JOHN E. PANCOAST. Portland historic resources inventory. Augusta: Maine Historic Preservation Commission, 1976. 98 leaves. MeHi.

4463 SHETTLEWORTH, EARLE G., JR. "Portland, Maine, engravers of the 1820s." OTNE, 61 (1970-1971), 59-65, 105-110.

4464 _____. "The Radford brothers, Portland cabinetmakers of the Federal period." Antiques, 106 (1974), 285-289.

4464A SILLIMAN, VINCENT BROWN. "An early Unitarian Society in Portland, Maine." UHSP, 2 Pt. 1, (1931), 31-36.
Unitarian Society of the town of Portland.

4465 _____. "Portland, Biddeford and early American Unitarianism." The Maine Unitarian, (Spring, 1946), [24-37].

4466 SILLS, CHARLES MORTON. Historical sketch of St. Luke's Parish, Portland, Me., delivered ... July 4th, 1886. Portland: B. Thurston, 1886. Pp. 16. MeHi.

4467 "SISTERS of Mercy, fifty years in Portland." MeCathHM, 8 (1919-1928), 89-106.

4468 "SIXTIETH anniversary, Portland Board of Trade." BTJ, 26 (1913-1914), 891-893, 895, 897, 899-901, 903.

4469 "SIXTY years in Woodfords: the history of Trinity Parish." The Northeast, 79 (January, 1952), 3-9.

4470 SLEEPER, FRANK. "Portland, Maine." Sun Life Review, 23 (October-November, 1966), 6-9.

4471 SMALL, CARLETON POTTER. "Church bells." The Maine Unitarian, (Spring, 1946), [10-11].

4472 _____, ed. The diaconate of the First Parish Church in Portland, Maine. n.p., 1944. Pp. 40. MeHi.

4473 _____. Notes on music in the First Parish, Portland, Maine, 1740-1942. Portland: Fred L. Tower, [1942?]. Pp. 20. MB.

4474 _____. The sextons, bells, and ringers of the First Parish Church of Portland. Portland: Fred L. Tower, 1943. Pp. 36. MBNEH.

4475 SMITH, ALONZO W. "Portland's parks and promenades." BTJ, 19 (1906-1907), 455, 457, 459, 461.

4476 SMITH, ELMER J. "Good spirit and hard work further God's work: a short history of St. Peter's East Deering." The Northeast, 76 (September, 1949), 7-9.

4477 SMITH, FRANCIS ORMOND JONATHAN. A statement of facts, concerning the history and management of the Portland Gas Light Company.... [Portland, 1852]. Pp. 20.

4478 SMITH, JOSEPH COBURN. "Portland Camera Club: 75 years of photographic fun in Maine." Down East, 20 (March, 1974), 41, 76-77.

4479 SMITH, MASON PHILIP. "Tate House in Stroudwater, Maine." Antiques, 84 (1963), 172-174.

4480 SMITH, THOMAS. Journals of the Rev. Thomas Smith, and the Rev. Samuel Deane, pastors of the First Church in Portland; with notes and biographical notices, and a summary history of Portland. (1821) 2d ed. William Willis, ed. Portland: Joseph S. Bailey, 1849. Pp. vi, 483.
   First edition was edited by Samuel Freeman.

4481 SOCIETY OF COLONIAL WARS. MAINE. Fort New Casco.... n.p., 1929. Pp. 24. Me.
   Includes historical address by Clarence Hale.

4482 "SOMETHING of Portland's history." BTJ, 27 (1914-1915), 53, 55, 57, 59.

4483 SPEAR, PEARL S. The old sailor's story of his life, written by himself. Portland: Southworth Bros., 1888. Pp. 133.

4484 STANSBURY, HELEN. "The Victoria Mansion." Down East, 2 (May, 1956), 20-25.

4485 STERLING, ROBERT THAYER. "The Portland Head Light." Yankee, 2 (March, 1936), 23-24.

4486 STEWART, KATHERINE WALLACE. Peaks Island--as it was; a memory-tour of the island--in its heyday. Portland: H. S. Kinsman, 1962. 25 leaves. MeP.

4487 THE STORY of the landing of Capt. Moodey and his soldiers on Falmouth Neck (Portland) in June 1716. [Portland]: Southworth Printing, 1916. Pp. 15. MeHi.

4488 STRATTON, ARTHUR. "The Anthoenson Press, 105 Middle Street, Portland 6, Maine." BA, 21 (February, 1947), 2-6.

4489 STUART, JESSIE. A short history of Little Diamond Island. [Portland?], 1961. 20, 3 leaves. Me.

4490 SWAN, FRANK HERBERT. Portland glass. (1949) Rev. and enl. by Marion Dana. Des Moines: Wallace-Homestead, [1969?]. Pp. xiii, 106.

4491 _____. Portland Glass Company. Providence, R.I.: Roger Williams Pr., 1939. Pp. 127.

4492 THOMAN, RICHARD S. "Portland, Maine: an economic-urban appraisal." Economic Geography, 27 (1951), 349-367.

4493 THOMAS, WILLIAM WIDGERY, 1873-1946. 115th anniversary; being a brief history of the Canal National Bank of Portland. Portland: Canal National Bank, [1941]. Unpaged. MeHi.

4494 THOMPSON, FLORENCE WHITTLESEY. "Early churches in Portland." SJMH, 9 (1921), 81-83.

4495 THOMPSON, WINFIELD MARTIN. "A Confederate raid." The Rudder, 16 (1905), 130-136, 243-250.
   An 1863 attack on the revenue cutter 'Caleb Cushing.'

4496 THURSTON, NORMAN W. "Cape Steam was built on old dry dock site." Exciter, 43 (November, 1961), 6-7, 16.

4497 THWING, EDWARD PAYSON. "Portland churches." CongQ, 16 (1874), 259-263.
   Limited to Congregational churches.

4498 TOBIE, WALTER E. "According to their lights, MGH--O.S." Maine Medical Association. Journal, 36 (1945), 23-29.
   Maine General Hospital.

4499 TODD, ALDEN. A spark lighted in Portland: the record of the National Board of Fire Underwriters. N.Y.: McGraw-Hill, 1966. Pp. 231.
   The Board was established as a result of the Portland fire of 1866.

4500 TODD, JOHN M. A sketch of the life of John M. Todd (sixty-two years in a barber shop) and reminiscences of his customers. Portland: W. W. Roberts, 1906. Pp. vii, 322.
Social life and customs.

4501 TREFETHEN, JESSIE B. A history of Brackett Memorial Church. n.p., [1961]. Pp. 9. MeHi.

4502 _____. Trefethen, the family and the landing. Portland: House of Falmouth, 1960. Pp. 61.

4503 TREMBLAY, WILFRID. "A trip through the Portland organ." Maine's Own Magazine, 7 (September, 1929), 11, 43, 46.

4504 TRUE, LATHAM. Ten years of the Kotzschmar Club.... Portland: Kotzschmar Club, 1910. Pp. 28. MeHi.
Musical society.

4505 U. S. ENGINEER DEPARTMENT. BOARD OF ENGINEERS FOR RIVERS AND HARBORS. The port of Portland, Maine. Washington: Govt. Print. Off., 1937. Pp. x, 125.

4506 VAN TRUMP, JAMES D. and ARTHUR P. ZIEGLER, JR. "Thomas Bird Mosher: publisher and pirate." Book Collector, 11 (1962), 295-312.

4507 VERRILL, ROBINSON. Story of the firm of Verrill, Dana, Walker, Philbrick & Whitehouse, 1862-1962. Rockland: Seth Low Pr., 1962. Pp. 77.
Law firm.

4508 VIRGIN, HARRY R. "The Constitutional Convention of 1819." MeHSC, 3 Ser., 2 (1906), 416-464.

4509 "THE WADSWORTH-Longfellow House and its distinguished occupants." BTJ, 15 (1902-1903), 240-241.

4510 WALZ, WILLIAM EMMANUEL. "Our law school: its origin, its life, and its work." Maine Law Review, 6 (1912-1913), 309-317.
University of Maine, Portland-Gorham; the school was located in Bangor when this article was published.

4511 WARREN, JOHN C. "The burning of Falmouth." Pine Tree Magazine, 7 (1907), 152-157.

4512 _____. "Portland privateers of the past." Pine Tree Magazine, 6 (1906-1907), 296-299.
War of 1812.

4513 WEISS, HARRY B. "Twelve toy books of the past mid-century." American Book Collector, 1 (1932), 91-93.
Bailey & Noyes, printers.

4514 WENTWORTH, HOWARD L., JR. History of the Portland Marine Society. n.p., [1969?]. 21 leaves. MeHi.

4515 "WEST Congregational Chapel, Portland, Me." CongQ, 6 (1864), 134-137.

4516 WESTBROOK JUNIOR COLLEGE, PORTLAND, ME. 125th anniversary celebration, 1831-1956. n.p., [1956]. Unpaged. MeP.

4517 WESTON, ISAAC. "The theater in Portland; sixty years ago." Northern Monthly, 1 (1864), 387-389.

4518 WEYGAND, JAMES LAMAR. "The Yellow Kid Press." American Book Collector, 19 (March, 1969), 26-27.

4519 "THE WHARVES of Portland, Maine." BTJ, 25 (1912-1913), 179, 181-182.

4520 WHEELER, WILLIAM A. The Maine Central Railroad, 1847-1947. [Portland]: Maine Central Railroad Company, 1947. Pp. 23. MeBa.

4521 "WHEN Lafayette came to Portland." Sun Up, 9 (June, 1931), 29.
1825.

4522 WILLARD, BENJAMIN J. Captain Ben's book: a record of the things which happened to Capt. Benjamin J. Willard, pilot and stevedore, during some sixty years on sea and land, as related by himself. Portland: Lakeside Pr., 1895. Pp. 204.
Seafaring life.

4523 NO ENTRY.

4524 WILLIS, WILLIAM. The history of Portland; a facsimile of the 1865 ed. with a new foreword by Gerald Morris. 2d ed., rev. and enl. Somersworth, N.H.: New Hampshire Publishing, 1972. Pp. xiii, 928.
First edition was published in two volumes, 1831-1833.

4525 _____. "Introductory address before the Maine Historical Society, February 2, 1855, at Augusta." MeHSC, 4 (1856), 3-28.
History of the Society.

4526 _____. "The Maine Historical Society." HistMag, 2 Ser., 3 (1868), 13-17.

4527 _____. "Old Falmouth in 1749." SJMH, 2 (1914-1915), 87-88.

4528 WOOD, ELSIE. "The Portland Public Library." Pine Cone, 6 (Autumn, 1950), 13-17.

4529 "WRECKING of the Annie C. MacGuire." Sun Up, 2 (June, 1925), 10, 25, 27.
An 1886 shipwreck.

4530 WRITERS' PROGRAM. MAINE. Portland city guide. Portland: Forest City Printing, 1940. Pp. xlv, 337.

4531 NO ENTRY.

4532   YERXA, DONALD A. "The burning of Falmouth, 1775: a case study of British imperial pacification." MeHSQ, 14 (1974-1975), 119-160.

4533   YOUNG MEN'S REPUBLICAN CLUB, PORTLAND, ME. Young Men's Republican Club, its history, by laws, committee rules, list of officers, list of members, etc. Portland: Brown Thurston, 1890. Pp. 52. MeHi.

SEE ALSO entries 168, 799, 1483, 1487, 1492, 1512, 1514, and 1534.

POWNAL (CUMBERLAND CO.)

4534   BRITT, BENJAMIN H. The ranger's history of Bradbury Mt. State Park, Pownal, Maine. [Freeport]: Freeport Pr., [1942?]. Pp. 15. Me.

4535   LATHAM, ETTIE J. History of the town of Pownal written for its centennial, Sept. 2, 1908. Lewiston: Lewiston Journal, 1908. Pp. 40.

4536   TRUE, NATHANIEL TUCKERMAN. "The Merrill Road, Pownal, Maine." Old Times, 4 (1880), 589-591.

4537   _____. "Peculiar people." Old Times, 3 (1879), 417-422.
       Biographies.

4538   _____. "Sketch of the pioneers of the Merrill Road, Pownal, Maine." Old Times, 8 (1884), 1135-1138.

PRENTISS PLANTATION (PENOBSCOT CO.)

4539   No items located.

PRENTISS TOWNSHIP (SOMERSET CO.)

4540   No items located.

PRESQUE ISLE (AROOSTOOK CO.)

4541   BARTER, J. MALCOLM. "The horse John R. Braden." Down East, 21 (October, 1974), 46-47, 65.

4542   CARTER, BERTHA. "Not bear, nor all potatoes. ..." Maine Teachers' Digest, 2 (1941-1942), 84-85, 88.
       Aroostook State Normal School, now University of Maine at Presque Isle.

4543   DUNN, CHARLES, JR. Cloudman Hill heritage. Northampton, Mass.: Marion E. Dodd, 1939. Pp. 37. MeHi.

4544   FLIGHT of the snowgoose, a history of the Presque Isle USO. n.p., [1946?]. Variously leaved. [MePriT].
       United Service Organization.

4545   LAMOREAU, MRS. PAUL DAVID. History, 1865-1965, Congregational Church, Presque Isle, Maine. n.p., [1965]. Pp. 52. MBC.

4546   PATTEN, ROLAND TAYLOR. 1783-1931, important data in the history of Presque Isle. Presque Isle: Star-Herald, [1932]. Unpaged. Me.

4547   PRESQUE ISLE CIVIC ROUNDTABLE, INC. Presque Isle centurama, 1859-1959. Edith Fairweather, ed. n.p., [1959]. Unpaged. Me.

4548   ROLFE, DAVID. "Presque Isle: city with a spirit." Down East, 5 (July, 1959), 42-45.

4549   TAYLOR, STANLEY R., C. RAYMOND WARD, and A. ERNEST SMITH. History of Trinity Lodge, No. 130, Presque Isle, Maine, from July 28, 1865 to December 31, 1954. n.p., [1955?]. Pp. 118. MeU.
       Freemasons.

4550   WELSH, STANLEY. "A Christian harvest in agricultural Aroostook: Saint John's Parish, Presque Isle." The Northeast, 77 (May, 1950), 12-14.

4551   [WHITE, MYRTLE T. M.]. Presque Isle, 1820-1920. [Presque Isle: Star Herald Publishing, 1920]. Unpaged. MeHi.
       Authorship and imprint from a newspaper clipping mounted in a copy at the Maine Historical Society.

SEE ALSO entry 50.

PRINCETON (WASHINGTON CO.)

4552   BELMORE, BRUCE WEATHERBY. Early Princeton, Maine. Princeton, 1945. Pp. 219.

4553   FREEMASONS. PRINCETON, ME. LEWY'S ISLAND LODGE, NO. 138. History of Lewy's Island Lodge, No. 138, of Free and Accepted Masons, Princeton, Maine, from 1866 to [1890]. Portland: Stephen Berry, 1870-1893. 3v. MeBa.

SEE ALSO entry 1840.

PROSPECT (WALDO CO.)

4554   DUNNACK, HENRY ERNEST. A history of Fort Knox State Park. Augusta: State Park Commission, [1960?]. Pp. 22. Me.

RAINBOW TOWNSHIP (PISCATAQUIS CO.)

4555   No items located.

RANDOLPH (KENNEBEC CO.)

4556   RANDOLPH, ME. 75th anniversary celebration, town of Randolph, Maine, August 9, 10, and 11, 1962. Gardiner: Knight Printing, 1962. Unpaged. MeP.

   SEE ALSO entries 1624, 1629, and 1648-1649.

RANGELEY (FRANKLIN CO.)

4557   GOLDER, ARTHUR L. "The Rangeley Lakes." NEM, New Ser., 22 (1900), 565-586.

4558   HAINES, ZENAS THOMPSON and BARBARA A. BRUCE, eds. Squire Rangeley's township, the early days--1837 to 1849. Rangeley: Highland Publishers, 1970. Pp. 72. Me.

4559   HOAR, JOEL SHERMAN. Pioneer days of Rangeley, Maine. Rangeley, 1928. Pp. 46.

4560   LAMBERT, SAMUEL W., JR. The Oquossoc Angling Association, 1870-1970. Meriden, Conn.: Meriden Gravure, 1970. Pp. 84. MeHi.

4561   WILLARD, LAWRENCE F. "Boobytown." Yankee, 28 (November, 1964), 94-97, 137-138, 141-143.
   Shipment of Lewiston's poor to Rangeley in 1850.

RANGELEY PLANTATION (FRANKLIN CO.)

4562   No items located.

RAYMOND (CUMBERLAND CO.)

4563   DINGLEY, THEDA C. "Hawthorne's boyhood in Raymond, Maine." Sun Up, 8 (October, 1930), 24-25.

4564   DOLLEY, MIRA L. 150th anniversary, town of Raymond, Maine, 1803-1953. n.p., 1953. Pp. 24. Me.

4565   KNIGHT, ERNEST HARMON. The origin and history of Raymondtown. Norway: Oxford Hills Pr., 1974. Pp. v, 106. Me.

4566   RAYMOND, ME. 150th anniversary, town of Raymond, Maine, 1803-1953. Raymond, 1953. Pp. 24. MeP.

   SEE ALSO entries 1508 and 1514.

READFIELD (KENNEBEC CO.)

4567   FRENCH, EDWIN RUTHVEN. History of Maine Wesleyan Seminary. Portland: Smith & Sale, 1919. Pp. 42.

4568   GREENE, JONAS. The crown won but not worn; or, M. Louise Greene, a student of five years at Kent's Hill, Me. Boston, 1868. Pp. iv, 162.

4569   KENT'S HILL SCHOOL, READFIELD, ME. Kent's Hill, 1824-1974, sesquicentennial. n.p., [1974?]. Pp. 36. MeU.

4570   "MAINE Wesleyan Seminary." American Quarterly Register, 2 (1829-1830), 110-112.

4571   "MAINE Wesleyan Seminary and Female Collegiate Institute." Maine Teacher and School Officer, 4 (1861-1862), 65-68.

4572   NEWTON, JOHN O. and OSCAR E. YOUNG. Kent's Hill and its makers. Farmington: Knowlton & McLeary, 1947. Pp. 228.
   Kent's Hill School.

4573   PAGE, MARY SCHULTZE. Reflections of Readfield. Farmington: Knowlton & McLeary, 1975. Pp. 56. Me.

REDINGTON TOWNSHIP (FRANKLIN CO.)

4574   No items located.

REED PLANTATION (AROOSTOOK CO.)

4575   No items located.

RICHARDSONTOWN TOWNSHIP (OXFORD CO.)

4576   No items located.

RICHMOND (SAGADAHOC CO.)

4577   FERRISS, LLOYD. "Richmond, 1823-1973." Down East, 19 (April, 1973), 44-49.

4578   FLEMING, JOHN DALY. Richmond on the Kennebec. Compiled from the manuscripts of Walter H. Sturtevant and Ruie L. Curtis.... Richmond: Richmond Historical Committee, 1966. Pp. viii, 198.

4579   LIBBY, ABIAL. History of Richmond Lodge, No. 63, of Free and Accepted Masons, from January 1st, 1850, to January 10th, 1886. Richmond: Ray Thompson, 1886. Pp. 34. Me.

4580　RICHARDS, CHARLES W.　A historical almanac, 1888, containing historical matter concerning the town of Richmond, collected from town records and other sources, and arranged by months, under each date.... Richmond: Bee Steam Job Print, 1887. Unpaged.

4581　RICHMOND HISTORICAL AND CULTURAL SOCIETY. Richmond, a long view, 1823-1973: pictorial supplement to "Richmond on the Kennebec." Richmond, 1973. Unpaged. Me.

4582　STURTEVANT, WALTER HENRY.　Old Richmond on the Kennebec, a history. Richmond, 1938. Unpaged. MeHi.
　　A prospectus for a work which was "to be published in the summer of 1938" but which never appeared; includes a brief historical synopsis.

4583　THAYER, HENRY OTIS.　"Fort Richmond, Maine." MeHSC, 2 Ser., 5 (1894), 129-160.

　　SEE ALSO entry 3532.

RILEY TOWNSHIP (OXFORD CO.)

4584　No items located.

RIPLEY (SOMERSET CO.)

4585　No items located.

ROBBINSTON (WASHINGTON CO.)

4586　KEENE, F. W.　"Maine's only counterfeiters." Yankee, 7 (November, 1941), 18, 37.
　　1829-1831.

4587　YOUNG, NORMA.　"Murder at Moneymaker Lake." Down East, 5 (June, 1959), 39, 55.
　　Ebenezer Ball, counterfeiter, killed deputy John Tileston Downes; trial held in Castine.

　　SEE ALSO entries 2705 and 2745.

ROCKLAND (KNOX CO.)

4588　AVERILL, ALBERT E.　"A Maine boy at sea in the eighties." AmNep, 10 (1950), 203-219.
　　Lime-coasting fleet of schooners.

4589　BACON, GEORGE FOX.　Rockland, Belfast and vicinity: its representative business men and its points of interest, embracing Rockland, Belfast, Camden, Rockport, Bucksport, Ellsworth, Thomaston, Waldoboro', Warren, Damariscotta, Wiscasset, Newcastle. Newark, N.J.: Glenwood Publishing, 1892. Pp. 176.

4590　BOWEN, ROGER.　"Lucy's gift to Rockland." Yankee, 31 (June, 1967), 140-148, 150-151.
　　Home of Lucy Farnsworth, now a museum.

4591　DIETZ, LEW.　"The great Rockland bank robbery." Down East, 17 (April, 1971), 40-43, 61-62.
　　1870.

4592　DRINKWATER, NORMAN, JR.　"The stone age of Dix Island." Down East, 10 (September, 1963), 43-47.
　　Granite industry.

4593　DUNTON, ALVIN ROBBINS.　The true story of the Hart-Meservey murder trial, in which light is thrown upon dark deeds, incompetency, and perfidy; and crime fastened upon those whose position, if not manhood, should have commanded honest dealing. Boston, 1882. Pp. 309.
　　Murder occurred in 1877.

4594　FINCH, GRANT E. and GEORGE F. HOWE.　"The lime industry at Rockland, Maine." Economic Geography, 6 (1930), 389-397.

4595　FORBES-ROBERTSON, DIANA.　"The Dermot sisters of Rockland, Maine." Down East, 11 (September, 1964), 16-21, 42-43.

4596　HAVILAND, THOMAS P.　"Rockland's ring-tailed Fourth." Yankee, 28 (July, 1964), 62-63, 85-87.
　　Fourth of July, 1914.

4597　HEALEY, EDITH P.　"Fire in the white city." NEG, 10 (Summer, 1968), 31-36.
　　Fire in a lime-processing factory in March, 1896; also includes accounts of other lime firm fires.

4598　HEBERT, RICHARD A.　"Rockland." Pine Cone, 2 (Autumn, 1946), 14-19.

4599　MEARA, EMMETT.　"It breaks a feller's heart." Yankee, 36 (April, 1972), 38-46.
　　Samoset Hotel.

4600　MERRILL, DAPHNE WINSLOW.　"Rockland--lime city, U.S.A." Down East, 17 (November, 1970), 40-44, 62-63.

4601　NEWBERT, ALBERT H.　History of Aurora Lodge, No. 50, F. & A. M., from the date of its charter July 18, 1826 to July 19, 1926. Rockland: Bald Mountain Pr., [1926]. Pp. 228. MeHi.

4602　RAWLINGS, CHARLES.　"Mystery of Lucy Farnsworth." Saturday Evening Post, 225 (May 2, 1953), 32-33, 102-104.
　　Farnsworth Art Museum.

4603　"A ROCK of the faith in Peterland: milestones of St. Peter's Parish, Rockland." The Northeast, 77 (January, 1950), 11-15.

4604 "ROCKLAND, Maine." BTJ, 3 (1890-1891), 274-275.
Signed: Winkle.

4605 ["ROCKLAND, Maine."] BTJ, 22 (1909-1910), 213-257.

4606 ROTARY INTERNATIONAL, ROCKLAND, ME. Rotary Club of Rockland, Maine, a history, 1924-1944. n.p., [1944?]. Pp. 15. MeBa.

4607 SHAFTER, TOBY. "The fleshpots of Maine: portrait of a Down-East Jewish community." Commentary, 7 (January, 1949), 60-67.

4608 _____. "The well-kept synagogue." Midstream, 2 (Winter, 1956), 4, 109.

4609 TRIPP, O. H. Our fine law library. n.p., [1922?]. Pp. 4. Me.
Knox County Bar and Library Association.

4610 VOGT, PETER S. "The Farnsworth House, Rockland." Down East, 20 (May, 1974), 66-67.

4611 WASSON, GEORGE SAVARY. "The old Rockland, Maine lime trade." OTNE, 21 (1930-1931), 156-167.

SEE ALSO entries 20, 1659-1660, 1666, 1673, and 2082.

ROCKPORT (KNOX CO.)

4612 CARLSON, SHIRLEE CONNORS. Rockport, Camden, Lincolnville, 1776-1976, the life and times of its people. [Camden]: Town Crier, 1975. Pp. 99. MeU.

4613 CRAMER, MARY MEEKER and ISABEL CURRIER. "Spite House." Down East, 7 (September, 1960), 24-29, 48.
Moved from Phippsburg in 1925.

4614 DIETZ, LEW. "Goose River portrait." Down East, 10 (October, 1963), 16-19, 22-23.
Goose River is the former name of Rockport.

4615 WALL, ARTHUR W. "Boyhood sailing days at Rockport." Down East, 21 (January, 1975), 50-53, 70, 72-73.

4616 _____. "Lime kilns of Rockport." Down East, 15 (May, 1969), 32-35, 54-55.

SEE ALSO entries 1653, 1659, 1666, 1668, 1671, 1673, 2082, 2641, and 4589.

ROCKWOOD STRIP (SOMERSET CO.)

4617 No items located.

ROME (KENNEBEC CO.)

4618 No items located.

ROQUE BLUFFS (WASHINGTON CO.)

4619 No items located.

ROXBURY (OXFORD CO.)

4620 No items located.

RUMFORD (OXFORD CO.)

4621 "THE DEVELOPMENT of Rumford Falls." Maine. Bureau of Industrial and Labor Statistics. Annual Report, 16 (1902), 116-154.

4622 FREEMASONS. RUMFORD, ME. BLAZING STAR LODGE, NO. 30. History of Blazing Star Lodge, Number Thirty, Free and Accepted Masons from 1819 to 1919. James B. Stevenson, comp. Auburn: Merrill & Webber, [1920?]. Pp. 169. MeU.

4623 GOULD, DANIEL. History of Rumford in 1826. Randy L. Bennett and Peter A. McKenna, eds. Rumford: Pennycook Pr., 1975. Pp. 79. MeHi.

4624 LAPHAM, WILLIAM BERRY. History of Rumford, Oxford County, Maine, from its first settlement in 1779, to the present time. Augusta: Maine Farmer, 1890. Pp. xv, 432.

4625 LEANE, JOHN J. A history of Rumford, Maine, 1774-1972. Rumford: Rumford Publishing, 1972. Pp. 160.

4626 _____. The Oxford story: a history of the Oxford Paper Company, 1847-1958. [Rumford]: Oxford Paper, 1958. Unpaged.

4627 MARTIN, GEORGE A. "Churches of Rumford Falls." BTJ, 18 (1905-1906), 597-598.

4628 TAYLOR, PEARL. "What happened on August 2, exactly fifty years ago." Yankee, 37 (August, 1973), 146-149.
Fire at the Oxford Paper Company.

4629 "A 'WELFARE' institution on a novel plan." American Review of Reviews, 45 (1912), 325-328.
Rumford Mechanics' Institute.

RUSSELL POND TOWNSHIP (SOMERSET CO.)

4630 No items located.

SABATTUS (ANDROSCOGGIN CO.)

4631   No items located.

SACO (YORK CO.)

4632   BEATTY, HAZEL. "Three hundred years for the
faith: the history of Trinity Parish, Saco."
The Northeast, 77 (March, 1950), 14-17.

4633   COGSWELL, JONATHAN. "A topographical and
historical sketch of Saco, county of York,
District of Maine." MHSC, 2 Ser., 4 (1816),
184-189.

4634   DEERING, FRANK CUTTER. The proprietors of
Saco and a brief sketch of the years following the first settlement of the town, also a
little about an old bank in Saco, Maine.
Saco: York National Bank, 1931. Pp. 59.

4635   DUNN, CHARLES, JR. "The mansion of Col.
Thomas Cutts." Pine Tree Magazine, 6 (1906-
1907), 332-339.

4636   DWIGHT, EDWARD STRONG. An address delivered
in Saco, Oct. 12, 1862, on the one hundredth
anniversary of the organization of the First
Church in Saco, Me. Saco: William Noyes,
1862. Pp. 27.

4637   FAIRFIELD, ROY P. "Labor conditions at the
old York: 1831-1900." NEQ, 30 (1957), 166-
180.
   York Manufacturing Company; textiles.

4638   _____. Sands, spindles, and steeples. Portland: House of Falmouth, 1956. Pp. xi, 461.

4639   FREY, LUELLA A. An historical paper: First
Parish Congregational Church, Saco, Maine.
Biddeford: Biddeford Journal, [1912?].
Pp. 15.

4640   LOMBARD, LUCINA HAYNES. "Saco block-house."
Pine Tree Magazine, 7 (1907), 133-139.

4641   LORD, ELVIRA M. First Parish Congregational
Church, Saco, Maine and its leadership (a
200th anniversary memoir), 1762-1962. n.p.,
[1962]. Pp. 44. MBC.

4642   MELCHER, BURDUS REDFORD. York Institute:
something of its past, present, and future.
Saco: Biddeford Journal, 1884. Pp. 24.
   Technical education.

4643   MOLLOY, ANNE. "Since 1872--the Saco Company,
the firm a wooden water pump created." Down
East, 19 (November, 1972), 58-59.
   Wooden products; primarily spools.

4644   NATIONAL ARCHIVES PROJECT. Ship registers
and enrollments of Saco, Maine, 1791-1915.
Rockland, 1942. xiii, 108 leaves.

4645   OWEN, DANIEL EDWARD. Old times in Saco: a
brief monograph on local events.... Saco:
Biddeford Times Print, 1891. Pp. viii, 172.

4646   SACO, ME. Saco's tercentenary program, Saco,
Maine, June 22 to July 4. n.p., [1931].
Pp. 22. MeHi.

4647   SACO, ME. FIRST PARISH CONGREGATIONAL CHURCH.
Manual of the First Congregational Church in
Saco, Maine, 1886. Biddeford: Daily Times
Print, 1886. Pp. 76. MeHi.
   Contains historical sketch.

4648   _____. Manual of the First Parish Congregational Church in Saco, Maine, 1903. Saco:
W. L. Streeter, 1903. Pp. 67.
   Includes chronological list of members,
1762-1903.

4649   "THE SECOND Parish in Saco." The Church Exchange, 4 (1896-1897), 10-11.

4650   SUTTON, KATHARINE AUGUSTA and ROBERT FRANCIS
NEEDHAM. Universalists at Ferry Beach: a
history. Boston: Universalist Publishing,
1948. Pp. 137.

4651   "TRINITY Church, Saco." The North East, 37
(September, 1909), 3-5; 38 (September, 1910),
5.

   SEE ALSO entries 556, 799, 1265, 1881, 1890,
1893, 1901, 1904, and 4181.

ST. AGATHA (AROOSTOOK CO.)

4652   ST. AGATHA PARISH. St. Agatha diamond jubilee, 1889-1964. n.p., 1964. Pp. 76.

4653   "ST. AGATHA'S Church, St. Agatha, Aroostook
County." MeCathHM, 3 (November, 1914), 19-20.

ST. ALBANS (SOMERSET CO.)

4654   No items located.

ST. CROIX TOWNSHIP (AROOSTOOK CO.)

4655   No items located.

ST. FRANCIS (AROOSTOOK CO.)

4656   ST. FRANCIS, ME. BICENTENNIAL COMMITTEE.
Memories. Madawaska: St. John Valley Printers, 1976. Pp. 38. [MeMaHi].

ST. GEORGE (KNOX CO.)

4657 ALLEN, ELMER E. History of Eureka Lodge at St. George, Maine, from 1870-1909. Rockland: Courier-Gazette, 1909. Pp. 44. MeBa.
Freemasons.

4658 MERRIAM, KENDALL A. "Wreck of the concrete steamer 'Polias.'" Down East, 17 (April, 1971), 50-52, 57.
At old Cilley Ledge on February 6, 1920.

4659 MESERVEY, ROY E. Coaster days, shipping in the town of St. George, Maine. Christopher Fahy, ed. [St. George], 1976. Pp. 33. MeU.

4660 MILLER, FRANK BURTON. Soldiers and sailors of the plantation of lower St. Georges, Maine, who served in the war for American independence. Rockland, 1931. Pp. 66.

4661 NEESON, MARGARET GRAHAM. On solid granite: the story of St. George's Church, its village, priests, and people. Long Cove: St. George's Episcopal Chapel, 1974. Pp. 154.

4662 ST. GEORGE chronicles, containing an historical sketch from 1605 to 1932, together with names, ages and dates of birth; a complete business directory. Joseph T. Simmons and Mabelle Andrews Rose, comps. Augusta: C. E. Nash & Son, 1932. Pp. 78.

SEE ALSO entry 5003.

ST. JOHN PLANTATION (AROOSTOOK CO.)

4663 No items located.

ST. JOHN TOWNSHIP (SOMERSET CO.)

4664 No items located.

SALEM TOWNSHIP (FRANKLIN CO.)

4665 OUR first old home day at Salem, Maine, August seventeenth, 1904. Boston: D. C. Heath, 1905. Pp. xvi, 227.
A town history.

SANDBAR TRACT (SOMERSET CO.)

4666 No items located.

SANDWICH ACADEMY GRANT (SOMERSET CO.)

4667 No items located.

SANDY BAY TOWNSHIP (SOMERSET CO.)

4668 No items located.

SANDY RIVER PLANTATION (FRANKLIN CO.)

4669 No items located.

SANFORD (YORK CO.)

4670 BETCHER, J. A. "Churches of Sanford and Springvale." BTJ, 21 (1908-1909), 399-402.

4671 BLAGDEN, CHARLES W. "The secret societies of Sanford and Springvale." BTJ, 21 (1908-1909), 404-406.
Differs slightly from following article.

4672 _____. "Secret societies of Sanford and Springvale." BTJ, 27 (1914-1915), 213, 215-216.
Differs slightly from previous entry.

4673 CHADBOURNE, BENJAMIN F. "The story of the Goodwill industries." BTJ, 21 (1908-1909), 375-377, 379, 381, 383, 385.
Sanford Mills, textiles.

4674 COLBY, D. W. "Schools of Springvale and Sanford." BTJ, 21 (1908-1909), 393, 395-396.

4675 DAVIS, W. E. "'Velmo'--its history and manufacture." Maine Association of Engineers. Journal, No. 11 (April, 1930), 30-38.
Sanford Mills.

4676 EMERY, EDWIN. The history of Sanford, Maine, 1661-1900. William Morrell Emery, ed. Fall River, Mass.: William M. Emery, 1901. Pp. xvi, 537.

4677 FLINT, GEORGE B., JR. "Goodall-Sanford Mills." Shoreliner, 2 (August, 1951), 50-59.
Textiles.

4678 GAY, ROGER CROWELL. Nasson College, 1912-1957: a modern parable of the mustard seed. N.Y.: Newcomen Society in North America, 1958. Pp. 24.

4679 GILE, HUGH. "Springvale and Sanford: past, present, and future." BTJ, 21 (1908-1909), 357, 359, 361, 363, 365, 367, 369, 371.

4680 HEBERT, RICHARD A. "The making of Maine: Goodall-Sanford industries." Pine Cone, 1 (Spring, 1945), 23-27.
Woolen and worsted.

4681 HERRICK, MARY DARRAH. "Nasson College Library." MeLAB, 7 (June, 1946), 4-5.

4682 McKINLEY, ALAN R. "With hands and hearts reaching heavenward: a brief historical survey of St. George's, Sanford." The Northeast, 77 (July, 1950), 12-17.

4683 "NORTH Parish Congregational Church of Sanford celebrates 175th anniversary." MeCP, 49 (January 15, 1962), 4-5.

4684 PHILBROOK, EUGENE S. "Churches of Sanford and Springvale." BTJ, 27 (1914-1915), 197, 199, 201.

4685 PROSSER, ALBERT L. A history of North Parish Congregational Church of Sanford, Maine, 1786-1961. n.p., [1961]. Pp. 134. MBC. Errata sheet inserted.

4686 SANFORD HISTORICAL COMMITTEE. Sanford, Maine: a bicentennial history; published in commemoration of the anniversary of the incorporation of the town in 1768. Albert L. Prosser, ed. Sanford, 1968. Pp. x, 504.

4687 "SANFORD, Maine." Sun Up, 2 (January, 1926), 28-29, 31-32.

4688 "SANFORD, Maine's largest town." BTJ, 27 (1914-1915), 185, 187, 189, 191, 193, 195.

4689 SEEMAN, BERNARD. "The town that refused to die." Coronet, 39 (January, 1956), 65-69. Industry.

4690 SMITH, ISAAC A. "Schools of Sanford and Springvale." BTJ, 27 (1914-1915), 204-205.

4691 STONE, HENRY J., ed. The Messenger, devoted to interests of the Congregational Church, at Sanford, Me., containing a history of the great fire of 1878.... Portland: Stephen Berry, 1879. Pp. 16. MeHi.

4692 WARD, ELMER L. A healthy tradition: the colorful romance of the horse blanket, the Angora goat, and Goodall-Sanford, Inc. N.Y.: Newcomen Society in North America, 1951. Pp. 32.

SANGERVILLE (PISCATAQUIS CO.)

4693 KNOWLTON, WILLIAM SMITH. Sangerville, centennial poem.... Augusta, [1914]. Pp. 24.

4694 SANGERVILLE, ME. 150th anniversary, Sangerville sesquicentennial, 1814-1964. n.p., [1964]. Unpaged. Me.

4695 "SANGERVILLE centennial: 1814-1914." SJMH, 2 (1914-1915), 103-182.

SEE ALSO entry 1782.

SAPLING TOWNSHIP (SOMERSET CO.)

4696 No items located.

SCARBOROUGH (CUMBERLAND CO.)

4697 BEAM, PHILIP C. Winslow Homer at Prout's Neck. Boston: Little, Brown, 1966. Pp. xxii, 282.

4698 CHAPMAN, LEONARD BOND. Monograph on the Southgate family of Scarborough, Maine, their ancestors and descendants. Portland: H. W. Bryant, 1907. Pp. viii, 60.

4699 HOLLAND, RUPERT SARGENT. The story of Prouts Neck. Prouts Neck: Prouts Neck Association, 1924. Pp. 67.

4700 HUTCHINSON, GLORIA. "Atlantic House, a summer refuge." Down East, 21 (June, 1975), 50-55. Hotel.

4701 LEAMON, JAMES S. "The Stamp Act crisis in Maine: the case of Scarborough." MeHSN, 11 (1971-1972), 74-93.

4702 LIBBEY, DOROTHY SHAW. Scarborough becomes a town. Portland: Bond Wheelwright, 1955. Pp. 282.

4703 MOULTON, AUGUSTUS FREEDOM. Grandfather tales of Scarborough. Augusta: Katahdin Publishing, 1925. Pp. 209.

4704 _____. Old Prouts Neck. Portland: Marks Printing, 1924. Pp. 123.

4705 _____. "The settlement of Scarborough." MeHSC, 2 Ser., 6 (1895), 415-440.

4706 MOULTON, FRED E. History of the organization of the Universalist Church at Scarborough and South Buxton, Maine. n.p., [1939?]. 7 leaves. MeHi.

4707 PINES and surf, Higgins Beach, Maine. n.p., n.d. Pp. 13. MeHi.

4708 PROUTS NECK ASSOCIATION. Prouts then and now, 1888-1970. Prouts Neck, 1971. Pp. 96.

4709 SCARBOROUGH, ME. Scarborough, Maine, 300th anniversary, 1658-1958. n.p., [1958]. Pp. 71. MeHi.

4710 SCARBOROUGH PUBLIC LIBRARY. FRIENDS. History of Scarborough. [Scarborough, 1973]. 26 leaves.

4711   SOCIETY OF COLONIAL WARS. MAINE. The Scottow
        stockade fort located on Black Point, Scar-
        borough, Maine, 1681-1690. n.p., 1931.
        Pp. 16. MBNEH.

4712   SOUTHGATE, WILLIAM SCOTT. "The history of
        Scarborough from 1633-1783." MeHSC, 3 (1853),
        9-237.

4713   THORNTON, JOHN WINGATE. "Formation and early
        records of the church in Scarborough, Me."
        CongQ, 8 (1867), 188-194.
            First Parish Congregational Church.

4714   _____. "The Kings of Scarborough and New
        York." HistMag, 2 Ser., 5 (1869), 50-51.
            King family.

4715   VAN RENSSELAER, MRS. J. K. "The Kings of
        Owascoag." American Historical Register, 1
        (1894-1895), 461-463.
            King family.

4716   WARREN, JOHN C. "The attack on Black Point
        Garrison." Pine Tree Magazine, 8 (1907), 31-
        33.
            King Philip's War.

        SEE ALSO entry 1265.

SEARSMONT (WALDO CO.)

4717   CUNNINGHAM, CHARLES M. and OTIS D. WILSON.
        History of Quantabacook Lodge, No. 129, Free
        and Accepted Masons, Searsmont, Me., from
        1871 to 1881. Belfast: George W. Burgess,
        1881. Pp. 18. [MePGLM].

4718   CUNNINGHAM, CHARLES M., WILLIAM S. COX, and
        W. H. WOODCOCK. History of Quantabacook
        Lodge of Free and Accepted Masons, Searsmont,
        Maine, from 1865 to 1871. Belfast: George
        W. Burgess, 1871. Pp. 18. [MePGLM].

4719   GARBUS, BETTY. "The Robbins family mill at
        Searsmont." Down East, 23 (November, 1976),
        48-51, 69.
            Sawmill.

4720   WHITING, BARTLETT J. "Incident at Quantaba-
        cook, March, 1764." NEQ, 20 (1947), 169-196.
            Hunting rights controversy with the Indians.

SEARSPORT (WALDO CO.)

4721   APPLEBEE, ROBERT B. Sailing ship history.
        Searsport: Penobscot Marine Museum, 1956.
        Pp. 14. MeBa.
            Ships built in Searsport.

4722   BLACK, FREDERICK FRASIER, comp. Searsport sea
        captains: a collection of photographs with
        brief biographical sketches, including the

ships they commanded. Searsport: Penobscot
Marine Museum, 1960. Pp. 226.

4723   CARVER, CLIFFORD NICKELS. John Carver (1799-
        1867) builder of wooden ships upon the Penob-
        scot Bay! N.Y.: Newcomen Society in North
        America, 1957. Pp. 32.

4724   EASTMAN, JOEL WEBB. A history of Sears Is-
        land, Searsport, Maine. [Searsport]: Sears-
        port Historical Society, 1976. Pp. 72. MeHi.

4725   KUHNERT, DALE WILLIAM. "Searsport: seaport
        to superport." Down East, 20 (November,
        1973), 28-35, 67-68.

4726   SEARSPORT, ME. FIRST CONGREGATIONAL CHURCH.
        Congregational centennial at Searsport, Maine,
        1815-1915. Portland: Southworth Printing,
        1916. Pp. 77. MBC.

4727   SEARSPORT, ME. 125TH ANNIVERSARY COMMITTEE.
        125th anniversary, Searsport, Maine, 1845-
        1970. n.p., [1970]. Unpaged. Me.

4728   SEARSPORT HISTORICAL SOCIETY. Around our town,
        Volume 1, 1967. Searsport, 1967. 130 leaves.
        MeHi.
            No more published.

4729   SULLIVAN, J. H. Searsport ships and captains,
        a list of ships commanded by Searsport men,
        1834-1927 [and a list of] vessels built in
        Searsport. [Searsport?], 1927. Broadside,
        19 x 12 inches. MeU.

4730   THURSTON, STEPHEN. Semi-centennial: a sermon
        on the fiftieth anniversary of the organiza-
        tion of the First Congregational Church in
        Searsport ... delivered October 4th, 1865.
        Portland: Brown Thurston, 1866. Pp. 24.
        MeBa.

SEBAGO (CUMBERLAND CO.)

4731   MESERVE FRED L., comp. Centennial history of
        Sebago, Maine, 1826-1926; containing the cen-
        tennial celebration of 1926, and historical
        matter. [Sebago?, 1926]. Pp. 54.

4732   NASON, LAWRENCE. Two stories from Sebago his-
        tory. n.p., [1957?]. Unpaged. MeHi.
            Potter Academy and the Spaulding Memorial
        Library.

SEBEC (PISCATAQUIS CO.)

4733   CUSHING, WAINWRIGHT. "Early history of the
        town of Sebec." PCHSC, 1 (1910), 10-34.

SEBOEIS PLANTATION (PENOBSCOT CO.)

4734 No items located.

SEBOOMOOK TOWNSHIP (SOMERSET CO.)

4735 No items located.

SEDGWICK (HANCOCK CO.)

4736 "ACCOUNT of the Baptist Church lately constituted at Sedgwick, District of Maine."
Massachusetts Baptist Missionary Magazine, 1
(1803), 124-127, 144-146.

4737 FREEMASONS. SEDGWICK, ME. EGGEMOGGIN LODGE.
History of Eggemoggin Lodge of Free and Accepted Masons, Sedgwick, Me., 1872. Ellsworth: N. K. Sawyer & Son, 1872. Pp. 15.
MeHi.

4738 LEE, JOHN R. "Maine Lake Ice Company." Down
East, 17 (March, 1971), 44-47.

4739 LOVETT, ROBERT WOODBERRY. "Storekeeping in a
Maine seacoast town: records of the W. G.
Sargent Company." BBHS, 27 (1953), 121-123.
1834-1927.

4740 NEESE, ABBY SARGENT. Sargentville: historical reminiscences. Rockland: Courier-
Gazette, 1975. Pp. 50.

4741 SEDGWICK, ME. BICENTENNIAL COMMITTEE. Sedgwick, Maine, bicentennial, 1763-1963, August
2-3-4. n.p., 1963. Pp. 88. Me.

4742 SEDGWICK, ME. FIRST BAPTIST CHURCH. Centen-
nial of the First Baptist Church, Sedgwick,
Maine, June 11-18, 1905; two historical pa-
pers: I. Historical sketch of the town of
Sedgwick by Rev. Arthur Warren Smith; II.
Rev. Daniel Merrill, A.M.--an appreciation by
Samuel P. Merrill. n.p., [1905]. Pp. 64.

4743 "SEDGWICK and settlers." MeHistMag, 8
(1893), 16-17.
Includes ecclesiastical history.

4744 "SEDGWICK Public Library--its history and
dedication." MeLB, 16 (1930-1931), 43-44.

4745 STRAND, MARK. The Sargeantville notebook.
Providence, R.I.: Burning Deck, 1973. Unpaged.

SEE ALSO entry 1561.

SEVEN PONDS TOWNSHIP (FRANKLIN CO.)

4746 No items located.

SHAPLEIGH (YORK CO.)

4747 LORING, AMASA. A history of Shapleigh.
Portland: B. Thurston, 1854. Pp. 40.

4748 VON KRUMREIG, EDWARD LUDWIG. An historical
address of the First Baptist Church of Shapleigh, Maine. n.p., [1903]. Pp. 66. MeHi.

SHAWTOWN TOWNSHIP (PISCATAQUIS CO.)

4749 No items located.

SHERMAN (AROOSTOOK CO.)

4750 SHERMAN MILLS, ME. WASHBURN MEMORIAL CHURCH.
History of the Washburn Memorial Church,
Sherman Mills, Maine, and the program of the
centennial observance, August 13 to 20, 1961.
n.p., [1961]. Pp. 15. MBC.

SHIRLEY (PISCATAQUIS CO.)

4751 "THE SHIRLEY House at Shirley Corner, Maine."
SJMH, 4 (1916-1917), 53.

SIDNEY (KENNEBEC CO.)

4752 SEE entry 1645.

SILVER RIDGE TOWNSHIP (AROOSTOOK CO.)

4753 No items located.

SKINNER TOWNSHIP (FRANKLIN CO.)

4754 SEE entry 3377A.

SKOWHEGAN (SOMERSET CO.)

4755 ANDERSON, THOMAS H. and FRANK A. NOLIN. History of Somerset Lodge, No. 34, Free and Accepted Masons, Skowhegan, Me., from January 1,
1875 to December 31, 1889. Skowhegan: J. O.
Smith, 1891. Pp. 36.

4756 COBURN, LOUISE HELEN. History of the Skowhegan Woman's Club, read at the birthday dinner of the Skowhegan Woman's Club held at
Lakewood, September 21, 1932 during the annual
meeting of the Maine Federation of Women's
Clubs. n.p., [1932]. Unpaged.

4757 _____. The passage of the Arnold Expedition through Skowhegan. Skowhegan, 1922. Pp. 24.

4758 _____. Skowhegan on the Kennebec. Skowhegan: Independent-Reporter Pr., 1941. 2v.

4759 DANFORTH, EDWARD F. Skowhegan lawyers, 1803-1927. Hinckley: Good Will Publishing, 1927. Pp. 58. Me.

4760 DIETZ, LEW. "The Skowhegan School of Painting and Sculpture." Down East, 16 (June, 1970), 40-43, 70, 72.

4761 DOWNER, ALAN S. "The Down East screamer." NEQ, 42 (1969), 181-200.
     Amos Angier Mann; journalist.

4762 ESTES, WILLIAM ROSCOE GREENE. History of Somerset Chapter, No. 15, Royal Arch Masons, Skowhegan, Maine, from 1863 to 1910. [Skowhegan]: Independent Reporter, 1910. Pp. 98. MeB.

4763 _____. History of Somerset Lodge, No. 34, of Free and Accepted Masons, Skowhegan, Me., from June 27, 1820, to January 1, 1875. Portland: Berry, 1875. Pp. 66.

4764 FIRST NATIONAL BANK OF SKOWHEGAN. A century of service, 1825-1925. [Skowhegan, 1925?]. Pp. 95. MH-BA.

4765 FOLSOM, EMMA B. "Historical church that has become an armory." Sun Up, 10 (March, 1932), 17.
     First Baptist Church.

4766 LAWRENCE, FRED F. "Progressive and beautiful Skowhegan." BTJ, 23 (1910-1911), 221-223, 225, 227.

4767 MERRILL, J. N. "Preventive medicine in Skowhegan." JMS, 2 (1895-1896), 647-649.

4768 NASH, HARRIET A. "A type of Bloomfield." NEM, New Ser., 20 (1899), 472-480.
     Social life and customs.

4769 PERKINS, DEFOREST H. "The schools and school system of Skowhegan." BTJ, 23 (1910-1911), 247-249.

4770 SKOWHEGAN, ME. 1724-1926, important data in the history of Skowhegan. [Skowhegan]: Independent-Reporter, [1926]. Unpaged. Me.

4771 "SKOWHEGAN." BTJ, 3 (1890-1891), 267-272.

     SEE ALSO entries 1816 and 3532.

SMITHFIELD (SOMERSET CO.)

4772 No items located.

SMYRNA (AROOSTOOK CO.)

4773 No items located.

SOLDIERTOWN TOWNSHIP (PENOBSCOT CO.)

4774 No items located.

SOLDIERTOWN TOWNSHIP (SOMERSET CO.)

4775 No items located.

SOLON (SOMERSET CO.)

4776 CUMMINGS, MILDRED H. South Solon: the story of a meeting house. [Solon]: South Solon Historical Society, 1959. Pp. 54.

4777 DAVIS, ISAAC FRANKLIN. A history of Solon, Maine. n.p., [1973?]. Pp. 77. Me.

4778 DIETZ, LEW. "The South Solon Meeting House." Down East, 3 (November, 1956-January, 1957), 21-23.

4779 RUSSELL, CHARLOTTE M. Scenes from Solon's history. [Solon]: Rusmer-linc, [1959]. 35 leaves.

4780 SOLON, ME. SESQUICENTENNIAL HISTORY COMMITTEE. Sketches from Solon's history. n.p., 1959. Pp. 95.

SOMERVILLE (LINCOLN CO.)

4781 No items located.

SOPER MOUNTAIN TOWNSHIP (PISCATAQUIS CO.)

4782 No items located.

SORRENTO (HANCOCK CO.)

4783 CHAFFEE, ZECHARIAH. Sorrento, Maine. Providence, R.I.: Livermore & Knight, 1911. Unpaged.

4784 LEWIS, LAWRENCE. Torna a Sorrento, 1938-1973. Worcester, Mass.: Commonwealth Pr., 1973. Pp. 74. MeBa.
     In English.

     SEE ALSO entry 1588.

SOUTH BERWICK (YORK CO.)

4785 BAER, ANNIE WENTWORTH. "Captain Nathan Lord's house." Granite Mo, 59 (1927), 201-206.

4786 BERWICK ACADEMY, SOUTH BERWICK, ME. A memorial of the 100th anniversary of the founding of Berwick Academy, July 1, 1891. Sarah Orne Jewett, ed. Cambridge, Mass.: Riverside Pr., 1891. Pp. xv, 118.
Historical address by John Lord.

4787 _____. 175th anniversary sampler: a collection of essays by alumni and friends of Berwick Academy. Jean M. Goodwin, ed. South Berwick, 1966. Pp. vi, 100.

4788 BROWN, FRANK CHOUTEAU. "Interior details and furnishings of the Sarah Orne Jewett dwelling, built by John Haggins in 1774 at South Berwick, Maine." Pencil Points, 21 (1940), 115-130.

4789 CARROLL, GLADYS HASTY. "Schooling in the early nineteen hundreds." NEG, 14 (Fall, 1972), 15-23.

4790 DONAHUE, MARIE. "Hamilton House on the Piscataqua." Down East, 22 (October, 1975), 36-39, 65-66.

4791 _____. "Maine's oldest private academy." Down East, 13 (October, 1966), 26-29, 40-42.
Berwick Academy.

4792 "GENERAL Lafayette in Maine." MHGR, 4 (1887), 229-235.
1815.

4793 GEORGES, JUSTINE FLINT. "Mementos of a great lady." Shoreliner, 1 (September, 1950), 10-13.
Sarah Orne Jewett House.

4794 HAMBLEN, ABIGAIL ANN. "Beloved village." Down East, 2 (August, 1955), 33, 45.

4795 HAWTHORNE, HILDEGARDE. "A garden of romance: Mrs. Tyson's, at Hamilton House, South Berwick, Maine." Century, 80 (1910), 778-786.
Emily D. Tyson.

4796 HENNESSY, WILLIAM G. "The house of Hamilton." Shoreliner, 3 (July, 1952), 9-16.
Jonathan Hamilton.

4797 HILTON, FANNIE MULLOY. Memories of a little country church or a brief history of the South Berwick & Wells Christian Church. South Berwick: Chronicle Print Shop, 1969. Pp. 54. Me.

4798 JEWETT, SARAH ORNE. Letters. (1956) Richard Cary, ed. Enl. and rev. ed. Waterville: Colby College Pr., 1967. Pp. viii, 186.

4799 KENISTON, AMANDA M. A history of the South Berwick Village Baptist Church from 1823 to 1926. n.p., [1926]. Pp. 14. MeHi.

4800 KINGSBURY, EDITH. "Hamilton House: historic landmark in South Berwick, Maine." House Beautiful, 65 (1929), 782-787, 874, 876.

4801 LEWIS, GEORGE. Address delivered by Rev. George Lewis, D.D., Wednesday, June 4th, 1902, at the two hundredth anniversary of the founding of the Congregational Church in South Berwick, Maine. South Berwick: Independent Pr., 1902. Pp. 30.

4802 RICKER, JENNIE DE R. South Berwick, Me., pages from the past. n.p., [1936?]. Pp. 17. MB.

4803 SCATES, JOHN CLARK. "Records of the First Church of Berwick (South Berwick), Me." NEHGR, 82 (1928), 71-98, 204-218, 312-333, 500-511; 83 (1929), 9-20, 147-156.

4804 SHELTON, LOUISE. "The garden at Hamilton House." American Homes and Gardens, 6 (1909), 422-425.

4805 SLOAN, ALEX. "South Berwick Church." Congregationalism in Maine, 13 (1926), 27-29.

4806 SOUTH BERWICK, ME. FIRST PARISH CHURCH. A brief history of the First Parish Church, South Berwick, Maine, 1702-1952. n.p., [1952]. Unpaged. MBC.

4807 STACKPOLE, EVERETT SCHERMERHORN. "The first permanent settlement in Maine." SJMH, 14 (1926), 190-215.
Great Works.

4808 TRAFTON, BURTON W. F., JR. "Hamilton House, South Berwick, Maine." Antiques, 77 (1960), 486-489.

4809 _____. "Hamilton House, South Berwick, Maine." OTNE, 48 (1957-1958), 57-64.
Differs from previous entry.

SEE ALSO entries 1322 and 1911.

SOUTH BRISTOL (LINCOLN CO.)

4810 GAMAGE, NELSON W. A short history of South Bristol, Maine. [South Bristol: Everett W. Gamage, 1953?]. Pp. 49.
Even numbered pages are on rectos.

SEE ALSO entry 1706.

SOUTH PORTLAND (CUMBERLAND CO.)

4810A FREEMASONS. CAPE ELIZABETH, ME. HIRAM LODGE, NO. 180. History of Hiram Lodge, No. 180, Free and Accepted Masons, Cape Elizabeth, Maine, and a full abstract from the records from its organization, November, 1875 to November 10, 1891. Stephen Scamman, comp. Portland: Smith & Sale, 1892. Pp. 107.
Due to a boundary change, the lodge is now in South Portland.

4811 FREEMASONS. SOUTH PORTLAND, ME. HIRAM LODGE, NO. 180. History of Hiram Lodge, No. 180, F. & A. M., South Portland, Maine, 1876-1976. n.p., [1976]. Pp. 224. MeHi.

4812 JONES, HERBERT GRANVILLE. Portland ships are good ships: the building of thirty British and 236 liberty ships by the New England Shipbuilding Corporation, South Portland, Maine. Portland: Machigonne Pr., 1945. Pp. ix, 60.

4813 LEAGUE OF WOMEN VOTERS OF SOUTH PORTLAND. MAINE. South Portland, Maine, a brief history. Portland: Maine Printers, 1960. Unpaged. MeP.

4814 _____. South Portland, Me., an All-American city. South Portland, 1971. Pp. 69.
Includes historical sketch.

4815 PRIDE TRAINING SCHOOL, SOUTH PORTLAND, ME. Pride Training School for retarded children: report on ten years' progress. n.p., [1960]. Pp. 52. MeP.

4816 SLEEPER, FRANK. "South Portland: Maine's fastest growing industrial city." Down East, 13 (March, 1967), 8-12, 15-16, 60.

4817 SOUTH PORTLAND, ME. Centennial program, old home day celebration, city of So. Portland, Maine, Saturday, August 21, 1920. n.p., [1920]. Unpaged. MeHi.
Includes a brief history of the city.

4818 SOUTH PORTLAND, ME. CHURCH OF THE NAZARENE. 50th anniversary, South Portland Church of the Nazarene. n.p., [1950]. Unpaged. MeP.
Includes history by Ada F. MacDonald.

4819 SOUTH PORTLAND, ME. 50TH ANNIVERSARY COMMITTEE. Souvenir program, 50th anniversary, city of South Portland, Maine, August 28-29, 1948. n.p., [1948]. Pp. 36. MeHi.
Includes history by Rosella A. Loveitt.

4820 SOUTH PORTLAND, ME. FIRST CONGREGATIONAL CHURCH. Historical address, sermon, poem and hymn read at the one hundred and seventy-fifth anniversary of the First Congregational Church and Parish (Old North Church) of South Portland and Cape Elizabeth, celebrated August 14-16, 1909, in the church, Meeting House Hill, 1734-1909. Portland: Southworth Printing, 1909. Pp. 34.
Historical address by Fritz H. Jordan.

4821 SOUTH PORTLAND, ME. FIRST METHODIST CHURCH. First Methodist Church, Church Street, (Brown's Hill), South Portland, Maine, 150th anniversary, 1803-1953, souvenir history and church directory. n.p., 1953. Unpaged. MBNEH.
History is by Wilson L. Lyon.

SEE ALSO entries 1487 and 1512.

SOUTH THOMASTON (KNOX CO.)

4822 CLARKE, WINFIELD S. History of Knox Lodge, No. 189, F. & A. M., from its organization, October 4, 1884, to January 31, 1910. Rockland: Opinion Pr., 1910. Pp. 49.

4823 NEESON, MARGARET GRAHAM. "The favored rock." Down East, 22 (September, 1975), 58-59, 82-83.
On Spruce Head Island and called "Date Rock."

SEE ALSO entry 1660.

SOUTHPORT (LINCOLN CO.)

4824 LEPPER, RUTH RHOADS. A pictorial history of Southport. West Southport: Ruth Lepper Gardner, 1976. Unpaged. MeU.

4825 "MAINE claims the only existing autograph library in the world." Sun Up, 3 (August, 1927), 33, 56.
All books are autographed by either the author or the donor.

4826 MERRILL, JOHN P. and SUZANNE MERRILL, eds. Squirrel Island, Maine: the first hundred years. Freeport: Bond Wheelwright, 1973. Pp. 66.

4827 MERRILL, SAMUEL PEARCE. Souvenir of Squirrel Island. Waterville: E. A. Pierce, 1895. Pp. 31. MeU.

4828 SOUTHPORT HISTORY COMMITTEE. Historical gleanings from Cape Newagen, Townsend, Southport. Boothbay Harbor: Harbor Print Shop, 1976. Pp. 96. Me.

4829 SQUIRREL ISLAND, ME. LIBRARY. Squirrelana. Squirrel Island, 1954. Unpaged.

4830 WHEELER, EDITH H. "Squirrel Island's first hundred years." Down East, 17 (July, 1971), 52-55, 81, 83.

SEE ALSO entries 1681-1682 and 1689-1690.

SOUTHWEST HARBOR (HANCOCK CO.)

4831   BARTER, J. MALCOLM. "Henry R. Hinckley & Co. --Maine builder of fiberglass sail yachts." Down East, 14 (April, 1968), 28-33.

4832   THE CLAREMONT Hotel--my story, 1884-1964. n.p., [1964?]. Pp. 7. MeU.

4833   PARKER, JESSE L. Recollections of Southwest Harbor, Maine, 1885-1894. n.p., 1955. 49 leaves. MeU.

4834   STEWART, ALICE ROSE. "Russians in Maine." Down East, 8 (September, 1961), 44-47, 54.
     Visit of the 'Cimbria' in 1878.

SEE ALSO entries 1587 and 1617.

SPENCER BAY TOWNSHIP (PISCATAQUIS CO.)

4835   No items located.

SPRINGFIELD (PENOBSCOT CO.)

4836   BRADBURY, OSGOOD NATHAN. History of Forrest Lodge, No. 148, of Free and Accepted Masons, of Springfield, Maine, from July 4, A.D. 1868, to December 31, A.D. 1869. Portland: Stephen Berry, 1872. Pp. 15. MeBa.

SQUAPAN TOWNSHIP (AROOSTOOK CO.)

4837   No items located.

SQUARETOWN TOWNSHIP (SOMERSET CO.)

4838   No items located.

STACYVILLE (PENOBSCOT CO.)

4839   No items located.

STANDISH (CUMBERLAND CO.)

4840   DINGLEY, ROBERT JORDAN. Boating in the Switzerland of America ... the Sebago-Long Lake Waterway, the Songo River Line. [Naples]: Naples Historical Society, [1970?]. Unpaged. MeHi.

4841   DRUMMOND, JOSIAH HAYDEN. History of Standish Lodge, No. 70, Free and Accepted Masons, Standish, Me., from June 10, 1852, to Oct. 1, 1874. Portland: Harmon, Paine, 1874. Pp. 38.

4842   STANDISH OLD HOME ASSOCIATION. The record of the first observance of Old Home Day ... on Thursday, August 9th, 1900.... Portland: Tucker Printing, 1900. Pp. 35. MeHi.

4843   USHER, HELEN, et al. Facts about Standish. Standish: Hartford Printing, 1922. Pp. 16. Me.

SEE ALSO entry 1494.

STARKS (SOMERSET CO.)

4844   SEE entries 1419, 1816, and 3362.

STETSON (PENOBSCOT CO.)

4845   DANIELS, LILLA WOOD. History of Stetson, Maine, 1800-1931. Bangor: Furbush Printing, [1931?]. Pp. 66.

STETSONTOWN TOWNSHIP (FRANKLIN CO.)

4846   No items located.

STEUBEN (WASHINGTON CO.)

4847   COBLENS, GLENORE ORRIS. All Souls by the Sea, Petit Manan Point, Maine: the history of a little church. Cherryfield: Narraguagus Printing, 1972. Pp. 14.

4848   HARRIS, HERBERT. History of Ionic Lodge, of Free and Accepted Masons, Steuben, Maine, from its organization, in 1806, to its close in 1813. Portland: The Grand Lodge, 1894. Pp. 23.

SEE ALSO entries 1855 and 1864.

STOCKHOLM (AROOSTOOK CO.)

4849   STOCKHOLM, ME. Town of Stockholm, Maine-- 90th anniversary, 1881-1971. n.p., [1971?]. Pp. 56. [MeHoR].
     Includes history by Fritz Anderson.

SEE ALSO entry 1456.

STOCKTON SPRINGS (WALDO CO.)

4850   CAREY, ROGER. "Fort Pownall." Down East, 19 (October, 1972), 54-56, 61.

4851 ELLIS, ALICE V. The story of Stockton Springs, Maine. [Stockton Springs]: Historical Committee of Stockton Springs, 1955. Pp. 223.

4852 HICHBORN, FAUSTINA. Historical sketch of Stockton Springs. Herbert C. Libby, ed. Waterville: Central Maine Publishing, 1908. Pp. 133.

4853 PIKE, RICHARD. "Building and occupancy of Fort Pownall." NEHGR, 14 (1860), 4-10.

4854 PORTER, JOSEPH WHITCOMB. "The expedition to Penobscot and the erection of Fort Pownal." MeHistMag, 7 (1891-1892), 61-65.

STONEHAM (OXFORD CO.)

4855 No items located.

STONINGTON (HANCOCK CO.)

4856 CURRIER, ISABEL. "The granite-bound town of Stonington." Down East, 13 (November, 1966), 16-21, 46, 48.

4857 _____. "A Maine quarry's fabulous feat." Down East, 14 (May, 1968), 22-25, 48-49.
The Rockefeller Bowl, the largest object to be cut from a single piece of granite anywhere in the United States.

SEE ALSO entries 1553, 1561, 2834-2836, and 2840-2843.

STOW (OXFORD CO.)

4858 No items located.

STRONG (FRANKLIN CO.)

4859 BUTLER, NATALIE STURGES and BENJAMIN BUTLER. Souvenir program, Republican centennial celebration, 1854-1954, Strong, Maine, August 7, 1954. n.p., [1954]. Unpaged. MeHi.
Includes a brief history of the town by Christine Richardson.

SEE ALSO entry 1419.

SUGARLOAF TOWNSHIP (FRANKLIN CO.)

4860 No items located.

SULLIVAN (HANCOCK CO.)

4861 GALLISON, WILLIAM W., EDWIN F. CLAPHAM, and SETH A. JOHNSON. History of David A. Hooper Lodge, No. 201, West Sullivan, Maine from the founding of the lodge to January 1, 1935. Ellsworth: American Print, 1935. Pp. 30. Me.

4862 SARGENT, WINTHROP. Colonel Paul Dudley Sargent, 1745-1827. [Philadelphia?, 1920]. Pp. 46.

SEE ALSO entries 1579 and 1588.

SUMMIT TOWNSHIP (PENOBSCOT CO.)

4863 No items located.

SUMNER (OXFORD CO.)

4864 SUMNER, ME. Centennial history of the town of Sumner, Me., 1798-1898. West Sumner: Charles E. Handy, Jr., 1899. Pp. 202, xxx.

SURRY (HANCOCK CO.)

4865 DODGE, ERNEST STANLEY. "The last days of coasting on Union River Bay." AmNep, 9 (1949), 169-179.
Ships and shipping.

4866 SURRY, ME. Surry's centennial souvenir, 1903. Ellsworth: Campbell Publishing, 1903. Unpaged. MBNEH.

SEE ALSO entry 1578.

SWANS ISLAND (HANCOCK CO.)

4867 "BURNT Coat or Swan's Island and other islands contiguous thereto." BHistMag, 3 (1887-1888), 21-26.

4868 SMALL, HERMAN WESLEY. A history of Swan's Island, Maine. Ellsworth: Hancock Publishing, 1898. Pp. 244.

4869 WESTBROOK, PERRY DICKIE. Biography of an island. N.Y.: T. Yoseloff, 1958. Pp. 224.

SWANVILLE (WALDO CO.)

4870 No items located.

SWEDEN (OXFORD CO.)

4871   No items located.

T3 INDIAN PURCHASE (PENOBSCOT CO.)

4872   No items located.

T4 INDIAN PURCHASE (PENOBSCOT CO.)

4873   No items located.

TALMADGE (WASHINGTON CO.)

4874   No items located.

TAUNTON & RAYNHAM ACADEMY GRANT (SOMERSET CO.)

4875   No items located.

TEMPLE (FRANKLIN CO.)

4876   SEE entry 1419.

THOMASTON (KNOX CO.)

4877   AYERS, BLANCHE WALDO. "The Knox memorial."
DARMag, 56 (1922), 293-295.
        Montpelier.

4878   CILLEY, JONATHAN PRINCE. "The Burtons of
Thomaston." Maine Bugle, 5 (1898), 200-212.
        Burton family.

4879   DEMERS, MABEL GOULD. "Doorways and beyond:
Montpelier." Pine Cone, 6 (Summer, 1950),
25-30.

4880   DUNNACK, HENRY ERNEST. "General Henry Knox,
American patriot." DARMag, 59 (1925), 354-
357.
        Primarily concerned with Montpelier, Knox's
home.

4881   ELKINS, L. WHITNEY. "Montpelier: the old
mansion home at Thomaston, Maine where General Knox lived during the Revolution." Sun
Up, 3 (August, 1926), 66, 69, 71, 74.

4882   FIELDS, J. E. "The mistress of Montpelier."
DARMag, 87 (1953), 525-528.
        Lucy Knox.

4883   FOWLER, HENRY THATCHER. General Knox and his
home in Maine: Montpelier. Rockland:
Courier-Gazette Pr., 1931. Pp. 26.

4884   FREEMASONS. THOMASTON, ME. ORIENT LODGE, NO.
15. History of Orient Lodge, No. 15, of F.
& A. Masons, located at Thomaston. Sanford:
Jas. H. Goodall, 1895. Pp. 38. MeHi.

4885   GREEN, SAMUEL M. "The architecture of Thomaston, Maine." SocArchHistJ, 10 (December,
1951), 24-32.

4886   GRIFFITHS, THOMAS MORGAN. Major General
Henry Knox and the last heirs to Montpelier.
Arthur Morgan Griffiths, ed. Monmouth: Mon-
mouth Pr., 1965. Pp. 130.

4887   HIGGINSON, MARY P. THACHER. "Two ancient
landmarks." Scribner's Monthly Magazine, 9
(1874-1875), 615-618.
        Montpelier in Thomaston and the Cornwallis
House, Camden, South Carolina.

4888   HUSSEY, MRS. LEROY FOGG. "Montpelier."
DARMag, 83 (1949), 579-580.
        Home of Henry Knox.

4889   KARL, ALICE W. "The new Montpelier." Sun
Up, 9 (July, 1931), 4, 28.
        The present Montpelier is a reproduction of
the home built by General Knox in 1793.

4890   LEFFINGWELL, B. H. "Montpelier, the home of
General Henry Knox at Thomaston, Me." Hobbies, 65 (August, 1960), 58-59.

4891   LETTERS to Christopher Prince, 1855-1865.
Journals of Eliza Prince, 1859-1860. Arthur
Spear, ed. Middletown, N.Y.: Whitlock Pr.,
1969. Pp. ix, 215.

4892   LINDLEY, E. MARGUERITE. "Montpelier: historic home of Major-General Henry Knox."
MagAmHist, 16 (1886), 121-132.

4893   MILES, CARLTON E. "Beautiful Montpelier, the
rebuilt Knox home." Sun Up, 10 (May, 1932),
12-13, 17.

4894   "'MONTPELIER,' once the residence of Gen'l
Knox at Thomaston, Me." BTJ, 6 (1893-1894),
241-242.

4895   NEALLEY, EDWARD BOWDOIN. "Oration delivered
at the centennial celebration of the incorporation of the town of Thomaston, July 4,
1877." MeHistMag, 8 (1893), 121-137.

4896   PACKARD, AUBIGNE LERMOND. A town that went
to sea. Portland: Falmouth Publishing,
1950. Pp. viii, 416.

4897   PARKER, W. J. LEWIS. "Sails, ships & cargoes:
Dunn & Elliot of Thomaston, Maine." Down
East, 17 (March, 1971), 48-52, 77, 80, 85-86,
90-91, 93.

4898   PORTER, JOSEPH WHITCOMB. "An abstract of the
history of the Maine State Prison, 1822-1886."
BHistMag, 6 (1890-1891), appendix, 1-15.

4899   _____. "An abstract of the history of the
Maine State Prison to the present time, 1882."
Maine State Prison. Annual Report, (1882),
45 pages of appendix at end.
    This article is more detailed than the
above entry.

4900   PRINCE, HEZEKIAH. Journals of Hezekiah
Prince, Jr., 1822-1828. Arthur Spear, ed.
N.Y.: Crown Publishers, 1965. Pp. xxii,
448.

4901   ROBBINS, ALLAN L. Information regarding the
Maine State Prison, Thomaston, 1824-1953.
Thomaston, [1953]. Pp. 55. MeBa.

4902   STARRETT, LEWIS FREDERICK. General Henry
Knox: his family, his manor, his manor
house, and his guests; a paper read before
the 12mo Club, Rockland, Maine, March 3,
1902. Rockland: Huston's Bookstore, 1902.
Pp. 34.

4903   STIMPSON, MARY STOYELL. "Thomaston--the home
of Knox." NEM, New Ser., 29 (1903-1904),
730-740.

4904   TEETERS, NEGLEY K. "Early days of the Maine
State Prison at Thomaston." Journal of Crim-
inal Law and Criminology, 38 (July-August,
1947), 104-108.

4905   THOMASTON CONGREGATIONAL CHURCH. The 150th
anniversary of the Thomaston Congregational
Church, Thomaston, Maine, 1809-1959. n.p.,
[1959]. Unpaged. MBC.

4906   THOMASTON HISTORICAL SOCIETY. Tall ships,
white houses, and elms: Thomaston, Maine,
1870-1900. Thomaston, 1976. Pp. 154. Me.
    Pictorial history.

4907   WILLIAMS, HARRIET R. "Montpelier, the Maine
home of Major General Henry Knox." DARMag,
98 (1964), 582-585.

        SEE ALSO entries 1659-1660, 1663, 1666, 1753,
2082, and 4589.

THORNDIKE (WALDO CO.)

4908   THORNDIKE, ME. A brief history of Thorndike,
Maine, 1819-1919. Thorndike: Newell White,
1919. Pp. 29. MBNEH.

4909   _____. Sesquicentennial celebration, town of
Thorndike, county of Waldo, State of Maine,
August 9, 10, 1969. n.p., [1969]. Pp. 36.
Me.

THORNDIKE TOWNSHIP (SOMERSET CO.)

4910   No items located.

TIM POND TOWNSHIP (FRANKLIN CO.)

4911   No items located.

TOMHEGAN TOWNSHIP (SOMERSET CO.)

4912   No items located.

TOPSFIELD (WASHINGTON CO.)

4913   No items located.

TOPSHAM (SAGADAHOC CO.)

4914   SMALL, CHARLES H. The state seal. Pills-
bury's soliloquy. When I was a lad; or The
second Jackson, M.D.... Topsham, 1880.
Pp. 8.

4915   SMITH, LINCOLN. "Leadership in local govern-
ment--the New England town." Social Science,
29 (June, 1954), 147-157.

4916   TOPSHAM, ME. Topsham, Maine: 200th anniversary, July 17, 18, 19, 1964. [Brunswick:
Brunswick Publishing, 1964]. Pp. 37.

4917   WILSON, ADAM. Historical discourse, delivered
before the Baptist church in Topsham, at the
close of the first half-century of their history, September 2, 1865. Waterville: Maxham
& Wing's Print, 1866. Pp. 15. MB.

        SEE ALSO entries 1315 and 2573.

TOWNSHIP C (OXFORD CO.)

4918   No items located.

TOWNSHIP D (FRANKLIN CO.)

4919   No items located.

TOWNSHIP E (FRANKLIN CO.)

4920   No items located.

TOWNSHIP 6 (FRANKLIN CO.)

4921   No items located.

TREMONT (HANCOCK CO.)

4922   COUSINS, EDGAR M. The Mt. Desert Congrega-
        tional Church, Tremont, Maine: historical
        sermon and notes. n.p., [1895]. Pp. 29.

4923   "HISTORY of McKinley and town of Tremont on
        Mount Desert Island." SJMH, 10 (1922), 233-
        235.
            McKinley is a village in Tremont.

4924   KEENE, WILLIAM R. History of Tremont Lodge,
        No. 77, of Free and Accepted Masons, Tremont,
        Maine, from 1881 to 1891, inclusive. Ells-
        worth: Campbell's Job Print, 1891. Pp. 21.
        [MePGLM].

4925   LURVEY, C. H. History of Tremont Lodge, No.
        77, of Free and Accepted Masons, Tremont,
        Maine, from 1871 to 1881. Ellsworth: Camp-
        bell Bros., 1881. Pp. 26. [MePGLM].

4926   TARR, ANDREW. History of Tremont Lodge, No.
        77, of Free and Accepted Masons, Tremont,
        Me., from 1854 to 1871. Portland: Stephen
        Berry, 1874. Pp. 19. MeHi.

        SEE ALSO entry 1587.

TRENTON (HANCOCK CO.)

4927   "REVIVAL in Trenton, Maine." The Sabbath
        School Treasury, 6 (1833), 32.

        SEE ALSO entries 1569 and 1579.

TRESCOTT TOWNSHIP (WASHINGTON CO.)

4928   No items located.

TROUT BROOK TOWNSHIP (PASCATAQUIS CO.)

4929   No items located.

TROY (WALDO CO.)

4930   No items located.

TURNER (ANDROSCOGGIN CO.)

4931   FRENCH, WILLIAM RILEY. A history of Turner,
        Maine, from its settlement to 1886. Port-
        land: Hoyt, Fogg & Donham, 1887. Pp. viii,
        312.
            Manuscript indices by Ethel P. Hall and
        Margaret Z. Garrett are at the Maine Histori-
        cal Society.

4932   GILBERT, WASHINGTON. Address ... delivered at
        the centennial celebration of the town of
        Turner, July 7th, 1886. Portland: B. Thurs-
        ton, 1886. Pp. 16. MeHi.

4933   HALE, CLARENCE. "Turner, Maine, centennial,
        November 23, 1923." SJMH, 12 (1924), 149-158.

4934   RICH, CAROLINE WEBSTER D. STOCKBRIDGE. Poem
        written for the centennial celebration of the
        town of Turner, Maine. Portland: B. Thurs-
        ton, 1886. Pp. 14.

        SEE ALSO entries 405 and 549.

UNION (KNOX CO.)

4935   MATTHEWS, EDWARDS A. Horse and buggy days:
        a brief history of Union, Maine. Belfast:
        Kelley Pr., 1950. Pp. 381.

4936   NASH, CHESTER and PATRICIA KAHN. 200 years
        in Union: a pictorial history of Union,
        Maine. [Union]: Union Historical Society,
        1974. Pp. 95. MeU.

4937   SIBLEY, JOHN LANGDON. A history of the town
        of Union, in the county of Lincoln, Maine, to
        the middle of the nineteenth century; with a
        family register of the settlers before the
        year 1800, and of their descendants. Boston:
        Benjamin B. Mussey, 1851. Pp. ix, 540.

4938   UNION, ME. A brief story and census of Union.
        Union: G. H. Cameron & J. R. Meservey, 1929.
        Unpaged. MeHi.

4939   _____. Union register: census, history,
        statistics, business directory.... Union:
        Union Publishing, 1888. Pp. 31. MeHi.

4940   UNION WEEKLY TIMES. Union, past and present:
        an illustrated history of the town of Union,
        Maine, from earliest times to date. Union,
        1895. Pp. 96.

UNITY (WALDO CO.)

4941   MURCH, EDMUND. A brief history of the town of
        Unity, written and read ... at a meeting of
        Harvest Moon Grange, Thorndike, 1892. Belfast:
        G. W. Burgess, 1893. Pp. 18.

4942   TABER, JAMES R. History of Unity, Maine.
Augusta: Maine Farmer Pr., 1916. Pp. 144.

4943   UNITY, ME. BICENTENNIAL BOOKLET COMMITTEE.
Unity today, 1975-76. n.p., [1976].
Pp. 48. Me.

4944   UNITY SESQUICENTENNIAL SOCIETY. Sesquicentennial of the town of Unity, Maine, 1804-
1954. n.p., [1954]. Pp. 26. Me.

4945   VICKERY, JAMES BERRY, III. A history of the
town of Unity, Maine. Manchester: Falmouth
Publishing, 1954. Pp. 254.
An enlargement of the author's master's
thesis at the University of Maine.

UNITY TOWNSHIP (KENNEBEC CO.)

4946   No items located.

UPPER CUPSUPTIC TOWNSHIP (OXFORD CO.)

4947   No items located.

UPPER ENCHANTED TOWNSHIP (SOMERSET CO.)

4948   No items located.

UPPER MOLUNKUS TOWNSHIP (AROOSTOOK CO.)

4949   No items located.

UPTON (OXFORD CO.)

4950   HEYWOOD, CHARLES ERROL. History of Upton,
Maine. Norway: Oxford Hills Pr., 1973.
Pp. 14.

VAN BUREN (AROOSTOOK CO.)

4951   DUNN, CLAIRE MARY DEVEAU. There need never
be discouragement. [Madawaska: Valley Publishing, 1972?]. Pp. 177. MeU.
Deveau family.

4952   PELLETIER, MARTINE. "In God we trust": Van
Buren, Maine. Madawaska: St. John Valley
Printers, 1976. Pp. 132. [MeMaHi].

4953   VAN BUREN, ME. PAROISSE ST. BRUNO. Album-
souvenir du centenaire de la fondation de la
Paroisse St. Bruno, Van Buren, Maine, 1838-
1938. n.p., [1938]. Pp. 103. MBC.

VANCEBORO (WASHINGTON CO.)

4954   LOW, ELIZABETH ARMSTRONG. "The bridge over
the River St. Croix." Down East, 20 (March,
1974), 66-67.
Attempt by a German spy, Werner Horn, to
blow up the bridge during World War I.

VASSALBORO (KENNEBEC CO.)

4955   "HISTORY of the Vassalboro Free Public Library." MeLAB, 20 (August, 1959), 13-14.

4956   MANSON, RAYMOND RUSSELL and ELSIA HOLWAY BUR-
LEIGH. First seventy years of Oak Grove Sem-
inary. [Vassalboro]: Vassalboro Historical
Society, 1965. Pp. 38.

4957   MARTIN, DON. "East Vassalboro's old water
mill still going strong." Down East, 18
(November, 1971), 38-41.

4958   MASSE, HERMAN CHARLES. History of the old
water power grist and saw mill at East Vassalboro, Maine, 1797-1971; owned and operated
by the Masse family since 1912.... n.p.,
[1971]. 15 leaves.

4959   ROBBINS, ALMA PIERCE. The history of Vassal-
borough, Maine. [Vassalboro?, 1971?].
Pp. 62.

4960   WRIGHT, LAURIE ROBESON. "Maine Quakers with
E.S.P." Maine Dig, 1 (Summer, 1967), 83-84.

SEE ALSO entry 1645.

VEAZIE (PENOBSCOT CO.)

4961   TODD, HELEN HATHORNE. Veazie in review....
[Veazie]: Ladies Aid Society of the Veazie
Congregational Church, 1953. Pp. 10. MeU.

VEAZIE GORE (PENOBSCOT CO.)

4962   No items located.

VERONA (HANCOCK CO.)

4963   "Orphan's Island." MeHistMag, 8 (1893), 67-
68.

VIENNA (KENNEBEC CO.)

4964   BRADLEY, IRVING R. History of Vienna, Maine
from 1782 to 1952 ... as given on town's 150th
anniversary. n.p., [1952?]. Unpaged. Me.

VINALHAVEN (KNOX CO.)

4965 CALDERWOOD, IVAN E. Days of Uncle Dave's fish house: Vinalhaven seafarers are recalled. Rockland: Courier-Gazette, 1969. Pp. 274.

4966 _____. The saga of Hod. Rockland: Courier Gazette, 1971. Pp. 197. MeP.
Social life and customs.

4967 _____. Sequel ... days of Uncle Dave's fish house: Vinalhaven seafarers are recalled. Rockland: Courier-Gazette, 1972. Pp. 266.

4968 CUMMINGS, MILDRED H. "When granite was king on Vinalhaven." Down East, 17 (September, 1970), 42-47.

4969 FLAGG, PALUEL JOSEPH. Maine holiday. N.Y.: Chad-Ohre Pr., 1947. Pp. 27. Me.

4969A GRINDLE, ROGER LEE. "Bodwell Blue: the story of Vinalhaven's granite industry." MeHSQ, 16 (1976-1977), 51-112.

4970 "LIFE and death of an island." Down East, 3 (February-March, 1957), 14-17, 29.
Hurricane Island.

4971 MASON, JOHN. "The wreck of the 'Royal Tar.'" Yankee, 29 (October, 1965), 85, 110-113.
1836.

4972 VINALHAVEN, ME. CENTENNIAL COMMITTEE. A brief historical sketch of the town of Vinalhaven, from its earliest known settlement; prepared by order of the town, on the occasion of its one hundredth anniversary. (1889) Rockland: Star Job Print., 1900. Pp. 84.
Present edition continued to 1900 by Albra J. Vinal.

4973 WINSLOW, SIDNEY L. Fish scales and stone chips. Portland: Machigonne Press, 1952. Pp. 256. Me.

SEE ALSO entry 1656.

WADE (AROOSTOOK CO.)

4974 No items located.

WAITE (WASHINGTON CO.)

4975 No items located.

WALDO (WALDO CO.)

4976 No items located.

WALDOBORO (LINCOLN CO.)

4977 BARTER, J. MALCOLM. "Waldoboro." Down East, 11 (June, 1965), 37-39, 49-50, 52.

4978 BROWN, GILBERT PATTEN. "New England's oldest Lutheran church." The Pennsylvania German, 11 (1910), 731-733.

4979 GROSS, ESTHER. Waldoborough, 1773-1973: 200 anniversary, a pictorial history. Waldoboro: Waldoboro Bicentennial Committee, 1973. Pp. 96.

4980 JORDAN, JOHN WOOLF. "A historical sketch of the Moravian Mission at Broad Bay, Maine, 1760-1770." Moravian HST, 4 (1891-1895), 1-12.

4981 KEENE, JESSIE L. History of Waldoboro Village Methodist Church, Waldoboro, Maine. n.p., 1957. Pp. 12. MeHi.

4982 LOCKE, JOHN LYMBURNER. "Translation of Gen. Waldo's circular--1753." MeHSC, 6 (1859), 319-332.
Includes an introduction; Samuel Waldo.

4983 McVICAR, C. WARNER, ed. Waldoboro's history: brief history of a beautiful Downeast town on Maine's midcoast. Waldoboro: Waldoboro Historical Society, 1971. Pp. 16. Me.

4984 MILLER, FRANK BURTON. The Miller family: an address delivered before the Miller Family Re-union Association of North Waldoboro, Maine, September 7, 1904. Rockland: Caslon Pr. Print, 1909. Pp. 47.

4985 _____. "The Waldoboro Millers." MHGR, 8 (1895), 238-241.
Miller family.

4986 MILLER, SAMUEL LLEWELLYN. History of the town of Waldoboro, Maine. Wiscasset: Emerson, 1910. Pp. 281.

4987 "A MORAVIAN colony in Maine." MeHSC, 2 Ser., 2 (1891), 333.

4988 PAYNE, FREDERICK G. 200th anniversary, Old German Church and meetinghouse. Waldoboro: Ladies Auxiliary and the Trustees of the German Protestant Society, [1972?]. Unpaged. Me.

4989 PITCHER, FRED A. Sketch of Waldoboro, Maine. [Boston?]: Waldoboro Club of Boston, n.d. Pp. 35. MBNEH.

4990 POHLMAN, HENRY N. The German colony and Lutheran Church in Maine: an address delivered before the Historical Society of the Lutheran Church, at its meeting in Washington, D.C., May 14th, 1869.... Gettysburg, Pa.: J. E. Wible, 1869. Pp. 24.

4991 "THE REED Mansion in Waldoboro as a source of history." Sun Up, 9 (July, 1931), 5.

4992 ROGGENBAUER, JOSEF. "Über die schweren Anfänge einer deutschen Siedlung in Neu-England aus der Mitte des 18. Jahrhunderts." Institut für Auslandsbeziehungen. Stuttgart. Zeitschrift für Kulturaustausch, 19 (1969), 297-302.
  Title in English: Difficult beginnings of a mid-eighteenth-century German settlement in New England; a copy is in the Special Collections Department, University of Maine at Orono.

4993 STAHL, JASPER JACOB. "Diary of a Moravian missionary at Broad Bay, Maine, in 1760." NEQ, 12 (1939), 747-759.
  George Soelle.

4994 _____. History of old Broad Bay and Waldoboro. Portland: Bond Wheelwright, 1956. 2v.

4995 THOMPSON, GARRETT W. "The Germans in Maine." SJMH, 5 (1917-1918), 3-7, 140-146.
  "To be continued," but no more appeared.

4996 WALDOBORO, ME. The centennial celebration of the incorporation of Waldoboro', Maine, July 4, 1873. Bangor: B. A. Burr, 1873. Pp. 52.

4997 WALDOBORO folks. [Boston]: Waldoboro-Boston Club, 1917. Pp. 35. MeHi.

4998 WALDOBORO HIGH SCHOOL. Waldoboro. [Waldoboro, 1934]. Pp. 42. Me.

4999 WILLIAMSON, WILLIAM DURKEE. "Lutherans." American Quarterly Register, 13 (1840-1841), 162-169.
  German settlers at Waldoboro.

  SEE ALSO entries 1216, 1282, 1706, 4589, and 5003.

WALES (ANDROSCOGGIN CO.)

5000 SEE entry 3769.

WALLAGRASS PLANTATION (AROOSTOOK CO.)

5001 No items located.

WALTHAM (HANCOCK CO.)

5002 SOME history of the town of Waltham and the Jordan family. n.p., [1966]. v.p. Me.

WARREN (KNOX CO.)

5003 EATON, CYRUS. Annals of the town of Warren, in Knox County, Maine, with the early history of St. George's, Broad Bay, and the neighboring settlements on the Waldo Patent. (1851) Emily Eaton, ed. 2d ed. Hallowell: Masters & Livermore, 1877. Pp. xvi, 680.
  For index, see entry 5010.

5004 FROM Warren to the sea, 1827-1852: letters of the Counce and McCallum families. Bertha K. Drewett and Arthur Spear, eds. Middletown, N.Y.: Whitlock Pr., 1970. Pp. xix, 203.

5005 GOULD, EDWARD KALLOCH. Historical address; delivered August 30, 1936 at bi-centennial of the town of Warren, Maine. [Rockland, 1936]. Pp. 19.

5006 MOODY, LINWOOD W. "Warren Depot." Down East, 16 (October, 1969), 50-51, 53-55.
  History of the village of Warren Depot.

5007 PORTER, LILLIAN RUSSELL. Bicentennial pageant, Warren, Maine, 1736-1936. n.p., 1972. Pp. 18. MeU.

5008 REIMS, GORDON A. "Waterway in the wilderness." NEG, 17 (Fall, 1975), 32-38.
  Georges River Canal.

5009 WARREN, ME. Warren history.... Union: Union Publishing, 1888. Pp. 44. MBNEH.

5010 WARREN HISTORICAL SOCIETY. Index [to] Annals of Warren, 1605-1876. n.p., [1970?]. Pp. 47. Me.
  See entry 5003.

  SEE ALSO entries 1659, 1666, and 4589.

WASHBURN (AROOSTOOK CO.)

5011 WASHBURN, ME. Washburn, one hundred years of progress. n.p., [1961]. Pp. 39. Me.

WASHINGTON (KNOX CO.)

5012 WALWORTH, ARTHUR CLARENCE. The Medomak way: the story of the first fifty years of an American summer camp for boys. Lancaster, N.H.: Bisbee Pr., 1953. Pp. 116.

5013 WASHINGTON, ME. HISTORICAL COMMITTEE. Sesquicentennial celebration, Washington, Maine, 1811-1961. n.p., [1961]. Unpaged. Me.

WASHINGTON TOWNSHIP (FRANKLIN CO.)

5014   No items located.

WATERBORO (YORK CO.)

5015   HAMILTON, SAMUEL KING. The Hamiltons of Waterborough (York County, Maine), their ancestors and descendants ... 912-1912. Boston: Murray and Emery, 1912. Pp. xiii, 407.
   Contains an account of the Massabesick Plantation and the town of Waterboro.

5016   KNIGHTS, ERNEST G. "The accursed brook." Yankee, 20 (March, 1956), 48-50.
   Thomas Hanson's smelt brook.

5017   _____. Waterboro, York County, Maine, 1768-1955. n.p., 1955. Unpaged. Me.

5018   SMITH, MRS. H. A. "God of all creation faithfully worshipped: Church of St. Stephen the Martyr, Waterboro Center." The Northeast, 79 (July, 1952), 4.

WATERFORD (OXFORD CO.)

5019   DOUGLASS, JOHN ABBOT. A discourse delivered before the Congregational Church and Society of Waterford, Me., Nov. 7th, 1871, at the semi-centennial anniversary of the settlement of the pastor. Bridgton: News Pr., [1871]. Pp. 15.

5020   FREEMASONS. WATERFORD, ME. MT. TIRE'M LODGE, NO. 132. Mt. Tire'm Lodge, No. 132, Free and Accepted Masons, Waterford, Me. Norway: Oxford County Advertiser, 1893. Pp. 32. MeHi.

5021   GAGE, THOMAS HOVEY, ed. Notes on the history of Waterford, Maine. Worcester, Mass., 1913. Pp. 87.

5022   RIPLEY, LINCOLN. "A description and history of Waterford, in the county of York." MHSC, 9 (1804), 137-147.

5023   WATERFORD, ME. The history of Waterford, Oxford County, Maine, comprising historical address, by Henry P. Warren; record of families, by Rev. William Warren, D.D.; centennial proceedings, by Samuel Warren. Portland: Hoyt, Fogg & Donham, 1879. Pp. vi, 371.

WATERVILLE (KENNEBEC CO.)

5024   BANGS, ISAAC SPARROW. Military history of Waterville, Maine, including the names and record, so far as known, of all soldiers from Waterville, in the several wars of the republic; a portion of the records of the Waterville Monument Association, and a sketch of W. S. Heath Post, No. 14, G. A. R. Augusta: Kennebec Journal Print, 1902. Pp. 75.

5025   "BASEBALL at Colby." Colby Alumnus, 1 (1911-1912), 124-125.

5026   BIXLER, JULIUS SEELYE. Colby College (1813-1953): a venture of faith. N.Y.: Newcomen Society in North America, 1953. Pp. 32.

5027   _____. "To grasp the budding growth--nettle and all." Colby Alumnus, 63 (Fall, 1973), 17-32, (Winter, 1974), 13-28.
   Colby College, 1942-1959.

5028   BUISSON, EMMA. Lettres de Mère Marie du Sacré-Coeur, fondatrice des Ursulines de Waterville, Maine, Etats Unis; précédées d'une notice biographique par U. T. R. Québec: L'Action sociale limitée, 1917. Pp. 238.

5029   BURRAGE, HENRY SWEETSER. "The beginnings of Waterville College, now Colby University." MeHSC, 2 Ser., 4 (1893), 124-145.

5030   CHAMPLIN, JAMES TIFT. A historical discourse delivered at the fiftieth anniversary of Colby University, August 2d, 1870. Waterville, 1870. Pp. 30.

5031   CHAPMAN, ALFRED KING. "Contrasts in curriculum." Colby Alumnus, 51 (Fall, 1961), 7-9.
   Colby College.

5032   CHIPMAN, CHARLES PHILLIPS. The formative period in Colby's history. Waterville, 1912. Pp. 29.

5033   "COBURN Classical Institute." BTJ, 19 (1906-1907), 313-317.

5034   "COBURN Classical Institute, Waterville, Maine." BTJ, 23 (1910-1911), 629, 631.

5035   COLBY COLLEGE, WATERVILLE, ME. General catalogue of officers, graduates and former students of Colby College. Charles P. Chipman, ed. Centennial ed., 1820-1920. Waterville, 1920. Pp. 470.

5036   _____. The history of Colby College. By Ernest Cummings Marriner. Waterville, 1963. Pp. 659.

5037   _____. Twelve years of transition, 1942-1954; report of the president of Colby College. Waterville, 1954. Pp. 16. MeP.
   The president was Julius S. Bixler.

5038   "THE COLBY College Press: an anniversary report." ColbLibQ, 4 (1955-1958), 6-16.

5039   "COLBY in the old days." Colby Alumnus, 1 (1911-1912), 112-116.

5040 "COLBY'S first football team." Colby Alumnus, 26 (October, 1936), 2.

5041 CUMMINGS, OSMOND RICHARD. "Waterville, Fairfield and Oakland Railway Company." Transportation Bulletin, No. 72 (April-December, 1965), 1-40.

5042 CUSTOM and practice in medical care: a comparative study of two hospitals in Arbroath, Scotland, U.K., and Waterville, Maine, U.S.A. by J. Simpson et al. N.Y.: Oxford Univ. Pr., 1968. Pp. 119.
Thayer Hospital.

5043 DUNN, REUBEN WESLEY. "The early days of baseball." Colby Alumnus, 15 (1925-1926), 49-50.
Colby College.

5044 DYER, RICHARD NYE. "Colby on Mayflower Hill." Down East, 4 (May, 1958), 20-23.

5045 ELKS, BENEVOLENT AND PROTECTIVE ORDER OF, WATERVILLE, ME., WATERVILLE LODGE, NO. 905. Waterville Lodge 905, fiftieth anniversary, 1904-1954, souvenir program. n.p., [1954]. Unpaged. MeHi.
Includes a history of the lodge by Ernest C. Simpson.

5046 "FOOTBALL at Colby." Colby Alumnus, 2 (1912-1913), 36-38.

5047 FOSS, H. WARREN. "Colby in the 90's." Colby Alumnus, 39 (February, 1950), 10, 12, 24.

5048 ____. "The gay nineties--the golden age." Colby Alumnus, 33 (April, 1944), 5-6.
Colby College.

5049 FRYE, ROBIE G. "A diary in 1878." Colby Alumnus, 22 (1932-1933), 188-190.
Colby College.

5050 GIVEEN, CLEMENT MARTIN, ed. A chronology of municipal history and election statistics, Waterville, Maine, 1771-1908. Augusta: Maine Farmer Pr., 1908. Pp. 278.

5051 ____. "Waterville as a railroad center." BTJ, 23 (1910-1911), 588-589, 591, 603.

5052 "A GREAT manufacturing institution." BTJ, 26 (1913-1914), 786-788.
Lockwood Company, textiles.

5053 HALL, JON F., ed. Old Waterville: a picture book. Waterville: Waterville Historical Society, [1976?]. Unpaged. MeU.

5054 HALL, OLIVER A. "Some early Colby ball players." Colby Alumnus, 32 (May, 1943), 9-10, (July, 1943), 10-13.
Baseball.

5055 HARTHORN, DREW THOMPSON. "Coburn Classical Institute." Colby Alumnus, 15 (1925-1926), 116-120.

5056 HATCH, BENTON LE ROY. A preliminary check list of Waterville, Maine, imprints through 1850. Waterville: Colby College Library, 1952. Pp. 23.

5057 HAYNES, GEORGE HENRY. Souvenir of Waterville, the university city of Maine. N.Y.: Kellogg, 1898. Pp. 32.

5058 HERRICK, MARY DARRAH and NIXON ORWIN RUSH. "Early literary societies and their libraries in Colby College, 1824-1878." College and Research Libraries, 6 (1944), 58-63.

5059 HERRICK, MARY DARRAH. "Forerunners of Colby fraternities." Colby Alumnus, 31 (March, 1942), 6-8.
Literary societies.

5060 ____. "Two Colby clubs of the 80s." Colby Alumnus, 34 (May, 1947), 9.
Munchausen Club and the Anti-Lingo League.

5061 HILL, J. F. "Brief account of the Waterville Clinical Society." JMS, 1 (1894-1895), 52.

5062 "HISTORY of Waterville Lodge, No. 33, of Maine." New England Freemason, 1 (1874), 393-401.

5063 JOHNSON, FRANKLIN WINSLOW. Exercises in celebration of the seventy-fifth anniversary of the opening of the Coburn Classical Institute, Waterville, Maine, June 19-25, 1904. Portland, 1904. Pp. 73.

5064 JORDAN, ARCHER. "Football in the nineties." Colby Alumnus, 2 (1912-1913), 38-40.
Colby College.

5065 KING, GEORGE MELLEN PRENTISS. "Memories of Waterville College, 1853-1857." Colby Alumnus, 3 (1913-1914), 29-32.

5066 KNIGHT, JOHN T. "Maine's newest parish: the history of Saint Mark's Church, Waterville." The Northeast, 75 (September, 1948), 12-17.

5067 KNOWLTON, WILLIAM SMITH. "Some reminiscences." Colby Alumnus, 15 (1925-1926), 152-153.
Colby College.

5068 LIBBY, HERBERT CARLYLE. "An historical address." Colby Alumnus, 21 (1931-1932), 61-75.
Colby College.

5069 ____. "The public schools of Waterville, Maine." BTJ, 23 (1910-1911), 599, 601, 603.

5070 "LOOKING backward fifty years." Colby Alumnus, 37 (May, 1948), 10-11.
Colby College in 1898.

5071 "THE MAN in the Hathaway shirt." Pine Cone, 8 (Winter, 1952-1953), 3-7.
C. F. Hathaway Shirt Company.

5072 MARRINER, ERNEST CUMMINGS. "A century of achievement." Colby Alumnus, 37 (July, 1948), 8-12.
Colby Alumni Association.

5073 _____. "Money is not all." Colby Alumnus, 50 (Spring, 1961), 7-9.
Colby Alumni Association.

5074 _____. "Room and board in shillings." Colby Alumnus, 60 (Winter, 1971), 20-21.
Colby in the 1830s.

5075 _____. "Some pointers from Colby's past." Colby Alumnus, 52 (Spring, 1963), 2-6.

5076 _____. "The tradition of scholarship at Colby." Colby Alumnus, 48 (Summer, 1959), 20-24.

5077 MOORE, KATRINA. "Waterville, Kennebec Valley town." Down East, 6 (October, 1959), 22-26, 42-43.

5078 OWEN, FRED K. "Colby fifty years ago." Colby Alumnus, 26 (March, 1937), 13-14.

5079 PAINE, ALBERT WARE. "Recollections of the early days." Colby Alumnus, 35 (April, 1946), 8-9.
Colby College as recalled in 1902 by an alumnus of 1832.

5080 _____. "One hundred years ago." Colby Alumnus, 22 (1932-1933), 18-20.
Colby College, 1826-1832; written in 1895.

5081 PHI BETA KAPPA. MAINE BETA, COLBY COLLEGE. Handbook of the Beta Chapter of Maine, Colby College. J. William Black, comp. Waterville, 1901. Pp. 39. Me.

5082 PHILBRICK, MINNIE LAMBERT SMITH. Centennial history of the First Baptist Church of Waterville, Maine. Waterville: Frank B. Philbrick, 1925. Pp. 129.
1818-1918.

5083 POTTLE, FREDERICK A. "Colby's second half-century." Colby Alumnus, 34 (March, 1945), 7-9, (April, 1945), 7-10.

5084 PREBLE, FRED MYRON. The educational abbey of Maine Baptists. Waterville, [1904?]. Pp. 32.
Colby College.

5085 RAMSDELL, T. J. "Colby in the 80's." Colby Alumnus, 39 (April, 1950), 4, 15.

5086 REDINGTON, FRANK. "Waterville, the city of progress." BTJ, 23 (1910-1911), 571-573, 575, 577, 579, 581, 583-584.

5087 REID, DICK. "Fifty years of Colby football." Colby Alumnus, 32 (November, 1942), 11-14.

5088 RUSH, NIXON ORWIN. "Historical sketch of the Colby library." Colby Alumnus, 28 (November-December, 1938), 3-4.

5089 _____. "Maine's first circulating library." MeLAB, 3 (August, 1942), 13-14.
Waterville Circulating Library, 1826.

5090 ["SIGNIFICANT moments in Colby history."] Colby Alumnus, 64 (Spring, 1975), entire issue.

5091 SKINNER, JOSEPH O. History of Waterville Lodge, No. 33, of Free and Accepted Masons, of Waterville, Me., from its foundation to 1874. Portland: Stephen Berry, 1874. Pp. 104. MeBa.

5092 SMALL, ALBION WOODBURY. "Colby University." NEM, 6 (1887-1888), 309-320.

5093 SMITH, JOSEPH COBURN. "The good old days and now." Colby Alumnus, 20 (1930-1931), 226-230.
Colby College, 1920-1930.

5094 _____. "150 honorable years." Colby Alumnus, 50 (Spring, 1961), 11-12.
Colby College.

5095 SMITH, WILLIAM A. "The Congregational Church of Waterville." MeCP, 30 (May, 1943), 6-8.

5096 SOULE, BERTHA LOUISE. "Colby in the eighties." Colby Alumnus, 43 (April, 1954), 6-10.

5097 "A TWENTIETH birthday for the 'Colby Library Quarterly.'" Colby Alumnus, 53 (Fall, 1963), 11-12.

5098 LES URSULINES à Waterville, précis historique, 1888-1913. Waterville: Elm City Publishing, [1913]. Pp. 23. MBC.

5099 WATERVILLE, ME. Waterville centennial, 1802-1902, June 22-23-24, the official programme. Waterville: W. M. Ladd, [1902]. Pp. 36. MeHi.

5100 WATERVILLE, ME. FIRST BAPTIST CHURCH. Centenary, 1818-1918, First Baptist Church, Waterville, Maine. n.p., [1918]. Pp. 15. MeHi.
Includes brief historical sketch by Minnie Lambert Smith Philbrick.

5101 _____. A history of the First Baptist Church, Waterville, Maine, articles of faith, church government, and list of present members. Portland: B. Thurston, 1872. Pp. 32. MeHi.

5102 "WATERVILLE claims one of the oldest banks in Maine." Sun Up, 4 (September, 1927), 36.
   Ticonic National Bank.

5103 "WATERVILLE, Maine." BTJ, 3 (1890-1891), 329-335.

5104 WATERVILLE PUBLIC LIBRARY. The fiftieth anniversary, 1896-1946: historical facts covering the half century.... [Waterville?, 1946]. Pp. 21. Me.

5105 _____. Waterville Public Library, souvenir program of the fiftieth anniversary of the dedication of the library building, 1905-1955. n.p., [1955?]. Unpaged. MeU.
   Includes brief history.

5106 "WATERVILLE Public Library, 1896-1946." MeLAB, 8 (February, 1947), 5-6.

5107 "THE WATERVILLE Street Railway group." Railroad Magazine, 47 (November, 1948), 82-87.

5108 "WATERVILLE, the heart of Maine." Sun Up, 3 (March, 1927), 19-20, 22, 26.

5109 "WATERVILLE'S modern public library." BTJ, 26 (1913-1914), 783.
   Includes history.

5110 WEBER, CARL J. "Lowell's visit to Waterville." Colby Alumnus, 25 (May, 1936), 10.
   1853.

5111 WHITE, CLARENCE H. Historical address delivered by Dr. Clarence H. White, on the occasion of the centennial celebration of the First Congregational Church, Waterville, Maine, October 21, 1928. n.p., [1928?]. Pp. 20. Me.

5112 _____. "Linking the old and new Colby." Colby Alumnus, 31 (October, 1941), 5-6.
   Colby College architecture.

5113 WHITTEMORE, EDWIN CAREY, ed. The centennial history of Waterville, Kennebec County, Maine including the oration, the historical address and the poem presented at the celebration of the centennial anniversary of the incorporation of the town, June 23d, 1902. Waterville: Executive Committee of the Centennial Celebration, 1902. Pp. vii, 592.

5114 _____. "The churches of Waterville." BTJ, 23 (1910-1911), 621-622.

5115 _____. Colby College, 1820-1925: an account of its beginnings, progress and service. Waterville: The Trustees of Colby College, 1927. Pp. x, 276.

5116 _____. "The development of Colby College." Sun Up, 8 (November, 1930), 12-15.

5117 _____. "A new chapter in Colby history." Sun Up, 8 (December, 1930), 3, 31.

   SEE ALSO entries 1421, 1639, and 3532.

WAYNE (KENNEBEC CO.)

5118 BRYANT, JUDSON B. A historical sketch of the Baptist Church of Wayne, Maine, read at the centennial exercises of the church, August 10, 1894. Portland: Brown Thurston, 1894. Pp. 17. MeHi.

5119 JOHNSON, JENNIE THORNE. "Picturesque 'Pocasset.'" Pine Tree Magazine, 7 (1907), 437-442.

5120 PERKINS, JACK. Illustrated history of Wayne, Maine; being a contemporary and past history of a small New England town. Wayne, 1968. Pp. 242.

5121 WALTON, GEORGE W., ed. History of the town of Wayne, Kennebec County, Maine, from its settlement to 1898. Augusta: Maine Farmer Publishing, 1898. Pp. iv, 354.

5122 WAYNE, ME. Centennial celebration of the town of Wayne, Kennebec County, Maine, August 18, 1898. Augusta: Maine Farmer Job Print, 1899. Pp. 38. Me.

WEBBERTOWN TOWNSHIP (AROOSTOOK CO.)

5123 No items located.

WEBSTER PLANTATION (PENOBSCOT CO.)

5124 No items located.

WELD (FRANKLIN CO.)

5125 CURRIER, GEORGE F. "One hundred fiftieth anniversary at Weld." MeCP, 46 (September 15, 1959), 9.
   First Congregational Church.

5126 FOSTER, E. J. "Early settlers of Weld." MHGR, 1 (1884), 119-123, 172-179; 2 (1885), 38-44, 94-99, 181-186, 240-243.

5127 ODLIN, JOHN W. Weld, Maine. Milford, N.H.: Cabinet Pr., [1940?]. Unpaged. MeHi.

5128 WELD, ME. Weld sesquicentennial, 1816-1966, history and program. n.p., [1966]. Pp. 24. Me.

WELLINGTON (PISCATAQUIS CO.)

5129 No items located.

WELLS (YORK CO.)

5130 CUSHING, JAMES ROYAL. Historical discourse; delivered Oct. 29, 1851, at the one hundred and fiftieth anniversary of the organization of the First Congregational Church, (the second in the state), in Wells, Maine. Portland, 1851. Pp. 22.

5131 DEAN, JOHN. A narrative of the shipwreck of the Nottingham Galley, in her voyage from England to Boston; with an account of the miraculous escape of the captain and his crew, on a rock called Boone-Island, the hardships they endured there, and their happy deliverance. Mason Philip Smith, ed. Portland: Provincial Pr., 1968. Pp. 23.

5132 "THE FIRST Congregational Church of Wells." Congregationalism in Maine, 13 (1926), 29-30.

5133 FRYER, ROBERT. "Lessons at Ogunquit." National Theatre Conference Bulletin, 9 (October, 1947), 10-19.
    Ogunquit Playhouse.

5134 HUBBARD, JEREMIAH and JONATHAN GREENLEAF. "An account of Wells." MeHSC, 1 (1831), 255-268.

5135 PERKINS, ESSELYN GILMAN. History of Ogunquit Village, with many interesting facts of more recent interest. Portland: Falmouth Publishing, 1951. Pp. 66.

5136 _____. A new history of Ogunquit, Maine. n.p., 1974. Pp. vi, 64. Me.

5137 _____. Wells: the frontier town of Maine. Ogunquit, 1970-1971. 2v.

5138 STEELE, WILLIAM. "Ogunquit Playhouse." Down East, 20 (July, 1974), 82-85.

5139 WELLS, ME. Programme of the celebration of the 250th anniversary of the town of Wells, Maine, August 26th, 1903. Kennebunk: Eastern Star Print, 1903. Pp. 11. Me.
    Includes historical sketch by William M. Tripp.

5140 WELLS, ME. 300TH ANNIVERSARY COMMITTEE. 300th anniversary, Wells, Maine, 1653-1953. n.p., [1953]. Pp. 60. Me.

    SEE ALSO entries 1322, 1884, and 5320.

WESLEY (WASHINGTON CO.)

5141 No items located.

WEST BATH (SAGADAHOC CO.)

5142 "REMINISCENCES of a former resident of New Meadows." PejHSC, 1 Pt. 1 (1889), 46-53.

WEST FORKS PLANTATION (SOMERSET CO.)

5143 No items located.

WEST GARDINER (KENNEBEC CO.)

5144 LYFORD, ELMORE B. "The only house of its kind?" Yankee, 33 (May, 1969), 40-43.
    An octagon house.

5145 MARTIN, BUD. West Gardiner's hundred years. Augusta: Kennebec Journal, 1950. Pp. 73. Me.

    SEE ALSO entries 1633 and 1649.

WEST MIDDLESEX CANAL GRANT (SOMERSET CO.)

5146 No items located.

WEST PARIS (OXFORD CO.)

5147 HAMMOND, GEORGE WARREN, et al. History of Granite Lodge, No. 182, Free and Accepted Masons, West Paris, Me., from its organization, September 16, 1878 to 1895. Portland: Stephen Berry, 1895. Pp. 24. MeBa.

5148 "HISTORY in West Paris." Sun Up, 9 (March, 1931), 24.

5149 MORTON, AGNES L. "West Paris, Maine." Sun Up, 3 (March, 1927), 14-16.

WESTBROOK (CUMBERLAND CO.)

5150 BURROUGHS, ADELINE R. "Westbrook, the paper city." Sun Up, 5 (December, 1927), 10-11.

5151 CHAPMAN, LEONARD BOND. "The first occupancy by Europeans of Saccarappa Falls on the Presumpscot River, now Westbrook." MeHSC, 2 Ser., 10 (1899), 282-300.

5152 "THE CITY of Westbrook." BTJ, 13 (1900-
1901), 73-88.

5153 COBB, OLIVER A. "A city of flourishing
lodges." BTJ, 19 (1906-1907), 710-711.

5154 CUMBERLAND MILLS, ME. WARREN CONGREGATIONAL
CHURCH. Manual of Warren Church of Cumber-
land Mills, Maine. Cumberland Mills: Henry
S. Cobb, 1911. Pp. 91. MeHi.
Includes history.

5155 [DESJARDINS, PHILIPPE E.]. Jubilee, a chronicle, 1899-1949. Lewiston: Echo Publishing,
[1950]. Pp. 52. MBC.
St. Hyacinth Parish; in English and French.

5156 ILSLEY, GEORGE BOARDMAN. "Westbrook, a city
of churches." BTJ, 19 (1906-1907), 700-704.

5157 LEWIS, JOHN R. An early history of Pride's
Corner Congregational Church, 1968. Pp. 69.
Me.

5158 MILLIONS, JEAN. Warren Congregational Church,
1869-1969. n.p., [1969]. Pp. 65. MeHi.

5159 ODD FELLOWS. INDEPENDENT ORDER OF. WESTBROOK,
ME., SACCARAPPA LODGE, NO. 11. 100th anni-
versary, Saccarappa Lodge, No. 11, I.O.O.F.,
Westbrook, Maine, May 22, 1944. [Westbrook]:
H. S. Cobb, [1944]. Pp. 36. MeHi.

5160 RAND, LEROY H. "History of Westbrook."
Westbrook Board of Trade Enterprise, 1 (June,
1911), 34, 36, (September, 1911), 34, 36,
(January, 1912), 24, 26, 28, 30, 32.

5161 RAY, ISABEL T. Historical pageant of Westbrook, 1820-1920. Westbrook: H. S. Cobb,
[1920]. Pp. 19. MeHi.

5162 _____. History of Westbrook Congregational
Church, 1832-1932. One hundred years of ser-
vice. [Westbrook]: H. S. Cobb, 1932.
Pp. 22. MeHi.

5163 ROWE, ERNEST RAY, comp. Highlights of Westbrook history. Marian B. Rowe, ed. [West-
brook]: Westbrook Woman's Club, 1952.
Pp. 237.

5164 STONE, KENNETH G. "The Dana Mills--a Bowdoin
institution." BA, 16 (1941-1942), 19-21.
Cotton; many Bowdoin Alumni have been associated with the firm.

5165 "THREE quarters of a century." MeCP, 31 (November, 1944), 6, 41.
Warren Congregational Church.

5166 WARREN, S. D. CO. A history of the S. D. War-
ren Company, 1854-1954. Westbrook, 1954.
Pp. vi, 120. MH-BA.
Paper.

5167 WESTBROOK, ME. Official program of the commemorative exercises of the one hundredth anniversary of the town of Stroudwater, name
changed to Westbrook, June 9th, 1814....
Westbrook: H. S. Cobb, 1914. Pp. 40. MeHi.
Includes history by Leroy H. Rand.

5168 WESTBROOK, ME. CHAMBER OF COMMERCE. Who's
who in Westbrook, Maine in 1964. Westbrook:
Wiggin Pr., 1964. 25 leaves. Me.

5169 "WESTBROOK." BTJ, 4 (1891-1892), 104-110.

5170 WESTBROOK, Maine. Westbrook: Rich Bros.,
[1923?]. Unpaged. MeHi.
Includes history by Isabel T. Ray.

5171 WESTBROOK CONGREGATIONAL CHURCH. Jubilee
year, 125th anniversary of the Westbrook Con-
gregational Church, January 17-18-20, 1957.
[Westbrook]: Wiggin Pr., [1957?]. Pp. 20.
MBC.
Includes a chronology of the church.

SEE ALSO entries 1483, 1492, and 1512.

WESTFIELD (AROOSTOOK CO.)

5172 No items located.

WESTMANLAND PLANTATION (AROOSTOOK CO.)

5173 SEE entry 1456.

WESTON (AROOSTOOK CO.)

5174 No items located.

WESTPORT (LINCOLN CO.)

5175 No items located.

WHITEFIELD (LINCOLN CO.)

5176 KEALY, JOHN E. "An ancient country rectory."
America, 42 (1930), 520-521.
Roman Catholic rectory erected in the nine-
teenth century.

5177 WHITEFIELD

5177 WATERS, HENRY C. A history of the town of Whitefield, Maine. Elizabeth Hardwick, ed. n.p., 1959. 10 leaves. Me.

5178 WHITEFIELD, ME. Sesquicentennial celebration, 1809-1959, Whitefield, Maine. n.p., 1959. Unpaged. Me.

WHITING (WASHINGTON CO.)

5179 FORSLUND, GLADYS HALL. History of Whiting, Maine. Calais: Advertiser Publishing, 1975. Pp. 94. Me.

WHITNEYVILLE (WASHINGTON CO.)

5180 SEE entry 1863.

WILLIAMSBURG TOWNSHIP (PISCATAQUIS CO.)

5181 No items located.

WILLIMANTIC (PISCATAQUIS CO.)

5182 PACKARD, MARLBOROUGH. A history of Packard's Camps, 1894-1916. D'Arcy Van Bokkelen and Elizabeth R. Cawley, eds. n.p., 1974. Pp. 30. MeU.

WILTON (FRANKLIN CO.)

5183 ADAMO, RUTH. A history of the town of Wilton. Rumford: Rumford Publishing, 1971. Pp. 60.

5184 BASS, STREETER. G. H. Bass Company, 1876-1976. n.p., 1976. Unpaged. MeU.
Shoes.

5185 BEAN, DEARBORN GORHAM. The history of Wilton Lodge, No. 156, of Free and Accepted Masons, Wilton, Maine, from its organization to September 15th, 1880. Farmington: Knowlton & McLeary, 1880. Pp. 14. [MePGLM].

5186 GIFFORD, ROY. "Wilton, Maine." Sun Up, 3 (June, 1926), 51-52, 54.

5187 [HEBERT, RICHARD A.] "The making of Maine: G. H. Bass & Co." Pine Cone, 1 (Autumn, 1945), 30-34.
Shoes.

5188 NOTTAGE, W. A. The history of Wilton Lodge, No. 156, of Free and Accepted Masons, Wilton, Maine, from September, 1880, to September, 1890. Farmington: Knowlton, McLeary, 1890. Pp. 13. [MePGLM].

5189 "SETTLEMENT of Wilton, Maine." Maine Genealogist and Biographer, 3 (1877-1878), 107-109.

5190 WILTON, ME. FIRST CONGREGATIONAL CHURCH. Manual of the First Congregational Church in Wilton, Maine. Wilton: J. W. Nelson, 1912. Pp. 28. MeHi.
Historical sketch by Mary E. Eaton.

5191 _____. Manual of the First Congregational Church in Wilton, Maine, containing a brief historical sketch.... Wilton: R. A. Carver, 1888. Pp. 20.
A copy is held by the church.

SEE ALSO entry 1419.

WINDHAM (CUMBERLAND CO.)

5192 BODGE, GEORGE MADISON. "New Marblehead, now Windham, Maine: grant, survey and settlement of the township." MHGR, 4 (1887), 35-47, 98-104, 197-203, 248-256; 5 (1888), 44-52, 90-105, 178-183, 225-233; 6 (1889), 270-275; 7 (1893), 108-115, 156-165, 210-218; 8 (1895), 8-18, 108-114, 168-174; 9 (1898), 22-29, 53-61, 103-108, 138-143, 167-173, 214-221, 333-340.

5193 DOLE, FREDERICK HOWARD. Sketches of the history of Windham, Maine, 1734-1935: the story of a typical New England town. Westbrook: H. S. Cobb, 1935. Pp. 155.

5194 DOLE, PHOEBE. An historical poem about Windham, Maine. [Windham]: Windham Historical Society, 1970. Unpaged. MeHi.

5195 DOLE, SAMUEL THOMAS. "Ancient Naguamqueeg." MeHSC, 2 Ser., 7 (1896), 405-412.

5196 _____. "Early schools in New Marblehead, now Windham." MeHSC, 2 Ser., 9 (1898), 391-403.

5197 _____. Historical address delivered at the one hundred and fiftieth anniversary of the Congregational Church at Windham Hill, December 14, 1893. Portland: Libby & Smith, [1894?]. Pp. 10.

5198 _____. "The meeting-house war in New Marblehead." MeHSC, 2 Ser., 10 (1899), 175-185.
Controversy as to the location of the meeting-house.

5199 _____. "An old time burial ground." MeHSC, 3 Ser., 2 (1906), 245-260.

5200 _____. Windham in the past. Frederick Howard Dole, ed. Auburn: Merrill & Webber, 1916. Pp. 611.

5201 DUMONT, EMMA L. Heritage "76" soldiers of the American Revolution, Windham, Maine. Windham: Windham Historical Society, 1975. Pp. 114. MeHi.

5202 ELDER, ISAAC L. and CHARLES JONES. History of Presumpscot Lodge, No. 127 of F. and A. M., at North Windham, Maine from 1864 to 1880. Portland: Dresser, McLellan, 1882. Pp. 32. MeHi.

5203 GOOLD, NATHAN. "Stephen Manchester, the slayer of the Indian chief Polin, at New Marblehead, now Windham, Maine, in 1756, and a soldier of the Revolution, with his ancestry." MeHSC, 2 Ser., 8 (1897), 313-330.

5204 _____. Windham, Maine, in the war of the Revolution, 1775-1783. Portland: H. W. Bryant, 1900. Pp. 16.

5205 GOOLD, WILLIAM. "Thomas Chute, the first settler of Windham, Maine, and his descendants." MeHSC, 2 Ser., 7 (1896), 412-423.

5206 SMITH, THOMAS LAURENS. A historical address, delivered on the Fourth of July, 1839, at the centennial anniversary, of the settlement of Windham. Portland: Arthur Shirley, 1840. Pp. 32.

5207 _____. History of the town of Windham. Portland: Hoyt & Fogg, 1873. Pp. 104.

5208 SPILLER, NELLIE D. "The Parson Smith homestead, South Windham, Maine." OTNE, 48 (1957-1958), 48-56.
   Peter Thatcher Smith.

5209 WINDHAM, ME. BICENTENNIAL BOOKLET COMMITTEE. Windham 1976. [Windham, 1976]. Pp. 107. MeHi.

5210 WINDHAM, ME. BICENTENNIAL COMMITTEE. Report of the Windham Bicentennial Committee, July 30, 1938 together with a copy of the historical address by Frederick H. Dole. Auburn: Merrill & Webber, [1938]. Pp. 37. Me.

5211 "WINDHAM, Maine." American Pioneer, 2 (1843), 42-45.

SEE ALSO entries 1493-1494.

WINDSOR (KENNEBEC CO.)

5212 MILLETT, MARGARET, SHIRLEY DEWAR, and DAVID SWEARINGEN, comps. History of Windsor, Maine, 1822-1972. n.p., [1972]. Pp. 50. Me.

WINN (PENOBSCOT CO.)

5213 COOPER, ARTHUR M. "The 75th anniversary of St. Thomas, Winn, and the rural Church in America." The Northeast, 71 (October, 1944), 5-7.

5214 REILLY, M. W. "Parish of the Sacred Heart, Winn, Maine." MeCathHM, 2 (March, 1914), 7-14.

5215 WINN, ME. ST. THOMAS' CHURCH. Centennial, St. Thomas' Church, Episcopal, Winn, Maine, 1868-1968. n.p., [1968]. Unpaged. MeHi.

SEE ALSO entry 50.

WINSLOW (KENNEBEC CO.)

5216 FISHER, CARLETON EDWARD. History of Fort Halifax. Winthrop: Courier-Gazette, 1972. Pp. 28.

5217 GOOLD, WILLIAM. "Fort Halifax: its projectors, builders and garrison." MeHSC, 8 (1881), 199-289.

5218 STEWART, ARTHUR W. "Fort Halifax, 1754." SJMH, 9 (1921), 132-134.

5219 WILSON, CHARLES B. "Indian relics and encampments in Maine." American Antiquarian and Oriental Journal, 5 (1883), 181-183.

5220 WINSLOW, ME. 200th anniversary, 1771-1971. n.p., [1971]. Pp. 76. Me.

5221 WIXSON, MRS. ELDWIN A., SR. "Fort Halifax in the State of Maine." DARMag, 92 (1958), 558, 561.

SEE ALSO entry 1639.

WINTER HARBOR (HANCOCK CO.)

5222 CLEAVES, SAMUEL W. "Historical sketch of Iron Bound Island, Frenchman's Bay." MeHist Mag, 8 (1893), 168-172.

5223 HAHN, NATHALIE WHITE. A history of Winter Harbor, Maine. n.p., 1974. Pp. 92. Me.

5224 HASKINS, STURGIS. "The Winter Harbor 21s." Down East, 23 (September, 1976), 48-51.
   Winter Harbor Yacht Club.

5225 RICH, LOUISE DICKINSON. "All this and fishing, too!" Outdoor Life, 128 (August, 1961), 44-46, 100-103.
   Schoodic Point.

5226 SMALLIDGE, ALLAN L. "Winter Harbor's one time elegance." Down East, 18 (September, 1971), 46-50, 103-104, 108, 112.

WINTERPORT (WALDO CO.)

5227 ATWOOD, CHARLES FRANCIS. History of Howard Lodge, No. 69, Free and Accepted Masons, Winterport, Maine, for the decade from 1879 to 1890. Bangor: Benjamin Burr, 1890. Pp. 11. [MePGLM].

5228 LITTLEFIELD, ADA DOUGLAS. An old river town; being a history of Winterport, (old Frankfort), Maine. N.Y.: Calkins, 1907. Pp. xiii, 249.

5229 MANTER, EZRA. History of Howard Lodge, No. 69, of Free and Accepted Masons, Winterport, Maine, from its organization, A.D. 1851, to January 1, 1870. Portland: Berry, 1874. Pp. 21.

5230 _____. History of Howard Lodge of Free and Accepted Masons, Winterport, Me., continued from the end of the year 1869, at which time the former history closed. Bangor: Samuel Smith & Son, 1881. Pp. 10. [MePGLM].

5231 MORGAN, SETH H. History of Howard Lodge, No. 69, Free and Accepted Masons, Winterport, Maine, for the decade from 1910 to 1920. Winterport: Lougee, [1920?]. Pp. 28. MeHi.

5232 REILLY, M. W. "St. Gabriel's Parish, Winterport." MeCathHM, 2 (June, 1914), 12-23.

5233 WILLIAMSON, JOSEPH. "Albert Livingston Kelly and Webster Kelly, of Winterport (Frankfort), Maine." BHistMag, 4 (1888-1889), 230-233.

5234 WINTERPORT, ME. 100th anniversary, town of Winterport ... July 3-July 9, 1960. William K. Dunham and Philip D. Sherwood, eds. Belfast: Eastern Illustrating and Publishing, [1960?]. Unpaged. MeU.

SEE ALSO entry 3091.

WINTERVILLE PLANTATION (AROOSTOOK CO.)

5235 No items located.

WINTHROP (KENNEBEC CO.)

5236 BRAGDON, CHARLES R. "Oilcloth pioneers in Maine." Interchemical Review, 5 (Winter, 1946-1947), 102-109.
       Wadsworth & Woodman.

5237 PARLIN, W. HARRISON. Reminiscences of East Winthrop. East Winthrop: Banner Publishing, 1891. Pp. 98. MBNEH.

5238 STACKPOLE, EVERETT SCHERMERHORN. History of Winthrop, Maine. Auburn: Merrill & Webber, 1925. Pp. 741.

5239 THURSTON, DAVID. A brief history of Winthrop, from 1764 to October 1855. Portland: Brown Thurston, 1855. Pp. xi, 247.

5240 TOWLE ACADEMY, WINTHROP, ME. Reunion of students at Towle Academy, Winthrop, Maine ... Thursday and Friday, July 30-31, 1908. Portland: Smith & Sale, 1909. Pp. 80. MeHi.

5241 WINTHROP, ME. An account of the centennial celebration at Winthrop, Me., May 20, 1871, embracing the historic address and poem in full.... Augusta: Sprague, Owen & Nash, 1871. Pp. 69.
       Address is by Samuel P. Benson and poem is by John W. May.

5242 WINTHROP, ME. CONGREGATIONAL CHURCH. Centennial of the Congregational Church in Winthrop, Maine, September 4, 1876. Portland: B. Thurston, 1876. Pp. 24. MeHi.
       Address by Thomas Newman Lord.

5243 WINTHROP, ME. WINTHROP BICENTENNIAL COMMITTEE. Winthrop, 1771-1971. Charles I. Foster, ed. Augusta: Kennebec Journal, 1971. Pp. 138. Me.

5244 "THE WOOLWORTH Farms at Winthrop." Down East, 9 (October, 1962), 20-23, 44.

5245 YORK, LOTTIE E. "Winthrop, the playground of central Maine." Sun Up, 3 (April, 1927), 38-40, 42-43, 45-46, 48.

SEE ALSO entry 3532.

WISCASSET (LINCOLN CO.)

5246 BRADFORD, ALDEN. "A description of Wiscasset and of the river Sheepscot." MHSC, 7 (1797), 163-171.

5247 BRIGGS, MAUD FULLER SMITH. Wiscasset, the home of my ancestors and the place of my birth. n.p., [194-?]. Pp. 26.

5248 CHASE, FANNIE SCOTT. Wiscasset in Pownalborough: a history of the shire town and the salient historical features of the territory between the Sheepscot and Kennebec Rivers. (1941) 2d ed., rev. Wiscasset, 1967. Pp. xvi, 546.

5249 ERSKINE, AMY ALBEE. "Governor Smith mansion, Wiscasset historic home." Sun Up, 10 (June, 1932), 11, 36.
       Samuel E. Smith.

5250 FEMALE CHARITABLE SOCIETY OF WISCASSET. Centenary of the Female Charitable Society of Wiscasset, 1805-1905. Wiscasset: Emerson, [1905?]. Pp. 32. MBNEH.

5251 GOLDSMITH, MARGARET O. "Some old houses in Wiscasset, Maine." Architectural Forum, 45 (1926), 265-272.

5252 HUTCHINSON, GLORIA. "Wiscasset's Musical Wonder House." Down East, 23 (August, 1976), 52-55, 96-97.

5253 LOWNDES, MARION. "Yankee mansion." House and Garden, 77 (June, 1940), 40, 66, 69.
Lee-Payson-Smith House.

5254 MacFARLANE, MRS. JOHN. "Our church in a New England village, St. Philip's Parish in Wiscasset." The Northeast, 77 (September, 1950), 8-10.

5255 MAST, ALAN. "Castle Tucker, the house on Windmill Hill." Down East, 22 (August, 1975), 58-63, 91.

5256 _____. "The great house on Main Street." Down East, 20 (July, 1974), 58-63.
Nickels-Sortwell House.

5257 MOODY, ROBERT EARLE. "The Lincoln County Court House." OTNE, 56 (1965-1966), 61-62.

5258 NORMAN-WILCOX, GREGOR. "Jane Gove, her rug." Antiques, 35 (1939), 182-183.

5259 PACKARD, ALPHEUS SPRING. Address delivered on the occasion of the centennial celebration of the Congregational Church at Wiscasset, Aug. 6th, 1873. Wiscasset: Joseph Wood, 1873. Pp. 27.

5260 PATTERSON, WILLIAM DAVIS. An architectural monograph: Wiscasset, Maine. N.Y.: R. F. Whitehead, 1926. Pp. 4.

5261 _____. "A contribution to the history of Lincoln Lodge of F. & A. M. of Wiscasset." MeHistMag, 8 (1893), 25-36.

5262 _____. "The old house of Timothy Langdon in Wiscasset, 1771-1891." MeHistMag, 7 (1891-1892), 108-111.

5263 NO ENTRY.

5264 PATTERSON, WILLIAM DAVIS. Old Wiscasset. (1931) Revised by J. B. Doggett. Augusta: Augusta Pr., 1951. Pp. 51. Me.

5265 _____. Wiscasset in early days: historical notes pertaining to the old town on the Sheepscot River. Bath: The Times Co., 1929. Pp. 32.

5266 PINKHAM, CHARLES E. "The old Lincoln County jail." Down East, 2 (August, 1955), 28-29, 37.

5267 SEE, ANNA PHILLIPS. "A grandmother among women's clubs." DARMag, 54 (1920), 285-292.
Female Charitable Society of Wiscasset.

5268 SEWALL, RUFUS KING. History of Lincoln Lodge, at Wiscasset. Portland: Bailey & Noyes, 1863. Pp. 54.
Freemasons.

5269 _____. History of Lincoln Lodge, supplemental, from A.D. 1862, to A.D. 1870, inclusive. Portland: S. Berry, 1871. Pp. 59-68.
Pagination continued from previous entry.

5270 _____. Wiscasset Point: the old meeting house and interesting incidents connected with its history. Wiscasset: Chas. E. Emerson, 1883. Pp. 18. Me.

5271 "THE STORY of a century." Wiscasset Fire Society. Proceedings, (January 22, 1901), 7-38.
Wiscasset Fire Society.

5272 THAYER, HENRY OTIS. "The Indians' administration of justice: the sequel to the Wiscasset tragedy." MeHSC, 2 Ser., 10 (1899), 185-211.
Attack on Indians on December 2, 1749.

5273 _____. "A page of Indian history: the Wiscasset tragedy." MeHSC, 2 Ser., 10 (1899), 81-103.
Attack on Indians on December 2, 1749.

5274 WHITTEMORE, MARGARET. "America's first woman's club." Yankee, 19 (November, 1955), 32-33.
Female Charitable Society of Wiscasset, 1805.

5275 "WISCASSET ... the town that has made its past live." Down East, 6 (August, 1959), 28-31.

5276 WRENN, TONY P. "Documenting an 1824 court house: Lincoln County, Wiscasset, Maine." Pioneer America, 3 (1971), 3-18.

SEE ALSO entries 801, 1153, 1322, 1677, 1704, and 1937.

WOODLAND (AROOSTOOK CO.)

5277 WOODLAND, ME. Woodland, Maine, 50 years of progress, 1906-1956. n.p., [1956?]. Pp. 32. MeU.

WOODSTOCK (OXFORD CO.)

5278   BACON, RALPH M. The old village of Woodstock,
Maine, 1808--1840-50. Bryant Pond: Woodstock
Chamber of Commerce, 1970. Pp. 10. MeHi.

5279   CHASE, A. MONT. Reunion of the teachers and
scholars of Woodstock, held at Bryant's Pond,
October 9, 1890. Bryant's Pond, 1891.
Pp. 113. MeHi.

5280   LAPHAM, WILLIAM BERRY. History of Woodstock,
Me., with family sketches and an appendix.
Portland: Stephen Berry, 1882. Pp. 315.

5281   [PERHAM, SIDNEY]. Recollections of the Chase
School House, Woodstock, burned on the night
of Jan. 26, 1883. Paris: Oxford Democrat,
1883. Unpaged. MeHi.
        Author attribution by Joseph Williamson.

5282   WHITNEY, STEPHEN T. "To reach the operator--
turn the crank." Yankee, 38 (January, 1974),
58-63, 119.
        Bryant Pond Telephone Company.

WOODVILLE (PENOBSCOT CO.)

5283   No items located.

WOOLWICH (SAGADAHOC CO.)

5284   JEWELL, MARGARET H. "The Corliss Pottery at
Woolwich, Maine." OTNE, 22 (1931-1932),
180-183.

5285   MONTSWEAG FREE BAPTIST CHURCH. Sesquicentennial of beginnings, 1780-1930. n.p., [1930].
Pp. 31. MeHi.

        SEE ALSO entry 1808.

WYMAN TOWNSHIP (FRANKLIN CO.)

5286   No items located.

YARMOUTH (CUMBERLAND CO.)

5287   BARROWS, JOHN HENRY. History of the First
Baptist Church, Yarmouth, Maine, centennial
discourse, June 16, 1897. n.p., [1897].
Pp. 16. MeHi.

5288   CURTIS, JOSEPH R. and NICHOLAS DRINKWATER.
History of Casco Lodge, No. 36, Free and Accepted Masons, Yarmouth, Maine, from A.D.
1821 to 1870. Portland: Berry, 1870.
Pp. 54.

5289   DRINKWATER, NICHOLAS. "History of Cumberland
Royal Arch Chapter, No. 35, Yarmouth, Maine."
Old Times, 3 (1879), 361-364.
        Freemasons.

5290   GARNISS, GEORGE W. Profiles of Yarmouth
heritage. Yarmouth: Yarmouth Historical
Society, 1967. Pp. v, 69. MeHi.

5291   "GETTING acquainted with Yarmouth, Maine."
CCJM, 28 (1915-1916), 339, 341-343, 345-347.

5291A   GURNEY, LEWIS. "Casco Lodge of Free and Accepted Masons, North Yarmouth, Maine." Old
Times, 1 (1877), 57-58.
        The lodge is in Yarmouth despite the title.

5292   HAMMOND, GEORGE WARREN. A mill-built dwelling house. Boston: Parkhill, 1892. Pp. 27.

5293   HUMPHREY, WASHINGTON I. Origin and progress
of the Baptist church in Yarmouth, Maine.
Portland: B. Thurston, 1861. Pp. 26. MeHi.

5294   KASTER, KATHERINE PRESCOTT. Cousins and
Littlejohn's Islands, 1645-1893. Portland:
Loring Printing, [1942?]. Pp. iv, 128.

5295   PLUMMER, EDWARD CLARENCE. Reminiscences of
a Yarmouth schoolboy. Portland: Marks
Printing, 1926. Pp. 263.

5296   ROGERS, ORVILLE F. Grandma's island and
grandma's ocean. [New Haven, Conn.], 1970.
33 leaves. MeHi.
        Littlejohn's Island.

5297   ROWE, WILLIAM HUTCHINSON. History of Casco
Lodge, No. 36, 1821-1950. n.p., [1950?].
Unpaged. MeHi.
        Freemasons.

5298   _____. The Yarmouth poets. n.p., [1914?].
Unpaged. MeHi.
        Includes biographical sketches.

5299   "TOWN of Yarmouth, Maine: its rise, progress,
and prosperity." BTJ, 13 (1900-1901), 9-20.

5300   YARMOUTH, ME. FIRST CONGREGATIONAL CHURCH.
Exercises of the 150th anniversary of the
First Church in Yarmouth, Me. 1730-1880.
Portland: William M. Marks, 1881. Pp. 52.
MeHi.
        Historical sermon by J. Torrey.

5301   _____. Second manual of the First Congregational Church in Yarmouth, Maine.... Portland: B. Thurston, 1878. Pp. 27. MBNEH.
        Includes historical sketch.

5302   "YARMOUTH." BTJ, 3 (1890-1891), 234-240.

5303 "YARMOUTH Corner." Old Times 5, (1881), 753-760; 6 (1882), 797-801, 946-952; 8 (1884), 1130-1133.
"To be continued," but periodical ceased publication.

SEE ALSO entries 440, 1521-1522, and 1524.

YORK (YORK CO.)

5304 BAER, ANNIE WENTWORTH. "Stories of an ancient city by the sea." Granite Mo, 11 (1888), 143-148, 188-192.

5305 BANKS, CHARLES EDWARD. History of York, Maine, successively known as Bristol (1632), Agamenticus (1641), Gorgeana (1642), and York (1652), with contributions on topography and land titles by Angevine W. Gowen. Boston: Calkins Pr., 1931-1935. 2v.
The title page states "in three volumes," but the third volume was never published.

5306 _____. "The Weare family of York, Maine." MHGR, 7 (1893), 90-99.

5307 BARDWELL, JOHN D. The York Militia Company, 1642-1972. York, 1972. Pp. 57. MeHi.

5308 BAXTER, JAMES PHINNEY. Agamenticus, Bristol, Gorgeana, York: an oration delivered by the Hon. James Phinney Baxter ... in York, Maine, on the two hundred and fiftieth anniversary of the town; together with a brief history of York and a descriptive account of the celebration of this anniversary, with a complete index of names and historic events August 5, 1902. York: Old York Historical and Improvement Society, 1904. Pp. 136.
Historical sketch by Frank D. Marshall.

5309 _____. Christopher Levett, of York, the pioneer colonist in Casco Bay. Portland: The Gorges Society, 1893. Pp. xii, 166.

5310 BOUVÉ, PAULINE CARRINGTON. "Old York, a forgotten seaport." NEM, New Ser., 26 (1902), 679-696.

5311 BRAGDON, KATHERINE. The York and Boston Tea Parties. [York]: Society for the Preservation of Historic Landmarks in York County, 1970. Unpaged. Me.

5312 CADWALADER, CAROLINE, ELIZABETH S. WINTON, and MARION P. HOSMER, eds. York, Maine, then and now. York: Old Gaol Museum Committee and the Old York Historical and Improvement Society, 1976. Pp. 97. MeHi.

5313 CATALOGUE of the relics and curiosities in the old gaol, York, Maine. York Corner: York Courant Printing House, 1901. Pp. 71 MeHi.
Includes a history of the prison.

5314 EMERY, GEORGE ALEXANDER. Ancient city of Georgeana and modern town of York (Maine), from its earliest settlement to the present time; also its beaches and summer resorts. Boston, 1873. Pp. xii, 192.

5315 ERNST, GEORGE. New England miniature: a history of York, Maine. Freeport: Bond Wheelwright, 1961. Pp. 284.

5316 FREEMASONS. YORK, ME. ST. ASPINQUID LODGE, NO. 198. History of Saint Aspinquid Lodge, No. 198, A. F. and A. M., York Village, Maine, 1892-1912. York Village: York Publishing, 1912. Pp. 62. Me.

5317 GOOLD, NATHAN. "Capt. Johnson Moulton's company; the first to leave the District of Maine in the Revolution." MeHSC, 2 Ser., 10 (1899), 300-308.

5318 HAYES, ADA. "The Clan McIntire." Shoreliner, 2 (October, 1951), 14-19.

5319 HUTCHINSON, GLORIA. "The house beside the Burying Ground." Down East, 21 (May, 1975), 36-39, 68-71.
Emerson-Wilcox House.

5320 _____. "Jefferds Tavern." Down East, 21 (October, 1974), 36-39, 68, 72, 74.
Built in Wells in 1754 and moved to York in 1939.

5321 JAMES, DONALD GRANT. This is my York. Albert Boulanger, ed. Haverhill, Mass.: B. & J. Yankee Guides, [1947?]. Pp. 39. MeHi.

5322 LABRIE, ROSE CUSHING. "Fifty years of faith." Shoreliner, 2 (August, 1951), 42-43.
Star of the Sea Church.

5323 _____. Sentinel of the sea, Nubble Light: a history of Cape Neddick Light Station. [Hampton, N.H.]: Hampshire Publishing, 1958. Unpaged.

5324 LITTLE, ELIZABETH N. "Nor' east by east." Newton, Mass., 1885. 13 leaves.

5325 MARSHALL, EDWARD WALKER. Old York, proud symbol of colonial Maine, 1652-1952. N.Y.: Newcomen Society in North America, 1952. Pp. 24.

5326 MARSHALL, FRANK DENNETT. An address before Old York Chapter, Daughters of the American Revolution, May 13, 1938, at the unveiling of tablet which marks the site of the first church in York, Maine, 1636-1667. n.p., 1938. Pp. 15. MeHi.

5327 MARSHALL, NATHANIEL GRANT. An address delivered at the dedication of the new Town Hall in York, Maine, on Monday evening, February 23, 1874. Portsmouth, N.H.: Journal Steam Pr., 1874. Pp. 31.

5328 YORK

5328 MARTIN, STELLA. "The captive of York." Graham's Magazine, 35 (1849), 113-120.
Amy Wakefield, 1692.

5329 MOODY, EDWARD C. Handbook history of the town of York, from early times to the present. Augusta: York Publishing, [1914]. Pp. 251.

5330 MOODY, THOMAS. Diary of Thomas Moody, campaign of 1760 of the French and Indian War. P. M. Woodwell, ed. South Berwick: Chronicle Print Shop, 1976. Pp. 56.

5331 NO ENTRY.

5332 NICHOLSON, NETTIE. "Candlemas Day in York, Maine, 1692." Ancestry: Quarterly Bulletin of the Palm Beach County Genealogical Society, 3 (April, 1968), 13-16.
Indian raid.

5333 "THE OLD gaol at York." Sun Up, 5 (August, 1928), 10-13.
Prison.

5334 PATTERSON, HELEN B. and PHILLIP DANA ORCUTT. "The saving of Sewall's Bridge." OTNE, 24 (1933-1934), 100-103.
Saved from demolition.

5335 PERKINS, ELIZABETH B. "An old village school at York, Maine." OTNE, 35 (1944-1945), 63-66.

5336 _____. "Sabby Day at York, Maine, 1750-1951." Shoreliner, 2 (July, 1951), 50-51.
First Parish Church.

5337 PREBLE, GEORGE HENRY. "The Garrison houses of York, Maine." NEHGR, 28 (1874), 268-272.

5338 REPPLIER, AGNES. "Where all roads lead." Harper's Magazine, 145 (1922), 501-512.

5339 REYNOLDS, JAMIE. York as Agamenticus, Bristol and Gorgeana. [York]: Society for the Preservation of Historic Landmarks in York County, 1969. Unpaged. Me.

5340 ROLDE, NEIL. York is living history. Brunswick: Harpswell Pr., 1975. Pp. 88. Me.

5341 SARGENT, WILLIAM MITCHELL. "The division of the 12,000 acres among the patentees at Agamenticus." MeHSC, 2 Ser., 2 (1891), 319-327.

5342 _____. "A topographical surmise: locating the houses of Gorges and Godfrey at York, Me." MeHSC, 2 Ser., 1 (1890), 133-135.

5343 SAWYER, RUFUS MORRILL. "Agamenticus, Georgiana, or York, Maine." CongQ, 8 (1866), 141-149, 267-276.

5344 SHAW, JUSTIN HENRY. "'Agamenticus majestic.'" SJMH, 11 (1923), 71-84.
Legend of "Saint" Aspenquid.

5345 SHERMAN, ARTHUR J. "Midsummer paradise." NEM, New Ser., 40 (1909), 485-495.

5346 STAR OF THE SEA CHURCH, YORK BEACH, ME. Golden jubilee, Star of the Sea Church, 1901-1951. n.p., [1951?]. Pp. 60. MeU.

5347 SYLVESTER, HERBERT MILTON. Ye romance of old York. Boston: Stanhope Pr., 1916. Pp. 427.
Also published in 1909 as volume two of the author's "Maine pioneer settlements."

5348 VAUGHAN, DOROTHY M. "The Sayward-Barrell House on York River, York Harbor, Maine." OTNE, 29 (1938-1939), 15-19.

5349 WARBURTON, SYBIL. The silent watcher; or, York as seen from Agamenticus, giving a glimpse into its past history as the city of Gorgeana, with a few suggestive pictures of the town at the present time. Boston: Heintzemann Pr., 1897. Pp. 70.

5350 WEBBER, LAURANCE E. "Maine's colonial warehouse on the York River." Down East, 19 (October, 1972), 62-63.
John Hancock stored contraband goods there during Revolution.

5351 WIGHTMAN, IDA MAY. The Indian massacre at York, Maine, January 25, 1691-2. [Newton?, N.H., 1917?]. Pp. 8.

5352 WILLOUGHBY, MALCOLM F. "The last of the 'Empire Knight.'" Down East, 21 (April, 1975), 20-21, 23-27.
A 1944 shipwreck off Boon Island Ledge.

5353 WINN, RALPH H. Legends of Cape Neddick. Freeport: Bond Wheelwright, 1964. Pp. xi, 99.

5354 _____. "Old Cape Neddick." Shoreliner, 3 (July, 1952), 56-58.
Cape Neddick House, hotel.

5355 YORK TERCENTENARY COMMITTEE. Three hundredth anniversary, 1652-1952, town of York, Maine. n.p., 1952. Unpaged. MeHi.

SEE ALSO entries 801, 962, and 987.

Supplementary Bibliographies and Guides

It is assumed that the user of this bibliography is familiar with such basic reference works as Constance M. Winchell's <u>Guide to Reference Books</u>. Bibliographies and guides relating to Maine subjects and places appear in the text proper. Listed below are a few additional subject bibliographies and guides to related materials which are either partially or wholly excluded from the bibliography, and which have geographical access.

ARNDT, KARL JOHN RICHARD and MAY E. OLSON. German-American newspapers and periodicals, 1732-1955: history and bibliography. 2d rev. ed. N.Y.: Johnson Reprint Corp., 1965. Pp. 810.
    Reprint of 1961 edition with the addition of an appendix.

BRIGHAM, CLARENCE SAUNDERS. History and bibliography of American newspapers, 1690-1820. Worcester: American Antiquarian Society, 1947. 2v.

_____. Additions and corrections. In the <u>Proceedings</u> of the American Antiquarian Society for April 1961 and reprinted separately.

COMPREHENSIVE DISSERTATION INDEX, 1861-1972. Ann Arbor, Mich.: Xerox University Microfilms, 1973. 37v.
    Volume 28, "History," has access under Maine locales.

_____. SUPPLEMENT. Ann Arbor, Mich.: Xerox University Microfilms, 1974-.

DICKINSON, ARTHUR TAYLOR. American historical fiction. 3d. ed. N.Y.: Scarecrow Pr., 1971. Pp. 380.

DICTIONARY OF AMERICAN BIOGRAPHY. Allen Johnson and Dumas Malone, eds. N.Y.: Charles Scribner's Sons, 1928-1937. 20v and index.
    Includes birthplace index and subject access under "Maine."

_____. SUPPLEMENTS 1-4. N.Y.: Charles Scribner's Sons, 1944-1974.
    Edited by Harris E. Starr, Robert L. Schuyler, Edward T. James, and John A. Garraty. Together, the entire set covers persons deceased as of December 1950.

DISSERTATION ABSTRACTS INTERNATIONAL. Ann Arbor, Mich.: University Microfilms, 1938-.
    Covers dissertations written since 1935. Volumes 1-11 have title "Microfilm Abstracts" and volumes 12-29 have title "Dissertation Abstracts." Indexes in each volume provide geographical access.

DORNBUSCH, CHARLES EMIL. Military bibliography of the Civil War. N.Y.: New York Public Library, 1971-1972. 3v.
    Volume one is a reprint of the 1961-1962 edition published as: Regimental publications and personal narratives of the Civil War.

DRAKE, MILTON. Almanacs of the United States. N.Y.: Scarecrow Pr., 1962. 2v.
    Covers 1639-1850.

EDWARDS, EVERETT EUGENE. A bibliography of the history of agriculture in the United States. Washington: Govt. Print. Off., 1930. Pp. iv, 307.

FORBES, HARRIETTE MERRIFIELD. New England diaries, 1602-1800: a descriptive catalog of diaries, orderly books, and journals. Topsfield, Mass.: Priv. Print., 1923. Pp. viii, 439.

GOHDES, CLARENCE H. Literature and theater of the United States and regions of the U. S. A.: an historical bibliography. Durham, N.C.: Duke Univ. Pr., 1967. Pp. ix, 275.

GREGORY, WINIFRED, ed. American newspapers, 1821-1936: a union list of files available in the United States and Canada. N.Y.: H. W. Wilson, 1937. Pp. 791.

GRIFFIN, APPLETON PRENTISS CLARK. Bibliography of American historical societies. 2d. ed. rev. and enl. Washington: Govt. Print. Off., 1907. Pp. 1374
    Issued as volume two of the annual report of the American Historical Association for 1905.

GUERRA, FRANCISCO. American medical bibliography, 1639-1783. N.Y.: Lathrop C. Harper, 1962. Pp. 885.

HAYWOOD, CHARLES. A bibliography of North American folklore and folksong. N.Y.: Greenberg, 1951. Pp. xxx, 1292.

KUEHL, WARREN F. Dissertations in history, and index to dissertations completed in history departments of United States and Canadian universities. Lexington: Univ. of Kentucky Pr., 1965-1972. 2v.
    Covers 1873-1970.

LARSON, HENRIETTA MELIA. Guide to business history: materials for the study of American business history.... Cambridge: Harvard Univ. Pr., 1948. Pp. 1181.

LE GEAR, CLARA EGLI. United States atlases: a list of national, state, county, city, and regional atlases in the Library of Congress. Washington: Govt. Print. Off., 1950-1953. 2v.

LOVETT, ROBERT WOODBERRY. American economic and business history information sources: an annotated bibliography of recent works pertaining to economic, business, agricultural and labor history, and the history of science and technology for the United States and Canada. Detroit: Gale Research, 1971. Pp. 323.

MILLER, GENEVIEVE. Bibliography of the history of medicine in the United States and Canada, 1939-1960. Baltimore: John Hopkins Univ., 1964. Pp. xvi, 428.
    Includes a section on local history arranged geographically.

NATIONAL CYCLOPEDIA OF AMERICAN BIOGRAPHY. N.Y.: White, 1892-.
    Volume 56 is 1975.

_____. CURRENT SERIES. N.Y.: White, 1930-.
    Volumes A-L have appeared as of 1977.

_____. REVISED INDEX. H. A. Harvey and Raymond D. McGill, comps. N.Y.: James T. White, 1971. Pp. 537.
    Subject index to events and institutions under "Maine."

ROOS, FRANK JOHN. Bibliography of early American architecture: writings on architecture constructed before 1860 in eastern and central United States. Urbana: Univ. of Illinois Pr., 1968. Pp. 389.

SCHLEBECKER, JOHN T. Bibliography of books and pamphlets on the history of agriculture in the United States, 1607-1907. Santa Barbara, Calif.: Clio Pr., 1969. Pp. 183.

SPEAR, DOROTHEA N. Bibliography of American directories through 1860. Worcester, Mass.: American Antiquarian Society, 1961. Pp. 389.
    Business, city, and county directories arranged by place. Many large libraries have in microform the directories listed herein.

STRATMAN, CARL J. Bibliography of the American theater excluding New York City. Chicago: Loyola Univ. Pr., 1965. Pp. x, 397.

TANSELLE, GEORGE THOMAS. Guide to the study of United States imprints. Cambridge: Harvard Univ. Pr., 1971. 2v.

Index

In using the index, a reader interested in a particular town or civil division as it relates to a subject should remember that he can locate entries for that town or civil division under subject headings if he keeps in mind the inclusive entry numbers for that locale.

Bellamy, Samuel, 3663
Bellgrade, former name of Belgrade
Bells, 685, 703, 2097, 3217, 4471, 4474
Belmont, Me., 2277
Belmore, Bruce Weatherby, 4552
Belvedere, locality in Crystal
Bemis, locality in Rangeley Plantation
Benedicta, Me., 2278
Benjamin, Asher, 3018
Benjamin, Charles H., 4077
Benner Corner, locality in Waldoboro
Bennett, Alberto A., 3384
Bennett, Ernest Nathaniel, 4183
Bennett, Gertrude Allinson, 3698
Bennett, Jacob, 3460A
Bennett, Mary E., 4149
Bennett, Randy L., 97, 3744, 4623
Bennett, Wells, 2262
Bensen, Richard A., 3099
Benson, Earl M., 3389, 3732
Benson, Louise M., 3963
Benson, Samuel Page, 5241
Benton, Me., 1421, 2279
Benton, Me. 100th Year Historical Survey Committee, 2279
Berean Baptist Church, Brunswick, Me., 2467, 2521
Berchen, William, 98
Berlin, alternate name of Township Six
Bernard, Francis, 1611
Bernard, John, 1608
Bernard, locality in Tremont
Bernardstown, former name of Cornville
Bernardstown plus Mile-and-a-Half Strip, former name of Madison
Berry, Clyde G., 3185
Berry, George Stillman, 2818
Berry, George W., 3580
Berry, Ira, 4184
Berry Stephen, 4185-4187
Berry Mills, locality in Carthage
Berrys Corner, locality in Garland
Berthiaume, Juniper, 3665
Berube, Jose Hyacinthe, 3086
Berwick, Me., 1911, 2280-2284
Berwick Academy. South Berwick, 4786-4787, 4791
Berwick Academy Grant, former name of Athens
Beston, Elizabeth Coatsworth, see Coatsworth, Elizabeth Jane
Beston, Henry, 99-100
Betcher, J. A., 4670
Beth Israel Congregation, Bangor, see Congregation Beth Israel, Bangor
Bethel, Me., 2285-2291
Bethel Savings Bank, 2287
Beveridge, Norwood P., 1652, 3911
Biard, Pierre, 1556, 1565, 1606, 1609
Bible Society of Maine, 523, 4188
Bibliographies, 7-8, 49, 57, 69, 101-102, 118, 144-145, 173, 215-216, 218, 221, 300, 345, 428, 492, 518, 543-545, 554, 598-599, 627, 629-630, 681, 687, 744-745, 752, 760, 769, 773, 775, 784, 804, 807, 821, 932-934, 936, 959, 1047, 1096, 1140, 1142, 1144, 1192-1193, 1247A, 1261, 1303, 1311, 1366, 1382, 1400, 1417, 1590, 1646, 1741, 1789, 1986, 2059, 2273, 2610, 3809, 3927, 4126, 4133
Bickford, Cora Belle, 799, 2310

Bickford, Gail H., 3124-3125
Bicknell, Henry S., 103
Biddeford, Me., 799, 1265, 1881, 1890, 1893, 1901, 2292-2311, 4181, 4465
Biddeford, Me. First Universalist Church, 2293
Biddeford, Me. Paroisse St. Joseph, 2294
Biddeford, Me. Public Library, 2295-2296, 2303
Biddeford, Me. Second Congregational Church, 2297, 2308
Biddeford and Saco Railroad, 1890
Biddeford Pool, Me., 3974
Big Island, locality in Seven Ponds Township
Big Lake Camp Ground, locality in No. 21 Plantation
Big Six Township, 2312
Big Squaw Township, 2313
Big Ten Township, 2314
Big Twenty Township, 2315
Big W Township, 2316
Bigelow, locality in Sugarloaf Township
Bigelow Township, 2317
Billias, George Athan, 104
Bingham, Millicent Todd, 2369
Bingham, William, 22, 25, 443, 1222
Bingham, Me., 2318-2319
Bingham, former name of Mariaville
Bingham, former name of Solon
Bingham Purchase, 22, 25, 443, 1222
Bingo, locality in Waite
Biography, collected, 21, 42-43, 50, 74, 96, 105-111, 126, 128, 138, 162, 177-178, 206, 210, 240, 326, 347, 377, 389, 398, 422-423, 446, 474, 495-496, 524, 546, 557, 587, 666, 690, 787, 800, 828, 831, 867, 910, 919, 948, 958, 960, 979, 986, 991, 1008, 1044-1045, 1146, 1187, 1204, 1206, 1235, 1237, 1248, 1272, 1345, 1347, 1359-1360, 1377, 1383-1384, 1387, 1428, 1482, 1485, 1506, 1524, 1584, 1593, 1597, 1610, 1634, 1741, 1750, 1758, 1765, 1782, 1797, 1840, 1864, 1880, 1882, 1886, 1897, 1907, 1909, 1957, 2003, 2018, 2027, 2047, 2082, 2104, 2120, 2131, 2154, 2236, 2248, 2326, 2332, 2348, 2376, 2384, 2442, 2463, 2476, 2506, 2519, 2586, 2594, 2780, 2837, 2839, 2854, 2880, 2910, 2924, 2967-2968, 2983, 2991, 2998, 3024, 3069, 3081, 3123, 3156, 3169, 3232, 3238, 3309, 3363, 3416, 3421, 3424, 3487, 3498, 3519, 3532, 3558, 3594, 3597, 3622, 3669, 3695, 3742, 3837, 3889, 3915-3916, 3944, 3950, 3956, 3980, 4060, 4072, 4128, 4155, 4169, 4181, 4357, 4537-4538, 4589, 4595, 4660, 4662, 4676, 4722, 4868, 5126, 5168, 5205, 5233, 5298, 5305, 5307
Biology-study and teaching, 3571
Biondi, Arnold S., 112
Birch Harbor, locality in Gouldsboro
Birch Island, locality in Harpswell
Birch Knolls, locality in Cape Elizabeth
Birch Point, locality in West Bath
Birch Stream, former name of Argyle Township
Bird, Harrison, 113
Births, see Vital records
Bisbee, Ernest Emerson, 114
Bisbeetown, locality in Waterford
Bischoff, Carl H., 3533
Bishop, Frank A., 3321
Bishop, William Henry, 115-116
Bishop, locality in Caribou
Bixler, Julius Seelye, 5026-5027, 5037

Fort Hill, locality in Gorham
Fort Josselyn, 4711
Fort Kent, Me., 1437, 3086-3089
Fort Kent, Me. Centennial Book Committee, 3088
Fort Kent Pit, locality in Wallagrass Plantation
Fort Kent State College, see University of Maine at Fort Kent
Fort Knox State Park, 4554
Fort Loyall, 4288
Fort McClary Memorial, 3468
Fort McKinley, 4243
Fort Mary, 2305
Fort New Casco, 4178A, 4481
Fort Pemaquid, 2409
Fort Pentagoet, 2739
Fort Point, 198
Fort Popham Memorial, 4110
Fort Pownall, 198, 364, 4850, 4853-4854
Fort Richmond, 4583
Fort St. George, 2300, 2427, 4115, 4130
Fort Scottow, 4711
Fort Sullivan, 2931
Fort Western, 1986; 1991, 1996, 2022, 2033
Fort William Henry, 2405, 2407
Fort Williams, locality in Cape Elizabeth
Fortier, Moyse, 1007
Fortifications, 41, 774, 1275, 1483, 1712, 1986, 1991, 1996, 2022, 2033, 2300, 2305, 2405, 2407, 2409, 2413, 2427, 2716, 2727, 2739, 2931, 2943, 2947-2947A, 3210, 3468, 4110, 4115, 4178A, 4282, 4288, 4303, 4375, 4481, 4554, 4583, 4640, 4711, 4716, 4850, 4853, 5216-5218, 5221, 5337
Fortunes Rocks, 2307
Foss, H. Warren, 5047-5048
Foss, Thomas, 1579
Fossett, Mildred B., 3157
Foster, Benjamin Browne, 420
Foster, Charles H., 420
Foster, Charles I., 5243
Foster, E. J., 5126
Foster, Elizabeth, 421
Foster Point, locality in West Bath
Fosters Corner, locality in Knox
Fosters Corner, locality in Windham
Four Corners, locality in Edgecomb
Four Corners, locality in Kennebunk
Four Corners, locality in Limestone
Fournier, Paul J., 3381
Fournier, locality in Madawaska
Fowler, Henry Thatcher, 4883
Fowler, William J., 2617
Fowler, William S., 3155
Fowler Township, 3090
Fox Islands, 1656
Fox Isle, former name of North Haven
Foxcroft, Joseph Ellery, 2879
Foxcroft, Me., see Dover-Foxcroft, Me.
Foxcroft, locality in Littleton
Foxcroft Academy, Dover-Foxcroft, 2883
Foxcroft Academy Grant, former name of Lincoln
Foxcroft Academy Grant, former name of Springfield
Framingham, locality in Littleton
Framingham Academy and Williams College Grants, former name of Littleton
Francisborough, former name of Cornish
Francistown, former name of Cornish

Franco-Americans, 17-18, 135, 316, 441, 502, 666, 722, 1007, 1324, 1402, 1431, 1441, 1443, 1987, 2294, 2301, 3554-3556, 3561-3562, 3687
Frankfort, Me., 1282, 3091
Frankfort, former name of Dresden
Franklin, Lynn, 422
Franklin, Me., 3092
Franklin and Megantic Railroad, 1542, 1550
Franklin County, 109, 555, 1025, 1537-1552
Franklin County Agricultural Society, 1545
Franklin Road, locality in Hancock
Fraternal organizations (see also Elks, Freemasons, Kiwanis, Odd Fellows, Rotary and United Fellowship), 426-427, 647, 654, 939, 981, 1034, 1172, 1342, 1788, 1947, 1966, 2095, 2148, 2215, 2266, 2269, 2298, 2338, 2381, 2389, 2441, 2596, 2646, 2649, 2651, 2706, 2754, 2770, 2772-2773, 2778, 2796, 2822, 2824-2825, 2844, 2867, 2870, 2907-2908, 2995, 2999, 3009, 3085, 3151, 3175, 3191, 3247, 3252, 3278, 3346, 3383, 3412, 3419, 3435-3436, 3535, 3579-3580, 3610, 3615-3617, 3624, 3645, 3717-3719, 3734, 3779, 3792-3793, 3846, 3943, 3954, 3965, 3968, 3984, 3987, 4056-4057, 4079-4080, 4088-4089, 4142, 4165, 4185-4186, 4198, 4228, 4246-4248, 4267, 4293, 4440, 4452, 4549, 4553, 4579, 4601, 4606, 4622, 4657, 4671-4672, 4717-4718, 4737, 4755, 4762-4763, 4810A-4811, 4822, 4836, 4841, 4848, 4861, 4884, 4924-4926, 5020, 5045, 5062, 5091, 5147, 5153, 5159, 5185, 5188, 5202, 5227, 5229-5231, 5261, 5268-5269, 5288-5289, 5291A, 5297, 5316
Fraternities, see Greek letter societies
Fraternity Club, Portland, Me., 4244
Fredericks, Katherine M. E., 1688
Fredyma, James P., 423
Free Democratic Party, 1093
Free ports and zones, 133
Free Soil Party, 1093
Free Street Baptist Church, Portland, 4300, 4327, 4392-4395
Free Will Baptist Meeting House, Augusta, 1989
Freedom, Me., 3093
Freeman, Charles, 424-425, 3584
Freeman, Frederic William, 4245
Freeman, Melville Chase, 3411, 3434
Freeman, Samuel, 4480
Freeman Township, 3094-3095
Freemasons, 426-427, 981, 1172, 1342, 1947, 1966, 2095, 2177, 2215, 2266-2267, 2269, 2298, 2338, 2381, 2441, 2596, 2646, 2649, 2651, 2654, 2706, 2754, 2770, 2772-2773, 2778, 2796, 2822, 2824-2825, 2844, 2867, 2870, 2907-2908, 2995, 2999, 3009, 3085, 3151, 3175, 3191, 3247, 3252, 3278, 3346, 3383, 3412, 3419, 3435-3436, 3535, 3579-3580, 3610, 3615-3617, 3624, 3645, 3717-3719, 3734, 3779, 3792-3793, 3830, 3846, 3954, 3965, 3968, 3987, 4056-4057, 4079-4082, 4088-4089, 4142, 4165, 4185-4187, 4198, 4228, 4246-4248, 4267, 4293, 4452, 4549, 4553, 4579, 4601, 4622, 4657, 4717-4718, 4737, 4755, 4762-4763, 4810A-4811, 4822, 4836, 4841, 4848, 4861, 4884, 4924-4926, 5020, 5062, 5091, 5147, 5185, 5188, 5202, 5227, 5229-5231, 5261, 5268-5269, 5288-5289, 5291A, 5297, 5316
Freeport, Me., 3096-3113, 3532
Freeport, Me. First Parish Church, Congregational, 3101

Lewiston, Me. Paroisse Saint-Pierre et Saint-Paul, 3554-3555
Lewiston, Me. Sainte Marie, 3556
Lewiston, Me. Trinity Church, 3528, 3557
Lewiston Historical Commission, 3558
Lewiston Junction, locality in Auburn
Lewiston Weekly Journal, 3559
Lewistown, former name of Lewiston
Lewy's Island Lodge, Freemasons, Princeton, 4553
Lexington Township, 3578
Libbey, Dorothy Shaw, 4702
Libby, Abial, 4579
Libby, Charles Freeman, 4308
Libby, Charles Thornton, 738, 3483
Libby, E. H., 957
Libby, F. Wayne, 3313
Libby, Herbert Carlyle, 4852, 5068-5069
Libby, Hilda, 2416
Libby, John E., 1969
Libby, Richard J., 683
Libby, Steve, 684, 3853
Libbytown, locality in Portland
Liberty, Me., 3579-3582
Liberty, Me. Historical Committee, 3582
Liberty Corner, locality in Denmark
Liberty Lodge, Freemasons, 3579
Librarians, 74, 4025
Libraries, 190, 838, 1068, 1270, 1347, 1932, 2007-2008, 2013, 2089, 2166, 2227-2230, 2260, 2486-2487, 2579, 2632, 2873, 2944, 2977, 3250, 3538, 3553, 3771, 3917, 4400-4401, 4457, 4528, 4609, 4681, 4732, 4744, 4825, 4955, 5058, 5088-5089, 5104-5106, 5109
Library associations, 44
Ligertwood, Margaret, 2830
Lighthouses, 1243, 1480, 1496, 1596, 1602, 2415-2416, 2665, 3179, 3731, 4044, 4347, 4485, 5323
Lille, locality in Grand Isle
Lily Bay Township, 3583
Lime industry, 371, 499, 4588, 4594, 4597, 4600, 4605, 4611, 4616
Limeburner, Grace M. Grindle, 2443, 2445
Limerick, Me., 3584-3587
Limerick Baptist Church, 3585
Limerick Mills, locality in Limerick
Limestone, Me., 3588-3589
Limington, Me., 3590-3593
Limington, Me. Congregational Church, 3592
Limington Academy, 3590
Lincoln, Charles Stuart Fessenden, 2524-2525
Lincoln, Edward Joshua, 2823
Lincoln, Enoch, 3137
Lincoln, J. J., 685
Lincoln family, 2853
Lincoln, former name of Thorndike
Lincoln, Me., 50, 3594-3598
Lincoln Academy, Newcastle, 3879
Lincoln Academy Grant, former name of Jefferson
Lincoln Baptist Association, 1692
Lincoln County, 16, 107, 907, 966, 1677-1712
Lincoln County Bicentenary Committee, 1696
Lincoln County Courthouse, Dresden, see Pownalborough Courthouse, Dresden
Lincoln County Court House, Wiscasset, 5257, 5276
Lincoln County Jail, 5266
Lincoln Lodge, Freemasons, Wiscasset, 5261, 5268-5269

Lincoln Mills, locality in Corinna
Lincoln Park, Portland, 4377
Lincoln Plantation, 3599
Lincolntown, former name of Garland
Lincolnvil, former name of Lincolnville
Lincolnville, Me., 1833, 3600-3601, 4612
Lincolnville Volunteer Fire Department, 3601
Lindley, E. Marguerite, 4892
Lindquist, Vernon R., 2122
Linekin, locality in Boothbay
Link, Eugene P., 4305
Linnell, William Shepherd, 4306
Linneus, Me., 3602
Linscott, Edward Lyon, 686
Liquor industry, 1408
Liquor laws, 33, 37, 232, 328, 1403
Lisbon, Me., 3603-3606
Lisbon Falls, Me., 3606
Litchfield, Me., 3607-3611
Litchfield, Me. Bicentennial Committee, 3608
Literary history, 167, 208, 254, 329, 497, 528, 674-675, 698, 885, 900, 913, 919, 956, 1397, 1514, 2122, 2157, 2466, 2499, 2553, 3138, 3171, 3202, 3971, 4229-4230, 4236, 4250, 4260, 4295, 4298, 4307, 4357, 4563, 5110
Literary societies, 2146, 2479, 2530, 2536, 3563, 4176, 5058-5059
Lithgow, Robert, 1272
Lithgow, William, 940, 1272
Lithgow Library and Reading Room, Augusta, 2008
Litoff, Hal, 688
Litoff, Judy Barrett, 688
Little, Dana A., 601
Little, Elizabeth N., 5324
Little, George Barker, 689
Little, George Thomas, 690, 2477, 2497, 2526
Little, Henry, 2595
Little Deer Island and Isles of Holt, former name of Deer Isle
Little Deer Isle, locality in Deer Isle
Little Diamond Island, 4489
Little Falls, Me., 3190
Little Falls, former name of Hollis
Little Falls, former name of Limington
Little Machias, locality in Cutler
Little Ossipee, former name of Limington
Little River, former name of Freeman Township
Little River, former name of Salem Township
Little River, locality in Lebanon
Little Squaw Mountain, former name of Little Squaw Township
Little Squaw Township, 3612
Little W Township, 3613
Littleborough, former name of Greene
Littleborough, former name of Leeds
Littlefield, Ada Douglas, 5228
Littlefield, Edith, 2830
Littlefield, Otis, 2338
Littlefield Corner, locality in Auburn
Littlejohn's Island, 5294, 5296
Littleton, Me., 3614
Livermore, Me., 3615-3624
Livermore Falls, Me., 3625-3627
Livermore Falls, Me. First Baptist Church, 3625
Livermore Falls Trust Company, 3626
Liverton, former name of Livermore

Military Order of the Loyal Legion of the United
    States. Maine Commandery, 876
Military service, Compulsory, 3455
Military training camps, 4243
Militia, 229, 517, 733, 741-742, 749, 764-765,
    1354, 1499, 1501-1502, 1894, 2698, 2709, 2962,
    3914, 5307, 5317
Millard, Kera C., 2794-2795
Miller, Alan R., 876A
Miller, Alice M., 3012
Miller, C. S. S., 877
Miller, Frank Burton, 4660, 4984
Miller, Samuel Llewellyn, 1698, 4986
Miller, William B., 249
Miller family, 4984-4985
Miller Corner, locality in Acton
Miller Corner, locality in Palmyra
Millerites, 1219
Millet, Joshua, 878
Millett, Margaret, 5212
Millgård, Per-Olof, 3859
Milligan, D. Winfield, 2626
Milliken, Fred G., 2930
Milliken, James Alphonso, 1864, 2760
Milliken, Philip I., 879
Milliken Mills, locality in Old Orchard Beach
Milliken Road, locality in Bridgewater
Milliken, Tomlinson Co., Portland, 4332
Millinocket, Me., 3737-3741
Millinokett, former name of Millinocket
Millions, Jean, 5158
Mills, Dudley A., 880
Mills, Hiram Francis, 881
Mills, William Howard, 882
The Mills, locality in Springfield
Mills, 358, 883, 2142, 2887, 3302, 3490, 3834, 4719,
    4957-4958
Milltown, Me., 1840, 2624
Milltown, New Brunswick, 2624
Millvale, locality in Bucksport
Millville, locality in Camden
Milnokett, former name of Millinocket
Milo, Me., 3742-3743
Milton, former name of Orneville Township
Milton Township, 3744
Minchassett, former name of Wells
Mineral water, 4151, 4156, 4159
Mineralogy, 1721, 1724
Mines and mineral resources, 974, 3277
Mingo Springs, locality in Rangeley
Ministerial associations, 425, 1489, 1533, 1554
Ministers, see Clergymen
Minot, John Clair, 885, 2537-2539
Minot, Me., 1425, 3745-3748
Minturn, locality in Swans Island
Misery Gore, 3749
Misery Township, 3750
Missions, 223, 886, 888, 1337, 1556, 1606, 1694,
    2692, 3889, 3891-3892, 3900
Missouri Compromise, 899
Mitchell, David, 3922
Mitchell, Dorothy, 887
Mitchell, Edwin Valentine, 888-890
Mitchell, George O., 2596
Mitchell, Harry Edward, 1865
Mitchell, Horace, 3485-3486

Mitchell, Jeanette Gordon, 3487
Mitchell, Jonathan, 2709
Mitchell, William H., 3885
Mitchell, Wilmot Brookings, 2540-2541
Mitchell Corner, locality in Cornville
Mitchell Corner, locality in Troy
Moffett, Ross, 891
Moldenhauer, Joseph J., 1800
Molloy, Anne, 4333, 4643
Mollusca, 681
Molunkus House, 3751
Molunkus Township, 3751
Monarda, locality in Silver Ridge Township
Money, 4263
Monhegan Plantation, 611, 962, 1712, 2425, 3752-3766
Monk, Guy Maxwell, 2388
Monks, John Peabody, 3394-3395
Monmouth, Me., 3767-3772
Monmouth Academy Grant, former name of Detroit
Monmouth Academy Grant, former name of Ripley
Monroe, Ira Thompson, 3619
Monroe, James, 1371
Monroe, Me., 3773
Monson, Me., 3773A-3780
Monson Academy and Hebron Academy Grants, former
    name of Monson
Monson Junction, locality in Abbot
Monson Maine Slate Company, 3775
Monson Mill, locality in Fort Fairfield
Monson Railroad Company, 3773A, 3774A, 3776
Montague, Henry Burt, 892
Montawamkeag, former name of Mattawamkeag
Monteith Road, locality in Bridgewater
Monterey, former name of Mount Chase Plantation
Montgomery, Job Herrick, 893, 4084
Montgomery, former name of Troy
Montgomery and St. Bernard Chapter, Royal Arch
    Masons, Bath, 2215
Monticello, Me., 3781
Montpelier, Thomaston, 4877, 4879-4883, 4886-4890,
    4892-4894, 4902-4903, 4907
Montrésor, John, 1101
Monts, Pierre du Guast, sieur de, 403, 1118, 2623-
    2625, 4100
Montsweag, Me., 5285
Montsweag Free Baptist Church, 5285
Montville, Me., 3782
Montville, former name of Liberty
Monument Lodge, Freemasons, Houlton, 3346
Monument Square, Portland, 4205
Monuments (see also Statues), 1330, 1573, 2385,
    2590
Moodey, Samuel, 4487
Moody, Edward C., 5329
Moody, Linwood W., 894-895, 1550-1551, 1667-1668,
    5006
Moody, Ralph, 896
Moody, Robert Earle, 738, 897-898, 1893, 5257
Moody, Samuel, 5336
Moody, Thomas, 5330
Moody, locality in Corinna
Moody, locality in Wells
Moody Beach, locality in Wells
Moody Corner, locality in Brighton Plantation
Moody Point, locality in Wells
Moor, John Louder, 3013

New Town, former name of Gray
New Vineyard, Me., 3362, 3872-3873
New Waterford, former name of Windsor
New Worcester, former name of Brewer
New Worcester, former name of Orrington
New York, 4714
New York Industrial Recorder, 4342
Newagen, locality in Southport
Newberg, former name of Newburgh
Newbert, Albert H., 4601
Newbert, E. E., 2017
Newburgh, Me., 3874
Newcastle, Me., 644, 1678, 1683-1684, 1709, 3875-
    3882, 4589
Newcastle, Me. Second Congregational Church, 3882
Newell, William Stark, 923
Newfield, Me., 3883
Newhall, Me., 1493
Newichawannock, former name of Berwick
Newman, Walter S., 1180
Newmarket, former name of Parsonsfield
Newport, Me., 3884-3886
Newport, former name of Blue Hill
Newry, Me., 3887
Newspapers, 492; 373, 395, 493, 713, 1097-1098,
    1407, 1423, 1429-1430, 1436, 1442, 1450-1452,
    1469, 1473, 1484, 1497, 1504, 1520, 1525, 1527,
    1531, 1535, 1538, 1547-1549, 1562, 1603, 1612,
    1622, 1627, 1630, 1632, 1635, 1638, 1640, 1643,
    1647, 1655, 1665, 1669-1670, 1672, 1675, 1685,
    1698, 1700, 1711, 1714, 1717, 1720, 1725, 1754-
    1755, 1757, 1774, 1776, 1795, 1803-1804, 1810,
    1817-1818, 1820, 1825, 1827-1828, 1831-1832,
    1835-1836, 1850, 1889, 1891-1892, 2149, 2158,
    2248, 2535, 2884, 2925, 2934, 3032, 3169, 3559,
    3676, 3849, 4059, 4251, 4328, 4345, 4423, 4450,
    4761
Newton, John C., 4572
Newton, Roger Hale, 4343
Newton Road, locality in Biddeford
Nicatow, former name of Medway
Nichols, Charles Joseph, 924, 1183
Nichols, George E., 925
Nichols, Ichabod, 1384, 4344
Nichols, L. Nelson, 926
Nicholson, Nettie, 5332
Nickels-Sortwell House, Wiscasset, 5256
Nickerson, Kermit S., 750
Nicolar, Joseph, 365
Nicolet, C. C., 4345
Nicolin, locality in Ellswroth
Nile, Le Roy, 1749, 2828
Niles, Margaret, 799
Nimscoscook, former name of Wells
Niscassett, former name of Wells
Nitkin, Nathaniel, 927, 3808
Nixon, Milton, A., 928
Nixon, Paul, 2542
Noble, Arthur, 940
Noble, John, 929, 2423
Noble, Robert E., 4346
Nobleboro, Me., 1678, 1708, 3888
Nobles Corner, locality in Norway
Noe, Sydney Philip, 2722
Nolin, Frank A., 4755
Nondenominational churches, see Churches, nondenomi-
    national

Norberg, Gard E., 3865
Norcross, locality in T3 Indian Purchase
Nordica, Lillian, 3045, 3056
Noridgewoc, former name of Norridgewock
Norigwok, former name of Norridgewock
Norland, locality in Livermore
Normal schools, see Teachers, training of
Norman-Wilcox, Gregor, 5258
Norridgewock, Me., 171, 1799, 1816, 3889-3902
Norridgewock Indians, 1030, 3889, 3891-3894, 3896-
    3898
Norridgewogg, former name of Norridgewock
Norrigeawok, former name of Norridgewock
Norris, Jane P., 1968
North, James William, 2018, 2543
North Anson, Me., 1947
North Bangor, former name of Veazie
North Berwick, Me., 3903-3910
North Berwick Bicentennial Committee, 3906
North Bridgton, Me., 2379, 2388, 2390
North Brownville, Me., 2461
North Chapel, locality in Arundel
North Church, Belfast, 2258
North Deering, locality in Portland
North Gray, Me., 3227
North Hancock, Me., 1579
North Haven, Me., 1656, 3911-3913
North Hill, former name of Brighton Plantation
North Island, 3911
North Lovell, Me., 3634
North New Portland, locality in New Portland
North Oak Hill, locality in Litchfield
North Parish Congregational Church, Sanford, 4683,
    4685
North Parish of Kittery, former name of Eliot
North Parish of Sanford, former name of Alfred
North Precinct of Pownalborough, former name of Alna
North Road, locality in Gilead
North Road, locality in Springfield
North Salem, former name of Salem
North Windham, Me., 5202
North Yarmouth, Me., 3927; 1521-1522, 1524, 3914-
    3937
North Yarmouth, Me. First Church, 3918, 3924, 3926
North Yarmouth Academy, 3935, 3937
North Yarmouth Academy Grant, 3938
North Yarmouth and Falmouth Social Library, North
    Yarmouth, 3917
Northeast Boundary, 544, 1247A; 4, 38, 58, 148, 157,
    159, 203, 225, 267; 283, 327, 334, 432-434, 445,
    461, 513-515, 542, 572, 608-610, 623-625, 672,
    713, 716, 749, 788, 853, 868, 872, 880, 930, 983,
    988, 1208, 1220, 1267, 1321, 1333, 1340, 1346,
    1393, 1866, 1871, 1876, 2924, 3690
Northeast Carry Township, 3939
Northeast Harbor, Me., 3795-3797
Northeast Harbor, Me. Union Church, 3795
Northeastern Boundary, see Northeast Boundary
Northern Maine Junction, locality in Hermon
Northern Star Lodge, Freemasons, North Anson, 1947
Northfield, Me., 3940
Northmen, 306, 585, 656, 1021, 1129, 1370, 2426
Northport, Me., 1833
Northwest Carry, former name of Seboomook
North-west Religious Society, North Yarmouth, 3930
Norton, Alton Ackley, 3395A

Walker, Ernest George, 3024
Walker, Elinor Stevens, 1325
Walker, George R., 2159
Walker, Harold S., 1676, 1763
Walker, Howell, 1472
Walker, John, 304
Walker, John E., 4082
Walker, Raymond J., 1473
Walker, Willard, 1326-1327
Walker Corner, locality in Thorndike
Walkers Mill, locality in Bethel
Wall, Arthur W., 4615-4616
Wallace, Charlotte, 3042
Wallace, Donald, 3042
Wallace, John, see Davis, Will R.
Wallace, Joseph, 3732
Wallagrass Plantation, 5001
Wallston, locality in St. George
Walnut Hill, locality in North Yarmouth
Walpole, Me., 1706
Walpole, former name of Nobleboro
Walpole Meeting House, 1706
Walsh, Louis Sebastian, 1328, 2270, 2737
Waltham, Me., 5002
Walton, George W., 5121
Walton, Octavia, see Goodbar, Octavia Walton
Waltons Mills, locality in Cornville
Walworth, Arthur Clarence, 5012
Walz, William Emmanuel, 4510
War of 1812, 150, 693, 799, 842, 1121, 1173-1174,
    1229, 1341, 1680, 1691, 1703, 1705, 1710, 2397,
    2647, 2686, 2695, 2712, 2924, 2926, 2933, 2936,
    3273, 4512, 5238
Warburton, Sybil, 5349
Ward, C. Raymond, 4549
Ward, Elmer L., 4692
Ward, Ernest E., 3311
Ward, Julius Hammond, 1801
Ward, Kent, 1764
Ward Hill, locality in Madison
Ward Hill, locality in Troy
Wards Cove, locality in Standish
Wardtown, locality in Freeport
Wardwell, Hosea B., 4086-4089
Ware, Ashur, 1302
Ware, Joseph, 1329
Warehouses, 5350
Warner, Maurice J., 1330
Warren, Henry Pelt, 5023
Warren, John C., 4511-4512, 4716
Warren, Juliet Marion Stanley, 1331
Warren, (S. D.) Co., Westbrook, 5166
Warren, Samuel, 5023
Warren, William, 5023
Warren, Me., 1659, 1666, 4589, 5003-5010
Warren Academy Grant, former name of Katahdin Iron
    Works
Warren Congregational Church, Cumberland Mills,
    5154, 5158, 5165
Warren Depot, 5006
Warren Historical Society, 5010
Warren Lodge, Freemasons, East Machias, 2907-2908
Warrenstown, former name of Hartland
Warsaw, former name of Pittsfield
Warships, 2186
Washburn, Algernon Sidney, 3621, 3623
Washburn, Cadwallader Colden, 1414, 3618, 3621,
    3623

Washburn, Charles, 3621, 3623
Washburn, Elihu Benjamin, see Washburne, Elihu
    Benjamin
Washburn, Emory, 4100
Washburn, Fremont E., 1332
Washburn, Israel (1784-1826), 3621, 3623
Washburn, Israel (1813-1883), 1333, 1414, 3618,
    3621-3623, 4218
Washburn, Jennie M., 3445
Washburn, Lilian, 3623
Washburn, Martha, 3621
Washburn, Monty, see Washburn, Fremont E.
Washburn, Reuel, 3624
Washburn, Samuel, 3621, 3623
Washburn, W. H. H., 2654
Washburn, William D., 1414, 3621, 3623
Washburn family, 3621, 3623
Washburn, Me., 5011
Washburn Memorial Church, Sherman Mills, 4750
Washburne, Elihu Benjamin, 1414, 3618, 3621, 3623
Washington, George, 3505
Washington, Me., 5012-5013
Washington, Me. Historical Committee, 5013
Washington, former name of Belgrade
Washington, former name of Brooks
Washington, former name of Limerick
Washington, former name of Mount Vernon
Washington, former name of Newfield
Washington, Treaty of (1842), see Webster-Ashburton
    Treaty
Washington Academy, East Machias, 2909-2910
Washington Academy Grant, former name of Cherryfield
Washington Academy Grant, former name of Cutler
Washington County, 108, 686, 1251, 1839-1876
Washington County Conference of Congregational
    Churches, 1860
Washington Junction, locality in Hancock
Washington Lodge, Freemasons, Lubec, 3645
Washington State Teachers College, see University of
    Maine at Machias
Washington Township, 5014
Wassataquoik, 1768
Wasson, George Savary, 1334, 3460A, 4611
Wasson, Mildred, 3021
Wasson, Samuel, 1619
Water resources development, 294
Water supply, 75-76, 172, 762, 1234, 1396, 2065,
    2118, 3159, 4337, 4433-4434
Waterboro, Me., 5015-5018
Waterborough, former name of Waterboro
Waterford, Me., 5019-5023
Waterman, Charles Elmer, 1335-1336, 1436, 1724,
    3723, 4050, 4065, 4152
Waterman, John Anderson, 3194
Watermans Beach, locality in South Thomaston
Waters, Henry C., 5177
Waterville, Me., 1421, 1639, 3532, 5024-5117
Waterville, Me. First Baptist Church, 5099-5101
Waterville Academy, see Coburn Classical Institute,
    Waterville
Waterville Circulating Library, 5089
Waterville Classical Institute, see Coburn Classical
    Institute, Waterville
Waterville Clinical Society, 5061
Waterville College, see Colby College
Waterville Fairfield and Oakland Railway, 5041

Westford Academy Grant, former name of Linneus
Westmanland Plantation, 1456
Weston, Hannah Watts, 1851
Weston, Isaac, 1345, 1533, 2813, 4517
Weston, Jonathan Delesdernier, 2924, 2937
Weston family, 1851
Weston, Me., 5174
Westport, Me., 5175
Westquatagoe, former name of North Yarmouth
Weston, Nathan, 2033
Wetherell, Alice M., 1347
Wetmore Isle, former name of Verona
Weygand, James Lamar, 4518
Wetherbe, R. L., 1346
Weygandt, Cornelius, 2826
Weymouth, George, see Waymouth, George
Weymouth, Gorham N., 2310
Whaling, 336, 852
Wharves, 2575, 2714, 3972, 4519
Wheatland, Stephen, 1348
Wheelden, Mrs. L. B., 2164
Wheeler, Amos Dean, 4100
Wheeler, Edith H., 4830
Wheeler, George Augustus, 1621, 2573, 2706, 2738-2739
Wheeler, Henry Warren, 2573-2575, 4136
Wheeler, W. C., 265-266
Wheeler, William A., 2576, 4520
Wheelersborough, former name of Hampden
Whipple, George Chandler, 75
Whipple, Joseph, 1350
Whitcombs Corner, locality in Waldo
White, Bruce H. M., 2577
White, Clarence H., 5111-5113
White, Jessie Wing, 3044
White, John, 3146
White, John W., 1351, 1475
White, Myrtle T. M., 4551
White, Stella King, 2674
White, Thomas R., 4034
White, William, 2271
White Mountain Club, Portland, 4241
White Oak Hill, locality in Poland
White Rock, locality in Gorham
White School Corner, locality in Madison
Whitefield, Me., 5176-5178
Whitehead, Russell Fenimore, 707
Whiteoak Corner, locality in Warren
White's Bridge, 1494
Whites Bridge, locality in Standish
Whites Corner, locality in Montville
Whites Corner, locality in New Gloucester
Whites Corner, locality in Winterport
Whiteside, William B., 1352
Whitin, Ernest Stagg, 1353
Whiting, Bartlett J., 4720
Whiting, Me., 5179
Whitman, Charles, Foster, 2584, 3955-3956
Whitman, Vic, 3957
Whitman, William Edward Seaver, 1354, 2759
Whitmore, Allan R., 3021A
Whitney, Clinton, 1355-1356
Whitney, Seth Harding, 1357-1358
Whitney, Stephen T., 5282
Whitney, Wendell, 4099
Whitney Corner, locality in Warren

Whitney Corner, locality in Newburgh
Whitney Lodge, Freemasons, Canton, 2654
Whitneyville, Me., 1863
Whitneyville and Machiasport Railroad, 1863
Whittaker, Frederick W., 2162
Whittemore, Edwin Carey, 3888, 5113-5117
Whittemore, James O., 2598
Whittemore, Margaret, 5274
Whitten, Albion, 4142
Whittier, Charles, 2850-2851
Whittier, Henry Smith, 2911
Whittier, Isabel Mary Skolfield, 2578
Whittier, John Greenleaf, 698
Whittier, L. H., 3247
Widber, Mrs. J. O., 799, 801
Wieden, Clifford, 3870
Wieden, Marguerite, 3870
Wiggin, Edward, 1476-1477
Wiggin, Frances Turgeon, 1360
Wiggin, Ruby Crosby, 1361, 1921
Wight, Carrie, 3887
Wight, Charles A., 3269
Wight, Denham Bartlett, 1726
Wightman, Ida May, 5351
Wilcox Settlement, locality in Cary Plantation
Wild River Railroad, 473
Wilde, Oscar, 2157
Wilder, Elizabeth F., 865
Wilder, Gerald G., 2579
Wilder, Philip S., 2493, 2580-2582
Wilder Young Hill, locality in Freedom
Wildes District, locality in Kennebunkport
Wildwood, locality in St. Albans
Wildwood Park, locality in Cumberland
Wiley Corner, locality in Lincolnville
Wilkins, Austin Horatio, 1362-1363
Wilkins, Raymond S., 1364
Will, Richard T., 3307
Willard, Benjamin J., 4522
Willard, Lawrence F., 3446, 4561
Willard, locality in South Portland
Willardham, locality in St. George
Willey, A. S., 1875
Willey, Austin, 1365
Williams, Anson R., 2194
Williams, Harriet R., 4907
Williams, Henry Clay, 106
Williams, Margaret, 2194
Williams, Myron R., 3958
Williams, Nathaniel West, 2609
Williams, Reuel, 1990
Williams, Stephen Guion, 3850
Williams College Grant, former name of Garland
Williams College Grant, former name of Lee
Williamsburg Township, 5181
Williamson, Joseph, 1366-1374, 1578, 2034, 2272-2273, 2740-2745, 3901, 4523, 5233
Williamson, Robert B., 1375
Williamson, William Durkee, 1376-1377, 1765, 2163, 4999
Willimantic, Me., 5182
Willis, John Lemuel Murray, 1378-1380, 2959, 2987-2992
Willis, William, 656, 1381-1388, 1534, 2666, 3878, 4100, 4269, 4480, 4524-4527
Willis Corners, locality in Thomaston